ASP.NET and VB.NET Web Programming

ASP.NET and VB.NET Web Programming

Matt J. Crouch

Addison-Wesley
Boston • San Francisco • New York • Toronto • Montreal
London • Munich • Paris • Madrid
Capetown • Sydney • Tokyo • Singapore • Mexico City

The publisher offers discounts on this book when ordered in quantity for special sales.
For more information, please contact:

Pearson Education Corporate Sales Division
201 W. 103rd Street
Indianapolis, IN 46290
(800) 428-5331
corpsales@pearsoned.com

Visit AW on the Web: www.aw.com/cseng/

Library of Congress Cataloging-in-Publication Data

Crouch, Matt J., 1974–
ASP.NET and VB.NET Web programming / Matt J. Crouch.
p. cm.
ISBN 0-201-73440-0 (Paperback : alk. paper)
1. Internet programming. 2. Active server pages. 3. Microsoft Visual BASIC. I. Title.
QA76.625 .C75 2002
005.2'76—dc21 2002002448

For information on obtaining permission for use of material from this work, please submit a written request to:

Pearson Education, Inc.
Rights and Contracts Department
75 Arlington Street, Suite 300
Boston, MA 02116
Fax: (617) 848-7047

ISBN: 0-201-73440-0
Text printed on recycled paper
1 2 3 4 5 6 7 8 9 10—MA—0605040302
First printing, May 2002

Contents

Preface

It was bound to happen sooner or later.

We've come to take for granted the Internet and all it has to offer. We can research, shop, entertain ourselves, and communicate with others worldwide without leaving our computers. The average Web surfer doesn't think about the magic behind the scenes of these Web sites that enable us to carry out these activities, but you are a Web application developer who provides these experiences for the Web-surfing masses. For many businesses, Web sites are not just attractive marketing tools but mission-critical pieces of their revenue streams. Your job is to ensure the best possible user experiences for Web surfers but, unfortunately, the time-to-market for these important Web applications shrinks with each passing day.

So how are you, the software developer, planning to cope with this trend? Fortunately, Web application development has taken turns for the better in recent years. Many new tools make life easier when programming interactive Web applications.

One of these tools is a Microsoft platform called .NET (pronounced *dot-net*). In short, the .NET platform is a new framework, based on industry standards, for creating Internet applications that deliver on Microsoft's promise to make information available "any time, any place and on any device."* To take Internet functionality to the next level, it must be decoupled from desktop and laptop computers. Devices like cell phones and PDAs now provide Internet connectivity, giving mobile users the freedom to recreate the rich user experience of desktop computers. The .NET platform makes developing applications for these mobile devices easier. It also eliminates the problems of connecting and sharing data across devices that would normally be incompatible due to differences in operating systems, network protocols, or programming languages. But most important, .NET applications make computers easier to use and users more productive. As the Internet becomes more and more a part of our daily lives, the more approachable,

* Taken from Microsoft's statement on *http://www.microsoft.com/presspass/inside_ms.asp*, December 2001.

productive, and responsive it needs to be. The .NET application platform can make that happen.

Active Server Pages.NET (ASP.NET), an integral part of the .NET Framework, is the key focus of this book. ASP.NET enables developers to create dynamic Web applications much in the same way desktop applications are created. Web applications can now share the same flow and feel as desktop applications; thus, users can do more with the computer skills they already have. For software developers, ASP.NET provides many advantages over other Web application development models, in particular the speed at which Web application and services can be developed.

This book also covers Web Services, the faceless applications that run on Internet servers everywhere. You can write .NET applications that aggregate Web Services. These Web Services, located in various locations in the Internet cloud (as well as your local area network), all work together to deliver on the promise of a rich and productive Internet experience for users.

Who This Book Is For

By now, you may have noticed that I have referred to you, the reader, as a software developer. This book is geared for those software developers who need to deliver first-rate Web applications and Web Services as quickly as possible. I take a unique approach with this book: I don't expect you to be an expert in Web application development. In fact, I assume that you have little or no knowledge of how Web applications or Web Services work. I'll discuss these topics in a tutorial format, so you can follow and learn while being productive.

This book is also intended for students and hobbyists who want to learn about programming Web applications and Web Services using the .NET platform. I've arranged the text of this book in a discussion/laboratory format, so students and teachers can effectively pick and choose topics and sections that are most relevant to their curriculum.

This book is geared toward beginner and intermediate developers alike. Even though I'm assuming minimal knowledge of Web programming methodologies, I am forced to set a few prerequisites. Since we are focusing on Web pages for a majority of this book, a working knowledge of basic HTML is very helpful—you should understand the common HTML tags as well as HTML forms. You should also be familiar with URLs. It's a good idea to be comfortable with the Windows operating system fundamentals, such as file operations (moving, copying, and so on) and navigation.

We will be programming Web Services using Visual Basic.NET (VB.NET). While I don't specifically require that you have used any previous version of Visual Basic, such experience will certainly be helpful. Ideally, you should have some programming experience with a high-level language, be it Visual Basic, C++, COBOL, Pascal, or some other language. You should also be familiar with language concepts such as procedures, loops, conditionals, variables, and so on. All the samples in this book are coded in VB.NET.

In addition, exposure to the fundamentals of relational database management systems will be beneficial when reading the material dealing with the "database-enabling" of your Web application. If you are comfortable working with tables, records, and key constraints and have basic database administration skills, you should be ready for the database sections in the book.

Focus and Goals of This Book

Why does this book focus on ASP.NET and the .NET platform? To put it simply, I believe the .NET platform will carry Internet applications to the next level. The .NET platform has set a new standard for programming ease for both browser-based applications and Web Services. My goal is to make you productive in the least amount of time using these technologies.

This book is a follow-up of sorts to *Web Programming with ASP and COM*, my first book. I was surprised by the radical differences between the ASP and ASP.NET technologies. Also, COM+ and .NET now overshadow traditional COM. For readers of my first book, you will need a paradigm shift in thinking to understand the programming model of .NET. If you are a first-time reader, you're in luck. We approach the material as if you've never been exposed to Web application programming—ASP and COM for that matter.

Above all, my ultimate goal is to provide you with a flying start toward developing world-class Web applications easily and quickly. ASP.NET and the .NET Framework provide the best environment for this. With easy-to-understand development languages (like Visual Basic) and the code modules in the .NET Framework, developing Web applications becomes very easy.

Software and Hardware Tools Used in This Book

At the time of this writing, the Microsoft .NET platform requires Windows NT/2000/XP (Professional and Server versions will work) for server-based applications. The final release of the .NET platform will support legacy versions of Windows (98/NT) for client applications, making the .NET platform more interoperable with older operating systems. When choosing hardware, make sure you have a computer that meets or exceeds the minimum hardware requirements for Windows 2000/XP. This should suffice for your development activities. When in doubt about your particular system configuration, just remember: It will not hurt to add more RAM or hard-drive space to your computer!

As a bare minimum, you can program for the .NET Framework using Windows 98, but with some restrictions. For example, you cannot host any Web-based server applications (ASP.NET and Web Services) using Windows 98 (or Windows ME). Such hosting requires Windows NT, Windows 2000, or Windows XP. However, any other "client" .NET application can be developed and run on Windows 98 and higher systems. This includes console applications, consumers/clients for Web Services, and Windows Forms applications. (Windows Forms applications are not covered in this book.)

Development with the .NET platform on Windows requires the .NET Framework. We'll also make use of the great tools that the Visual Studio.NET (VS.NET) environment provides. In this book, we will be developing with the VB.NET portion of the product. The examples in the book are oriented around using VS.NET as our primary development tool. If obtaining a copy of VS.NET is not feasible, you may still download the .NET Framework SDK for free from Microsoft's Web site. The .NET Framework SDK contains all the development tools you'll need to work with the examples in this book but is limited as far as graphical-based development tools, and it doesn't have VS.NET's ease of use. In support for those readers using the .NET Framework SDK by itself, I provide instructions on how to compile and run many of the samples in this book using the command-line tools that ship with the .NET Framework.

Other Essential Software

There is some essential software that you'll need to have while you develop .NET and ASP.NET applications. The examples in the book use SQL Server 7.0/2000, a powerful, scalable, and robust database management system. Chapter 7 deals with examples that interact with SQL Server, so access to SQL Server is a requirement. Microsoft offers a trial download of SQL Server 2000 at *http://www.microsoft.com/sql*.

Conventions and Styles Used in This Book

This book uses many design features to help you get the most out of the information presented. The text is organized in such a way that no matter your skill level, you'll be able to find the information you need quickly.

This book follows a tutorial format and is geared toward readers with little or no experience with ASP.NET and the .NET Framework. Discussions of specific concepts are followed by lab exercises. Screenshots guide you through every step of the development process.

Section Headings and Text References

Section headings are numbered to make it easier to find relevant portions of the text. Code samples may contain line markers to help you reference source code discussed in the text. Here's a sample source code listing with a line marker.

```
Function DoThatThingYouDo(n As Integer)
   Dim x As Integer
   For x = 1 to n
㉓        DoIt(x)
   Next
End Function
```

In the text, an inline reference to the source code line would appear like this: ㉓. This allows you to quickly locate the source code under discussion.

Helpful Stuff

Occasionally I'll mention special tips that will make your development efforts easier. These are highlighted like this:

> **TIP:** Make sure you stop and smell the roses.

Warnings . . . Watch Out!

I'm also watching out for you. There are plenty of opportunities to "shoot yourself in the foot" when developing software. When I see possible danger heading your way, I'll notify you with a warning section:

> **WARNING:** Running with scissors is not a good idea.

Tech Talk

Some discussions may not have direct relevance to the topic at hand but may interest the more industrious programmer. Some folks prefer not to listen to technical talk (like me—I enjoy simplicity), but I include it for the sake of completeness. I segregate these discussions from the main text like this:

> **TECHTALK**
> Here's where a geeky discussion happens. You can just skip over it if you've forgotten your pocket protector or if this sort of talk doesn't interest you.

Miscellaneous

Certain unfamiliar terms in the text are set in *italic* text. Menu commands (such as those in Windows and the VS.NET development environment) appear in **boldface** text. Also note that some reference tables, particularly long ones such as those for the .NET Framework Class Library, have been placed in appendixes for better readability of the text.

Electronic Source Code Files

When a code sample in the text is available in electronic form online, the file is named `csn-nn.ext`, where `n-nn` is the code sample number and `.ext` is one of the following: `.vb`, `.aspx`, `.asmx`, or `.ascx`. Code examples for the lab exercises are similarly labeled as `Lcsn-nn.vb`. For example, `cs2-02.vb` refers to the second code sample in Chapter 2, and `Lcs5-02.vb` refers to the second lab code sample in Chapter 5. These source code samples are available online at *http://www.awprofessional.com/titles/0201734400.* Not all source code sections are numbered. Those that do not have numbers (or captions) are not available in electronic format, due to either their short length or their lack of complexity.

Some code samples are followed by a line that shows how to build (compile) the program using the VB.NET command-line utility, `vbc.exe`. This information is provided for those readers who do not have access to VS.NET and are using the .NET Framework SDK by itself. Note that code samples for ASP.NET and Web Services do not have build instructions since these files are automatically compiled by the .NET Framework.

Talk to Me, Baby!

I mean it! I've received quite a bit of feedback from readers of my first book, *Web Programming with ASP and COM*, and your continued feedback is very important. I do my best to answer each e-mail personally. While I can't help you with general programming questions, I can certainly respond to any queries you have about material that relates directly to this book. Please send me your comments, suggestions, rants, raves, and ramblings. My e-mail address is matt_crouch@hotmail.com.

I've written the code in this book using the release candidate of VS.NET. Since the generally available release of VS.NET won't be ready until sometime after this writing (Microsoft is aiming for February 2002), I've prepared this text with the most current version of VS.NET I could find. This ensures that you have the most accurate code at your disposal. However, expect a few changes as Microsoft hammers out the final details of the .NET Framework.

Acknowledgments

This is the section where I thank people, and I can't thank them enough. First, thanks to my readers who sent all the kind words about my first book. You've provided much motivation to continue my writing career. *Grazie!*

Addison-Wesley is full of many wonderful people, most notably my editor, Mary O'Brien, whose continued support makes the long hours of putting together a book worthwhile. Alicia Carey and Elizabeth Ryan were a pleasure to work with as well; they always took care of the very important little details that accompany a complex project such as this one.

Many thanks go to my mentor and friend, Mark Hayton. I owe him for his brutal honesty, both at work and elsewhere.

The Addison-Wesley editorial group assembled a great team of reviewers for the text: Brad Abrams of Microsoft Corporation, Doug Thews (thanks for cleaning up my code and for your insightful submittals!), Daryl Ritcher, and Don Browning. I'm very grateful for their extremely valuable input. These individuals played a large part in the success of this project.

Copyeditors are the unsung heroes of the publishing world. My satisfaction with this book comes from the efforts of my copyeditor, Chrysta Meadowbrooke. She has an incredible talent for helping me to express what's really inside my head. Not to mention, she's the best "nonprogrammer programmer" I've met to date.

I also owe my gratitude to my friends Meagan (thanks, sweetie), Clinton, Vijay, Alia, Steven, Jamie, and Shannon for their support, encouragement, and friendship.

Most of all, thanks to my parents, Pam and John.

Matt J. Crouch
Indianapolis, IN
December 2001

CHAPTER 1

The .NET Platform and the Web

Welcome to Web programming with the .NET Framework! In this chapter, you will gain a basic understanding of various topics:

- Historical overview of Web technologies
- General Web server and Web client (browser) architecture, the foundation of any Web application system
- TCP/IP and HTTP
- Overview of ASP.NET, including Web Forms and Web Services
- Internet Information Server
- The .NET Framework, including the Common Language Runtime (CLR)
- COM+ Component Services

1.1 The Pathway to Web Applications

The phrase "The Web means business" has become such a cliché that it's hard to imagine a time when the World Wide Web was just about serving up static documents (back in the early 1990s). Indeed, the Web has developed into an interactive medium of global proportions and has presented a wealth of opportunity for businesses to become more profitable. However, many obstacles stood in the way of achieving the high level of interactivity that Web sites commonly feature today. Highly skilled programmers had to crank out arcane code to access a corporation's data and intellectual assets and present that material in a Web format. To make matters worse, effective tools for Web development were in short supply. As a result, Web development projects ranked as some of the most expensive software projects. Early Web applications were restricted mainly to the UNIX operating system, which confined their development and maintenance to a small group of privileged individuals with specialized skills. The road traveled to create highly interactive Web sites was certainly treacherous, but it paved the way for wonderful technologies like Active Server Pages.NET (ASP.NET) and the .NET platform.

1.2 The Web Client/Server Model

Before we begin to discuss ASP.NET and the .NET platform, let's discuss how all the components of a Web-based network environment fit together.

1.2.1 Web Clients and Web Servers

At the highest level, communication in a Web-based environment takes place between two entities:

- A Web client, which is the software that requests files, data, and services
- A Web server, which fulfills the client's requests for content

In most cases, the Web client is the ubiquitous Web browser, such as Microsoft Internet Explorer or Netscape Navigator. The Web server software could be software such as Microsoft Internet Information Server (see Section 1.4 for an overview).

1.2.2 Protocols for Web Client/Server Communication

The Web client (browser) and the Web server send information back and forth using the Transmission Control Protocol/Internet Protocol (TCP/IP). This is the same network protocol used by many other Internet services, such as e-mail and the File Transfer Protocol (FTP). It's a common language that all computers connected to the Internet (and some local area networks) speak. A digital software conduit, or socket, connects computers using TCP/IP.

A socket is a line of "plumbing" established by either the client or the server software that is used to move packets of data back and forth between the client and the server. It is through this "channel" that requests and responses are sent inside packets of data. A packet is a fragment of data that includes information about its origination, its destination, and so forth. TCP/IP handles the encapsulation of user data into these packets for transmission. Packets transmitted along sockets arrive at their destination in exactly the order in which they were transmitted. Web applications communicate over sockets using a higher-level protocol—the HyperText Transfer Protocol (HTTP).

HTTP is a simple command–response system used for communication on the Web. It functions just as described: a command is issued by the client to the server, then the server sends a response, thus completing the data exchange. HTTP contains roughly ten commands in its instruction set (in version 1.1 of the protocol). Typically, the commands sent by the client are requests for files, such as HyperText Markup Language (HTML) documents and images. HTTP is stateless, which means that when a client request is completed, the Web server normally closes the socket connection with the browser and "forgets" the details of the exchange (except for a possible system log entry). Later we will discuss why this is an obstacle when developing a Web application.

The first version of HTTP (version 0.9) was extremely limited, so much so that it implemented only one client command—the GET method. This command accepted one parameter (the file pathname) and requested that document from the Web server. In those early days, content was static text only. No multimedia, interactivity, or persistency was supported until the next revision of HTTP was adopted.

So, HTTP 0.9 was depreciated, and HTTP 1.0 emerged in its place. This upgraded version provided commands not only to retrieve documents but also to allow the client to send additional information to the server. (HTTP 1.1, the latest incarnation, added more features, such as the ability to host more than one Web host on the same physical server.) Some of this information could include parameters to an executable program residing on the Web server. Given this information, the external executable program can send data back to the client based on processing the program did on the information sent. This method of encoding data to be sent from Web client to Web server is called the Common Gateway Interface (CGI). Applications and scripts that read the CGI encoding scheme are called CGI scripts or CGI applications (or simply CGIs).

1.2.3 Server-Side Processing with CGI Programs

CGI works by processing the data sent by the Web browser (typically data that originate from an HTML form) to the Web server. The data contained in the form fields are encoded by the browser using the `x-url-encoding` system before transmission. The data is sent by one of two methods:

- Encoding the data in the body of an HTTP POST command (a POST request)
- Passing the data as arguments to a script file in the URL (a GET request)

The Web server receives this data and passes it to a CGI application for processing. The CGI application processing can include any programming logic and code necessary to produce the desired output. The CGI application then sends the results to the Web browser as HTML or other data that the browser can render.

1.2.4 Disadvantages of Using CGI

CGI provides the "plumbing" functionality for Web client/server communication, but interpreting the CGI encoding can be difficult. Although this architecture may seem simple and elegant on the surface, it is very much at a disadvantage when compared to programming with ASP.NET. Let's do two brief comparisons of ASP.NET and CGI to illustrate.

1. Writing CGI programs is the least cost-effective method of Web development. Since CGI is simply an encoding scheme for passing data back and forth between Web clients and Web servers, CGI programs typically need extra code to interpret the encoding. This is only a preliminary step; after decoding the CGI data, we must then process it. ASP.NET solves both of these problems by (1) making it extremely easy to parse CGI data using built-in code objects designed for CGI decoding and (2) providing a framework for using many different programming languages, like Visual Basic.NET (VB.NET) and JScript.NET, to process the data. Using ASP.NET clearly eliminates many monotonous programming steps associated with CGI development, thus freeing programmers to concentrate more on the main application logic of the program. ASP.NET also makes building Web applications easier by utilizing reusable component control for many common user interface elements.

2. CGI programs run separately from the Web server process in a separate application. When the Web browser makes a request for a CGI program, the CGI executes in another system process independently

from the Web server. On the Windows platform, CGI applications are typically implemented as executables (EXEs). The largest problem with this is the CPU resources involved in launching the application. In most cases, valuable CPU time and memory are stolen from the Web server when resources are at a premium. This occurs because one EXE process is created for each request of the CGI program—a very costly operation in Windows. When coupled with a high number of users requesting files from the Web server, the server's resources can be exhausted quickly. ASP.NET is designed to use minimal system resources by executing in the process space of the Web server, thereby sharing its system resources. The underlying runtime engine for .NET also minimizes memory leaks, thus providing further stability. ASP.NET also has the ability to execute in a separate process space, much like traditional EXEs.

1.3 Components of ASP.NET and the .NET Framework

The following component pieces of ASP.NET and .NET are discussed in greater depth in Sections 1.4 through 1.8.

- *Internet Information Server* is the core server software that delivers Web content to the user's browser.
- *ASP.NET pages* are typically HTML pages that host static content and executable code that dynamically generates content. They act as a "glue" between the presentation layer (content) and the application services (data). *Web Forms* are the framework used to build Web applications. Web Forms provide rich user interfaces and are similar in functionality to traditional Visual Basic applications.
- *Common Language Runtime* and the *.NET Framework Class Library* provide the runtime environment for managed code (code that executes in the CLR). The .NET Framework Class Library offers a set of components for developing applications with rich functionality.
- *Managed components* enable modularity and allow sharing of these modules among many different applications.
- *Web Services* provide component-based functionality that can be accessed over the network by any machine using a variety of protocols. In other words, it's a programmatic way to access Web resources that isn't tied to an HTML page.

1.4 Overview of Internet Information Server

Internet Information Server (IIS) is Microsoft's software for serving up content on the Web. In addition to supporting delivery of Web content via HTTP, IIS also supports FTP and the Simple Mail Transfer Protocol (SMTP) for sending Internet e-mail. The functionality of IIS is extendable through the Internet Server Application Programmer's Interface (ISAPI). ISAPI programs come in two flavors: ISAPI extensions and ISAPI filters.

1.4.1 ISAPI Extensions

ISAPI extensions bear a striking resemblance to traditional CGI programs. Both programs are invoked in much the same manner. They can receive URL-encoded form data from an HTTP POST request as well as from an HTTP "get" request. However, unlike CGI programs, which are EXEs, ISAPI extensions exist as Windows dynamic link libraries (DLLs). DLLs are compiled code modules whose functions are called by another program during runtime. DLLs share the memory of the program that is calling the DLL. In this case, the program calling the ISAPI DLL extension is IIS. Therefore, ISAPI extensions don't incur the overhead associated with EXEs when they allocate memory. ISAPI extensions are also multithreaded, which enables them to run many times concurrently without impacting the precious resources of the server. ISAPI extensions can be used when a problem calls for a CGI-like program but performance must remain paramount.

1.4.2 ISAPI Filters

ISAPI filters differ from CGIs and ISAPI extensions. Like ISAPI extensions, ISAPI filters exist as DLLs, can perform many operations at once, and run in the memory space of IIS. However, these programs are not directly invoked by a request from a Web browser. An ISAPI filter's job is to intercept requests from a Web browser and send back some kind of alternative response. In effect, an ISAPI filter modifies the default behavior of the Web server and how it returns data—hence the name *filter*. To illustrate how this works, let's look at what happens during a normal request–response transaction between a Web server and a Web browser.

When a Web server has no ISAPI filter, the following sequence occurs.

1. The user requests a URL, and the Web browser sends the appropriate HTTP command to the Web server.

2. The Web server receives the command and requests the file in the URL. This could be either a static HTML file or a server-side script or program.
3. The server sends the content of the file (or output of the script program) back to the client (browser), and the connection is closed.

When a Web server has an ISAPI filter, the procedure changes somewhat.

1. The user requests a URL, and the Web browser sends the appropriate HTTP command to the Web server.
2. The Web server receives the request and passes that request data as parameters to the ISAPI filter code. This step is transparent to the user. The user has no knowledge of the ISAPI filter at work on the server.
3. The ISAPI filter performs some server-side processing and then sends back customized data through the IIS server and back out to the Web browser. The connection is then closed.

ISAPI filters have many applications, including the following:

- Customized logging of user activity on the server
- Advanced security systems that examine the origin of each HTTP request and determine whether the user is allowed to enter
- On-the-fly decryption of files on the Web server based on a password
- Modification of the output stream of the Web server

In essence, ISAPI filters do exactly as their name implies—they filter incoming requests from Web clients.

1.5 Overview of ASP.NET

ASP.NET provides a framework for building Web applications. ASP.NET is unique among Web application development platforms in two main ways.

1. ASP.NET applications are fully compiled. Other Web application development platforms, including classic ASP, use interpreted code to dynamically generate content. ASP.NET applications use programming languages such as VB.NET, C#, and JScript.NET (plus many others provided by third-party vendors), which increases flexibility during development since different languages can be used based on a programmer's skills and experience.

2. ASP.NET ships with many reusable controls that make common programming tasks easy, providing a framework that encourages a rich third-party market of reusable controls for a variety of tasks. Basic user interface controls like buttons, text fields, and drop-down lists are included, plus advanced ones like calendar controls and editable data grids. These controls can be used in a declarative manner; you can simply drag-and-drop the controls (or type in their definitions by hand) in your ASP.NET applications and they'll function with no or very little supplemental code.

1.5.1 Web Forms

Web Forms allow programmers to build form-based Web applications designed around an event-driven application model. An event-driven application is constructed by placing user-interface objects onto a form and assigning behaviors to the objects in response to certain object events, such as a mouse-click.

ASP.NET Web Forms are very powerful for a number of reasons.

- Web Forms can run on any browser. Web Forms are controlled server-side and rendered using standard HTML 3.2 code. This ensures maximum compatibility with older browsers while providing enhanced functionality for Internet Explorer by using Dynamic HTML when appropriate. ASP.NET determines what content to serve back to the user based on an automatic browser detection.
- Any .NET-compatible language (for example, VB.NET) can be used to code ASP.NET applications.
- Web Forms execute inside the CLR, which brings all of its advantages to Web Forms, including the .NET Framework Class Library, type-safety, and other features.

1.6 The .NET Common Language Runtime and Class Library

The .NET CLR controls execution of programs. Any program written for .NET executes within this environment. Code that runs in the CLR is known as *managed code*. The CLR enables programmers to write code that is interoperable across different languages. The CLR also provides features such as automatic memory management, which frees programmers from the task of managing their own memory allocation and deallocation (a process that can introduce errors in program execution). The CLR enables language code to interact with code written in other languages at the object level. In addition, the CLR can provide self-describing objects (making deployment and reuse easier) and enable code to run on any CPU that provides an implementation of the CLR.

The .NET Framework Class Library is an extensive collection of data types and objects intended to give programmers a start in developing their applications. The data type and objects are designed and categorized to make accessing system functionality such as input/output (I/O), graphics, database access, and other system-level services easy. The objects come with all the benefits and features of object-oriented languages, such as inheritance and polymorphism. We'll talk more about inheritance and polymorphism in Chapter 2; these features allow us to customize many of the objects in the .NET Framework Class Library to make them most useful for the programming task at hand. The .NET Framework Class Library also supports objects like basic data types (for example, integers, strings, and so on) as well as more abstract data types (for example, user interface controls). Also note that the .NET Framework Class Library is available no matter what language you choose to use, and it works for client and server applications. You'll find yourself using it quite often, so it's worth learning all you can about its capabilities.

1.7 Managed Components in .NET

Many times throughout the text, we'll be talking about components. A *component* is an independent unit of code that encapsulates a task (such as e-mailing a message) or critical business rules and logic (like a voter registration process). To illustrate the concept of a component, let's examine the basic programmatic steps that a hypothetical order-entry system performs to fulfill a customer order.

1. A clerk fills out shipping information, billing information, and order detail in a computerized form. On completion, the clerk sends the data to the server.
2. The server receives the data. The system compares the order detail with a list of current product inventory. If all the items requested are in stock, the system logs the order to a database showing that the order was received and is pending. If any items requested are out of stock, the system informs the customer that the order can't be fully filled at that time.

3. The system then calculates total cost and shipping charges and sends the order to the company's distribution warehouse via e-mail. The customer's credit card information is sent for processing. If credit is approved, the system informs the customer that the order is now being processed.
4. The order e-mail is received at the warehouse, and the products needed are picked. Once the order is fulfilled, the system sends an e-mail message to the customer that the order has been shipped.

Although the complexity involved in making a complete order-entry system is not apparent in the preceding four steps, they nonetheless serve as a good example of how the steps of this order-processing system can be "wrapped up" into an order entry component.

The .NET Framework helps us not only by making these components easy to program but also by providing many code engineering and organization benefits as well. By creating a component that performs the functionality of the ordering system, we gain the advantage of having the code completely hidden inside a compiled assembly. The component is object-oriented in the true sense. The component has information hiding, which makes the details of the component's implementation unavailable to the user of the object. We can enhance the functionality of the object through inheritance, and the component can be reused in many different programming environments. The .NET Framework also makes deployment of the object easy with the use of embedded *metadata* that describe the details of the component to clients.

1.8 Web Services

Some of the problems that developers face when making distributed applications are the lack of standard communication protocols and the issues of how to deploy the applications and make the application's services available to different clients. Web applications have traditionally had their data and services tied directly to HTML and Web browsers. For a time, this was a good way to obtain information like stock quotes and to order goods and services. Users simply navigated to the appropriate Web site and used the site's HTML pages as their interface to the data they wished to view and the tasks they wished to accomplish.

With the "next generation" of the Web, this process for meeting informational needs has largely become inefficient. Users must learn a whole new interface for each Web site or service they use. Furthermore, if they want to use the information obtained from these Web sites in other applications, they most likely have to resort to a manual process of cutting and pasting the data into those applications. Then there's the issue of the availability of Web sites and services. Users are demanding that this information be available on devices other than their desktop computers. Before .NET, getting Web services data to PDAs, cell phones, and other Internet-enabled appliances proved very difficult or even impossible in some cases.

XML Web Services takes a giant leap toward solving these problems. To attack the communication dilemma, Web Services relies on using HTTP as the network transport. This eliminates the need for proprietary communication protocols that are common with other distributed object models, plus it is easier to operate across Internet firewalls since it uses the same network port as normal Web traffic. Web Services also uses the Extensible Markup Language (XML) to facilitate the formatting of requests and responses from Web Services. Again, this eliminates the need for a proprietary solution since virtually any software system can understand a text-based language like XML. It also provides a mechanism for describing the programming interface to potential clients of Web Services. These features allow many different applications and devices to act as consumers of data from the Web Service without having to navigate a user interface to extract data.

1.9 Language Independence in the .NET Framework

One great advantage of the .NET Framework platform is the ability to use any language to write applications. Actually, this is not a new concept. The Component Object Model (COM) already allows reuse of COM components in any COM-aware language and allows for COM components to be written in languages such as Visual Basic and C++. COM has proved very successful, but the superior capabilities of the .NET Framework's language interoperability features shine. With COM, interoperability is possible only when the components adhere to a binary standard for interaction. That is, every component has to follow rules of communication established for sending information to compiled components. The .NET CLR takes this interoperability a step further by allowing cross-language inheritance and standardized exception handling.

Cross-language interoperability has many benefits, such as allowing for enhancements to existing objects coded in one language to be added using a different language. In team environments, developers can be free to use whatever language they choose to develop objects. When it comes time to integrate the team members' components, we can be sure that they can talk to each other seamlessly on the runtime/binary level as well as on the source-code level.

1.10 COM+ Component Services and .NET

At the foundation of many Microsoft-based distributed Web applications is COM+ Component Services. COM+ Component Services provide transaction processing, object pooling, queued components, and other features. COM+ is an integral part of Windows and distributed computing. COM+ provides a runtime environment for components, which include traditional COM+ components and .NET assemblies. Within this runtime environment, you can do several things.

- Manage *automatic transactions*: You can commit or roll back changes made to data in an automatic fashion when certain events happen in program code, such as thrown exceptions or failure of business rules.
- Use declarative *role-based security*: You can assign execute permissions to certain components based on logical groups to which the active user has been assigned. COM+ handles this elegantly without requiring you to write complex security code.
- Make components use *object pooling*: You can precreate object instances and keep them in a pool awaiting use by a client program. This provides a considerable performance gain since objects are not being created from scratch for every request (an expensive process).
- Create *queued components*: You can immediately execute components over a live network connection or provide delayed execution of components for disconnected situations, such as a dial-up connection that is not always available.

When you write .NET components, you can take advantage of all the features COM+ Component Services has to offer. Microsoft recommends COM+ Component Services to develop secure, scalable, and responsive Web applications. We'll cover this in Chapter 5.

1.11 Direction and Plans for .NET

.NET has enormous potential. At the heart of .NET is Web Services, the technology that enables a user experience never before seen. With the availability of faster Internet connections and devices like cell phones and PDAs, Microsoft plans to deliver on the promise of a user-centered computing experience with data available "any time, any place and on any device."* Since Web Services uses open standards for communication and encoding of data

* Taken from Microsoft's statement on *http://www.microsoft.com/presspass/inside_ms.asp*, December 2001.

exchanges (HTTP, XML, SOAP, and WSDL), this opens the door for any computer system to interface with any device the user has. For example, personal information management (PIM) software, such as Microsoft Outlook, running on a desktop computer can automatically sync with PIM software running on a PDA. The PDA is Internet- and .NET-enabled, so it can consume information from Web Services deployed throughout the Internet. The PIM software running on the PDA can receive an e-mail alert indicating a change in, say, a travel itinerary due to a delayed airline flight. The PDA automatically takes the information about the flight change and updates the user's calendar in the PIM software. Taking the process a step further, the PIM software can notify the user's colleagues via e-mail that the flight was delayed and the scheduled meeting will have to be postponed. Web Services enables this type of seamless integration and automation, and the sky's the limit to what can be created using the Web Services technology.

One particularly exciting initiative for Web Services, developed by Microsoft, is called .NET My Services. It is often referred to as a "digital safe-deposit box" for the user. Inside this personal information space the user can store many things. In the initial rollout of .NET My Services, the following features will be included:

- .NET Profile—name, nickname, special dates, picture, and address
- .NET Contacts—electronic relationships/address book
- .NET Locations—electronic and geographical locations
- .NET Alerts—subscription, management, and routing of alerts
- .NET Presence—connection status (online, offline, busy, free) and specification of which device(s) to send alerts to
- .NET Inbox—inbox items like e-mail and voice mail, including existing mail systems
- .NET Calendar—time and task management
- .NET Documents—raw document storage
- .NET ApplicationSettings—application settings
- .NET FavoriteWebSites—favorite URLs and other Web identifiers
- .NET Wallet—receipts, payment instruments, coupons, and other transaction records
- .NET Devices—device settings and capabilities
- .NET Services—services provided for an identity
- .NET Lists—general-purpose lists
- .NET Categories—a way to group lists

The most important fact about .NET My Services is that the user is in direct control of this information at all times. Since other Web sites, individuals, and Web services will request data from the user's "safe-deposit box," there must be strict security controls in place that the user can adjust. The user can designate who is allowed to gain access to his or her personal information. Organizations accessing a user's .NET My Services can also (with the user's consent) add items to the user's personal information. For example, if the user wants to purchase an airline ticket, the user can give a particular airline access to a credit card located in the .NET Wallet, make the purchase, and add the flight itinerary to the .NET Calendar automatically. The airline can then issue notifications about flight changes through the .NET Alerts system and, if applicable, alter the .NET Calendar information to reflect time and date changes to the itinerary.

In summary, Web Services and .NET My Services open up several opportunities for rich application integration that make the user's online experience more productive and more enjoyable.

1.12 What's Ahead

This book is designed to get you started on creating great .NET solutions for the Web. Focusing on solutions based on browsers and Web Services, the remaining chapters cover the following topics.

- ✔ Chapter 2: **The VB.NET Crash Course**. This chapter introduces the concepts of the VB.NET programming language, including language constructs such as procedures, looping, conditionals, error handling, and object-oriented programming concepts. This chapter is intended to get you up to speed quickly on VB.NET. Keep in mind that it is not a replacement for a good reference book on the subject.
- ✔ Chapter 3: **Working with ASP.NET**. This chapter provides a background on building browser-based Web applications using the ASP.NET Server Controls.
- ✔ Chapter 4: **Using the .NET Framework Class Library**. This chapter describes how to use the .NET Framework Class Library to get a good start on building applications. Topics covered include common programming tasks such as file I/O, text manipulation, messaging, and other topics as they relate to Web development.
- ✔ Chapter 5: **Building .NET Managed Components for COM+**. This chapter discusses the construction of .NET components and provides a

background on the .NET CLR, the Common Type System, and other general .NET platform topics. We'll also explore COM+ Component Services and how to program your .NET components to use these services.

- ✔ Chapter 6: **Building Web Services**. As mentioned before, Web Services is the most important feature of the .NET platform. In Chapter 6, we'll discuss the construction of Web Services and review code samples and labs to help you get a jump start into making your own Web Services.
- ✔ Chapter 7: **Accessing Data with ActiveX Data Objects.NET**. Data access is probably the single most important task that a Web application or service performs. This chapter shows you how to use a powerful data access method to work with a variety of data stores.
- ✔ Chapter 8: **Securing Your .NET Applications**. This chapter covers miscellaneous security topics as they relate to application development. We'll also briefly discuss cryptography and how you can implement it in your applications.

Further Reading

Here are some helpful resources for further study of the topics discussed in this chapter.

- Microsoft COM+ Web site (*http://www.microsoft.com/complus*): This site provides an executive overview of COM+ and also includes links to white papers on COM+.
- Microsoft IIS Web site (*http://www.microsoft.com/windows2000/technologies/web/default.asp*): This site offers resources related to IIS and other Web and application services included in Windows 2000/XP.
- Microsoft .NET Web site (*http://www.microsoft.com/net*): This is Microsoft's Web site dedicated to all things .NET. You'll find resources for developers, information technology personnel, and business professionals.
- CGI Web site (*http://hoohoo.ncsa.uiuc.edu/cgi*): This site at the University of Illinois explains CGI very well.

CHAPTER 2

The VB.NET Crash Course

2.1 What Is VB.NET?

VB.NET is Microsoft's latest update to its very popular programming language, Visual Basic (VB). Since the early 1990s, VB has enabled thousands of developers to rapidly build applications for PCs (first with DOS, then with Windows). To usher in the new era of .NET and the Internet, Microsoft substantially updated VB to include new features that take advantage of the .NET Framework, Microsoft's strategy for delivering application services over the Web to many different devices. Plus, VB.NET contains "modern" language features like true object-oriented programming (OOP). I'll talk about OOP in this chapter and throughout the book.

In writing this book I've assumed that you have no previous experience with VB or VB.NET, so together we'll approach VB.NET from the beginner's point of view. If you have worked with previous versions of VB, read the headings in this chapter to determine which sections you want to concentrate on to learn new features of the language.

You will learn some essential fundamentals in this chapter:

- Using variables, constants, and operators
- Working with variable types
- Creating functions and subroutines to modularize code
- Executing conditional processing, looping, and flow control
- Handling errors and exceptions
- Using object-oriented programming techniques
- Using threading techniques
- Writing simple .NET console applications using VB

It's important to note that this chapter is no substitute for a good book or reference manual on VB. Documenting every feature of the language is beyond the scope of this book. The purpose of this chapter is to bring you up to speed with VB.NET if you are a new programmer and to introduce VB veterans to the new features of the language. My recommendation is to read several books on VB to increase your understanding of its abilities. Of course, there is also no substitute for hands-on experience developing applications with VB.

2.2 Hello World (Yet Again)

It may seem premature to begin the chapter with a lab exercise, but there's no better way to get comfortable with VB.NET than to just dive in. When you're done with this lab, you will have learned:

- The basics of the VS.NET Integrated Development Environment (IDE)
- How to edit and build an application

Don't fret over the mechanics of the code in this lab. I'll explain all that soon enough. Right now, let's get your first program working.

LAB 2-1
YOUR FIRST VB APPLICATION

STEP 1. Launch the VS.NET IDE.

a. From the Windows Start button, select **Programs→Microsoft Visual Studio.NET 7.0→Microsoft Visual Studio.NET 7.0.** The VS.NET home page appears after launching finishes (Lab Figure 2-1).

STEP 2. Create the VB console application project.

a. To begin a new VS.NET project, select **File→New→Project** from the menu bar. The New Project dialog appears with options for the new project. For this exercise, you're building what is known as a *console application,* a simple program that displays its output in a text-only window (reminiscent of the days of MS-DOS). I chose a console application for your first program

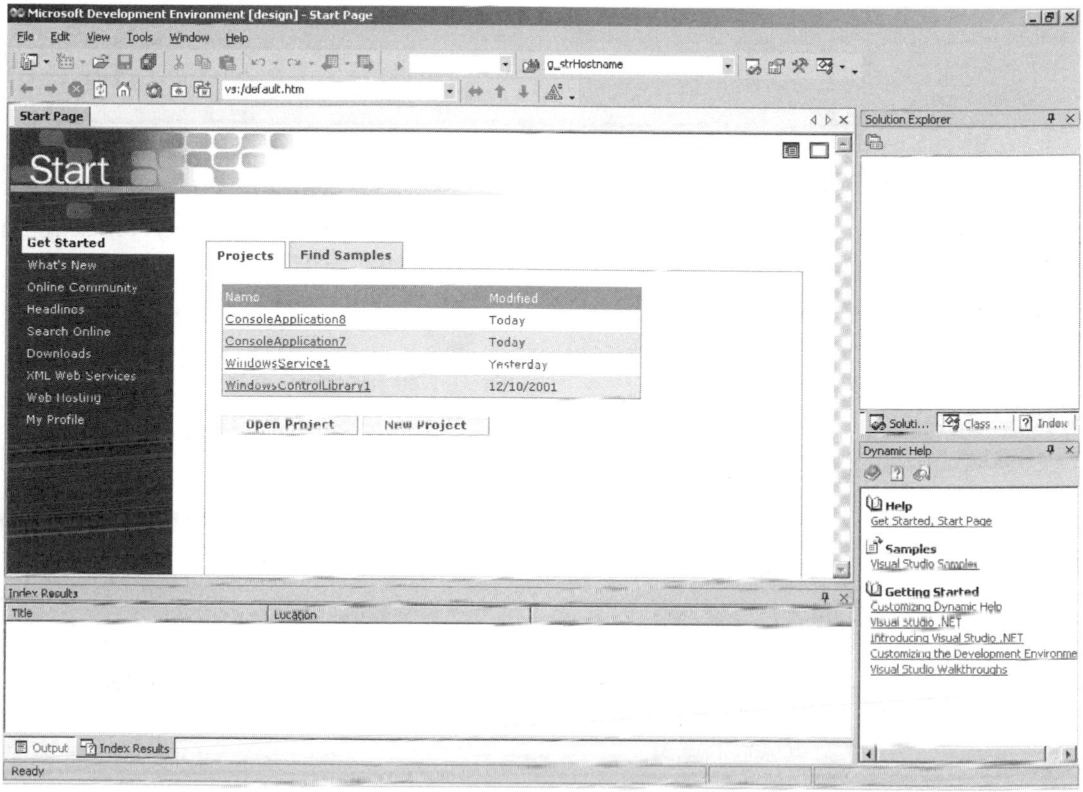

Lab Figure 2-1 The VS NET home page

(and many of the subsequent programs in this book) because of its low complexity. This allows you to concentrate on the core language features of VB.NET and the relevant .NET Framework concepts. Highlight the Console Application icon in the New Project dialog; you may need to scroll down to find it (Lab Figure 2-2).

b. Once you locate and highlight the Console Application icon, you need to give your new project a name. To do this, enter a name for the project in the Name text box. Call your project "HelloWorld." You can select a location for the project files by clicking the Browse button or you can use the default location.

c. Now click on the OK button to create the new project.

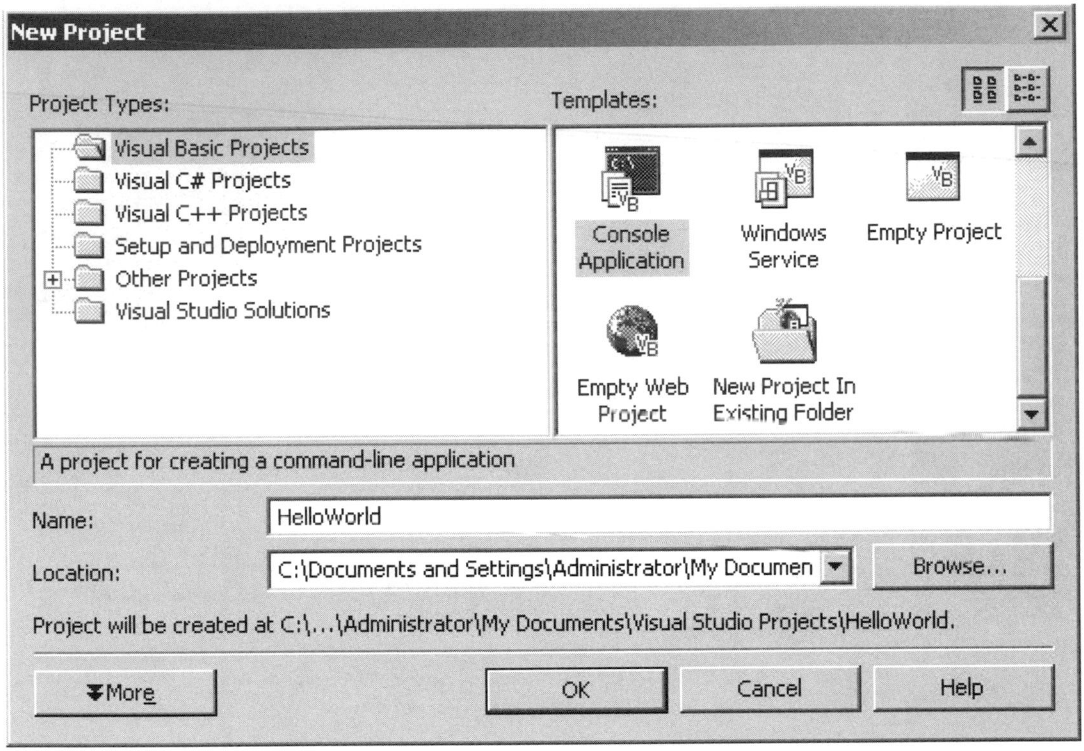

Lab Figure 2-2 The New Project dialog

STEP 3. Enter the program code.

a. You should now see the code window for `Module1`, a default code module created by VS.NET. You will modify the default code in this window to create your first application. If VS.NET is not showing the `Module1` code in the front window, click the Module1.vb tab to bring the code to the front window (Lab Figure 2-3).

b. Now you're ready to type in some code to make the HelloWorld project say "hello" to its user. Type in the code shown below.

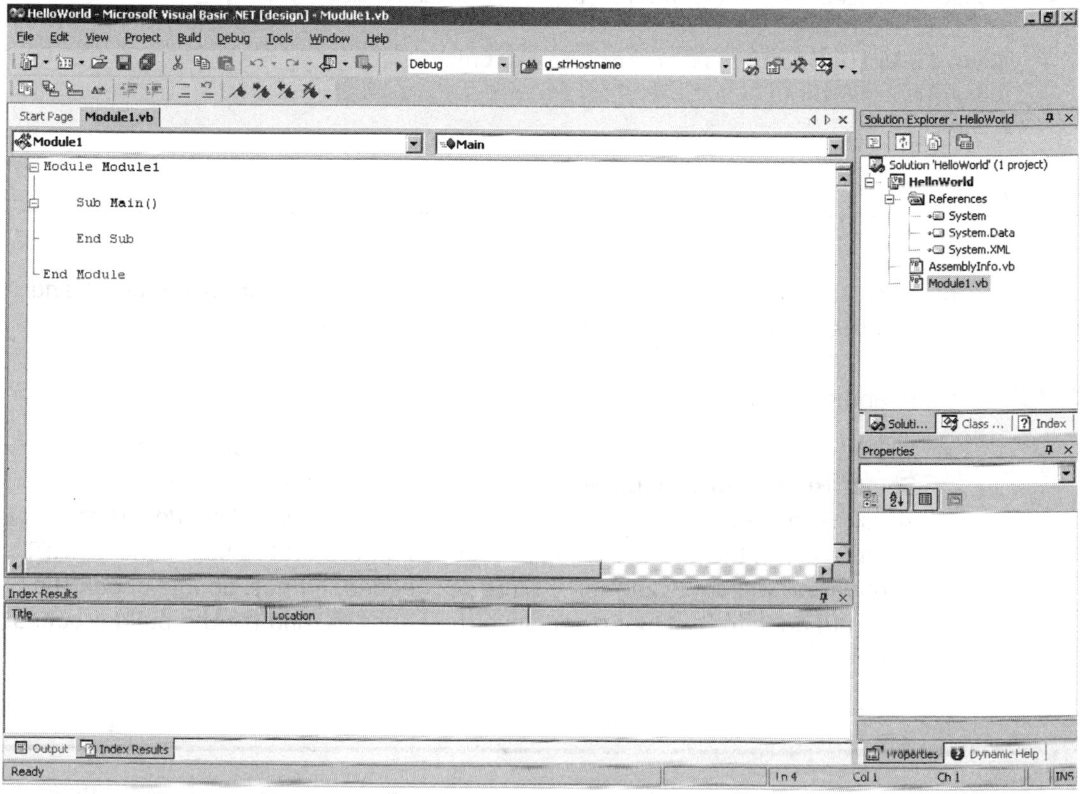

Lab Figure 2-3 The VS.NET Code Editor window

LAB CODE SAMPLE 2-1

```
Imports System
Module Module1

   Sub Main()
      Dim strUserName As String

      Console.WriteLine("Welcome to Visual Studio.NET!")
      Console.Write("Whom do I owe this pleasure to? ")

      strUserName = Console.ReadLine()
```

```
        Console.WriteLine("Well, hello {0}! It's good to meet you!", _
            strUserName)
        Console.WriteLine("Press <enter> to continue")
        Console.ReadLine()
    End Sub

End Module
```

c. Click the Save All button on the tool bar. This saves your code module and all other modified files associated with the project.

STEP 4. Build and run the project.

a. You're almost done. Now you're ready to build your application and run it. Select **Build→Build Solution** from the menu. After a few moments, you should see some system messages displayed in the Build window (Lab Figure 2-4). If the build process is successful, the status bar of the VS.NET application will say "Solution update succeeded." If not, double-check the program code for typing errors, save the changes, and try the build process again.

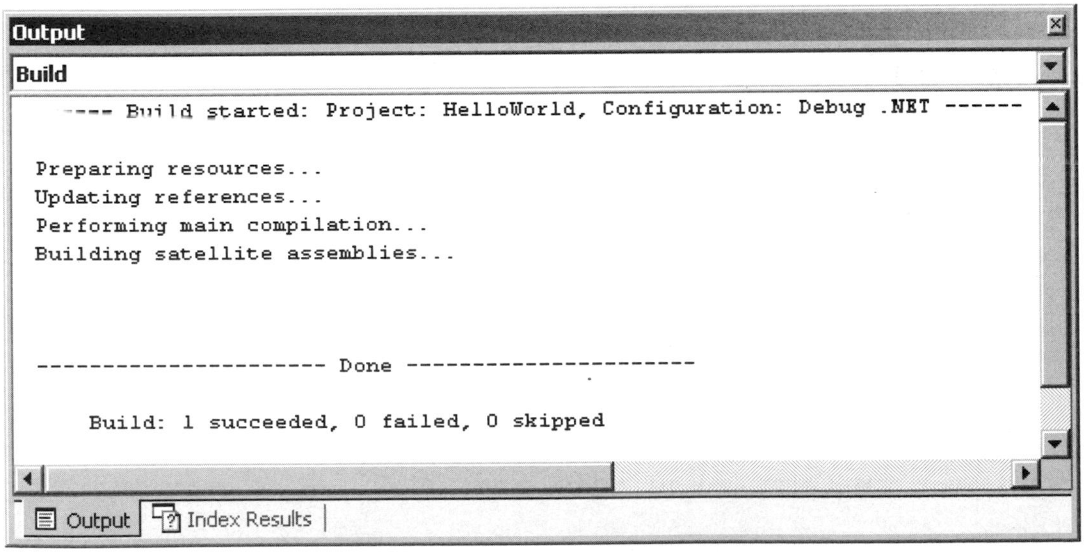
Output
Build
------ Build started: Project: HelloWorld, Configuration: Debug .NET ------
Preparing resources...
Updating references...
Performing main compilation...
Building satellite assemblies...
---------------------- Done ----------------------
Build: 1 succeeded, 0 failed, 0 skipped
Output
Index Results

Lab Figure 2-4 The Build window

Lab Figure 2-5 HelloWorld in action

b. To run the program, click the Start button on the tool bar. You can also simply press the F5 key. After a moment or two, the console window will appear with your running program. So, introduce yourself. . . . (See Lab Figure 2-5.)

c. When the program terminates (after you press <enter> to continue), the system returns to VS.NET.

Congratulations! You've just written your first VB.NET application!

2.3 Variables, Constants, and Operators

Most programming languages store data for later use. It's helpful to be able to store intermediate results of calculations to pass to other processing routines. We may also want to store data that we use over and over again. In addition, we may need temporary data storage for our programs. That's when variables are used.

Constants are similar to variables. They hold data, but unlike variables, their data cannot be modified once the constant is first defined in a program. For example, if you are writing a program to compute the area of a circle, you could use a constant to hold the value of pi (the ratio of the circumference of a circle to its diameter—remember high school math?), which does not change regardless of the circle's size. Using a constant allows you to assign a friendly name to a value that could otherwise easily be forgotten. (Which is easier to remember: "pi" or "3.14159 . . ."?)

Performing arithmetic operations is central to almost any program, so most programming languages provide arithmetic operators. The operators in VB.NET basically correspond to their mathematical counterparts (+ for addition, – for subtraction, * for multiplication, and / for division).

2.3.1 Variable Types

Variables in VB.NET have three characteristics.

1. *Name*: Programmers assign variable names, typically choosing a name for each variable that describes the data it contains. For instance, you could name a variable "price" to reflect that it holds a dollar amount.
2. *Data type*: Variables also hold different types of data, for example, textual, numeric, date-based, or arbitrary binary data. The programmer designates what type of data the variable will hold when it is created.
3. *Scope*: Variables also exhibit a behavior called scope, which defines where in a program the variables can be accessed. (Scope is discussed further in Section 2.3.3.)

If you completed Lab 2-1, you had a brief exposure to variables. The HelloWorld program contains the following line of code:

```
Dim strUserName As String
```

This VB.NET statement creates a variable called `strUserName`. It's used to hold the name that the user types into the program. Such text information calls for the use of a `String` data type, which holds any combination of alphanumeric data.

The code illustrates the use of the `Dim` command. The `Dim` command tells VB.NET that you intend to use a variable in your program with the supplied name and data type. This makes VB.NET set aside memory to hold values in the variable.

As mentioned before, variables can hold many different types of data. VB.NET natively provides a selection of variable types that can accommodate most storage tasks. Let's look at the different data types available.

First, there are numeric data types. VB.NET has numeric data types to handle integer numbers (for example, 1, 2, –5, 23) and fractional data types (for example, 4.23, 3.14, –0.12). Depending on your program's requirements, you may need different levels of precision for your numbers. Table 2-1 shows the different integral types. Pay special attention to the range of valid values.

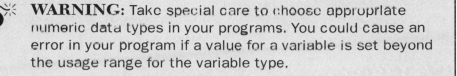

> **WARNING:** Take special care to choose appropriate numeric data types in your programs. You could cause an error in your program if a value for a variable is set beyond the usage range for the variable type.

Use integral data types in your programs for storing only whole number values (no decimals, no fractions). Watch out; storing fractional values causes VB.NET to either round or truncate values, which could lead to unexpected results.

VB.NET also provides data types for noninteger numbers (decimals and fractions). According to your programming requirements, you may need to

Table 2-1 VB.NET Integral Data Types

Integral Data Type	Storage Used	.NET Class/ Structure	Range of Valid Values
`Byte`	8 bits	`System.Byte`	0 to 255
`Short`	16 bits	`System.Int16`	–32,678 to 32,767
`Integer`	32 bits	`System.Int32`	–2,147,483,648 to 2,147,483,647
`Long`	64 bits	`System.Int64`	–9,223,372,036,854,775,808 to 9,223,372,036,854,775,807

use fractional numeric data types that offer varying levels of precision. The fractional data types are listed in Table 2-2.

> **WARNING:** `Single` and `Double` should not be used for calculations involving financial figures. Use the `Decimal` type for those calculations.

The `Char` data type in VB.NET is used to hold a single alphanumeric Unicode character. Unicode is a standard for encoding most of the symbols used by languages around the world. It's an important element in the multilingual capabilities of VB.NET and of Windows itself. Older software systems represented characters from the ASCII character set, which includes symbols used

Table 2-2 VB.NET Fractional Data Types

Fractional Data Type	Storage Used	.NET Class/ Structure	Range of Valid Values
`Single`	32-bit floating point	`System.Single`	–3.402823e38 to –1.401298e-45 for negative values 1.401298e-45 to 3.402823e38 for positive values
`Double`	64-bit floating point	`System.Double`	–1.79769313486231e308 to –4.94065645841247e-324 for negative values 4.94065645841247e-324 to 1.79769313486232e308 for positive values
`Decimal`	96-bit fixed point	`System.Decimal`	Largest and smallest values can be obtained from the `MaxValue` and `MinValue` fields of the `System.Decimal` structure.

by the English language only. This makes Unicode a better solution for applications targeted for international markets. A Unicode character uses 16 bits (2 bytes) of memory storage.

The `String` data type is used to hold text information. The data in a string is stored as a series of Unicode characters. Strings can be any length; their storage is managed automatically for you by VB.NET.

The `Date` data type is used to store calendar date and time information. A `Date` type holds both a date and a time in a 64-bit format. The `Date` type has a resolution of 100 nanoseconds and can keep dates as far back as January 1, 1 CE, 12:00 A.M. (based on the Gregorian calendar). The maximum date is December 31, 9999 CE. The `Date` data type maps to the `System.DateTime` structure. Yes, the `Date` type is Y2K compliant, in case you're wondering!

Another class of VB.NET data types is the binary data types. These include the `Boolean` type and the `Byte` type. The `Boolean` type holds data such as true/false, yes/no, on/off, and so on. The `Byte` type holds 8 bits of unsigned data. Typically, the `Byte` data type is used to store arbitrary binary data. Several bytes clumped together as an array (see Section 2.3.4) can be used by your program to store things such as images, audio, and so on. The `Byte` and `Boolean` types map to .NET Framework structures `System.Byte` and `System.Boolean`, respectively.

The `Object` type is a special data type used to reference any other type. It maps to the `System.Object` class. Any class that you create in VB.NET inherits from the `System.Object` class. (Inheritance is discussed in Section 2.7.4.)

2.3.2 Declaring and Assigning Variables

To use variables, you must define storage for them in your program. This code shows how to declare a variable by using the `Dim` statement:

```
Dim strUserName As String
```

This tells VB.NET to create storage for a `String` data type and to call it `strUserName`.

When declaring a variable, you can also assign it an initial value. To do this, declare a variable with the `Dim` command and then add an assignment operator (=) along with the value you wish to assign to the variable, as shown in the example below:

```
Dim strUserName As String = "Testing 1 2 3"
```

2.3.3 Scope and Lifetime of Variables

When you declare a variable, the value that it holds has limitations on where and when it can be accessed—the *scope* and *lifetime* of the variable, respectively. To illustrate these concepts, it's best to look at some existing code.

Turning again to Lab 2-1, consider the variable `strUserName`. The variable holds the text string that the user types at the console. Once the text string is stored in the variable, the program accesses it once again to display the response to the user. Since we declared the variable within the bounds of the program's main subroutine, it is accessible at any time during the execution of the code in the main subroutine. Variables that are declared inside subroutines and functions are called *local variables.*

Some variables are declared outside of any subroutine or function. These variables are known as *global variables.* Global variables can be accessed from anywhere in the program's code, and their lifetime exists for the entire duration of the program's execution.

Here's an example that uses both global and local variables. It's a modification of the program in Lab 2-1.

Code Sample 2-1 Build instructions: `vbc /r:system.dll cs2-01.vb`

```
Imports System
Module Module1
  Dim g_intTestGlobal As Integer

  Sub Main()
    Dim strUserName As String

    Console.WriteLine("Welcome to Visual Studio.NET!")
    Console.Write("Whom do I owe this pleasure to? ")

    strUserName = Console.ReadLine()

    Console.WriteLine("Well, hello {0}! It's good to meet you!", _
                strUserName)

    AnotherSubroutine()
    Console.WriteLine("AnotherSubroutine() has been executed")
    Console.WriteLine("The value of g_intTestGlobal is: {0}", _
                g_intTestGlobal)

    Console.WriteLine("Press <enter> to continue")
    Console.ReadLine()
  End Sub
```

```
    Sub AnotherSubroutine()
      g_intTestGlobal = 100
      Console.WriteLine(_
        "We have set the g_intTestGlobal variable")
    End Sub

End Module
```

When you run this program, you'll see the output shown in Figure 2-1.

> **TIP:** It's good programming style to limit the use of global variables. Try to use local variables whenever possible. Your code will be easier to understand, and it will help you avoid problems associated with multithreaded applications.

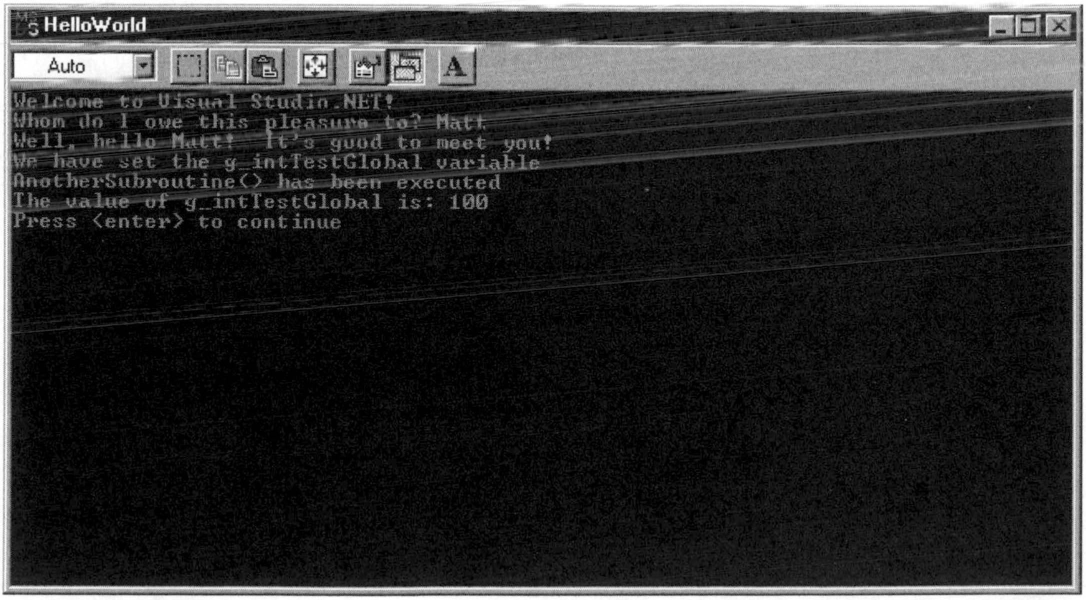

Figure 2-1 Output of modified HelloWorld program

2.3.4 Arrays

Arrays are a collection of data elements that all have the same data type. Arrays are useful for processing large sets of data without having to declare a separate variable for each data element.

Arrays have dimensionality, which refers to the number of subscripts used to access each element in the array. All arrays have at least one dimension and can support up to sixty dimensions, but you'll probably deal with arrays that have a maximum of only three dimensions since we tend to conceptualize data (and our physical world) that way.

Arrays also have defined minimums and maximums for the subscripts used to reference the array elements. Array dimensions usually begin with 0 and have a maximum value of what an `Integer` (`Int32`) data type can hold.

Figure 2-2 shows a representation of a one-dimensional array. It contains five elements, each element a string.

When we declare an array, we usually give it an initial size. In the following two code examples, one declares an array of strings with five initial elements, and the other a two-dimensional array of `Boolean` values (100 values arranged in 10 rows and 10 columns):

```
Dim aryStringArray(5) As String
Dim aryGrid(10, 10) As Boolean
```

Once you declare an array, you can either increase or decrease its size. The `ReDim` statement is used to change the size of an array after it has been declared using `Dim`:

```
ReDim aryStringArray(15) As String
```

When `ReDim` is used in this fashion, all the data contained in the array are lost. However, you can retain the contents of an array you are resizing by supplying the `Preserve` keyword after the `ReDim` command, like this:

```
ReDim Preserve aryStringArray(15) As String
```

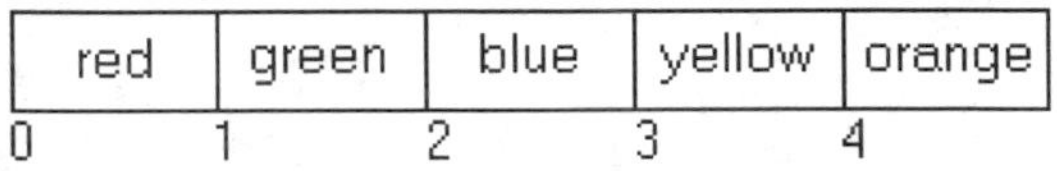

Figure 2-2 One-dimensional array with five elements

You can resize any dimension of an array. However, you can use the `Preserve` keyword only on the last dimension of the array.

You may not always know the size of an array, but you can determine it by using the `UBound()` function:

```
lngArraySize = UBound(aryMyArray)
```

You can also initialize the contents of an array in your code at the time the array is declared. Here's how it's done:

```
Dim aryStringArray() As String = {"ff", "aa", "bb"}
Dim aryIntArray() As Integer = {1, 2, 3}
```

This sample shows how to declare two arrays, one for holding `String` variables and the other for holding `Integer` variables. Notice that there is no explicit size declared for the arrays. This is not allowed by VB.NET when explicit array initialization is used as shown above.

2.3.5 Converting Data Types

Variables can be converted from one data type to another. In many cases, VB.NET performs what's called an *implicit conversion.* An implicit conversion process makes assumptions on behalf of the programmer about how the data should be treated during the conversion. For example, if we wish to convert an `Integer` data type to a `Long` data type, we can assume that we are dealing with numeric data. Consider this code fragment:

```
Dim intA As Integer = 3
Dim lngB As Long

lngB = intA
```

The variable `lngB` now contains the value "3" stored in a `Long` data type. A conversion like this is considered "safe" because a `Long` data type has greater precision than the `Integer` data type. If we did the reverse (converted a `Long` variable to an `Integer` variable), we'd run the risk of losing data since the value that the `Long` variable is holding may be beyond the maximum range of an `Integer` variable. In many cases, VB.NET won't even allow this type of implicit conversion.

Explicit conversion may also be used to convert data types. Explicit conversion involves the use of special VB.NET functions to convert one data type to another.

> **TIP:** Explicit conversions are always preferable to implicit conversions since explicit conversions remove any ambiguities and force VB.NET to make a conversion according to your intentions.

2.3.6 Using Constants

VB.NET uses constants to assign meaningful, easily recognizable names to pieces of data. Unlike variables, the value of a constant cannot be changed once it is defined. VB.NET provides a number of predefined constants to make programming easier. You may also define your own constants throughout your VB.NET code.

The syntax for defining a constant is as follows:

```
Const myConstantName = value As typename
```

Constants can be strings or numbers. The data type must also be specified. Strings must be enclosed in double quotation marks:

```
Const g_strName As String = "Matt"
```

You can also specify date and time values by enclosing a properly formatted date and time within pound signs (#):

```
Const g_dteDDay As Date = #6/4/1944 5:30:00 AM#
```

2.3.7 Arithmetic and Comparison Operators

Arithmetic Operators

All programming languages need the ability to perform arithmetic operations and comparison operations. VB.NET includes all the necessary arithmetic operators, as shown in Table 2-3.

When using arithmetic operators, use a format such as the following, which shows addition:

```
Variable = numericExpression1 + numericExpression2
```

Table 2-3 Arithmetic Operators in VB.NET

Operator	Use
^ operator	Raises a number to the power of an exponent
* operator	Multiplies two numbers
/ operator	Divides two numbers and returns a floating-point result
\ operator	Divides two numbers and returns an integer result
`Mod` operator	Divides two numbers and returns only the remainder
+ operator	Sums two numbers
- operator	Finds the difference between two numbers or indicates the negative value of a numeric expression

All arithmetic operators are binary, meaning that they operate on two expressions. The subtraction operator (–) can also be applied in a unary fashion to negate the value of an expression:

```
Variable = -numericExpression
```

Assignment Operators

There are several forms of assignment operators, as shown in Table 2-4.

Past versions of VB had only one type of assignment operator, the equal sign (=). To perform certain operations, such as incrementing a value, you had to write code such as this:

```
intMyVar = intMyVar + 1
```

Code like this can be overly verbose. VB.NET allows you to shorten this operation to:

```
intMyVar += 1
```

The other assignment operators work similarly, such as the division assignment operator. This line of code divides an `Integer` variable's value by 2:

```
intMyVar /= 2
```

Table 2-4 Assignment Operators in VB.NET

Operator	Use
= operator	Assigns a value to a variable or property
^= operator	Raises the value of a variable to the power of an exponent and assigns the result back to the variable
*= operator	Multiplies the value of a variable by the value of an expression and assigns the result to the variable
/= operator	Divides the value of a variable by the value of an expression and assigns the result to the variable
\= operator	Divides the value of a variable by the value of an expression and assigns the integer result to the variable
+= operator	Adds the value of an expression to the value of a variable and assigns the result to the variable
-= operator	Subtracts the value of an expression from the value of a variable and assigns the result to the variable
&= operator	Concatenates a string expression to a string variable and assigns the result to the variable

Bit-Wise Operators

Many languages allow bit-wise operations. Bit-wise operations compare the bit values of numeric expressions and evaluate them according to the rules of Boolean logic: AND, OR, NOT, and XOR (Exclusive OR). Tables 2-5 through 2-8 present the truth tables for these rules.

Table 2-5 AND Truth Table

Value 1	Value 2	Result
False	False	False
False	True	False
True	False	False
True	True	True

Table 2-6 OR Truth Table

Value 1	Value 2	Result
False	False	False
False	True	True
True	False	True
True	True	True

Table 2-7 NOT Truth Table

Value	Result
False	True
True	False

Table 2-8 XOR Truth Table

Value 1	Value 2	Result
False	False	False
False	True	True
True	False	True
True	True	False

VB.NET includes four different bit-wise operators, as shown in Table 2-9.

Here's a quick example of a bit-wise operation using OR on the numbers 21 and 40:

```
Dim int1 As Integer = 21
Dim int2 As Integer = 40

Console.WriteLine(int1 BitOr int2)
```

The binary representation of 21 is 010101 and 40 is 101000. Performing an OR operation on each bit pair, we get 111101, which is 61 in decimal and the output of the above code.

Table 2-9 Bit-Wise Operators in VB.NET

Bit-Wise Operator	Use
`BitAnd` operator	Performs a logical conjunction on two numeric expressions
`BitNot` operator	Performs a logical negation on a numeric expression
`BitOr` operator	Performs a logical disjunction on two numeric expressions
`BitXor` operator	Performs a logical exclusion on two expressions

Logical Operators

In VB.NET code there is another group of similar Boolean operators called logical operators—`And`, `Or`, `Not`, and `Xor`. Like their counterparts, the bitwise operators, they perform the same Boolean operations. However, instead of performing Boolean operations on the bits themselves, logical operators compare true/false expressions.

For example, suppose we want to take the XOR of two separate Boolean expressions. We can write two such expressions like this:

```
Dim blnVal1 As Boolean = False
Dim blnVal2 As Boolean = True
Console.WriteLine((blnVal1 Or blnVal2) Xor (blnVal1 And blnVal2))
```

This code fragment outputs a value of "true" since the left-hand expression in the boldface code line is true and the right-hand expression is false.

Comparison Operators

Comparison operators test whether or not expressions are equal to, less than, greater than, less than or equal to, or greater than or equal to each other (see Table 2-10). Expressions can hold numeric, string, date/time, and object data.

VB.NET includes two more comparison operators, `Like` and `Is`. These special comparison operators work on strings and objects, respectively. The `Like` operator is especially useful for matching string patterns. Comparing

Table 2-10 Truth Table for Comparison Operators

Operator	True If	False If
< (less than)	expression1 < expression2	expression1 >= expression2
<= (less than or equal to)	expression1 <= expression2	expression1 > expression2
> (greater than)	expression1 > expression2	expression1 <= expression2
>= (greater than or equal to)	expression1 >= expression2	expression1 < expression2
= (equal to)	expression1 = expression2	expression1 <> expression2
<> (not equal to)	expression1 <> expression2	expression1 = expression2

against string patterns has several advantages over simply testing for equality. For example, suppose you are searching through an array of strings to match names that begin with a certain letter combination. In the following example, we'll compare various string values against a string pattern.

```
Dim str1 As String = "Crouch, Matt"
Dim str2 As String = "Crowley, John Doe"
Dim str3 As String = "Crow, Sam"
Dim str4 As String = "Smith, Joe"

Console.WriteLine(str1 Like "Cro*") ' Displays "True"
Console.WriteLine(str2 Like "Cro*") ' Displays "True"
Console.WriteLine(str3 Like "Cro*") ' Displays "True"
Console.WriteLine(str4 Like "Cro*") ' Displays "False"
```

The string pattern used is designed to match strings that begin with "Cro." The asterisk (*) instructs VB.NET to match any number of characters. It's called the *wildcard character*. In addition to matching strings by wildcards, you can also use character ranges and character lists (see Table 2-11).

You can change how string patterns operate with two different options. Two statements, `Option Compare Text` and `Option Compare Binary`, determine whether string comparisons are treated with case sensitivity in mind. If `Option Compare Text` is placed in your code before your string pattern comparisons, VB.NET will disregard case sensitivity and follow the rules

Table 2-11 Pattern-Matching Characters in VB.NET

Symbol	Meaning	Example
?	Matches any single character	`"Cow" Like "C?w"` (true)
*	Matches zero or more characters	`"Matt" Like "M*"` (true)
#	Matches a single numeric character (0–9)	`"317-555-1212" Like "###-###-####"` (true)
`[charlist]`	Matches any single character in a character list	`"A" Like "[A-Z]"` (true)
`[!charlist]`	Matches any single character not in a character list	`"Z" Like "[!A-C]"` (true)

of sorting/comparisons that are applicable to your system locale. `Option Compare Binary` will sort characters according to the binary representation.

> **TECHTALK: SYSTEM LOCALE**
> Windows is a multilingual operating system, which means that several different world languages can be used. Applications you create may be targeted to international markets, so you should add support for local languages. By default, VB.NET uses the system locale that is the default for your installation of Windows. This can be changed in code as well.

While we're on the subject of strings, you should be aware of the very useful concatenation operators. Concatenation takes two strings and combines them into one string. The concatenation operator is the ampersand (&). Thus, concatenation is performed as follows:

```
Dim strFirstName as String = "Matt"
Dim strLastName as String = "Crouch"
Console.Write(strFirstName & " " & strLastName)
```

2.4 Modularizing Your Code—Functions and Subroutines

Functions and subroutines allow logical organization of your program's code. The aim of using functions and subroutines is not only to improve readability of code but also to engineer your code for greater modularity. Typically, functions and subroutines are used to group together code statements that make up a task. For example, calculating the amount to bill a customer for an order of goods requires several steps. The amounts of the items ordered must be totaled, the sales tax calculated, and the shipping and handling charges applied. This involves several different calculations, but the end result is the amount to bill the customer. It would make good design sense to group together the code that performs these tasks. That's the job for procedures and functions.

Using procedures and functions also eliminates a phenomenon called "spaghetti code." Spaghetti code arises when code execution flows from one area of the code to another without regard for organization. Spaghetti code was more of a problem back in the first days of BASIC, when functions and subroutines were not supported. You can still write spaghetti code today, but using functions and subroutines makes this less likely.

2.4.1 Using Functions

A *function* is a group of code statements that are executed and give a result back to the code that invoked the function. To define a function in VB.NET, place any code statements between the `Function` and `End Function` keywords:

```
Function MyFunction() As Integer
   ' Your code statements go here
   '
End Function
```

Each function is referred to by a name; in the example above, the function is called `MyFunction`. As mentioned before, a function returns a result back to the code that invoked the function. VB.NET requires that you designate the data type of that result. In the example, the code `As Integer` designated the result as an `Integer` value.

Most functions need input parameters. You define those parameters by placing their names and types in parentheses following the function name. Here's a function that calculates the area of a triangle:

```
Function TriangleArea(ByVal Base As Double, _
            ByVal Height As Double) As Double

   TriangleArea = 0.5 * Base * Height

End Function
```

To invoke the function, we can write:

```
Dim dblArea As Double

dblArea = TriangleArea(3, 8)
Console.WriteLine(dblArea)
```

Notice the use of the keyword `ByVal` in the function code. This tells the program that the parameter that follows should be treated as *call by value*.

Call by value means that the actual value of the parameter supplied in the invocation of the function is passed into the function. Any updates made to the value passed into the function will be discarded.

Parameters can also be *call by reference*. Call by reference passes the memory location of the variable used for the parameter. To designate a parameter as call by reference, use the `ByRef` keyword before the parameter name. Be sure when you call a function with the call by reference parameter that you supply a variable for the parameter instead of a constant expression. This gives VB.NET a location to hold data for the parameter. Call by reference parameters are useful when you want your function to return more than one value to the invoking code and also for performance reasons when passing objects or structures of large size.

Functions, unlike subroutines, return a value to the caller. You set that value by making an assignment to the function name. In the `TriangleArea` function, we assigned the return value to the area of the triangle (based on the length of the base and height).

2.4.2 Using Subroutines

Sometimes you might not need to return a value from a function. In this case, a subroutine is a good choice. Subroutines provide the same features and are called in the same manner as functions, but they are intended for executing blocks of code when no specific value is needed as output. You define subroutines almost the same way as functions. Here's an example:

```
Sub DisplayHeader()
   Console.WriteLine("Welcome to .NET Web Programming with VB")
   Console.WriteLine("Enjoy your stay!")
End Sub
```

When defining parameters for a subroutine or function, you may find that some parameters are not used in all calls to that subroutine or function. When this is the case, you can designate such parameters as *optional parameters*. To mark a parameter as optional simply supply the `Optional` keyword before `ByRef` or `ByVal`.

```
Function CalculateTotalCharges(ByVal LineItemTotal As Double, _
                    Optional ByVal SalesTax As Double = 0.525) _
                       As Double
   CalculateTotalCharges = LineItemTotal * SalesTax
End Function
```

You'll need to follow a couple of rules when using optional parameters.

1. Optional parameters must specify a default value. The default value is used by the subroutine or function when the caller supplies no value for the parameter. In the example above, the default value specified is 0.525.
2. Parameters defined after an optional parameter must also be defined as optional.

2.5 Controlling Program Flow

An application needs to be able to change its flow of execution based on certain conditions that occur within the application code. VB.NET provides a complete set of control structures for controlling program flow: conditional processing, flow control statements, and loops.

2.5.1 Conditional Processing

Conditional processing tests an expression and executes code based on the value of that expression.

`If . . . Then . . . Else` *Statements*

The first type of conditional processing is the `If . . . Then . . . Else` statement. The general syntax of a `If . . . Then . . . Else` statement is shown below.

```
If expression1 Then
   statements1
ElseIf expression2
   statements2
   . . . more ElseIf statements
Else
   statements3
End If
```

where *expression1* is any expression that evaluates to true or false. If *expression1* is true, then the statements in the *statements1* block are executed and program flow resumes with the statement following the `End If` line. The `ElseIf` and `Else` clauses are optional. If *expression1* is false, the `ElseIf` statement performs an expression check on *expression2*. If *expression2* is true, then the statements in the *statements2* block are executed. If *expression2* is false, then any `ElseIf` statements that follow are each evaluated in turn. If the `Else` clause is supplied, the statements in the *statements3* block are executed if *expression1* is false. Here's a quick example.

```
Dim intA As Integer = 5

If intA > 0 And intA <= 10 Then
   Console.WriteLine("{0} is within range", intA)
Else
   Console.WriteLine("{0} is out of range", intA)
End If
```

Select Case Statements

If you must check the value of an expression against several values and execute code based on each of those choices, then a `Select Case` statement is most appropriate. The `Select Case` statement was designed to eliminate the overly complex code that results from using `ElseIf` statements to conditionally branch on the value of an expression. The general syntax of a `Select Case` statement is shown below.

```
Select Case test-expression
   Case expression1
   .
   . [statements1]
   .
   Case expression2
   .
   . [statements2]
   .
   Case expression n
   .
   . [statements n]
   .
   Case Else
   .
   . [statements]
   .
End Select
```

VB.NET first evaluates *test-expression*. If *test-expression* equals the value of *expression1*, then the statements in the *statements1* block are executed and program flow resumes with the statement following the `End Select` line. If the comparison of *test-expression* and *expression1* is false, then *test-expression* is compared against *expression2*, *expression n*, and so on. If *test-expression* does not match any of the expressions in any of the `Case` clauses, the statements after the `Case Else` line are executed.

> **WARNING:** Although optional, including the `Case Else` clause in your `Select Case` is a good idea because you want your code to catch unexpected values in *test-expression.*

Let's look at an example.

```
Dim strSomebody As String = "Matt"

Select Case strSomebody
Case "Matt"
  Console.WriteLine("It's Matt!")   ' This should be _
                    ' printed to the console
Case "Joe"
  Console.WriteLine("It's Joe!")
Case "David"
  Console.WriteLine("It's David!")
Case Else
  Console.WriteLine("Wassup?! Who are you?")
End Select
```

2.5.2 Flow Control Statements

VB.NET's flow control statements can enable you to branch to different areas in your code unconditionally. There are two such statements: `Exit` and `Goto`.

`Exit` Statements

`Exit` is used to leave a function, subroutine, or loop (see Section 2.5.3). Use `Exit` when you want to stop code execution within these code structures based on some circumstances that happened previously. `Exit` takes the following keywords: `Do`, `For`, `Sub`, `Function`, `Property`, and `Try`. For now, let's look at `Sub` and `Function`. These statements cause code execution to flow out of a subroutine or function, respectively.

Here's `Exit` being used within a subroutine.

```
Sub CheckPassword(ByVal Password As String)
   If Password <> g_strPassword Then
      Exit Sub
   Else
      Console.WriteLine("You guessed the password! Good job!")
   End If
End Sub
```

Goto Statements

The other unconditional branch function is `Goto`. It transfers execution to a labeled line of code. Here's an example of code using `Goto`. Notice the code label `Here`.

```
Sub DisplayHeader()
   Console.WriteLine("Welcome to Web Programming with .NET")

   Goto Here

   Console.WriteLine("Enjoy your stay!")

Here:
   Console.WriteLine("How'd we get here??")
End Sub
```

This function will never display "Enjoy your stay" since the `Goto` statement skips over that code line.

> **WARNING:** If you've been a programmer for a while, you've heard many times that `Goto` is bad. And why is it bad? Because modern programming languages with features like functions, subroutines, and object-oriented programming have virtually eliminated the need for `Goto`. `Goto` also contributes to "spaghetti code," which I warned you about earlier. There are only two situations when the use of `Goto` is acceptable: to write error-handling code and to escape from a deeply nested `If . . . Then` statement or loop structure. Even then, using `Goto` is still not recommended.

2.5.3 Loops

Loops execute a block of code a predetermined number of times or until a particular test condition has been met.

Do . . . Loop Loops

The `Do . . . Loop` comes in two flavors. It can execute statements either until the test expression is true (`Do Until`) or as long as the test expression is true (`Do While`).

Here's an example using `Do While`.

```
Do While EnergyLevel() > 50
   WriteInBook()
   If BookComplete() Then
      Exit Do
   End If
Loop
```

The code in the block is executed while the `EnergyLevel()` function returns a value greater than 50. Notice the use of the `Exit` statement. This causes an early termination of the loop if the `BookComplete()` function returns true. This type of loop is known as a *top-driven loop* since the test expression is checked before code execution.

If you prefer, you can use the following syntax instead. It works the same as the previous example, except that this loop is a *bottom-driven loop*. This means that the code in the loop is executed first, and then the continuation expression is evaluated.

```
Do
   WriteInBook()
   If BookComplete() Then
      Exit Do
   End If
Loop While EnergyLevel() > 50
```

For . . . Next Loops

The `For . . . Next` loop is used to execute a group of statements a specified number of times. A `For . . . Next` loop has a counter variable that increments or decrements with each pass through the loop. The statements inside the loop are executed until the designated value for the counter is reached.

This code will print a string a given number of times.

```
Sub Repeater(ByVal DisplayString As String, _
             ByVal Count As Integer)

   Dim intCounter As Integer

   For intCounter = 1 To Count
      Console.WriteLine(DisplayString)
   Next

End Sub
```

There is an optional keyword for the `For . . . Next` statement called `Step`, which controls how the counter variable is incremented or decremented. If no `Step` is specified in a `For . . . Next` loop, VB.NET assumes that you are incrementing the counter by 1 for each iteration through the loop. By specifying a `Step` clause, you can control the direction and the amount the counter is incremented or decremented. The best way to illustrate this is with an example of code that prints out a sequence of numbers.

```
Sub CounterDemo()

   Dim intCounter As Integer

   For intCounter = 0 To 10 Step 2
      Console.Write(intCounter & " ")
   Next

   Console.WriteLine()

   For intCounter = 10 To 0 Step -1
      Console.Write(intCounter & " ")
   Next

   Console.WriteLine()

End Sub
```

This will output the following:

0 2 4 6 8 10

10 9 8 7 6 5 4 3 2 1 0

Notice that if the value for `Step` is negative, it causes the loop to count backward, and positive values cause the loop to count forward.

For Each . . . Next Loops

Sometimes you may want to step or count through a collection of items, such as the elements in an array. VB.NET provides the `For Each . . . Next` statement for that purpose.

Suppose you have an array of strings and you wish to process each element in the array. The array is declared in the usual manner:

```
Dim aryStringArray() As String = {"Red", "Green", "Blue"}
```

You can write the following code to access each element in the array.

```
Dim strSingleString As String

For Each strSingleString In aryStringArray
   Console.WriteLine("*** " & strSingleString)
Next
```

Notice that a `For Each . . . Next` loop contains an iterator (in the example, `strSingleString`) used to store an array element for each iteration through the loop. Generally, this iterator variable can be of any type, but it is usually set to whatever data type matches the elements in the array.

The `For Each . . . Next` statement is also used for looping through *collections* (see Section 4.3).

While . . . End While Loops

`While . . . End While` is another top-driven loop construct. It works much like the `Do While` loop but its syntax looks like this:

```
While ImNotDone()
   ' do something here
End While
```

The expression following the `While` keyword is evaluated, and if true, the program executes the loop's code block.

2.6 Handling Errors and Exceptions

Catching errors and other extraordinary conditions in code has always been a problem for programmers. Often errors occur and go unnoticed during program execution. When this occurs, subsequent code that executes after the erroneous code will most likely fail, especially if the subsequent code relies on accurate results from the previous code. What's needed is an efficient, straightforward process for identifying errors and handling subsequent code execution gracefully.

2.6.1 Unstructured Error Handling

Old-style error handling often relies on return values from functions. This is a simple and sometimes effective way to handle errors. It works like this: You call a function and check the return value. If the return value corresponds to a defined error result code, you can display an error message or perform whatever action is appropriate for the type of error that occurred. Here's an example.

```
If TotalLineItems() = c_Successful Then
   Success = WriteTotalToDatabase(total)
   If Success Then
      If SendNotificationEmail() Then
         ' Some processing here
      Else
         Success = NotifySysAdmin()
         If Success Then
            ' Error noted. Now What?
         Else
            ' Error not reported!!
         End If
      End If
   Else
      DisplayErrorMessage()
   End If
End If
```

As you can see, handling errors can be quite complex and can complicate your code considerably. What's worse is that many programmers skip placing error-handling code altogether because of the complexity it adds to their code. That's clearly not a good thing since this would make finding bugs a tedious process.

Fortunately, VB.NET provides a few options for error handling. Suppose you want to tell VB.NET to execute a common error-handling routine whenever an error occurs in the code. You want this to be as automatic as possible since you want to avoid the code abomination discussed previously. VB.NET provides a statement called `On Error Goto` for this purpose. Here it is in code.

```
Sub ErrorHandlingDemo()
   On Error Goto Err_handler

   Dim intA As Integer = 3
   Dim intB As Integer = 0
   Dim intResult As Integer

   ' do some work
   TotalLineItems()
   WriteTotalToDatabase(total)
   SendNotificationEmail()

   intResult = intA \ intB
   ' You can't divide by zero, but you knew that . . .
   ' so this code should cause an error

Done:
   Exit Sub

Err_handler:
   '* Handle error
   Console.WriteLine(Err.Description)
   Goto Done
End Sub
```

This code introduces a couple of new VB.NET concepts—code labels and the `Err` object.

Notice we defined two code labels in the example subroutine: `Done` and `Err_handler` (these are arbitrary names that you define). Labels allow us to assign identifiers to individual lines of code. At the top of the subroutine, we placed an `On Error Goto` statement. This instructs VB.NET to jump to the `Err_handler` label whenever a runtime error occurs. In that area we placed error-handling code. After the error is handled, the code unconditionally branches to the `Done` label where the subroutine exits. If no error is encountered in the subroutine, execution will end once the `Exit Sub` command is encountered at the `Done` label.

The `Err` object gives runtime error information. In the example, the error handler simply displays the error description to the console:

```
Attempted to divide by zero.
```

2.6.2 Structured Exception Handling

Programmers who have used C++ frequently use *structured exception handling*, which provides much flexibility and offers greater control over what kinds of exceptions are handled and how. Compare this with error handling in the last section using `On Error Goto`. That type of error handling is *unstructured*. It provides no facility for distinguishing the types of exceptions that occur. This is important since some exceptions raised by the system may not be relevant to the code's functionality and purpose. Conversely, some exceptions, such as system errors, are top priority and should be handled appropriately.

Consider the following example of structured exception handling. We're going to try to divide by zero again. (Maybe it'll work this time?)

```
Sub StructuredErrorHandler()
   Dim intA As Integer = 3
   Dim intB As Integer = 0
   Dim intResult As Integer

   Try
      ' Division is futile...
      intResult = intA \ intB

   Catch e As DivideByZeroException
      Console.WriteLine("EXCEPTION CAUGHT: " & (e.toString))
   Finally
      Console.WriteLine("Division attempt complete.")
   End Try
End Sub
```

When we call the `StructuredErrorHandler()` function, we get the output shown in Figure 2-3.

A structured error handler begins with the `Try` keyword; this is known as the *`Try` block*. Code that you think might cause an error goes there. Following the `Try` block are one or more *`Catch` blocks*. This is where you discriminate the types of errors that occur within the `Try` block. Each catch has an associated exception type, and its declaration follows the `Catch` keyword. The .NET Framework has several types of predefined exceptions. One such exception type, `DivideByZeroException`, is used in the example to catch when the code attempts to divide a value by zero. There is also an exception called `Exception`, which can catch any exception regardless of type. You should place appropriate error-handling code inside each `Catch` block that you

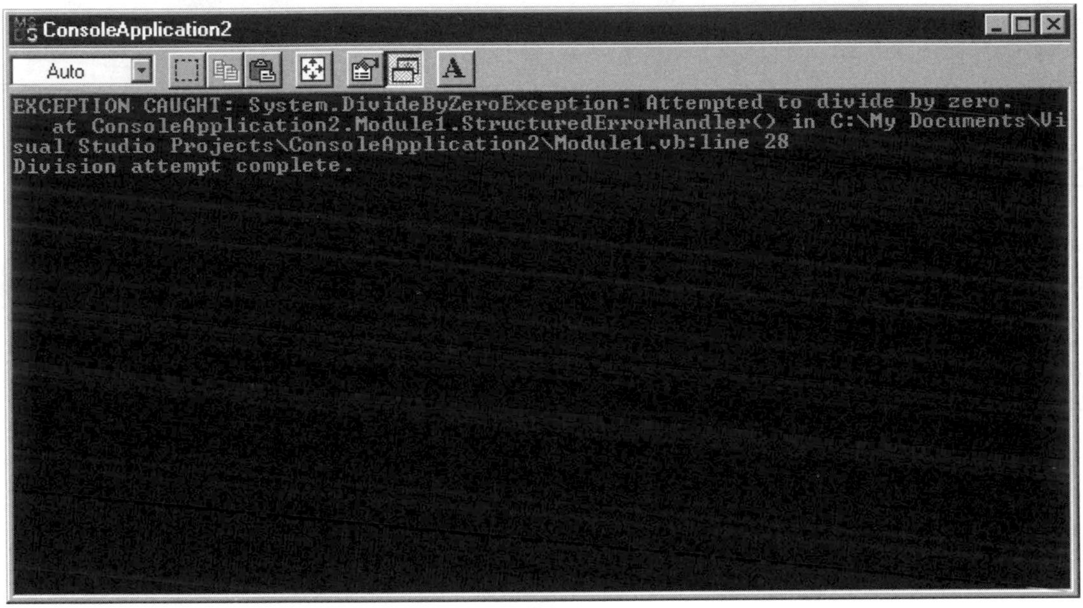

Figure 2-3 Output of the `StructuredErrorHandler()` function

define. Error-handling code typically includes displaying error messages to the user, resetting variables, exiting the function, or other code housekeeping tasks. After all exceptions have been tested and caught, code in the ***`Finally`* block** is executed. Code in this block can contain a success message (if the `Try` code was indeed successful), housekeeping code, or another terminating message.

VB.NET provides the ability for you to throw (that is, produce or raise) your own exceptions. Whenever an application-defined error occurs or some other extraordinary event occurs, you may elect to throw an exception. Here's an example.

```
Dim intTestValue As Integer = 1000

Try
   If intTestValue >= 1000 Then
      Throw New Exception("x is out of range")
   End If
Catch
   Console.WriteLine("Error!")
```

```
Finally
   Console.WriteLine("Executing finally block.")
End Try
```

2.7 Object-Oriented Programming

Once upon a time, programmers worked with programming languages that could not abstract data and processes into code in an easy and logical manner. Those languages did have features such as functions, which allowed programmers to divide a program into several small subprograms. This type of programming is called *structured programming*. It helps organization of code somewhat, but still it is difficult to model real-life processes that apply to corresponding data.

Enter object-oriented programming (OOP). Not surprisingly, the central element to OOP is the *object*. An object is a collection of data and operations performed on the data.

What types of things can be objects? Well, the short answer is, basically, anything. Machines make good examples for objects. For instance, consider a gasoline engine. A gasoline engine has several physical characteristics of importance, such as the number of cylinders, its horsepower, the manufacturer's serial number, and torque. Several actions may be taken on the gasoline engine, such as starting it, stopping it, and increasing or decreasing the throttle. This description defines what the object is and what it does.

2.7.1 Class Basics

Now let's take the object-oriented concept to code. Here's how we can define a gasoline engine as an object in VB.NET.

```
❶ Public Class GasolineEngine

❷    Private m_intHorsepower As Integer
   Private m_strSerialNumber As String
   Private m_intNumberOfCylinders As Integer
   Private m_intRPMs As Integer


   Public Sub New(ByVal intHorse As Integer, _
                  ByVal intCylinders)
      MyBase.New()
```

```
    m_intRPMs = 0
    m_intNumberOfCylinders = intCylinders
End Sub

Public Sub Finalize()

End Sub
❸   Public Sub StartEngine()
    m_intRPMs = 1500
End Sub

Public Sub StopEngine()
    m_intRPMs = 0
End Sub

Public Function AdjustThrottle(ByVal intAmount As Integer) _
                As Boolean
    If m_intRPMs + intAmount > 10000 Then
        AdjustThrottle = False
    Else
        m_intRPMs += intAmount
        AdjustThrottle = True
    End If
End Function

Public ReadOnly Property Tachometer() As Integer
    Get
        Tachometer = m_intRPMs
    End Get
End Property

Public Property Horsepower() As Integer
    Get
        Horsepower = m_intHorsepower
    End Get
    Set(ByVal Value As String)
        m_intHorsepower = Value
    End Set
End Property

❹   Public Property SerialNumber() As String
    Get
        SerialNumber = m_strSerialNumber
    End Get
```

```
      Set(ByVal Value As String)
         m_strSerialNumber = Value
      End Set
   End Property

   Public Property NumberOfCylinders() As Integer
      Get
         NumberOfCylinders = m_intNumberOfCylinders
      End Get
      Set(ByVal Value As String)
         m_intNumberOfCylinders = Value
      End Set
   End Property

End Class
```

This is a simple example of how an entity (in this case, a simple gasoline engine) can be modeled in software with a class declaration. It describes the characteristics of the gasoline engine (tachometer, horsepower, serial number, and number of cylinders), plus the actions that can be applied to the gasoline engine (starting, stopping, and adjusting the throttle). The characteristics become class member variables and the actions become member functions of the class.

Creating classes starts with a class definition. In line ❶, the `Class` keyword starts the class definition. Notice the use of the keyword `Public`. This is an *access modifier* that designates the type of access allowed on the class. `Public` indicates that the class doesn't have any access restrictions in regards to where it can be used in the code (that is, the class can be used anywhere in the current module). There are other access modifiers such as `Private`, `Protected`, and `Friend`; Table 2-12 shows the complete list.

The class block terminates with the `End Class` statement.

Inside the class block are member variable and member function declarations. The example above defines member variables for each of the gasoline engine's characteristics. In line ❷, the horsepower member variable is defined as an `Integer` data type. The `Private` access modifier also appears, making the variable accessible only to code inside the class declaration. The VB.NET compiler will not allow any other attempted access, for example, from the main program code. The code block defines member variables for the other engine characteristics (serial number, number of cylinders, and tachometer) in a similar manner.

Defining member functions is similar to defining regular functions. Line ❸ shows how to define the `StartEngine()` member function. As with the

Table 2-12 VB.NET Class Access Modifiers

Access Modifier	Description
`Private`	Member can be used only from within the class in which the member is defined.
`Public`	Member can be used globally (within the current code module).
`Protected`	Member can be used within the class in which the member is defined plus any derived classes.
`Friend`	Member can be accessed from modules that are outside the class but part of the project/assembly within which the class is defined.
`Protected Friend`	Member has `Protected` and `Friend` access combined.

previous member variable declarations, an access modifier can be applied to the function definition. In the example, the access modifiers for the member functions are `Public`. This means that they can be called from outside the class code.

2.7.2 Class Properties

Class *properties* are similar to class member variables but have added flexibility. Suppose that a user of your class assigns a value to a member variable. Ordinarily there's no way to check, for instance, whether the value assigned is within the variable's acceptable range. Furthermore, once the variable is assigned, additional tasks may need to be performed as a consequence of assigning that variable. It would be nice if VB.NET provided a facility to make implementing this behavior straightforward. Fortunately that's exactly what class properties do. Using properties to access members of a class gives good encapsulation of the data in the class.

Take a look at line ❹, which defines the property for the engine's serial number. A property definition begins with an access modifier and the `Property` keyword, followed by a name for the property and an `As` clause to designate the data type for the property (`String` in the example). Inside the property block are the defined `Get` and `Set` behaviors (each forms a code block of its own). The code for the `Get` block is very simple. Treat the

`Property` keyword just like a function whose value is being returned. The property name, `SerialNumber`, is assigned to the value in the private class member variable `m_strSerialNumber`. The `Set` code is just as simple: assign the private member variable `m_strSerialNumber` to the value that was included in the assignment. The code in the `Set` block is invoked whenever an assignment is made to the property. The value used in the assignment is kept in the special reserved variable called `Value`.

Class methods, member variables, and properties are accessed using the dot (`.`) operator. It follows these general forms:

```
Variable = object.membervariable
Returnvalue = object.functionname()
Object.membervariable = value
```

2.7.3 Constructors and Destructors

Now that the class is defined, how do you actually use it? Using a class requires creating an instance of it and then destroying it when you're done using it. That's the job of constructors and destructors. Let's create a short program using the `GasolineEngine` class to demonstrate how this is done. The following code shows the class example in its entirety.

Code Sample 2-2 Build instructions: vbc /r:system.dll cs2-02.vb

```
Module Module1

   Public Class GasolineEngine

      Private m_intHorsepower As Integer
      Private m_strSerialNumber As String
      Private m_intNumberOfCylinders As Integer
      Private m_intRPMs As Integer


      Public Sub New(ByVal intHorse As Integer, _
                     ByVal intCylinders As Integer)
         MyBase.New()
5           m_intRPMs = 0
         m_intNumberOfCylinders = intCylinders
      End Sub
```

```
Public Sub Finalize()

End Sub

Public Sub StartEngine()
   m_intRPMs = 1500
End Sub

Public Sub StopEngine()
   m_intRPMs = 0
End Sub

Public Function AdjustThrottle(ByVal intAmount As Integer) _
                As Boolean
   If m_intRPMs + intAmount > 10000 Then
      AdjustThrottle = False
   Else
      m_intRPMs += intAmount
      AdjustThrottle = True
   End If
End Function

Public ReadOnly Property Tachometer() As Integer
   Get
      Tachometer = m_intRPMs
   End Get
End Property

Public Property Horsepower() As Integer
   Get
      Horsepower = m_intHorsepower
   End Get
   Set(ByVal Value As String)
      m_intHorsepower = Value
   End Set

End Property

Public Property SerialNumber() As String
   Get
      SerialNumber = m_strSerialNumber
   End Get
   Set(ByVal Value As String)
      m_strSerialNumber = Value
```

```
            End Set
        End Property

        Public Property NumberOfCylinders() As Integer
            Get
                NumberOfCylinders = m_intNumberOfCylinders
            End Get
            Set(ByVal Value As String)
                m_intNumberOfCylinders = Value
            End Set
        End Property

    End Class

    Sub Main()
6       Dim objEngine As GasolineEngine
7       objEngine = New GasolineEngine(100, 4)

        objEngine.SerialNumber = "123"

        objEngine.StartEngine()
        Console.WriteLine("Started Engine No. {0} ", _
                          objEngine.SerialNumber)

        Console.WriteLine(“Speed: {0}”, objEngine.Tachometer)

        objEngine.AdjustThrottle(100)
        Console.WriteLine("Speed: {0}", objEngine.Tachometer)

        objEngine.StopEngine()

        Console.ReadLine()
    End Sub

End Module
```

A *constructor* is a code statement that creates an instance of a new variable. An *instance* of a variable or object is an in-memory and actively used image of an object or variable. All classes must have a constructor in order to be used. A class constructor in VB.NET is simply a subroutine called `New()` that you define anywhere inside the `Class` block.

There's one important requirement for a constructor: the `MyBase.New()` statement. `MyBase` refers to the current class. The `New` portion of the command calls the constructor on the base class. Don't forget to include it so VB.NET can properly instantiate the class. Inside the `New()` subroutine, you can place additional code to execute upon creation of a new class instance. In the `GasolineEngine` class example, we set the initial RPMs of the engine to zero on line ❺.

Lines ❻ and ❼ show how to create the class. First, the `Dim` command declares a new variable that is the type of the class. Then, the `New` command actually creates the new instance of the class. Two parameters are used as part of the constructor: the horsepower and the number of cylinders. These are used to complete the initialization of the class.

Invoking the destructor for the class can occur in two ways.

1. If the class object falls out of scope (for example, a locally declared class in an exiting function or subroutine), the `Finalize()` subroutine is called.
2. The destructor can be called immediately when the class object is set to a special constant called `Nothing`:

```
myClassObject = Nothing
```

> **TIP:** Even though VB.NET features automatic garbage collection (cleanup of unused allocated memory), you can explicitly set class objects to `Nothing` when they are no longer needed. This helps the garbage collector clean up orphaned objects that have a lifetime longer than the garbage collector can detect them.

2.7.4 Inheritance

Inheritance is an important topic in object-oriented programming. Inheritance allows one class to take on the characteristics of another class. The new class, called the *derived class*, assumes the behavior of the *base class* (the original class). Derived classes can also contain new class members, which act as a superset of the base class.

Why and how should inheritance be used? Inheritance enables code reuse. When designing systems, think about common operations that are performed on different classes. If you find lots of operations in common, it's best to make a generic class that covers the functionality of all those classes.

Suppose that we work for a retailer who sells different pieces of furniture, say, chairs and tables. We want to be able to track the merchandise by stock number, color, and price. We also want a function to display that data. We could treat a chair and a table as separate classes with member functions and variables that include the tracking information, but this isn't necessary. Since both a chair and a table are pieces of furniture, they share common characteristics. Stock number, color, and price all describe a piece of furniture.

Inheritance eliminates redundant class definitions. We could begin the furniture program with a generic furniture class, as shown below.

```
Public Class FurniturePiece

   Public StockNumber As String
   Public Color As String
   Public Price As Double

❽  Public Sub New(ByVal strStockNumber As String, _
                 ByVal strColor As String, _
                 ByVal dblPrice As Double)
      StockNumber = strStockNumber
      Color = strColor
      Price = dblPrice
   End Sub

❾  Public Overridable Sub DisplayInfo()

      Console.WriteLine(StockNumber & " " & Color & _
                " " & Price)
   End Sub

End Class
```

This class, `FurniturePiece`, is the base class. The `New` constructor in line ❽ contains initialization code for the common furniture characteristics. We've also defined the member function that displays the furniture data. There's a new keyword in line ❾, `Overridable`, that we'll discuss further in the next section.

Let's define the `Chair` and `Table` classes, using inheritance from the base class.

```
Public Class Chair
   Inherits FurniturePiece

   Public FabricStyle As String
   Public ChairType As String
```

```
    Public Sub New(ByVal strStockNumber As String, _
        ByVal strColor As String, _
        ByVal dblPrice As Double, _
        ByVal strFabricStyle As String, _
        ByVal strChairType As String)

        MyBase.New(strStockNumber, strColor, dblPrice)

        FabricStyle = strFabricStyle
        ChairType = strChairType

    End Sub

❿   Public Overrides Sub DisplayInfo()
        Console.WriteLine("Overridden for Chair: " & _
                StockNumber & "  " & _
                Color & "  " & _
                Price & "   " & _
                FabricStyle & " " & _
                ChairType)
    End Sub
End Class

Public Class Table
    Inherits FurniturePiece
    Public Wood As String
    Public Sub New(ByVal strStockNumber As String, _
            ByVal strColor As String, _
            ByVal dblPrice As Double, _
            ByVal strWood As String)

        MyBase.New(strStockNumber, strColor, dblPrice)

        Wood = strWood
    End Sub

End Class
```

To define a derived class, we placed the `Inherits` keyword in the code line after the `Class` statement. Following `Inherits`, we specified the base class name (`FurniturePiece` in the example). Since a chair and a table have unique characteristics, we defined new class members inside the derived classes. Keep in mind that we also have full access to the base class members in the new derived classes.

2.7.5 Overridden Functions

When derived classes are defined, you'll sometimes want to alter the behavior of class member functions in the base class. Since a derived class represents a new kind of object with its own unique behavior, you need a mechanism to change that behavior, that is, to override it. This brings us to the topic of overridden functions.

The `FurniturePiece` class contains the `DisplayInfo()` function, which we wish to override because we want to display the unique member variables for fabric style and chair type (for the `Chair` class). To designate a function to be overridden, we supplied the `Overridable` keyword as part of the function definition in line ❾. Then, we defined the new `DisplayInfo()` member function, placing the keyword `Overrides` in the function definition in line ❿.

Here's a quick piece of code that demonstrates our creation.

```
Sub Main()
   Dim myChair As Chair
   myChair = New Chair("123", "Brown", 299.99, _
         "Paisley", "Rocker")
   myChair.DisplayInfo()

   Console.ReadLine()
End Sub
```

This code, which calls the overridden `DisplayInfo()` function defined in the `Chair` class, generates the output shown in Figure 2-4

Table 2-13 shows the different class modifiers you can use when you define derived classes using inheritance.

Table 2-14 lists several options available for applying inheritance modifiers to class methods and properties.

> **WARNING:** Derived classes can inherit from only one base class. Attempts to inherit from more than one base class result in a compiler error.

Sometimes you'll need to access base class members inside a derived class. Use the `MyBase` keyword for that. As an example, let's modify the overridden `DisplayInfo()` function of the `Chair` class to include a call to the base class `DisplayInfo()` function.

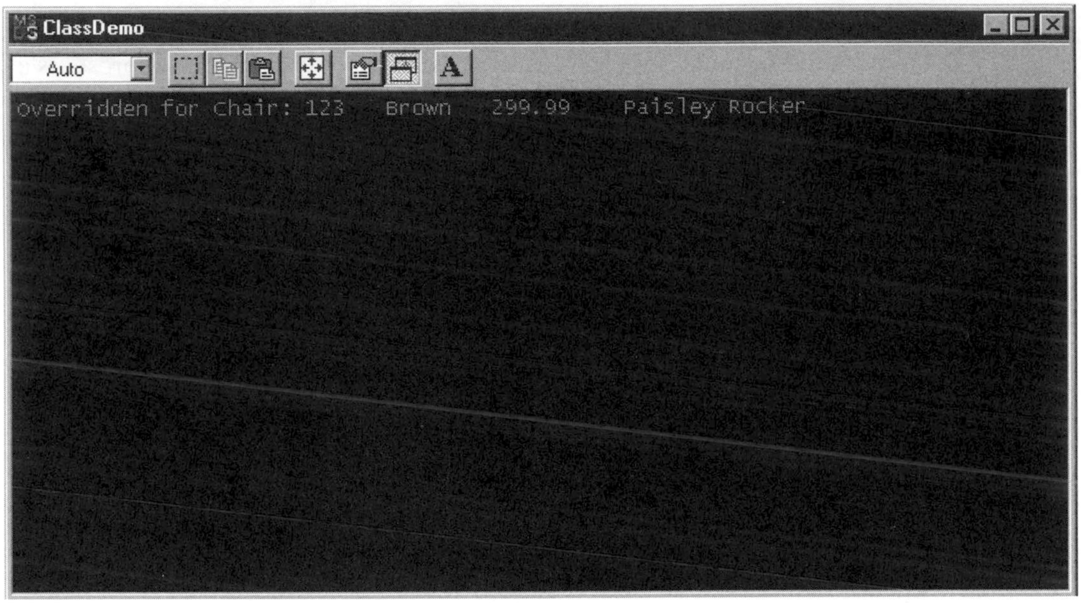

Figure 2-4 Sample output from the furniture class demo

Code Sample 2-3 Build instructions: `vbc /r:system.dll cs2-03.vb`

```
Public Overrides Sub DisplayInfo()

   MyBase.DisplayInfo()

   Console.WriteLine("Overridden for Chair: " & _
      StockNumber & "  " & _
      Color & "  " & _
      Price & "   " & _
      FabricStyle & " " & _
      ChairType)
End Sub
```

Now the test program will display the output shown in Figure 2-5.

Another special keyword used in inheritance is `MyClass`. Use it when you want to refer to the class you are currently "in"—that is, if you wish to call a

Table 2-13 Class Modifiers and Statements Used in Inheritance

Modifier/Statement	Use
`Inherits` *classname*	Designates that the current class will inherit *classname*
`NotInheritable`	Specifies that the current class can't be inherited by another class
`MustInherit`	Specifies that the class cannot be created on its own (using `New`)—a derived class must be created from this class

Table 2-14 Property/Method Modifiers Used in Inheritance

Modifier	Use
`Overridable`	Allows the method or property to be overridden in the derived class
`Overrides`	Designates that the function/property overrides a function/property in the base class
`NotOverridable`	Prevents a method/property defined in the base class from being overridden in a derived class; the default for class properties/methods
`MustOverride`	Designates that the function/property must be overridden and implemented in the derived class and that `MustInherit` must be defined for the class

> **WARNING:** You can't use `MyBase` to access private base class members. You also cannot treat `MyBase` as a real object, which is confusing since it behaves like one as far as syntax goes. It is simply a keyword.

function or subroutine that is inside a class block and you are currently writing code within that block, use the `MyClass` keyword to reference it. Here's how it works in this example class.

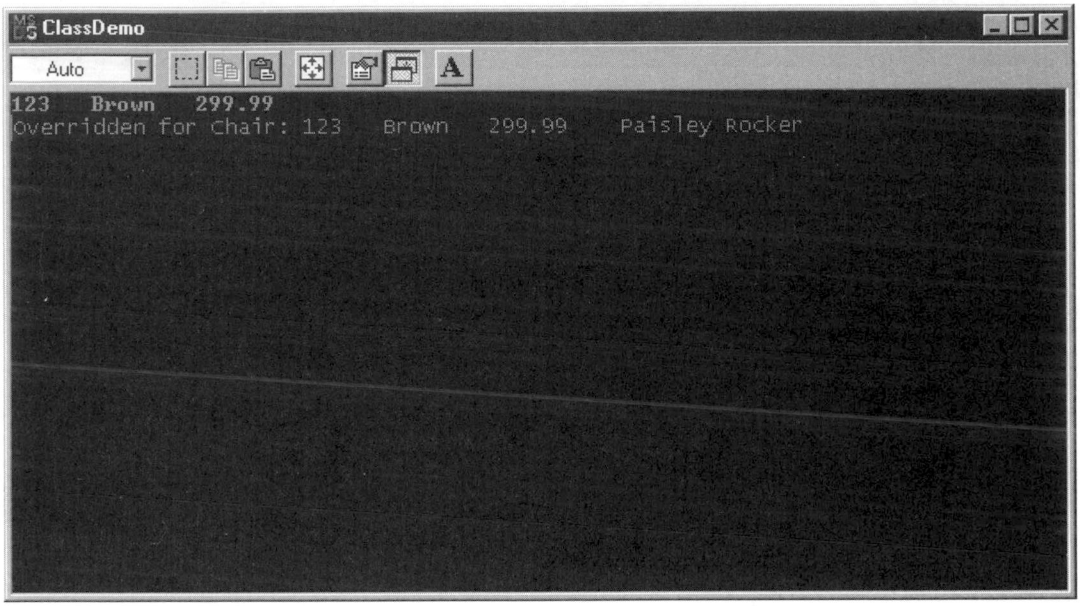

Figure 2-5 Output of the furniture class demo with call to base class `DisplayInfo()` function

```
Public Class Chair
   Inherits FurniturePiece

   Public FabricStyle As String
   Public ChairType As String

   Public Function SomeFunction() As Boolean
      ' Do something here . . .
   End Function

   Public Sub New(ByVal strStockNumber As String, _
      ByVal strColor As String, _
      ByVal dblPrice As Double, _
      ByVal strFabricStyle As String, _
      ByVal strChairType As String)

      MyBase.New(strStockNumber, strColor, dblPrice)
```

```
        FabricStyle = strFabricStyle
        ChairType = strChairType

    End Sub

    Public Overrides Sub DisplayInfo()

        MyBase.DisplayInfo()

        MyClass.SomeFunction()

        Console.WriteLine("Overridden for Chair: " & _
                    StockNumber & "  " & _
                    Color & "  " & _
                    Price & "   " & _
                    FabricStyle & " " & _
                    ChairType)
    End Sub

End Class
```

You can also use the keyword `Me` in place of `MyClass`. These keywords are equivalent, so use whichever form makes most sense to you.

2.7.6 Overloading

Normally, procedure and property names must have a unique name. However, there might be circumstances in which you must create duplicate procedure and property names. This OOP concept is known as *overloading*.

Overloading a function is necessary when you want to have a common name for a procedure or property that operates on different data types. This allows simplification of code since you don't have to write separate procedures with different names for each data type you're handling. Here's an example.

```
Public Overloads Function SomeFunction(ByVal intA As Integer) _
   As Boolean
   ' Do something here with the integer parameter . . .
End Function

Public Overloads Function SomeFunction(ByVal strB As String) _
```

```
   As Boolean
   ' Do something here with the string parameter . . .
End Function
```

When the overloaded function is called, VB.NET invokes the function for the correct parameter type passed to it. Semantically, these functions should perform the same type of operation. In other words, both of these example functions should contain the same application logic.

2.7.7 Polymorphism Overview

Polymorphism means "many forms" and is an important concept in OOP. Imagine that we have defined several different classes that have the same properties and methods. All the things that the classes represent have similar operations and characteristics (for example, trucks, cars, and minivans). For starters, we could define a `Vehicle` as a base class. Then, for each type of vehicle we can define classes that derive from the `Vehicle` class.

Code Sample 2-4 Build instructions: `vbc /r:system.dll cs2-04.vb`

```
Imports System
Module Module1

(11)     Public MustInherit Class Vehicle
         Public MustOverride Function StartEngine() As Boolean
         Public MustOverride Sub StopEngine()
         Public MustOverride Function Accelerate(_
                  ByVal intAmount As Integer) As Boolean
   End Class

   Public Class Truck
(12)        Inherits Vehicle

(13)        Overrides Function StartEngine() As Boolean
          Console.WriteLine("Starting TRUCK engine . . .")
      End Function

      Overrides Sub StopEngine()
         Console.WriteLine("TRUCK engine stopped")
      End Sub

(14)        Overrides Function Accelerate(ByVal intAmount As Integer) _
                          As Boolean
```

```
            Console.WriteLine("Accelerating TRUCK engine by {0}", _
                              intAmount)
            Accelerate = True
        End Function

    End Class

    Public Class Minivan
15      Inherits Vehicle

        Overrides Function StartEngine() As Boolean
            Console.WriteLine("Starting MINIVAN engine . . .")
        End Function

        Overrides Sub StopEngine()
            Console.WriteLine("MINIVAN engine stopped")
        End Sub

        Overrides Function Accelerate(ByVal intAmount As Integer) _
                                      As Boolean
            Console.WriteLine("Accelerating MINIVAN engine by {0}", _
                              intAmount)
            Accelerate = True
        End Function

    End Class

16  Sub DoVehicleOperations(ByVal objVehicle As Vehicle)

        Dim blnDidEngineDied As Boolean

17      objVehicle.StartEngine()
18      blnDidEngineDied = objVehicle.Accelerate(5)
19      objVehicle.StopEngine()

    End Sub

    Sub DoPolymorphismDemo()

        Dim objMinivan As New Minivan()
        Dim objTruck As New Truck()

        Console.WriteLine("VB.NET Polymorphism Demo")
        Console.WriteLine()
```

```
20          DoVehicleOperations(objMinivan)
21          DoVehicleOperations(objTruck)

    End Sub

    Sub Main()
        DoPolymorphismDemo()
        Console.ReadLine()
    End Sub

End Module
```

It's no surprise that we're using inheritance here. It makes sense in this case since a truck and a minivan are both vehicles. But unlike the previous inheritance examples, the base class `Vehicle` provides no implementation of its own, hence the class modifier `MustInherit` in line 11. We define member functions here, but we do not implement them. That's the job of the derived classes, `Truck` and `Minivan`.

Now comes the inheritance part. `Truck` and `Minivan` both inherit from `Vehicle` in the usual way using the `Inherits` keyword in lines 12 and 15. Since the `Vehicle` class is marked as `MustInherit`, we need to make implementations for each function that we define in `Vehicle`. That's a requirement of a class marked as `MustInherit`. We create those implementations in lines 13 and 14. For the sake of this demonstration, the implementations are very simple. The only goal is to provide console output that identifies whether we are dealing with a truck or a minivan.

The subroutine `DoPolymorphismDemo()` does the real work of the demonstration program. We begin by declaring and instantiating new `Truck` and `Minivan` class objects. We then call the `DoVehicleOperations()` function in line 16. Pay close attention to the parameter of this function, `objVehicle`. Its type is `Vehicle`, which is the name of the base class. We then call each method of the `objVehicle` object. Then the magic of polymorphism happens (see lines 17 through 21). Without any logic on our part, VB.NET determines the type of object passed to `DoVehicleOperations()` and calls the appropriate overridden subroutine or function based on the "real" type of `objVehicle`.

The output of the polymorphism demonstration program appears in Figure 2-6.

This type of polymorphism is called *inheritance polymorphism*. This is not the only way you can implement polymorphism in VB.NET. You can also implement polymorphism by using interfaces, a technique covered in the next two sections.

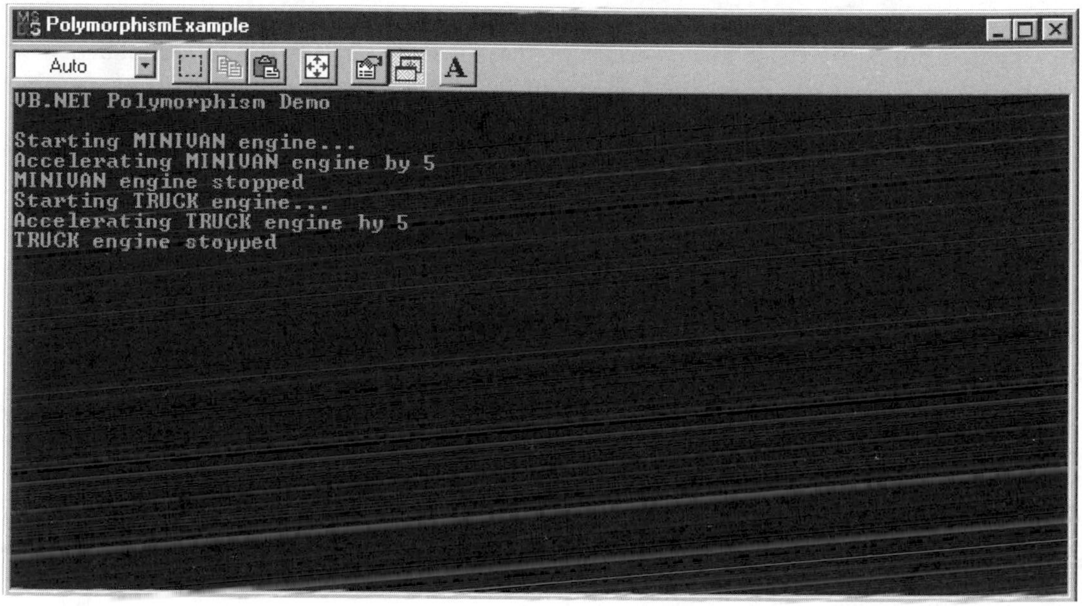

Figure 2-6 Output of the polymorphism demo

2.7.8 Interfaces

Interfaces are similar to classes; they group together members, properties, and methods but do not provide any implementations of those members, properties, and methods. Interfaces allow you to implement a contract that specifies how a programmer can communicate with a class. Interfaces have been a central part of Microsoft's component strategy, in particular the popular Component Object Model (COM). All the design advantages that interfaces brought to COM have been carried over into the .NET Framework.

Interfaces specify a protocol of communication between the implementer and the caller of the class. An interface is a contract that cannot be broken (without consequences, like breaking the application). This may seem limiting, but in reality it is quite powerful.

To illustrate, let's imagine that we designed a class with some particular features. Afterward, the class is coded, tested, and deployed in a production environment. After the customers have used the application for a while, they request that new features be implemented. Also, testing after deployment discovers some bugs due to logic errors. The features and bugs are tied to our class. Our job is to implement the new features and fix the bugs.

This scenario presents a common problem for software that is currently used in the field. In order to successfully deploy a patch that fixes the problems, we need to make certain we don't disable any current functionality. Without interfaces, a code fix requiring a change to the parameters of member functions would cause other code in the application to break since it is expecting the original parameter format. This could quickly make an easy fix a lot of work.

Interfaces alleviate the problem of breaking code in this fashion. If changes to the architecture of the class are required at a later time, a new interface can be added simply. Code that used the original interface to communicate with the class can continue to do so, but newer code can use an entirely different interface to access the same class. The solution to our bug scenario is to simply implement a new interface to the class with the required features.

Interfaces are implemented in VB.NET through use of the `Interface . . . End Interface` notation. This works almost the same as defining classes.

```
Interface IMyClassInterface
   Sub MyProc(ByVal intParam1 As Integer)
   Sub YourProc(ByVal strText1 As String)
   Function AnybodysProc(ByVal intSomeParam As Integer) _
         As Boolean
End Interface


Public Class CMyClass
(22)     Implements IMyClassInterface

(23)Public Sub MyProc(ByVal intParam1 As Integer) _
   Implements IMyClassInterface.MyProc
   Console.WriteLine("Calling MyProc() . . .")
End Sub

(24)Public Sub YourProc(ByVal strText1 As String) _
   Implements IMyClassInterface.YourProc
   Console.WriteLine("Calling YourProc() . . .")
End Sub

(25)Public Function AnybodysProc(ByVal intSomeParam As Integer) _
         As Boolean Implements IMyClassInterface.AnybodysProc
   Console.WriteLine("Calling AnybodysProc() . . .")
   AnybodysProc = True
```

```
End Function

End Class
```

Remember that unlike classes, interfaces provide no implementation for their members. We take care of the implementation step in line ㉒; that is, the class implementation. We use the `Implements` keyword here to signal to VB.NET that we are providing an implementation of the interface `IMyClassInterface`. (Interface names are generally prefixed with the letter *I*, although this is not a requirement.) Lines ㉓, ㉔, and ㉕ show the actual implementation of the interface subroutines and function. Again, notice the use of the `Implements` keyword. The `Implements` keyword is followed by the name of the interface and the subroutine or function name (in the form `Interfacename.SubroutineName`).

Now that we have defined the class and interface, we need to be able to create a new instance of the class and obtain a "handle" to the desired interface (in this case, it's `IMyClassInterface`). We can do that with the code shown below.

```
㉖ Dim objMyClass As IMyClassInterface
Dim blnReturnValue As Boolean

㉗ objMyClass = New CMyClass()

objMyClass.MyProc(1)
objMyClass.YourProc("test")
blnReturnValue = objMyClass.AnybodysProc(1)
```

We start with the `Dim` statement in line ㉖. This creates a variable to hold an object reference to our interface `IMyClassInterface`. We create an instance of `CMyClass` in line ㉗, but instead of assigning the return value of `New` to a variable of type `CMyClass`, we assign it to a variable of type `IMyClassInterface`. This causes VB.NET to use the interface we defined rather than the default one provided by `CMyClass`.

Now let's go back to the code modification scenario we discussed previously. We want to define an alternative interface to our class to allow client software (program code that uses the class) to use either interface depending on design requirements. We can define an alternative interface as shown below.

```
Interface IMyAlternativeClassInterface
   Inherits IMyClassInterface
```

```
   Sub MyAltSub()
End Interface
```

We want to construct our new interface, `IMyAlternativeClassInterface`, so that it has the same functionality as our original interface, `IMyClassInterface`. This is simple because VB.NET allows us to inherit from an existing interface in the same way that we create derived classes (that is, by using the `Inherits` keyword). Our new interface includes one new subroutine called `MyAltSub()`, which is included in the `Interface` code block.

We need to make a small change to the `Class` statement to tell `CMyClass` about the new interface. We add the new interface to the `Implements` statement.

```
Public Class CMyClass
   Implements IMyClassInterface, IMyAlternativeClassInterface
```

> **TIP:** The `Implements` statement can take any number of class names or interface names. Each one is followed by a comma (,).

Then we add the implementation of the new function, `MyAltSub()`, to the class.

```
Public Sub MyAltSub() _
   Implements IMyAlternativeClassInterface.MyAltSub
   Console.WriteLine("Calling MyAltSub() . . .")
End Sub
```

Now we can reference the new interface and call the new subroutines. Since the new interface inherited from `IMyClassInterface`, we can still call all of the subroutines and functions from that interface.

```
(28) Dim objMyClass As IMyAlternativeClassInterface
Dim blnReturnValue As Boolean

objMyClass = New CMyClass()

(29) objMyClass.MyAltSub()
objMyClass.MyProc(1)
```

```
objMyClass.YourProc("test")
blnReturnValue = objMyClass.AnybodysProc(1)

Console.ReadLine()
```

We change the `Dim` statement to declare `objMyClass` as the interface `IMyAlternativeClassInterface` in line ㉘. Then we simply add a call to `objMyClass.MyAltSub()` in line ㉙ to invoke the subroutine.

2.7.9 Implementing Polymorphism by Using Interfaces

Let's return to the topic of polymorphism. As mentioned earlier, there are two ways to implement polymorphism. We explored how we can use inheritance principles to treat classes with a common base class the same way. By using interfaces, we can implement inheritance in much the same way. Not surprisingly, this is called *interfaced-based inheritance*. The objective is to have two classes that are unrelated by inheritance yet share some common behavior. This is particularly important since we are restricted to using single inheritance in VB.NET.

To implement polymorphism via interfaces, we define an interface and implement it in different classes. As an example, suppose we're programming a game in which players can use two kinds of weapons: a machine gun and a rocket launcher. Players want, of course, to be able to fire the weapons and reload them when ammunition has been exhausted. Our implementation starts with an interface that contains two functions called `Fire()` and `Reload()`, plus a property for checking how much ammunition remains. We define the interface as follows.

```
Interface IGameWeapon
   ReadOnly Property NumOfRounds() As Double
   Function Fire(ByVal TargetLocationX As Double, _
                 ByVal TargetLocationY As Double, _
                 ByVal TargetLocationZ As Double) _
                 As Boolean
   Sub Reload(ByVal Rounds As Integer)
End Interface
```

We provide an implementation of the machine gun and rocket launcher using two classes, `CMachineGun` and `CRocketLauncher`, respectively. In the code below, notice the use of the `Implements` keyword followed by the interface name and function name in lines ㉚, ㉛, and ㉜. This signals VB.NET that we are providing an implementation for the named interface and function.

```
Public Class CMachineGun
   Implements IGameWeapon

   Private m_intMagazine As Integer

   ReadOnly Property NumOfRounds() As Double _
30          Implements IGameWeapon.NumOfRounds
      Get
         NumOfRounds = m_intMagazine
      End Get
   End Property

   Public Function Fire(ByVal TargetLocationX As Double, _
                    ByVal TargetLocationY As Double, _
                    ByVal TargetLocationZ As Double) _
31                    As Boolean Implements IGameWeapon.Fire

      Dim rndRandomGen As New Random()
      Dim intRndNumber As Integer

      If m_intMagazine > 1 Then
         m_intMagazine -= 1
         Fire = True
      Else
         Console.WriteLine("Out of ammo!")
         Fire = False
      End If

      intRndNumber = rndRandomGen.Next(1, 10)
      Console.Write("{0} ", intRndNumber)
      If intRndNumber <= 5 Then
         Console.WriteLine("Machine gun: Target missed!")
      End If

      If intRndNumber >= 6 Then
         Console.WriteLine("Machine gun: Target hit!")
      End If
   End Function

   Public Sub Reload(ByVal Rounds As Integer) _
32                Implements IGameWeapon.Reload
      If Rounds + m_intMagazine > 50 Then
         Console.WriteLine("Machine gun magazine at capacity")
      Else
```

```
            m_intMagazine += Rounds
         End If

      End Sub

End Class


Public Class CRocketLauncher
   Implements IGameWeapon

   Private m_intTubeCount As Integer

   ReadOnly Property NumOfRounds() As Double _
      Implements IGameWeapon.NumOfRounds
      Get
         NumOfRounds = m_intTubeCount
      End Get
   End Property

   Public Function Fire(ByVal TargetLocationX As Double, _
                  ByVal TargetLocationY As Double, _
                  ByVal TargetLocationZ As Double) _
                  As Boolean Implements IGameWeapon.Fire
      Dim rndRandomGen As New Random()
      Dim intRndNumber As Integer

      If m_intTubeCount > 1 Then
         m_intTubeCount -= 1
         Fire = True
      Else
         Console.WriteLine("Out of rockets!")
         Fire = False
      End If

      intRndNumber = rndRandomGen.Next(0, 10)

      Console.Write("{0} ", intRndNumber)

      If intRndNumber <= 3 Then
         Console.WriteLine("Rocket: Target missed!")
      End If

      If intRndNumber >= 4 Then
```

```
            Console.WriteLine("Rocket: Target hit!")
        End If

    End Function

    Public Sub Reload(ByVal Rounds As Integer) _
        Implements IGameWeapon.Reload

        If Rounds + m_intTubeCount > 5 Then
            Console.WriteLine("No more rockets can be loaded")
        Else
            m_intTubeCount += Rounds
        End If

    End Sub

End Class
```

I'll skip explaining the details of the implementation of `CMachineGun` and `CRocketLauncher` since they are straightforward. Let's move on to some sample code that uses our classes.

Code Sample 2-5 Build instructions: `vbc /r:system.dll cs2-05.vb`

```
Sub ReloadAndAttack(ByVal Weapon As IGameWeapon)

    Weapon.Reload(5)
    If Not Weapon.Fire(1, 2, 3) Then
        Console.WriteLine("Run for cover!")
    End If

End Sub

Sub Main()
    Dim objMachineGun As New CMachineGun()
    Dim objRocketLauncher As New CRocketLauncher()

    ReloadAndAttack(objMachineGun)
    ReloadAndAttack(objRocketLauncher)
    Console.ReadLine()
End Sub
```

Figure 2-7 Output of interface polymorphism demo

In the main subroutine, we create two objects, one for each weapon. The subroutine `ReloadAndAttack()` demonstrates the polymorphism of interfaces. The subroutine takes a single parameter, `Weapon`, which is of type `IGameWeapon` (the interface we defined). We call `ReloadAndAttack()` with both `objMachineGun` and `objRocketLauncher`. Remember that this is legal since both classes implement the `IGameWeapon` interface.

Inside the `ReloadAndAttack()` function, we call `Fire()` and `Reload()` for `Weapon`. VB.NET polymorphism ensures that the correct implementations for these procedures are called (see Figure 2-7).

2.8 Multithreaded Programming

So far the programs we have written start execution at some predefined starting point (such as the `Main()` subroutine), execute some statements, call some functions, and exit. Execution follows a single path, commonly known as a *thread*. Applications that use a single thread are known as *single-threaded* applications.

Many applications, however, are not single-threaded. In some cases, single-threaded applications are not particularly efficient. Applications typically involve several tasks, for example, handling user input, sorting large data lists, sending data to other applications, and so on. A single-threaded application performing each of these tasks would have to execute each one sequentially, even if the tasks are totally independent of each other. Imagine another scenario: a hypothetical single-threaded Web server. Each request for a document from the Web server would have to be completely fulfilled before another request could be processed. This clearly can't work; Web servers typically need to handle hundreds of simultaneous requests. The solution to maximizing hardware resources for CPU-intensive applications is to make the applications *multithreaded*. In the .NET Framework, these applications are referred to as *free-threaded*.

> **WARNING:** Multithreading is an advanced programming topic and is not for the faint of heart. Although we discuss some multithreading concepts here, they are not essential to our discussions of forthcoming topics, such as Web Forms. Many beginning programmers may become frustrated when faced with difficulties that come with multithreaded programming, such as debugging and synchronization issues.

VB.NET and the .NET Framework include provisions for making free-threaded applications. The .NET Framework is massive and contains hundreds of class objects that perform many functions. For now, we will consider a particular class, `System.Threading.Thread`, which is used to "spawn," or create, a new thread.

To understand the concept of free-threading, it helps to see a visual example of how code follows an execution path when it is running on a separate thread. Let's create a program with two threads. Each thread prints out a message that identifies itself 200 times. This is handled in two separate functions, `ThreadOneProc()` and `ThreadTwoProc()`, which execute simultaneously.

Code Sample 2-6 Build instructions: `vbc /r:system.dll cs2-06.vb`

```
Imports System
Module Module1

   Public Sub ThreadOneProc()
      Dim intCount As Integer
```

```
        For intCount = 1 To 200
            Console.WriteLine("This is thread ONE")
        Next
    End Sub

    Public Sub ThreadTwoProc()
        Dim intCount As Integer

        For intCount = 1 To 200
            Console.WriteLine("This is thread TWO")
        Next
    End Sub

    Sub Main()
33          Dim thd1 As New _
            System.Threading.Thread(AddressOf ThreadOneProc)

34          Dim thd2 As New _
            System.Threading.Thread(AddressOf ThreadTwoProc)

35          thd1.Start()
36          thd2.Start()

    End Sub

End Module
```

Try running this program. The resulting output should be illuminating (your output may vary from that shown in Figure 2-8).

When the program runs, notice that sometimes messages repeat and sometimes they alternate between one and the other. This is how free-threaded applications work. The operating system is allocating processor time for each thread and switching quickly between each thread. Each thread ends when 200 iterations through the `For . . . Next` loop have occurred. At that point, the main program (main thread) ends, and the program exits.

Creating and starting a thread takes two steps: declaring a thread and calling the `Start()` function. The two `Dim` statements in lines 33 and 34 create two thread objects. The constructor for the thread object is the address in memory of the procedure to run for the thread. We use the VB.NET statement `AddressOf` to determine the address in memory for a procedure.

Figure 2-8 Output of simple free-threading example

> **WARNING:** Procedures you are running in a separate thread cannot contain any parameters. Passing of data in and out of the thread must be done using global variables (which is not recommended) or class members.

Calling the `Start()` method of the thread object, as shown in lines ㉟ and ㊱, starts execution of the thread. The current thread (in this case, the main program) continues and starts the second thread. When both threads have finished, the program exits.

2.8.1 Thread Synchronization

The first threading example illustrates how simultaneous execution of procedures can occur by using threads. However, one of the problems with free-threaded applications is being able to coordinate threads that operate on the same set of data. Sometimes a program must wait until termination of a thread so the other thread will have accurate data that was processed by the first thread. Coordinating threads is called *thread synchronization*.

Generally two methods are used to synchronize threads in VB.NET: by using the `IsAlive()` function of `System.Threading.Thread` or by using *events*. Let's start by looking at `IsAlive()`. (We'll explore events in the next section.)

In this example, we will create a large array of random numbers and sort them in ascending order using a sort procedure. If you were ever a computer science student, you most certainly have been exposed to the *bubble sort* algorithm. The bubble sort works by visiting each element in the array and comparing its value to the adjacent element's value. If one is greater than (or less than, depending on how the elements are to be sorted) the other, the values are swapped. This process repeats throughout the array until all the elements are ordered correctly. There are many sort algorithms, but the bubble sort is the easiest to understand. It is also the slowest. Choosing bubble sort enables the sample program to run slowly enough so we can observe its behavior easily while the program runs.

The code example below contains a class named `CNumberList`. This class contains an array of integers to sort and two member subroutines called `Sort()` and `PrintList()`, which are self-explanatory. The constructor for `CNumberList` takes a parameter for the size of the array to create. The array is then filled with random numbers in the range of 0 to 10,000. The program creates a large array so the program will run long enough for us to observe its execution in the console window.

Code Sample 2-7 Build instructions: `vbc /r:system.dll cs2-07.vb`

```
Imports System
Imports Microsoft.VisualBasic

Module Module1
   Dim objList As CNumberList

   Public Class CNumberList
      Private m_aryNumbers() As Integer

      Public Sub New(Optional ByVal intSize As Integer = 10)
         Dim intCounter As Integer
         Dim intRandomNumber As Integer
         Dim objRandom As New System.Random()
```

```
      ReDim m_aryNumbers(intSize + 1)

      For intCounter = 0 To intSize
         m_aryNumbers(intCounter) = _
            objRandom.Next(0, 10000)
      Next
   End Sub

   Public Sub Sort()
      Dim intCounter As Integer
      Dim intTmpValue As Integer
      Dim intCounter2 As Integer

      Dim blnSorted As Boolean = False

      For intCounter2 = 1 To UBound(m_aryNumbers)
         For intCounter = 0 To UBound(m_aryNumbers) - 1
            If m_aryNumbers(intCounter) > _
                  m_aryNumbers(intCounter + 1) Then
               intTmpValue = m_aryNumbers(intCounter)
               m_aryNumbers(intCounter) = _
                  m_aryNumbers(intCounter + 1)
               m_aryNumbers(intCounter + 1) = _
                  intTmpValue
            End If

         Next
      Next

   End Sub

   Public Sub PrintList()
      Dim intCounter As Integer

      For intCounter = 0 To UBound(m_aryNumbers)
         Console.WriteLine(m_aryNumbers(intCounter))
      Next

   End Sub
End Class

Sub Main()

37          objList = New CNumberList(1500)
```

```
(38)        Dim thdSortThread As New _
            System.Threading.Thread(AddressOf objList.Sort)

        Console.WriteLine("Starting sort . . .")

(39)        thdSortThread.Start()
(40)        Do While thdSortThread.IsAlive()
            Console.Write(".")
        Loop

        objList.PrintList()

    End Sub

End Module
```

The main program creates a new `CNumberList` object with 1,500 integers in line (37). Then, a thread is created for the `Sort()` function in line (38). In line (39), the thread is started. Before we call the `PrintList()` method to display the sorted list, we need to wait until the `Sort()` function/thread is finished sorting the numbers. So, we make a `Do . . . While` loop in line (40) that continually checks to see if the sort thread is still running. If the thread is still alive, the program will output a period (.) to the console to visually indicate that the sort is running. On termination of the thread, the `Do . . . While` loop exits and the sorted array is displayed. In effect, we've synchronized the sort thread with the main thread of the application.

Using `IsAlive()` is easy, but it is not very efficient. A better way to synchronize threads is to use events.

2.8.2 Events and Thread Synchronization

An event is a type of signal that you can attach to a class. That signal can be activated when some set of circumstances happens inside the class. The event can then be handled by the host (that is, the code that created the class object). For example, an event may be fired when data changes to a particular value inside the class.

An event is simple to define. Just put some code like this inside your class:

```
Public Event SomethingHappened()
```

When you want to raise an event (and subsequently notify the hosting code of the event), simply call the`RaiseEvent` statement:

```
RaiseEvent SomethingHappened()
```

A class that contains events should be declared in the following way:

```
Dim WithEvents objMyClass As CMyClassThatHasEvents
```

`WithEvents` tells VB.NET that you wish to use the events defined by the class. Using `Dim WithEvents` works only on nonlocal declarations. In other words, declarations like this need to be made at the global level or at the module level.

Let's modify the previous example to synchronize the threads by using events. The boldface lines indicate the changes made to the previous code.

Code Sample 2-8 Build instructions: `vbc /r:system.dll cs2-08.vb`

```
Imports System
Imports Microsoft.VisualBasic

Module Module1
   Dim WithEvents objList As CNumberList

   Public Class CNumberList
      Private m_aryNumbers() As Integer

41    Public Event Progress(ByVal intPercentDone As Integer)
      Public Event Done()

      Public Sub New(Optional ByVal intSize As Integer = 10)
         Dim intCounter As Integer
         Dim intRandomNumber As Integer
         Dim objRandom As New System.Random()

         ReDim m_aryNumbers(intSize + 1)

         For intCounter = 0 To intSize
            m_aryNumbers(intCounter) = _
               objRandom.Next(0, 10000)
```

```
            Next
        End Sub

        Public Sub Sort()
            Dim intCounter As Integer
            Dim intTmpValue As Integer
            Dim intCounter2 As Integer

            Dim blnSorted As Boolean = False

            For intCounter2 = 1 To UBound(m_aryNumbers)
                For intCounter = 0 To UBound(m_aryNumbers) - 1
                    If m_aryNumbers(intCounter) > _
                            m_aryNumbers(intCounter + 1) Then
                        intTmpValue = m_aryNumbers(intCounter)
                        m_aryNumbers(intCounter) = _
                            m_aryNumbers(intCounter + 1)
                        m_aryNumbers(intCounter + 1) = _
                            intTmpValue
                    End If

                Next
                RaiseEvent Progress(CInt(intCounter2 / _
                            UBound(m_aryNumbers) * 100))
            Next
          RaiseEvent Done()

        End Sub

        Public Sub PrintList()
            Dim intCounter As Integer

            For intCounter = 0 To UBound(m_aryNumbers)
                Console.WriteLine(m_aryNumbers(intCounter))
            Next

        End Sub
    End Class

    Sub Main()

        objList = New CNumberList(15000)
```

```
        Dim thdSortThread As New _
           System.Threading.Thread(AddressOf objList.Sort)

        Console.WriteLine(_
           "Starting sort . . . Press <enter> to cancel")
        Console.WriteLine("Percent Complete:")
        thdSortThread.Start()

        Console.ReadLine()
        Console.WriteLine("Ending . . .")
        thdSortThread.Abort()

    End Sub

(42) Public Sub objList_Progress(ByVal intPercentDone As Integer)  _
                         Handles objList.Progress
        Dim chrBS As New Char()
        chrBS = Chr(8)

        Console.Write(chrBS & chrBS & chrBS & intPercentDone)
    End Sub

(43) Public Sub objList_Done() Handles objList.Done
        Console.WriteLine()
        Console.WriteLine("Sort Complete! Printing list . . .")
        objList.PrintList()
    End Sub
End Module
```

Beginning at line (41), we define two events for our class: `Progress()` and `Done()`. `Progress()` is fired for every complete pass through the number array loop. We use `Progress()` as a way to provide visual feedback about the completeness of the sort. Events can also contain parameters. `Progress()` contains one integer parameter, `intPercentDone`, which we use to tell the hosting code what percentage of the sort is complete. The `Done()` event signals the end of the sort operation (and the end of thread execution).

Events have corresponding event-handling procedures, as shown in lines (42) and (43). These procedures, which reside in the hosting code, are called when `RaiseEvent` is invoked for the event. The `Handles` keyword tells VB.NET that the procedure is to be used as an event handler for the given object procedure.

The modified example contains two new features, thanks to the convenience that free-threading and events provide.

1. The user can cancel a sort operation already in progress by hitting the Enter key. After the sort thread is started, main execution continues on to a call to `Console.ReadLine()` in the main thread. The program waits for the user to hit the Enter key. If this happens, the program calls `thdSortThread.Abort()` to immediately terminate execution of the sort thread.
2. The user sees a visual indicator about the progression of the sort. The `Progress()` event is raised periodically to indicate progression of the sort operation. Finally, when the `Done()` event is raised, the user knows that the sort thread has ended and can print out the sorted list.

Figure 2-9 shows the program in action.

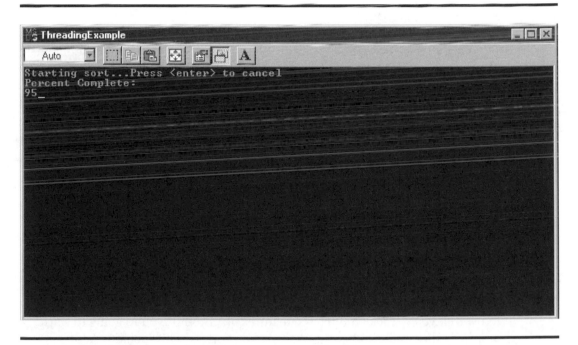

Figure 2-9 Output from the event-based thread synchronization program

2.9 Summary

Take a deep breath. We covered quite a lot in this VB.NET crash course, including basic concepts about:

- The role of VB.NET as part of Microsoft VS.NET and as the .NET-enabled version of Visual Basic, a language with a rich history on the Windows platform
- The VS.NET Integrated Development Environment
- Variables and data types
- Conditional processing, looping, and flow control statements
- Object-oriented programming techniques
- Simple free-threading concepts

As a result, by working through this chapter you have learned how to:

- Create a new project, enter code, compile code, and run sample programs
- Make console applications
- Use the `Console.WriteLine()` and `Console.ReadLine()` statements to display output to and get keyboard input from users, respectively
- Write procedures (functions and subroutines) to modularize your code and make it more readable
- Convert variables from one type to another
- Control program flow
- Use classes, inheritance, overloading, polymorphism, interfaces, and free-threading

Congratulations! You're ready to move on to the next step in Web programming with VB.NET.

2.10 What's Ahead

Now that you've tackled the basic features of VB.NET, you're going to start applying those skills to making Web-based projects. This includes Active Server Pages.NET (ASP.NET) Web pages, which we'll cover in Chapter 3. Later in the book, you'll learn how to make .NET Framework Class Libraries (Chapter 4) and .NET Web Services (Chapter 6) using VB.NET.

Further Reading

- *Visual Basic Language Reference* (.NET Framework SDK documentation): *Visual Basic Language Reference* provides a detailed reference for the Visual Basic language.
- *Design Guidelines for Class Library Developers* (.NET Framework SDK documentation): *Design Guidelines* provides suggestions for good programming practices to follow when developing classes.

CHAPTER 3

Working with ASP.NET

ASP.NET is the framework you'll use to build Web applications for the .NET Framework. One of the design goals of ASP.NET was to bring to the Web the same rich application features (as close as possible) used in traditional desktop applications. ASP.NET achieves this by providing a flexible development methodology that allows the use of any .NET-capable language to code dynamic Web pages. ASP.NET also frees up the Web application developer from many mundane programming tasks by providing built-in code objects for many common Web-programming tasks.

3.1 The Features of ASP.NET

ASP.NET provides a programming model that contains many features to support rich application functionality. In this chapter, you'll learn how you can apply these features to your own Web applications.

Compatibility with Any .NET Language

Many Web application development environments don't allow for many of the features that traditional programming languages provide, which is why one of the primary design goals of ASP.NET was to make Web applications as rich in features as their desktop counterparts.

Compiled Code

Many Web application development environments don't provide an environment that takes advantage of features available to desktop applications, primarily because Web development languages are generally interpreted. Prior versions of ASP are an example of this. ASP in its previous incarnations consisted of an interpreted environment based on ActiveX scripting languages such as VBScript and JScript. Interpreted languages have a distinct disadvantage—they are subject to the inefficiency of code interpretation each time the code is executed (that is, every time the page is requested from the Web server).

ASP.NET addresses the inefficiency of interpreted code. When a user first requests a Web page with ASP.NET code, ASP.NET compiles the code embedded in the Web page. This not only provides great speed enhancement but also allows for other features such as strong variable typing and early binding to objects. In addition, ASP.NET applications can cache data for faster delivery through special Application Programmer's Interfaces.

Easy Application Deployment

Many Web applications are tightly integrated with the Web server, which makes deployment and maintenance of the application difficult. Before the development of ASP.NET, replacing Web application components sometimes required a restart of the Web server, and some components (like COM objects) needed to be registered with the operating system in order to be used. ASP.NET addresses these issues by removing those prohibitive requirements and making deployment and maintenance as simple as copying files to the appropriate directories on the server. In some cases, no further configuration is required. ASP.NET also solves the problem of swapping out new components or pages, not by locking them, as other systems do, but by making copies of the existing pages and components for the pending requests. Then, after all pending requests have been fulfilled, the new pages and components become active.

Simple Application Configuration

Many Web applications have distinctive application settings that control various parts of the Web application, such as page request time-outs. Unlike many Web application development environments (including prior versions of ASP), ASP.NET stores these settings in human-readable XML configuration files. These XML configuration files are placed in common directories, making them easy for administrators to locate. New settings can be added easily to XML-based files, and the settings are stored in a hierarchical fashion for easy referencing.

Advanced Session and Application State Management

Applications, be they desktop-based or Web-based, need to retain information about current conditions in the application. Given that the Web client/Web server model is inherently stateless (no data are saved between requests for pages), it becomes the job of the application environment to track the application state. ASP.NET has several offerings for maintaining application state, and some are even compatible with older versions of ASP. And, of course, ASP.NET offers advanced state management that improves on the legacy methods of state management.

Integrated Security Features

Security is an important concern in Web programming. ASP.NET leverages the security features of server versions of Windows (.NET/XP/2000/NT), which enable you to implement security in a variety of ways. Users can be authenticated using traditional methods provided by IIS like BASIC and Windows (formerly known as challenge/response authentication) as well as newer methods like Microsoft Passport. Protecting the site's files can be done by assigning user and group access to the individual files and directories. In addition, authorized users and groups can be stored in an XML file.

Direct Low-Level HTTP Support

Modern Web applications usually consist of HTML and executable code interspersed within the HTML. But Web applications are sometimes supplemented by lower-level programs that interact with the Web server through a tight integration. Typically, these programs modify the default behavior governing how requests for documents are handled by the Web server. In the past, such low-level programs needed to be written in low-level languages such as C++. But with the advent of ASP.NET, these programs can now be written as normal ASP.NET pages in languages like VB.NET.

Backward Compatibility with ASP

If you have experience with prior versions of ASP, you'll be glad to know that ASP.NET works quite nicely with regular ASP. In fact, applications written in classic ASP can run alongside ASP.NET applications without any ill effects. This makes upgrading and transitioning your existing ASP code base to ASP.NET less difficult by allowing a gradual phasing out of old ASP application code.

3.2 The Anatomy of ASP.NET Pages

3.2.1 The Code Structure of ASP.NET

ASP.NET pages begin with a plain-text file that has an `.aspx` extension. IIS uses this extension to identify particular files that contain executable code and should be processed as ASP.NET pages (as opposed to plain HTML files or other file types).

The contents of the `.aspx` file are called the *page*. The page consists of visual markup (HTML) and application logic (executable code written in a .NET language). ASP.NET also has the ability to store application code in separate files rather than grouping it with the HTML. For organizational and structural reasons, placing application code in a separate file is usually a good idea. This concept is called *code behind*, and we'll see how it works in just a moment.

The page I referred to earlier is actually an ASP.NET class. When an ASP.NET class is compiled, a new class that derives from the `Page` class is generated automatically. In reality, this new class is an executable program. Once it is initially compiled by ASP.NET, it is run each time a request for its corresponding `.aspx` file is made. For compatibility with all Web browsers, the output of the executable can be HTML 3.2. If the `.aspx` file changes, the page is recompiled into a new class. The dynamically generated class also contains the page elements (HTML elements, controls, and so on) as class members of the generated class. The compilation occurs only during the first request of a page and after modifications have been made to the page's code.

Let's take a quick look at a very simple `.aspx` file to familiarize you with its structure. The following code listing shows a typical `.aspx` file.

Code Sample 3-1

```
<%@ Page Language="vb"
❶    AutoEventWireup="false"
%>

<html>
<body>
<form id=WebForm1
   method=post
❷    runat="server">

<h1>Example .aspx File</h1>
Enter a value:

❸ <asp:TextBox id=txtEnteredVal
   runat="server">
</asp:TextBox><br>
```

```
❹ <asp:Button id=cmdSend
     runat="server"
     Text="Send">
  </asp:Button><br>

❺ <asp:Label id=lblDisplay
     runat="server"
     Width="101"
     Height="19">
  </asp:Label>

  </form>
  </body>
  </html>
```

At first glance, this `.aspx` file looks much like an ordinary HTML file, but on closer inspection, you'll see several items that you won't recognize as standard HTML (see the numbered lines). This `.aspx` file contains three new items of interest:

1. ASP.NET page directives (shown in line ❶)
2. The `runat="server"` attribute (shown in line ❷)
3. Web Controls (shown in lines ❸, ❹, and ❺)

Page directives provide ASP.NET with information about the code contained in the file. They can be located anywhere in the file, but they are generally placed at the top. Page directives allow for customization of compiler settings. We'll investigate page directives in detail in Section 3.16.

I stated earlier that ASP.NET allows you to separate content (HTML) from application logic. Often you will want to expose some HTML elements to the ASP.NET object model. These HTML items, in a sense, are executed on the server. The `runat="server"` attribute instructs the page compiler to preprocess these HTML elements on the server rather than simply serving up the HTML text back to the browser. The HTML `<form>` tag that appears just above line ❷ shows the use of the `runat="server"` attribute.

Web Controls are server-side code pieces that perform a variety of functions. We'll talk about Web Controls in depth in Sections 3.8 through 3.14, but for now, let's say that the Web Controls defined in lines ❸ through ❺ are user-interface elements that interact with the server.

When a browser requests the `.aspx` file shown above, the result returned to the browser looks something like Figure 3-1.

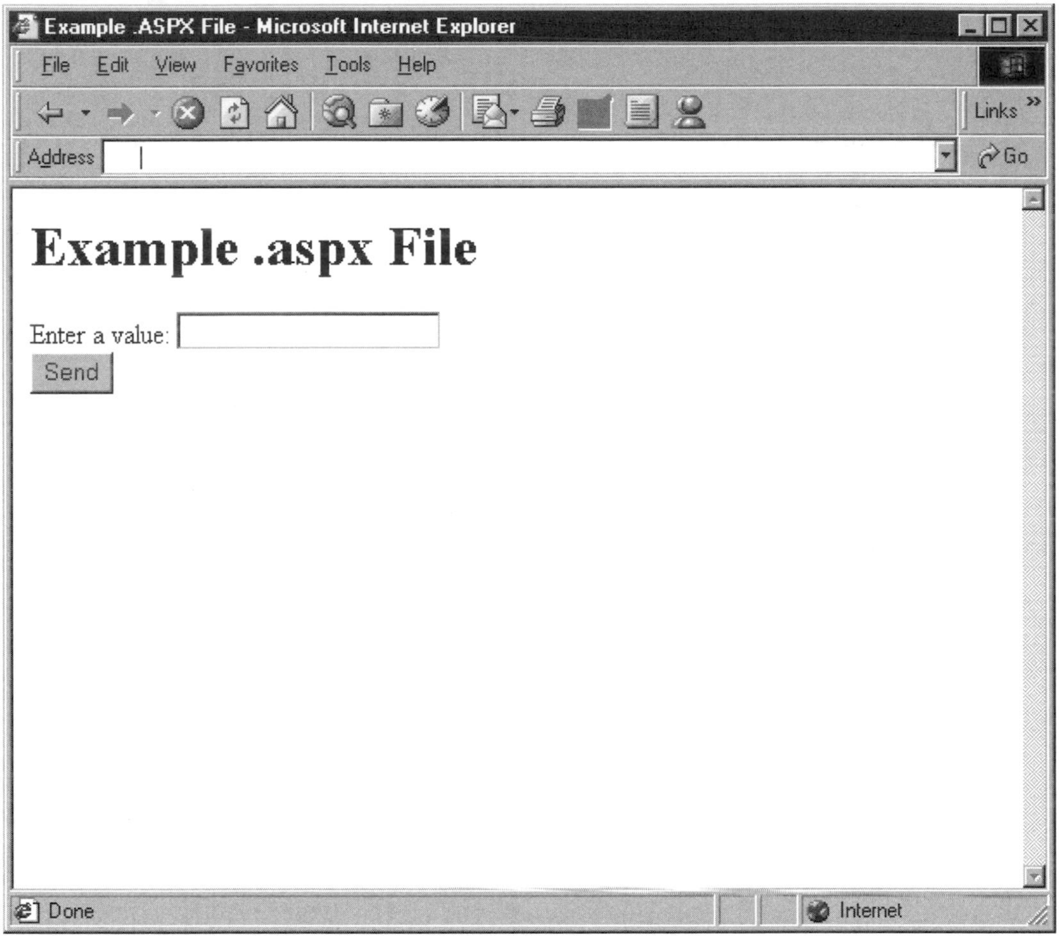

Figure 3-1 Sample `.aspx` file rendered in a Web browser

The HTML delivered to the browser should look familiar since it is plain HTML 3.2 (some formatting has been added for readability).

```
<html>
<head>
<title>Example .ASPX File</title>
</head>
```

```
<body>
<form name="WebForm1" method="post"
   action="Webform1.aspx" id="WebForm1">
<input type="hidden" name="__VIEWSTATE"
   value="YTB6LTEwNzAyOTU3NjJfX1949e1355cb" />

<h1>Example .aspx File</h1>
Enter a value:

<input name="txtEnteredVal"
   type="text" id="txtEnteredVal" /><br>

<input type="submit" name="cmdSend"
   value="Send" id="cmdSend" /><br>

<span id="lblDisplay"
   style="height:19px;width:101px;"></span>

</form>
</body>
</html>
```

By serving back only HTML 3.2, we provide maximum compatibility with whatever Web browser the end user is using.

3.2.2 Execution Stages and State Management

What steps really occur when a Web browser requests an ASP.NET page? It's important to understand that Web applications (be they ASP.NET or another type) don't behave like traditional desktop applications. Web applications use a request–response model of communication: the Web browser requests a document from the Web server and the Web server responds with the data from that document. Web applications also contain HTML forms, which allow for user input. The Web browser must package up the data entered in the form before sending it to the server. The data in the form can then be used as input for an ASP.NET program. The program is executed using the form data as input, and the results are returned to the browser as HTML. This sequence of steps is referred to as a *round-trip*.

Round-trips are usually required when the user of the Web application expects a meaningful response to a query issued from an HTML form. In some instances, round-trips are not required. If the Web browser is capable, it can provide immediate feedback from form input. This type of feedback is generally limited to simple data validation and is handled using client-side scripts. Data validation using this method can check for conditions such as form completeness, numerical ranges, and correct data formatting. Functions such as searching a database require a round-trip to the server since the data to be searched is stored on the server.

I mentioned in Chapter 1 that an inherent characteristic of Web servers is their stateless nature. This means that once a request of a document or program is made of the Web server, the Web server normally discards all information that was sent as input. As a result, the Web page must be regenerated from scratch for every round-trip. Keeping state is valuable because subsequent requests to other pages may want to access data values returned from other pages. Traditional desktop applications never had a problem keeping state. Because desktop applications are typically loaded into memory once and are kept in memory until the user exits the application, the program can freely store any values it needs in the memory allocated for the application. As Web applications become more advanced and function more like desktop applications, a reliable state-management system is required.

Fortunately, many state-management tasks in ASP.NET are done for you, and other state-management tasks can be accomplished in a number of ways. The ASP.NET Web Controls and HTML Controls, for instance, can maintain their associated values between round-trips without any coding effort on your part. This is called the *view state*.

View state is maintained using the `__VIEWSTATE` hidden form field, which is automatically generated by ASP.NET for every `.aspx` file that contains a server-side form. In the previous section, the source generated by ASP.NET showed the `__VIEWSTATE` hidden field with an encoded text string as its value. This encoded text string contains information about the state (values) of the server-side controls on the form. When the form is posted back to the server, the `__VIEWSTATE` will be posted along with the other form values. Form values that haven't been changed by the user are restored with values encoded in the `__VIEWSTATE` value from the previous post.

3.2.3 The Events Model for the Page Class

The `Page` class contains events that fire when (1) the page loads into the browser and (2) when server code execution ends and page rendering has finished. These events are `Page_Load` and `Page_Unload`, respectively.

You can specify event-handling code for these events in your `.aspx` file. Consider the following `.aspx` file with code in place for responding to the `Page_Load` and `Page_Unload` events.

Code Sample 3-2

```
<%@ Page Language="vb"%>
<html>
<head>

<script language="vb" runat="server">
   Sub Page_Load(Sender as Object, E as EventArgs)
      lblSampleLabel.Text = "Loaded!"
   End Sub

   Sub Page_Unload(Sender As Object, E as EventArgs)
      ' Cleanup code goes here
   End Sub
</script>
</head>

<body>
<form id="WebForm2"
   method="post"
   runat="server">

Page state:
<asp:Label id-lblSampleLabel
   runat="server">
</asp:Label>

</form>
</body>
</html>
```

When we request this page, we get the output shown in Figure 3-2.

The `Page_Load` event is fired when the page and all its controls are rendered. The code then displays the message "Loaded!" in the `lblSampleLabel` Control. `Page_Unload` is fired when the page is about to be discarded. This is where cleanup code is placed (freeing objects and so on). Any references made to visual elements in this event are not recognized since `Page_Unload` is fired after page processing is complete.

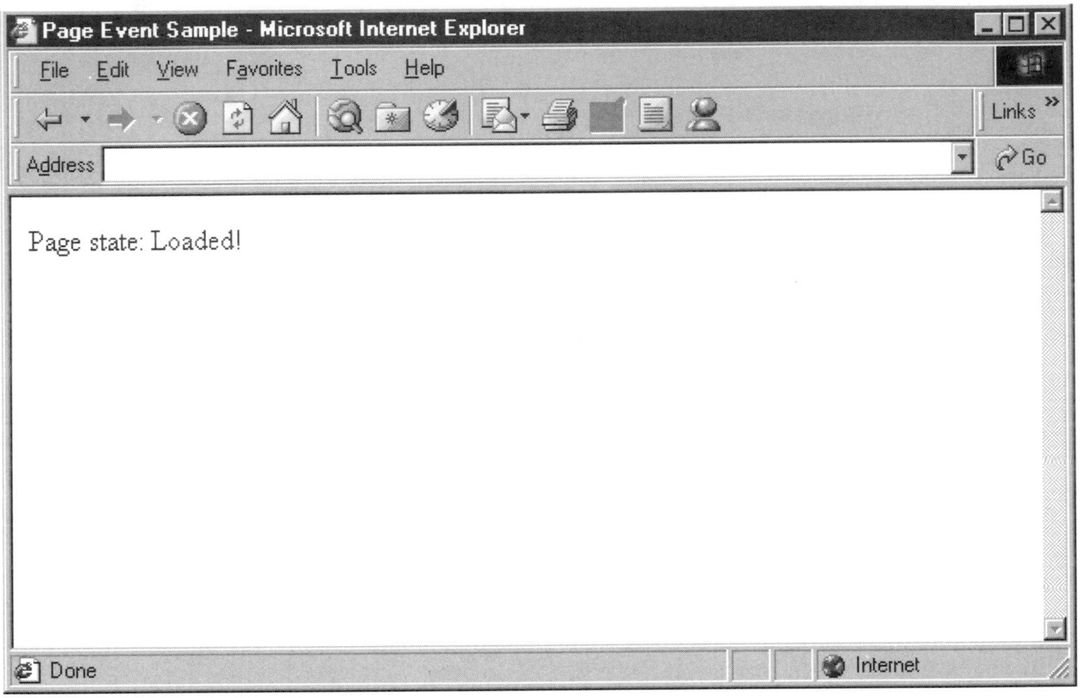

Figure 3-2 Output of the Page events sample code

3.3 Introducing Web Forms

Web Forms is the name given to the technology that provides dynamic Web pages with ASP.NET. In a sense, Web Forms allow programmers to code against the page itself in an object-oriented manner. The Web page and all the objects contained within it (controls, text, and so on) can be accessed using an object model.

Web Forms provide many distinct programming advantages. They provide an event-based programming model. This means that objects on Web Forms such as buttons, controls, and text have behaviors as well as appearances. For example, a button can exhibit a particular behavior when it is clicked. The clicking of the button is an event. Events cause certain sections of code to execute inside the program, like displaying new data to the user or submitting data to the server. Event-based programming models are common with desktop application development, but ASP.NET Web Forms deliver, for the first time, this type of functionality to the Web browser.

Web Forms allow for the separation of application logic from content. On older Web-development systems, application code (typically script code) was interspersed with HTML. The main advantage of this separation is to facilitate better team-based development. Designers who work with layout and content can create the visual look and feel of the page without interrupting the work of the Web programmers who place the application logic that drives the page's functionality.

Web Forms work closely with the VS.NET Integrated Development Environment (IDE) to provide an easy design-time development experience. Users of Visual Studio have long enjoyed the benefits of rapid application development (RAD) by combining event-based programming with easy-to-use form design tools. With VS.NET, you can use those same RAD features to construct ASP.NET pages with greater ease than ever before. In addition, if you've programmed applications using Visual Basic's Forms Designer in the past, you'll be pleased to find a similar interface in VS.NET.

ASP.NET frees developers from having to write less routine code typically associated with Web applications. It accomplishes this by providing a standard set of server-based controls for many common tasks, such as data entry validation. We'll investigate these great timesaving controls in coming sections.

3.4 VS.NET Web Applications and Other IDE Basics

VS.NET offers an easy way to create new ASP.NET Web application projects. You can create a new ASP.NET Web application in the same way you create other types of applications in VS.NET: by selecting **File→New→Project** from the menu bar and clicking the ASP.NET Web Application button (see Figure 3-3).

Adding new Web Forms to the application is simple. In the Solution Explorer window, right-click on the icon for your Web application and select **Add→Add Web Form** . . . as shown in Figure 3-4. Then select the Web Form icon in the Templates section of the screen and give your new Web Form a file name (see Figure 3-5). The new Web Form is saved and becomes part of the current solution.

Whenever you want to view the code or when you place a Web Control on the Web Form for the first time, a new code module is added to the solution that serves as the code-behind module for the Web Form. A newly created code-behind module looks like the sample below. (Some formatting has been added for readability.)

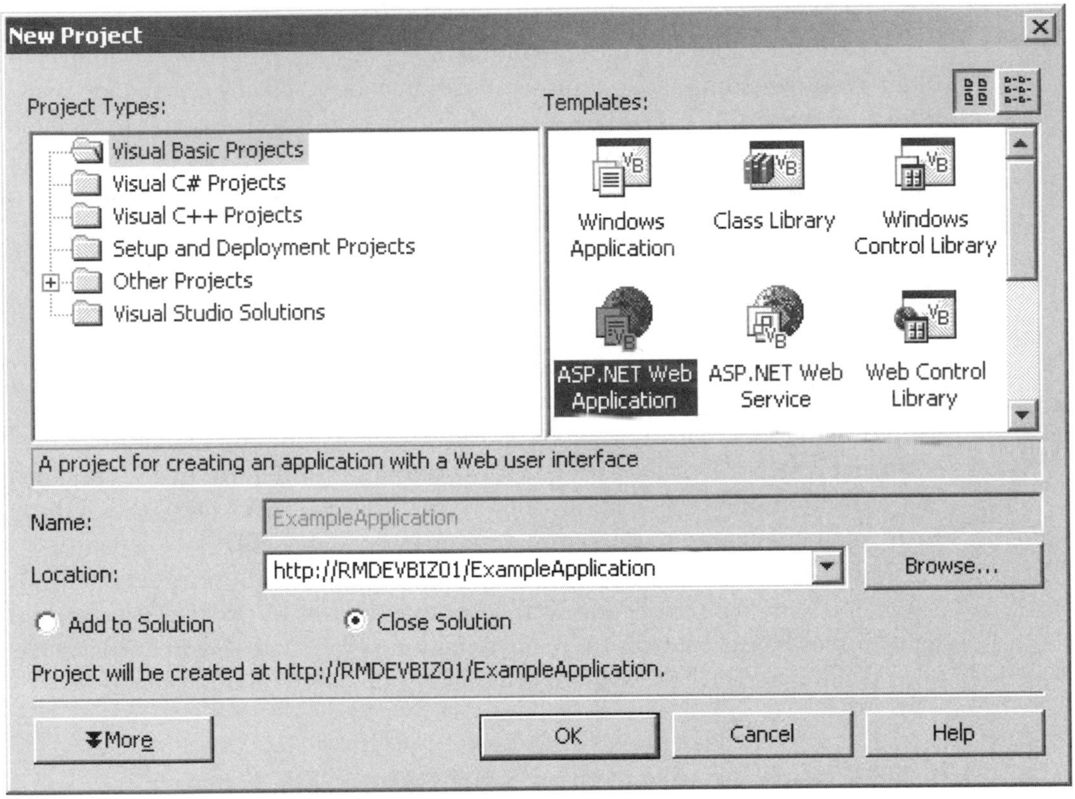

Figure 3-3 Creating a new Web application in VS.NET

```
❻Public Class MyWebForm
❼   Inherits System.Web.UI.Page

#Region " Web Form Designer Generated Code "

    ' This call is required by the Web Form Designer.
    <System.Diagnostics.DebuggerStepThrough()> _
    Private Sub InitializeComponent()

    End Sub

❽     Private Sub Page_Init(ByVal sender As System.Object, _
      ByVal e As System.EventArgs) Handles MyBase.Init
          InitializeComponent()
```

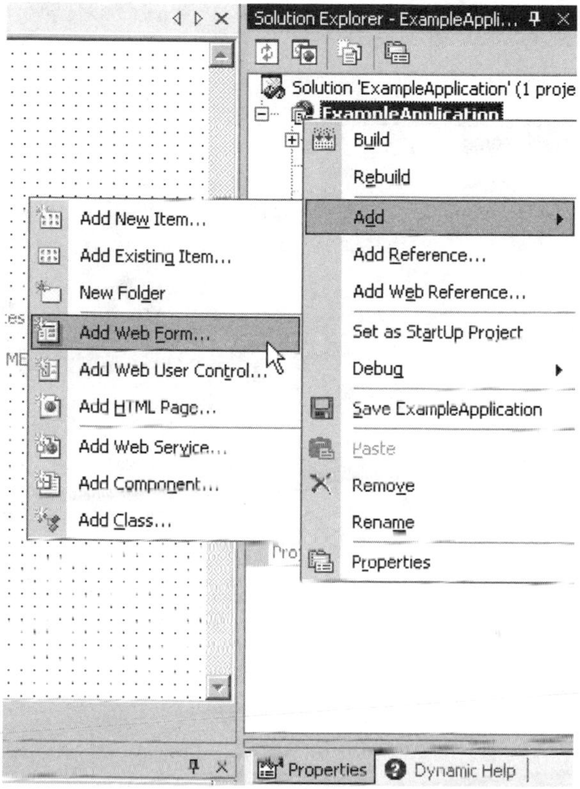

Figure 3-4 Adding a new Web Form to the Web application

```
    End Sub

#End Region

❾   Private Sub Page_Load(ByVal sender As System.Object, _
        ByVal e As System.EventArgs) Handles MyBase.Load

    End Sub

End Class
```

This code-behind module defines a new class for the Web Form and creates plumbing code. Notice that VS.NET assigned the class the same name

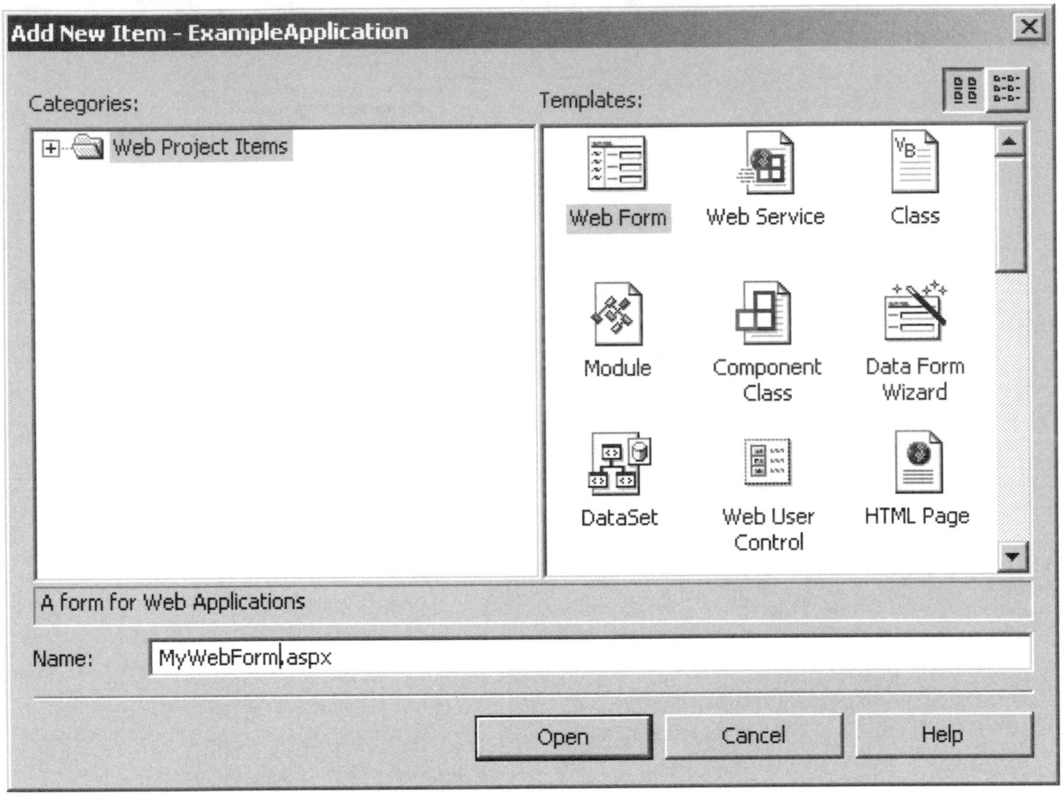

Figure 3-5 Saving the new Web Form

given to the Web Form in Figure 3-5, `MyWebForm` (see line ❻). This class inherits from the `Page` class (see line ❼), which is a predefined ASP.NET class. This exposes the `Page` class's events and other properties and methods so they can be used within the new class. Two inherited `Page` event handlers are defined for us, `Page_Init and Page_Load`, in lines ❽ and ❾, respectively.

As you develop a Web Form using the VS.NET IDE, you will see code added to the code-behind module. In particular, code will be generated in response to new Web Controls placed on the Web Form. During the discussions of Web Controls that appear later in this book, we will constantly be referring back to the code-behind file, so it's important to familiarize yourself with its structure.

3.5 Separating Content and Code—the Code-Behind Feature

When building Web applications with VS.NET, you can greatly simplify the amount of code that you'll actually have to type. VS.NET also offers many features to keep your code organized, such as the code-behind feature.

Code behind came about when design and organizational issues arose from mixing application code with HTML (that is, mixing logic with presentation). Many programmers combined the two elements within the same file (as many did with ASP 3.0). The result was a code base that was difficult to maintain and understand due to the chaotic mixture of HTML and script. The code-behind feature alleviates that problem by completely separating HTML from the program code; they are, in fact, in separate files.

The two files are linked together using a special page directive, `Codebehind`, which is defined in the `.aspx` file. `Codebehind` specifies the pathname to a code module file. If the pathname is omitted, the class is assumed to be in the `/bin` directory of the Web application's virtual Web directory. Here's a sample page directive line that contains `Codebehind`.

```
<%@ Page Language="vb"
   AutoEventWireup="false"
   Codebehind="SampleWebButton.vb"
   Inherits="WebApplication1.SampleWebButton"
%>
```

When you use the VS.NET IDE to create Web applications, the IDE is configured to generate the above code for you. Whenever you create a new Web Form (from the **New** menu), this and other "boilerplate" Web Form code is placed in the file. The code-behind module (the `.vb` file) is also generated with some event-handling code (we'll discuss this in a moment).

You have other options when specifying a code-behind class. You may also specify an `Src` attribute, which tells ASP.NET where your class file is located. If omitted, ASP.NET assumes that the class is located in the `/bin` directory of the Web application. Looking at the previous example, we can represent the same thing using this form.

```
<%@ Page Language="vb"
   AutoEventWireup="false"
   Src="SampleWebButton.vb"
   Inherits="WebApplication1.SampleWebButton"
%>
```

3.6 Application Configuration

Applications in ASP.NET are comprised of a virtual Web directory and pages, files, and assemblies contained within the directory and subdirectories. You can define settings for this application plus write event handlers for application-wide events. A special file called the `Global.asax` file controls these settings and events.

3.6.1 Structure and Configuration of the `Global.asax` File

There is exactly one `Global.asax` file per application, and it is optional. The file is always located at the root level of the virtual directory for the ASP.NET Web application. At first this may seem like a security risk since the `Global.asax` file is a file like any other in the Web application directory that users may request. The `Global.asax` file can also contain code that may compromise the security of the Web server. Because of this potential vulnerability, ASP.NET places a restriction on the `Global.asax` file so that any direct HTTP request for it is automatically denied.

When VS.NET creates a new Web application, a `Global.asax` file is created automatically. The `Global.asax` file contains a code-behind file named `Global.asax.vb`. Here's how a typical VS.NET-generated `Global.asax` file looks:

```
<% Application Codebehind="Global.asax.vb" Inherits="Lab3_1.Global" %>
```

The code-behind file, `Global.asax.vb`, looks like this:

```
Imports System.Web
Imports System.Web.SessionState

Public Class Global
   Inherits System.Web.HttpApplication

   Sub Application_Start(ByVal Sender As Object, _
      ByVal e As EventArgs)

   End Sub

   Sub Session_Start(ByVal Sender As Object, ByVal e As EventArgs)

   End Sub
```

```
    Sub Application_BeginRequest(ByVal Sender As Object, _
       ByVal e As EventArgs)

    End Sub

    Sub Application_EndRequest(ByVal Sender As Object, _
       ByVal e As EventArgs)

    End Sub

    Sub Session_End(ByVal Sender As Object, ByVal e As EventArgs)

    End Sub

    Sub Application_End(ByVal Sender As Object, _
       ByVal e As EventArgs)

    End Sub

End Class
```

The `Global.asax.vb` file defines a class called `Global`, which inherits from `System.Web.HttpApplication`. This class defines all the methods, properties, and events that all application objects use within an ASP.NET application. In this file, VS.NET places overridden stubbed functions that handle events of the `HttpApplication` class. Those events are associated with the beginning and ending of user sessions and of the ASP.NET application.

3.7 Using HTML Controls

Most controls in ASP.NET are server-based. Server-based controls are chunks of server-side code that exist in a Web page. The code outputs standard HTML 3.2 for compatibility with all Web browsers. ASP.NET Controls come in two varieties: HTML Controls and Web Controls. We'll discuss the HTML Controls in this section and the Web Controls in Sections 3.8 through 3.14.

Using HTML Controls is easy since they correspond directly to standard HTML 3.2 elements. That is, elements such as buttons, input boxes, tables, and so on can be rendered on the server and then served up to the Web browser. The advantage of this is that HTML element properties can be referenced programmatically, whereas standard client-side HTML cannot. Table 3-1 lists the HTML Controls and their HTML 3.2 equivalents. Existing

HTML and pre-.NET ASP pages can be migrated over to ASP.NET easily by simply adding a `runat="server"` attribute to each tag.

The method for programming with HTML Controls should be familiar to anyone who has worked with the corresponding HTML elements. In effect, an HTML Control becomes an object you can reference using the usual

Table 3-1 ASP.NET HTML Controls

HTML Control Name	HTML 3.2 Representation
HTMLAnchor	<a>
HTMLButton	<button>
HTMLForm	<form>
HTMLGenericControl	<div> or <>span>
HTMLImage	<img>
HTMLInputButton	<input type="button">
HTMLInputCheckBox	<input type="check">
HTMLInputFile	<input type="file">
HTMLInputHidden	<input type="hidden">
HTMLInputImage	<input type="image">
HTMLInputRadioButton	<input type="radio">
HTMLInputText	<input type="button"> or <input type="password">
HTMLSelect	<select>
HTMLTable	<table>
HTMLTableCell	<td>
HTMLTableRow	<tr>
HTMLTextArea	<textarea>

`object.member` notation. In the following discussions of the different HTML Controls, you will see several examples of this.

All HTML Controls must contain an `ID` attribute. The `ID` attribute is used by ASP.NET to uniquely identify the control. It also is the way to programmatically reference the control. For example, if an HTML Control contains an `ID` attribute named `txtMyTextField`, then the VB.NET code for referencing the object members would look like this:

```
txtMyTextField.Text = "sometext"
```

Let's look at each of the individual HTML Controls in more detail.

3.7.1 The HTMLForm Control

ASP.NET Web Forms always begin with an `HTMLForm Control. The HTMLForm` Control is just like its HTML equivalent, but it contains the `runat="server"` attribute. For other server controls to be recognized by the ASP.NET Framework, they must be placed between beginning and ending `<form>` tags. The syntax for an `HTMLForm` Control appears below.

```
<form
   runat="server"
   id="programmaticID"
   method=POST | GET
   action="srcpageURL"
>
other HTML and server controls go here
</form>
```

In most cases you should set the method attribute to `POST`. ASP.NET relies on values posted back to the server in a hidden form variable for control state management. The server recognizes this hidden data only when it is sent via the `POST` mechanism.

3.7.2 The HTMLAnchor Control

An HTML anchor serves as a hyperlink to other documents or to another position within the document. The syntax for the `HTMLAnchor` Control is shown below.

```
<a
   runat="server"
   id="programmaticID"
   href="linkurl"
   name="bookmarkname"
   OnServerClick="onserverclickhandler"
   target="linkedcontentframeorwindow"
   title="titledisplayedbybrowser"
>
linktext
</a>
```

The `href`, `name`, `target`, and `title` properties can be set at runtime. The `OnServerClick` procedure is fired when the anchor link text is clicked. For example, here's how to dynamically generate anchor tags and change the `title` attribute based on the anchor clicked.

Code Sample 3-3

```
<%@ Page Language="vb"%>
<html><head>
<title>HTMLAnchor Sample</title>
<script language=vb runat="server">
   Sub Page_Load(Source as Object, E As EventArgs)
      AChoice1.name = "Choice1"
      AChoice1.title = "Choice 1"
      AChoice2.name = "Choice2"
      AChoice2.title = "Choice 2"
      AChoice3.name = "Choice3"
      AChoice3.title = "Choice 3"
   End Sub

   Sub AChoice1_click(Source as Object, E as EventArgs)
      AChoice1.title = "CLICKED: Choice 1"
   End Sub

   Sub AChoice2_click(Source as Object, E as EventArgs)
      AChoice2.title = "CLICKED: Choice 2"
   End Sub

   Sub AChoice3_click(Source as Object, E as EventArgs)
      AChoice3.title = "CLICKED: Choice 3"
   End Sub
```

```
</script>
</head>
<body>

<form id="HtmlAnchorSample"
   method="post"
   runat="server">

<h1>HtmlAnchor Example</h1>

<p><a href="htmlanchorsample.aspx"
   id=AChoice1
   onserverclick="AChoice1_click"
   runat="server">Choice 1</a>
</p>
<p><a href="htmlanchorsample.aspx"
   id=AChoice2
   onserverclick="AChoice2_click"
   runat="server">Choice 2</a>
</p>
<p><a href="htmlanchorsample.aspx"
   id=AChoice3
   onserverclick="AChoice3_click"
   runat="server">Choice 3</a>
</p>

</form>
</body>
</html>
```

Notice in Figure 3-6 that the title attribute is not the default title string we set in the `Page_Load` event but the new "CLICKED" string set by the `OnServerClick` event-handler code. In most current Web browsers, the HTML title attribute text serves as the floating "tool-tip" text for the anchor.

3.7.3 The HTMLButton Control

The `HTMLButton` Control works only with Web browsers that support HTML 4.0, so keep in mind the audience of your Web site when choosing to implement the `HTMLButton` Control in your pages. Its main purpose is to provide a

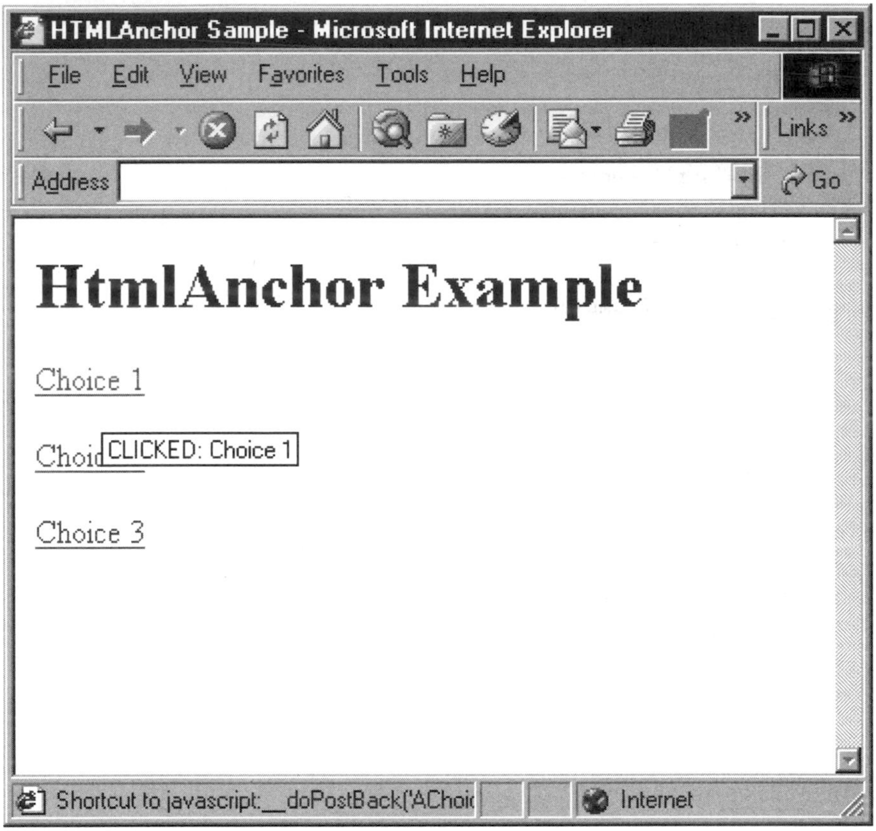

Figure 3-6 Output of the HTMLAnchor Control example

button whose appearance is very customizable. Its general syntax appears below.

```
<button
   runat="server"
   id="programmaticID"
   OnServerClick="onserverclickhandler"
>
inner HTML goes here
</button>
```

Cascading Style Sheet (CSS) styles change the default appearance of the button. You can use many different style combinations to achieve the exact look you desire. Here's code for a button that is yellow with bold, italic blue text.

Code Sample 3-4

```
<%@ Page Language="vb" %>
<html><head>
</head>
<body>

<form id="HTMLButtonExample"
   method="post"
   runat="server">
<h1>HTML Button Sample</h1>

<button runat="server"
   style="FONT-WEIGHT:
      bolder;
      COLOR: blue;
      FONT-STYLE:
      italic;
      FONT-FAMILY:
      Verdana;
      BACKGROUND-COLOR: yellow">
Click this button
</button>

</form>
</body>
</html>
```

3.7.4 The `HTMLGenericControl` Control

Some HTML tags don't correspond to a specific control like a button, hyperlink, or text box. In fact, controls in this particular category don't have a visual representation by themselves. The HTML tags `<span>`, `<div>`, `<body>`, and `<font>` are examples of this. The `HTMLGenericControl` Control is used as follows.

```
<span | body | div | font | others
   runat="server"
   id="programmaticID"
>
```

```
your HTML goes here
</span | body | div | font | others>
```

The typical use for `HTMLGenericControl` is to display dynamic text in the page. For example, you may want to display the results of a query that executed on the server in a certain area on the page. That area can be defined by using the `<span>` tag and can be server-side enabled by supplying the `runat="server"` attribute. Here's an example.

Code Sample 3-5

```
<%@ Page Language="vb"%>
<html>
<head>
<TITLE>HTMLGenericControl Example</TITLE>
<script language=vb runat="server">

Sub Page_load(Source As Object, E As EventArgs)

   Dim strOutputString as String
   Dim intCount as Integer

   strOutputString = "<OL>"
   For intCount = 1 To 5
      strOutputString &= "<LI>Numbered list"
   Next
   strOutputString &= "</OL>"

   lblMyText.InnerHTML = strOutputString
End Sub

</script>


</head>
<body>

<form id="HTMLGenericControl"
   method="post"
   runat="server">

<h1>HTMLGenericControl Example</h1>
```

```
Span text:

<span id=lblMyText
   runat="server">
</span>

</form>
</body>
```

This example builds a simple HTML ordered list and puts the HTML text into a string when the `Page_Load` event fires. Then the `InnerHTML` property is set for the `HTMLGenericControl lblMyText`. This dynamically inserts the ordered list between the `<span>` tags. The output appears in Figure 3-7.

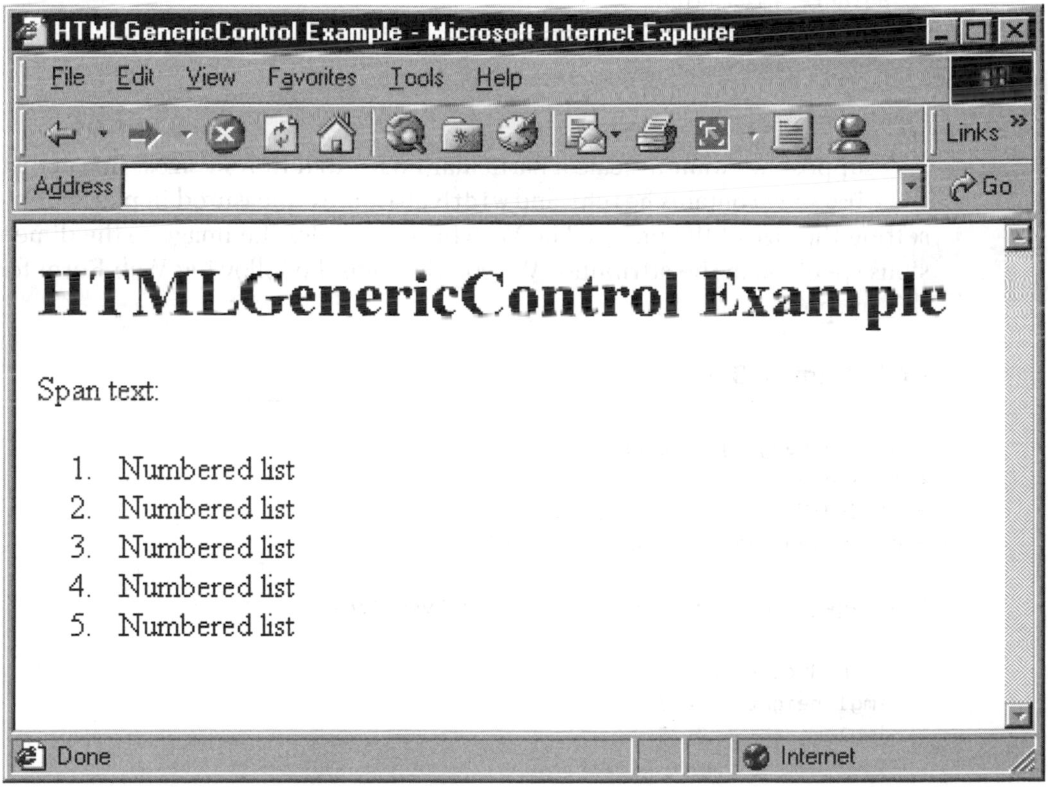

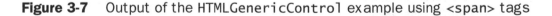

Figure 3-7 Output of the `HTMLGenericControl` example using <span> tags

3.7.5 The HTMLImage Control

Inline images are an essential part of most Web pages. The images are often subject to change with each page visit. This is especially true of banner advertisements, which must change according to user demographics or product popularity. Whatever the reason for manipulating inline images on a Web page, ASP.NET provides the HTMLImage Control for changing <img> tag characteristics on the server. All of the <img> tag attributes are made available on the server. Here's the complete syntax showing those attributes.

```
<img
   id="programmaticID"
   runat="server"
   alt="alttext"
   align= top | middle | bottom | left | right
   border="borderwidth"
   height="imageheight"
   src="imageURI"
   width="imagewidth"
>
```

Suppose we want to scale a particular image to different sizes. Recall that the <img> tag contains height and width attributes (measured in pixels) for setting the size of the image. The Web browser scales the image to the dimensions specified in the attributes. We could design the following Web Form for this purpose.

Code Sample 3-6

```
<%@ Page Language="vb"%>
<html><head>
<TITLE>HTMLImage Example</TITLE>
<script language=vb runat="server">

Sub Page_Load(Source As Object, E As EventArgs)

   '* Reduce to 25%
   img1.height *= 0.25
   img1.width *= 0.25
   img1.alt = "Image at 25%"

   '* Reduce to 50%
   img2.height *= 0.50
```

```
    img2.width *= 0.50
    img2.alt = "Image at 50%"

    '* Reduce to 75%
    img3.height *= 0.75
    img3.width *= 0.75
    img3.alt = "Image at 75%"

End Sub

</script>
</head>
<body>

<form id="HTMLImageSample"
    method="post"
    runat="server">

<h1>HTMLImage Sample</h1>
<p>This will display an image at three
    different sizes from the original: 25%,
    50%, and 75%
</p>
<p>
<table cellspacing=1 cellpadding=1 width=300 border=1>
    <tr>
        <td><img id=imgOriginal height=266
            alt="mountain (Original Size)"
            src="mountain.jpg"
            width=366
            runat="server"></td>
        <td><img id=img1 height=266
            alt=""
            src="mountain.jpg"
            width=366
            runat="server"></td>
    </tr>
    <tr>
        <td><img id=Img2 height=266
            alt=""
            src="mountain.jpg"
            width=366
            runat="server"></td>
        <td><img id=Img3
```

```
            height=266
            alt=""
            src="mountain.jpg"
            width=366
            runat="server"></td>
    </tr>
</table>
</p>

</form>
</body>
</html>
```

The `Page_Load` subroutine/event contains the resizing code. All that's required to resize the image is to multiply the height and width values of each image by the desired percentage. In addition, we set the `alt` tag of each image to a caption denoting the size reductions that we performed. (This caption appears when the user holds the mouse pointer over the images.) Figure 3-8 shows the final browser output.

3.7.6 The `HTMLInputButton` Control

Buttons are used frequently on Web pages. Their typical purpose is to invoke an application command. In Web applications, this usually means that a round-trip to the server is required to retrieve information. The ASP.NET HTML Controls provide three types of buttons: general-purpose buttons, submit buttons, and form-reset buttons.

The following general syntax is used to define a button.

```
<input
    type=button | submit | reset
    runat="server"
    id="programmaticID"
    OnServerClick="onserverclickhandler"
>
```

In HTML 3.2, submit buttons cause the contents of the form to be sent to the server at the location specified in the enclosing `<form>`'s `action` URL. Reset buttons cause all the values entered in input elements on the form to be erased or set back to their default values. General-purpose buttons are used for customized actions that don't necessarily behave like form submittals, typically in conjunction with client-side script.

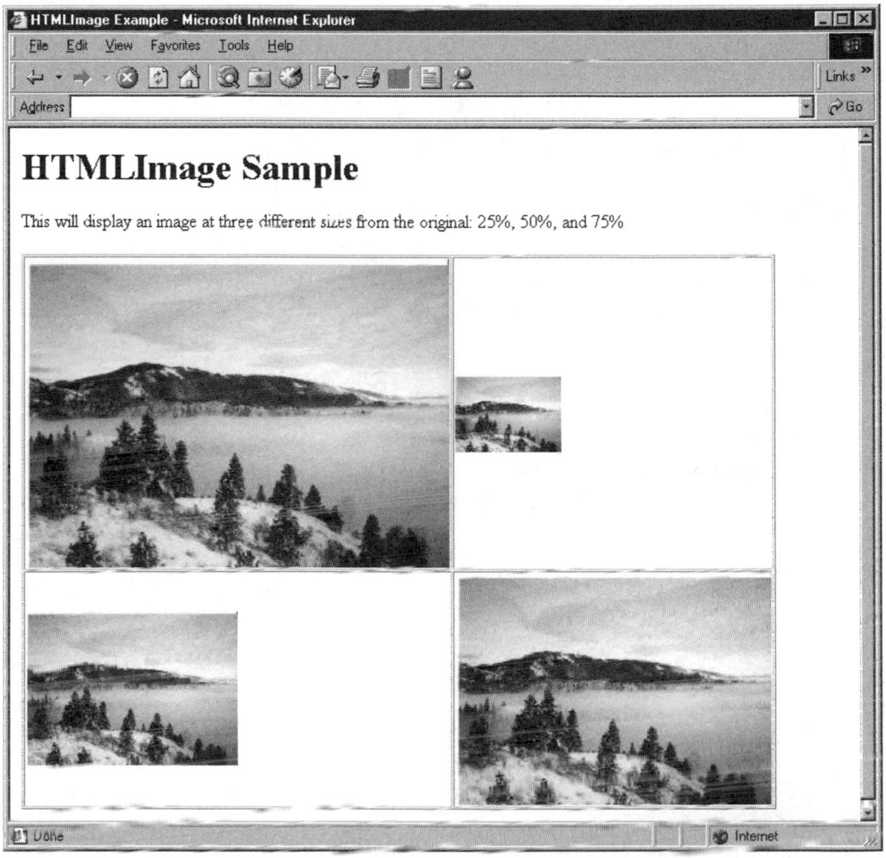

Figure 3-8 Output of the `HTMLImage` example

Whatever type of button is used on a form, ASP.NET can respond by executing an event-handling procedure designated in `OnServerClick`. When the user clicks the button, a post-back goes to the server.

> **WARNING:** The reset button does not cause a post-back to the server for a click event.

The example below shows a typical use of the `HTMLInputButton` Control. The sample displays a single button. When the button is clicked, the text of the button toggles to a different display value.

Code Sample 3-7

```
<%@ Page Language="vb"%>
<html><head>
<title>HTMLInputButtonSample</title>
<script language=vb runat="server">

Sub btnReset_Click(Source as Object, E As EventArgs)

   If btnInputButton.Value = "Value One" Then
      btnInputButton.Value = "Value Two"
      Exit Sub
   End If

   If btnInputButton.Value = "Value Two" Then
      btnInputButton.Value = "Value One"
      Exit Sub
   End If
End Sub

</script>
</head>

<body>

<form id="HTMLInputButtonSample"
   method="post"
   runat="server">

<h1>HTMLInputButton Example</h1>
<p>
<input type=button
   value="Value One"
   id="btnInputButton"
   OnServerClick="btnReset_Click"
   runat="server">
</p>

</form>
</body>
</html>
```

3.7.7 The HTMLInputCheckBox Control

Checkboxes are used to indicate a series of independent options within the same category. They are often encountered in HTML forms to allow users to select several choices from a list of options. The syntax of an HTMLInputCheckBox Control is shown below.

```
<input
   type=checkbox
   runat="server"
   id="programmaticID"
   checked
>
```

Let's make a form with some sample checkbox entries and a submit button.

Code Sample 3-8

```
<%@ Page Language="vb"%>
<html>
<head>
<title>HTMLInputCheckBoxSample</title>
<script language=vb runat="server">

Sub btnSubmit_Click(Source As Object, E As EventArgs)

   Dim strResponse as String

   If ckbRed.Checked Then
      strResponse &= "Red "
   End If
   If ckbYellow.Checked Then
      strResponse &= "Yellow "
   End If

   If ckbGreen.Checked Then
      strResponse &= "Green "
   End If

   If ckbBlue.Checked Then
      strResponse &= "Blue "
   End If
```

```
   If Page.IsPostBack Then
      lblText.InnerHTML = "You selected: " & strResponse
   End If

End Sub

</script>
</head>
<body>

<form id="HTMLInputCheckBoxSample"
   method="post"
   runat="server">
<h1>HTMLInputCheckBox Example</h1>
<p>Please make your color selections:</p>
<p>
<input id=ckbRed
   type=checkbox
   runat="server"> Red</p>
<p>
<input id=ckbYellow
   type=checkbox
   runat="server"> Yellow</p>
<p>
<input id=ckbBlue
   type=checkbox
   runat="server"> Blue</p>
<p>
<input id=ckbGreen
   type=checkbox
   runat="server"> Green</p>
<p>
<input id=btnSubmit
   runat="server"
   type=submit
   onserverclick="btnSubmit_Click"
   value=Submit>
</p>
</form>
<div id="lblText" runat="server"></div>
</body>
</html>
```

This page displays a series of four checkboxes (see Figure 3-9). The user can select any number of these boxes. By using the Boolean `Checked` property of the `HTMLInputCheckBox` Control the program tests each checkbox to see if it was selected. The property is true if the user checks the box.

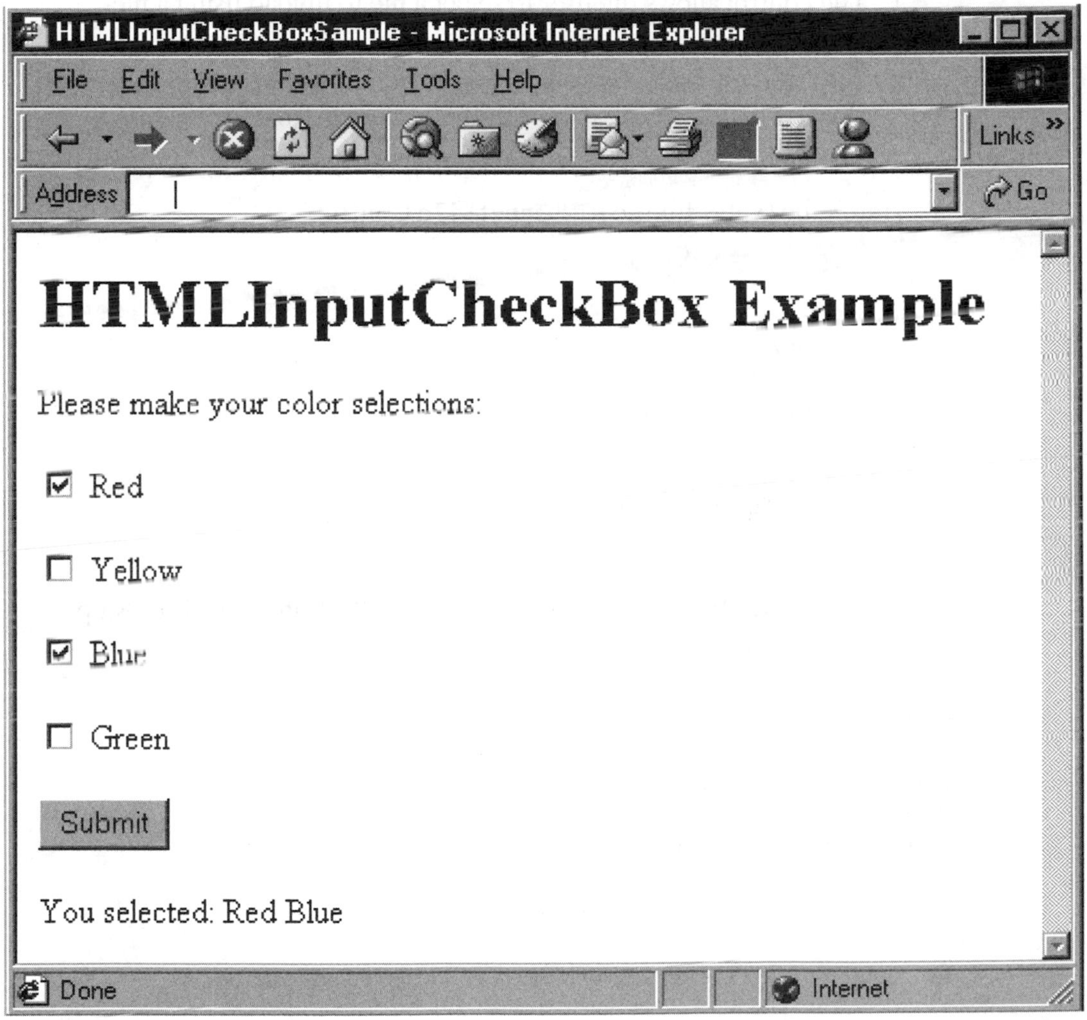

Figure 3-9 Output of the `HTMLInputCheckBox` example

3.7.8 The `HTMLInputFile` Control

Many Web sites can accept files transmitted from users' computers. Examples of such sites include those that host photo albums, provide backup facilities, or accept file attachments for Web-based e-mail. In ASP.NET, the `HTMLInputFile` Control enables this capability.

Uploading a file using the `HTMLInputFile` Control is a three-step process.

1. The control allows the user to select a file to upload using a file-browsing dialog box.
2. Once the user selects the file, it is encoded for transmission and sent along with other form data with the server post-back.
3. The file is saved to disk on the server.

Here's the syntax for the `HTMLInputFile` Control.

```
<input
   type=file
   runat="server"
   id="programmaticID"
   accept="MIMEencodings"
   maxlength="maxfilepathlength"
   size="widthoffilepathtextbox"
   postedfile="uploadedfile"
>
```

A simple form that accepts a file for posting illustrates this three-step process. Let's start with the posting form.

Code Sample 3-9

```
<%@ Page Language="vb"%>
<html><head>
<TITLE>HTMLInputFile Example</TITLE>

<script language=vb runat="server">

10  Function GetFileNameFromPath(ByVal PathName as String)

   Dim intFirstPos As Integer

   intFirstPos = InStrRev(PathName, "\") + 1
   GetFileNameFromPath = Mid(PathName, intFirstPos)
```

```
End Function

⓫ Sub btnSubmit_Click(Source As Object, E As EventArgs)

   Dim strSavePath as String
   Dim strFileName as String

   strFileName = GetFileNameFromPath(_
      filSelectFile.PostedFile.FileName)

   lblFileInfo.InnerHTML = "You selected: " & strFileName

   strSavePath = Server.MapPath("\Samples2")
⓬    filSelectFile.PostedFile.SaveAs(strSavePath & "\" & _
      strFileName)

End Sub

</script>

</head>
<body>

⓭ <form id="HTMLInputFileSample"
   method="post"
   enctype="multipart/form-data"
   runat="server">

<h1>HTMLInputFile Example</h1>
<p>Please select a file to upload to the server:</p>
<p>
<input id=filSelectFile
   type=file
   runat="server">
</p>
<p>
⓮  <INPUT id=btnSubmit
   type="submit"
   value="Submit"
   OnServerClick="btnSubmit_Click"
   runat="server">
</p>
<p>
```

```
<span id=lblFileInfo
   runat="server">
</span>
</p>

</form>
</body>
</html>
```

In the code block that starts at line ⓮, we show the declaration of an `HTMLInputFile` Control. This will display a file browse button that will allow the user to select a file to upload to the server. Note that the `enctype` for the form is set to `"multipart/form-data"`, and the `method` is set to `"post"` (see the code block beginning at line ⓭). This is required because files uploaded via a form post are encoded in a special way that differs from regular form submissions (that is, forms that contain only simple controls such as input boxes, radio buttons, checkboxes, and so on).

> **TECHTALK: ENCODING SCHEME FOR FILE POSTS**
> The encoding scheme and standard used to upload files to a Web server via an HTML form post are described in Internet Request for Comments document #1867. Go to *http://www.ietf.org* to obtain this document.

The form resulting from this code looks similar to that shown in Figure 3-10.

The file is uploaded with a post-back to the server (that is, when the user clicks the submit button). The `btnSubmit_Click` event procedure coded in line ⓫ handles that form-submission event. In this procedure, retrieving the file data that was posted and saving it to the server's storage area is a two-step process.

1. Obtain the file name from the posted file. Information about the posted file is contained in the `PostedFile` object (see line ⓬), which is a member of the `HTMLInputFile` Control. `FileName` holds the complete pathname of the file selected on the user's workstation. The `GetFileNameFromPath()` function defined on line ❿ extracts the file name from the absolute path in `FileName`.

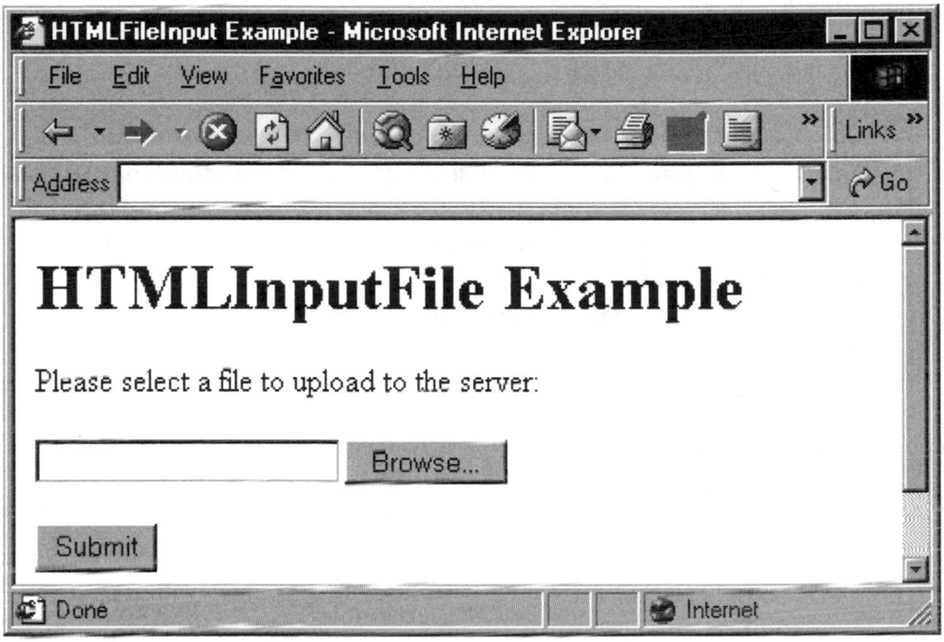

Figure 3-10 Output of the `HTMLInputFile` example

2. Save the file on the server. To save the file, we need to obtain the absolute, physical path to the location to which we wish to save the file. We obtain this location by using the `MapPath()` method of the ASP.NET `Server` object. I'll explain this object in detail in Section 3.23, but for now I'll just explain the `MapPath()` method. It returns the physical path for a given virtual path (for example, `c:\inetpub\wwwroot\images` for `\images`). Then, the `SaveAs()` method of the `PostedFile` object saves the actual file with the file name extracted from the `POST` request into the directory obtained from `MapPath()`.

> **WARNING:** Uploading files successfully to the server through the method described here is contingent on the user holding sufficient file permissions (write permissions) for the directory to which the file is being saved.

3.7.9 The HTMLInputHidden Control

Hidden form variables behave much like text input fields except they do not have any visible appearance. Hidden input fields have many uses. The primary use is to retain values across page requests. A server-side program can echo back a posted value in the form of a hidden input field. When the page is posted a second time, the value is sent again along with the other form data. This effectively persists data (or "state" as we call it in Web applications). We've discussed application state already; ASP.NET uses hidden input fields to preserve application state.

The syntax for the `HTMLInputHidden` Control appears below.

```
<input
   type="hidden"
   runat="server"
   id="programmaticID"
   value="contentsofhiddenfield"
>
```

Whatever the purposes for using hidden form variables, ASP.NET makes it just as easy to use them as it is to use other HTML Controls. The quick example below provides a simple demonstration of the `HTMLInputHidden` form variable, showing how to increment the value of a hidden variable with each post-back to the server.

Code Sample 3-10

```
<%@ Page Language="vb"%>
<html><head>
<title>HTMLInputHidden Example</title>
<script language=vb runat="server">
⓯  Sub Page_Load(Source As Object, E As EventArgs)
   If Page.IsPostBack Then
      lblCounter.InnerHTML = _
⓰              CInt(hdnHiddenField.Value) + 1
      hdnHiddenField.Value = _
         CInt(hdnHiddenField.Value) + 1
   End If
End Sub
</script>
</head>
<body>
```

```
<form id="HTMLInputHidden"
   method="post"
   runat="server">

<h1>HTMLInputHidden Example</h1>
<p>
<input id=hdnHiddenField
   type=hidden
   runat="server"
   value="0">
</p>

<p>
<input type="submit"
   runat="server"
   value="Submit">
</p>

<p>
<span id=lblCounter
   runat="server">
</span>
</p>

</form>
</body>
</html>
```

Page_Load in line ⓯ handles the counter increment contained in the hdnHiddenField. Since HTML Control properties are not strongly typed, conversion using the VB.NET function CInt() is required before incrementing the value (see line ⓰). The incremented value is updated in the HTMLGenericControl lblCounter.

3.7.10 The HTMLInputImage Control

Often images are used as buttons on Web pages. The HTML specification defines a type of <input> element that uses a type of image. You may opt to use the HTMLInputImage Control when your design requirements don't allow for the standard button provided by the HTMLInputButton Control or others. The HTMLInputImage Control uses the following syntax.

```
<input
   type=image
   runat="server"
   id="programmaticID"
   src="imagepath"
   align="imagealignment"
   alt="alttext"
      OnServerClick="onserverclickhandler"
   width="borderwidthinpixels"
>
```

The `HTMLInputImage` Control shares the same attributes as the HTML `<img>` tag, so the same formatting options are available in the `HTMLInputImage` Control. The `HTMLInputImage` Control responds to a click event and executes the procedure set for `OnServerClick`. An example page using the `HTMLInputImage` Control follows.

Code Sample 3-11

```
<%@ Page Language="vb"%>
<html><head>
<title>HTMLInputImage Example</title>
<script language=vb runat="server">

Sub imgImage1_Click(Source As Object, _
      E As ImageClickEventArgs)
   imgImage1.src = "wb2.gif"
   imgImage2.src = "wb1.gif"
   imgImage3.src = "wb1.gif"
End Sub

Sub imgImage2_Click(Source As Object, _
      E As ImageClickEventArgs)
   imgImage1.src = "wb1.gif"
   imgImage2.src = "wb2.gif"
   imgImage3.src = "wb1.gif"
End Sub

Sub imgImage3_Click(Source As Object, _
      E As ImageClickEventArgs)
   imgImage1.src = "wb1.gif"
   imgImage2.src = "wb1.gif"
   imgImage3.src = "wb2.gif"
```

```
End Sub

</script>
</head>
<body>

<form id="WebForm1"
   method="post"
   runat="server">
<h1>HTMLInputImage Example</h1>
<p>Click a button below to highlight your choice:</p>

<input id=imgImage1
   type=image
   src=wb1.gif
   runat="server"
   OnServerClick="imgImage1_Click">Choice 1
<br>
<input id=imgImage2
   type=image
   src=wb1.gif
   runat="server"
   OnServerClick="imgImage2_Click">Choice 2
<br>
<input id=imgImage3
   type=image
   src=wb1.gif
   runat="server"
   OnServerClick="imgImage3_Click">Choice 3

</form>
</body>
</html>
```

This example presents the user with three graphical buttons. Each of the buttons responds to a user click, which in turn causes a post-back to the server. The event-handling procedure for each button changes the button's graphic to an alternate image (showing that the button has been selected). The other buttons' images are then reverted back to their original images.

3.7.11 The HTMLInputRadioButton Control

HTML radio buttons allow the user to select from a group of mutually exclusive options. In other words, use radio buttons when you want the user to make only one choice from a set of choices.

It's important to group together related radio buttons by using the **name** attribute. This instructs the browser to treat the buttons as a group. When the user clicks on one radio button to highlight it, the previous selection becomes unhighlighted.

ASP.NET provides the `HTMLInputRadioButton` Control for programmatically controlling HTML radio buttons. The code selection below shows the typical syntax for the `HTMLInputRadioButton` Control.

```
<input
   type=radio
   runat="server"
   id="programmaticID"
   checked
name="radiobuttongroup"
>
```

Here's a sample page that demonstrates the use of the `HTMLInputRadioButton` Control.

Code Sample 3-12

```
<%@ Page Language="vb" %>
<html><head>
<title>HTMLInputRadio Example</title>

<script language=vb runat="server">

Sub cmdSendSurvey_Click(Source As Object, E As EventArgs)

   Dim strResults as String = _
      "<b>You answered: <br>"

   If rdbYearlyIncome1.Checked Then
      strResults &= "Less than $25,000/yr"
   End If

   If rdbYearlyIncome2.Checked Then
```

```
        strResults &= "$26,000 - $50,000/yr"
    End If

    If rdbYearlyIncome3.Checked Then
        strResults &= "$51,000 or more/yr"
    End If

    strResults &= "<br>"

    If Radio1.Checked Then
        strResults &= "E-mail newsletter"
    End If
    If Radio2.Checked Then
        strResults &= "Magazine Ad"
    End If
    If Radio3.Checked Then
        strResults &= "Other"
    End If

    strResults &= "</b>"
    lblResults.InnerHTML = strResults

End Sub
</script>
</head>
<body>

<form id="HTMLInputRadio"
    method="post"
    runat="server">

<h1>HTMLInputRadio Example</h1>
<p>Please answer our short survey:</p>
<ol>
<li><b>What is your yearly income?</b><br>
<input id=rdbYearlyIncome1
    checked name="YearlyIncome"
    type=radio
    runat="server">Less than $25,000/yr<br>
<input id=rdbYearlyIncome2
    name="YearlyIncome"
    type=radio
    runat="server">$26,000 - $50,000/yr<br>
<input id=rdbYearlyIncome3
```

```
   name="YearlyIncome"
   type=radio
   runat="server">$51,000 or more/yr<br>
<li><b>How did you hear about our Web site?</b><br>
<input id=Radio1
   name="HearAboutUs"
   type=radio
   checked runat="server">E-mail newsletter<br>
<input id=Radio2
   name="HearAboutUs"
   type=radio
   runat="server">Magazine Ad<br>
<input id=Radio3
   name="HearAboutUs"
   type=radio
   runat="server">Other<br>
<li>

<INPUT id=cmdSendSurvey
   type="submit"
   value="Send Survey"
   runat="server"
   onserverclick="cmdSendSurvey_Click">

</form>
</LI>
</OL>
<p>
<span id=lblResults
   runat="server">
</span>
</p>
</body>
</html>
```

The results of this sample code are shown in Figure 3-11. The code has two groups of radio buttons: `YearlyIncome` and `HearAboutUs`. This way, only one choice can be made for each question. We set the subroutine `cmdSendSurvey_Click` to be the event handler for the `OnServerClick` event for the Send Survey button. The `Checked` property of the `HTMLInputRadioButton` Control is of particular interest. This is how the program checks to see which option was selected for a particular radio button group. The code in the subroutine checks each button individually

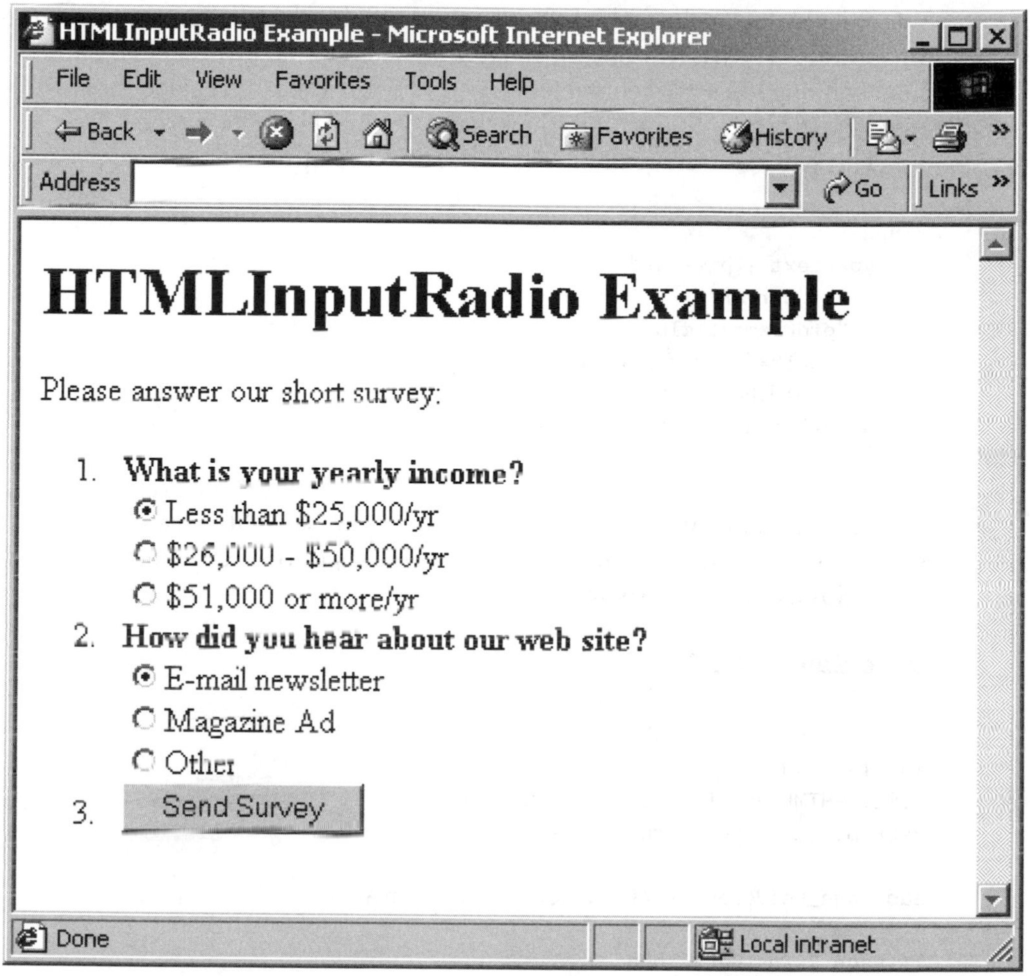

Figure 3-11 Output of the `HTMLInputRadioButton` example

and simultaneously builds a result string. This result string contains the text of the options that were selected. Finally, the result string is assigned to the `InnerHTML` property of `lblResults`, which displays the result.

3.7.12 The `HTMLInputText` Control

The most common HTML form input element is the text box. The HTML text box is a single-line input field that can accept either any number of characters or a defined number of characters. HTML text boxes can also be set with a default value, which displays in the field when the page is rendered. In addition, HTML text boxes can be designated as password fields. Rather than echoing the actual characters typed, these text boxes replace them with asterisks (or other characters) to mask the original characters typed.

The syntax for usage of the `HTMLInputText` Control follows.

```
<input
   type=text | password
   runat="server"
   id="programmaticID"
   maxlength="max#ofcharacters"
   size="widthoftextbox"
   value="defaulttextboxcontents"
>
```

Programming with the `HTMLInputText` field is straightforward. The sample page below shows how to use the `HTMLInputText` Control for regular text fields as well as password fields.

Code Sample 3-13

```
<%@ Page Language="vb" %>
<html><head>
<title>HTMLInputText Example</title>
<script language=vb runat="server">

Sub Page_Load(Source As Object, E As EventArgs)

If Page.IsPostBack Then
   If Len(txtPassword.Value) <= 4 Then
      lblResults.InnerHTML = _
      "<font color=red>Password must be longer than 4 characters</font>"
   Else
      lblResults.InnerHTML = "Welcome, " & _
         txtUsername.Value
   End If
End If

End Sub

</script>
</head>
```

```
<body>
<form id=frmMain
   runat="server">

<h1>HTMLInputText Example</h1>

<p>Create a new account with our system.
Just follow the steps below:
</p>

<span id=lblResults
   runat="server">
</span>

<ol>
   <li>Choose a username
   (maximum of 10 characters)<br>
   <INPUT id=txtUsername
   type="text"
   maxlength=10
   runat="server">

   <li>Now, choose a password
   (maximum of 8 characters)<br>

   <INPUT id=txtPassword
   type="password"
   maxlength=8
   runat="server">
   <li><INPUT id=cmdSubmit
   type="submit"
   value="Submit"
   runat="server"></li>
</ol>
</form>
</body>
</html>
```

3.7.13 The `HTMLSelect` Control

HTML `<select>` input elements allow the user to select a choice from a list of options. The options appear in one of two ways: in a drop-down menu or in a list box. Each of these types of input elements is implemented with the HTMLSelect Control.

The difference between the two types of lists is controlled by the size attribute of the control. If the size attribute is set to 1 or is not specified, a drop-down list is rendered. If the size attribute is greater than 1, a list box is rendered that displays size number of items at a time.

The HTMLSelect Control also supports a new type of event: the OnServerChange event. This event is fired when the user makes a change in the selection. Note that a selection change does not cause a post-back to the server. The event handler subroutine specified in the OnServerChange event is executed only upon a post-back to the server. The post-back can occur due to any event designed to perform a post-back, such as clicking a submit button, or due to an OnServerClick event from another control.

The HTMLSelect Control can also be bound to a data source. We'll explore data access in Chapter 7, where I'll provide a demonstration of binding data to the HTMLSelect Control as well as others. For now, here is the complete syntax for the HTMLSelect Control.

```
<select
   runat="server"
   id="programmaticID"
   OnServerChange="onserverchangehandler"
   DataSource="databindingsource"
   DataTextField="fieldtodatabindoptiontext"
   DataValueField="fieldtodatabindoptionvalue"
   Multiple
   Items="collectionofoptionelements"
   SelectedIndex="indexofcurrentlyselecteditem"
   Size="#ofvisibleitems"
   Value="currentitemvalue"
>
<option>value1</option>
<option>value2</option>
</select>
```

To demonstrate the capabilities of the HTMLSelect Control, let's review a page that allows the user to add text items to a drop-down list and a list box. The Display Selection button also shows how to get the selected value from the HTMLSelect Control. (The Display Selection button causes a post-back.)

Code Sample 3-14

```
<%@ Page Language="vb"%>
<html><head>
<title>HTMLSelect Example</title>
<script language=vb runat="server">

Sub btnAddToDDLB_Click(Source as Object, E As EventArgs)
   ddlbDropDown.Items.Add(txtItem.Value)
   ddlbDropDown.SelectedIndex = ddlbDropDown.Items.Count - 1
End Sub

Sub btnAddToLB_Click(Source as Object, E As EventArgs)
   lstListBox.Items.Add(txtItem.Value)
   If lstListBox.Items.Count < 5 Then
   .lstListBox.size = lstListBox.Items.Count
   End If
End Sub

Sub btnDisplaySelection_Click(Source As Object, E As EventArgs)
   lblResults.InnerHTML = "Drop Down: " & _
      ddlbDropDown.Value & _
      "<br>List Box: " & _
      lstListBox.Value & _
      "<br>"
End Sub

</script>
</head>

<body>
<h1>HTMLSelect Example</h1>

<form id=HTMLSelect
   method=post
   runat="server">
<p>

<span id=lblResults
   runat="server">
</span>

<select id=ddlbDropDown
   runat="server">
```

```
   <option selected></option>
</select>

<select id=lstListBox
   size=2
   runat="server">
   <option></option>
</select>
</p>

<p>
<input id=txtItem
   type=text
   runat="server">
</p>
<p>
<input id=btnAddToDDLB
   type=button
   value="Add to Drop-Down List Box"
   runat="server"
   onserverclick="btnAddToDDLB_Click">

<input id=btnAddToLB
   type=button
   value="Add to List Box"
   runat="server"
   onserverclick="btnAddToLB_Click">
</p>
<p>
<input id=btnDisplaySelection
   type=button
   value="Display Selection"
   runat="server"
   onserverclick="btnDisplaySelection_Click">
</p>

</form>
</body>
</html>
```

3.7.14 The `HTMLTable`, `HTMLTableCell`, and `HTMLTableRow` Controls

HTML tables are an important Web design element. Tables enable content to be displayed in a tabular format, like a spreadsheet, using rows and columns. Tables are also useful as a page layout tool. They facilitate more precise positioning of HTML than do other tags. Allowing the appearance and placement of tables to be controlled on the server further enhances the power of tables. This functionality is provided by the `HTMLTable` Controls.

Up to this point, all our ASP.NET examples use controls that were created at design time (that is, when using VS.NET to place the controls on a new Web Form). We adjusted the properties and even the HTML associated with these controls (the `InnerHTML` property) at runtime. But we usually have not known the results of server-side execution before running the program, as is usually the case when generating tables dynamically based on the results of server side code execution.

ASP.NET Controls are objects in the traditional sense; they have the same general characteristics as the objects we created in Chapter 2 using VB.NET. We created new instances of these objects dynamically at runtime (using the `New` command). Thus it follows that we can do the same with ASP.NET Controls. The example below is a good illustration of this new ASP.NET programming concept. This code generates a new table in the browser from dimensions that the user specifies. The user enters the number of rows and columns into the Web Form, posts it to the server, and renders the table. Here's an overview of that code.

Code Sample 3-15

```
<%@ Page Language="vb" %>
<html><head>
<title>HTMLTable Example</title>

<script language=vb runat="server">
Sub btnGenerateGrid_Click(Source As Object, E As EventArgs)

   Dim tr as HTMLTableRow
   Dim td as HTMLTableCell
   Dim intRowCounter As Integer
   Dim intCellCounter As Integer
   tr = New HTMLTableRow()
```

```
   For intRowCounter = 1 To CInt(txtRows.Value)

17        tr = New HTMLTableRow()

18        For intCellCounter = 1 To CInt(txtCols.Value)
19           td = New HTMLTableCell()
20           td.align = "center"
        td.InnerHTML = "HTML goes here"
21           tr.Cells.Add(td)
      Next

22       tblGridTable.Rows.Add(tr)

   Next

End Sub
</script>
</head>
<body>

<form id="HTMLTable"
   method="post"
   runat="server">

<h1>HTMLTable Example</h1>

<p>Enter the size of the table
grid you wish to generate:</p>

Rows: <input id=txtRows
   type=text
   runat="server">
<br>
Columns: <input id=txtCols
         type=text
         runat="server">
<br>

<INPUT id=btnGenerateGrid
   type="button"
   value="Generate Table Grid"
   onserverclick="btnGenerateGrid_Click"
   runat="server">
```

```
<table id=tblGridTable
   border=2
   runat="server">
</table>

</form>
</body>
</html>
```

This page begins with a Web Form that contains two text boxes for entering a number of rows and a number of columns. The Web Form also includes a blank HTML table with no rows. The values that the user enters for rows and columns in the text boxes specify the dimensions of the table to create when the user clicks the Generate Table Grid button.

The subroutine `btnGenerateGrid_Click` handles the generation of the new table. The HTML table is made up of rows and cells generated by two separate HTML Controls called `HTMLTableRow` and `HTMLTableCell`, respectively. These types of HTML Controls are known as *child controls* since they exist only within the context of a parent control, in this case `HTMLTable`. The subroutine uses nested `For . . . Next` loops to create new cells and rows. The inner loop that begins in line ⓲ creates new table cells. The loop runs as many times as specified by the value entered by the user for the number of cells. On each iteration through the loop, the `New` operator creates a new `HTMLTableCell`. Then we set the `align` and `InnerHTML` properties for the newly created cells.

Notice that before we entered the cell creation loop, we created an `HTMLTableRow` Control in line ⓱. This serves as the container for the `HTMLTableCell` Controls. As the table cells are created, they are added to a table row through its `Cells` collection (see line ⓳).

Once the row is filled with the specified number of cells, it is added to the HTML table through the `Rows` object in line ⓴. Then the nested loop repeats until the remaining rows are added to the table.

3.7.15 The `HTMLTextArea` Control

Another type of text input field, similar to `HTMLInputText`, is the `<textarea>` input element. Both of these HTML input elements accept text entered into them, but the `<textarea>` element can accept multiple lines of text. It is best suited for typing in long messages rather than short strings.

Here is a code sample using the `HTMLTextArea` Control.

Code Sample 3-16

```
<%@ Page Language="vb"%>
<html><head>
<title>HTMLTextArea Example</title>

<script language=vb runat="server">

Sub cmdSendComments_Click(Source As Object, E As EventArgs)
   lblResults.InnerHTML = "You entered: <I>" & _
   txaFeedback.Value & _
   "</I>"
End Sub

</script>
</head>
<body>

<form id="HTMLTextArea"
   method="post"
   runat="server">

<h1>HTMLTextArea Example</h1>

<p>Tell us why you like ASP.NET
and you can win yourself a nice prize!</p>

<textarea id=txaFeedback
   rows=10
   cols=30
   runat="server">
[Type your comments here]
</textarea>
<br>
<INPUT id=cmdSendComments
   type="submit"
   value="Send Comments"
   onserverclick="cmdSendComments_Click"
   runat="server">

<p>
<span id=lblResults
   runat="server"></span>
</p>
```

```
</form>
</body>
</html>
```

Like the `HTMLInputText` Control, the `HTMLTextArea` Control stores the value entered by the user in the `Value` property. The code in the `cmdSendComments_Click` subroutine uses this property to echo the text back to the user.

> **TIP:** You can find a complete reference to the ASP.NET HTML Controls in the VS.NET documentation or in the MSDN Library .NET Framework SDK documentation.

3.8 Using Web Controls

Web Controls provide richer functionality than their HTML Control counterparts. By using Web Controls instead of HTML Controls, substantial gains in functionality and visual appearance definition are gained. In this section and Sections 3.9 through 3.14, we'll explore the different types of Web Controls and their uses.

3.8.1 Shared Web Control Properties

All the ASP.NET Web Controls share rich formatting options. Some of the characteristics you can programmatically adjust include color, border styles, fonts, text styles, and many more (see Table 3-2). See Section 3.9.1 for an example of how to adjust the shared Web Control properties.

Table 3-2 Shared Web Control Properties

Property	Description
`AccessKey`	Sets the control's accelerator key, used to jump to a control (set focus) by pressing an ALT + *key* combination. Specify a single letter for this property, such as *A*. Access keys are not supported on all browsers.
`Attributes`	A runtime-only property that sets the control's persistence format.

(continued)

Table 3-2 Shared Web Control Properties *(continued)*

Property	Description
`BackColor`	Sets the background color of the control. You can specify the name of standard Web colors (for example, red, yellow, green) or an RGB hex value (for example, #3F3023).
`BorderWidth`	Specifies the width of the control's border in pixels. Not compatible with some down-level browsers (those other than Microsoft Internet Explorer).
`BorderStyle`	Sets the style of the control's border. Can be one of the following: `NotSet`, `None`, `Dotted`, `Dashed`, `Solid`, `Double`, `Groove`, `Ridge`, `Inset`, or `Outset`.
`CSSClass`	Specifies a cascading style sheet class to apply to the control.
`Enabled`	Enables or disables the control (true/false value).
`Font.Bold`	Sets the text to boldface (true/false value).
`Font.Italic`	Sets the text to italic (true/false value).
`Font.Name`	Specifies the font to use for the control.
`Font.Names`	Specifies a list of fonts to use for the control. Starting from the beginning of the list, if a particular font isn't available, the text is rendered using the next available font.
`Font.Overline`	Sets whether a line is displayed above the text (true/false value).
`Font.Size`	Specifies the HTML size of the font (a number from 1 to 7).
`Font.Strikeout`	Sets the text to strikeout (true/false value).
`Font.Underline`	Sets the text to underline (true/false value).
`ForeColor`	Sets the color of the text, specified as an HTML color or hex value.
`Height`	Sets the height of the control in pixels.

Property	Description
TabIndex	Specifies the tab order of the control; defaults to 0. Supported only in Microsoft Internet Explorer 4.0 or greater.
ToolTip	Specifies the text to use as a "floating" tool tip. Does not work with down-level browsers.
Width	Sets the width of the control in terms of characters, pixels, or percentage. Specified as a number (*n*px or *n*%).

3.9 Web Controls for Displaying and Formatting Data

You can use several Web Controls for displaying and formatting data within the browser window. The simplest of these is the Label Control.

3.9.1 The `Label` Control

The `Label` Control is used to display any arbitrary HTML within a predefined area. Labels are static, meaning that the `Label` Control is used primarily to display information that users can't edit. The `Label` Control appears in the VS.NET Control Toolbox under the Web Forms category (see Figure 3-12).

To place any Web Control on a Web Form, simply select the one you want in the Control Toolbox and drag it to the Web Form. Figure 3-13 shows this operation in progress using the `Label` Control.

After you've placed the `Label` Control on the Web Form, you can resize it to your wishes and requirements. You can also adjust its design-time properties, which are located in the Properties window (see Figure 3-14).

The most common property you will adjust for any Web Control is the `ID` property. Recall that you use the `ID` property to programmatically reference the Web Control in your code. VS.NET will automatically assign an ID property to any Web Control you drag onto the Web Form, but it's to your advantage to assign the Web Control a new name that's meaningful to your application.

When you drag a `Label` Control onto a Web Form, VS.NET generates the code necessary to display the label in the page. If you click on the HTML tab (located at the bottom of the main window that contains the Web Form), you'll switch to a source-code view of the `.aspx` file. Here you'll see the

Figure 3-12 VS.NET Control Toolbox with the `Label` Control option selected

generated code for the `Label` Control you placed on the Web Form. The code below in boldface shows the `Label` Control code.

Code Sample 3-17

```
<%@ Page Language="vb"
   AutoEventWireup="false"
   Inherits="MyWebForm"
   Src="cs3-17.aspx.vb"
```

```
%>

<html>
<head>
<title>Web Control - Label Control</title>
</head>

<body>

<form id="MyWebForm" method="post" runat="server">
<h1>Web Control - Label Control</h1>
<p>

<asp:Label
   id=lblTestLabel
   runat="server">Label
</asp:Label>

</p>

</form>
</body>
</html>
```

Here's the complete syntax for the `Label` Control.

```
<asp:Label id="Label1" runat="server"
   Text="label"
/>
```

or

```
<asp:Label id="Label1" runat="server">
Text
</asp:Label>
```

As you can see from the syntax example, the `Label` Control can have two different forms. The first has a `Text` attribute that specifies the text to display. The second syntax form has a closing tag, and any text placed inside the tags becomes the text for the label. VS.NET uses the first syntax form.

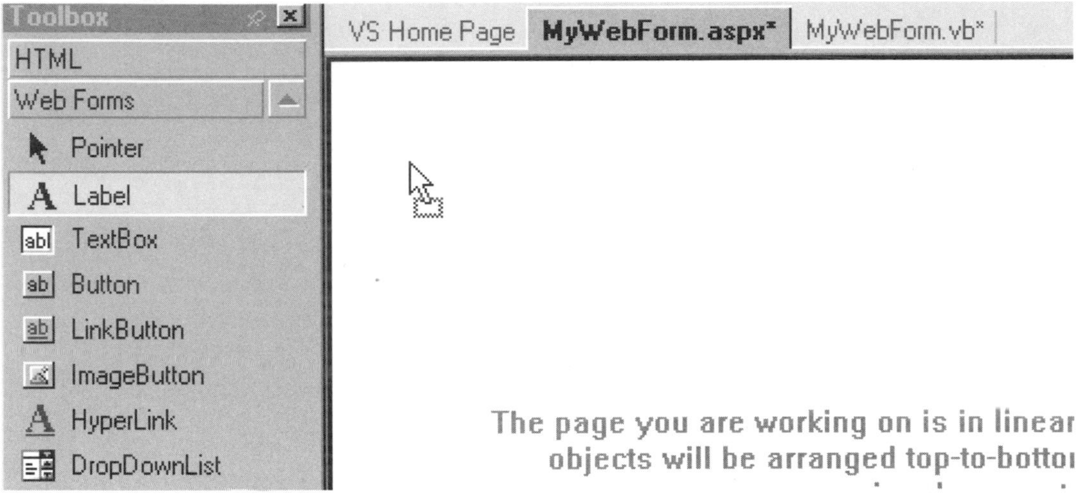

Figure 3-13 Dragging the `Label` Control onto a Web Form

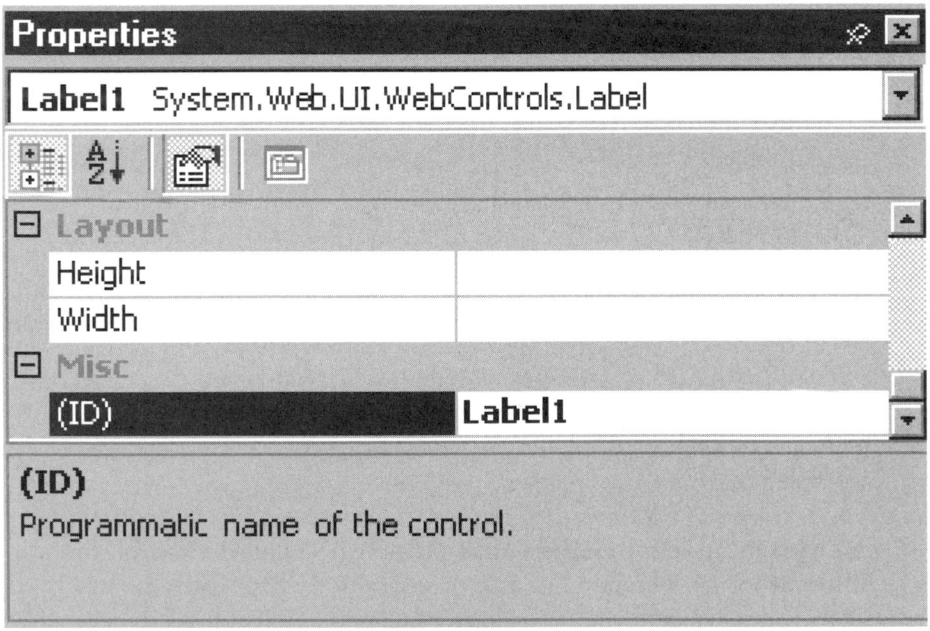

Figure 3-14 The VS.NET Properties window

Adjusting the Shared Properties for Web Controls

As mentioned in Section 3.8.1, you can use shared properties to control the visual appearance of Web Controls. The `Label` Control example below contains a code-behind module and demonstrates how to set the different shared properties of Web Controls.

```
Imports System
Imports System.Web
Imports System.Drawing
Imports System.Web.UI
Imports System.Web.UI.WebControls
Imports System.Web.UI.HtmlControls

Public Class MyWebForm
   Inherits System.Web.UI.Page

   Protected WithEvents lblTestLabel As _
      System.Web.UI.WebControls.Label

   Private Sub Page_Load(ByVal Sender As System.Object, _
         ByVal e As System.EventArgs) _
         Handles MyBase.Load

㉑     lblTestLabel.BorderStyle = BorderStyle.Dashed
㉒     lblTestLabel.BorderWidth = Unit.Pixel(5)
      lblTestLabel.Height = Unit.Pixel(30)
      lblTestLabel.Width = Unit.Pixel(100)
㉓     lblTestLabel.BackColor = Color.Yellow
      lblTestLabel.Enabled = False
㉔     lblTestLabel.Font.Name = "Arial"
㉕     lblTestLabel.Font.Bold = True
      lblTestLabel.ToolTip = "This is a tool tip"
      lblTestLabel.Text = "This is a test of the Label Web Control"

   End Sub

End Class
```

Programmatically changing the values of the shared Web Control properties sometimes involves structures and classes from the `System.Drawing` and `System.Web.UI.WebControls` namespaces. In this example, `BorderStyle` and `Unit` come from the `System.Web.UI.WebControls` namespace, and `Color` and `Font` come from the `System.Drawing` namespace. In line ㉑, we set the

BorderStyle of the label for a Dashed outline. Dashed is a field of the BorderStyle structure. We also set the thickness of the border by supplying a value for BorderWidth in line ㉒. The Unit structure's Pixel() method is used to return a Unit structure from a 32-bit signed integer value that specifies a pixel measurement. Other methods of the Unit structure include Percentage() and Point(), which return Unit structures expressed in percentages and points (for fonts), respectively.

Line ㉓ shows how to specify a color (in this case, yellow) for the background of the label. The Color structure contains properties for all the standard Web colors. If you wish to specify a custom RGB color, you can use the FromARGB() method of the Color structure. One form of this function takes three parameters: the byte values for red, green, and blue. Call it like this:

```
lblTestLabel.BorderColor = Color.FromARGB(123, 29, 55)
```

The Font class controls the appearance of the Label Control's text. This includes the font face as well as text styles (bold, italic, underline, and so on). Lines ㉔ and ㉕ set the label text for the Arial font in bold.

The rendered Label Control from this code appears in Figure 3-15.

Many of the shared properties can be set at design time for Web Controls. Also, being able to programmatically set them is a powerful feature. Programmatically set control properties will override properties set at design time.

3.9.2 The Panel Control

Web pages can contain many different elements and controls. Sometimes those controls and elements need to be contained as a group. The Panel Control provides server-side control over the HTML <div> element. The Panel Control is used primarily as a page-layout tool.

The syntax for the Panel Control follows.

```
<asp:Panel id="Panel1" runat="server"
   BackImageUrl="url"
   HorizontalAlign="Center | Justify | Left | NotSet | Right"
   Wrap="True | False"
/>
   (Other controls declared here)
</asp:Panel>
```

The demonstration below of the Panel Control dynamically displays swatches of all the colors in the Web-safe palette. The Web-safe palette contains 216 distinct RGB colors guaranteed not to cause pixel dithering

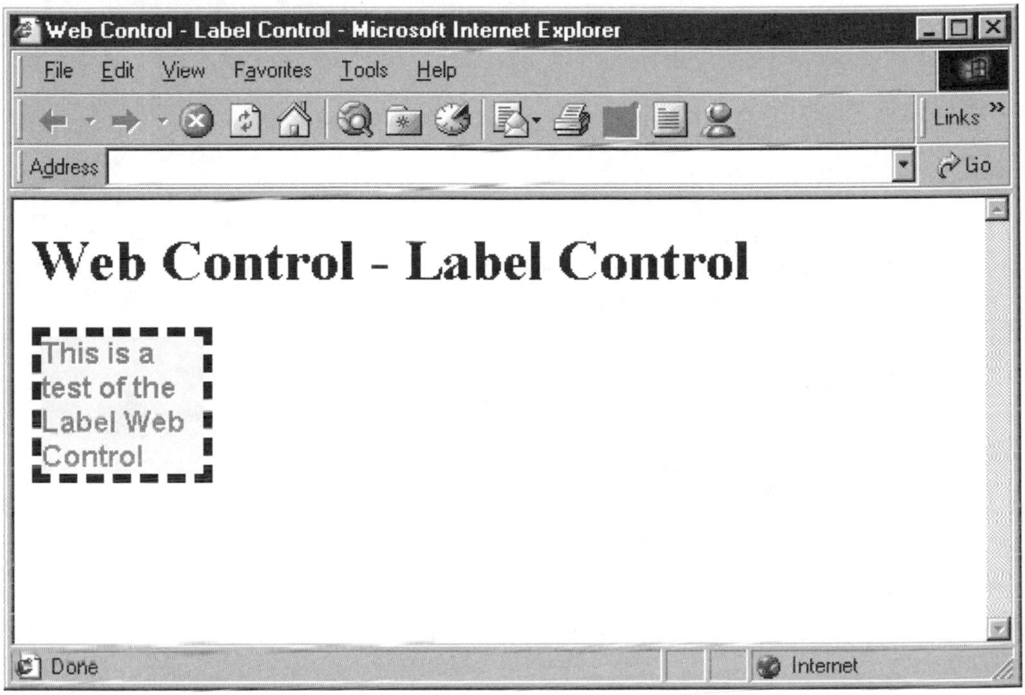

Figure 3-15 Output of the `Label` Control example

regardless of the video hardware used to display them. Web designers often refer to Web-safe palette charts such as the one we're about to construct. Each color swatch in our chart will contain tool-tip text signifying the hex color value used in HTML.

The Web form is simple. The boldface text in the sample code below shows how to declare a `Panel` Control on a Web Form. For visual clarity, we give the panel for the color chart a width equal to the maximum width of the browser window.

Code Sample 3-18

```
<%@ Page Language="vb"
   AutoEventWireup="false"
   Src="cs3-18.aspx.vb"
   Inherits="WebControlPanel"%>
<html><head>
```

```
<TITLE>Web Control - Panel Control</TITLE>
</head>
<body>

<form id="WebControlPanel"
   method="post"
   runat="server">

<h1>Web Control - Panel Control</h1>
This will display all the "web-safe"
colors as Labels inside a Panel Web Control:

<p>

<asp:Panel id=pnlColorPanel
   runat="server"
   Width="100%">
</asp:Panel>

</p>

</form>
</body>
</html>
```

The code-behind file for the resulting Web Form follows.

```
Imports System
Imports System.Drawing
Imports System.Web
Imports System.Web.UI
Imports System.Web.UI.WebControls
Imports Microsoft.VisualBasic


Public Class WebControlPanel
   Inherits System.Web.UI.Page

   Protected WithEvents pnlColorPanel As _
      System.Web.UI.WebControls.Panel

   Private Sub Page_Load(ByVal Sender As System.Object, _
            ByVal e As System.EventArgs) _
            Handles MyBase.Load
```

```
      Dim intRed As Integer
      Dim intGreen As Integer
      Dim intBlue As Integer
      Dim strColor As String
      Dim lblColorLabel As Label

      If Not IsPostback Then

(26)     For intRed = 0 To 255 Step 51
            For intGreen = 0 To 255 Step 51
               For intBlue = 0 To 255 Step 51
(27)                 strColor = "#" & _
                        ZeroPad(Hex(intRed)) & _
                        ZeroPad(Hex(intGreen)) & _
                        ZeroPad(Hex(intBlue))

(28)                 lblColorLabel = New Label()
(29)                 With lblColorLabel
                    .ToolTip = strColor
                    .BackColor = Color.FromARGB(intRed, _
                          intGreen, intBlue)
                    .Width = Unit.Pixel(10)
                    .Height = Unit.Pixel(10)
(30)                    pnlColorPanel.Controls.Add(lblColorLabel)
                  End With
               Next
            Next
         Next

      End If
   End Sub

   Private Function ZeroPad(ByVal HexValue As String) _
                     As String
      If Len(HexValue) = 1 Then
         ZeroPad = "0" & HexValue
      Else
         ZeroPad = HexValue
      End If
   End Function

End Class
```

The **Page_Load** event contains the code to create the color chart. This code demonstrates two important concepts: creating new Web Controls dynamically and working with child controls. First, I'll explain the logic for generating the color values.

An HTML color is an RGB value. Each component (red, green, and blue) of the color has a number assigned to it (0–255). To iterate through the entire RGB color space, we create three nested `For . . . Next` loops beginning in line ㉖. The program steps through the loop every 51 iterations. That gives us hex values of `00`, `33`, `66`, `99`, `CC`, and `FF`. Every color in the Web-safe palette contains RGB values that are from this set of hex values. When all three loops have exited, the program has covered each RGB combination. In the code block beginning in line ㉗, each RGB integer value is converted to a two-character hexadecimal string and concatenated to form a complete color string

Line ㉘ starts the creation of a new `Label` Control. This label will become a color swatch. In line ㉙, we begin a `With . . . End With` block to set the properties of the newly created label. These include setting the tool-tip text to the color string, sizing the label to a 10 × 10 pixel rectangle, and setting the background color with the current RGB values.

The `Panel` Control is used as a container for other Web Controls. Recall the discussion about the `HTMLTable` Control (see Section 3.7.14) and how it contained child controls (`HTMLTableRow` and `HTMLTableCell`). The `Panel` Control works in a similar fashion. Take note of the code in line ㉚. The `pnlColorPanel` code contains a `Controls` collection. Part of that `Controls` collection is an `Add()` method. The parameter to the `Add()` method is a control object (`System.Web.UI.WebControls`). Since the `Label` Control inherits from `System.Web.UI.WebControls`, we can pass our dynamically created `Label` Control to this method. At that point, each label is positioned sequentially inside the panel we created.

The output of the code written above is shown in Figure 3-16.

3.9.3 The `Table`, `TableRow`, and `TableCell` Controls

The `Table`, `TableRow`, and `TableCell` Web Controls provide rich functionality for generating tables. The syntax below shows the constructs used to create a new `Table` Control.

```
<asp:Table id="Table1" runat="server"
   BackImageUrl="url"
   CellSpacing="cellspacing"
   CellPadding="cellpadding"
   GridLines="None | Horizontal | Vertical | Both"
```

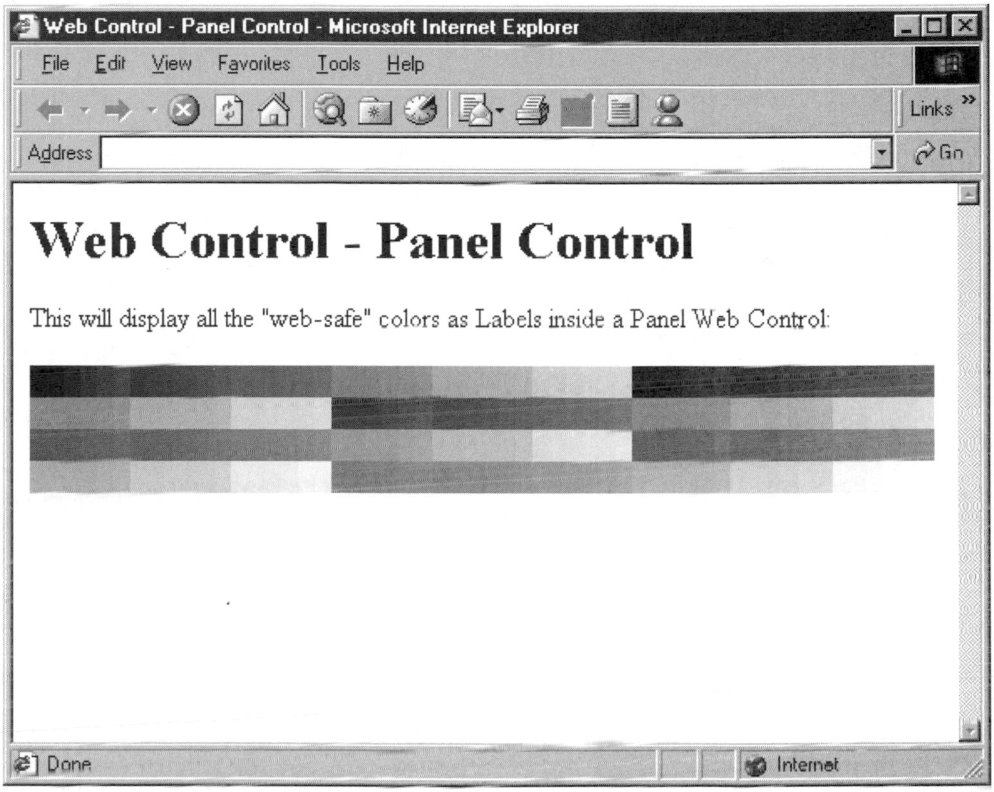

Figure 3-16 Output of the `Panel` Control example

```
   HorizontalAlign="Center | Justify | Left | NotSet | Right"
/>
   <asp:TableRow>
      <asp:TableCell>
         Cell text
      </asp:TableCell>
   </asp:TableRow>
</asp:Table>
```

The `TableRow` and `TableCell` Controls are usually used as child controls to the `Table` Control. Much like their HTML Control equivalents, you can programmatically create new rows and cells using the VB.NET

New() command. The syntax for the TableRow and TableCell commands appears below.

```
<asp:TableRow id="TableRow1" runat="server"
   HorizontalAlign="Center | Justify | Left | NotSet | Right"
   VerticalAlign="Bottom | Middle | NotSet | Top"
/>
(cells go here)
</asp:TableRow>
```

```
<asp:TableCell id="TableCell1" runat="server"
   ColumnSpan="colcount"
   RowSpan="rowcount"
   HorizontalAlign="Center | Justify | Left | NotSet | Right"
   VerticalAlign="Bottom | Middle | NotSet | Top"
   Wrap="True | False"
/>
   Cell text
</asp:TableCell>
```

Using tables, you can construct some interesting shapes and define some advanced page layouts. On some Web sites, you may see a figure that looks like a desktop window. You can simulate this look by using HTML tables. The `Table`, `TableRow`, and `TableCell` Controls make creating these windows easy and allow you to control their style characteristics with just minor code changes.

Here's the example code, starting with the `.aspx` file that contains the HTML. The boldface text shows the use of the `Table` Control.

Code Sample 3-19

```
<%@ Page Language="vb"
   AutoEventWireup="false"
   src="cs3-19.aspx.vb"
   Inherits="WebControlTable"%>
<html><head>
<TITLE>Web Control - Table, TableRow,
```

```
TableCell Controls</TITLE>
</head>
<body>

<form id="WebControlTable"
   method="post"
   runat="server">

<h1>Web Control - Table,
TableRow, TableCell Controls
</h1>

<p>
This page demonstrates how to
create HTML tables dynamically using
the Table, TableRow, and
TableCell Web Controls.
</p>

<p>
<asp:Table id=tblDisplayWindow
      runat="server">
</asp:Table>
</p>


</form>
</body>
</html>
```

Notice that the initial `Table` Control does not have any rows, cells, or base properties set. The following VB.NET code sets up those things.

```
Imports System
Imports System.Drawing
Imports System.Web
Imports System.Web.UI
Imports System.Web.UI.WebControls
Imports Microsoft.VisualBasic
```

```
Public Class WebControlTable
   Inherits System.Web.UI.Page

   Protected WithEvents tblDisplayWindow As _
         System.Web.UI.WebControls.Table

   Private Sub Page_Load(ByVal Sender As System.Object, _
               ByVal e As System.EventArgs) _
      Handles MyBase.Load

         CreateDisplayWindow(200, 300, "Test Window")

   End Sub

   Private Sub CreateDisplayWindow(ByVal h As Integer, _
                        ByVal w As Integer, _
                        ByVal TitleString As String)

      Dim trRow As TableRow
      Dim tdCell As TableCell

31    With tblDisplayWindow
         .Width = Unit.Pixel(w)
         .Height = Unit.Pixel(h)
         .CellPadding = 2
         .BackColor = Color.Gray
      End With

32    trRow = New TableRow()
33    tdCell = New TableCell()
      tdCell.BackColor = Color.Navy
      tdCell.ForeColor = Color.White
      tdCell.Text = "<B>" & TitleString & "</B>"
34    trRow.Height = Unit.Percentage(10)
      trRow.Cells.Add(tdCell)

35    tblDisplayWindow.Rows.Add(trRow)

      trRow = New TableRow()
      tdCell = New TableCell()
      With tdCell
         .BackColor = Color.White
         .BorderWidth = Unit.Pixel(3)
         .BorderColor = Color.White
```

```
            .VerticalAlign = WebControls.VerticalAlign.Top
            .Text = "Content is displayed here"
        End With

        trRow.Cells.Add(tdCell)

(36)    tblDisplayWindow.Rows.Add(trRow)

    End Sub

End Class
```

The subroutine `CreateDisplayWindow()` performs the rendering work for the Web window. The window is composed of a main table and two rows (one for the title bar and another for the content). The subroutine takes three parameters: `h` and `w`, which specify the main table's height and width, respectively, in pixels, and `TitleString`, which is the text to display in the title bar.

Let's start with the construction of the main table. We define the main `Table` Control in the HTML in the `.aspx` file. This `Table` Control has an `ID` of `tblDisplayTable`. In the code block beginning with line (31), we set the size and the background color of the table. Notice the use of the `Unit` structure to specify pixel units and the `Color` structure to select one of the predefined Web colors. We're also allowing a two-pixel padding of the table cells. This will give the content cell (which we'll define in a moment) the appearance of being surrounded by a gray outline.

Moving on, we define the row that will make up the title bar. Starting with the creation of a new row in line (32) and a new cell in line (33), we set the color and text properties of the single cell in the row. To make sure that the new row doesn't inadvertently occupy more of the table's height than we need for the title text, in line (34) we explicitly set the height of the row to 10% of the table's total height. Since we define only two rows for this table, the other row will occupy the remaining 90% of the height. In line (35) the row is added to the `Rows` collection.

The content portion of the window follows a similar definition. The content row is added at line (36).

The final look of the page appears something like that shown in Figure 3-17.

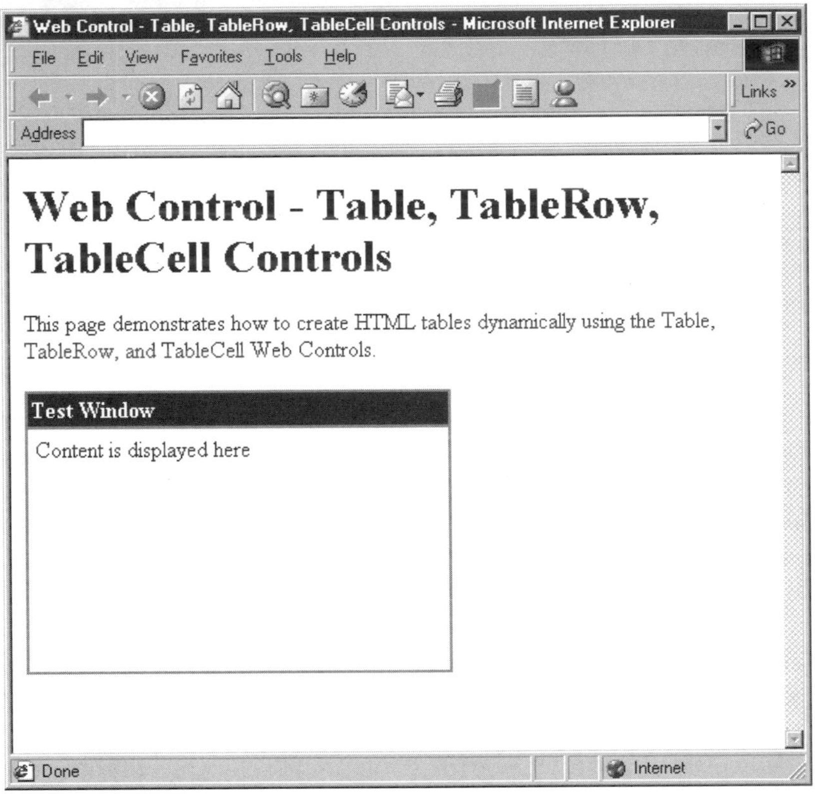

Figure 3-17 Output of the `Table`, `TableRow`, and `TableCell` Controls example

3.10 Web Controls for Creating Buttons

In this section, we'll be talking about the different buttons available in ASP.NET. All the buttons in this section cause a post-back to the server. Whenever you need the server to respond to a user click, use one of the button Web Controls. Which button you use depends on the design requirements of your site. Buttons can be a graphic image, a hyperlink, or a regular push button.

3.10.1 The `Button` Control

The `Button` Control renders a regular push button, the most common type of button seen on Web pages, as an HTML button (`<INPUT type=button>`). Here's the syntax to use.

```
<asp:Button id="MyButton" runat="server"
   Text="label"
   Command="command"
   CommandArgument="commandArgument"
   OnClick="OnClickMethod"
/>
```

In addition to the shared Web Control properties, the `Button` Control contains some unique properties. The `Text` property specifies the text to display on the button itself, such as "Submit Form." The `OnClick` property sets the procedure name to call when the button is clicked. As shown in the code above, there are also two other properties, `Command` and `CommandArgument`, which are discussed further below.

Bubbled-Up Events

The `Command` and `CommandArgument` properties bring up a new Web Control concept called *bubbled-up events*. You've already seen with the `Table`, `TableRow`, and `TableCell` Controls how you can embed child controls inside another container control. If one of the child controls can fire events (such as a button firing an `OnClick` event), you may want to notify the parent control of that event occurring. The event fired by the child control event can be sent or "bubbled up" to the parent control through a message contained in the `Command` property. An optional command parameter can be passed in the `CommandArgument` property. The `Button` Control example in Section 3.10.4 shows a sample implementation of bubbled-up events.

3.10.2 The `ImageButton` Control

The `ImageButton` Control allows you to use a graphical image as a button for causing a post-back. You can use the `ImageButton` Control to create clickable icons as well as image maps, with which the coordinates of where the click took place (in relation to the x/y coordinate system that frames the image) can be reported to the `OnClick` subroutine. The syntax for using the `ImageButton` Control appears below.

```
<asp:ImageButton id="ImageButton1" runat="server"
   ImageUrl="string"
   Command="command"
   CommandArgument="commandArgument"
   OnClick="OnClickMethod"
/>
```

In the `ImageUrl` property, you can specify a URL to an image to use for the button. The `Command`, `CommandArgument`, and `OnClick` properties function the same way they do for the `Button` Control.

3.10.3 The `LinkButton` Control

The `LinkButton` Control appears just like a hyperlink to the user, but instead of simply navigating to another URL, which is the default behavior, the `LinkButton` Control can cause a post-back to the server just like the `Button` and `ImageButton` Controls. Here is the `LinkButton` Control syntax.

```
<asp:LinkButton id="LinkButton1" runat="server"
   Text="label"
   Command="command"
   CommandArgument="commandArgument"
   OnClick="OnClickMethod"
/>

<asp:LinkButton id="LinkButton1" runat="server"
   Command="command"
   CommandArgument="commandArgument"
   OnClick="OnClickMethod"
/>
   Text
</asp:LinkButton>
```

3.10.4 Demonstration of Web Button Controls

This demonstration shows the usage of all three types of button controls. The `.aspx` file includes the creation of each type of button at design time.

Code Sample 3-20

```
<%@ Page Language="vb"
   AutoEventWireup="false"
   src="cs3-20.aspx.vb"
   Inherits="WebControlButtonSample"%>
<html>

<head>
<title>Web Control - Button Example</title>
</head>
```

```
<body>

<form id="WebControlButtonSample"
   method="post"
   runat="server">

<h1>Web Control - Button Example</h1>

<p>Demonstration of Button,
LinkButton, and ImageButton:
</p>

<p>
<asp:Button id=btnWebControlButton
   runat="server"
   Text="Button">
</asp:Button>
</p>

<p>
<asp:LinkButton id=lbtWebLinkButton
   runat="server">
   LinkButton
</asp:LinkButton></p>

<p>
<asp:ImageButton id=igbWebImageButton
   runat="server"
   ImageUrl="mountain.jpg">
</asp:ImageButton>
</p>

<p>
<asp:Label id=lblResults
   runat="server"
   Width="202"
   Height="84">
</asp:Label>
</p>

</form>
</body>
</html>
```

The code-behind file provides some routines for handling the `Click` events for each button.

```
Imports System
Imports System.Drawing
Imports System.Web
Imports System.Web.UI
Imports System.Web.UI.WebControls
Imports Microsoft.VisualBasic

Public Class WebControlButtonSample
   Inherits System.Web.UI.Page
   Protected WithEvents lblResults As _
      System.Web.UI.WebControls.Label
   Protected WithEvents igbWebImageButton As _
      System.Web.UI.WebControls.ImageButton
   Protected WithEvents lbtWebLinkButton As _
      System.Web.UI.WebControls.LinkButton
   Protected WithEvents btnWebControlButton As _
      System.Web.UI.WebControls.Button

37 Public Sub igbWebImageButton_Click(ByVal sender As Object, _
            ByVal e As System.Web.UI.ImageClickEventArgs) _
            Handles igbWebImageButton.Click
      lblResults.Text = "You clicked ImageButton at: " & _
         e.X.ToString() & ", " & e.Y.ToString()
   End Sub

   Public Sub lbtWebLinkButton_Click( _
            ByVal sender As Object, _
            ByVal e As System.EventArgs) _
            Handles lbtWebLinkButton.Click
      lblResults.Text = "You clicked the LinkButton!"
   End Sub

   Public Sub btnWebControlButton_Click( _
            ByVal sender As Object, _
            ByVal e As System.EventArgs) _
            Handles btnWebControlButton.Click
      lblResults.Text = "You clicked the Button control!"
   End Sub
End Class
```

Of particular interest is the `Click` event code for the `igbWebImageButton` Control in line (37). As mentioned before, you can treat the `ImageButton` Control as an image map that returns the coordinates of where the click event occurred. To retrieve the coordinates, the code above makes the second parameter of the `Click` event handler `System.Web.UI.ImageClickEventArgs`. This class contains two members specific to image maps: `X` and `Y`. They correspond to the x/y coordinates of the click event location.

The output of the demonstration is shown in Figure 3-18.

Figure 3-18 Output of the button controls demonstration

3.11 Web Control for Inputting Text

The ability to input text is central to any interactive Web site. The HTML standard provides three forms of text input: the <input type=text> tag, the <input type=password> tag, and the <textarea> tag. Both <input> tags function much the same way, but the <textarea> tag is used for multiline input and is generally used for typing in larger amounts of text. In ASP.NET, this distinction between all three different input mechanisms is removed and is replaced by the TextBox Control.

3.11.1 The TextBox Control

The TextBox Control's actual rendering is determined by the TextMode property. The syntax for the TextBox Control appears below.

```
<asp:TextBox id=value runat="server"
   AutoPostBack="True | False"
   Columns="characters"
   MaxLength="characters"
   Rows="rows"
   Text="text"
   TextMode="Single | Multiline | Password"
   Wrap="True | False"
   OnTextChanged="OnTextChangedMethod"
>
</asp:TextBox>
```

Table 3-3 lists the properties of the TextBox Control.

The TextBox Control can also respond via an event, when the text contents have changed. According to how the AutoPostBack property is set, this may cause an immediate post-back to the server. Otherwise, the event is processed upon the next post-back to the server (for example, when a submit button is clicked). The event is called OnTextChanged.

The following example shows the variety of text boxes you can create along with demonstrations of event handling.

Code Sample 3-21

```
<%@ Page Language="vb"
   AutoEventWireup="false"
   src="cs3-21.aspx.vb"
   Inherits="WebControlTextBoxSample"%>
```

```
<html>
<head>
<TITLE>Web Control - TextBox Example</TITLE>
</head>
<body>

<form id="WebControlTextBoxSample"
   method="post"
   runat="server">
<h1>Web Control - TextBox Example</h1>

<p>Enter any text into these text boxes:</p>

<p>Single-line text box:
<asp:TextBox id=txtSingle
   runat="server">
</asp:TextBox>
</p>

<p>Password text box:
<asp:TextBox id=txtPassword
   textmode="password"
   runat="server">
</asp:TextBox>
</p>

<p>Multiline text box (delayed event).
<asp:TextBox id=txtDelayedEvent
   runat="server"
   TextMode="MultiLine"
   Rows="3"
   Columns="30">
</asp:TextBox>
</p>

<p>Multiline text box (AutoPostBack):
<asp:TextBox id=txtAutoPost
   runat="server"
   TextMode="MultiLine"
   Rows="3"
   Columns="30"
38     autopostback="True">
</asp:TextBox>
</p>
```

```
<p>
<asp:Button id=btnSubmit
   runat="server"
   Text="Submit Data">
</asp:Button>
</p>

<p>
<asp:Label id=lblSingleTxtResult
   runat="server">
</asp:Label>
</p>

<p>
<asp:Label id=lblPasswordTxtResult
   runat="server">
</asp:Label>
</p>

<p>
<asp:Label id=lblMultiDelayedResult
   maintainstate="False"
   runat="server">
</asp:Label>
</p>

<p>
<asp:Label id=lblMultiAutoResult
   runat="server">
</asp:Label>
</p>

</form>
</body>
</html>
```

This code demonstrates four different `TextBox` Controls, each one with different `TextMode` and `AutoPostBack` attributes. The purpose of the example is to show the behavior of these text boxes under different circumstances.

The `OnTextChanged` event of the `TextBox` Control shows, for the first time, how client-side events can trigger a post-back to the server. In order to trigger an immediate post-back when text changes in a text box, you need to

Table 3-3 Properties of the TextBox Control

Property	Description
AutoPostBack	Indicates whether changes to the control's text made by a user in his or her browser will cause an immediate post-back to the server. `True` causes a post-back. The default value is `False`.
Columns	Specifies how many characters wide the control should be.
MaxLength	Indicates the maximum number of characters a user is allowed to type into the field. Works only for single-line input and password fields.
Rows	Indicates for multiline text boxes the number of rows to display at one time.
Text	Sets the default text to display in the text box or the text that a user enters into the text box.
TextMode	Specifies the kind of text box to render: single-line, multiline, or password.
Wrap	Indicates for multi-line text boxes whether or not to let the text wrap around to the next line when a line reaches the width of the text box; a Boolean value.

use the client-side event to trigger a form post. Client-side JavaScript can accomplish this. Whenever a Web Control like a text field loses focus (that is, when the Web Control becomes unhighlighted because the user switches to another one), its contents are checked for changes. If there is a client-side event handler for that change, you can configure that client-side event handler to trigger a form post if changes have occurred. That's exactly what happens when you set the `AutoPostBack` property to `True` as shown in line ㊳.

The appearance of a text box is controlled by several factors: the `TextMode` property, the `Rows` property, and the `Columns` property. The `Rows` and `Columns` properties apply only to multiline text boxes. Conversely, some `TextBox` Control properties (for example, `MaxLength`) have meaning for only single-line input text boxes.

The code-behind file for this HTML demonstrates the event-handling mechanism of `OnTextChanged`, the event raised when the contents of the text box have changed.

```
Imports System
Imports System.Drawing
Imports System.Web
Imports System.Web.UI
Imports System.Web.UI.WebControls

Public Class WebControlTextBoxSample
   Inherits System.Web.UI.Page
   Protected WithEvents lblMultiAutoResult As _
      System.Web.UI.WebControls.Label
   Protected WithEvents lblMultiDelayedResult As _
      System.Web.UI.WebControls.Label
   Protected WithEvents lblPasswordTxtResult As _
      System.Web.UI.WebControls.Label
   Protected WithEvents lblSingleTxtResult As _
      System.Web.UI.WebControls.Label
   Protected WithEvents btnSubmit As _
      System.Web.UI.WebControls.Button
   Protected WithEvents txtAutoPost As _
      System.Web.UI.WebControls.TextBox
   Protected WithEvents txtDelayedEvent As _
      System.Web.UI.WebControls.TextBox
   Protected WithEvents txtPassword As _
      System.Web.UI.WebControls.TextBox
   Protected WithEvents txtSingle As _
      System.Web.UI.WebControls.TextBox

39   Public Sub txtAutoPost_TextChanged(ByVal sender As Object, _
        ByVal e As System.EventArgs) _
        Handles txtAutoPost.TextChanged

      lblMultiAutoResult.Text = "AutoPostBack: New Value: " & _
        txtAutoPost.Text
   End Sub

40   Public Sub txtDelayedEvent_TextChanged( _
        ByVal sender As Object, _
        ByVal e As System.EventArgs) _
        Handles txtDelayedEvent.TextChanged

      lblMultiDelayedResult.Text = "DelayEvent: New Value:" & _
        txtDelayedEvent.Text

   End Sub
```

```
    Public Sub btnSubmit_Click(ByVal sender As Object, _
          ByVal e As System.EventArgs) _
          Handles btnSubmit.Click
       lblSingleTxtResult.Text = "Single line: New Value: " & _
          txtSingle.Text
       lblPasswordTxtResult.Text = "Password: New Value: " & _
          txtPassword.Text
    End Sub
End Class
```

The `txtAutoPost` text box in line ㊴ has the `AutoPostBack` attribute set, so whenever text changes in the text box (and whenever the text box loses focus), a post-back is executed. The `txtDelayedEvent` text box in line ㊵, on the other hand, does not cause an immediate post-back. The `TextChanged` event is raised upon a post-back that is initiated from elsewhere, namely the `btnSubmit` button.

3.12 Web Controls for Selecting Choices

Selection Controls, including radio buttons and checkboxes, allow users to select from a series of predefined values. These Selection Controls are usually grouped together to represent choices in the same category. For example, an online survey might ask to what types of industries your company sells products. Possible choices could include health care, aerospace, and hospitality, each accompanied by a checkbox. Checkboxes represent independent options since more than one (or none) can be selected.

Radio buttons, like checkboxes, allow users to select from a list of options. However, radio buttons are intended to represent mutually exclusive options, that is, only one choice in a category can be selected. For example, an online survey may ask about your income level. Radio buttons for different income ranges allow you to select only one choice.

3.12.1 The CheckBox Control

The `CheckBox` Control renders an HTML `<input type=checkbox>` element to the browser. Each checkbox can have a label, which can appear to the right or to the left of the checkbox, according to the `TextAlign` property. The default state of the checkbox and its current state are indicated by the `Checked` property. Here is the syntax for the `CheckBox` Control.

```
<asp:CheckBox id="CheckBox1" runat="server"
   AutoPostBack="True | False"
   Text="label"
   TextAlign="Right | Left"
   Checked="True | False"
   OnCheckedChanged="OnCheckedChangedMethod"
/>
```

Like the `TextBox` Control, the `CheckBox` Control can respond to changes made to itself. A change event can be raised and handled by an event-handling procedure passed into `OnCheckedChanged`. `AutoPostBack` works as described before; when set to `True`, a post-back occurs when the box is checked or unchecked.

Here is the HTML for a page that asks a few simple questions of the user.

Code Sample 3-22

```
<%@ Page Language="vb"
   AutoEventWireup="false"
   Src="cs3-22.aspx.vb"
   Inherits="WebControlCheckBox"%>
<html>
<head>
   <title>Web Control - CheckBox Example</title>
</head>
<body>

<form id="Form1" method="post" runat="server">
<h1>Web Control - CheckBox Example</h1>

<p>Please take our "Geek Test":</p>

<p>
<asp:CheckBox id=ckbKnowHTTP
   runat="server"
   Text='You know what "http://" really means'>
</asp:CheckBox>
</p>

<p>
<asp:CheckBox id=ckbCanCount
   runat="server"
   Text="You can count to 50 in binary">
```

```
</asp:CheckBox>
</p>

<p>
<asp:CheckBox id=ckbTransporter
   runat="server"
   Text='You can explain the physics of the
   "Transporter"'>
</asp:CheckBox>
</p>

<p>
<asp:Button id=btnSubmit
   runat="server"
   Text="Geek Out!">
</asp:Button>
</p>

<p>
<asp:Label id=lblResponse
   runat="server"
   Width="393px">
</asp:Label>
</p>

</form>
</body>
</html>
```

The results of this example appear in Figure 3-19. Here is the code to generate the page.

```
Imports System
Imports System.Drawing
Imports System.Web
Imports System.Web.UI
Imports System.Web.UI.WebControls

Public Class WebControlCheckBox
   Inherits System.Web.UI.Page
   Protected WithEvents ckbKnowHTTP As _
      System.Web.UI.WebControls.CheckBox
   Protected WithEvents lblResponse As _
```

```
      System.Web.UI.WebControls.Label
   Protected WithEvents btnSubmit As _
      System.Web.UI.WebControls.Button
   Protected WithEvents ckbTransporter As _
      System.Web.UI.WebControls.CheckBox
   Protected WithEvents ckbCanCount As _
      System.Web.UI.WebControls.CheckBox

41  Public Sub ckbTransporter_CheckedChanged( _
      ByVal sender As Object, _
      ByVal e As System.EventArgs) _
      Handles ckbTransporter.CheckedChanged

      If ckbTransporter.Checked Then
         lblResponse.Text = "It's science fiction, remember?"
      Else
         lblResponse.Text = ""
      End If
   End Sub

   Public Sub btnSubmit_Click(ByVal sender As Object, _
      ByVal e As System.EventArgs) _
      Handles btnSubmit.Click

      Dim strResponse As String

      If ckbCanCount.Checked Then
         strResponse = strResponse & _
            "Really? What's 3.14159 in binary? :-)<BR>"
      End If

      If ckbKnowHTTP.Checked Then
         strResponse = strResponse & _
            "Hypertext Transfer Protocol . . . very good . . . <BR>"
      End If

      If ckbTransporter.Checked Then
         strResponse = strResponse & _
            "A Trekkie, are you?!<BR>"
      End If

      lblResponse.Text = strResponse

   End Sub
End Class
```

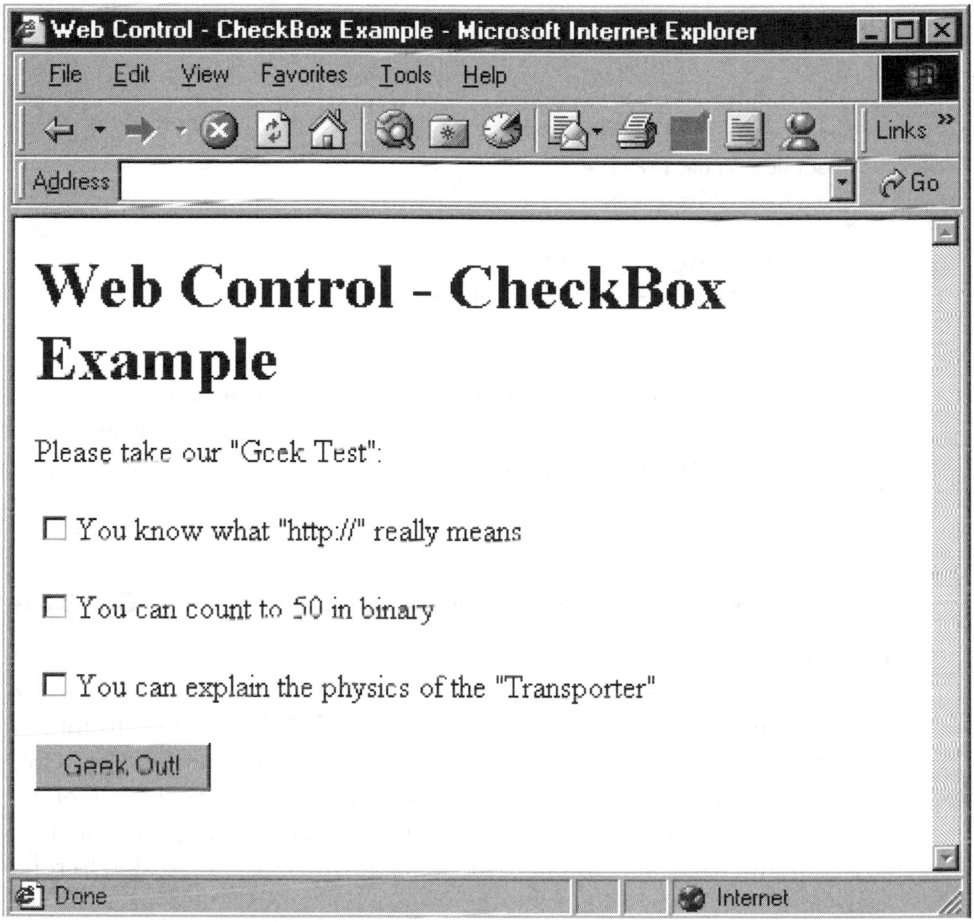

Figure 3-19 Output of the CheckBox Control demonstration

In this code-behind file, the primary objective beginning in line ❹❶ is to collect the checked responses from the user. The event handler for the `CheckedChanged` event causes a message to be displayed in the `lblResponse Label` Control.

3.12.2 The RadioButton Control

The RadioButton Control works much like the CheckBox Control.

```
<asp:RadioButton id="RadioButton1" runat="server"
   AutoPostBack="True | False"
   Checked="True | False"
   GroupName="GroupName"
   Text="label"
   TextAlign="Right | Left"
   OnCheckedChanged="OnCheckedChangedMethod"
/>
```

Something special to note: The GroupName property is used to assign a name to a collection of radio buttons. This is required since radio buttons are normally used to group mutually exclusive options. So, when one radio button in the group is clicked, the others flip to their "off" position.

3.12.3 The CheckBoxList and RadioButtonList Controls

You may have noticed that creating CheckBox Controls, assigning names to them, and retrieving and setting their on/off state can require lots of code. This becomes apparent especially when the Web page design calls for many of these Web Controls. This statement also holds true for RadioButton Controls.

Another situation may arise when you need to generate these Web Controls dynamically from a data source. The data source may contain a fairly large amount of data. It would be beneficial in this case to be able to reference each Web Control by an index rather than a name. ASP.NET provides the CheckBoxList and RadioButtonList Controls for this purpose.

Let's begin with the CheckBoxList Control. Its syntax appears below.

```
<asp:CheckBoxList id="CheckBoxList1" runat="server"
   AutoPostBack="True | False"
   CellPadding="Pixels"
   DataSource='<% databindingexpression %>'
   DataTextField="DataSourceField"
   DataValueField="DataSourceField"
   RepeatColumns="ColumnCount"
   RepeatDirection="Vertical | Horizontal"
   RepeatLayout="Flow | Table"
   TextAlign="Right | Left"
```

```
    OnSelectedIndexChanged="OnSelectedIndexChangedMethod"
/>

</asp:CheckBoxList>
```

The CheckBoxList and RadioButtonList Controls share many of the same properties (see Table 3-4).

Table 3-4 Properties of the CheckBoxList and RadioButtonList Controls

Property	Description
AutoPostBack	Causes an immediate post-back to the server when a user checks an item if this property is set to True. The default value is False.
CellPadding	Sets the spacing between controls, measured in pixels or a Unit quantity.
DataSource	Indicates the data source to use to bind to the control.
DataTextField	Designates the field or property of the object in the data source to be used for the Text property of each control.
DataValueField	Designates the field or property of the object in the data source to be used for the Value property of each control.
Items	Defines a collection representing the controls. Each item in the collection is of type ListItem.
RepeatColumns	Sets the number of columns used to display the controls. The default value is 1.
RepeatDirection	Sets the direction, Vertical or Horizontal, that the controls are displayed in the list. If Vertical, the checkboxes are ordered top to bottom. If Horizontal, the checkboxes are ordered left to right.
RepeatLayout	The list can be rendered using Flow or Table. Flow displays the controls in-line, without formatting. Table displays the controls inside cells of an HTML table. Default is Table. Set this property using the RepeatLayout enumeration.

(continued)

Table 3-4 Properties of the CheckBoxList and RadioButtonList Controls *(continued)*

Property	Description
SelectedIndex	Specifies the index of the currently selected control.
SelectedItem	Gets the Value property value for the currently selected control.
SelectedItems (applies only to CheckBoxList Control)	Indicates a collection of the selected checkboxes.
TextAlign	Designates how text (the caption) should be displayed next to the controls, to the Right or to the Left.

Although we won't go into much detail about data sources and data binding yet (we'll cover that topic further in Chapter 7), the example of the RadioButtonList Control shown below contains data binding. We won't actually bind to a database system, but we will use an array as our data source. Individual items can also be added by inserting a ListItem object into each list at design time. We'll do examples of both.

Demonstration of the CheckBoxList Control

Let's begin by exploring how the CheckBoxList Control is populated manually.

Code Sample 3-23

```
<%@ Page Language="vb"
   AutoEventWireup="false"
   src="cs3-23.aspx.vb"
   Inherits="WebControlCheckBoxListSample"%>

<html><head>
<title>Web Control - CheckBoxList Example</title>
</head>
<body>

<form id="WebControlCheckBoxListSample"
```

```
   method="post"
   runat="server">

<h1>Web Control - CheckBoxList Example</h1>

<p>This CheckBoxList is populated at
design time with ListItems:</p>

<p>

<asp:CheckBoxList id=cblTestCheckBoxList
   maintainstate=False
   runat="server">
<asp:ListItem Value="Item1">
Item #1
</asp:ListItem>
<asp:ListItem Value="Item2">
Item #2
</asp:ListItem>
<asp:ListItem Value="Item3">
Item #3
</asp:ListItem>
</asp:CheckBoxList>
</p>
<p>

<asp:Button id=btnSendResponse
   runat="server"
   Text="Send Response">
</asp:Button>

</p>

<p>
<asp:Label id=lblResponse
   runat="server"
   Width="36"
   Height="19">
</asp:Label>
</p>

</form>
</body>
</html>
```

This code uses the usual Web Form, with a submit button and a `CheckBoxList` Control (the code for which is shown in boldface). A new class object is introduced here: the `ListItem` object. The `ListItem` object can be used in different Web Controls, like `RadioButtonList`, `ListBox` (see Section 3.13.1), and `DropDownList` (see Section 3.13.2). The `ListItem` class object allows you to programmatically reference any individual item. When you have access to a `ListItem` object, you can query its `Value`, `Text`, and `Selected` properties.

Each `ListItem` object placed inside the `CheckBoxList` Control contains a value for `Text` and a value for `Value`. The text located between the opening and closing `asp:ListItem` tags becomes the value for the `Text` property when referenced programmatically. Remember that you can use the alternate notation for specifying the text label by assigning the `Text` property directly and not use a closing `asp:ListItem` tag.

Now we're ready to check the submitted data. The code-behind file iterates through each `ListItem` and tests to see if the `ListItem` was checked.

```
Imports System
Imports System.Drawing
Imports System.Web
Imports System.Web.UI
Imports System.Web.UI.WebControls

Public Class WebControlCheckBoxListSample
   Inherits System.Web.UI.Page
   Protected WithEvents lblResponse As _
      System.Web.UI.WebControls.Label
   Protected WithEvents btnSendResponse As _
      System.Web.UI.WebControls.Button
   Protected WithEvents cblTestCheckBoxList As _
      System.Web.UI.WebControls.CheckBoxList

   Public Sub btnSendResponse_Click(ByVal sender As Object, _
         ByVal e As System.EventArgs) _
         Handles btnSendResponse.Click

      Dim liListItem As ListItem
      Dim strResponse As String

      strResponse = "Selections made: <BR>"

42       For Each liListItem In cblTestCheckBoxList.Items
         If liListItem.Selected Then
```

```
43              strResponse &= liListItem.Text & "<BR>"
            End If
        Next

        lblResponse.Text = strResponse

    End Sub
End Class
```

Web Controls that deal with collections of `ListItem` objects have a property called `Items`. This is the property used to test the items in the list. `Items` is a collection, so beginning in line 42 the code uses a `For . . . Each` loop to retrieve each `ListItem`. The `Selected` property, a Boolean value, is set to `True` if the `ListItem` is selected. The response back to the user is formatted in line 43 so the `Text` property of the `ListItem` is echoed back.

Data Binding to Web Controls Using Class Objects and the `ArrayList`

When you perform data binding, you are passing into Web Controls a set of data—data in the general sense, since bindable data can come from a variety of sources. A data-bound Web Control is usually bound to database data, but ASP.NET is flexible enough to treat an `ArrayList`, XML data, or a class object as a bindable data source.

Binding data from a class object to a Web Control is quite powerful yet easy to do. In the example below, we first create a class object to contain members we'll use as data to bind to the Web Control. The class, `CMyItemClass`, is very simple and contains two public string properties.

```
Public Class CMyItemClass
    Private m_strMember1 As String
    Private m_strMember2 As String

    Public Sub New(ByVal Member1 As String, _
                ByVal Member2 As String)

        m_strMember1 = Member1
        m_strMember2 = Member2
    End Sub

    Public Property Member1() As String
        Set
            m_strMember1 = Value
        End Set
```

```
      Get
         Member1 = m_strMember1
      End Get
   End Property

   Public Property Member2() As String
      Set
         m_strMember2 = Value
      End Set
      Get
         Member2 = m_strMember2
      End Get
   End Property
End Class
```

Reusing the previous CheckBoxList example, we place this class definition in the code-behind file.

Next, we modify the `Page_Load` subroutine and place this new code.

```
Protected Sub WebControlCheckBoxListSample_Load( _
            ByVal Sender As System.Object, _
            ByVal e As System.EventArgs)

44  Dim aryArray As New System.Collections.ArrayList()
   Dim liListItem As ListItem
   Dim strResponse As String
   Dim intCounter As Integer


   If Not IsPostback Then

45    With aryArray
         .Add(New CMyItemClass("Item1", "Item #1"))
         .Add(New CMyItemClass("Item2", "Item #2"))
         .Add(New CMyItemClass("Item3", "Item #3"))
      End With

46    With cblTestCheckBoxList
         .DataTextField = "Member2"
         .DataValueField = "Member1"
         .DataSource = aryArray
         .DataBind()
      End With
   Else
```

```
      strResponse = "Selections made: <BR>"

47    For Each liListItem In cblTestCheckBoxList.Items
         strResponse &= liListItem.Text & " " & _
         liListItem.Selected & "<BR>"
      Next

      lblResponse.Text = strResponse

   End If

End Sub
```

In line (44) this code introduces a new object, the `ArrayList` object. The `ArrayList` object is a class in the `System.Collections` namespace (see Chapter 4) that encapsulates an array of objects that can be sized dynamically. The `ArrayList` object is one of the data sources that Web Controls can bind against.

Beginning in line (45) we add `CMyItemClass` objects to `aryArray`, the `ArrayList`. When we defined the `CmyItemClass` objects, we defined a constructor that populated the two property values `Member1` and `Member2` (`m_strMember1` and `m_strMember2`). We will use the values of those two properties to bind to the Web Control later.

In the next block of code beginning in line (46), we call the necessary functions to bind the class objects to the `CheckBoxList` Control. This is done when the browser first requests the page. Beginning with the `DataTextField` and `DataValueField` properties, we set each with the name of the `CMyItemClass` properties. When the individual checkboxes are rendered in HTML, the `DataTextField` property is used as shown below. (The white space in the HTML has been edited for clarity.)

```
<span>
<input type="checkbox"
   id="cblTestCheckBoxList_0"
   name="cblTestCheckBoxList:0" />

(This becomes the value for DataTextField.)
<label for="cblTestCheckBoxList_0">Item #1
</label>
</span>

<span>
```

```
<input type="checkbox"
   id="cblTestCheckBoxList_1"
   name="cblTestCheckBoxList:1" />

(This becomes the value for DataTextField.)
<label for="cblTestCheckBoxList_1">Item #2
</label>
</span>

<span>
<input type="checkbox"
   id="cblTestCheckBoxList_2"
   name="cblTestCheckBoxList:2" />

(This becomes the value for DataTextField.)
<label for="cblTestCheckBoxList_2">Item #3
</label>
</span>
```

Next, we specify the expression to be used for `DataSource`. In our case, this is simply the name of the `ArrayList` object, `aryArray`. Finally, to actually bind the data, we call the `DataBind()` method of the `CheckBoxList` Control.

When a post-back occurs, each checkbox is tested to see if it was set (see line ㊼). A `For . . . Each` loop is used to iterate through the `Items` `ListItemCollection` of the `CheckBoxList` Control. For each `ListItem`, we concatenate the `Text` and `Selected` properties to the response string `strResponse`. Finally, the output is displayed by setting the `Text` property of the `lblResponse` `Label` Control.

Demonstration of the RadioButtonList Control

The code for the `RadioButtonList` Control example is very similar to the code for the `CheckBoxList` Control example. The main difference is that we check only for the single selected value, using the `SelectedItem` property. But first, here's the syntax for the `RadioButtonList` Control.

```
<asp:RadioButtonList id="RadioButtonList1" runat="server"
   AutoPostBack="True | False"
   CellPadding="Pixels"
   DataSource="<% databindingexpression %>"
   DataTextField="DataSourceField"
```

```
    DataValueField="DataSourceField"
    RepeatColumns="ColumnCount"
    RepeatDirection="Vertical | Horizontal"
    RepeatLayout="Flow | Table"
    TextAlign="Right | Left"
    OnSelectedIndexChanged="OnSelectedIndexChangedMethod"
/>
    <asp:ListItem text="label" value="value" selected="True | False" />
</asp:RadioButtonList>
```

Let's modify the previous `Page_Load` subroutine to include this code.

```
Protected Sub Page_Load( _
   ByVal Sender As System.Object, _
   ByVal e As System.EventArgs)

   Dim aryArrayList As New System.Collections.ArrayList()

   If Not IsPostback Then

      With aryArrayList
         .Add("Radio Button #1")
         .Add("Radio Button #2")
         .Add("Radio Button #3")
      End With

      With rblRadioButtonList
         .DataSource = aryArrayList
         .DataBind()
      End With

   Else
      lblResponse.Text = _
         rblRadioButtonList.SelectedItem.Text
   End If
End Sub
```

Inside this `Page_Load` code (executed upon a post-back to the server), the boldface code shows the use of the `SelectedItem` property. The `RadioButtonList` Control allows for only one selection, so the `SelectedItem` property evaluates to only a single `ListItem`.

3.13 Web Controls for Creating Lists

The ASP.NET List Controls allow users to select textual items from a list. List Controls are rendered as drop-down menus or boxes that contain a list of text items. Depending on the configuration, single or multiple items can be selected.

3.13.1 The `ListBox` Control

The `ListBox` Control shares many of the same properties of the other List Controls (for example, the `CheckBoxList` and `RadioButtonList` Controls). The `ListBox` Control also uses `ListItem` objects to represent the available choices in the list. The syntax of the `ListBox` Control appears below.

```
<asp:ListBox id="Listbox1" runat="server"
   DataSource="<% databindingexpression %>"
   DataTextField="DataSourceField"
   DataValueField="DataSourceField"
   AutoPostBack="True | False"
   Rows="rowcount"
   SelectionMode="Single | Multiple"
   OnSelectedIndexChanged="OnSelectedIndexChangedMethod"
/>
   <asp:Listitem value="value" selected="True | False">
      Text
   </asp:Listitem>
</asp:ListBox>
```

`SelectionMode` determines whether or not the `ListBox` Control allows selection of multiple items. The example (see Figure 3-20) shows how to use the `ListBox` Control in either multiple- or single-select modes. Each `ListBox` Control is designed to render the available choices as a list, which displays `Rows` number of choices at a time. If the number of available choices exceeds the visible capacity of the `ListBox` Control, a vertical scroll bar allows users to scroll to see the other selections.

Here is the code used to create the `ListBox` Control example.

Code Sample 3-24

```
<%@ Page Language="vb"
   AutoEventWireup="false"
   src="cs3-24.aspx.vb"
```

```
   Inherits="WebControlCheckBoxListSample"%>
<html><head>
<title>Web Control - ListBox Control Example</title>
</head>
<body>

<form id="WebControlListBoxSample"
   method="post"
   runat="server">

<h1>Web Control - ListBox Control Example</h1>

<p>The ListBox control can allow for
single or multiple selections:</p>

<p>Select a single item:
<asp:ListBox id=lbSingleSelection runat="server">
   <asp:ListItem Value="Grape"
   .Selected="True">Grape
   </asp:ListItem>
   <asp:ListItem Value="Apple">Apple
   </asp:ListItem>
   <asp:ListItem Value="Orange">Orange
   </asp:ListItem>
   <asp:ListItem Value="Banana">Banana
   </asp:ListItem>
</asp:ListBox>
</p>

<p>Select multiple items:

<asp:ListBox id=lbMultipleSelections
   runat="server"
   Rows="3"
   selectionmode="Multiple">
<asp:ListItem Value="Red">Red
   </asp:ListItem>
<asp:ListItem Value="Green">Green
   </asp:ListItem>
<asp:ListItem Value="Blue">Blue
   </asp:ListItem>
<asp:ListItem Value="Yellow">Yellow
   </asp:ListItem>
<asp:ListItem Value="Orange">Orange
   </asp:ListItem>
```

```
<asp:ListItem Value="Brown">Brown
   </asp:ListItem>
</asp:ListBox>
</p>

<p>
<asp:Button id=btnSendSelections
   runat="server"
   Text="Send Selections">
</asp:Button>
</p>

<p>
<asp:Label id=lblSelections
   runat="server"
   Width="199"
   Height="19">
</asp:Label></p>

</form>
</body>
</html>
```

Retrieving the selected items from the `ListBox` Control is relatively straightforward, similar to the procedure for the `CheckBoxList` and `RadioButtonList` Controls. Here is the `Page_Load` (`WebControlListBoxSample_Load`) event handler, which demonstrates how to retrieve the selected items from a multiple-select `ListBox` Control as well as for a `ListBox` Control that allows just one selection.

```
Imports System
Imports System.Drawing
Imports System.Web
Imports System.Web.UI
Imports System.Web.UI.WebControls

Public Class WebControlCheckBoxListSample
   Inherits System.Web.UI.Page
   Protected WithEvents lbSingleSelection As _
      System.Web.UI.WebControls.ListBox
   Protected WithEvents lbMultipleSelections As _
      System.Web.UI.WebControls.ListBox
   Protected WithEvents lblSelections As _
```

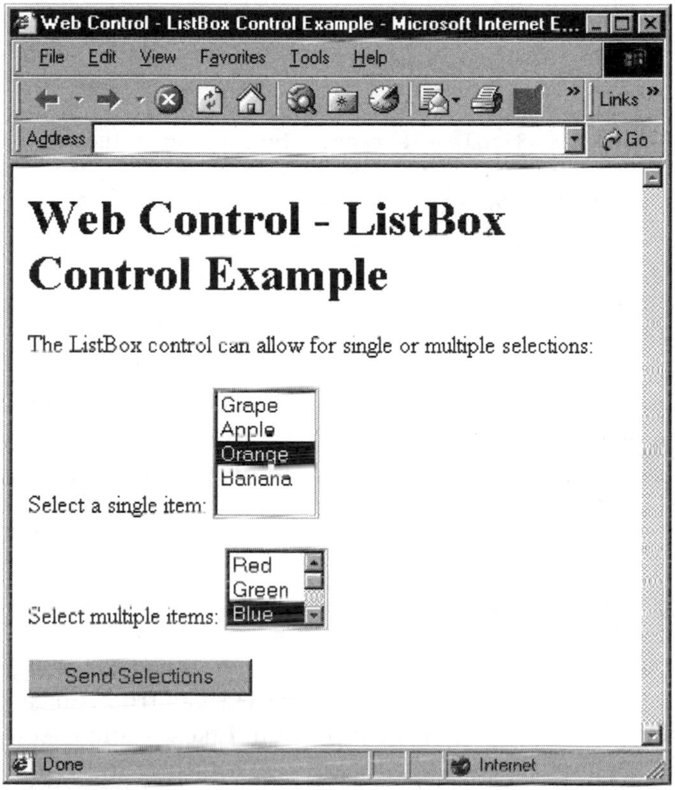

Figure 3-20 Output of the `ListBox` Control example

```
   System.Web.UI.WebControls.Label

Protected Sub Page_Load(ByVal Sender As System.Object, _
          ByVal e As System.EventArgs) _
          Handles MyBase.Load

   Dim strSelections As String
   Dim liListItem As ListItem

   If Not IsPostback Then

   Else
48    For Each liListItem In lbMultipleSelections.Items
         If liListItem.Selected Then
```

```
                strSelections &= liListItem.Value & " "
            End If
        Next

        strSelections &= "<BR>" & _
            lbSingleSelection.SelectedItem.Value

        lblSelections.Text = strSelections

    End If
  End Sub
End Class
```

The `ListBox` Control contains an `Items` collection beginning in line 48 that can be used to check each `ListItem` for selection. In the case of a single-selection `ListBox` Control, we simply reference the `SelectedItem` property and obtain the `Value`.

3.13.2 The `DropDownList` Control

Almost identical in functionality to the single-select `ListBox` Control but differing in appearance is the `DropDownList` Control. You can think of the `DropDownList` Control as a pop-up menu. Like the single-select `ListBox` Control, it allows for only one selection. The syntax for the `DropDownList` Control follows.

```
<asp:DropDownList id="DropDownList1" runat="server"
   DataSource="<% databindingexpression %>"
   DataTextField="DataSourceField"
   DataValueField="DataSourceField"
   AutoPostBack="True | False"
   OnSelectedIndexChanged="OnSelectedIndexChangedMethod"
/>
   <asp:ListItem value="value" selected="True | False">
      Text
   </asp:ListItem>
</asp:DropDownList>
```

The example for the single-selection `ListBox` Control can easily be converted to a `DropDownList` Control with just a few changes to the code. First, we change the Web Control type from `ListBox` to `DropDownList` in the HTML.

```
<asp:DropDownList id=lbSingleSelection runat="server">
   <asp:ListItem Value="Grape"
   .Selected="True">Grape
   </asp:ListItem>
   <asp:ListItem Value="Apple">Apple
   </asp:ListItem>
   <asp:ListItem Value="Orange">Orange
   </asp:ListItem>
   <asp:ListItem Value="Banana">Banana
   </asp:ListItem>
</asp:DropDownList>
```

Then, we update the code-behind file to reflect the change made in the HTML.

```
Protected WithEvents lbSingleSelection As _
   System.Web.UI.WebControls.DropDownList
```

3.14 Miscellaneous Basic Controls

Two Web Controls we haven't covered yet are the `Hyperlink` Control and the `Image` Control.

3.14.1 The `Hyperlink` Control

The `Hyperlink` Control provides server-side functionality for the HTML anchor <A> tag. This Web Control is useful for dynamically generating hyperlinks in your code.

```
<asp:Hyperlink id="Hyperlink1" runat="server"
   NavigateUrl="url"
   Text="HyperlinkText"
   ImageUrl="url"
   Target="window"
/>

<asp:Hyperlink id="Hyperlink1" runat="server"
   NavigateUrl="url"
   ImageUrl="url"
   Target="window"
/>
</asp:Hyperlink>
```

Here's a quick overview of the properties of the `Hyperlink` Control. `NavigateUrl` specifies the target for the hyperlink. `Text` is the text that makes up the clickable part of the hyperlink. `ImageUrl` specifies an image to use for the hyperlink instead of text. When an `ImageUrl` is specified, whatever text is assigned to the `Text` property becomes the HTML `alt` attribute for the `<img>` tag.

3.14.2 The Image Control

The `Image` Control provides a design-time and programmatic way to display images.

```
<asp:Image id="Image1" runat="server"
   ImageUrl="string"
   AlternateText="string"
   ImageAlign="NotSet | AbsBottom | AbsMiddle
       | BaseLine | Bottom | Left | Middle |
      Right | TextTop | Top"
/>
```

`ImageAlign` controls the horizontal and vertical positioning of any HTML adjacent to the image.

3.15 Creating a Simple ASP.NET Application

Now that you've learned about the HTML and Web Controls, you're ready to build your first Web application with VS.NET! You'll quickly see how easy it is to create useful applications in a short time.

The objective of Lab 3-1 is to familiarize you with the basics of building a Web application with Visual Basic.NET. This lab involves

- Launching the VS.NET IDE
- Creating a new Web application
- Adding a Web Form
- Using the Toolbox and Properties windows
- Building the Web application
- Running the Web application

This lab is a Web version of the HelloWorld project created in Lab 2-1. It allows a user to enter his or her name into a text box and then click a button to receive a greeting from the application.

LAB 3-1
YOUR FIRST ASP.NET PROJECT

STEP 1. Launch VS.NET.

a. To launch VS.NET, click the **Start** menu and locate the Visual Studio.NET 7.0 program group (see Lab Figure 3-1).

STEP 2. Create a new project.

a. To create a new Web application, select **File→New→Project** from the menu bar (see Lab Figure 3-2). This displays the New Project dialog box, where you select the project type and give the new project a name.

b. Under Project Types, select the Visual Basic Projects folder, then select ASP.NET Web Application (see Lab Figure 3-3). Call the new project "Lab3-1" by typing this text into the Name field. Next, choose a Web server that has the Front Page Server 2000 extensions installed. Type the URL to the Web server in the Location field or select a Web server from the list by clicking the Browse button. A new Web page will be created on the target Web server. Lab Figure 3-4 shows the progress message for setting up the Web application's Front Page Web page as well as the starter files.

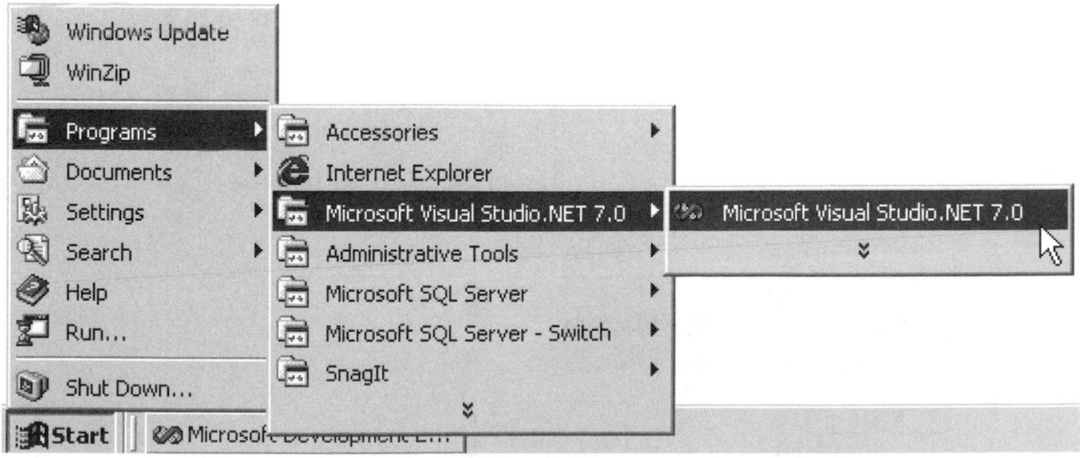

Lab Figure 3-1 Launching VS.NET

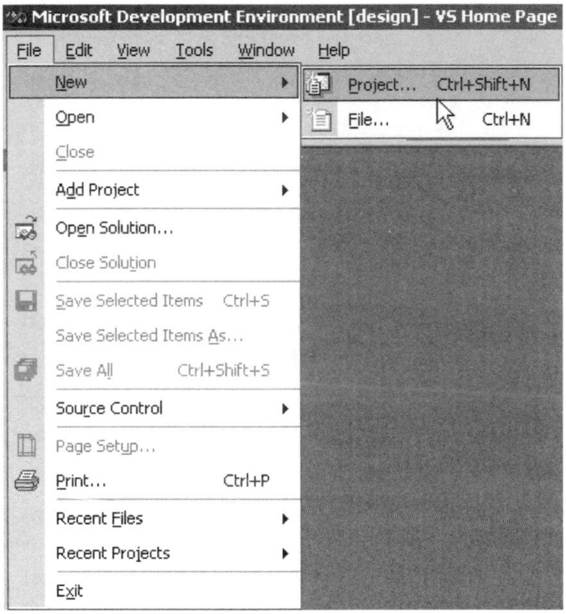

Lab Figure 3-2 Creating a new project

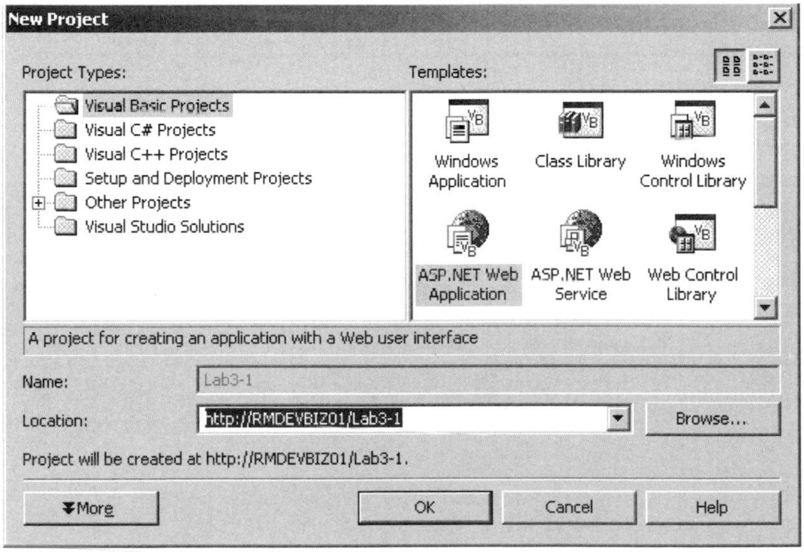

Lab Figure 3-3 The New Project window

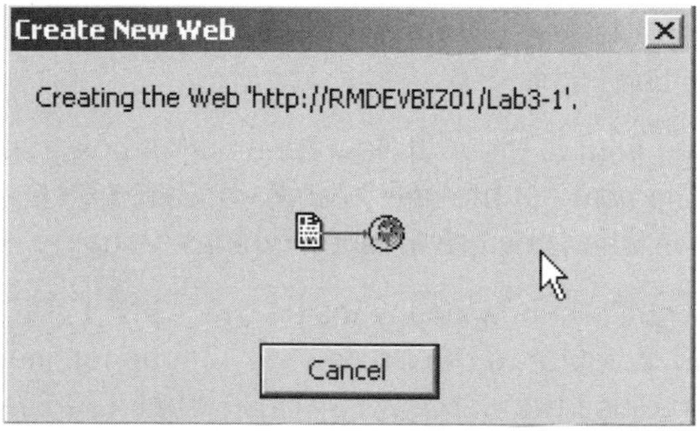

Lab Figure 3-4 Progress message displayed while VS.NET creates a new Web page

STEP 3. Add a Web Form to the project.

a. After the Web page is created, VS.NET creates the initial project files and a solution file. The solution file contains information about the project, its files, and the code references. Open the Solution Explorer window (if it's not already open), shown in Lab Figure 3-5, to view this information.

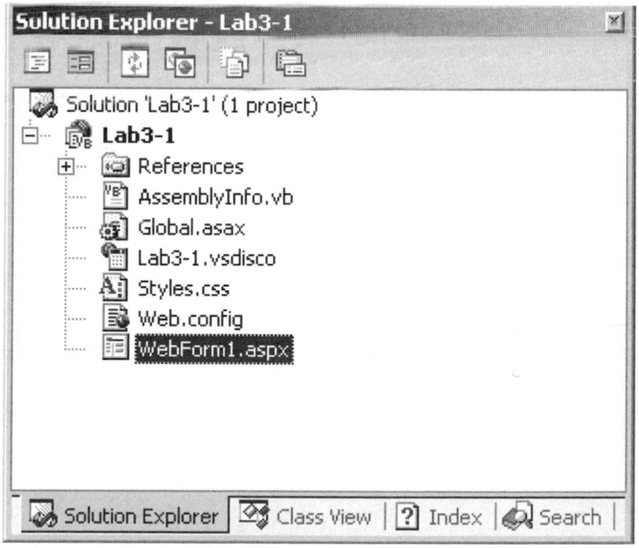

Lab Figure 3-5 The Solution Explorer window

b. To add a new Web Form to the solution, right-click on the Lab3-1 icon inside the Solution Explorer window and select **Add→Add Web Form . . .** from the menu (see Lab Figure 3-6).

c. In the Name field of the Add New Item dialog box, type "Lab3-1_FirstPage.aspx" as the name of the new Web Form (see Lab Figure 3-7). Click the Open button when you are finished typing the name.

The new Web Form now opens inside the VS.NET IDE and is ready for editing. VS.NET defaults to the Design View mode for the Web Form. This mode allows you to use the HTML WYSIWYG (What You See Is What You Get) editor and to place Web Controls onto the Web Form. The Toolbox window shows the available HTML and Web Controls plus other components and controls (see Lab Figure 3-8).

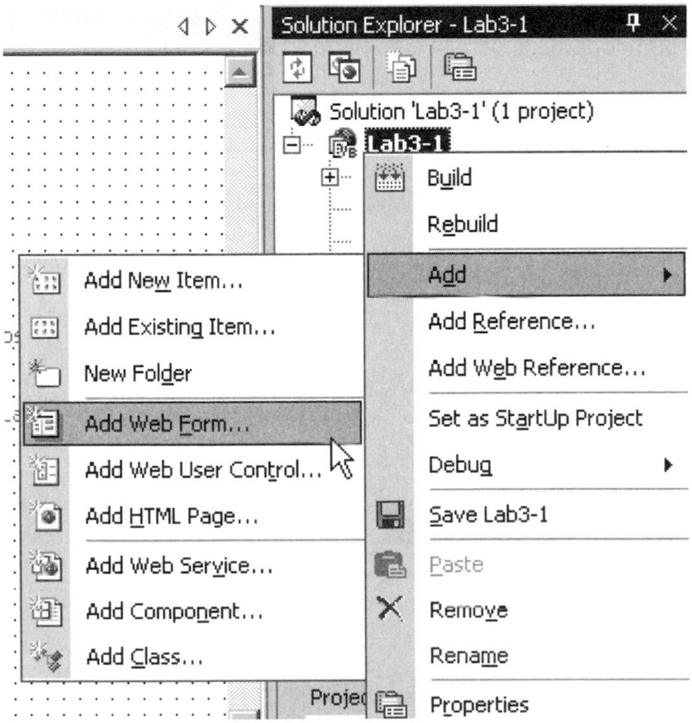

Lab Figure 3-6 Adding a new Web Form to the project

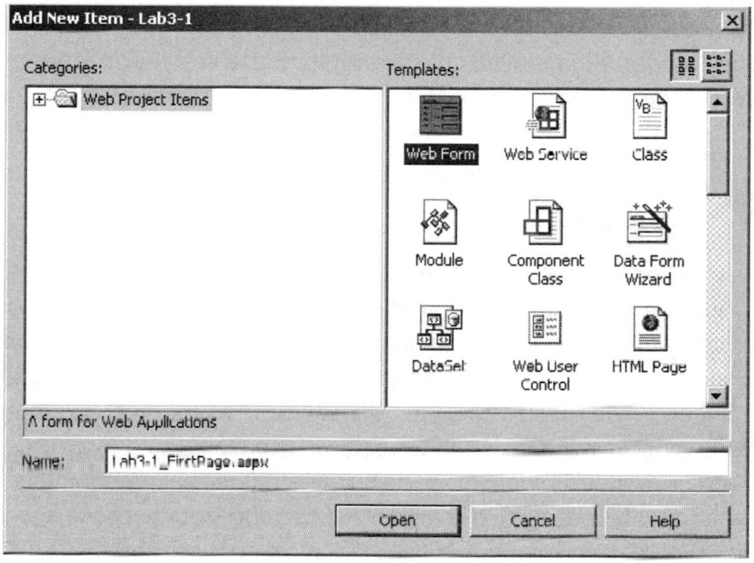

Lab Figure 3-7 The Add New Item dialog box

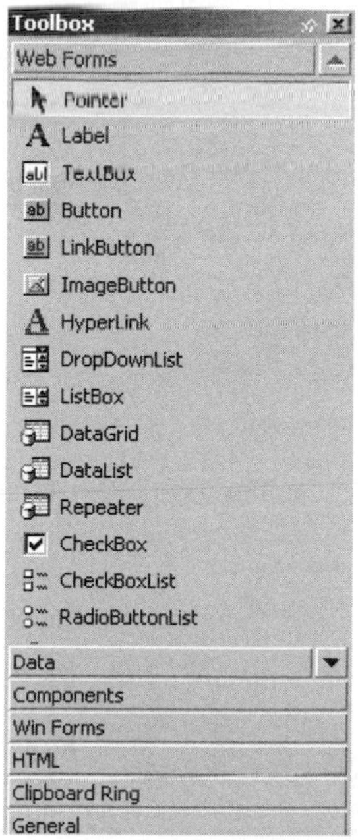

Lab Figure 3-8 The Toolbox window

STEP 4. Edit the Web Form.

a. To add a Web Control to the Web Form, drag the desired Web Control from the Toolbox window onto the location on the Web Form where you want the Web Control to appear. In this lab you'll use three Web Controls:

1. A `Label` Web Control
2. A `TextBox` Web Control
3. A `Button` Web Control

Drag one of each of these Web Controls onto the Web Form.

Whenever you drag new Web Controls or objects onto a Web Form, VS.NET assigns the new object a default name, usually in the format `ControlNameX`, where `ControlName` is the name of the Web Control and X is a sequential number. Since this name doesn't describe the Web Control's purpose, it's good programming practice to rename it to something more meaningful. A good convention to follow is to choose a name that is a combination of the type of Web Control plus a name that describes its purpose or functionality. For example, you can call a `Label` Control `lblUserResponse`. This serves as a reminder that the Web Control is a `Label` Control (`lbl`) and that it is used to display a response message to the user (`UserResponse`).

b. Assign the name of the Web Control and adjust other design-time properties by right-clicking the Web Control in the Design View and selecting **Properties** from the menu (see Lab Figure 3-9). This displays the Properties win-

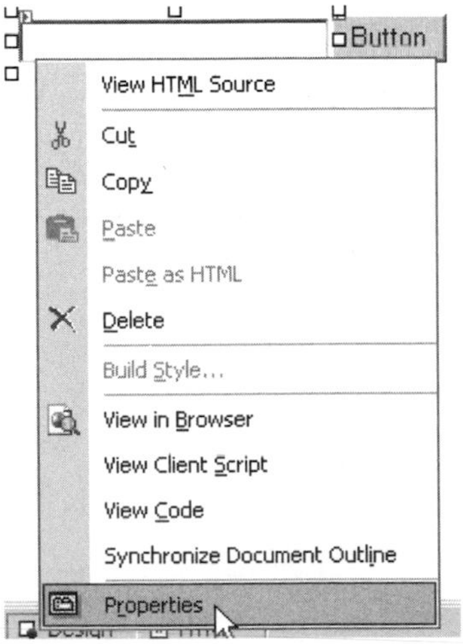

Lab Figure 3-9 Activating the Properties window

dow, which contains properties for the Web Control. Lab Figure 3-10 shows the Properties window.

To change the name of the Web Control, click in the (ID) field and type a new name. This value will be used to programmatically reference the Web Control in application code. You can adjust other properties using the same procedure. For this lab, name the Web Controls as follows:

- The TextBox Control: txtYourName
- The Label Control: lblReply
- The Button Control: cmdSayHello

c. As an optional step, try experimenting with the properties that control visual appearance, like the BackColor property of the TextBox Control. Also, feel free to get creative with the page design. This will help you become more comfortable working with the VS.NET IDE.

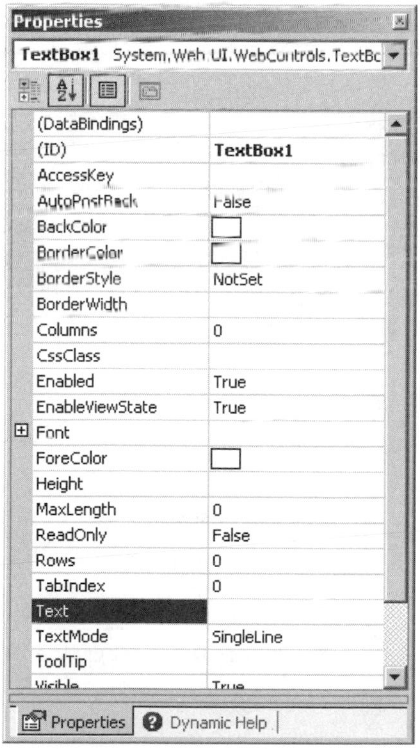

Lab Figure 3-10 The Properties window

STEP 5. Edit the Code-Behind file for the Web Form.

a. To add functionality to the Web Form, you need to add a code-behind file for the Web Form. There are two ways you can do this.

- Method 1: Double-click the Web Control for which you wish to write code. This allows you to write event handlers for the Web Control.
- Method 2: Simply right-click anywhere inside the Web Form and select **View Code** from the menu (see Lab Figure 3-11).

b. To edit the code-behind file, select the desired Web Control from the new menu that appears. For example, to write code to handle the `Click` event for the `cmdSayHello` `Button` Control, select `cmdSayHello` from the menu (see Lab Figure 3-12).

c. Select the event for which you wish to write code. In this case, select the `Click` event as shown in Lab Figure 3-13.

d. The code for the `Click` event of `cmdSayHello` is very simple. Assign the value entered in the `TextBox` Control, `txtYourName`, to the `Text` property

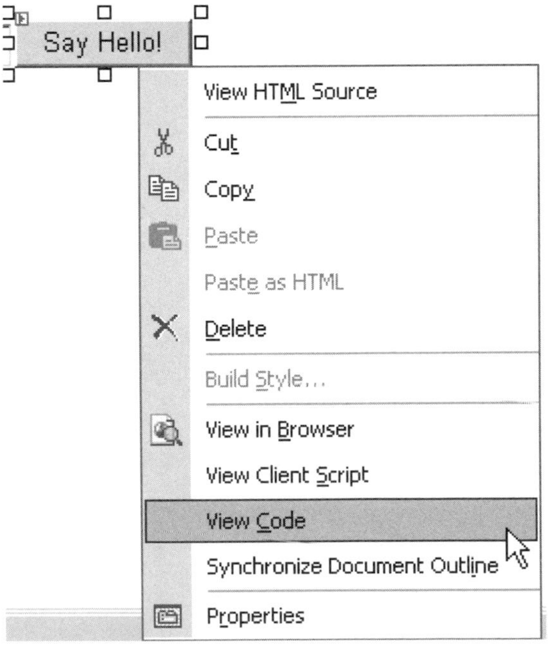

Lab Figure 3-11 Selecting View Code for the `Button` Control

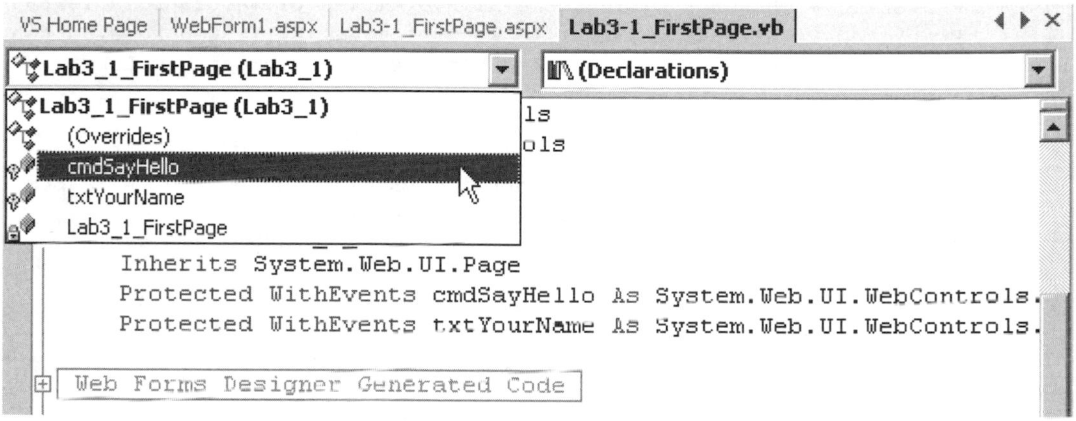

Lab Figure 3-12 Selecting the `cmdSayHello` `Button` Control for code-behind editing

of the `lblReply` `Label` Control. The entry of this code is shown in Lab Figure 3-14.

STEP 6. Build and run the Web application.

a. You are now ready to build the project (solution). In this step you'll compile all the necessary assemblies and prepare the Web application for execution. To build the solution, select **Build→Build Solution** from the menu bar (see Lab Figure 3-15).

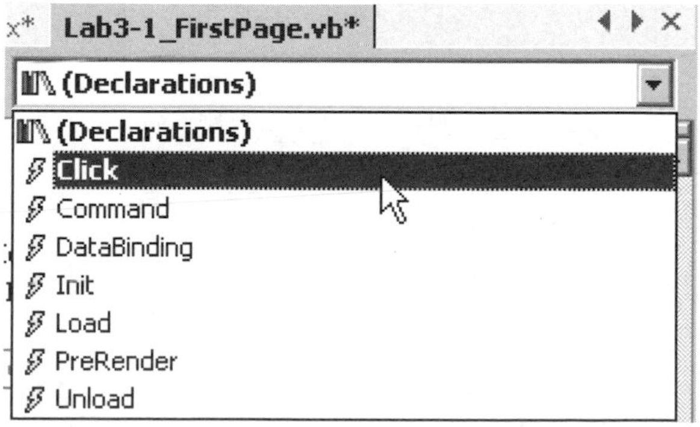

Lab Figure 3-13 Selecting an event for code-behind editing

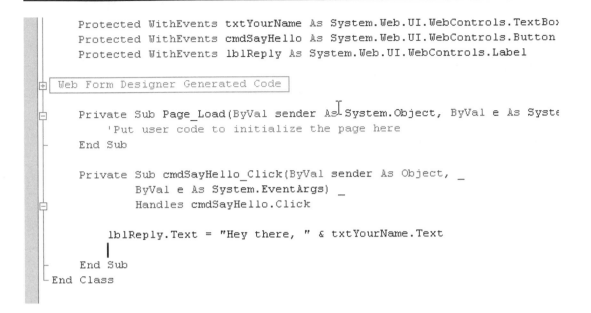

```
    Protected WithEvents txtYourName As System.Web.UI.WebControls.TextBo›
    Protected WithEvents cmdSayHello As System.Web.UI.WebControls.Button
    Protected WithEvents lblReply As System.Web.UI.WebControls.Label

[+] Web Form Designer Generated Code

    Private Sub Page_Load(ByVal sender As System.Object, ByVal e As Syste
        'Put user code to initialize the page here
    End Sub

    Private Sub cmdSayHello_Click(ByVal sender As Object, _
            ByVal e As System.EventArgs) _
            Handles cmdSayHello.Click

        lblReply.Text = "Hey there, " & txtYourName.Text

    End Sub
End Class
```

Lab Figure 3-14 Editing code for the `Click` event

b. Now that the solution is built, you need to tell VS.NET which Web page to use as the entry point into the application (the *start page*). You can designate any Web page in the solution as the start page by right-clicking it in the Solution Explorer window and selecting **Set As Start Page** from the menu (see Lab Figure 3-16).

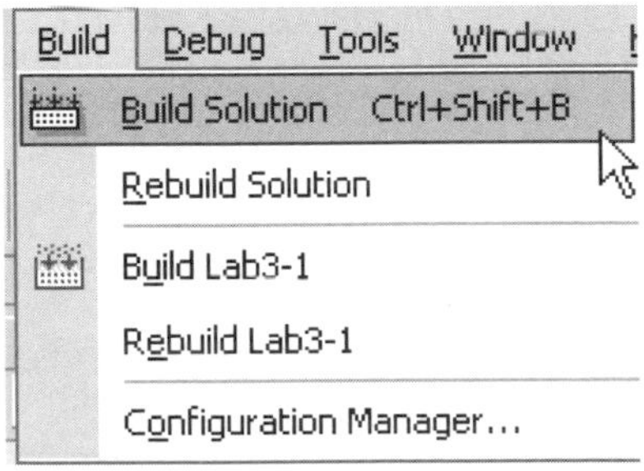

Lab Figure 3-15 Building the Web application

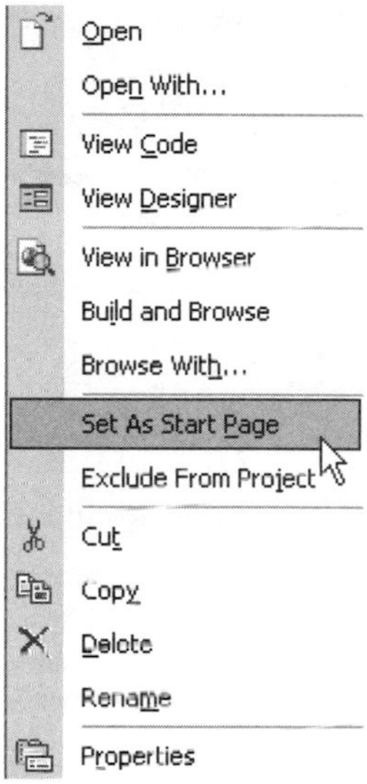

Lab Figure 3-16 Setting the start page for the Web application

c. Now you're ready to run the Web application. Select **Start Without Debugging** from the Debug menu (see Lab Figure 3-17). This runs the application without invoking the VS.NET debugger. Your first Web application in action should look something like the screen shown in Lab Figure 3-18.

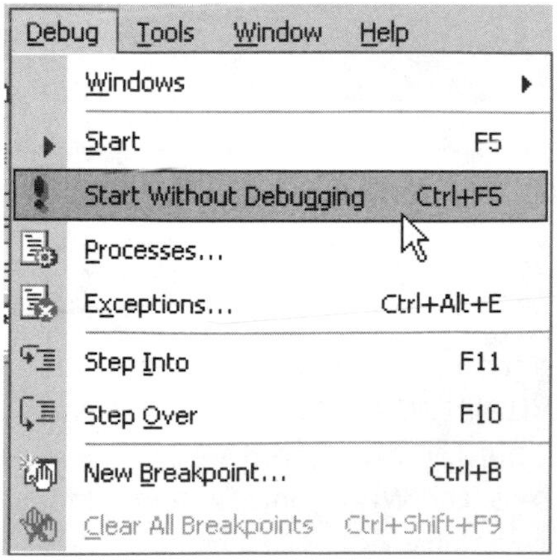

Lab Figure 3-17 Running the Web application

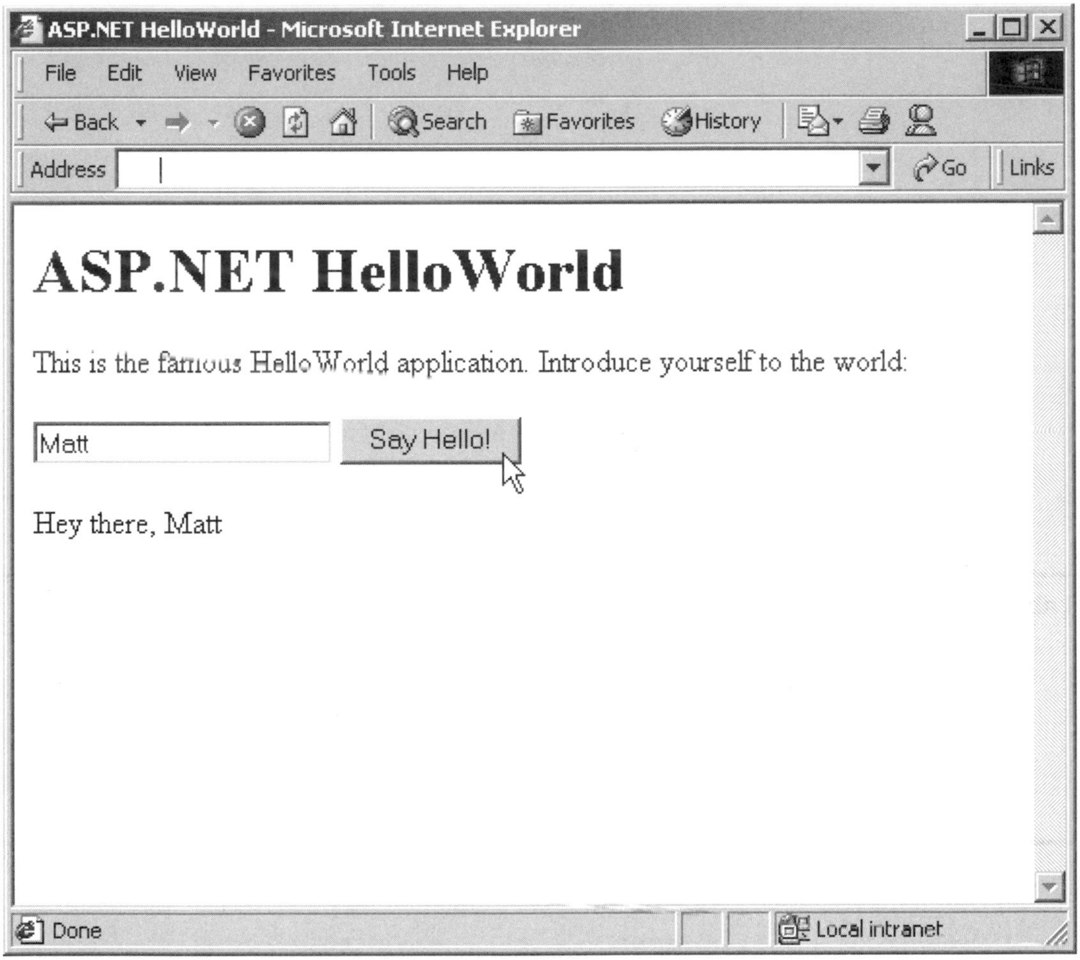

Lab Figure 3-18 Running the Lab3-1 Web application

Congratulations on finishing the lab! You've gained valuable experience for developing ASP.NET applications with VB.NET. Other Web applications in this book are, of course, considerably more complex, but the fundamentals are the same. In the next lab, you'll have the chance to use more of the Web Controls and add much more application code to provide rich application functionality.

3.16 ASP.NET Page Directives

When writing Web applications, there are times when you need to adjust settings that control page-specific compiler behavior. Page directives control settings for the code compiler like page settings (for example, the language to use) and namespaces to import into the page. The six types of page directives you can use are listed in Table 3-5.

Each of the page directives can have several different attributes associated with it. You may have noticed some of these page directive attributes already in the code for some of the sample Web Forms. The attributes usually set what language to use for the page and what class to use for the code-behind file, as in this example.

```
<%@ Page Language="vb"
   Codebehind="WebControlButtonSample.vb"
   Inherits="ExampleApplication.WebControlButtonSample"
%>
```

3.16.1 The `@ Page` and `@ Control` Directives

The `@ Page` and `@ Control` directives share many common attributes. Table 3-6 shows the possible attributes that can be used in the `@ Page` and `@ Control` directives and their functions.

Table 3-5 ASP.NET Page Directives

Page Directive	Description
`@ Assembly`	Links an assembly to the current page
`@ Control`	Defines control-specific attributes for ASP.NET user controls
`@ Import`	Imports a namespace into a page
`@ OutputCache`	Controls the output-caching policies of a page
`@ Page`	Controls page settings used by the page compiler
`@ Register`	Allows assignment of aliases to namespaces used with the page

Table 3-6 Attributes Used for the `@ Page` and `@ Control` Page Directives

Page Directive Attribute	Description
`AspCompat` (used only for `@ Page`)	Sets backward compatibility with classic ASP. The default is `False`, which means "not compatible."
`Buffer`	Turns HTTP buffering on or off. `True` is the default.
`CodePage`	Sets the locale code page for the page.
`ContentType`	Sets the MIME type for the HTTP response. Supports any valid MIME type.
`Culture`	Sets the culture setting for the page.
`Description`	Provides a text description of the page.
`EnableSessionState`	Turns session state support on or off. The default is `True`.
`ErrorPage`	Specifies the URL of the error page. A redirect to this URL occurs when an unhandled exception is encountered.
`Inherits`	Specifies the name of the code-behind class for the page to inherit. The specified class can be any class that inherits from the `Page` class.
`Language`	Sets the default language for the page. Valid languages are VB, C#, and JScript.
`LCID`	Sets the locale ID code.
`MaintainState`	Turns the view state of the HTML and Web Controls on and off on a page-wide level. The default is `True`.
`ResponseEncoding`	Enables response encoding of page content.
`SRC`	Indicates the path to the code-behind class to compile. If a code-behind class is used and this attribute is omitted, assemblies in the `/bin` directory are used to resolve the path to the class.

Page Directive Attribute	Description
`Trace` (used only for `@ Page`)	Turns on and off debug tracing for the page. The default is `False`.
`Transaction`	Indicates transaction support for the page. Possible values are `NotSupported`, `Supported`, `Required`, and `RequiresNew`.
`Warnings`	Generates a compiler error if the compiler encounters warnings and this attribute is set to `True`. The default is `False`.

3.16.2 The `@ Import` Directive

Use the `@ Import` directive like you would use the `Imports` statement in VB.NET: to add a reference to a namespace. Use one `@ Import` directive per namespace. To import multiple namespaces, write code like the following.

```
<%@ Import Namespace="System.Drawing" %>
<%@ Import Namespace="YourNamespace" %>
<%@ Import Namespace="System.Net.Sockets" %>
```

> **TIP:** All pages automatically include implicit references to the following namespaces, so you don't need to reference them using the `@ Import` directive: `System`, `System.Collections`, `System.IO`, `System.Web`, `System.Web.UI`, `System.Web.UI.HtmlControls`, and `System.Web.UI.WebControls`.

3.16.3 The `@ Register` Directive

The `@ Register` directive allows you to refer to namespaces and classes by an alias. This is especially useful when you want to associate with a namespace or class a "friendly" name that makes more sense to you. There are two forms of the `@ Register` directive:

```
<%@ Register Tagprefix="tagprefix" Namespace="namespace" %>

<%@ Register Tagprefix="tagprefix"
   Tagname="tagname" Src="pathname" %>
```

The `Tagprefix` attribute sets an alias for a namespace. The `Tagname` attribute specifies an alias to use for a class. `Namespace` is the namespace to associate with the specified tag prefix. Here are some examples.

```
<%@ Register Tagprefix="MyTag"
   Namespace="MyCompany:MyNameSpace" %>
<%@ Register Tagprefix="Acme"
   Tagname="AdRotator" Src="AdRotator.ascx" %>
```

Given these declarations, you can reference classes in aliased namespaces like this.

```
<MyTag:MyControl id="Control1" runat="server" />
<Acme:AdRotator file="myads.xml" runat="server" />
```

3.16.4 The `@ Assembly` Directive

Another way to include references to classes in a page is to specify the name of an assembly file directly. When you do this, all the classes and interfaces available inside the assembly can be used within the page. Any assemblies used by your Web application are included in the `/bin` directory of your application, so a fully qualified path to the assembly file isn't required. The syntax for the `@ Assembly` directive appears below.

```
<%@ Assembly Name="SomeAssembly.dll" %>
```

3.16.5 The `@ OutputCache` Directive

The output of pages can be cached for better application performance. You can control the settings for the output cache by using the `@ OutputCache` directive. Here is the syntax.

```
<%@ OutputCache Duration="cachetime" Vary="headers" %>
```

`Duration` is measured in seconds. This is the length of time during which the output cache for the page is kept active. `Vary` is a comma-separated list of HTTP headers used to vary the output cache.

3.17 ASP.NET Rich Controls

Some ASP.NET controls provide richer functionality and more interactivity than others. These Web Controls, which are sometimes referred to as *rich controls*, use Dynamic HTML and client-side script when appropriate to provide better user interaction. Like the other Web Controls, they feature automatic browser detection. If down-level browsers are used to visit a page that contains rich controls, the dynamic functionality of those controls are implemented using server round-trips. There are two such controls that ship with ASP.NET: the `Calendar` Control and the `AdRotator` Control.

3.17.1 The `Calendar` Control

The `Calendar` control is used to ease the problems caused by user input of dates. Many Web sites that require the user to enter date information need to take into account complex validation rules, such as valid formats, correct ranges, and so on. These problems are magnified if the site must be implemented in other languages, which can cause the rules for entering dates for one country to not match another country's rules for date entry.

The `Calendar` Control solves date-entry problems by allowing the user to select dates graphically. The `Calendar` Control displays dates in a one-month view, just like a traditional calendar. To select a date, the user first navigates to a month using scrolling buttons and then clicks on the desired date. Multiple dates can be selected as well as whole weeks or an entire month. This makes the `Calendar` Control very versatile for many different types of applications, such as appointment books and reservations systems. The `Calendar` Control's look can also be customized with a variety of styles, colors, and fonts, plus the output of individual days can be customized with user data from a database or other source.

The `Calendar` Control has many properties, but the default syntax is all you need to get started. The basic syntax for the `Calendar` Control follows.

```
<asp:Calendar id="calendar1" runat="server">
```

Using just the above syntax, the control renders in the browser with default styles and date selection enabled and displays the current month and date on the Web server, as shown in Figure 3-21.

Table 3-7 contains the complete listing of the `Calendar` Control's many properties. Remember that as a Web Control, the `Calendar` Control also inherits all the shared properties of other Web Controls.

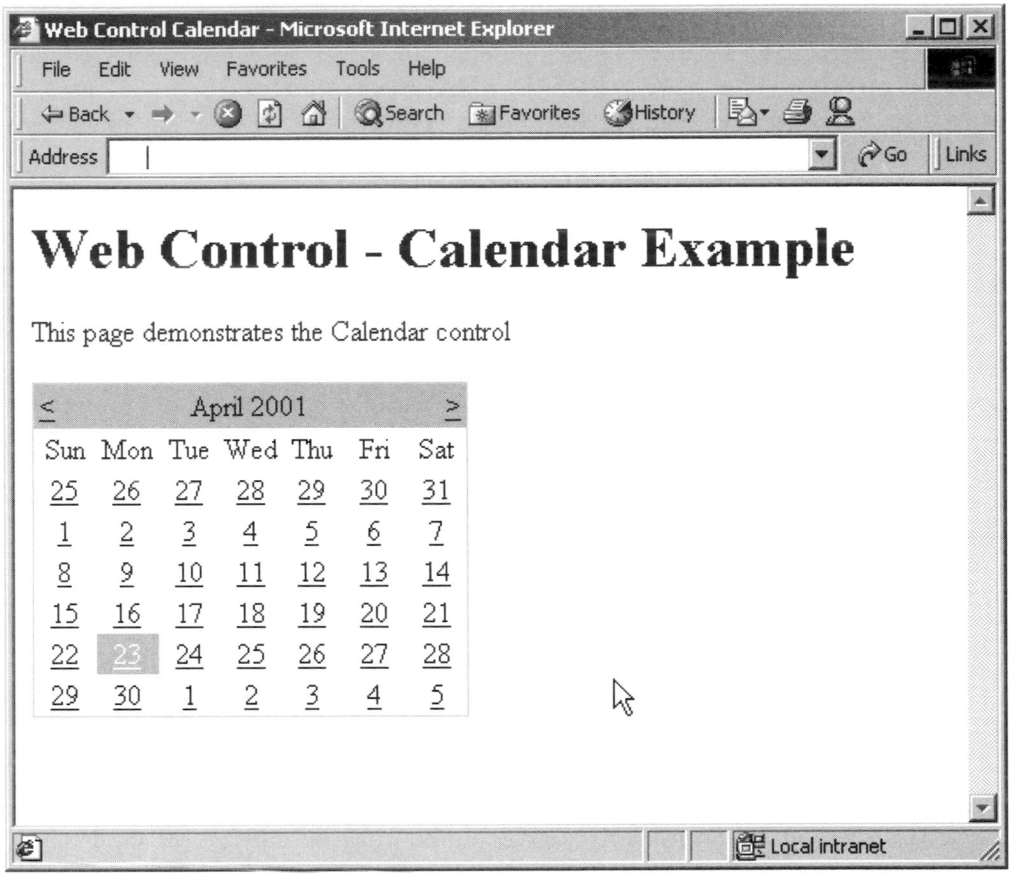

Figure 3-21 The `Calendar` Control with default styles

Table 3-7 Properties of the `Calendar` Control

Property	Description
`CellPadding`	Controls the amount of space between the cell border and the cell contents in the calendar (a cell contains a day).
`CellSpacing`	Gets or sets the amount of space between the borders of adjacent cells. Controls the amount of space between the borders of adjacent cells in the calendar.

Property	Description
DayHeaderStyle	Read-only property that returns an object (System.Web.UI.WebControls.TableItemStyle) that represents the style of the day-of-the-week header.
DayNameFormat	Sets or gets the format (as an object of type System.Web.UI.WebControls.DayNameFormat) for the day names.
DayStyle	Read-only property of type System.Web.UI.WebControls.TableItemStyle that gets style properties for the individual days in the calendar.
FirstDayOfWeek	Controls which day is displayed as the first day of the week in the calendar. Property is of type System.Web.UI.WebControls.FirstDayOfWeek.
NextMonthText	Controls the text displayed for the next month hyperlink if the ShowNextPrevMonth property is set to True.
NextPrevFormat	Controls the format for the next and previous month hyperlinks. Property is of type System.Web.UI.WebControls.NextPrevFormat.
NextPrevStyle	Read-only property that gets the style of the next/previous month navigators as an object of type System.Web.UI.WebControls.TableItemStyle.
OtherMonthDayStyle	Read-only property that returns the style property (as a System.Web.UI.WebControls.TableItemStyle object) of the months following and preceding the current month.
PrevMonthText	Controls the text for the previous month hyperlink.
SelectedDate	Sets or gets the currently selected date as an object of System.DateTime type.
SelectedDates	Read-only property that defines a collection of System.DateTime objects representing the selected dates on the calendar.

(continued)

Table 3-7 Properties of the `Calendar` Control *(continued)*

Property	Description
`SelectedDayStyle`	Read-only property that gets the style properties for the selected date as a `System.Web.UI.WebControls.TableItemStyle` object.
`SelectionMode`	Gets or sets the date selection capabilities on the calendar to allow the user to select a day, week, or month. Controls how date selections are made on the calendar using the `System.Web.UI.WebControls.CalendarSelectionMode` object.
`SelectMonthText`	Controls the text displayed for the month selection in the selector column if `SelectionMode` is set to `CalendarSelectionMode.DayWeekMonth`.
`SelectorStyle`	Read-only property that gets the style properties for the week and month selectors as a `System.Web.UI.WebControls.TableItemStyle` object.
`SelectWeekText`	Gets or sets the text shown for the week selection in the selector column if `SelectionMode` is `CalendarSelectionMode.DayWeek` or `CalendarSelectionMode.DayWeekMonth`.
`ShowDayHeader`	Indicates whether or not to show the days of the week on the calendar. Default is `True`.
`ShowGridLines`	Controls the display of grid lines in the calendar around the days.
`ShowNextPrevMonth`	Indicates with a Boolean value whether or not to display the next and previous month hyperlinks in the calendar title.
`ShowTitle`	Gets or sets a Boolean value indicating whether the calendar title is displayed.
`TitleFormat`	Controls the format for the calendar title as a `System.Web.UI.WebControls.TitleFormat` object.

Property	Description
`TitleStyle`	Read-only property that gets the style for the calendar title as a `System.Web.UI.WebControls.Style` object.
`TodayDayStyle`	Read-only property that gets the style for today's date as a `System.Web.UI.WebControls.Style` object.
`TodaysDate`	Controls today's date for use in the calendar.
`VisibleDate`	Gets or sets the date that specifies which month to display. The date can be any date within the month.
`WeekendDayStyle`	Read-only property that gets the style for weekend dates as a `System.Web.UI.WebControls.Style` object.

When you use VS.NET to put calendars on your pages, you can use a convenient feature to give your calendar a pleasing look. In the Properties window for the `Calendar` Control, click on the AutoFormat link (see Figure 3-22). This brings up the Calendar AutoFormat window shown in Figure 3-23. You can select a color and style scheme from a list of predefined styles.

> **TIP:** Using the Calendar AutoFormat feature provides you with a base for customizing your calendar. Since the Calendar AutoFormat feature fills in many properties for you, you can simply change them as desired to fit your design needs. For example, you can change the color of the heading to something different.

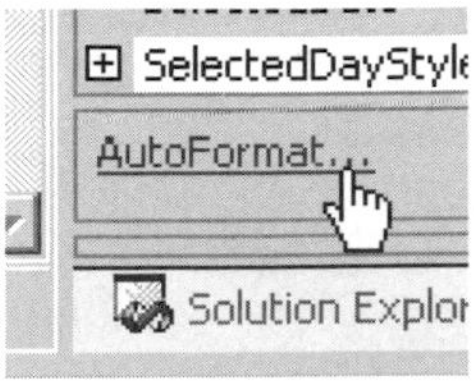

Figure 3-22 The Calendar AutoFormat option

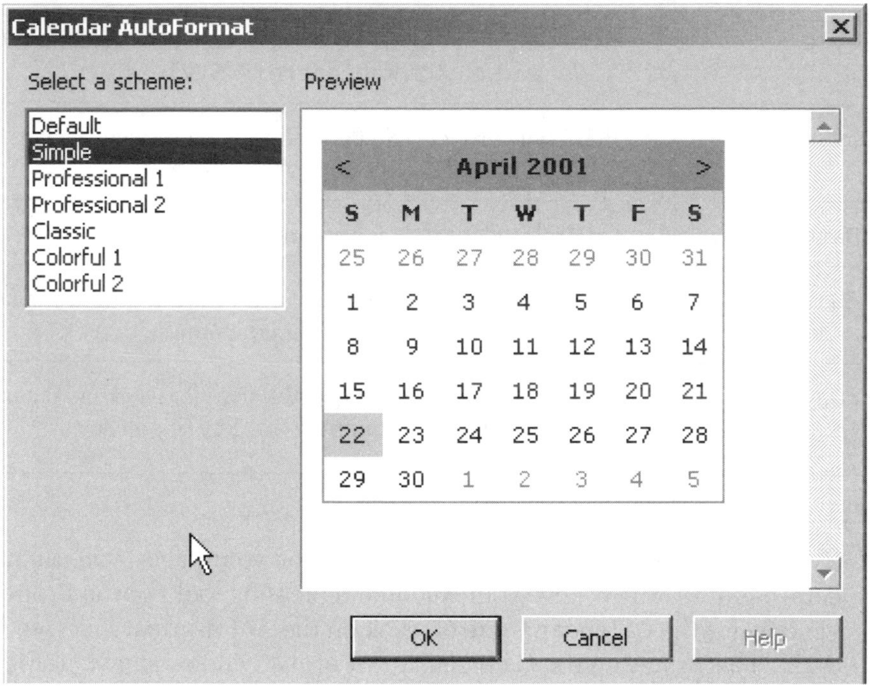

Figure 3-23 The Calendar AutoFormat window

Here's an example of how `Calendar` Control usage looks in HTML form. The Calendar AutoFormat feature generated this calendar. Notice the notation used to reference the fields in the object types, such as for the Font object (for example, `Font-Size="8pt"`).

Code Sample 3-25

```
<%@ Page Language="vb"
   AutoEventWireup="false"
   src="cs3-25.aspx.vb"
   Inherits="WebControlCalendar"
%>
<html>
   <head>
      <title>Calendar Demo</title>
```

```
   </head>
   <body>

<form id="Form1" method="post" runat="server">

<asp:calendar id=Calendar1
   runat="server"
   DayNameFormat="FirstLetter"
   BackColor="White"
   SelectorStyle-BackColor="#CCCCCC"
   NextPrevStyle-VerticalAlign="Bottom"
   TodayDayStyle-ForeColor="Black"
   TodayDayStyle-BackColor="#CCCCCC"
   DayHeaderStyle-Font-Bold="True"
   DayHeaderStyle-BackColor="#CCCCCC"
   Font-Size="8pt"
   Font-Names="Verdana"
   Height="180"
   OtherMonthDayStyle-ForeColor="#808080"
   TitleStyle-Font-Bold="True"
   TitleStyle-BorderColor="Black"
   TitleStyle-BackColor="#999999"
   WeekendDayStyle-BackColor="#FFFFCC"
   ForeColor="Black"
   BorderColor="#999999"
   Width="201"
   SelectedDayStyle-Font-Bold="True"
   SelectedDayStyle-ForeColor="White"
   SelectedDayStyle-BackColor="#666666"
   CellPadding="4">
</asp:Calendar>

<asp:Label id=lblSelectionMessage
   runat=server>
</asp:label>

</form>
</body>
</html>
```

The `Calendar` Control, like other Web Controls, also responds to events. The `Calendar` Control has three events, listed in Table 3-8, that are of particular interest.

Table 3-8 Events of the `Calendar` Control

Event	Description
`DayRender`	Occurs when each day is created in the control hierarchy for the calendar. Use this event to modify the contents of each date cell with custom data.
`SelectionChanged`	Occurs when the user clicks on a day, week, or month selector and changes the `SelectedDate` property.
`VisibleMonthChanged`	Occurs when the user clicks on the next or previous month controls on the calendar title.

As a quick example, let's write some code to echo back the date the user selects from the calendar. Using the definition created earlier in the Calendar AutoFormat example, we write an event handler for the `SelectionChanged` event in a code-behind file.

```
Imports System
Imports System.Drawing
Imports System.Web
Imports System.Web.UI
Imports System.Web.UI.WebControls

Public Class WebControlCalendar
   Inherits System.Web.UI.Page

   Protected WithEvents lblSelectionMessage As _
      System.Web.UI.WebControls.Label
   Protected WithEvents Calendar1 As _
      System.Web.UI.WebControls.Calendar

   Public Sub Calendar1_SelectionChanged( _
            ByVal sender As Object, _
            ByVal e As System.EventArgs) _
            Handles Calendar1.SelectionChanged

      lblSelectionMessage.Text = _
            Calendar1.SelectedDate.ToString()

   End Sub
End Class
```

The code is straightforward; we are simply taking the value of the SelectedDate property, which holds the user selection, and displaying the string contents to the lblSelectionMessage Label Control.

3.17.2 The AdRotator Control

Banner advertisements are as ubiquitous as Web sites themselves, and ASP.NET makes it easy to incorporate them into your pages. In order to maximize the effectiveness of banner advertisements, you want to display rotated advertisements that would be most relevant to each user browsing the site. For example, you may want to display advertisements for a particular product line when the user browses to an area of your site that features those products. In another situation, you may want to run a special promotion on a particular product or series of products. Advertisements for those special promotional products can appear with greater frequency than other advertisements. The AdRotator Control provides this functionality with minimal coding effort.

The AdRotator Control is just as easy to use as the other Web Controls. The syntax for the AdRotator Control appears below.

```
<asp:AdRotator
    id=value
    runat="server"
    AdvertisementFile="AdvertisementFile"
    OnAdCreated="OnAdCreatedMethod"
    KeywordFilter="keyword"
    Target="browserwindoworframename"
>
</asp:AdRotator>
```

As with the other Web Controls, the AdRotator Control inherits all the shared Web Control properties. The properties specific to the AdRotator Control are listed in Table 3-9.

The advertisement data file holds all the information about the banner ads to display. This includes for each ad the URL to the banner graphic, the URL link associated with the banner graphic, the graphic's ALT text, a keyword associated with the banner, and a rotation "weight." All of this data is contained within an XML format. In order for the AdRotator Control to function properly, the XML format must be valid. The path to the advertisement file is specified in the AdvertisementFile property. This is the format for the XML advertisement file.

Table 3-9 Properties of the `AdRotator` Control

Property	Description
`AdvertisementFile`	Specifies the relative path to the advertisement data file (in XML format).
`KeywordFilter`	Designates a keyword to use that filters the advertisements. If specified, only banner ads that have a keyword that matches the value in `KeywordFilter` are eligible for display.
`Target`	Specifies the name of the browser window or frame in which to display the advertisement. Keywords such as `_TOP`, `_NEW`, `_CHILD`, `_SELF`, `_PARENT`, or `_BLANK` can be used

```
<Advertisements>
   <Ad>
      <ImageUrl>URL of image to display</ImageUrl>
      <TargetUrl>URL of page to link to</TargetUrl>
      <AlternateText>
         Text to show as ToolTip
      </AlternateText>
      <Keyword>keyword used to filter</Keyword>
      <Impressions>relative weighting of ad</Impressions>
   </Ad>
</Advertisements>
```

TECHTALK: XML

XML stands for eXtensible Markup Language. For the uninitiated, XML is the talk of the whole software industry. XML allows you to package data in a hierarchical, self-describing format. XML has wide applications, from business-to-business e-commerce to providing an infrastructure for distributed Internet applications. It's no coincidence that all of the .NET Framework relies heavily on XML. XML is a World Wide Web Consortium standard and is embraced by many different software vendors. I'll mention XML again in the discussions of data access and Web Services. If you're curious about the technical details and specifications of XML, you can find more information at the World Wide Web Consortium's XML Web site at *http://www.w3.org/XML*.

Constructing an advertisement file is as simple as following the above format. The file can contain any number of banner entries. Here's a sample of an advertisement file that contains four banner ads, complete with ALT texts, hyperlinks, keywords, and impressions (relative rotation weights).

```
<Advertisements>
   <Ad>
      <ImageUrl>banner1.gif</ImageUrl>
      <TargetUrl>
      http://your-server/webcontroladrotator.aspx
      </TargetUrl>
      <AlternateText>Computer Classes for KIDS!</AlternateText>
      <Keyword>education</Keyword>
      <Impressions>100</Impressions>
   </Ad>
   <Ad>
      <ImageUrl>banner2.gif</ImageUrl>
      <TargetUrl>
      http://your-server/webcontroladrotator.aspx
      </TargetUrl>
      <AlternateText>Save NOW on Floppy Disks!</AlternateText>
      <Keyword>supplies</Keyword>
      <Impressions>150</Impressions>
   </Ad>
   <Ad>
      <ImageUrl>banner3.gif</ImageUrl>
      <TargetUrl>
      http://your-server/webcontroladrotator.aspx
      </TargetUrl>
      <AlternateText>
      Enroll for Typing Classes Now!
      </AlternateText>
      <Keyword>education</Keyword>
      <Impressions>150</Impressions>
   </Ad>
   <Ad>
      <ImageUrl>banner4.gif</ImageUrl>
      <TargetUrl>
      http://your-server/webcontroladrotator.aspx
      </TargetUrl>
      <AlternateText>Networkz 'R Us</AlternateText>
      <Keyword>consulting</Keyword>
      <Impressions>100</Impressions>
   </Ad>
</Advertisements>
```

Keyword and Impressions are two features you can use to selectively display ads based on importance or category. Keyword causes the AdRotator Control to display banner ads that have a keyword that matches the keyword specified in the KeywordFilter property. This is useful, for example, when the user is in an area of a site that is customized for a certain demographic (for example, you can display ads in the business section of a site that pertain to consulting and business services and filter out ads for entertainment). The Impressions feature allows you to make particular banner ads appear more often than others. This is useful when you want to draw attention to a special product or service. In banner hosting scenarios, you may want to give higher Impressions values to companies that have paid higher hosting fees in exchange for greater ad exposure. The values for Impressions are relative; higher values receive more rotation.

The AdRotator Control also defines an event called OnAdCreated. This event is raised upon the next post-back to the server whenever the advertisement changes. The OnAdCreated event is useful for adjusting the content of the rest of the page based on which banner ad the AdRotator Control picked.

The AdCreatedEventArgs object associated with the OnAdCreated event contains these members:

- e.AdProperties (IDictionary collection of all properties for the selected banner ad)
- e.AlternateText (corresponds to AlternateText in the XML file)
- e.ImageUrl (corresponds to ImageURL in the XML file)
- e.NavigateUrl (corresponds to TargetURL in the XML file)

Since the AdCreatedEventArgs object contains all the relevant information about the banner ad, you should be able to make good decisions about content changes to the page based on this information.

The AdRotator Control example below demonstrates these concepts. The .aspx file contains the AdRotator Control and a Label Control.

Code Sample 3-26

```
<%@ Page Language="vb"
   AutoEventWireup="false"
   Src="cs3-26.aspx.vb"
   Inherits="WebControlAdRotator"%>
<html><head>
<TITLE>Web Control - AdRotator Sample</TITLE>
</head>
<body>
```

```
<form id="WebControlAdRotator"
   method="post"
   runat="server">
<h1>Web Control - AdRotator Sample</h1>

<p>The AdRotator can rotate banner advertisements.
Click "Refresh" to see a new ad banner.
</p>

<p>
<asp:AdRotator id=adrotMyRotator
   runat="server"
   Width="470"
   Height="60"
   AdvertisementFile="adrot.xml">
</asp:AdRotator>
</p>

<p>
<asp:Label id=lblCurrentAd
   runat="server"
   Width="461"
   Height="19">
</asp:Label>
</p>

</form>
</body>
</html>
```

Here's the code-behind file.

```
Imports System
Imports System.Web
Imports System.Web.UI
Imports System.Web.UI.WebControls

Public Class WebControlAdRotator
      Inherits System.Web.UI.Page
      Protected WithEvents lblCurrentAd As _
   System.Web.UI.WebControls.Label
      Protected WithEvents adrotMyRotator As _
   System.Web.UI.WebControls.AdRotator
```

```
        Public Sub adrotMyRotator_AdCreated( _
           ByVal sender As Object, _
           ByVal e As System.Web.UI.WebControls.AdCreatedEventArgs)
           lblCurrentAd.Text = "The '" & _
                        e.AlternateText & _
                        "' ad was rendered."
        End Sub

End Class
```

Apart from the placement of the `AdRotator` Control in the `.aspx` file, no coding is required to display and rotate banner ads. The interesting code is in the code-behind portion of the example. We write an event handler for `AdCreated` (`OnAdCreated`) that sets the `lblCurrentAd` `Label` Control with the value of the `ALT` text for the banner's graphic.

Figure 3-24 shows the example in action, displaying one of the banner ads contained in the advertisement file.

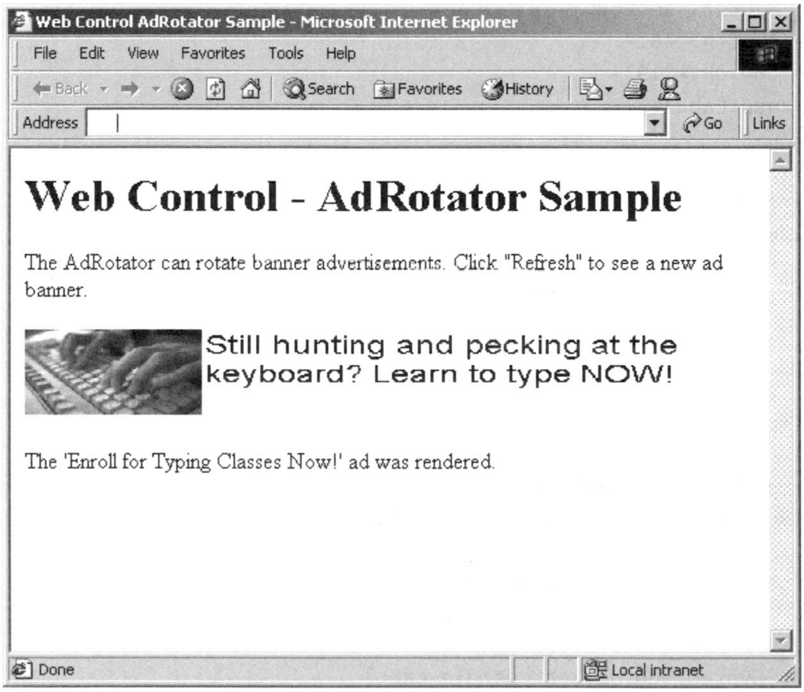

Figure 3-24 Output of the `AdRotator` Control example

3.18 Validation Controls

Whenever a user fills out an HTML form, you almost always want to check the data being entered for validity. Of course, what constitutes valid data varies greatly from application to application. The stability of a software system relies on the system's acceptance of valid data from the user. Validation code is cumbersome to write. Many sites also resort to writing code to do common tasks, like checking phone numbers and ZIP codes. Another problem is that some older browsers lack client-side script functionality to check values entered on a form. It would be beneficial to have a set of routines that make input validation less of a chore for application developers and that function on any browser.

Even through data validation is implemented in many different ways across many sites, those implementations share common characteristics. If you were filling out an order form to purchase goods online, you would make product selections and perhaps enter a credit card number. Since it would not make sense to process the order with incomplete information, fields like the ones described need to be checked to see if the user provided proper input. Some fields may accept only a certain value, while others expect values within a defined range. Other fields may require complex validation, such as checking for a valid numerical format (for example, social security and phone numbers). Still others may need to validate the data based on an entry provided in another field. If a particular form contains many fields for the user to fill in (such as a new user registration), a summary report of data entry errors made by the user would be helpful so he or she could complete the form accurately

ASP.NET provides a series of Web Controls that aid in the process of validating data. These Web Controls are collectively known as the Validation Controls. These controls operate with any Web browser and can provide client-side or server-side validation of data depending on the browser's capabilities.

3.18.1 The `BaseValidator` Control

All the validation controls inherit from a special Web Control called the `BaseValidator` Control. The `BaseValidator` Control isn't one you use directly (it is, in fact, an abstract class), but it contains properties and methods that all the Validation Controls use. Table 3-10 gives a list of properties you'll use often when working with the Validation Controls.

Table 3-10 Properties of the Validation Controls

Property	Description
`ControlToValidate`	Sets or gets the `ID` of the Control to validate.
`Display`	Determines how the Control is used in the page. Takes a type of `ValidationDisplay`. Possible values are `Static`, `None`, and `Dynamic`.
`Enabled`	Determines whether or not the Control is enabled (true/false value).
`ErrorMessage`	Gets or sets the text for error messages.
`ForeColor`	Gets or sets the text color of validation messages.
`IsValid`	Gets or sets a flag to indicate whether the referenced control passed validation.

3.18.2 The `RequiredFieldValidator` Control

The most basic validation you can perform is to make sure that a field contains data (that is, that the field isn't blank). This is the job of the `RequiredFieldValidator` Control. The `RequiredFieldValidator` Control inherits all the shared Web Control properties (as do all the other Validation Controls). Follow the sample syntax below to place the `RequiredFieldValidator` Control in your Web Forms. The properties listed here are required.

```
<asp:RequiredFieldValidator
   id="RequiredFieldValidator1" runat="server"
   ControlToValidate="id_of_control"
   ErrorMessage="Your error message here"
   ForeColor="Red">
</asp:RequiredFieldValidator>
```

`ControlToValidate` is the `ID` of any Web Control on the page. This is the property that the `RequiredFieldValidator` Control uses to check for data entry. (All the other Validation Controls use the `ControlToValidate` property in the same way.) If the validation fails, that is, if the user did not supply any data in the field, the text specified in ErrorMessage appears in the display area when data is posted back to the server. The post-back does not execute until the error (and all other validation errors on the page) are reconciled. This means that all other Validation Controls on the page must contain valid data before the post-back occurs. The ForeColor property specifies a color for the ErrorMessage text. It's a good idea to choose a color that stands out from the rest of the page so users can identify an error easily. For design purposes, the Display property can be used to designate how Validation Controls are displayed in the page. By default, Validation Controls take up space on the page even if the error message is not currently being displayed. Since this can cause difficulties in page layout, you can set the Display property to Dynamic, which causes the Validation Control to occupy space on the page only when an error is displayed. Setting Dynamic for the Display property is really applicable only to Web browsers that support DHTML (up-level browsers such as Internet Explorer 4.0 or above). This is because validation occurs on the client side, without a server post-back. Down-level browsers always perform server-side validation since they cannot reliably use client-side script in all types of data validation scenarios.

Below is a small example of a Web Form that uses the RequiredFieldValidator Control. The RequiredFieldValidator Control checks for an entry in the txtRequired text box when the btnSubmit button is clicked.

Code Sample 3-27

```
<%@ Page Language="vb" %>
<html><head>
<TITLE>Validation Demo</TITLE>
</head>
<body>

<form id="WebControlValidationDemo"
   method="post"
   runat="server">

<h1>Validation Demo</h1>
<p>You must type something here:

<asp:TextBox id=txtRequired
   runat="server">
</asp:TextBox>
```

```
<asp:RequiredFieldValidator id=rfvTxtRequired
   runat="server"
   ErrorMessage="You must enter something!"
   ControlToValidate="txtRequired">
</asp:RequiredFieldValidator>
</p>

<p>
<asp:Button id=btnSubmit
   runat="server"
   Text="Send Data">
</asp:Button>
</p>

</form>
</body>
</html>
```

3.18.3 The `CompareValidator` Control

Another type of validation to perform is checking an entry against a single value, and this is the job of the `CompareValidator` Control. You can perform any kind of comparison using logical operators. For example, you can check to see if an entry matches a particular value. You can also compare the value of one entry with that of another entry. You can check to see if a value is greater or less than another value. Any combination of greater-than-or-equal-to or less-than-or-equal-to checks are also possible. Plus, the `CompareValidator` Control can check a value to see if it is a particular data type.

To code the `CompareValidator` Control, you can use the minimum syntax.

```
<asp:CompareValidator
   id="CompareFieldValidator1"
   runat="server"
   ForeColor="Red"
   ControlToValidate="id_of_control"
   ErrorMessage="Your error message here.">
</asp: CompareValidator >
```

To perform different types of operations with the `CompareValidator` Control, you can set the specific properties shown in Table 3-11 to control how the data is compared.

Table 3-11 Properties of the `CompareValidator` Control

Property	Description
`ControlToCompare`	Specifies the `ID` of a control with which you wish to compare `ControlToValidate`.
`Operator`	Determines the type of comparison operation to perform. Can be one of the following: `Equal`, `NotEqual`, `GreaterThan`, `GreaterThanEqual`, `LessThan`, `LessThanEqual`, or `DataTypeCheck`.
`Type`	Specifies the data type to use for the comparison. Can be `String`, `Integer`, `Double`, `Date`, or `Currency`. Defaults to `String`.
`ValueToCompare`	Sets the value to compare against. Used if `ControlToCompare` is not set.

Let's look at two examples of the `CompareValidator` Control. In the first example, we perform a simple check for a specific value. We want the user to select a number from a list that contains a series of numbers (created using the `DropDownList` Control) before continuing on with the post-back.

Code Sample 3.28

```
<%@ Page Language="vb" %>
<html><head>
<TITLE>Validation Demo</TITLE>
</head>
<body>

<form id="WebControlValidationDemo"
   method="post"
   runat="server">


<p>Select the magic number:
<asp:DropDownList id=ddlNumberList runat="server">
<asp:ListItem Value="Please Select a Number">
   Please Select a Number
</asp:ListItem>
```

```
<asp:ListItem Value="31">31</asp:ListItem>
<asp:ListItem Value="42">42</asp:ListItem>
<asp:ListItem Value="123">123</asp:ListItem>
<asp:ListItem Value="44">44</asp:ListItem>
<asp:ListItem Value="784">784</asp:ListItem>
</asp:DropDownList>

<asp:CompareValidator id=cvMagicNumber
   runat="server"
   ErrorMessage="You must select a number!"
   ControlToValidate="ddlNumberList"
   ValueToCompare="Please Select a Number"
   Operator="NotEqual">
</asp:CompareValidator>
</p>

<p>
<asp:Button id=btnSubmit
   runat="server"
   Text="Send Data">
</asp:Button>
</p>

</form>
</body>
</html>
```

The `CompareValidator` Control, `cvMagicNumber`, uses a string comparison to see if the `ValueToCompare` choice "Please Select a Number" is selected. This is a `NotEqual` comparison, as specified in the `Operator` property, so this means that `ErrorMessage` is displayed when the "Please Select a Number" choice is left selected in the list upon an attempted post-back.

In the next example, the `CompareValidator` Control is used on two different controls. These controls contain numbers as well. The `DropDownList` Control is used twice with two different IDs to select a maximum and a minimum value. We want to implement a validation where the user cannot select a choice for the minimum value that is greater than the maximum or a maximum value that is less than the minimum. The boldface text below points out that section of code.

Code Sample 3-29

```
<%@ Page Language="vb" %>
<html><head>
<TITLE>Validation Demo</TITLE>
</head>
<body>

<form id="WebControlValidationDemo"
   method="post"
   runat="server">

<p>Select a minimum:
<asp:DropDownList id=ddlMinimum runat="server">
   <asp:ListItem Value="-10">-10</asp:ListItem>
   <asp:ListItem Value="0">0</asp:ListItem>
   <asp:ListItem Value="50">50</asp:ListItem>
   <asp:ListItem Value="100">100</asp:ListItem>
</asp:DropDownList>

Select a maximum:
<asp:DropDownList id=ddlMaximum runat="server">
<asp:ListItem Value="0">0</asp:ListItem>
<asp:ListItem Value="20">20</asp:ListItem>
<asp:ListItem Value="70">70</asp:ListItem>
<asp:ListItem Value="100">100</asp:ListItem>
</asp:DropDownList>
</p>

<p>
<asp:CompareValidator id=cvMinMax
   runat="server"
   ErrorMessage="Minimum must be less than maximum!"
   ControlToValidate="ddlMinimum"
   ControlToCompare="ddlMaximum"
   Type="Integer"
   Operator="LessThan">
</asp:CompareValidator>
</p>

<p>
<asp:CompareValidator id=cvMaxMin
   runat="server"
   ErrorMessage="Maximum must be greater than minimum!"
```

```
    ControlToValidate="ddlMaximum"
    ControlToCompare="ddlMinimum"
    Type="Integer"
    Operator="GreaterThan">
</asp:CompareValidator>
</p>

<p>
<asp:Button id=btnSubmit
    runat="server"
    Text="Send Data">
</asp:Button>
</p>

</form>
</body>
</html>
```

In these comparisons, we explicitly set the `Type` of the comparison to `Integer`, since we are dealing with numeric comparisons. Notice the use of `Operator` and `ControlToCompare` in both `CompareValidator` Controls. Each `CompareValidator` Control specifies the other for `ControlToCompare`. The `Operator` is set to `GreaterThan` or `LessThan`, keeping consistent with the meaning of the `ErrorMessage` value.

3.18.4 The `RangeValidator` Control

The `RangeValidator` Control allows you to check a value to see if it falls within a defined range. The syntax appears below.

```
<asp:RangeValidator id=RangeValidator1
    runat="server"
    ErrorMessage="Value is out of range!"
    ControlToValidate="txtRangeNumber"
</asp:RangeValidator>
```

The `RangeValidator` Control allows explicit range values or a minimum and maximum that come from two Web Controls. Table 3-12 lists the properties specific to the RangeValidator Control.

To demonstrate the `RangeValidator` Control, let's expand on the last example with the `CompareValidator` Control. In that example, a user selected a minimum and maximum value from two drop-down lists and the application

Table 3-12 Properties of the `RangeValidator` Control

Properties	Description
`MaximumValue`	The maximum value for the range
`MinimumValue`	The minimum value for the range

tested to make sure the selections were meaningful. Now we want to test whether an integer value entered into a text box falls within the range specified (1 through 10). The example begins with the two `DropDownList` Controls from the previous example. Then we add a `TextBox` Control along with a `RangeValidator` Control, as shown in the boldface text.

Code Sample 3-30

```
<%@ Page Language="vb"%>
<html><head>
<TITLE>Validation Demo</TITLE>
</head>
<body>

<form id="WebControlValidationDemo"
   method="post"
   runat="server">

<p>Select a minimum:
<asp:DropDownList id=ddlMinimum runat="server">
   <asp:ListItem Value="-10">-10</asp:ListItem>
   <asp:ListItem Value="0">0</asp:ListItem>
   <asp:ListItem Value="50">50</asp:ListItem>
   <asp:ListItem Value="100">100</asp:ListItem>
</asp:DropDownList>

Select a maximum:
<asp:DropDownList id=ddlMaximum runat="server">
<asp:ListItem Value="0">0</asp:ListItem>
<asp:ListItem Value="20">20</asp:ListItem>
<asp:ListItem Value="70">70</asp:ListItem>
<asp:ListItem Value="100">100</asp:ListItem>
</asp:DropDownList>
</p>
```

```
<p>
<asp:CompareValidator id=cvMinMax
   runat="server"
   ErrorMessage="Minimum must be less than maximum!"
   ControlToValidate="ddlMinimum"
   ControlToCompare="ddlMaximum"
   Type="Integer"
   Operator="LessThan">
</asp:CompareValidator>
</p>

<p>
<asp:CompareValidator id=cvMaxMin
   runat="server"
   ErrorMessage="Maximum must be greater than minimum!"
   ControlToValidate="ddlMaximum"
   ControlToCompare="ddlMinimum"
   Type="Integer"
   Operator="GreaterThan">
</asp:CompareValidator>
</p>

<p> . . . and enter a number between 1 and 10:
<asp:TextBox id=txtRangeNumber
   runat="server">
</asp:TextBox>
</p>

<p>
<asp:RangeValidator id=rvRangeValidator
   runat="server"
   ErrorMessage="Value is out of range!"
   ControlToValidate="txtRangeNumber"
   Type="Integer"
   MinimumValue="1"
   MaximumValue="10">
</asp:RangeValidator>
</p>

</form>
</body>
</html>
```

Now when the user enters a value in the `txtRangeNumber` text box, `rvRangeValidator` checks against a range defined by the `MinimumValue` and `MaximumValue` properties.

3.18.5 The `RegularExpressionValidator` Control

Sometimes you need to perform complex validation that is a step beyond simply comparing values, checking for nonblank entries, or other types of simple validation. There are many examples of complex data validation on the Web. For example, a form may require the user to enter data in a particular format, like a phone number with area code, a social security number, or a valid credit card number. These types of validation operations require checking for certain character sequences and patterns. A tool long known to computer scientists and academics aids in these types of validations: the *regular expression*.

Regular expressions are built using a sort of language made up of literal characters and special control characters called *metacharacters*. Regular expressions are compact and optimized for handling and searching text. When a regular expression is applied to text, literal characters in the regular expression are used to match their equivalents in the search text. Metacharacters are used to match certain sequences of characters. Metacharacters function as the commands in the regular expression language. Some metacharacters are used to match a series of any characters, a character or characters within a defined subset, or more complex comparisons. Regular expressions are, in all honesty, quite complex, and developing them is not for the faint of heart. Whole books have been written on the subject of regular expressions, so a detailed discussion of regular expressions is well beyond the scope of this book. Many programming languages (for example, PERL) make copious use of regular expressions.

Do you have to be an expert on regular expressions to use them effectively in your code? Certainly not! You can always write pattern-matching code in your preferred programming language (VB.NET, C++, and so on) if that proves effective for you. But the benefits of using regular expressions will be most realized when you notice the amount of code that you *don't* have to write if you use a general-purpose programming language instead. Regular expressions are widely used in many different environments and have broad programming support. In addition, VS.NET provides some prebuilt regular expressions for you to use in your projects. We'll look at those in a moment.

The general syntax for the `RegularExpressionValidator` Control appears below.

```
<asp:RegularExpressionValidator
   id=id_of_control runat="server"
   ControlToValidate="control_to_validate"
   ErrorMessage="Your Error Message here"
   ValidationExpression="your_regular_expression">
</asp:RegularExpressionValidator>
```

Here's a scenario for using a regular expression. Web sites often try to collect e-mail addresses. E-mail addresses follow a general form, typically *username@host.net*. In other words, an e-mail address contains at least four parts (in this order): a string of arbitrary length, an @ sign, any number of domain names delimited by a period (.), and an ending top-level domain. All valid e-mail addresses follow this pattern. (By *valid* I mean that the e-mail address follows the defined format, not that the e-mail belongs to an active user or exists at all.)

How do you build such a regular expression? Actually, for performing an e-mail address check as described above, you don't need to. VS.NET does that for you with the Regular Expression Editor. To see how this is done, first drag a `RegularExpressionValidator` Control to the Web Form. Then open the Properties window for the `RegularExpressionValidator` Control and click the button in the box for the `ValidationExpression`. This opens the Regular Expression Editor, pictured in Figure 3-25. Select the Internet E-Mail Address option. The Validation Expression box shows the syntax for validating a `TextBox` Control for a valid e-mail address entry.

The example below uses this syntax and also shows multiple Validation Controls (in the boldface code blocks) being applied to a single `TextBox` Control. We also use the `RequiredFieldValidator` Control to check for a blank entry. Any and all Validation Controls applied must pass the validation test before a valid post-back occurs.

> **TIP:** The double validation on the `TextBox` Control in this example isn't actually necessary since a blank entry would not pass the regular expression test of the e-mail address. The two validations simply illustrate the concept of using multiple Validation Controls. Always check for ways to optimize your own validation by keeping this fact in mind.

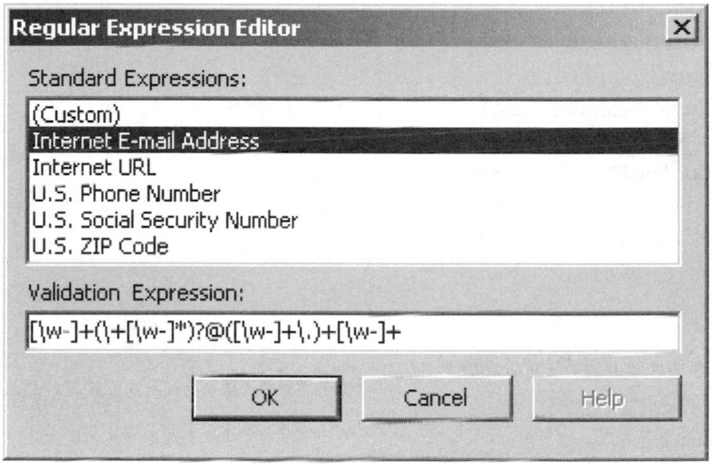

Figure 3-25 VS.NET Regular Expression Editor

Code Sample 3-31

```
<%@ Page Language="vb" %>
<html><head>
<TITLE>Validation Demo</TITLE>
</head>
<body>

<form id="WebControlValidationDemo"
   method="post"
   runat="server">

<p>
Enter an e-mail address:
<asp:TextBox id=txtEmailAddress
   runat="server">
</asp:TextBox>

<asp:RequiredFieldValidator id=rfvTxtEmailAddress
   runat="server"
   ErrorMessage="You must enter an e-mail address!"
   ControlToValidate="txtEmailAddress">
</asp:RequiredFieldValidator>
</p>
```

```
<p>
<asp:RegularExpressionValidator
   id=revTxtEmailAddress
   runat="server"
   ErrorMessage="That doesn't appear to be
   a valid e-mail address!"
   ControlToValidate="txtEmailAddress"
   ValidationExpression="[\w-]+(\+[\w-]*)?@([\w-]+\.)+[\w-]+">
   </asp:RegularExpressionValidator>
</p>

<p>
<asp:Button id=btnSubmit
   runat="server"
   Text="Send Data">
</asp:Button>
</p>

</form>
</body>
</html>
```

3.18.6 The CustomValidator Control

In some instances, a required validation is beyond the scope of the capabilities of the stock Validation Controls. You need the ability to supply a custom validation routine. The `CustomValidator` Control is as versatile as you want it to be.

Using the `CustomValidator` Control begins with the following syntax.

```
<asp:CustomValidator id=CustomValidator1
   runat="server"
   ErrorMessage="Your error message here">
</asp:CustomValidator>
```

The `CustomValidator` Control has the ability to perform validations on the client or on the server. The advantage, of course, of using client-side validation is that a post-back is not required to validate the data. However, if your validation requires checking data that exists only server-side, your choice should be obvious. Keep in mind the audience of your Web application and ask yourself questions like, "Will my users be using down-level browsers, such as Netscape Navigator?" and "Can I perform any validations written for server-side on the client-side?" Your answers to these questions affect which type of validation to use.

> **TIP:** As a general rule regarding where to place validation code, consider the following three questions and the guidelines given for each.
>
> 1. *Is there a chance that my users will use a down-level browser?* (The answer to this question will be invariably "yes" if your Web application will be used on the Internet.) Client-side validation can sometimes be performed on down-level browsers, but this requires that the code be written in JScript/JavaScript. Incompatibilities may be encountered between browsers running this script code. It is generally better to have validations run on the server whenever Internet Explorer 4.x or Netscape Navigator is being used.
> 2. *Is it possible to run my validation code on the client?* To determine this, you will need to analyze your application's requirements and determine whether values entered by the user need to be compared against a set of known values. If the set of known values is large enough that a database is required to store them, the validation code should be executed on the server. If, however, the set of values to check is small, consider placing the values in an array in client-side code and checking the entered value for a matching element in that array.
> 3. *What programming expertise is available for the project?* If your organization has many VB programmers, you may wish to opt for server-side validation since VB runs very reliably on the server. If JScript/JavaScript expertise is available and scalability and performance are paramount for your Web application, client-side validation with JScript/JavaScript may be the way to go.

If you plan to use client-side validation, make note of the `ClientValidationFunction` property listed in Table 3-13.

Performing a client-side validation involves writing a script code procedure to execute when validation is supposed to occur for the

Table 3-13 Properties of the `CustomValidator` Control

Property	Description
`ClientValidationFunction`	Specifies the function name and signature that performs the validation. Signature for the function should be *`ClientValidationFunction`*(*`source`*, *`value`*) (*where* `value` is of type `ServerValidateEventArgs`) and return a Boolean value. Function should return `True` upon a successful validation.
`OnServerValidate`	Specifies the name of the server-side function to execute as validation code. Signature for the function should be *`ClientValidationFunction`*(*`source`*, *`value`*) and return a Boolean value. Function should return `True` upon a successful validation.

`CustomValidator` Control's `ControlToValidate` property. Here's an example that tests whether a text box contains an even number.

Code Sample 3-32

```
<%@ Page Language="vb"%>
<html><head>
<TITLE>Validation Demo</TITLE>

<script language=javascript>
<!--
   function clientSideTest (source, arguments)
   {

      if ((arguments.Value % 2) == 0)
      {
         arguments.IsValid = true;
      }
      else
      {
         arguments.IsValid = false;
      }
   return arguments.IsValid;
   }
```

```
//-->
</script>

</head>
<body>

<form id="WebControlValidationDemo"
   method="post"
   runat="server">

<p>Enter an even number:
<asp:TextBox id=txtClientSideTest
   runat="server">
</asp:TextBox>

<asp:CustomValidator id=cvClientSideTest
   runat="server"
   controltovalidate="txtClientSideTest"
   ErrorMessage="You must enter an even number!"
   clientvalidationfunction="clientSideTest">
</asp:CustomValidator>
</p>

<p>
<asp:Button id=btnSubmit
   runat="server"
   Text="Send Data">
</asp:Button></p>

</form>
</body>
</html>
```

Notice the JScript/JavaScript function at the top of the page called `clientSideTest()`. This function is the validation function for the `txtClientSideTest` Control. As stated before, the signature of the validation function must contain two parameters. When the application determines that the value entered (obtained from the `value` property of the `ServerValidateEventArgs` object) is valid, the application sets the `IsValid` property of the `ServerValidateEventArgs` object.

Let's look at another example. This one performs a server-side validation in a code-behind file. In this example, we're writing a useful function to check whether a credit card number is valid (that is, properly formatted; the function does not check the customer's credit or even whether the number entered belongs to a real credit card). The code we use to place a `CustomValidator` Control on the page is similar to the last example.

Code Sample 3-33

```
<%@ Page Language="vb"
   AutoEventWireup="false"
   Src="cs3-33.aspx.vb"
   Inherits="WebControlValidationDemo"%>
<html><head>
<TITLE>Validation Demo</TITLE>
</head>
<body>

<form id="WebControlValidationDemo"
   method="post"
   runat="server">

<h1>Validation Demo</h1>

<p>
Give me your credit card number:
<asp:TextBox id=txtCreditCard
   runat="server">
</asp:TextBox>

<asp:CustomValidator id=cvCreditCardCheck
   OnServerValidate="IsCreditCardValid"
   runat="server"
   ControlToValidate="txtCreditCard"
   ErrorMessage="That's not a valid credit card number!"
   Width="119"
   Height="57"
   Display="Dynamic">
</asp:CustomValidator>

<asp:RequiredFieldValidator id=rfvCreditCard
   runat="server"
   ControlToValidate="txtCreditCard"
   ErrorMessage="You must enter a credit card number!"
   Display="Dynamic">
</asp:RequiredFieldValidator>
</p>
```

```
<p>
<asp:Button id=btnSubmit
   runat="server"
   Text="Send Data">
</asp:Button></p>

</form>
</body>
</html>
```

This code also makes use of the `RequiredFieldValidator` Control to make sure the user types in something for the `txtCreditCard` text box. The interesting code shows up in the code-behind file with the `IsCreditCardValid()` function. Notice that this function has the same type of signature as the last example (`source`, `args`).

```
Imports System
Imports System.Web
Imports System.Web.UI
Imports System.Web.UI.WebControls
Imports Microsoft.VisualBasic

Public Class WebControlValidationDemo
   Inherits System.Web.UI.Page

      Public Sub IsCreditCardValid(ByVal source As Object, _
                ByVal args As ServerValidateEventArgs)

         Dim intCounter As Integer
         Dim intTmpInt As Integer
         Dim intAnswer As Integer
         Dim strTmp As String

         strTmp = args.Value

         intCounter = 1
         intTmpInt = 0

         args.IsValid = False
         strTmp = Replace(strTmp, " ", "")

         If Not IsNumeric(strTmp) Then
            args.IsValid = False
```

```
            Exit Sub
         End If

         While intCounter <= Len(strTmp)
            If Len(strTmp) Mod 2 <> 0 Then
               intTmpInt = Val(CChar(Mid(strTmp, intCounter, 1)))
               If intCounter Mod 2 = 0 Then
                  intTmpInt = intTmpInt * 2
                  If intTmpInt > 9 Then intTmpInt = intTmpInt - 9
               End If
               intAnswer = intAnswer + intTmpInt
               intCounter = intCounter + 1
            Else
               intTmpInt = Val(CChar(Mid(strTmp, intCounter, 1)))
               If intCounter Mod 2 <> 0 Then
                  intTmpInt = intTmpInt * 2
                  If intTmpInt > 9 Then intTmpInt = intTmpInt - 9
               End If
               intAnswer = intAnswer + intTmpInt
               intCounter = intCounter + 1
            End If
      End While
      intAnswer = intAnswer Mod 10
      If intAnswer = 0 Then
         args.IsValid = True
      End If

   End Sub
End Class
```

3.19 Data List Controls

Many times you need to display information in a list format on Web pages. You may need to display a list containing product offerings and prices, a timetable of departures and arrivals from an airport, or maybe thumbnails from an online photo album. Building these types of lists with other Web development systems requires a significant amount of code, and many Web development systems lack facilities to generate these lists declaratively instead of programmatically.

ASP.NET shines again by making data lists easy to generate. The Web Controls that produce lists are called the List Controls. The data for the List Controls can come from a variety of sources, including flat files, XML, and relational databases.

In this section, we'll explore the three types of List Controls: `Repeater`, `DataGrid`, and `DataList`. We'll also see some data-binding examples, but we'll forgo examples using databases until Chapter 7.

3.19.1 The Repeater Control

The `Repeater` Control is the simplest of the List Controls. It allows for the display of data items by rendering each row in a data source as a row in the Web page. The `Repeater` control renders the rows in a list according to an HTML template you specify. Using these templates, you can control the total appearance of the list. A list header, list item, and list footer can each have different styles. You can also control how spacing between rows is rendered and how to render alternating rows in the list.

The `Repeater` Control uses the following syntax.

```
<asp:Repeater id="Repeater1" runat="server"
   DataSource="<% databindingexpression %>"
>

   <HeaderTemplate>
      Header template HTML
   </HeaderTemplate>
   <ItemTemplate>
      Item template HTML
   </ItemTemplate>
   <AlternatingItemTemplate>
      Alternating item template HTML
   </AlternatingItemTemplate>
   <SeparatorTemplate>
      Separator template HTML
   </SeparatorTemplate>
   <FooterTemplate>
      Footer template HTML
   </FooterTemplate>
<asp:Repeater>
```

Let's start by exploring how templates work. Templates allow you to specify arbitrary HTML to render for the template item. In other words, you can specify HTML for rows, headers, and footers for a particular list. Table 3-14 lists the possible template divisions for the `Repeater` Control.

Table 3-14 Templates Used in the `Repeater` Control

Template	Description
`AlternatingItemTemplate`	HTML to render for alternating rows in the list
`FooterTemplate`	HTML to render at the end of all the rows in the list
`HeaderTemplate`	HTML to render before any rows in the list are rendered
`ItemTemplate`	HTML to render for each row in the list
`SeparatorTemplate`	HTML to render between rows in the list

You'll typically want to display lists as HTML tables since this is the generally accepted way to display tabular data. A typical template for a list looks something like the code shown below.

Code Sample 3-34

```
<%@ Page Language="vb"
   AutoEventWireup="false"
   Src="cs3-34.aspx.vb"
   Inherits="WebFormRepeaterControl"%>
<html><head>
<TITLE>Web Controls - Repeater Control</TITLE>
</head>
<body>

<form id="WebFormRepeaterControl"
   method="post"
   runat="server">
<h1>Web Controls - Repeater Control</h1>

<p>
(49) <asp:Repeater id=rptTestRepeater
   runat="server">

(50)    <HeaderTemplate>
   <table border=1>
   <tr>
```

```
    <td bgcolor="Black">
    <font color="white"><b>Color</b></font>
    </td>
    <td bgcolor="Black">
          <font color="white"><b>Swatch</b></font>
       </td>
    </tr>
    </HeaderTemplate>
51      <ItemTemplate>
    <tr>
       <td></td>
       <td bgcolor=""></td>
    </tr>
    </ItemTemplate>
52      <FooterTemplate>
    <caption valign="bottom" align="left">
       <i>Table 1-1 Some colors</i>
    </caption>
    </table>
    </FooterTemplate>

</asp:Repeater>
</p>

</form>
</body>
</html>
```

We begin the template with the placement of the `Repeater` Control in line (49). To build a list based on an HTML table, we need to begin with a `<table>` tag as our `HeaderTemplate` in line (50) along with a header row that we define using a table row (using the `<tr>` tag) with two columns (using the `<td>` tag). In lines (51) and (52), we define how each item in the list will be rendered (using a table row with two columns) and how to close off the table (with an ending `</table>` tag and a `<caption>` tag).

That's all we need to define a template to display a list of data with two columns. But now we need to give the `Repeater` Control a data source to which to bind. For our example, we'll create a data source for the `Repeater` Control that's based on the `System.Collection.Hashtable` class (see Section 4.2.4). The hashtable is a sort of associative array. Each item in the hashtable contains a key and a corresponding value. We'll create a hashtable with some values in it and display the key–value pairs in the two-column template we just created. In the code-behind file (for the `Page_Load` event), we create the hashtable with some color values, as shown by the boldface text below.

```
Imports System
Imports System.Data
Imports System.Collections
Imports System.Drawing
Imports System.Web
Imports System.Web.UI
Imports System.Web.UI.WebControls

Public Class WebFormRepeaterControl
   Inherits System.Web.UI.Page
   Protected WithEvents rptTestRepeater As _
      System.Web.UI.WebControls.Repeater

   Private Sub Page_Load(ByVal Sender As System.Object, _
               ByVal e As System.EventArgs) _
                        Handles MyBase.Load

      Dim aryMyList As New Hashtable()

      With aryMyList
         .Add("Red", "#FF0000")
         .Add("Green", "#00FF00")
         .Add("Blue", "#0000FF")
         .Add("Yellow", "#FFFF00")
      End With

      rptTestRepeater.DataSource = aryMyList
      rptTestRepeater.DataBind()

   End Sub

End Class
```

After we create the `aryMyList` hashtable, we populate it with some key–value pairs. Then the data binding is established. We set the `DataSource` property of the `Repeater` Control, `rptTestRepeater`, and then call `DataBind()` to perform the data binding to the `Repeater` Control.

To actually display the items we put in the hashtable, we need to revisit the `ItemTemplate` section of the previously written `Repeater` Control's code and put in a template expression. The data items we added are Web color values along with the name of each color. Looking back at the code section beginning on line (51), we change the `ItemTemplate` section to the following code.

```
<ItemTemplate>
<tr>
<td><%# Container.DataItem.Key %></td>
<td bgcolor="<%# Container.DataItem.Value %>"></td>
</tr>
</ItemTemplate>
```

Figure 3-26 shows the `Repeater` Control in action.

Figure 3-26 Output of the `Repeater` Control example

Template expressions are placed inside special markers, the <%# and %> symbols. When you want to access the data bound to the Repeater Control, you need to access the RepeaterItem class that is associated with each template (ItemTemplate, HeaderTemplate, and so on). You do this by using the Container keyword. The Container keyword allows you to reference the parent control of whatever child control you are currently using. DataItem is a member of the RepeaterItem class. DataItem is of type Object. The exact type of object that DataItem is depends on the type of data that is bound to the control. In the case of the bound hashtable above, each DataItem object is a DictionaryEntry object. The DictionaryEntry object has two members of interest: Key and Item. These correspond to the key and value items we added to the hashtable with the Hashtable.Add method for the color name and color value.

Here's another example of template expressions. Suppose that we bound the Repeater Control to an array list instead of a hashtable. First, we replace the code that populates the hashtable with this code that fills an array list with some values.

```
Dim aryMyList As New Hashtable()

With aryMyList
   .Add("#00FF00")
   .Add("#FF0000")
   .Add("#0000FF")
   .Add("#FFFF00")
End With

rptTestRepeater.DataSource = aryMyList
rptTestRepeater.DataBind()
```

The ItemTemplate code also changes a bit.

```
<ItemTemplate>
<tr>
   <td><%# Container.DataItem %></td>
   <td bgcolor="<%# Container.DataItem %>"></td>
</tr>
</ItemTemplate>
```

This time, the object for DataItem is just a string, System.String, since that is the type of data we supplied when we populated the array list. Notice that we don't reference a member of System.String. We certainly can, if needed, call methods of System.String for purposes of formatting or trimming the string. The example relies on the default member of System.String, which returns the characters of the string. In summary, it's necessary to know how your bound data is structured so a properly declared template expression can be assigned.

3.19.2 The DataGrid Control

Displaying structured data in a tabular format is quite common on Web pages, and ASP.NET provides facilities, via the `DataGrid` Control, to display such data in a grid format. The `DataGrid` Control is ideal for displaying data such as price sheets, order forms, timetables, and any other type of structured data with just a little bit of code on the part of the developer. In addition to displaying the data in an aesthetically pleasing format, the `DataGrid` Control can also allow the user to edit the data in the grid. This makes the `DataGrid` Control quite usable for Web applications with rich functionality.

The `DataGrid` Control allows for full control over appearance of the data it contains. It renders the grid as an HTML table. In general, any CSS style can be applied to the headers, item rows, and footers. You can also specify visual characteristics such as spacing between cells, row navigation controls, and sorting and paging behaviors. The data to which the `DataGrid` Control binds are ActiveX Data Objects.NET (ADO.NET) `DataViews`, which are objects that represent a particular view of table data. For purposes of introducing the `DataGrid` control, we won't spend too much time now discussing ADO.NET since we'll revisit ADO.NET and the List Controls in Chapter 7 when we discuss data access in detail.

At its simplest, the `DataGrid` Control uses this syntax:

```
<asp:DataGrid id=your_control_id runat="server">
```

While this is the only syntax needed to display bounded data, you typically need to adjust the look and feel of the data grid to suit your application's design requirements. Consider this example that uses the `DataGrid` Control.

Code Sample 3-35

```
<%@ Page Language="vb"
   AutoEventWireup="false"
   Src="cs3-35.aspx.vb"
   Inherits="WebFormDataGrid1"%>

<html><head>
<title>Web Form - DataGrid Example 1</title>
```

```
</head>
<body>

<form id=WebFormDataGrid1
   method=post runat="server">
<h1>Web Form - DataGrid Example 1</h1>

<p>
(53) <asp:DataGrid id=dgMyDataGrid
   runat="server"
   AutoGenerateColumns="False"
   HeaderStyle-BackColor="#aaaadd"
   Font-Size="8pt"
   Font-Name="Verdana"
   CellSpacing="0"
   CellPadding="3"
   ShowFooter="false"
   BorderColor="black"
   BackColor="#ccccff">

(54) <Columns>
   <asp:boundcolumn headertext="Drawing Date"
      datafield="DrawingDate">
   </asp:boundcolumn>
   <asp:boundcolumn
      headertext="Winning Numbers"
      datafield="WinningNumbers">
   </asp:boundcolumn>
   <asp:boundcolumn
      headertext="Winner's Name"
      datafield="WinnersName">
   </asp:boundcolumn>
</Columns>
</asp:DataGrid>

</p>
</form>
</body>
</html>
```

The code block beginning in line (53) shows the placement of the `DataGrid` Control and also the adjustment of several visual properties. Many of these properties are simply the shared properties inherited from `Control` and

WebControl. Some are specific to the DataGrid Control, and those appear in Table 3-15.

Table 3-15 Properties of the DataGrid Control

Property	Description
AllowCustomPaging	Controls custom paging
AllowPaging	Sets whether or not paging is allowed
AllowSorting	Sets whether or not sorting is allowed
AlternatingItemStyle	Gets the style properties for alternating items in the data grid
AutoGenerateColumns	Determines whether the DataGrid Control is allowed to automatically generate columns for bound data
BackImageUrl	Sets the background image for the data grid
CellPadding	Sets the amount of space between cells in the data grid
CellSpacing	Sets the amount of space between the borders of adjacent cells
Columns	Returns a collection of the Column Controls in the data grid
CurrentPageIndex	Gets or sets the index of the current page
DataKeyField	Gets or sets the primary key field in the data source referenced by DataSource
DataKeys	Gets a collection of primary key field names created by evaluating the DataKeyField value against the data source
DataSource	Gets or sets the data source to which the control will bind; must support the System.Collections.ICollection interface
EditItemIndex	Gets or sets the index of the item to edit
EditItemStyle	Gets the style properties of the item to edit
FooterStyle	Gets the style properties of the footer item

(continued)

Table 3-15 Properties of the DataGrid Control *(continued)*

Property	Description
GridLines	Gets or sets the grid line style
HeaderStyle	Gets the style properties of the header item
HorizontalAlign	Sets how surrounding text flows around the data grid
Items	Gets a collection of DataGridItem objects representing the individual items within the grid
ItemStyle	Gets the style for the individual items in the data grid
PageCount	Gets the total page count of pages to display
PagerStyle	Gets the style of the pager buttons for the data grid
PageSize	Sets or gets the number of items to display per page
SelectedIndex	Sets or gets the index of the currently selected item
SelectedItem	Gets the currently selected item
SelectedItemStyle	Gets the style of the currently selected item
ShowFooter	Specifies whether or not to show the footer of the data grid
ShowHeader	Specifies whether or not to show the header of the data grid
VirtualItemCount	Gets or sets the total number of items in the data grid to calculate the index of the first item on the page when AllowCustomPaging is True

The DataGrid Control needs data to which to bind. We can create some new data "on the fly" by using ADO.NET's DataTable and DataRow objects in the code-behind file.

```
Imports System
Imports System.Data
Imports System.Drawing
Imports System.Web
```

```
Imports System.Web.UI
Imports System.Web.UI.WebControls
Imports Microsoft.VisualBasic

Public Class WebFormDataGrid1
   Inherits System.Web.UI.Page
   Protected WithEvents dgMyDataGrid As _
      System.Web.UI.WebControls.DataGrid

   Private Sub Page_Load(ByVal Sender As System.Object, _
         ByVal e As System.EventArgs) _
         Handles MyBase.Load

      If Not (IsPostBack) Then
         BindIt()
      End If

   End Sub

   Public Sub BindIt()
      Dim intCounter As Integer
      Dim workRow As DataRow
      Dim dteToday As Date
      Dim trTableRow As DataRow
      Dim tblTable As New DataTable()

      With tblTable.Columns
         .Add(New DataColumn("DrawingDate", _
               System.Type.GetType("System.String")))
         .Add(New DataColumn("WinningNumbers", _
               System.Type.GetType("System.String")))
         .Add(New DataColumn("WinnersName", _
            System.Type.GetType("System.String")))
      End With

      For intCounter = 1 To 10
         workRow = tblTable.NewRow()
         workRow("DrawingDate") = _
         FormatDateTime(dteToday.Today.AddDays(-intCounter), _
                  DateFormat.ShortDate)
         workRow("WinningNumbers") = CStr(intCounter * 100)
         workRow("WinnersName") = ""
         tblTable.Rows.Add(workRow)
      Next
```

```
        dgMyDataGrid.DataSource = tblTable.DefaultView
        dgMyDataGrid.DataBind()

    End Sub

End Class
```

In the `BindIt()` subroutine, we create a new `DataTable`, add `DataColumns` to the `DataTable`, and add `DataRow` objects containing data to the `DataTable`. The code adds a total of ten rows. Each row contains a date string, a number, and a string field that's initially left blank. After the rows have been added to the table, we set the `DataSource` to the `DefaultView` of the table, and call `DataBind()` to bind the data to the `DataGrid` Control.

Now that the data is bound to the `DataGrid` Control, we need to revisit the `.aspx` file and add columns to the visual part of the data grid. So, inside the tags for the `DataGrid` Control, we place the code below, which replaces code starting at line 54 of the `.aspx` file code.

```
<Columns>

<asp:boundcolumn headerstyle-font-bold=True
    headertext="Date"
    datafield="DrawingDate"/>
<asp:boundcolumn headerstyle-font-bold=True
    headertext="Winning Number"
    datafield="WinningNumbers"/>
<asp:boundcolumn headerstyle-font-bold=True
    headertext="Winner's Name"
    datafield="WinnersName"/>

</Columns>
```

The `DataGrid` Control can use any of the classes shown in Table 3-16 as columns for the grid.

For the above example, we use the `BoundColumn` class to create bindings between the visual column and the data field in the data source. There are many styles we can apply to the `BoundColumn` class. We can set style characteristics for the header, item, and footer portions of the column. In the example, we apply bold formatting to `headertext`, which is the string displayed in the top cell of the column. We also set a value for `datafield`, which tells the column which data field in the data source to use when displaying the item data.

Table 3-16 Valid Controls for the `Columns` Collection of the `DataGrid` Control

Class	Description
`BoundColumn`	Column whose value comes from a bound data field
`ButtonColumn`	Column that contains push buttons
`DataGridPagerStyle`	Style class for the paging controls
`EditCommandButton`	Column for `Edit`, `Update`, and `Cancel` commands used for editing data in the current row
`HyperlinkColumn`	Column that contains hyperlinks
`TableItemStyle`	Style class for individual table items
`TemplateColumn`	Column built from a template

When we run the code in this example, the output looks like that shown in Figure 3-27.

The `DataGrid` Control supports other features that we haven't covered yet, such as in-place editing of data. We'll cover that topic in Chapter 7 with the discussions of data access and ADO.NET. We'll revisit the `DataGrid` Control and add functionality, such as editing the data in the columns, updating the database, and other functions.

3.19.3 The `DataList` Control

The `DataGrid` Control is highly useful for displaying tabular-based data, but often you'll need to display data using a different layout. The `DataList` Control is designed to provide maximum flexibility when arranging your data on the screen. The primary advantage of using the `DataList` Control comes from the fact that you are not limited to displaying your data in columns. The `DataList` Control allows you to display data in a row-based format. It supports many templates and styles (the same as the `Repeater` Control). You can also include functionality for selecting rows. In addition, rich data-editing features are included as well. All features considered, the `DataList` Control proves the most flexible for displaying different types of data.

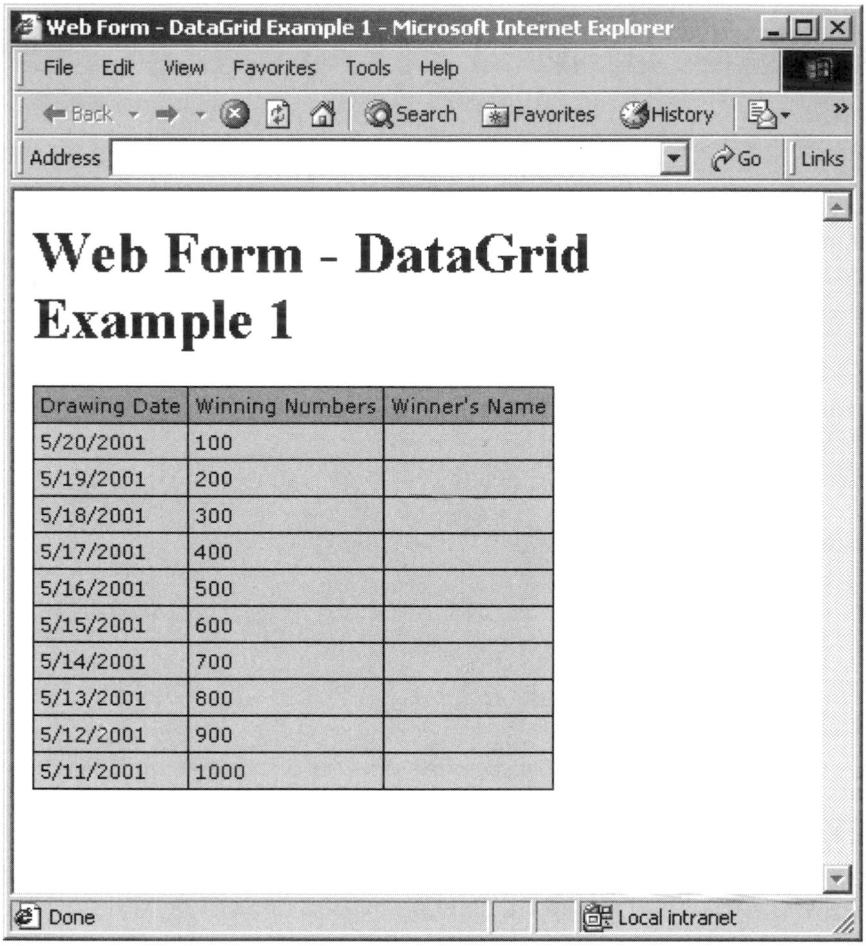

Figure 3-27 Output of the `DataGrid` Control example

To use the `DataList` Control, you need to place it on a Web Form, set the list format, set the list layout, and template the data. In the example, let's begin by placing the `DataList` Control on a Web Form.

Code Sample 3-36

```
<%@ Page Language="vb"
   AutoEventWireup="false"
```

```
   Src="WebFormDataListEx1.vb"
   Inherits="WebFormDataListEx1"%>
<html><head>
<TITLE>DataList Example</TITLE>
</head>
<body>

<form id="WebFormDataListEx1"
   method="post"
   runat="server">
<h1>DataList Example</h1>

<p>
<asp:DataList id=dlMyDataList
   runat="server"
   ForeColor="Black">

   <AlternatingItemStyle
      BackColor="Gainsboro">
   </AlternatingItemStyle>

   <FooterStyle
      BackColor="Silver"
      ForeColor="White">
   </FooterStyle>

   <ItemStyle
      BackColor="White">
   </ItemStyle>

   <HeaderStyle
      BackColor="Navy"
      Font-Bold="True"
      ForeColor="White">
   </HeaderStyle>

</asp:DataList>

</p>
</form>
</body>
</html>
```

As mentioned before, the `DataList` Control uses the same template styles as the `Repeater` Control, and we include some of them in the example. We define `Property` tags for `AlternatingItemStyle`, `FooterStyle`, `ItemStyle`, and `HeaderStyle`.

Now is a good time to make up some data to which the `DataList` Control can bind. Here is the code-behind file that accomplishes this.

```
Imports System
Imports System.Data
Imports System.Collections
Imports System.Web
Imports System.Web.UI
Imports System.Web.UI.WebControls
Imports Microsoft.VisualBasic

(55)Public Class CFileInformation
    Public Filename As String
    Public FileSize As Long
    Public Caption As String
    Public ImageURL As String
End Class

Public Class WebFormDataListEx1
      Inherits System.Web.UI.Page
      Protected WithEvents dlMyDataList As _
              System.Web.UI.WebControls.DataList

      Private Sub Page_Load(ByVal Sender As System.Object, _
         ByVal e As System.EventArgs) _
         Handles MyBase.Load
            If Not IsPostback Then
               BindTheData()
            End If
      End Sub

      Private Sub BindTheData()

         Dim strImagePath As String
         Dim strFilename As String
```

```
        Dim clsFileInfo As CFileInformation
        Dim aryArrayList As New ArrayList()

        strImagePath = Server.MapPath("images")

56      strFilename = Dir(strImagePath & "\*.jpg")
        Do While strFilename <> ""
           clsFileInfo = New CFileInformation()
           clsFileInfo.Filename = strFilename
           clsFileInfo.ImageURL = "images/" & strFileName
57         aryArrayList.Add(clsFileInfo)
           strFileName = Dir()
        Loop

58      dlMyDataList.DataSource = aryArrayList
        dlMyDataList.DataBind()

     End Sub

End Class
```

In the data-binding code we do two things: we create a class to hold file information and we write code to find all the .jpg images in a directory.

The class definition beginning in line 55 is simple. We want to keep track of a few items of information about the file, including the file name, the file size, a text caption, and the URL to the image.

The directory we are seaching is located using the `MapPath` command, a method of the ASP.NET Server intrinsic object (see Section 3.23), to query the physical pathname of a Web directory called "`/images`". The code in line 56 uses the VB.NET `Dir()` statement to locate all files in the directory with an extension of `.jpg`. Then for each file located, a new `CFileInformation` object is created and populated with the file's information. Each object is then placed into `aryArrayList` in line 57. The data binding is completed by setting the `DataSource` property of `dlMyDataList` in line 58 and subsequently calling `DataBind()` for the control.

Note the changes made to the `DataList` Control to facilitate the data binding.

```
<asp:DataList id=dlMyDataList
   runat="server"
   repeatlayout=Table
   repeatdirection=Horizontal
   repeatcolumns=3>

   <ItemTemplate>
59          <%# Container.DataItem.FileName %><br>
60          <img src="<%# Container.DataItem.ImageURL %>">
   </ItemTemplate>

   <AlternatingItemStyle
      BackColor="white">
   </AlternatingItemStyle>

   <FooterStyle
      ForeColor="White">
   </FooterStyle>

   <ItemStyle
      BackColor="White">
   </ItemStyle>

   <HeaderStyle
      BackColor="white"
      Font-Bold="True"
      ForeColor="White">
   </HeaderStyle>

</asp:DataList>
```

The interesting action takes place in the `ItemTemplate` code block in lines 59 and 60. We template the column that displays the HTML `<img>` tag that displays the data. The object in the `DataItem` for the `DataList` Control is the `CFileInformation` class, which holds the file name and URL for the image. We return each of those values and get output similar to that shown in Figure 3-28.

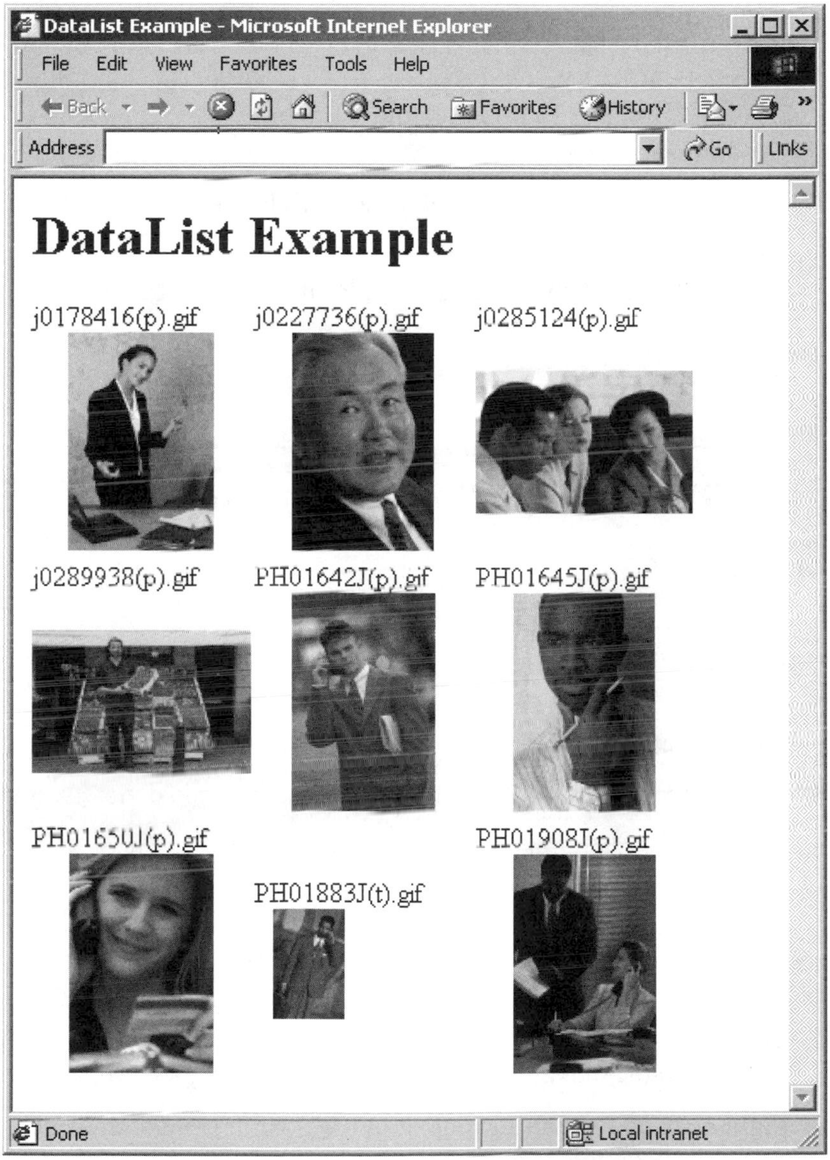

Figure 3-28 Output of the `DataList` Control example for displaying images

3.20 Building the XYZ Corporation Home Page

It's time to take what you've learned so far about Web Controls and build the home page for the XYZ Corporation. You'll be using several different Web Controls in this lab. After completing this lab you should be able to do the following in future projects:

- Create a new Web project using VS.NET
- Convert an HTML file into a Web Form
- Work with Web Controls and add functionality to them

LAB 3-2
THE XYZ CORPORATION HOME PAGE

STEP 1. Launch VS.NET.

a. Launch VS.NET from the Windows Start bar.

STEP 2. Create a new VB.NET Web application.

a. Select **File→New→Project** from the menu bar.

b. Highlight Visual Basic Projects in the Project Types pane.

c. Highlight the Web Application icon in the Templates pane. Name the project "Lab3-2".

STEP 3. Copy files for the XYZ Corporation home page.

a. Click the Solution Explorer button on the tool bar to show the Solution Explorer window. Files for the XYZ Corporation home page need to be added to the project; they're located in the "\Samples\Labs" folder.

b. Right-click on the Lab3-2 project in the Solution Explorer window and select **Add→Add Existing Item . . .** (see Lab Figure 3-19).

c. Next, select the files `compban.gif`, `mail.gif`, `banner1.gif`, `banner2.gif`, `banner3.gif`, `banner4.gif`, `adrot.xml`, and `xyz_home_TEMPLATE.htm` and click the Open button (see Lab Figure 3-20).

d. Rename the `xyz_home_TEMPLATE.htm` file to `xyz_home.aspx`. A warning appears as shown in Lab Figure 3-21 asking you to confirm the file rename

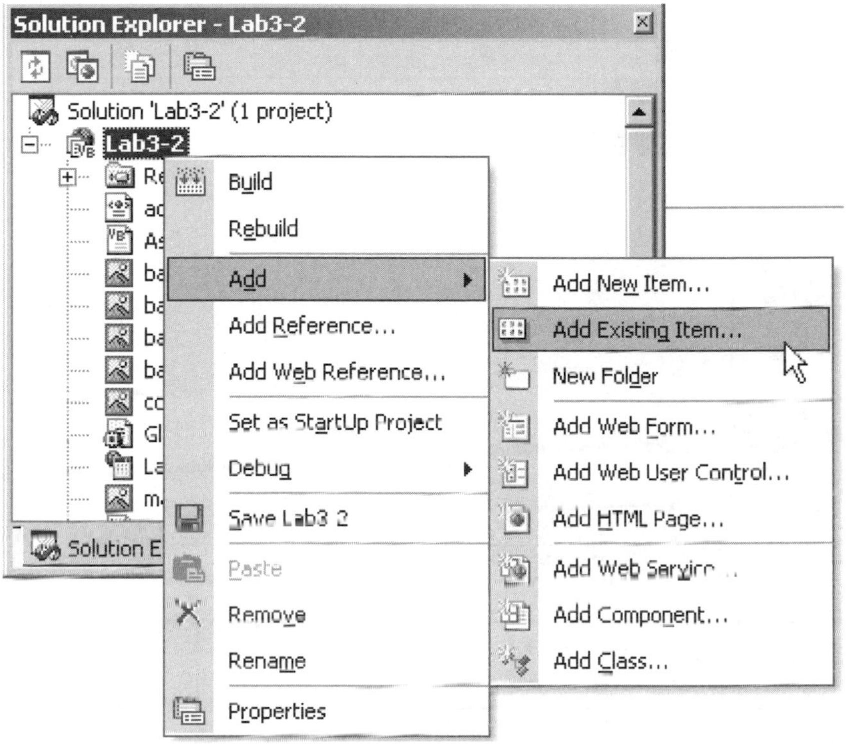

Lab Figure 3-19 Adding items to the project

since you're changing the file type. Click the Yes button to approve the change.

e. Another dialog box appears asking if you want to create a new class file associated with the newly renamed `.aspx` file (see Lab Figure 3-22). Click the Yes button to create the class file.

STEP 4. Add the Web Controls.

Now that the HTML file is converted to a Web Form, you can add Web Controls to the Web Form as required. Text placeholders in the file show the locations where the Web Controls should go (see Lab Figure 3-23).

The home page contains a small "quizlet" or survey in which the user selects a response to a multiple-choice question—a good candidate for using a `RadioButtonList` Control.

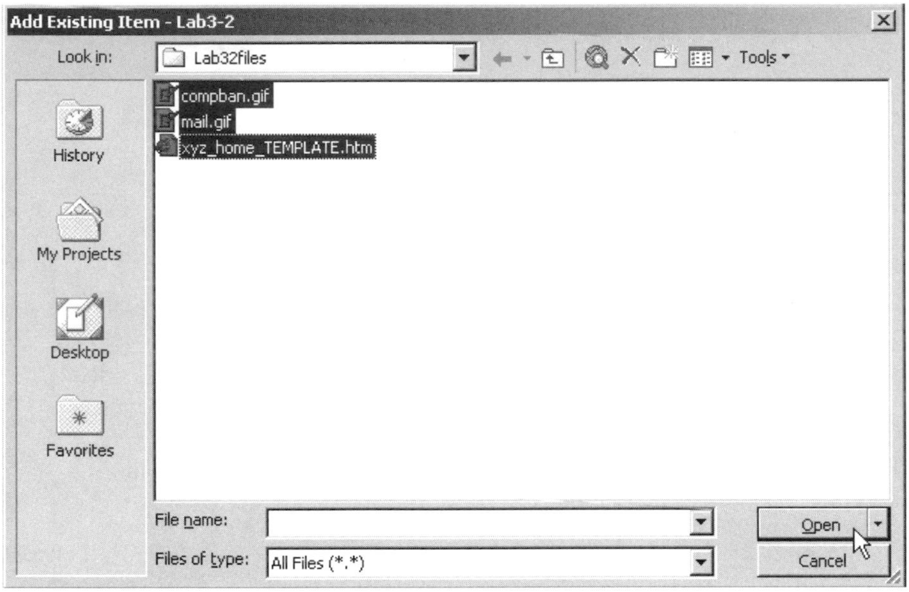

Lab Figure 3-20 Selecting files to add to the project

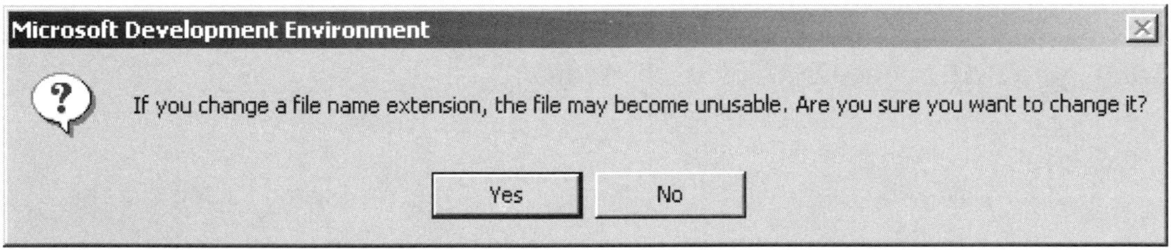

Lab Figure 3-21 Confirming the change to the file name extension

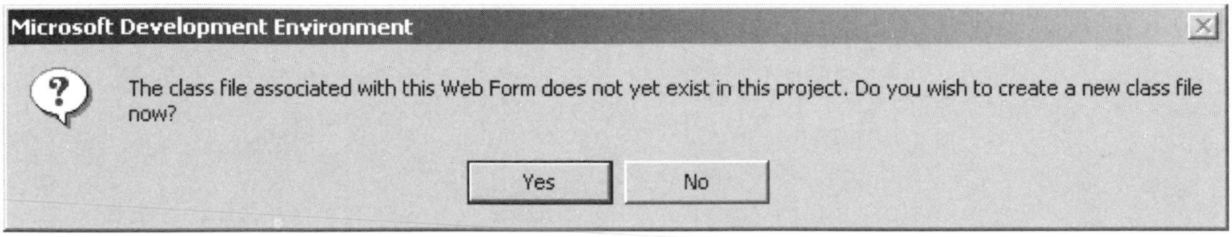

Lab Figure 3-22 Confirming the creation of a new class file

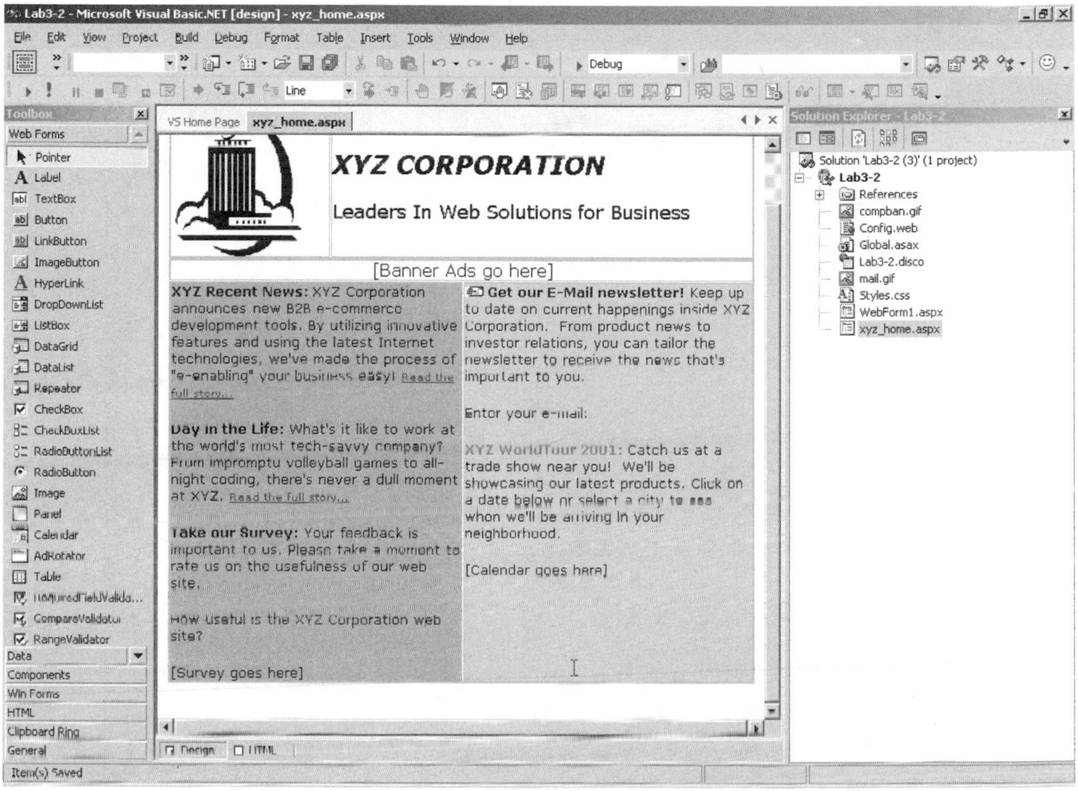

Lab Figure 3-23 The XYZ Corporation home page with placeholders for Web Controls

a. Drag a `RadioButtonList` Control from the Toolbox and place it on the Web Form near the survey placeholder. Right-click the newly placed `RadioButtonList` Control and select Properties from the pop-up menu.

b. To add radio buttons to the list, click the button in the `Items` property to bring up the ListItem Collection Editor. Click the Add button to add a `ListItem`. Edit the text and values of the `ListItem` as shown in Lab Figure 3-24. If you wish to make a particular `ListItem` the default choice, set the `Selected` property to `True`. Also, be sure to assign a meaningful name to the control (through the `ID` property).

c. Repeat Step b for as many choices as you want to add to the list of radio buttons.

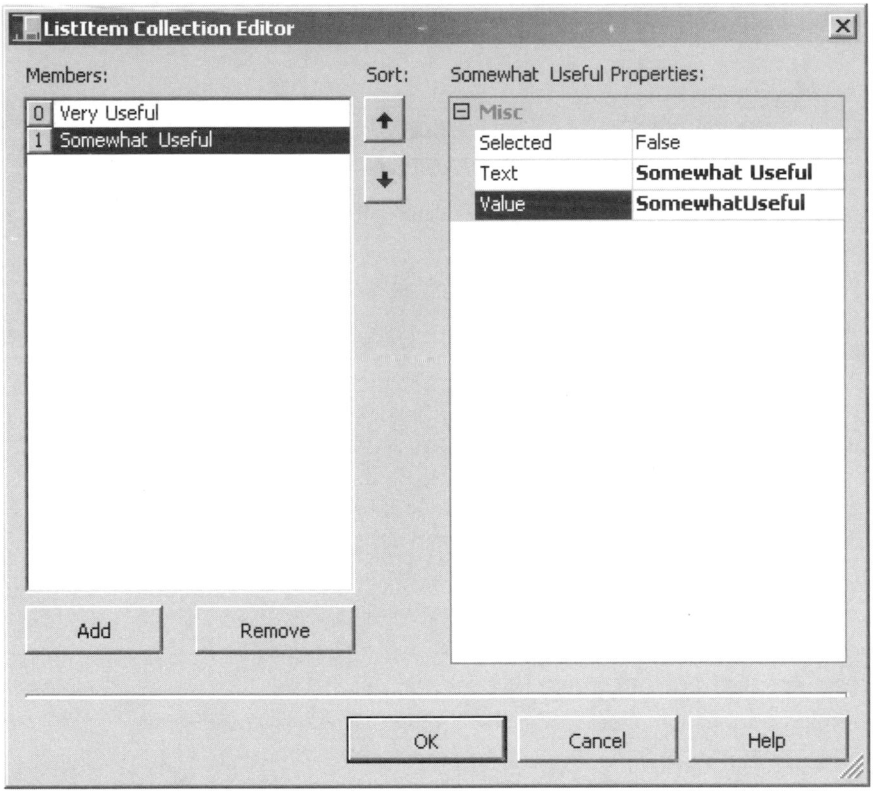

Lab Figure 3-24 The ListItem Collection Editor

d. Next, add a submit button somewhere underneath the list of radio buttons so the user can submit his or her survey response. Also, add a `Label` Control next to the button. This label will be used to display a message confirming that a selection was made. Assign an identifier (`ID` property) to each of these controls. Lab Figure 3-25 shows an example of this portion of the page.

e. On the other side of the page, there's a placeholder for giving the user the ability to enter his or her e-mail address to subscribe to the XYZ Corporation newsletter. You want to validate the e-mail address entered (as much as the `RegularExpressionValidator` Control allows you to) to ensure you're collecting "good data." This requres the `TextBox`, `RegularExpressionValidator`, `Label`, and `Button` Controls. Again,

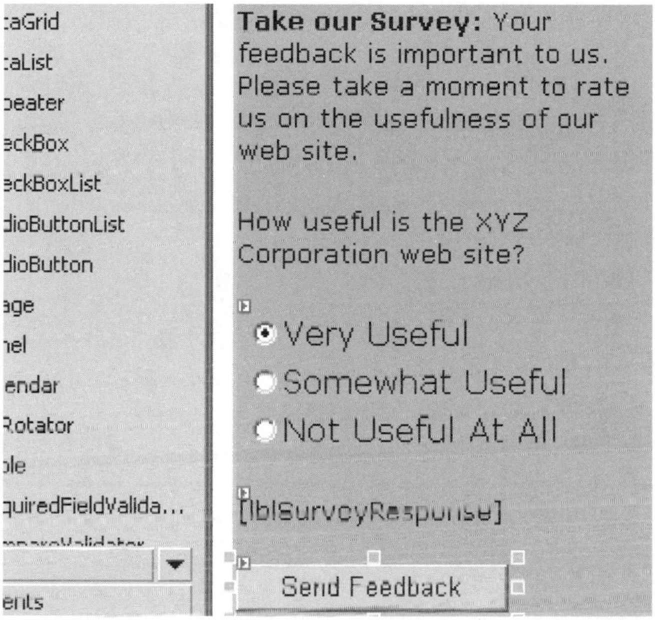

Lab Figure 3-25 Placing the `RadioButtonList`, `Label`, and `Button` Controls

set the `ID` properties for each to meaningful names. Lab Figure 3-26 shows a sample layout after completion of this step.

f. Now add the events calendar to the page by using the `Calendar` Control (see Lab Figure 3-27). You can quickly change the display style of the calendar, if you wish, by right-clicking the `Calendar` Control and selecting Auto Format. . . . AutoFormat provides a graphical interface for changing styles.

g. Place the `AdRotator` Control at the top of the page near the banner ads placeholder (see Lab Figure 3-28). Set the `AdvertisementFile` property to "adrot.xml".

STEP 5. Add code for the Web Controls.

a. Now you're ready to code the functionality behind the XYZ Corporation home page. Right-click the Send Feedback button you created and select View Code. Locate the name of the button (`cmdSendSurvey`) and select it from the drop-down list at the top of the code window. Then select the `Click` event for the button from the drop-down list to the immediate right. This "stubs out" the event-handling code.

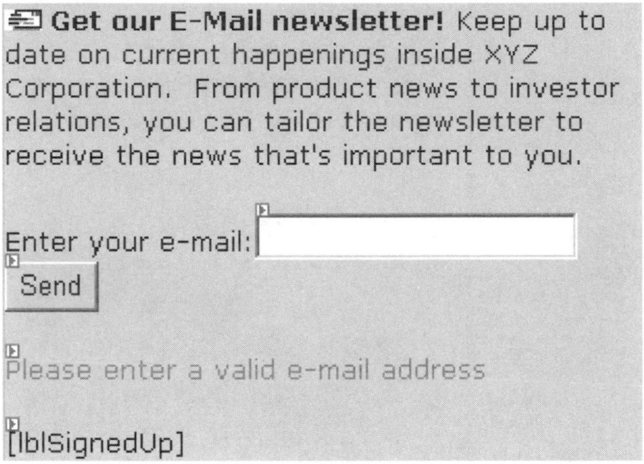

Get our E-Mail newsletter! Keep up to date on current happenings inside XYZ Corporation. From product news to investor relations, you can tailor the newsletter to receive the news that's important to you.
Enter your e-mail:

[lblSignedUp]

Lab Figure 3-26 Enabling entry of e-mail addresses

XYZ WorldTour 2001: Catch us at a trade show near you! We'll be showcasing our latest products. Click on a date below or select a city to see when we'll be arriving in your neighborhood.
May
June 2001
Jul
Sun
Mon
Tue
Wed
Thu
Fri
Sat
27 28 29 30 31 1 2
3 4 5 6 7 8 9
10 11 12 13 14 15 16
17 18 19 20 21 22 23
24 25 26 27 28 29 30
1 2 3 4 5 6 7

Lab Figure 3-27 Adding the `Calendar` Control

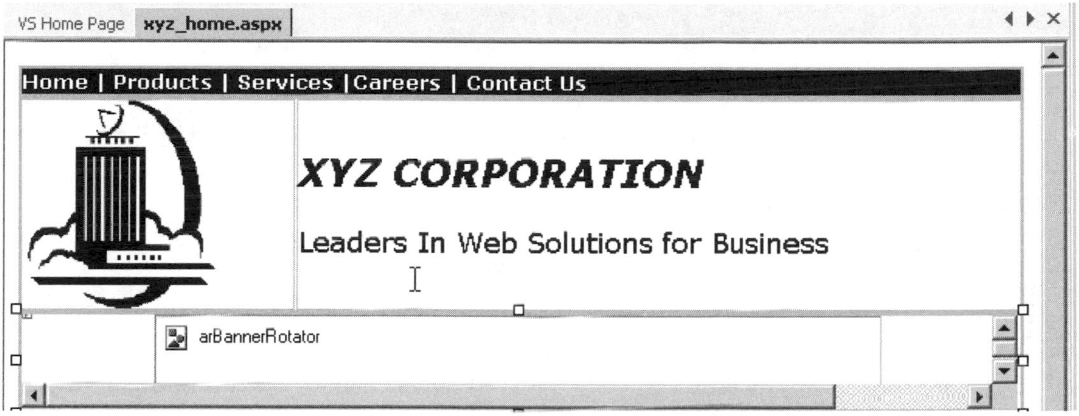

Lab Figure 3-28 Placing the AdRotator Control

b. Enter the following sample code.

```
Public Sub cmdSendSurvey_Click(ByVal sender As Object, _
        ByVal e As System.EventArgs) _
      Handles cmdSendSurvey.Click
   lblSurveyResponse.Text = "We recorded: " & _
   rblSurvey.SelectedItem.Text & _
   " Thank you!"
End Sub
```

c. Add some code to display information about XYZ Corporation events when the user clicks a particular date on the calendar: the selected date is checked, and an appropriate message is displayed in a `Label` Control.

```
Private Sub Calendar1_SelectionChanged( _
   ByVal sender As Object, _
   ByVal e As System.EventArgs) _
   Handles Calendar1.SelectionChanged

   Dim strDateString As String

   strDateString = FormatDateTime( _
            Calendar1.SelectedDate, _
            DateFormat.ShortDate)
```

```
        Select Case strDateString
            Case "6/4/2001"
                lblCorporateEvents.Text = strDateString & _
                    ": Product Demonstrations!"
            Case "6/20/2001"
                lblCorporateEvents.Text = strDateString & _
                    ": Launch of new product!"
            Case Else
                lblCorporateEvents.Text = strDateString & _
                    ": No events on this date."
        End Select
    End Sub
```

d. Now all that's left is to build the Web application by selecting **Build→Build Solution** from the menu bar. Set the Start Page to the home page file in the Solution Explorer. Click the Start button on the tool bar to run your project.

That's it for Lab 3-2! Of course, the coding for the XYZ Corporation Web site would be considerably more complex than what you created in this lab, and the site would contain many more pages. There are many different ASP.NET pages you can build on your own. Get creative and get practicing!

3.21 User Controls

The ASP.NET Controls allow you to build most Web applications with ease. But many Web applications use custom code that is specific to an organization or industry. This code is likely to be reused many times and in many different projects (think *components*). In the case of Web pages, designers strive to create a consistent look and feel. This places a burden on Web designers since much of the front-end Web code exists as HTML intermixed with script. Traditionally, this type of code is difficult to maintain and hard to keep modularized by function. With the introduction of User Controls, ASP.NET seeks to alleviate some of the troubles caused by these traditional code problems.

A User Control is a reusable piece of ASP.NET code. User Controls are built using many of the same techniques used to build Web Forms. When ASP.NET code is packaged up as a User Control, it makes reuse of the code in another Web Form as easy as supplying a new page directive at the top of the Web Form and placing the User Control in the page. User Controls are used within a Web Form similar to how other Web Controls are used.

3.21.1 Authoring a User Control

User Controls are simply a collection of other Web Controls and their behaviors. When you author User Controls, you can also expose your own properties to the User Control. This way, you can programmatically control the characteristics of the User Control.

Let's start by making a very simple User Control that allows us to pick a color and shows us the hex value for that color. (This User Control will be helpful for Web designers who need to know these values when designing Web pages.)

We can begin the process by starting with an ordinary Web Form. We then place other Web Controls on the Web Form that will serve as the basis for the User Control. For this example, let's create a `PasswordConfirm` User Control that will have two `TextBox` Controls, a `CompareValidator` Control, and a `Button` Control. The `PasswordConfirm` User Control will allow the user to enter a new password in the first text box and confirm it by retyping the same password in the second text box.

Here's the Web Form containing all the necessary Web Controls.

Code Sample 3-37

```
<html>
<head>
<title>User Control Sample 1</title>
</head>
<body>

<form id="UserControlSample1"
   method="post"
   runat="server">

<p>New Password:
<asp:TextBox id=txtNewPassword
   textmode=Password
   runat="server">
</asp:TextBox>
</p>

<p>Confirm Password:
<asp:TextBox id=txtOldPassword
   textmode=Password
   runat="server">
</asp:TextBox>
```

```
<asp:Button id=btnChangePassword
   runat="server"
   Text="Change Password">
</asp:Button>
</p>

<p>
<asp:CompareValidator id=cvPassword
   runat="server"
   ErrorMessage="Password not confirmed"
   ControlToValidate="txtOldPassword"
   ControlToCompare="txtNewPassword"
   Display="Dynamic">
</asp:CompareValidator>
</p>

</form>
</body>
</html>
```

Now the transformation from Web Form to User Control occurs. To make this Web Form into a User Control, the `<html>`, `<form>`, and `<body>` tag pairs need to be removed from the file. Also, the `<%@ Control %>` directive needs to be added. The attributes to the page directive (like the `Language` attribute) can remain the same. Finally, we need to rename the file so it has an `.ascx` extension, the extension for User Controls. The new code should read as shown below.

```
<%@ Control Language="vb" %>

<p>New Password:
<asp:TextBox id=txtNewPassword
   textmode=Password
   runat="server">
</asp:TextBox>
</p>

<p>Confirm Password:
<asp:TextBox id=txtOldPassword
   textmode=Password
   runat="server">
</asp:TextBox>
```

```
<asp:Button id=btnChangePassword
   runat="server"
   Text="Change Password">
</asp:Button>
</p>

<p>
<asp:CompareValidator id=cvPassword
   runat="server"
   ErrorMessage="Password not confirmed"
   ControlToValidate="txtOldPassword"
   ControlToCompare="txtNewPassword"
   Display="Dynamic">
</asp:CompareValidator>
</p>
```

That's all we need to do to finish the User Control, but let's take things just a step further. User Controls can have custom properties, so let's add one to ours. Suppose that we want users to specify their own custom error messages when the values for the two `TextBox` Controls do not match. We can add some code directly to the `.ascx` file that declares a property.

```
<script language=vb runat=server>

Public Property ErrMessage() as String
   Set
      cvPassword.ErrorMessage = Value
   End Set
   Get
      ErrMessage = cvPassword.ErrorMessage
   End Get
End Property

</script>
```

In this code, we declare a property called `ErrMessage`. This property will now act as a way to adjust the `ErrorMessage` property of the `CompareValidator` Control.

With this code in place, we are now ready to use the `PasswordConfirm` User Control in another Web Form, such as the one whose code appears below.

Code Sample 3-38

```
<%@ Page Language="vb" %>

(61) <%@ Register TagPrefix="MattsControls"
   TagName="PasswordConfirm"
   Src="cs3-37.ascx" %>

<html>
<head>
</head>
<body>
<h1>User Control Demonstration</h1>
The PasswordConfirm User Control appears below:

<form id="UserControl1Usage"
   method="post"
   runat="server">

(62) <MattsControls:PasswordConfirm
   id=pcMyPassword
   ErrMessage="The password was not correctly confirmed"
   runat="server"/>

</form>
</body>
</html>
```

Using a User Control in a Web Form starts with the `<%@ Register %>` page directive, shown above beginning in line (61). This directive informs ASP.NET how we wish to reference the User Control we created previously. User Controls, like Web Controls, have a `TagPrefix` and a `TagName`. You may specify any strings to be used for `TagPrefix` and `TagName`. In this example, we call the `TagPrefix` "MattsControls" and the `TagName` "PasswordConfirm". Most importantly, we tell ASP.NET where to find the `.ascx` file for the control in the `Src` attribute (a relative path).

Now we place the User Control on the page. This works just like the other Web Controls we've used before, as shown in line (62). Notice the use of the property `ErrMessage`. When we run this page, we see output like that shown in Figure 3-29.

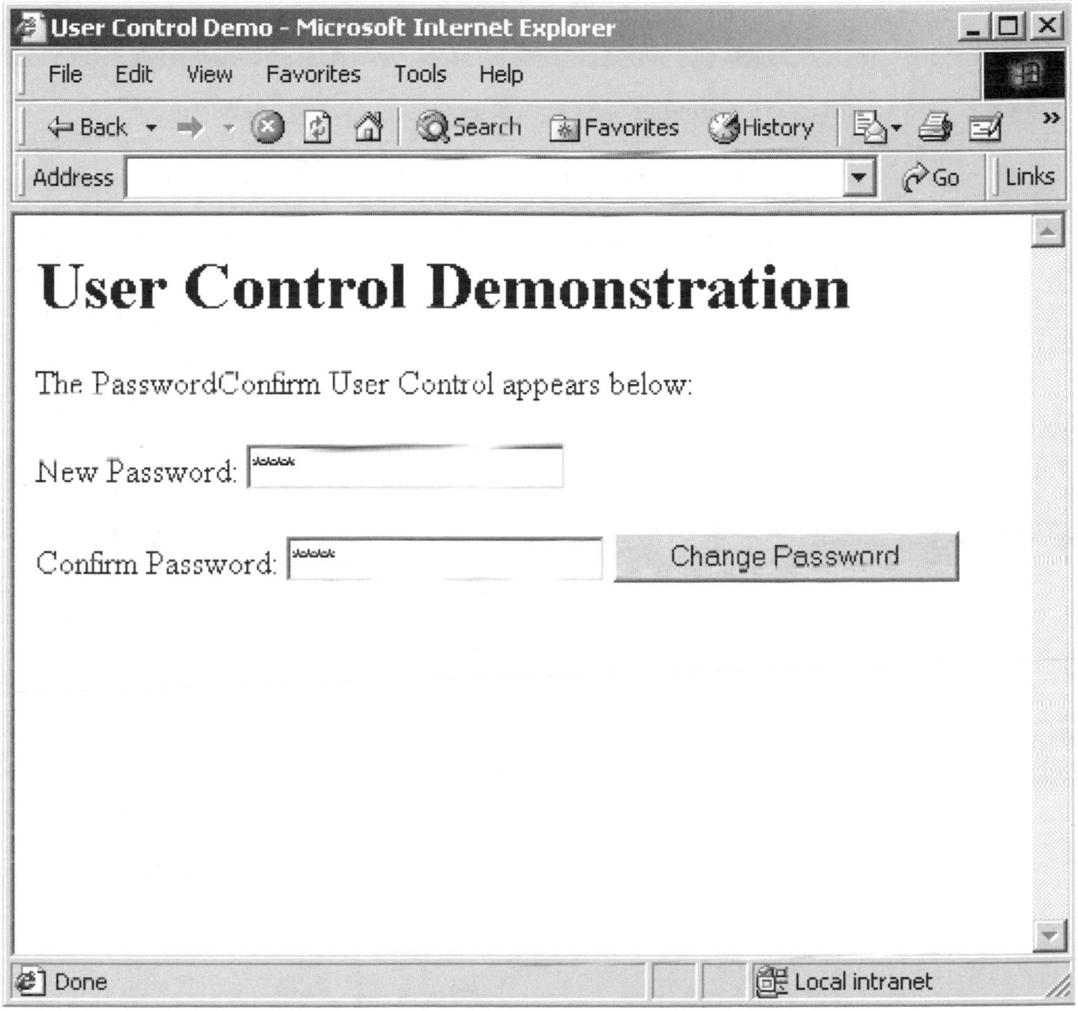

Figure 3-29 Output of the example showing a User Control used in a Web Form

3.22 Saving State with the `StateBag` Object

ASP.NET provides an option to save state across page requests without saving any information on the server. `ViewState` is a static object of type `StateBag` that can be used to store arbitrary values across page requests. Tables 3-17 and 3-18 list the properties and methods, respectively, of the `StateBag` class.

Table 3-17 Properties of the `StateBag` Class

Property	Description
`Count`	Gets the number of `StateItem` objects in the `StateBag` object
`Item`	Gets or sets the value of an item stored in the `StateBag` object
`Keys`	Gets a collection of keys representing the items in the `StateBag` object
`Values`	Gets a collection of the view state values stored in the `StateBag` object

Table 3-18 Methods of the `StateBag` Class

Method	Description	Syntax
`Add`	Adds a new `StateItem` object to the `StateBag` object. If the item already exists in the `StateBag` object, `Add` updates the value of the item.	`Add(ByVal` *`key`* `As String, ByVal` *`value`* `As Object) As StateItem`
`Clear`	Removes all items from the current `StateBag` object.	—
`GetEnumerator`	Returns an enumerator that iterates over all of the key–value pairs of the `StateItem` objects stored in the `StateBag` object.	`GetEnumerator() As IDictionaryEnumerator`
`IsItemDirty`	Checks a `StateItem` object stored in the `StateBag` object to evaluate whether it has been modified since the call to `Control.TrackViewState`.	`IsItemDirty(ByVal` *`key`* `As String) As Boolean`
`Remove`	Removes the specified `StateItem` object from the `StateBag` object.	`Remove(ByVal` *`key`* `As String)`

Every Web Form has access to the `ViewState` object, which is a static object you don't need to declare explicitly. You can store any values you wish in the `ViewState` collection. Here are some examples.

Writing to `ViewState`:

```
ViewState("MyStateVariable") = "Test"
```

Retrieving from `ViewState`:

```
StrMyVariable = ViewState("MyStateVariable")
```

3.23 ASP.NET Intrinsic Objects

One set of objects in ASP.NET provides low-level access to Web application protocols and frameworks. In classic ASP, these objects are collectively known as the ASP.NET *intrinsic objects*. With the intrinsic objects, you can work more directly with the underlying CGI, HTTP stream, and session-management capabilities of ASP.NET. The intrinsic objects also provide for compatibility with classic ASP, since these objects were the only way to get at Web server functionality through program code. This section won't go into too much detail about the intrinsic objects since it is unlikely that you'll be using them often in your ASP.NET applications.

3.23.1 The `HttpRequest` Object

The `Http`Request object is responsible for retrieving information sent in an HTML form. HTML form data can be sent using two methods: an HTTP GET and an HTTP POST. The CGI encoding scheme, which is used to encode data in fields, controls, and so on for transmission to the server, takes each field on the form and represents it as a *name–value* pair, with *name* being the name of the HTML form element and *value* being the data associated with that form element.

Tables 3-19 and 3-20 show the properties and methods, respectively, of the `HttpRequest` object.

Table 3-19 Properties of the `HttpRequest` Object

Property	Description
`AcceptTypes`	Gets a string array of client-supported MIME accept types.
`ApplicationPath`	Gets the ASP.NET application's virtual application root path on the server.
`Browser`	Gets information about the requesting client's browser capabilities.
`ClientCertificate`	Collection that contains the certification fields (specified in the X.509 standard) from a request issued by the Web browser. This is used when the Secure Sockets Layer (SSL) is used to connect to a Web server. The certificate that identifies the Web server is contained in this object.
`ContentEncoding`	Gets the character set of the entity body.
`ContentLength`	Specifies the length, in bytes, of content sent by the client.
`ContentType`	Gets the MIME content type of the incoming request.
`Cookies`	Specifies a collection of cookies sent in the HTTP request. Each cookie in the collection may contain a cookie dictionary, which contains keys. `HasKeys` is a Boolean attribute to a cookie that states whether or not the cookie contains subvalues (keys).
`FilePath`	Gets the virtual path of the current request.
`Files`	Gets the collection of client-uploaded files (Multipart MIME format).
`Filter`	Gets or sets the filter to use when reading the current input stream.
`Form`	Specifies a collection of name–value pairs for fields and values on an HTML form that were submitted to the server via an HTTP POST.
`Headers`	Gets a collection of HTTP headers.

Property	Description
HttpMethod	Gets the HTTP data transfer method (such as GET, POST, or HEAD) used by the client.
InputStream	Gets the contents of the incoming HTTP entity body.
IsAuthenticated	Gets a value indicating whether the user has been authenticated.
IsSecureConnection	Gets a value indicating whether the HTTP connection uses secure sockets (that is, HTTPS).
Params	Gets a combined collection of QueryString, Form, ServerVariables, and Cookies items.
Path	Gets the virtual path of the current request.
PathInfo	Gets additional path information for a resource with a URL extension.
PhysicalApplicationPath	Gets the physical file system path of the currently executing server application's root directory.
PhysicalPath	Gets the physical file system path corresponding to the requested URL.
QueryString	Gets the collection of HTTP query string variables.
RawUrl	Gets the raw URL of the current request.
RequestType	Gets or sets the HTTP data transfer method (GET or POST) used by the client.
ServerVariables	Gets a collection of Web server variables.
TotalBytes	Gets the number of bytes in the current input stream.
Url	Gets information about the URL of the current request.
UrlReferrer	Gets information about the URL of the client's previous request that linked to the current URL.

(continued)

Table 3-19 Properties of the `HttpRequest` Object *(continued)*

Property	Description
`UserAgent`	Gets the raw user agent string of the client browser.
`UserHostAddress`	Gets the IP host address of the remote client.
`UserHostName`	Gets the DNS name of the remote client.
`UserLanguages`	Gets a sorted string array of client language preferences.

Table 3-20 Methods of the `HttpRequest` Object

Method	Description	Syntax
`BinaryRead`	Performs a binary read of a specified number of bytes from the current input stream.	`BinaryRead(ByVal` *`count`* `As Integer) As Byte()`
`MapImageCoordinates`	Maps an incoming image-field form parameter to appropriate x/y coordinate values.	`MapImageCoordinates(ByVal` *`imageFieldName`* `As String) As Integer()`

`MapPath`	Maps the virtual path in the requested URL to a physical path on the server for the current request.	`MapPath(ByVal` *`virtualPath`* `As String) As String`
		
		`MapPath(ByVal` *`virtualPath`* `As String, ByVal` *`baseVirtualDir`* `As String, ByVal` *`allowCrossAppMapping`* `As Boolean) As String`

`SaveAs`	Saves an HTTP request to disk.	`SaveAs(ByVal` *`filename`* `As String, ByVal` *`includeHeaders`* `As Boolean)`

> **TECHTALK: THE CGI ENCODING SCHEME**
>
> The CGI encoding scheme represents some characters as escape sequences. To illustrate, let's look at how HTML form data is encoded.
>
> Consider an HTML form with three text fields named `COLOR`, `SIZE`, and `STYLE`. Suppose the user enters "green," "XL," and "sweater/V Neck," respectively, for each variable. The string of data that is sent in the HTTP request would be encoded in this manner:
>
> ```
> COLOR=green&SIZE=XL&STYLE=sweater%2FV+Neck
> ```
>
> A name–value pair in an HTTP request takes the format *`name=value`*. The ampersand (&) character delimits the name–value pairs. Notice that the forward-slash (/) and space characters in the value for STYLE have been "escaped out." The percent sign (%) is used to prefix a hexadecimal number that represents the ASCII value of the character being encoded (a forward-slash is ASCII 2F in hexadecimal). This is necessary because some characters, like a space character, are represented as other ASCII characters. In this case, a space is represented as a plus sign (+). CGI is a low-level encoding scheme, and many Web programmers (ASP.NET programmers in particular) don't need to write programs that parse CGI-encoded data.

3.23.2 The `HttpResponse` Object

The job of the `HttpResponse` object is to send data back to the user's browser and control the output of the HTTP stream in a programmatic way. Sometimes you may need to dynamically insert content into the HTTP stream. You may wish to set cookies as part of your script. You also may need to send customer HTTP headers as part of the output of a script, or you may need to log additional information about the client request. If your programming task involves sending output back to the client, the `HttpResponse` object is the vehicle for that task.

The properties of the `HttpResponse` object are listed in Table 3-21 along with descriptions of their functions.

Table 3-21 Properties of the `HttpResponse` Object

Property	Description
`Buffer`	Indicates whether or not to buffer the HTTP output stream (true/false value)
`BufferOutput`	Gets or sets a value indicating whether to buffer output and send it after the entire page is finished processing
`Cache`	Gets the caching policy (expiration time, privacy, vary clauses) of a Web page
`CacheControl`	Determines whether proxy servers are able to cache the output generated by ASP
`Charset`	Specifies the value of the character set in the HTTP Content-Type header
`ContentEncoding`	Gets or sets the HTTP character set of the output stream
`ContentType`	Specifies the MIME HTTP content type to use for the response
`Cookies`	Gets the response cookie collection
`Expires`	Sets the expiration date (after which the browser will refresh) for the page
`ExpiresAbsolute`	Sets the expiration date and time (after which the browser will refresh) for the page
`Filter`	Gets or sets a wrapping filter object used to modify the HTTP entity body before transmission
`IsClientConnected`	Indicates whether or not the Web browser still has an open connection to the server (true/false value)
`Output`	Enables output of text to the outgoing HTTP response stream
`OutputStream`	Enables binary output to the outgoing HTTP content body
`Status`	Specifies the value of the HTTP status line for the response

Property	Description
`StatusCode`	Gets or sets the HTTP status code of the output returned to the client
`StatusDescription`	Gets or sets the HTTP status string of the output returned to the client
`SuppressContent`	Gets or sets a value indicating whether to send HTTP content to the client

The `HttpResponse` object methods programmatically control the HTTP output stream. Using the `HttpResponse` object, you can control the flow of HTTP output, write to the output stream, redirect the browser, and append custom data to the Web server logs. Table 3-22 shows the `HttpResponse` object methods.

Table 3-22 Methods of the `HttpResponse` Object

Method	Description	Syntax
`AddFileDependencies`	Adds a group of file names to the collection of file names on which the current response depends	`AddFileDependencies(ByVal` *`filenames`* `As ArrayList)`
`AddFileDependency`	Adds a single file name to the collection of file names on which the current response depends	`AddFileDependency(ByVal` *`filename`* `As String)`
`AddHeader`	Sends an arbitrary HTTP header with the response	`AddHeader(ByVal` *`name`* `As String, ByVal` *`value`* `As String)`
`AppendHeader`	Adds an HTTP header to the output stream	`AppendHeader(ByVal` *`name`* `As String, ByVal` *`value`* `As String)`

(continued)

Table 3-22 Methods of the `HttpResponse` Object *(continued)*

Method	Description	Syntax
`AppendToLog`	Appends a string to the Web server log entry for this response	`AppendToLog(ByVal` *`param`* `As String)`
`ApplyAppPathModifier`	Adds a session ID to the virtual path and returns the combined path	`ApplyAppPathModifier(ByVal` *`virtualPath`* `As String) As String`
`BinaryWrite`	Writes raw binary data to the HTTP output stream	`BinaryWrite(ByVal` *`buffer()`* `As Byte)`
`Clear`	Clears buffered HTTP output from the current HTTP output stream	—
`ClearContent`	Clears all content output from the buffer stream	—
`ClearHeaders`	Clears all headers from the buffer stream	—
`Close`	Closes the socket connection to a client	—
`End`	Terminates the current script	—
`Flush`	Sends buffered output immediately	—
`Pics`	Appends a PICS-Label HTTP header to the output stream	`Pics(ByVal` *`value`* `As String)`

`Redirect`	Sends an HTTP redirect to the browser, causing the given URL to be requested from the server	`Redirect(ByVal` *`url`* `As String)`
		
		`Redirect(ByVal` *`url`* `As String, ByVal` *`endResponse`* `As Boolean)`

Method	Description	Syntax

`Write`	Writes output to the HTTP stream with character conversion	`Write(ByVal` *`ch`* `As Char)`
		`Write(ByVal` *`obj`* `As Object)`
		`Write(ByVal` *`s`* `As String)`
		`Write(ByVal` *`buffer()`* `As Char, ByVal` *`index`* `As Integer, ByVal` *`count`* `As Integer)`

`WriteFile`	Writes the specified file directly to an HTTP content output stream	`WriteFile(ByVal` *`filename`* `As String)`
		`WriteFile(ByVal` *`filename`* `As String, ByVal` *`readIntoMemory`* `As Boolean)`
		`WriteFile(ByVal` *`fileHandle`* `As IntPtr, ByVal` *`offset`* `As Long, ByVal` *`size`* `As Long)`
		`WriteFile(ByVal` *`filename`* `As String, ByVal` *`offset`* `As Long, ByVal` *`size`* `As Long)`

The `Http`Response object contains one collection, called `Cookies`, whose attributes are described in Table 3-23. This collection allows you to place cookies on the client machine. A cookie can have different attributes attached to it that control how the cookie is to be used.

3.23.3 The `HttpServerUtility` Object

The `HttpServerUtility` object contains some miscellaneous utility functions and accesses properties on the Web server. With the `HttpServerServer` object, you can perform HTML/URL encoding, resolve physical pathnames on the server, and create instances of COM software components.

Tables 3-24 and 3-25 list the properties and methods, respectively, of the `HttpServerUtility` object.

Table 3-23 Attributes of the `Cookies` Collection

Name	Description
`Domain`	Sets the limiting domain for the cookie. Request must come from the domain specified for the cookie to be returned.
`Expires`	Sets the date when the cookie expires. Must be set for the cookie to be written to the client's disk.
`HasKeys`	Specifies whether the cookie contains keys.
`Path`	If specified, the cookie is sent only to requests to this path. If this attribute is not set, the application path is used.
`Secure`	Specifies whether the cookie is secure.

Table 3-24 Properties of the `HttpServerUtility` Object

Property	Description
`MachineName`	Gets the server machine name
`ScriptTimeout`	Gets and sets the request time-out (in seconds)

Table 3-25 Methods of the `HttpServerUtility` Object

Method	Description	Syntax

`CreateObject`	Creates an instance of a COM server component.	`CreateObject(ByVal` *`progID`* `As String) As Object`
		
		`CreateObject(ByVal` *`type`* `As Type) As Object`

`CreateObjectFromClsid`	Creates a server instance of a COM object identified by the object's class identifier (CLSID).	`CreateObjectFromClsid(ByVal` *`clsid`* `As String) As Object`

Method	Description	Syntax

`Execute`	Executes a `.asp` file inline with other ASP script code.	`Execute(ByVal` *`path`* `As String)`
		
		`Execute(ByVal` *`path`* `As String, ByVal` *`writer`* `As TextWriter)`

`GetLastError`	Returns an `ASPError` object that describes the error condition. Information on runtime, script compiling, and preprocessing errors can be obtained using this method.	`GetLastError() As Exception`

`HtmlDecode`	Decodes a string that has been encoded to eliminate illegal HTML characters.	`HtmlDecode(ByVal` *`s`* `As String) As String`
		
		`HtmlDecode(ByVal` *`s`* `As String, ByVal` *`output`* `As TextWriter)`

`HtmlEncode`	Applies HTML encoding to the specified string for formatting non-ASCII characters for display.	`HtmlEncode(ByVal` *`s`* `As String) As String`
		
		`HtmlEncode(ByVal` *`s`* `As String, ByVal` *`output`* `As TextWriter)`

`MapPath`	Returns the actual system pathname for the given Web virtual path (for example, `/pictures` may return `c:\webroot\pictures`).	`MapPath(ByVal` *`path`* `As String) As String`

(continued)

Table 3-25 Methods of the `HttpServerUtility` Object *(continued)*

Method	Description	Syntax

`Transfer`	Performs a server-side redirect, sending all state information to the given path for processing.	`Transfer(ByVal` *`path`* `As String)`
		
		`Transfer(ByVal` *`path`* `As String, ByVal` *`preserveForm`* `As Boolean)`

`UrlDecode`	Decodes a string encoded for HTTP transmission and sent to the server in a URL.	`UrlDecode(ByVal` *`s`* `As String) As String`
		
		`UrlDecode(ByVal` *`s`* `As String, ByVal` *`output`* `As TextWriter)`

`UrlEncode`	Applies URL encoding rules, including escape characters, to the string.	`UrlEncode(ByVal` *`s`* `As String) As String`
		
		`UrlEncode(ByVal` *`s`* `As String, ByVal` *`output`* `As TextWriter)`

`UrlPathEncode`	Applies URL encoding rules to the path portion of a URL string and returns the encoded string.	`UrlPathEncode(ByVal` *`s`* `As String) As String`

3.23.4. The `HttpApplicationState` Object

The `HttpApplicationState` object is used to store application-persistent data available for all users of the Web application to access. The `HttpApplicationState` object stores all of its application variables in a collection. Each application variable constitutes one item in the `HttpApplicationState` object's collection.

To store an application variable, use the following syntax:

```
Application("variable_name") = value
```

The value assigned to the application variable can be of any type, including string, numeric, and object variables. To retrieve the value of an application variable, just reverse the notation:

```
variable = Application("variable_name")
```

Table 3-26 lists the available collections in the HttpApplicationState object.

The HttpApplicationState object also contains the methods described in Table 3-27.

3.23.5 The HttpSessionState Object

By using the HttpSessionState class, you can declare variables that have "session scope." That is, they are available for use in any .asp file within the application. You also need to be able to determine when the user has "left" (that is, stopped using the application). This is accomplished by examining how much time has elapsed since the user last requested a page inside the virtual directory. The session is considered ended if that time-out period has

Table 3-26 Properties of the HttpApplicationState Object

Property	Description
AllKeys	Gets the access keys in the HttpApplicationState collection.
Contents	Gets a reference to the HttpApplicationState object.
Count	Gets the number of objects in the HttpApplicationState collection.
Item	Gets access to an object in an HttpApplicationState collection. This property is overloaded to allow access to an object by name or numerical index.
Keys	Gets a NameObjectCollectionBase.KeysCollection instance that contains all the keys in the NameObjectCollectionBase instance.
StaticObjects	Gets all objects declared via an <object runat="server"></object> tag within the ASP.NET application.

Table 3-27 Methods of the `HttpApplicationState` Object

Method	Description	Syntax
`Add`	Adds a new object to the `HttpApplicationState` collection	`Add(ByVal` *`name`* `As String, ByVal` *`value`* `As Object)`
`Clear`	Removes all objects from an `HttpApplicationState` collection	—
`Get`	Gets an `HttpApplicationState` object by name or index	`Get(ByVal` *`index`* `As Integer) As Object` `Get(ByVal` *`name`* `As String) As Object`
`GetKey`	Gets an `HttpApplicationState` object name by index	`GetKey(ByVal` *`index`* `As Integer) As String`
`Lock`	Prevents other clients from modifying values contained in application variables	—
`Remove`	Removes an application variable from the collection	`Remove(ByVal` *`name`* `As String)`
`RemoveAll`	Removes all application variables from the collection	—
`RemoveAt`	Removes an application variable at the specified index	`RemoveAt(ByVal` *`index`* `As Integer)`
`Set`	Updates the value of an object in an `HttpApplicationState` collection	`Set(ByVal` *`name`* `As String, ByVal` *`value`* `As Object)`
`Unlock`	Unlocks access to an `HttpApplicationState` variable to facilitate access synchronization	—

elapsed. Unlike `HttpApplicationState` variables, which hold their value for the duration of the Web server process lifetime, `HttpSessionState` variables are destroyed after the time-out period.

The properties of the `HttpSessionState` object are listed in Table 3-28.

Table 3-28 Properties of the `HttpSessionState` Object

Property	Description
`CodePage`	Gets or sets the code page identifier for the current session
`Contents`	Gets a reference to the current `HttpSessionState` object
`Count`	Gets the number of items in the session state collection
`IsCookieless`	Gets a value indicating whether the session is managed using a cookieless session
`IsNewSession`	Gets a value indicating whether the session has been created with the current request
`IsReadOnly`	Gets a value indicating whether the session is read only
`IsSynchronized`	Gets a value indicating whether access to the collection of session state values is read-only (thread-safe)
`Item`	Gets or sets individual session values
`Keys`	Gets a collection of all session keys
`LCID`	Gets or sets the locale identifier (LCID) of the current session
`Mode`	Gets the current session state mode
`SessionID`	Gets the unique session ID used to identify a session
`StaticObjects`	Gets a collection of objects declared by `<object runat="server">` tags within the `Global.asax` application file
`SyncRoot`	Gets an object that can be used to synchronize access to the collection of session state values
`Timeout`	Gets and sets the time-out period (in minutes) allowed between requests before the session state provider terminates the session

`HttpSessionState` objects are added and removed in the same way as `HttpApplicationState` objects. For `HttpSessionState` objects there is also an additional method called `Abandon`, which causes an immediate termination of the session. Table 3-29 lists the methods of the `HttpSessionState` object.

3.23.6 The `ObjectContext` Object

The `ObjectContext` object is used in controlling transactions for COM+. With the `ObjectContext` object, you can abort and complete COM+ transactions and specify event handlers for when these transactions abort or complete. (More information about COM+ transactions appears in Chapter 5.)

The methods and events of the `ObjectContext` object are given in Tables 3-30 and 3-31, respectively.

Table 3-29 Methods of the `HttpSessionState` Object

Method	Description	Syntax
`Abandon`	Cancels the current session	—
`Add`	Adds a new item to the session state	`Add(ByVal` *`name`* `As String, ByVal` *`value`* `As Object)`
`Clear`	Clears all values from the session state	—
`CopyTo`	Copies the collection of session state values to a one-dimensional array, starting at the specified index of the array	`Sub CopyTo(ByVal` *`array`* `As Array, ByVal` *`index`* `As Integer)`
`GetEnumerator`	Gets an enumerator of all session state values in the current session	—
`Remove`	Deletes an item from the session state collection	`Remove(ByVal` *`name`* `As String)`
`RemoveAll`	Clears all session state values	—
`RemoveAt`	Deletes an item at a specified index from the session state collection	`Public Sub RemoveAt(ByVal` *`index`* `As Integer)`

Table 3-30 Methods of the `ObjectContext` Object

Method	Description
`SetAbort`	Marks the current transaction as "failed" and notifies COM+ to undo any changes made to database tables during the attempted transaction
`SetComplete`	Notifies COM+ that this step in the transaction executed without problems and the transaction can continue

Table 3-31 Events of the `ObjectContext` Object

Event	Description
OnTransactionAbort	Event-handling subroutine raised when the transaction is aborted within the page
OnTransactionCommit	Event-handling subroutine raised when the transaction completes within the page

3.24 Summary

Let's review what you've learned in this chapter.

- ASP.NET applications are compiled code. They can be written in a variety of .NET-capable languages and can be mixed freely. ASP.NET applications provide facilities for state management, interactive debugging, and integrated security features.
- ASP.NET pages have a `.aspx` extension, which IIS uses to identify ASP.NET pages. ASP.NET pages have an event model that allows you to determine when the page loads and unloads.
- ASP.NET Web applications are configured using an XML-based configuration file called `Global.asax`. Using `Global.asax`, you can define application event handlers that allow you to trap events such as session starts and expirations.
- The HTML Controls provide server-side functionality to standard HTML elements. They are intended to correspond to the programming model of HTML and make the migration of existing static HTML pages to ASP.NET easier.

- The Web Controls provide rich server and client-side functionality for displaying content in Web pages. Web Controls provided with ASP.NET include standard user interface elements (such as text boxes, buttons, and lists) and rich controls such as the `Calendar` and `AdRotator` Controls. Web Controls can have many different events for which you can write event handlers. Web Controls adjust their rendering behavior automatically according to the Web browser being used to display them.
- Validation Controls allow you to code client-side or server-side form validation by simply placing various Validation Controls onto a Web Form. Many types of validations can be performed, such as comparison operations, checks for required entries, and validation of range limits.
- List Controls are used to display data in tabular and free-form formats. You can use templates to customize the exact look of the formatted data. Data for the List Controls can come from a variety of sources. The `DataList` and `DataGrid` Controls have rich editing capabilities.
- You can program custom controls called User Controls. These snippets of ASP.NET code wrap up other server controls into a single control. This provides a good way to reuse code and aids in consistency within a Web site.
- The ASP.NET intrinsic objects are intended to provide low-level support for Web application development. By using the ASP.NET intrinsic objects you can query the Web server for environment variables, get low-level access to CGI-encoded data, and perform other functions.

3.25 What's Ahead

In the coming chapters, we'll cover more topics related to building Web applications, including the following:

- The .NET Class Library, a set of objects used for several common programming tasks
- Web Services, which allow programmatic access to classes you write over the Web
- Data access and ADO.NET, which is the technology used to access relational databases and other data stores

Further Reading

- MSDN Library (http://msdn.microsoft.com/library/default.asp): This is the definitive source for programming reference material with the Microsoft platform. Documentation for the .NET Framework is also included.

CHAPTER 4

Using the .NET Framework Class Library

4.1 Common Features of the .NET Framework Class Library

Modern software systems are not created by writing fully customized code, and .NET applications are no exception. The .NET Framework Class Library contains an assortment of classes and data types that can be used to develop .NET Framework applications. The advantage of this is that much of the code you would have to write to perform common programming tasks such as file I/O, graphics, and printing is provided as preassembled components that are ready to be used wherever required.

Due to the size and complexity of the .NET Framework, we'll limit our exploration of the .NET Framework Class Library to the more common features that you're likely to implement in Web applications. We'll cover the following topics:

- Data collections
- File I/O
- Event logging
- Message queuing
- Text handling
- Internet communication
- XML data handling
- Internet e-mail

4.2 Using Data Collections (`System.Collections`)

Programmers frequently have to work with sets of data and perform various operations on the sets. Some of these operations include adding data elements to the set, removing them, and searching for the existence of a certain item in the set. There are different types of sets, and each set has its own behavior and rules that govern how the data are accessed. In this section we'll explore the following common data set types.

- *Arrays*: Arrays are simple, ordered or unordered collections of objects. Each element in the array has an ordinal index. The first element has an index of 0. Random access of any element in the array is allowed.
- *Stacks*: A stack is a collection of elements that allows insertions or removals only from one end of the collection (the "top"). This makes a last-in-first-out (LIFO) structure. Stacks are an important concept in computer science. Techniques such as recursion rely on stacks to operate.
- *Queues*: Queues are structures that allow for insertion of elements at one end and removal of elements from the other. A queue is a first-in-first-out (FIFO) structure. A classic illustration of a queue involves customers waiting for service at a bank window. Customers enter at the end of the group and advance forward to the window as other customers are served and leave.
- *Hashtables*: A hashtable is a list of elements in which each element can have an associated unique key value rather than an ordinal index. This association is very useful because it allows for fast lookups of information without linearly searching a structure such as a simple array.

4.2.1 The `ArrayList` Class

The `System.Collections.ArrayList` class implements a dynamic array. Unlike static arrays used by other development languages, an `ArrayList` can grow or shrink in size as new elements are added or taken away. A complete list of `ArrayList` class methods are given in Appendix A.

Let's look at a quick example of the usage of the `ArrayList` class. This program creates two arrays of integers, merges the two, sorts the merged list, and lets the user search for an element in the list.

Code Sample 4-1 Build instructions: vbc /r:system.dll cs4-01.vb

```
Imports System
Imports System.Collections
Imports Microsoft.VisualBasic

Module Module1

   Sub Main()
      Dim aList1 As ArrayList
      Dim aList2 As ArrayList
      Dim intSearchChoice As Integer
      Dim intLocatedIndex As Integer

      '* Create the two lists
❶     aList1 = CreateArrayList()
      aList2 = CreateArrayList()

      '* Original two ArrayLists
❷     PrintArrayList(aList1)
      PrintArrayList(aList2)

      '* Show combined ArrayList
❸     aList1.AddRange(aList2)
      PrintArrayList(aList1)

      '* Sort the list
❹     aList1.Sort()
      PrintArrayList(aList1)

      '* Search the list
      Console.Write("Enter an element to search for: ")
      intSearchChoice = CInt(Console.ReadLine())
      intLocatedIndex = _
            aList1.BinarySearch(0, _
            UBound(aList1.ToArray()), _
            intSearchChoice, Nothing)

      If intLocatedIndex <> -1 Then
         Console.WriteLine("Match found at index: {0}", _
            IntLocatedIndex

      Else
         Console.WriteLine("No match found.")
```

```
      End If

   End Sub

   Sub PrintArrayList(ByVal AryLst As ArrayList)
      Dim intElement As Integer

      For Each intElement In AryLst
         Console.Write(intElement.ToString() & " ")
      Next
      Console.WriteLine()
   End Sub

   Function CreateArrayList() As ArrayList

      Dim aNewArrayList As New ArrayList()
      Dim intIndex As Integer
      Dim rndRandom As New Random()
      Randomize()
      For intIndex = 0 To 9
         aNewArrayList.Add(rndRandom.Next(0, 99))
      Next

      CreateArrayList = aNewArrayList
   End Function

End Module
```

This example shows various operations with `ArrayList` objects. The `CreateArrayList()` function initializes a new `ArrayList` object and populates it with ten integers. Our sample works with two `ArrayList` objects created at the beginning of the program (see line ❶). In line ❷ we use the `PrintArrayList()` function to traverse through an `ArrayList` object (using a `For . . . Each` loop) and display each element. Line ❸ shows the `AddRange()` function, which concatenates the contents of the two `ArrayList` objects so the contents of `aList2` are appended to `aList1`.

The `Sort()` method shown in line ❹ can be used to sort array elements that are members of any .NET object class (`System.Object`). Any sort algorithm needs to be able to compare values, but if we are sorting data that is beyond simple data types like integers or strings, we need to be able to tell the `Sort()` method how to compare two elements. To do this, the `Sort()` method internally uses the `CompareTo()` method of the `IComparable` interface to sort the items in ascending order. Some data types, like the VB.NET `Integer` type used in the example (which maps to the .NET `Int32` class) already contain implementations of `IComparable`, so we don't need to supply a class that implements `IComparable`. If we were to provide such an implementation, it would look something like the following code.

```
Public Class MyCustomDataType : Implements IComparable

   Public m_strStudentName As String
   Public m_intIDNumber As Long

   Public Function CompareTo(ByVal pObj As Object) As Integer _
      Implements IComparable.CompareTo

      Dim objTmpCustomDataType As MyCustomDataType

❺       objTmpCustomDataType = CType(pObj, MyCustomDataType)

      '* Descending order comparison
❻       CompareTo = objTmpCustomDataType.m_intIDNumber - _
               m_intIDNumber

      '* Ascending order comparison
❼       'CompareTo = m_intIDNumber - _
      '          objTmpCustomDataType.m_intIDNumber

   End Function

End Class
```

The `MyCustomDataType` class defined above encapsulates a `String` value and a `Long` value. In this sample implementation of the `CompareTo()` method of the `IComparable` interface, the one parameter of `CompareTo()` is a `System.Object` type. This value is converted to `MyCustomDataType` in line ❺ using `CType()`. Then we perform the actual comparison. In this example, we are choosing to compare the `m_intIDNumber` members of the object passed into `CompareTo()` and the base class. The first comparison in line ❻ and the commented-out second comparison in line ❼ show how the ordering of the operands in the subtraction operation can alter the sort order.

We can modify the `PrintArrayList()` and `CreateArrayList()` functions from the previous example to include support for `MyCustomDataType`.

```
Sub PrintCustomArrayList(ByVal AryLst As ArrayList)

   Dim objCustom As MyCustomDataType

   For Each objCustom In AryLst
      Console.WriteLine(objCustom.m_strStudentName & _
      ControlChars.Tab & objCustom.m_intIDNumber)
   Next

End Sub

Function CreateCustomArrayList() As ArrayList

   Dim aNewArrayList As New ArrayList()
   Dim intIndex As Integer
   Dim rndRandom As New Random()
   Dim objCustom As MyCustomDataType
   Dim intTmpInteger As Integer

   Randomize()
   For intIndex = 0 To 9

      objCustom = New MyCustomDataType()

      intTmpInteger = rndRandom.Next(1000, 5000)
      objCustom.m_intIDNumber = intTmpInteger
      objCustom.m_strStudentName = "Student" & _
                intTmpInteger.ToString()

      aNewArrayList.Add(objCustom)

   Next

   CreateCustomArrayList = aNewArrayList

End Function
```

Then it's a simple matter of creating the array, calling `Sort()` in the normal fashion, and displaying the items.

Code Sample 4-2 Build instructions: vbc /r:system.dll cs4-02.vb

```
Dim aCustomObjArray As ArrayList

aCustomObjArray = CreateCustomArrayList()
aCustomObjArray.Sort()
PrintCustomArrayList(aCustomObjArray)
```

> **TIP:** Another way to sort items in an ArrayList array in descending order is to call the Sort() method, then call the Reverse() method.

Using a binary search to find an element in an array is a popular as well as efficient technique. Recall that for a binary search to work correctly, the elements in the array must already be sorted. In the previous example, we sorted the integer array, so now we're ready to perform a binary search. Consider this sample usage of the BinarySearch() method of the ArrayList class.

```
Console.Write("Enter an element to search for: ")
intSearchChoice = CInt(Console.ReadLine())
intLocatedIndex = _
   aList1.BinarySearch(0, _
   UBound(aList1.ToArray()), _
   intSearchChoice, Nothing)

If intLocatedIndex <> -1 Then
   Console.WriteLine("Match found at index: {0}", _
      intLocatedIndex)
Else
   Console.WriteLine("No match found.")
End If
```

The BinarySearch() method allows us to search a portion of the array list. We do this by specifying a lower and upper index for the first two parameters. ArrayList indexes are zero-based, so we specify "0" for the lower index. To get the highest index, we use the ToArray() function to return an ordinary array containing the array list's elements and then use the UBound() return value to obtain the highest index. The third parameter specifies the element (or object) for which to search. The fourth parameter is not used since we are using the default implementation of IComparable. The BinarySearch() method returns an integer that is the index where the first item is located. If the search turns up nothing, "–1" is returned.

4.2.2 The Stack Class

The System.Collections.Stack class implements a stack data structure. Stacks have many different uses and can hold any System.Object type. The available properties and methods of the Stack class are listed in Appendix A.

Let's explore the use of a stack in a sample program. Many applications have an Undo feature that allows users to revert back to a previous state in case of a data-entry error or other unintentional action. Some programs offer a multiple Undo feature that can recall an application state from many steps ago (how many is determined by the application). A stack can be used to track that state information. In the elementary example below, we repeatedly prompt the user to enter a word or phrase to build a sentence. If the user makes a mistake, he or she can correct the last word or phrase and enter a new phrase.

Code Sample 4-3 Build instructions: vbc /r:system.dll cs4-03.vb

```
Imports System
Imports System.Collections
Imports Microsoft.VisualBasic

Module Module1

   Sub Main()

      Dim stkUndoStack As New Stack()

❽     Do While (AddPhrase(stkUndoStack))
      Loop

      Console.WriteLine("Final sentence is:")
      DisplayStackContents(stkUndoStack)
   End Sub

   Function AddPhrase(ByRef UndoStack As Stack) As Boolean

      Dim strWordOrPhrase As String
      Dim strPhrase As String
```

```
      AddPhrase = True

      Console.Write("Add a word or phrase: ")
      strWordOrPhrase = Console.ReadLine()

      Select Case strWordOrPhrase
         Case "."
            AddPhrase = False
            Exit Function
         Case "#"
            If UndoStack.Count > 0 Then
               Console.WriteLine("Undo phrase: " & _
9                    UndoStack.Peek())
10                strPhrase = UndoStack.Pop()
               AddPhrase = True
            Else
               Exit Function
            End If
         Case Else
11              UndoStack.Push(strWordOrPhrase)
      End Select

      DisplayStackContents(UndoStack)

   End Function

   Sub DisplayStackContents(ByRef UndoStack As Stack)
      Dim strPhrase As String
      Dim aryStandardArray As Object()
      Dim intIndex As Integer

      Console.Write("Current contents: ")
12        aryStandardArray = UndoStack.ToArray()

      For intIndex = UBound(aryStandardArray) To 0 Step -1
         Console.Write(aryStandardArray(intIndex) & " ")
      Next
      Console.Write(ControlChars.CrLf)

   End Sub

End Module
```

The main program consists of a loop beginning in line ❽ that accepts string entries. The `AddPhrase()` function handles pushing and popping phrases onto and off of the stack. Entering a single period (`.`) causes the loop to terminate. Upon receiving the "undo" command, which is a single pound character (`#`), the function pops that item off the stack. Notice the use of the `Peek()` method in line ❾. This allows the user to look at the value before it is popped off the stack. After displaying the value, the `Pop()` function called in line ❿ removes it from the top of the stack. This action restores the sentence to its composition one phrase or word earlier. Any other string is considered a phrase to add to the sentence, which we add by calling the `Push()` method in line ⓫.

After each entry of a phrase, the program displays the current sentence. Since we can't visit every item in the stack by popping or peeking each value (this would empty the stack), we copy the stack items to a `System.Array` class. In line ⓬, we use the `ToArray()` method to obtain a string array representation of the data in the stack. Then, in reserve order, we traverse the items in the array and display each string item.

4.2.3 The Queue Class

The `System.Collections.Queue` class implements a queue data structure. The properties and methods of the `Queue` class appear in tables in Appendix A.

As stated before, queues are used to model data that is stored in a FIFO manner. One example of this involves documents being submitted to a printer, appropriately called a *print queue*. We can create a simulation of such a queue using the `Queue` class, as shown in the code below.

Code Sample 4-4 Build instructions: `vbc /r:system.dll cs4-04.vb`

```
Imports System
Imports System.Collections
Imports Microsoft.VisualBasic

Module Module1

   Public Class DocRecord
      Public DocTitle As String
      Public DocOwner As String
      Public DateTimeSubmitted As Date
      Sub New(Optional ByVal DTitle = "", _
         Optional ByVal DOwner = "")
```

```
        DocTitle = DTitle
        DocOwner = DOwner
        DateTimeSubmitted = Now()
    End Sub
End Class

Function InitializeQueue() As Queue
    Dim objDocQueue As New Queue()
    Dim objDoc As DocRecord
    Dim intIndex As Integer

    For intIndex = 1 To 5
        objDoc = New DocRecord()

        With objDoc
            .DocOwner = "Joe"
            .DocTitle = "Document #" & _
                intIndex.ToString()
        End With

13          objDocQueue.Enqueue(objDoc)
    Next

    InitializeQueue = objDocQueue

End Function

Sub AddDocToQueue(ByVal DocQueue As Queue, _
        ByVal Doc As DocRecord)
    DocQueue.Enqueue(Doc)
    Console.WriteLine("{0} submitted to queue", _
        Doc.DocTitle)
End Sub

Sub PrintDoc(ByVal DocQueue As Queue)
    Dim objDoc As DocRecord
14      objDoc = DocQueue.Dequeue()
    Console.WriteLine("{0} has printed", _
          objDoc.DocTitle)
End Sub

Sub ShowDocsInQueue(ByVal DocQueue As Queue)
    Dim objDoc As DocRecord
```

```
    Console.WriteLine("Print Queue" & _
       ControlChars.CrLf)
⓯      For Each objDoc In DocQueue.ToArray()
       Console.WriteLine("{0}" & ControlChars.Tab & _
                       "{1}" & ControlChars.Tab & _
                       "{2}", _
                       objDoc.DocTitle, _
                       objDoc.DocOwner, _
                       FormatDateTime( _
                       objDoc.DateTimeSubmitted))
    Next
 End Sub


 Sub Main()
    Dim objPrtQueue As Queue
    objPrtQueue = InitializeQueue()
    ShowDocsInQueue(objPrtQueue)

    Console.WriteLine("2 documents printed . . . ")
    PrintDoc(objPrtQueue)
    PrintDoc(objPrtQueue)
    AddDocToQueue(objPrtQueue, _
       New DocRecord("New Document", "Sam"))
    ShowDocsInQueue(objPrtQueue)
 End Sub

End Module
```

We begin by initializing the queue with a set of five objects. Each time through the loop the program adds the newly created object to the queue using the `Enqueue()` method, as shown in line ⓭. The program then displays the current contents of the queue. This is handled by the function `ShowDocsInQueue()`. As with the `Stack` class (and other classes in `System.Collections`), we can return an array representation of the queue contents using `ToArray()`. We use the returned array with a `For . . . Each` loop that begins in line ⓯ to iterate through the array and display the members of the `DocRecord` class. Printing a document involves removing it from the queue, which we do by using the `Dequeue()` method in line ⓮. Finally, a new document is added, which is placed "behind" the existing documents already in the queue. The listing below shows the final output of the program to illustrate its ending state.

```
Print Queue

Document #1    Joe    7/15/2001 4:13:27 PM
Document #2    Joe    7/15/2001 4:13:28 PM
Document #3    Joe    7/15/2001 4:13:28 PM
Document #4    Joe    7/15/2001 4:13:28 PM
Document #5    Joe    7/15/2001 4:13:28 PM
2 documents printed . . .
Document #1 has printed
Document #2 has printed
New Document submitted to queue
Print Queue

Document #3    Joe    7/15/2001 4:13:28 PM
Document #4    Joe    7/15/2001 4:13:28 PM
Document #5    Joe    7/15/2001 4:13:28 PM
New Document   Sam    7/15/2001 4:13:28 PM
Press any key to continue
```

4.2.4 The Hashtable Class

The `System.Collections.Hashtable` class implements an associative name–value pair array of objects. Reference tables for the `Hashtable` class appear in Appendix A.

Hashtables are highly useful data structures. In many cases, particularly in simple applications, using a hashtable is a fast and convenient way to give the programmer search and retrieval operations without having to resort to the overhead of a database. For example, if we wanted to look up a contact in an information storage area by using a particular key (like last name or ID number), we could implement that search by using a hashtable. Let's look at such a system in the following code example.

Code Sample 4-5 Build instructions: vbc /r:system.dll cs4-05.vb

```
Imports System
Imports System.Collections
Imports Microsoft.VisualBasic

Module Module1

   Public Class ContactEntry
      Public m_strLastName As String
```

```
      Public m_strFirstName As String
      Public m_intAge As Integer

      Sub New(Optional ByVal LName = "", _
            Optional ByVal FName = "", _
            Optional ByVal Age = 0)
         m_strLastName = LName
         m_strFirstName = FName
         m_intAge = Age
      End Sub

   End Class

   Sub AddContact(ByRef ContactTable As Hashtable)

      Dim rndRandom As New Random()
      Dim intIDNumber As Integer
      Dim objContactEntry As New ContactEntry()

      Console.Write("Enter last name: ")
      objContactEntry.m_strLastName = Console.ReadLine()

      Console.Write("Enter first name: ")
      objContactEntry.m_strFirstName = Console.ReadLine()

      Console.Write("Enter age: ")
      objContactEntry.m_intAge = CInt(Console.ReadLine())

      Randomize()
      intIDNumber = rndRandom.Next(1, 1000)
16    Do While ContactTable.ContainsKey(intIDNumber)
         intIDNumber = rndRandom.Next(1, 1000)
      Loop

17    ContactTable.Add(intIDNumber, objContactEntry)
      Console.WriteLine("Added contact with ID: " & _
           intIDNumber.ToString())

   End Sub

   Sub QueryContact(ByRef ContactTable As Hashtable)
      Dim objContact As ContactEntry

      Console.Write("Enter ID number: ")
      objContact = ContactTable.Item(_
```

```
(18)                CInt(Console.ReadLine()))

        If Not objContact Is Nothing Then
           Console.WriteLine( _
              "Contact info: " & ControlChars.CrLf & _
              "Last Name: {0}" & ControlChars.CrLf & _
              "First Name: {1}" & ControlChars.CrLf & _
              "Age: {2}" & ControlChars.CrLf, _
              objContact.m_strLastName, _
              objContact.m_strFirstName, _
              objContact.m_intAge.ToString())
        Else
           Console.WriteLine("Contact not found")
        End If

     End Sub

     Sub ListContacts(ByRef ContactTable As Hashtable)

        Dim objContact As ContactEntry

(19)    For Each objContact In ContactTable.Values
           Console.WriteLine("{0}" & ControlChars.Tab & _
              "{1}" & ControlChars.Tab & _
              "{2}", _
              objContact.m_strLastName, _
              objContact.m_strFirstName, _
              objContact.m_intAge.ToString())
        Next

     End Sub

     Sub Main()
        Dim objMyContacts As New Hashtable()

        AddContact(objMyContacts)
        AddContact(objMyContacts)
        AddContact(objMyContacts)
        ListContacts(objMyContacts)
        QueryContact(objMyContacts)

     End Sub

  End Module
```

This simple program prompts the user to enter information about three contacts and stores those contacts in a hashtable. After completion of data entry, the contacts are displayed in a list, and the program prompts the user for a key value (ID number) to recall a contact's information.

A unique key value must be used to insert a new object into a hashtable. The key value for each contact is randomly generated. Line ⓰ shows how to generate this value. Beginning with a random number, the program searches the hashtable for an existing key with this randomly generated value by using the `ContainsKey()` method. Since the value needs to be unique, the program repeatedly generates a random number until an unused key value is found. Then, the new `ContactEntry` class object is added to the hashtable using the `Add()` method shown in line ⓱.

We can search a hashtable by using the `Item()` method. The single parameter to the `Item()` method in line ⓲ is the object (in this case it's an `Integer` type) that is the key value. The `Item()` method returns an object reference to the matching object or `Nothing` if the object can't be located.

Beginning in line ⓳ we include code to display the contacts in a list. By using the `Values()` method, we can obtain an `ICollection` interface handle that can be used by the `For . . . Each` loop. The `objContact` variable holds the current contact as we iterate through the loop, and we access its members to display the data to the console.

4.3 Handling File Input/Output and Directories (`System.IO`)

There is no doubt that file I/O will play a key role in many of the applications you will write. The `File` class encapsulates various operations that can be performed on a single file, such as creating, copying, deleting, moving, and opening files. Many of the methods of the `File` class return special classes that are used to read to and write files. These are collectively known as *stream classes*. We'll cover them in this section. We'll also discuss how to read and write files and how to create, move, delete, and rename files and directories. Finally, we'll explore how to perform operations with directories, such as listing their contents.

4.3.1 Reading Text Files

Text files contain only character data. They include ASCII and Unicode text files. By using the methods of the `File` class, you can read these files easily. Before we discuss the stream classes, let's begin with a simple example. This code reads an existing file and prints its output to the console.

Code Sample 4-6 Build instructions: vbc /r:system.dll cs4-06.vb

```
Imports System
Imports System.IO

Module Module1

    Sub Main()

        Dim objStreamReader As StreamReader

        Try
            objStreamReader = File.OpenText("test.txt")
            Console.Write(objStreamReader.ReadToEnd())
            objStreamReader.Close()
        Catch E As Exception
            Console.WriteLine("Error occurred: " & E.Message)
        End Try

    End Sub

End Module
```

This straightforward code starts by declaring a `StreamReader` class, the class returned from the call to the `OpenText()` method of the `File` class. Once the program successfully opens a stream to the `test.txt` file, the program reads the entire contents with the `ReadToEnd()` method, which returns a `String` object. Then the `StreamReader` class closes the file using the `Close()` method.

Note that the `New()` method of the `File` class is declared as `Private` and all the methods of the `File` class are static. This means that you don't explicitly use the `New()` method for a `File` class to use the class's methods.

Tables 4-1 and 4-2 give the details of the `StreamReader` class. The `StreamReader` class, whose purpose is to read text from a file stream, implements the base class `TextReader`.

4.3.2 Writing Text Files

You can write to a text file using the `StreamWriter` class. The `StreamWriter` class can write data to the stream in a number of ways, such as writing a single character, a character array, an object, a subset of a character array, miscellaneous simple data types (`Boolean`, `Decimal`, `Integer`, `Long`, `Double`, and so

Table 4-1 Properties of the `StreamReader` Class

Property	Description
`BaseStream`	Returns the stream object
`CurrentEncoding`	Gets the character encoding

Table 4-2 Methods of the `StreamReader` Class

Method	Description	Syntax
`Close`	Closes the file associated with the stream	—
`DiscardBufferedData`	Throws away the current data in the `StreamReader` class	—
`Peek`	Returns the next character from the stream but does not advance the file pointer	`Peek() As Integer`
`Read`	Reads the next character from the stream; returns "–1" at the end of the stream	`Read() As Integer`
`ReadLine`	Reads one line of characters from the stream	`ReadLine() As String`
`ReadToEnd`	Reads the entire contents of the stream	`ReadToEnd() As String`

on), or a more complex `String` data type. You have the flexibility to write formatted strings, like the ones used when specifying a `ParamArray` in `Console.Write()`. The following example demonstrates these various ways of writing to a stream using the `StreamWriter` class.

Code Sample 4-7 Build instructions: vbc /r:system.dll cs4-07.vb

```
Imports System
Imports System.IO

Module Module1
   Sub WriteToStream()
      Dim objStreamWriter As StreamWriter
      Dim intA As Integer = 100
      Dim intB As Integer = 200
      Dim blnSampleBoolean As Boolean = True
      Dim dSampleDecimal As Decimal = 3.14
      Try

         objStreamWriter = File.CreateText("c:\newfile.txt")

         With objStreamWriter
              .WriteLine("Log File for " & FormatDateTime(Now()))
              .WriteLine("-------------------------------------")
              .Write("This is a formatted string: {0} {1}", _
                   intA, intB)
              .WriteLine()
              .WriteLine(blnSampleBoolean)
              .WriteLine(dSampleDecimal)
              .Close()
         End With

         Catch E As Exception
            Console.WriteLine("Error occurred: " & E.Message)
      End Try
   End Sub

   Sub Main()
       WriteToStream()
   End Sub
End Module
```

Calling this function produces a file similar to the one below.

```
Log File for 7/17/2001 8:58:50 PM
------------------------------------
This is a formatted string: 100 200
True
3.14
```

> **TIP:** File write operations using `System.IO` classes are buffered in memory for performance enhancement. Call the `Flush()` method of any stream object to permanently write any buffered data to disk. Use the `Flush()` method when you require the most up-to-date contents of the file to which you're writing. `Flush()` is called implicitly when the class object is garbage-collected (a process by which memory is reclaimed from an object no longer in use).

Tables 4-3 and 4-4 list the properties and methods, respectively, of the `StreamWriter` class.

Table 4-3 Properties of the `StreamWriter` Class

Property	Description
`AutoFlush`	Causes all output bound for the stream to be written immediately when the value is `True`
`BaseStream`	Returns the underlying stream object
`Encoding`	Gets the encoding in which the output is written
`FormatProvider` (inherited from `extWriter`)	Gets an object that controls formatting
`NewLine` (inherited from `TextWriter`)	Gets or sets the line terminator string used by the current `TextWriter` class

Table 4-4 Methods of the `StreamWriter` Class

Method	Description	Syntax
`Close`	Closes the open stream.	–
`Flush`	Forces all buffered output to be written to the stream.	–

Method	Description	Syntax
`Write`	Writes data to the stream. Form 1 writes a single `Char` to the stream. Form 2 writes a `Char` array to the stream. Form 3 writes a string object to the stream. Form 4 writes a portion of a character array to the stream, starting at the specified index and continuing for the specified count.	Form 1: `Write(ByVal` *`value`* `As Char)` Form 2: `Write(ByVal` *`buffer()`* `As Char)` Form 3: `Write(ByVal` *`value`* `As String)` Form 4: `Write(ByVal` *`buffer()`* `As Char, ByVal` *`index`* `As Integer, ByVal` *`count`* `As Integer)`

`WriteLine` (inherited from `TextWriter`)	Writes data to the stream with an ending new line character. The various syntaxes show the use of different data types.	`WriteLine()`
		
		`WriteLine(Boolean)`
		
		`WriteLine(Char)`
		
		`WriteLine(Char())`
		
		`WriteLine(Decimal)`
		
		`WriteLine(Double)`
		
		`WriteLine(Int32)`
		
		`WriteLine(Int64)`
		
		`WriteLine(Object)`
		
		`WriteLine(Single)`
		
		`WriteLine(String)`
		
		`WriteLine(UInt32)`
		
		`WriteLine(UInt64)`
		
		`WriteLine(String, Object)`
		
		`WriteLine(String,Object())`
		
		`WriteLine(Char(), Int32, Int32)`

4.3.3 Using Binary File I/O with the FileStream Object

Most files you will encounter will not contain solely textual data. Many files, such as graphic images, contain binary data—that is, the bytes in the file extend beyond what can be represented using text-encoding methods such as ASCII. The `StreamReader` and `StreamWriter` classes are designed to handle only text data. Using these classes to read binary data files gives unpredictable and incorrect results. For reading binary files, the `FileStream` and `BinaryReader` objects should be used. For writing binary files, use the `BinaryWriter` object together with the `FileStream` object. Tables 4-5 and 4-6 list the properties and methods, respectively, of the `FileStream` object.

Table 4-5 Properties of the `FileStream` Object

Property	Description
`CanRead`	Returns a value of `True` if the stream supports read operations
`CanSeek`	Returns a value of `True` if the stream supports random access seeking
`CanWrite`	Returns a value of `True` if the stream supports write operations
`Handle`	Gets the operating system file handle for the file that the current `FileStream` object encapsulates; used with COM interoperability with unmanaged code
`IsAsync`	Returns a value of `True` if the file supports asynchronous read/write operations
`Length`	Sets the length of the stream in bytes
`Name`	Specifies the name supplied to the `FileStream` constructor
`Position`	Designates the current position of the stream

Table 4-6 Methods of the `FileStream` Object

Method	Description	Syntax
`BeginRead`	Begins an asynchronous read	`BeginRead(ByVal` *`array()`* `As Byte, ByVal` *`offset`* `As Integer, ByVal` *`numBytes`* `As Integer, ByVal` *`userCallback`* `As AsyncCallback, ByVal` *`stateObject`* `As Object) As IAsyncResult`
`BeginWrite`	Begins an asynchronous write	`BeginWrite(ByVal` *`array()`* `As Byte, ByVal` *`offset`* `As Integer, ByVal` *`numBytes`* `As Integer, ByVal` *`userCallback`* `As AsyncCallback, ByVal` *`stateObject`* `As Object) As IAsyncResult`
`Close`	Closes the file and releases any resources associated with the current file stream	–
`EndRead`	Waits for the pending asynchronous read to complete	`EndRead(ByVal` *`asyncResult`* `As IAsyncResult) As Integer`
`EndWrite`	Ends an asynchronous write, blocking until the I/O operation has completed	`EndWrite(ByVal` *`asyncResult`* `As IAsyncResult)`
`Flush`	Clears all buffers for this stream and causes any buffered data to be written to the underlying device	–
`Lock`	Prevents access by other processes to all or part of a file	`Lock(ByVal` *`position`* `As Long, ByVal` *`length`* `As Long)`

(continued)

Table 4-6 Methods of the `FileStream` Object *(continued)*

Method	Description	Syntax
`Read`	Reads a block of bytes from the stream and writes the data in a given buffer	`Read(ByVal` *`array()`* `As Byte, ByVal` *`offset`* `As Integer, ByVal` *`count`* `As Integer) As Integer`
`ReadByte`	Reads a byte from the file and advances the read position one byte	`ReadByte() As Integer`
`Seek`	Sets the current position of this stream to the given value	`Seek(ByVal` *`offset`* `As Long, ByVal` *`origin`* `As SeekOrigin) As Long`
`SetLength`	Sets the length of this stream to the given value	`SetLength(ByVal` *`value`* `As Long)`
`Unlock`	Allows access by other processes to all or part of a file that was previously locked	`Unlock(ByVal` *`position`* `As Long, ByVal` *`length`* `As Long)`
`Write`	Writes a block of bytes to this stream using data from a buffer	`Write(ByVal` *`array()`* `As Byte, ByVal` *`offset`* `As Integer, ByVal` *`count`* `As Integer)`
`WriteByte`	Writes a byte to the current position in the file stream	`WriteByte(ByVal` *`value`* `As Byte)`

4.3.4 Reading Binary Files

For our first example of reading a binary file, let's use the `FileStream` object to read song information from an MP3 music file.

The program beginning on page 325 reads ID3v1 information and encapsulates it into a class. The main program displays the ID3v1 information to the console.

TECHTALK: MP3

MPEG Layer 3 (commonly referred to as MP3) is a popular file format for encoding audio data into a highly compressed form. In spite of their small size, MP3 files have extraordinary sound quality and are well suited for playing back high-fidelity music.

As the popularity of the MP3 format increased, users began to collect large numbers of MP3 files. To facilitate indexing of these files (using a scheme other than the file name), the ID3v1 standard was created. The ID3v1 structure is a 128-byte data block appended to the end of the file that contains information about the song title, artist, album, year of publication, genre, and additional comments. You can find additional information about ID3v1 (including the updated standard, ID3v2) at *http://www.id3.org/id3v1.html*.

Code Sample 4-8 Build instructions: `vbc /r:system.dll cs4-08.vb`

```
Imports System
Imports System.IO

Module Module1

   Public Enum ID3Offsets
      intArtistOffset = 34
      intTitleOffset = 4
      intAlbumOffset = 64
      intYearOffset = 94
      intCommentOffset = 98
      intGenreCodeOffset = 128
   End Enum

   Public Class MP3ID3v1

      Private m_objFS As FileStream
      Public m_strTitle As String
      Public m_strArtist As String
      Public m_strAlbum As String
      Public m_strYear As String
```

```
Public m_strComment As String
Public m_strRawID3 As String
Public m_strGenreCode As String

Public Sub New(ByVal Filename As String)
   RefreshID3Info(Filename)
End Sub

Public Sub RefreshID3Info(ByVal FileName As String)
   Dim bytTag(128) As Byte

   Try
20          m_objFS = New FileStream(FileName, _
              FileMode.Open, _
              FileAccess.ReadWrite)
21          m_objFS.Seek(m_objFS.Length - 128, _
              SeekOrigin.Begin)
22          m_objFS.Read(bytTag, 0, 128)
23          m_strRawID3 = BytesToString(bytTag)

   Catch E As Exception
      Console.WriteLine("Error: " & E.Message)
   End Try

24     If Left(m_strRawID3, 3) = "TAG" Then
      m_strTitle = Trim(Mid(m_strRawID3, _
            ID3Offsets.intTitleOffset, 30))
      m_strArtist = Trim(Mid(m_strRawID3, _
            ID3Offsets.intArtistOffset, 30))
      m_strAlbum = Trim(Mid(m_strRawID3, _
            ID3Offsets.intAlbumOffset, 30))
      m_strYear = Trim(Mid(m_strRawID3, _
            ID3Offsets.intYearOffset, 4))
      m_strComment = Trim(Mid(m_strRawID3, _
            ID3Offsets.intCommentOffset, 30))
      m_strGenreCode = Asc(Mid(m_strRawID3, _
            ID3Offsets.intGenreCodeOffset, 1))
   Else
      m_strRawID3 = Space(128)
   End If
End Sub

Private Function BytesToString( _
      ByVal bytBytes() As Byte) As String
```

```
            Dim byt As Byte
            Dim strReturnString As String
            For Each byt In bytBytes
               If byt <> 0 Then
                  strReturnString &= ChrW(byt)
               Else
                  strReturnString &= " "
               End If
            Next
            BytesToString = strReturnString
         End Function
      End Class


      Sub Main()
         Dim objMP3Info As New _
            MP3ID3v1("c:\Peter Murphy - Cuts You Up.mp3")

         With objMP3Info
            Console.WriteLine("Artist: {0}", .m_strArtist)
            Console.WriteLine("Title: {0}", .m_strTitle)
            Console.WriteLine("Album: {0}", .m_strAlbum)
            Console.WriteLine("Year: {0}", .m_strYear)
            Console.WriteLine("Comment: {0}", .m_strComment)
            Console.WriteLine("Genre Code: {0}", .m_strGenreCode)
         End With

      End Sub

   End Module
```

Let's investigate the source code. The `MP3ID3v1` class contains member variables for each of the ID3v1 segments that occur at different offsets in the file. The overloaded `New()` constructor calls the function that reads the song information, `RefreshID3Info()`.

The real work of reading the ID3v1 block begins with opening the file by creating a new `FileStream` object in line ⓴. In the constructor, we specify the file name, how we wish to open the file (open existing, open existing or create, open for append, and so on), and whether or not we want the stream to support read/write (in this example we specify read and write access). Once the stream is opened, we want to position it at the start of the ID3v1 data block. Since the data block is positioned at the end of the file and we know it's a fixed length (128 bytes), we calculate the required position by subtracting that length from the total length of the file (supplied by the `Length` property). The search starts at the beginning of the file, which we specified as the last parameter to the `Seek()` method in line ㉑.

With the stream in position, we use the `Read()` method in line ㉒ to read 128 bytes into byte array `bytTag`. We're using a byte array because we're reading binary data. To make the parsing work easier, we convert that byte array into a string so we can use VB.NET's useful string-manipulation functions. In line ㉓ the private function `BytesToString()` performs that conversion for us.

The rest of the code starting at line ㉔ parses the raw ID3v1 string. After checking for the identifying header (`"TAG"`), the parsing proceeds by extracting substrings using `Mid()` at the defined offsets and assigning the results to the member variables.

Finally, the `Main()` subroutine displays the member variable values to the console. Running this program on a test MP3 file produces sample output like the following. (This example uses an MP3 file I stored on my hard drive. To run the sample code yourself, replace the path in the source code with one to an appropriate MP3 file on your system.)

```
Artist: Peter Murphy
Title: Cuts You Up
Album: Deep
Year: 1989
Comment: Gothic Rock collection
Genre Code: 13
```

4.3.5 Writing Binary Files

To illustrate writing data to binary files, let's extend the MP3 ID3v1 reader program to include the ability to write new song information to an MP3 file. This involves building a string containing the ID3v1 string, converting the string to a byte array, and writing the byte array to the file. We add this functionality to the class with the following new public subroutine, `WriteID3Info()`.

```
Public Sub WriteID3Info( _
      Optional ByVal Title As String = "", _
      Optional ByVal Artist As String = "", _
      Optional ByVal Album As String = "", _
      Optional ByVal Year As String = "", _
      Optional ByVal Comment As String = "", _
      Optional ByVal GenreCode As Integer = 0)
```

```
Dim strNewRawID3 As String = "TAG"

(25)  If Title = "" Then
   strNewRawID3 &= m_strTitle.PadRight(30)
Else
   strNewRawID3 &= Title.PadRight(30)
End If

If Artist = "" Then
   strNewRawID3 &= m_strArtist.PadRight(30)
Else
   strNewRawID3 &= Artist.PadRight(30)
End If

If Album = "" Then
   strNewRawID3 &= m_strAlbum.PadRight(30)
Else
   strNewRawID3 &= Album.PadRight(30)
End If

If Year = "" Then
   strNewRawID3 &= m_strYear.PadRight(4)
Else
   strNewRawID3 &= Year.PadRight(4)
End If

If Comment = "" Then
   strNewRawID3 &= m_strComment.PadRight(30)
Else
   strNewRawID3 &= Comment.PadRight(30)
End If

If GenreCode = 0 Then
   strNewRawID3 &= Chr(CInt(m_strGenreCode))
Else
   strNewRawID3 &= Chr(GenreCode)
End If

Try
   With m_objFS
(26)         .Seek(m_objFS.Length - 128, SeekOrigin.Begin)
(27)         .Write(StringToBytes(strNewRawID3), 0, 127)
(28)         .Flush()
```

```
(29)          .Close()
        End With

    Catch E As Exception
        Console.WriteLine("Error writing ID3 info: " & E.Message)
    End Try

End Sub

Private Function StringToBytes( _
        ByVal strString As String) As Byte()

    Dim ch As Char
    Dim intIndex As Integer
    Dim bytReturnArray(128) As Byte

    For intIndex = 0 To 127
        bytReturnArray(intIndex) = _
            Asc(strString.Chars(intIndex))
    Next

    StringToBytes = bytReturnArray

End Function
```

The new subroutine allows us to modify part or all of the existing ID3v1 information by using `Optional` parameters for the subroutine. If a parameter is not specified, the existing value in the class member variable that corresponds to the parameter is used. The boldface code blocks beginning in line (25) show how we build the ID3v1 string. Each parameter is appended to the string and padded out to 30 characters with spaces (4 characters for the year) using the `String` object's `PadRight()` method.

As in the prior example, we use the `Seek()` method in line (26) to position the stream at the start of the ID3v1 block. In line (27), we use a private function to reverse the conversion we did previously; this time we convert the string into a byte array using `StringToBytes()`. This result is then used by the `Write()` method to write the binary block to the file. The `Flush()` method in line (28) ensures that the buffered writing persists to the disk. Then we finalize the process by closing the stream in line (29).

To call the new member subroutine, use the following example code. This changes the comment to the new string, leaving the other fields unmodified.

```
objMP3Info.WriteID3Info("", "", "", "", "Matt was here")
```

4.3.6 Performing File Operations

The `File` class helps you whenever you wish to change characteristics or manage files. We've taken a cursory look in the previous sections at the `File` class. For instance, we used the `OpenText()` method to return a `FileStream` object for writing text files. In addition to acting as the "object factory" for stream objects, the `File` class can be used to rename, delete, move, and copy files.

The `File` class methods are static, so the class has no constructor and is available at any time for use in your programs, assuming the `System.IO` namespace is imported properly. In addition to the `File` class, the `FileInfo` class offers instance methods of the same functionality as the `File` class. This, in effect, lets you specify a file name as part of the `FileInfo` class's constructor.

Tables in Appendix A list more information on the `File` and `FileInfo` classes.

4.3.7 Getting File Information

Here is an example of retrieving various pieces of information about a file. This example uses the `FileInfo` class.

Code Sample 4-9 Build instructions: vbc /r:system.dll cs4-09.vb

```
Imports System
Imports System.IO

Module Module1
   Sub DisplayFileInformation(ByVal FileSpec As String)
      Dim strFileInfo As String
      Dim fabFileAttribs As New FileAttributes()
30    Dim objFileInfo As New FileInfo(FileSpec)

31    Try
         If objFileInfo.Exists Then
         fabFileAttribs = objFileInfo.Attributes
32       If fabFileAttribs And FileAttributes.Archive Then
            Console.WriteLine("Archive flag set")
         Else
            Console.WriteLine("Archive flag set")
         End If
33          strFileInfo = "File information: {0}" & _
                      ControlChars.CrLf & _
                      "Size: {1}" & ControlChars.CrLf & _
```

```
                        "Created: {2}" & ControlChars.CrLf
         Console.WriteLine(strFileInfo, _
                        objFileInfo.Name, _
                        objFileInfo.Length, _
                        FormatDateTime( _
                       objFileInfo.CreationTime))
      End If
   Catch E As Exception
      Console.WriteLine("ERROR: " & E.Message)
   End Try

 End Sub

 Sub Main()
   DisplayFileInformation("test.txt")
 End Sub

End Module
```

This subroutine begins by creating a new `FileInfo` object in line ㉚ with the provided file name as a constructor. The subroutine proceeds with a `Try . . . Catch` block beginning in line ㉛ with a check for the existence of the file with the `Exists` property. When we know the file exists, we can proceed with other file operations.

Line ㉜ demonstrates how to obtain file attributes. File attributes are Boolean flags applied to files to indicate various characteristics about the file, such as read-only and archive. We can test individual flags to see if they are set by applying a bit-wise `And` operation with the `Attributes` property and the selected item from the `FileAttributes` enumeration. We check the `Archive` flag, which is used by backup systems to indicate that the file is ready to be backed up (in other words, that it has been modified since the last backup).

The code beginning at line ㉝ shows how to retrieve various characteristics about the file contained in the `FileInfo` class properties.

4.3.8 Copying, Moving, and Renaming Files

This example shows how you can make a copy of a file and rename it using the `CopyTo()` method and the `MoveTo()` method, respectively.

```
Sub CopyAndRename(ByVal FileToCopy As String)
   Dim objFileInfo As FileInfo
```

```
    Try
        objFileInfo = New FileInfo(FileToCopy)

        objFileInfo.CopyTo(objFileInfo.DirectoryName & _
                      "Copy of " & objFileInfo.Name, _
                      True)
        objFileInfo.MoveTo(objFileInfo.DirectoryName & _
                      "OLD_" & objFileInfo.Name)
    Catch E As Exception
        Console.WriteLine("ERROR: " & E.Message)
    End Try

End Sub
```

> **TIP:** Although there is no explicit method for renaming a file, you can emulate the same behavior using `MoveTo()`. Simply use the `DirectoryName` property plus the concatenated new file name for the destination name parameter.

4.3.9 Deleting Files

In this example, we delete a file using the static `Delete()` method of the `File` class.

```
Sub DeleteTheFile(ByVal FileToDelete As String)
    Try
        File.Delete(FileToDelete)
    Catch E As Exception
        Console.WriteLine("ERROR: " & E.Message)
    End Try

End Sub
```

4.3.10 Creating, Moving, and Renaming Directories

The methods and properties of the `Directory` and `DirectoryInfo` classes are organized in a manner similar to those of the `File` and `FileInfo` classes. The `Directory` class contains static versions of the instance methods found in the

DirectoryInfo class. Reference tables for the Directory and DirectoryInfo classes appear in Appendix A.

4.3.11 Creating and Getting Directory Information

The sample code below obtains basic directory information by using the DirectoryInfo object.

Code Sample 4-10 Build instructions: vbc /r:system.dll cs4-10.vb

```
Imports System
Imports System.IO
Imports Microsoft.VisualBasic

Module Module1

Sub DisplayDirectoryInfo(ByVal DirectoryName As String)

   Dim objDir As New DirectoryInfo(DirectoryName)
   Dim strDirInfo As String
   Dim objFile As FileInfo
   Dim strRootDir As String

   Try
34       If Not objDir.Exists Then
35           objDir.Create()
         End If

         strDirInfo = "Directory Name: {0}" & _
            ControlChars.CrLf & _
            "Creation Date: {1}" & ControlChars.CrLf & _
            "Last Accessed: {2}" & ControlChars.CrLf & _
            "Last Written: {3}" & ControlChars.CrLf

36       Console.WriteLine(strDirInfo, _
            objDir.FullName, _
            FormatDateTime(objDir.CreationTime), _
            FormatDateTime(objDir.LastAccessTime), _
            FormatDateTime(objDir.LastWriteTime))
```

```
            strRootDir = objDir.FullName

(37)        objDir = New DirectoryInfo(strRootDir & _
               "\sub1\sub2")
            objDir.Create()

(38)        objFile = New FileInfo(objDir.FullName & _
               "\fileone.txt")
            objFile.Create()

            objFile = New FileInfo(objDir.FullName & _
               "\filetwo.txt")
            objFile.Create()

      Catch E As Exception
            Console.WriteLine("Error: " & E.Message)
      End Try

   End Sub

   Sub Main()
      DisplayDirectoryInfo(".\")
   End Sub

End Module
```

As in the previous example with the `File` and `FileInfo` classes, we first check in line (34) for the existence of the directory. If the directory does not exist, it is created in line (35) by using the `Create()` method. The code block beginning in line (36) shows the use of the `DirectoryInfo` properties `CreationTime`, `LastAccessTime`, and `LastWriteTime` to retrieve the date and time the directory was created, when it was last accessed, and the last time files inside the directory were modified, respectively.

Next we create some new directories under the previously created directory. The code block that starts in line (37) shows the use of the `Create()` method, but this time we specify a path that contains a nested directory. Recall that the `Create()` method creates any directories in the path that do not yet exist. Finally, in line (38) we use the `FileInfo` class to create two new empty files in the innermost directory for use in the next example, which displays directory contents.

4.3.12 Accessing Directory Contents

This example lists the contents of a given directory.

Code Sample 4-11 Build instructions: `vbc /r:system.dll cs4-11.vb`

```
Imports System
Imports System.IO

Module Module1

Sub DisplayDirectoryContents(ByVal DirectoryName As String)
   Dim objDir As New DirectoryInfo(DirectoryName)
   Dim aFiles As FileInfo()
   Dim objFile As FileInfo

   Console.WriteLine("Contents of: " & DirectoryName)

   Try
      aFiles = objDir.GetFiles()

      For Each objFile In aFiles
         Console.WriteLine(objFile.Name)
      Next

   Catch E As Exception
      Console.WriteLine("Error: " & E.Message)
   End Try

End Sub

Sub Main()
   DisplayDirectoryContents(".\")
End Sub

End Module
```

The key statement in this example, the `GetFiles()` method, returns an array of `FileInfo` objects. The `For . . . Each` loop is then used as an iterator to get the information, in this case the file name, from each object.

4.4 Watching the File System for Changes (`System.IO.FileSystemWatcher`)

A powerful and very useful class that is part of the .NET Framework `System.IO` namespace is the `FileSystemWatcher` class. The `FileSystemWatcher` class allows you to set up a process that monitors a directory (or directories) for changes that occur to the files. These changes can include name changes, moves, and alterations of the file contents.

> **WARNING:** The `FileSystemWatcher` class works only on Windows NT 4.0 and above.

This class has many practical applications. For example, suppose that you have a back-end image-processing system that accepts user submissions for an online photo album. After an image is sent to the Web host, a server-side application could copy the image file to a particular processing directory. Whenever new files are added to this processing directory, the system could generate a thumbnail version of the image suitable for browsing in a Web page. The `FileSystemWatcher` class could provide the functionality to monitor the directory and direct application code to generate the thumbnail upon receipt of the file.

The `FileSystemWatcher` class works through either an asynchronous, event-driven mechanism or through a synchronous wait routine. In the event-driven model, event handlers are registered for different file events such as when files are changed, created, deleted, or renamed. Whenever a change occurs in the watched directory, a corresponding event is raised for that change. In the synchronous watching mechanism, a method is called that waits indefinitely until a change occurs.

Applications that use the `FileSystemWatcher` class are typically Windows Services or other "faceless" applications.

Table 4-7 lists the properties of the `FileSystemWatcher` class, and Table 4-8 lists the methods.

In the example on page 338, we use the event-driven mechanism of file-watching. The code watches a directory for files that are created, changed, renamed, or deleted.

Code Sample 4-12 Build instructions: vbc /r:system.dll cs4-12.vb

```
Imports System
Imports System.IO

Module Module1

   Sub Main()

39    Dim objWatcher As New FileSystemWatcher(".\")

40    objWatcher.NotifyFilter = NotifyFilters.FileName Or _
                      NotifyFilters.Attributes Or _
                      NotifyFilters.LastAccess Or _
                      NotifyFilters.LastWrite Or _
                      NotifyFilters.Security Or _
                      NotifyFilters.Size

41    AddHandler objWatcher.Changed, AddressOf OnChanged
      AddHandler objWatcher.Created, AddressOf OnChanged
      AddHandler objWatcher.Deleted, AddressOf OnChanged
      AddHandler objWatcher.Renamed, AddressOf OnRenamed

42    objWatcher.EnableRaisingEvents = True

      Console.WriteLine("Press Enter to quit")
      Console.WriteLine()
      Console.ReadLine()
   End Sub

   Public Sub OnChanged(ByVal source As Object, _
                      ByVal e As FileSystemEventArgs)
      Dim strChange As String
43    Select Case e.ChangeType
         Case WatcherChangeTypes.Changed
            strChange = "Changed"
         Case WatcherChangeTypes.Created
            strChange = "Created"
         Case WatcherChangeTypes.Deleted
            strChange = "Deleted"
      End Select

44    Console.WriteLine("File: {0} {1}", _
```

```
                        e.FullPath, strChange)

    End Sub

    Public Sub OnRenamed(ByVal source As Object, _
                         ByVal e As RenamedEventArgs)
45      Console.WriteLine("File: {0} Renamed to {1}", _
                        e.OldFullPath, e.FullPath)
    End Sub

End Module
```

We begin this program by creating a `FileSystemWatcher` object in line 39 and using the constructor to specify a path to a directory to watch. By default, this will watch the specified directory as well as nested directories. In the code

Table 4-7 Properties of the `FileSystemWatcher` Class

Property	Description
`EnableRaisingEvents`	Turns on (`True`) and turns off (`False`) file change notification.
`Filter`	Gets or sets the filter used to determine what subset of files to monitor for changes.
`IncludeSubdirectories`	Specifies whether subdirectories are to be included (`True`) when monitoring for changes.
`InternalBufferSize`	Sets the size (in bytes) of the buffer to use to store change data. Should be a minimum of 4096 bytes (4K) and a multiple of that value for best performance.
`NotifyFilter`	Gets or sets the type of changes to monitor. Can be any of the following: `Attributes`, `CreationTime`, `DirectoryName`, `FileName`, `LastAccess`, `LastWrite`, `Security`, and `Size`.
`Path`	Specifies the directory path to watch.
`SynchronizingObject`	Specifies the object used to marshal the event-handler calls issued as a result of a directory change.

Table 4-8 Methods of the `FileSystemWatcher` Class

Method	Description	Syntax
`BeginInit`	Starts the file watching for the component used on a Windows Form or by another component	–
`EndInit`	Stops the file watching for the component used on a Windows Form or by another component	–
`OnChanged`	Called when a file change occurs	`OnChanged(ByVal` *`e`* `As FileSystemEventArgs)`
`OnCreated`	Called when a file is created	`OnCreated(ByVal` *`e`* `As FileSystemEventArgs)`
`OnDeleted`	Called when a file is deleted	`OnDeleted(ByVal` *`e`* `As FileSystemEventArgs)`
`OnError`	Called when `InternalBufferSize` is exceeded	`OnError(ByVal` *`e`* `As ErrorEventArgs)`
`OnRenamed`	Called when a file is renamed	`OnRenamed(ByVal` *`e`* `As RenamedEventArgs)`
`WaitForChanged`	Synchronously watches for file system changes	`WaitForChanged(ByVal` *`changeType`* `As WatcherChangeTypes) As WaitForChangedResult` `WaitForChanged(ByVal` *`changeType`* `As WatcherChangeTypes, ByVal` *`timeout`* `As Integer) As WaitForChangedResult`

block that begins in line ⓴ we tell the `FileSystemWatcher` object what types of changes to monitor. In this case, we are watching for any changes to a file's attributes, last accessed time, last write time, security attributes, or size.

The next step is to configure the events of the `FileSystemWatcher` object. We do this with the help of the `AddHandler` statement. The parameters to the `AddHandler` statement are the event name and the name of the function that will handle the event, as demonstrated in the code beginning at line ㊶. We are registering event handlers for four different events of the `FileSystemWatcher` object: `Changed`, `Created`, `Deleted`, and `Renamed`. Notice the use of the required `AddressOf` operator. This creates a delegate (pointer) to the function name that handles the event. With all the configurations in place, we set `EnableRaisingEvents` to `True` in line ㊷ to activate file watching.

Two subroutines handle the different events raised by the `FileSystemWatcher` object, the first being `OnChanged()`. The signature of this event-handling subroutine must include two parameters: a `source` object variable and a `FileSystemEventArgs` object variable. Information about the change is contained in the `FileSystemEventArgs` object. Of particular importance is the `ChangeType` property, which contains the type of event that occurred. The possible events are contained in the `WatcherChangeTypes` enumeration, the values of which are given in Table 4-9.

In line ㊸ we use a `Select . . . Case` statement to detect the type of change made to the file. Line ㊹ shows the use of the `FullPath` property, which contains the full pathname to the file involved in the change event. The details of the change are output to the console.

The `OnRenamed()` event handler shows the use of the `OldFullPath` property of the `RenamedEventArgs` object , which is used specifically for rename events. The `RenamedEventArgs` object contains the original name of the file before the rename. The code in line ㊺ writes to the console both the old and

Table 4-9 Enumeration Values of the `WatcherChangeType` Property

Value	Description
`All`	The creation, deletion, change, or renaming of a file or folder
`Changed`	The change of a file or folder, including changes to size, attributes, security settings, last write time, and last access time
`Created`	The creation of a file or folder
`Deleted`	The deletion of a file or folder
`Renamed`	The renaming of a file or folder

new names of the file. Any event handler for rename events must have a signature using the `RenamedEventArgs` object.

4.5 Using the Windows Event Log (`System.Diagnostics`)

When production applications are deployed, it is important to be able to track errors and other anomalies that occur during execution. Information such as this is crucial to support staff members in diagnosing and correcting software problems encountered by users. Robust error and event logging is an important part of any production application.

Since the first versions of Windows NT, a common event log (simply named the Event Log) has been used as a tool to record application errors and events. Rather than having to write your own error logging and tracking system, you can code your applications to access the Windows Event Log and its common repository that all applications use to record application events. This section outlines the basics of the Windows Event Log.

The contents of the Windows Event Log are viewed using the Event Viewer application. To launch the Event Viewer (in Windows 2000), right-click on the My Computer icon and select Manage. The Computer Management console opens. Under **Computer Management→System Tools→Event Viewer,** you'll find the Event Viewer.

Notice that the Event Viewer is comprised of three different logs: the Application Log, the Security Log, and the System Log (see Figure 4-1). These are used to record program events, security events and audits, and low-level device and system events, respectively.

The Type column describes the type of the event. This is usually *Information*, *Warning*, or *Error*. The Date and Time columns indicate the date and time, respectively, that the event was posted to the log. The Source column denotes what application, service, or device originated the event. The Category column identifies what type of operation was being performed at the time the event was generated, and the Event column shows the ID number for the event. The User column shows which user account generated the event. Finally, the Computer column gives the name of the computer on which the event took place.

The `EventLog` object is very versatile and provides facilities to read, write, and query events. You can also access Windows Event Logs on remote computers. Tables in Appendix A outline the available properties and methods of the `EventLog` object.

Let's examine how to work with the Event Log by writing a simple program. This program writes a string to the Application Log and reads the current entries from the same log.

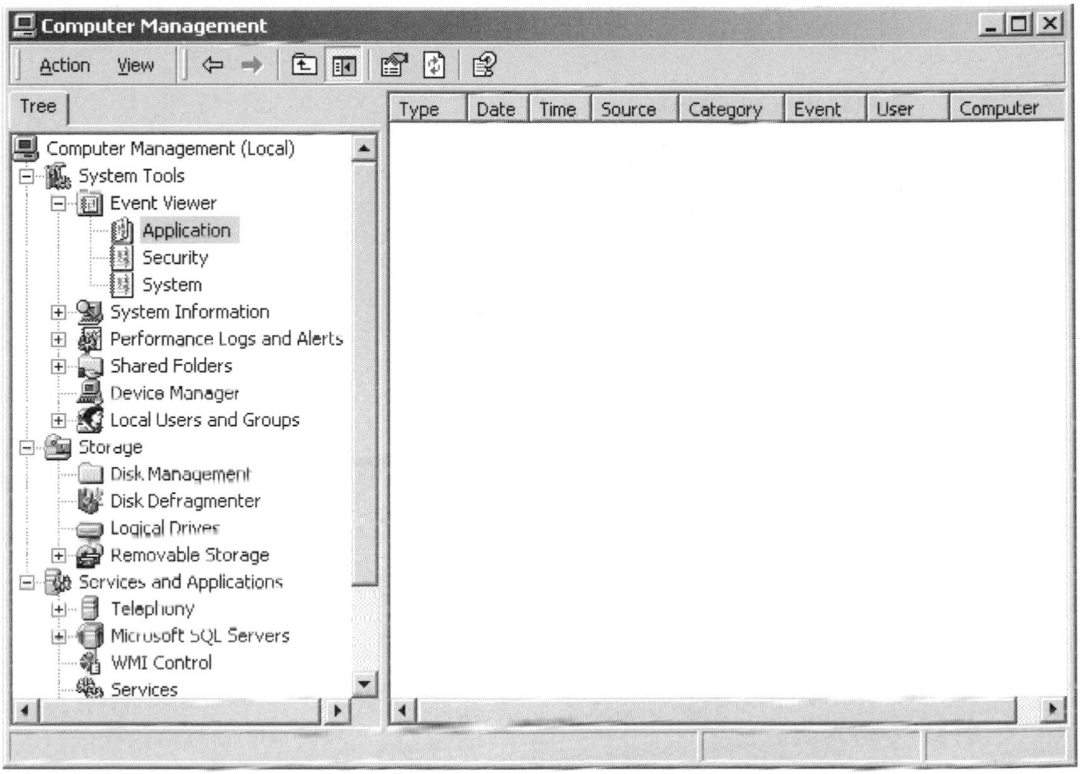

Figure 4-1 The Event Viewer

Code Sample 4-13 Build instructions: vbc /r:system.dll cs4-13.vb

```
Imports System
Imports System.Diagnostics
Imports Microsoft.VisualBasic

Module Module1

   Sub Main()
      Dim strLogStr As String

      Console.Write("Enter a string: ")
      strLogStr = Console.ReadLine()
```

```
        WriteToLog(strLogStr)
        ReadApplicationLog()
    End Sub

    Public Sub ReadApplicationLog()
        Dim strLog As String = "Application"
        Dim strMachine As String = "."

46      If (Not EventLog.Exists(strLog, strMachine)) Then
            Console.WriteLine("The log does not exist!")
            Exit Sub
        End If

47      Dim objLog As New EventLog()
48      objLog.Log = strLog
49      objLog.MachineName = strMachine

        Console.WriteLine("Entry count: " & _
50             CStr(objLog.Entries.Count))

        Dim objEntry As EventLogEntry

        Console.WriteLine("Type" & ControlChars.Tab & _
                 "Date" & ControlChars.Tab & _
                 "Source" & ControlChars.Tab & _
                 "Message" & ControlChars.Tab)

51      For Each objEntry In objLog.Entries
52             Console.WriteLine( _
            objEntry.EntryType & ControlChars.Tab & _
            objEntry.TimeWritten & ControlChars.Tab & _
            objEntry.Source & ControlChars.Tab & _
            objEntry.Message)
        Next


    End Sub

    Public Sub WriteToLog(ByVal StringToLog As String)

        Dim strLog As String
        Dim strSource As String

        strLog = "Application"
        strSource = "EventLogSample"
```

```
      If (Not EventLog.SourceExists(strSource)) Then
         EventLog.CreateEventSource(strSource, strLog)
      End If

      Dim objLog As New EventLog()
53       objLog.Source = strSource

      If (objLog.Log.ToUpper() <> strLog.ToUpper()) Then
         Console.WriteLine( _
            "Application in use. Choose another name.")
         Exit Sub
      End If

54       objLog.WriteEntry(StringToLog, _
         EventLogEntryType.Information)
   End Sub

End Module
```

This program reads and writes to the Event Log. Let's begin our discussion with the `ReadApplicationLog()` subroutine. We first need to check to see if the desired log exists on the target machine (the local machine) by using the static `Exists()` method in line 46. If that succeeds, we proceed to line 47 where we create a new `EventLog` object. In lines 48 and 49 we set the `Log` and `MachineName` properties with the values "`Application`" and "`.`", respectively, to denote the Application Log and the local machine.

With those properties set, we are ready to retrieve information about the log. Starting with line 50 we retrieve the number of entries in the log using the `Entries.Count` property. In line 51 we start a `For . . . Each` loop to iterate the collection of `EventLogEntry` objects in `Entries`. Each `EventLogEntry` object contains properties that correspond to the different fields in the Event Log. Beginning in line 52 we display the contents of the `EntryType`, `TimeWritten`, `Source`, and `Message` properties.

Writing to the Event Log is handled by the `WriteToLog()` subroutine. Taking a single `String` parameter, the subroutine repeats the process of `ReadApplicationLog()` that checks for the existence of the Application Log and the creation of a new `EventLog` object. Before the write to the log occurs, we set the `Source` property in line 53, which denotes what program is producing the event. Writing to the log is accomplished through a call to the `WriteEntry()` method in line 54.

Figure 4-2 shows some sample output from the program.

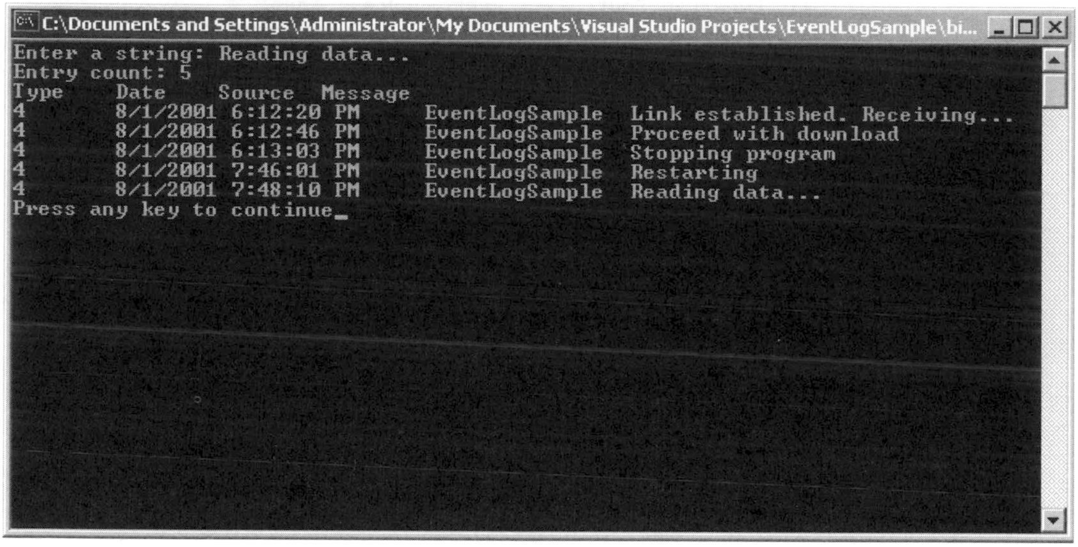

Figure 4-2 Output of the EventLog sample program

4.6 Working with Active Directory Services (System.DirectoryServices)

This section describes how to access Windows Active Directory Services. Active Directory Services encompasses a plethora of hierarchical storage systems made up of directories.

The term *directory*, as it relates to Active Directory Services, is a general one. It does not specifically refer to directories on your file systems (folders) but instead to any data stored in a hierarchical manner. Examples of directories include a name and address book, an employee roster, and a store of account information on a multiuser computer system. Each of these directories is referred to as a *namespace*. Specifically, a namespace is a root node in the directory service. The children of these nodes are called *container objects*. Container objects can contain other container objects and also *leaf objects* (which have no children).

Depending on the type of information you are querying, various protocols allow you to access that information through the use of a specific Active Directory Services provider. The following released providers can be used with Active Directory Services.

- **Windows NT 4.0 Directory Services**—This is the most widely used directory service. In short, Windows NT 4.0 Directory Services allow you to completely administer a Windows 2000/NT server or domain. You can perform all kinds of user and group management (including creation, modification, and deletion of users and groups plus group membership). You can control Windows 2000/NT services, including starting, stopping, and setting the start-up status. Management of print queues and print jobs is supported. You can also manage file shares on an NT server.
- **Lightweight Directory Access Protocol (LDAP) and Exchange Server**—LDAP is an Internet standard protocol for communicating with a wide variety of directory services. One application for LDAP is to provide access to data on Microsoft Exchange Server. Active Directory Services allows access to items such as message stores and recipient (user) data.
- **Internet Information Server (IIS)**—With the IIS provider, you can perform many administrative tasks relating to IIS. For example, you can manage virtual directories in the Web server filespace, set up other Internet services like FTP, manage log files, and configure settings for the servers.
- **Novell Directory Services (NDS)**—Active Directory Services also allows access to NDS. We won't be covering NDS in this book.

4.6.1 Displaying Active Directory Services Contents

To demonstrate querying Active Directory Services for information, let's start by using the Windows NT provider. We'll explore two examples of how to query for information about a computer and a user account on that computer. Here's the first example.

Code Sample 4-14 Build instructions: vbc /r:system.dll /r:system.directoryservices.dll cs4-14.vb

```
Imports System
Imports System.IO
Imports System.DirectoryServices
Imports Microsoft.VisualBasic

Module Module1
```

```
    Public Sub GetADInfo(ByVal ADPath As String)
       Dim strKey As String
       Dim objValue As Object
       Dim objDirEnt As DirectoryEntry

       Try
55        objDirEnt = New DirectoryEntry(ADPath)

56        Console.WriteLine("Name = " & _
                   objDirEnt.Name)
          Console.WriteLine("Path = " & _
                   objDirEnt.Path)
          Console.WriteLine("SchemaClassName = " & _
                   objDirEnt.SchemaClassName)
          Console.WriteLine("")
          Console.WriteLine("Properties:")

57        For Each strKey In _
                   objDirEnt.Properties.PropertyNames
             Console.Write(ControlChars.Tab & _
                   strKey & " = ")
             Console.WriteLine("")
             For Each objValue In _
58                    objDirEnt.Properties(strKey)
             Console.WriteLine(ControlChars.Tab & _
                   ControlChars.Tab & objValue.ToString())
             Next
          Next
       Catch E As Exception
          Console.WriteLine("Error: " & E.Message)
       End Try

    End Sub

    Sub Main()
       GetADInfo("WinNT://rmdevbiz01")
       Console.WriteLine("--------------------------")
       GetADInfo("WinNT://rmdevbiz01/matt")
    End Sub

End Module
```

Many inquiries of Active Directory Services begin with the `DirectoryEntry` object. The `DirectoryEntry` object contains a constructor that allows us to specify a path to a node in Active Directory Services. In the example above, we use the name of a computer on the network, RMDEVBIZ01, to construct a new `DirectoryEntry` object in line (55). After the constructor executes and the node is located, the properties of the `DirectoryEntry` object are populated in the code block beginning in line (56).

Nodes in Active Directory Services can contain any number of properties. These properties are housed in a `PropertyCollection` object. The `PropertyNames` and `Values` properties of the `PropertyCollection` object are of particular interest. They are both collections that contain the names and values, respectively, of the node. Each value in the `PropertyNames` collection can contain one or more `Values` objects. So, with that in mind, we use two nested `For . . . Each` loops to visit each value in the `PropertyCollection` object. The outer loop that begins in line (57) obtains all the names of the properties. Each property name is then used as an index into the `Properties` collection to obtain individual values for the property in the inner loop that starts in line (58).

The output of `GetADInfo()`, using a computer name as the path, gives results like the following.

```
Name = RMDEVBIZ01
Path = WinNT://rmdevbiz01
SchemaClassName = Computer

Properties:
      OperatingSystem =
            Windows NT
      OperatingSystemVersion =
            5.0
      Owner =
            SampleOwner
      Division =
            SampleDivision
      ProcessorCount =
            Uniprocessor Free
      Processor =
            x86 Family 6 Model 7 Stepping 2
```

For the next example, we take the previous code and change the Active Directory Services path to point to a user account on a particular machine. Here's sample output of that directory node for the user "matt."

```
Name = matt
Path = WinNT://rmdevbiz01/matt
SchemaClassName = User

Properties:
      RasPermissions =
            1
      UserFlags =
            66049
      MaxStorage =
            -1
      PasswordAge =
            323671
      PasswordExpired =
            0
      LoginHours =
            System.Byte[]
      FullName =
            Matt J. Crouch
      Description =
            Developer
      BadPasswordAttempts =
            0
      HomeDirectory =

      LoginScript =

      Profile =

      HomeDirDrive =

      Parameters =

      PrimaryGroupID =
            513
      MinPasswordLength =
            6
      MaxPasswordAge =
            5184000
      MinPasswordAge =
            86400
      PasswordHistoryLength =
            5
      AutoUnlockInterval =
```

```
        1800
LockoutObservationInterval =
        1800
MaxBadPasswordsAllowed =
        5
objectSid =
        System.Byte[]
```

4.6.2 Searching Active Directory Services Contents

Sometimes you need to locate a particular item in Active Directory Services by using a searching mechanism. Maybe you wish to locate a certain employee in a company and find his or her e-mail address. Often personnel directories are kept in an LDAP store made publicly available. LDAP is also a very popular way to locate individuals on the Internet.

> **WARNING:** Searches of Active Directory Services contents using the .NET Framework `System.DirectoryServices` classes are currently supported only for the LDAP provider.

> **TECHTALK: LDAP**
> Details on the Lightweight Directory Access Protocol (LDAP) can be found in RFC 1777 at http://www.ietf.org/rfc/rfc1777.txt including the syntax used for search queries strings.

In this example subroutine, we query for users in an LDAP directory who have a surname beginning with the supplied parameter `LastName`.

```
Public Sub SearchAD(ByVal LastName As String)

   Dim objDirEnt As DirectoryEntry
   Dim objADSearchResult As SearchResult
   Dim objSearchRSColl As SearchResultCollection
   Dim objTmpDirEnt As DirectoryEntry
   Dim objADSearch As DirectorySearcher
```

```
Try
59      objDirEnt = New DirectoryEntry( _
                "LDAP://ldap.yourserverhere.com")
60      objADSearch = New DirectorySearcher(objDirEnt, _
                "(sn=" & LastName & "*)")

61      objSearchRSColl = objADSearch.FindAll()

   For Each objADSearchResult In objSearchRSColl
      objTmpDirEnt = _
62                  objADSearchResult.GetDirectoryEntry()
63    Console.WriteLine(objTmpDirEnt.Name)
   Next

   Catch E As Exception
      Console.WriteLine("ERROR: " & E.Message)
   End Try

End Sub
```

The `SearchAD()` subroutine uses the `SearchResult`, `SearchResultCollection`, `DirectoryEntry`, and `DirectorySearcher` classes. Performing a search involves connecting to the LDAP server, which establishes a starting point for our search. Then, a search object (`DirectorySearcher`) is created along with a supplied LDAP query string. The search is then executed and the results are retrieved.

Line 59 starts the process of the search with the creation of a `DirectoryEntry` object. In the `DirectoryEntry` object's constructor, we supply a URL to the LDAP server in the form `LDAP://yourserverhere.com`. This establishes the connection. The code then moves on to line 60, where the `DirectorySearcher` object is created. One of the constructor forms of `DirectorySearcher` takes the previously created `DirectoryEntry` object and the LDAP query string, which we build from the supplied parameter `LastName`. The wildcard character (*) tells the program to include search results that match any number of characters following the value of `LastName`.

Line 61 executes the actual search. Since more than one user in the LDAP directory might match the query, the results are returned in the form of a `SearchResultCollection` object that implements the `ICollection` interface. The `SearchResultCollection` object is a collection of `SearchResult` objects, and we use a VB.NET `For . . . Each` loop to iterate through each search result.

Inside the `For . . . Each` loop, notice the call to the `GetDirectoryEntry()` method in line ❻❷. This method of the `SearchResult` class is used to obtain a `DirectoryEntry` object for each `SearchResult` object in the `objSearchRSColl SearchResultCollection`. After this `DirectoryEntry` object is retrieved, we can display information about it, such as its `Name` property (see line ❻❸). This returns the LDAP common name (`cn`) for the object, which usually contains the person's full name (depending on the organization of the LDAP directory).

The `SearchResult` object properties and method are listed in Tables 4-10 and 4-11, respectively.

The `SearchResultsCollection` class contains not only a collection but also useful operations such as dumping the objects in the collection into an array. Tables 4-12 and 4-13 describe the properties and methods, respectively, available in the `SearchResultsCollection` class.

Tables in Appendix A show the properties and methods of the `DirectoryEntry` and `DirectorySearcher` classes.

4.6.3 Modifying Active Directory Services Contents

The previous LDAP examples showed how you can display the contents of nodes and entries in Active Directory Services and how to search an LDAP store for particular items. What's left? Modifying the contents—the topic of the following example.

Let's return to the example of retrieving the account information of a Windows user. We'll modify the example to change the description property

Table 4-10 Properties of the `SearchResult` Class

Property	Description
`Path`	Gets the path for this `SearchResult` object
`Properties`	Gets a `ResultPropertyCollection` of properties set on this object

Table 4-11 Method of the `SearchResult` Class

Method	Description
`GetDirectoryEntry`	Gets the `DirectoryEntry` object that matches with the `SearchResult` object

Table 4-12 Properties of the `SearchResultsCollection` Class

Property	Description
`Count`	Counts the number of `SearchResult` objects in the collection
`Handle`	Gets the handle returned by `IDirectorySearch::ExecuteSearch` (called by `DirectorySearcher`)
`Item`	Gets the `SearchResult` object in the collection at the specified index
`PropertiesLoaded`	Gets the `DirectorySearcher` properties that were specified before the search was executed

Table 4-13 Methods of the `SearchResultsCollection` Class

Method	Description	Syntax
`Contains`	Indicates whether the specified `SearchResult` object is in the collection	`Contains(ByVal` *`result`* `As SearchResult) As Boolean`
`CopyTo`	Copies `SearchResult` objects in the collection to an array beginning with the specified index	`CopyTo(ByVal` *`results()`* `As SearchResult, ByVal` *`index`* `As Integer)`
`IndexOf`	Retrieves the index of a specified `SearchResult` object in this collection	`IndexOf(ByVal` *`result`* `As SearchResult) As Integer`

of the account. The code change is minimal; it requires setting one of the properties of a `DirectoryEntry` object with a new value, as shown in boldface text in the following code snippet.

```
Public Sub ChangeAcctDescription(ByVal AcctPath As String, _
            ByVal DescValue As String)

   Dim objDirEnt As DirectoryEntry

   Try
```

```
        objDirEnt = New DirectoryEntry(AcctPath)
        objDirEnt.Properties("Description")(0) = DescValue
        objDirEnt.CommitChanges()

    Catch E As Exception
        Console.WriteLine("ERROR: " & E.Message)
    End Try

End Sub
```

All that's involved in changing the property is obtaining the key name of a property in the `Properties` collection (a `PropertyCollection` class) and specifying the item index (in this case, `0`). Then we can assign a new value. Changes aren't permanent until the `CommitChanges()` method is called and the application has sufficient permissions to modify the directory.

4.7 Using Message Queues (System.Messaging)

Microsoft Message Queues (MSMQ) is an integral part of many enterprise applications. It plays a key role in the scalability and robustness of transaction-intensive systems. MSMQ facilitates communication between disparate components or systems by passing messages, which are segments of data that represent commands or arbitrary data. Its robustness comes from the fact that the sender and receiver don't need a currently active network connection to communicate.

Message queuing works by using a store-and-forward technique for communication between systems across the enterprise. To understand how message queuing works, it helps to look at a classic example of an implementation of MSMQ. Consider your e-mail system. It is a method of communication between two parties, but, unlike "live" forms of communication, like a telephone conversation that relies on the fact that both parties are actively connected, e-mail does not require you to be present to receive a message. An e-mail message to you is received by the mail server and is stored there until you retrieve it (that is, it is forwarded to your e-mail reader program)—hence, the name *store-and-forward communication*.

How does this relate to MSMQ in enterprise applications? Generally speaking, the concept is exactly the same, although the messages are typically not e-mail-style messages. Messages are sent to a message queue, a FIFO storage area where another application, called a *listener application*, retrieves them. To add robustness to the message-queuing process, there is a provision in the message-queuing system to ensure that the message is delivered only once. Again, this works like the e-mail example. When the user attempts to retrieve the messages from the server, he or she sends a message back to the server for each message indicating it was successfully retrieved and can be removed from the server (queue). Like e-mail systems, the MSMQ system has the ability to prioritize messages. Messages that are marked as urgent make their way through the queue much faster than messages of lower priority.

> **TECHTALK: MICROSOFT MESSAGE QUEUES**
> This discussion about MSMQ does not include detailed information about the administrative side of MSMQ, in particular the management of queues. You can obtain information about the administration of MSMQ from its Computer Management Console by right-clicking on Message Queuing in the Tree and selecting Help.

You can create four different types of queues in MSMQ.

1. *Public queues* are published in Active Directory Services, which enables any computer within the Active Directory Services forest to access the public queues.
2. *Private queues* can be accessed only on the local computer on which they were created. They are typically used by local applications as temporary storage areas. *System queues* are a type of private queue reserved by the operating system for storage of administrative messages.
3. *Dead-letter queues* are reserved for storing messages that cannot be delivered to their destination. This could be due to an unknown destination queue, storage constraints that prohibited delivery of the message, the maximum number of message hops was exceeded, or the expiration date of the message has passed.
4. *Transactional queues* receive messages within a transaction boundary. This means each message sent as part of a transaction must be delivered successfully and in the relative order it was sent. If any part of the transaction (any single message delivery) fails, none of the messages are delivered.

4.7.1 Creating a Queue

In this example we'll create a new public queue and a function, called - `CreatePublicQueue()`, that returns a `MessageQueue` object. The

MessageQueue object provides the functionality needed to access message queues. Tables in Appendix A list the properties and methods of the MessageQueue class.

Let's look at the CreatePublicQueue() function in the code below.

```
Public Function CreatePublicQueue(
        ByVal QName As String) As MessageQueue
   Dim objQueue As MessageQueue

   Try
64    If Not MessageQueue.Exists(".\" & QName) Then
         objQueue = MessageQueue.Create(".\" & QName)
      Else
65          objQueue = New MessageQueue(".\" & QName)
      End If

      CreatePublicQueue = objQueue

   Catch E As Exception
      Console.WriteLine("Error: " & E.Message)
   End Try

End Function
```

In line 64 the function checks to see if the queue already exists by using the static method Exists(). Notice that the pathname to the queue begins with ".\". This denotes that the queue we are attempting to look up would reside on the local computer. If the queue doesn't already exist, we use the static Create() method to make the new queue with the specified name. If the queue with the specified name already exists, we simply pass that name into the MessageQueue constructor in line 65, which returns a MessageQueue object pointing to the queue path.

4.7.2 Sending a Message to a Queue

Sending a message to a queue is simple. Keep in mind that although the following example sends a String object to the queue, you can send any object type (System.Object) to the queue using the Send() method.

```
Public Sub SendMessageToQueue( _
      ByVal Q As MessageQueue, ByVal Msg As String)
   Q.Send(Msg)
End Sub
```

4.7.3 Dequeuing a Message

Dequeuing a message (that is, receiving it) is done by calling the `Receive()` method. This method returns a `Message` object, which contains the body of the message queue plus many different message characteristics. In this example, the `Message` object contains a property called `Body` which is of the `System.Object` type. The `Body` property is implicitly converted to a `String` object as the return value of the function.

```
Public Function Dequeue(ByVal Q As MessageQueue) As String
   Dim objQMsg As Message
   objQMsg = Q.Receive()
   Dequeue = objQMsg.Body
End Function
```

4.8 Communicating with Servers on the Internet (`System.Web` and `System.Net`)

In this section we'll cover how to communicate with servers or peers on the Internet (and intranet) using standard TCP/IP, the same network protocol used by many other Internet services, including e-mail. It's a common language that all computers connected to the Internet speak. (For more on TCP/IP, see Section 1.2.2.)

The `System.Net.Sockets` namespace contains classes and types for establishing connections using TCP and also UDP (User Datagram Protocol), another method of network communication on the Internet. The Microsoft .NET Framework `System.Net.Sockets` class wraps functions of the Windows Sockets API, which was the standard (and difficult) way for writing Internet application software for many years. We'll explore this and other related classes in the following sections.

4.8.1 A Simple TCP Client Application

TCP client applications begin with establishing a connection to a server. The VB.NET application created in the example below establishes that connection by using the `TcpClient` class. The `TcpClient` class contains functionality to open and close connections and to obtain stream objects on which to send and receive data. The properties and methods of the `TcpClient` class are listed in Tables 4-14 and 4-15.

This example implements a very simple Web client. The program opens up a TCP socket connection to a server on port 80. Then an HTTP `GET` com-

Table 4-14 Properties of the TcpClient Class

Property	Description
Active	Indicates whether the TCP connection is still active (true/false value)
Client	Retrieves the underlying Socket object
LingerState	Sets the connection linger option
NoDelay	Causes a delay to be invoked when send and receive buffers are full if the value is set to True
ReceiveBufferSize	Sets the size of the receive buffer
ReceiveTimeout	Sets the time-out value (in milliseconds) of the connection
SendBufferSize	Specifies the size of the send buffer
SendTimeout	Sets the send time-out value (in milliseconds) of the connection

Table 4-15 Methods of the TcpClient Class

Method	Description	Syntax
Close	Closes the TCP connection	—
Connect	Opens a connection to a TCP server	Connect(ByVal *remoteEP* As IPEndPoint)
		Connect(ByVal *address* As IPAddress, ByVal *port* As Integer)
		Connect(ByVal *hostname* As String, ByVal *port* As Integer)
GetStream	Gets the stream used to read and write data to the server	GetStream() As NetworkStream

mand is sent over the socket connection and the response from the server is received and then displayed.

Code Sample 4-15 Build instructions: vbc /r:system.dll cs4-15.vb

```
Imports System
Imports System.IO
Imports System.Net
Imports System.Net.Sockets
Imports System.Text
Imports Microsoft.VisualBasic

Module Module1

   Public Sub Main()
      Dim objTCPClient As New TcpClient()
      Dim bytWrite() As Byte

      Dim objStream As NetworkStream
      Dim strHTTPCommand As String
      Dim intNumberOfBytes As Integer
      Dim strReceivedData As String
      Dim bytReceivedData(1024) As Byte
      Dim intTotalBytes As Integer = 0

      Try
66          objTCPClient.Connect("localhost", 80)
67          objStream = objTCPClient.GetStream()

            strHTTPCommand = "GET/home.htm HTTP/1.0" & _
                             ControlChars.CrLf & _
                             ControlChars.CrLf

68          bytWrite = Encoding.ASCII.GetBytes(strHTTPCommand)

69          objStream.Write(bytWrite, 0, bytWrite.Length)

70          intNumberOfBytes = objStream.Read(bytReceivedData, _
                             0, 1024)
            intTotalBytes += intNumberOfBytes
71       Do While intNumberOfBytes <> 0
            ReDim Preserve bytReceivedData( _
                           bytReceivedData.Length + 1024)
            intNumberOfBytes = objStream.Read( _
```

```
                             bytReceivedData, _
                             intTotalBytes, 1024)
             intTotalBytes += intNumberOfBytes
          Loop

          ReDim Preserve bytReceivedData(intTotalBytes)

          strReceivedData = _
(72)                      Encoding.ASCII.GetString(bytReceivedData)

          Console.WriteLine(strReceivedData)

(73)      objTCPClient.Close()

       Catch exc As Exception
          Console.WriteLine("Error: " & exc.Message)
       End Try

    End Sub

End Module
```

We begin this program with the `Connect()` method in line (66), which establishes a connection with the given host and the specified port. This initializes the `TcpClient` class and allows us to obtain a `NetworkStream` object in line (67) that represents the channel for sending and receiving data.

Once the connection has been successfully established, we proceed with preparing data to be sent to the server. We build an HTTP `GET` command string that instructs the Web server to retrieve the document `home.htm` from the Web server root directory. In order for any data to be written to the stream, that data must be in the format of a byte array. This is a requirement of the `Write()` method of the `NetworkStream` object. The `Encoding.ASCII` class provides a method called `GetBytes()` that converts a string into a byte array suitable for our purposes; we use this method in line (68). Then in line (69) we call the `Write()` method of the `NetworkStream` object, instructing it to write all of the data in the byte array (beginning with the offset `0` and ending with the length of the array).

Once the data has been written, we want to read the server's response. We do this by initiating a read operation on the stream using the `Read()` method in line (70). This is an initial read from the stream that retrieves a maximum of 1024 bytes from the stream. The `Do . . . While` loop that begins in line (71) performs a "chunked" read of the data in 1024-byte blocks. To accommodate the storage of the accumulated data, we increase the size of the array by 1K for each chunk read from the stream while keeping a running total of the number of bytes received. Once the loop completes, signaled by a `Read()` return value of `0`, the program truncates the byte array to the actual number of bytes stored in the array. In line ⑫ we use the `Encoding.ASCII` class to convert the data received in the byte array back into a `String` object using the `GetString()` method.

Finally, the program displays the data to the user and closes the connection with the `Close()` method in line ⑬. Here is some sample output from the program.

```
HTTP/1.1 200 OK
Server: Microsoft-IIS/5.0
Cache-Control: no-cache
Expires: Tue, 14 Aug 2001 02:13:55 GMT
Date: Tue, 14 Aug 2001 02:13:55 GMT
Content-Type: text/html
Accept-Ranges: bytes
Last-Modified: Tue, 14 Aug 2001 01:10:02 GMT
ETag: "2c6d3ad85d24c11:8d5"
Content-Length: 144

<html>
<head>
<TITLE>Matt's Home Page</TITLE>
</head>

<body>
<h1>Welcome to Matt's Home Page</h1>
Enjoy your stay.
</body>

</html>
```

4.8.2 A Simple TCP Server Application

The .NET Framework `System.Net.Sockets` classes also allow you to write TCP servers. This section demonstrates a program for a rudimentary TCP server that displays incoming data as it is received. Tables 4-16 and 4-17 show the properties and methods of the `TcpListener` class, which is used in the program.

Table 4-16 Properties of the `TcpListener` Class

Property	Description
`Active`	Gets or sets a value that indicates whether the listener's socket has been bound to a port and started listening
`LocalEndpoint`	Gets the active end point for the local listener socket
`Server`	Gets or sets the underlying network socket

Table 4-17 Methods of the `TcpListener` Class

Method	Description	Syntax
`AcceptSocket`	Accepts an incoming socket connection request	`AcceptSocket() As Socket`
`AcceptTcpClient`	Accepts an incoming connection request	`AcceptTcpClient() As TcpClient`
`Pending`	Determines whether there are pending connection requests	`Pending() As Boolean`
`Start`	Starts listening to network requests	–
`Stop`	Closes the network connection	–

The small server program below listens for connection requests and displays incoming data from the TCP client. This functionality is encapsulated in a class we call `TCPServ`.

> **TIP:** You can use Windows Telnet to test this program. Simply type *`telnet localhost 10000`* from the command prompt. It's best to test this server program locally (on your computer) since nonstandard ports (such as 10000) are normally blocked by firewalls.

Code Sample 4-16 Build instructions: `vbc /r:system.dll cs4-16.vb`

```
Imports System.Net
Imports System.Net.Sockets
Imports System.Text
Imports System.IO

Module Module1

   Public Class TCPServ
      Private m_objTCPListener As TcpListener
      Private m_bytRequest(128) As Byte
      Private m_bytResponse(128) As Byte

      Public Sub New()
(74)         m_objTCPListener = New TcpListener(10000)
(75)         m_objTCPListener.Start()
      End Sub

      Public Sub Run()
         Dim objTCPClient As TcpClient
         Dim objNetStream As NetworkStream
         Dim intBytesRead As Integer

         Dim strStringRequest As String

(76)     objTCPClient = m_objTCPListener.AcceptTcpClient()
(77)     objNetStream = objTCPClient.GetStream()

         Do While True
(78)        If objNetStream.DataAvailable Then
               intBytesRead = _
(79)                  objNetStream.Read(m_bytRequest, 0, _
                  m_bytRequest.Length)
               ReDim Preserve m_bytRequest(intBytesRead)
               strStringRequest = _
                  Encoding.ASCII.GetString(m_bytRequest)
               Console.WriteLine("Server received: " & _
                  strStringRequest)
            End If
         Loop

      End Sub
```

```
    End Class

    Sub Main()
        Dim objTCPServ As New TCPServ()
        objTCPServ.Run()
    End Sub

End Module
```

In the constructor of the TCPServ class we initiate the first step of setting up the server: creating a TcpListener object and setting it to listen on a TCP port (port 10000) in line (74). Then, to begin listening for connections, we call the Start() method in line (75).

In the Run() subroutine we accept an incoming connection to the server by using AcceptTcpClient() in line (76). This method, once called, waits (and blocks the current thread) until a connection is received. AcceptTcpClient() predictably returns a TcpClient object, just like the one used in the previous examples. From this object we obtain the NetworkStream object, which is used to read the incoming data from the TCP client using GetStream() in line (77).

Next we start a Do . . . While loop that receives the data from the TCP client until the program is terminated. First the program checks to see if there is data to receive on the stream by looking at the DataAvailable property in line (78). If ready to proceed with receiving data, the program calls Read() in line (79) to populate a byte array with the data. Then the byte array is converted into a String object for display to the console.

4.8.3 HTTP Communication

The TCP client example showed how you can use the TcpClient class to retrieve documents from a Web server using HTTP commands. While this is a perfectly acceptable way to perform this function, there are more elegant ways to accomplish the same task. Two classes in the .NET Framework, System.Net.WebRequest and System.Net.WebResponse, handle most of the low-level details of HTTP-based network communication (like HTTP redirections), which you would have to implement yourself if you resorted to using the System.Net.Sockets classes.

Tables 4-18 through 4-21 provide an overview of the WebRequest and WebResponse classes.

Table 4-18 Properties of the `WebRequest` Class

Property	Description
`ConnectionGroupName`	Specifies the connection group for the class
`ContentLength`	Sets the content length (in bytes) of the request data
`ContentType`	Specifies the MIME type of the request being sent
`Credentials`	Specifies the network credentials needed when requesting files that require authentication
`Headers`	Specifies a collection of HTTP headers
`Method`	Determines the HTTP protocol method used for the request (for example, `GET`, `POST`, `HEAD`)
`PreAuthenticate`	Indicates whether to preauthenticate the request
`Proxy`	Sets the network proxy to use for the request
`RequestUri`	Gets the URI of the Internet resource associated with the request when overridden in a descendant class
`Timeout`	Sets the time-out value for the request

Table 4-19 Methods of the `WebRequest` Class

Method	Description	Syntax
`Abort`	Cancels a request in progress	–
`BeginGetRequestStream`	Provides an asynchronous version of the `GetRequestStream` method	`BeginGetRequestStream( ByVal` *`callback`* `As AsyncCallback, ByVal` *`state`* `As Object) As IAsyncResult`

Method	Description	Syntax
BeginGetResponse	Begins an asynchronous request for an Internet resource	BeginGetResponse(ByVal *callback* As AsyncCallback, ByVal *state* As Object) As IAsyncResult
Create	Initializes a new WebRequest object instance with the given URI scheme	Create(ByVal *requestUriString* As String) As WebRequest Create(ByVal *requestUri* As Uri) As WebRequest
CreateDefault	Initializes a new WebRequest object instance with the given URI scheme	CreateDefault(ByVal *requestUri* As Uri) As WebRequest
EndGetRequestStream	Returns a Stream object for writing data to the Internet connection	EndGetRequestStream (ByVal *asyncResult* As IAsyncResult) As Stream
EndGetResponse	Returns a WebResponse object	EndGetResponse(ByVal *asyncResult* As IAsyncResult) As WebResponse
GetRequestStream	Returns a Stream object for writing data to the Internet resource	GetRequestStream() As Stream
GetResponse	Returns a response to an Internet request	GetResponse() As WebResponse
RegisterPrefix	Registers a WebRequest descendant for the specified URI	RegisterPrefix(ByVal *prefix* As String, ByVal *creator* As IWebRequestCreate) As Boolean

Table 4-20 Properties of the `WebResponse` Class

Property	Description
`ContentLength`	The content length of the received data (in bytes)
`ContentType`	The MIME type of the data being received
`Headers`	The collection of HTTP header name–value pairs from the response
`ResponseUri`	The URI of the Internet resource that responded to the request

Table 4-21 Methods of the `WebResponse` Class

Method	Description	Syntax
`Close`	Closes the response stream	–
`GetResponseStream`	Returns the data stream (`System.IO.Stream` object) from the Internet resource	`GetResponseStream() As Stream`

Here's a sample program that allows the user to enter a URL, retrieve textual data like an HTML or text file from a Web server, and view that data in the console. The program demonstrates the use of the `WebRequest` and `WebResponse` classes.

Code Sample 4-17 Build instructions: `vbc /r:system.dll cs4-17.vb`

```
Imports System
Imports System.Net.Sockets
Imports System.Net
Imports System.IO
Imports System.Text

Module Module1

   Sub Main()
      Console.WriteLine("Enter a URL to retrieve:")
```

```
      GetDocument(Console.ReadLine())
   End Sub

   Public Sub GetDocument(ByVal URL As String)
      Try
         Dim objReq As WebRequest
         Dim objResult As WebResponse
         Dim objReceiveStream As Stream
         Dim bytData(1024) As Byte
         Dim intCount As Integer
         Dim intTotalBytes As Integer

80       objReq = WebRequest.Create(URL)
81       objResult = objReq.GetResponse()
82       objReceiveStream = objResult.GetResponseStream()

         intCount = objReceiveStream.Read(bytData, 0, 1024)
         intTotalBytes += intCount

         Do While intCount > 0
            ReDim Preserve bytData(bytData.Length + 1024)
            intCount = objReceiveStream.Read(bytData, _
                  intTotalBytes, 1024)
            intTotalBytes += intCount
         Loop

         ReDim Preserve bytData(intTotalBytes)
         Console.WriteLine(Encoding.ASCII.GetString(bytData))

      Catch E As Exception
         Console.WriteLine("ERROR: " & E.Message)
      End Try
   End Sub

End Module
```

We begin with formulating the request from a URL string. In line 80 we use the `Create()` method of the `WebRequest` class to perform the preliminary initialization of the request. This step prepares the program to obtain a handle to the response from the server. The `GetResponse()` method in line 81 returns a `WebResponse` object. `GetResponse()`also actually sends the HTTP request to the Web server. To get at the actual data, we obtain a `Stream` object in line 82. Finally, as in previous examples, we perform a chunked read of all the data, then convert the resulting data collected in the byte array to a `String` object to display to the console.

4.9 Manipulating XML Data (`System.XML`)

So much has been said lately about XML that it may soon become a household name. Rightfully so, because XML is the technology that drives efficient data exchanges, enables elegant modeling of data, and provides many advantages over other text-based flat-file formats. Plus, XML is platform independent, and XML parsers exist for many platforms and operating systems.

Since much of the .NET architecture is based on XML, it comes as no surprise that the .NET Framework has extensive support for manipulating XML data. The .NET Framework includes two different XML parsers: a tree-based parser and a stream-based parser. We'll discuss both of them in this chapter.

TECHTALK: DOCUMENT OBJECT MODEL STANDARD

The `XmlDocument` class and its associated classes implement the W3C Document Object Model (DOM) Level 1 Core and the DOM Level 2 Core standard. This standard consists of a definition of an API used to manipulate XML-based data structures. You can find information on the specification at the W3C's DOM Web site, *http://www.w3.org/DOM/DOMTR#dom1.*

Note: This text covers only a subset of the capabilities of the `System.XML` classes that support XML in the .NET Framework. Most of the material presented in the examples applies to DOM Level 1 Core functionality.

4.9.1 Creating Tree-Based XML Documents

Let's cover the tree-based DOM parser first. The tree-based XML parser reads an entire XML document into memory to construct a tree data structure representation of the XML text. This is a good way to manipulate relatively small amounts of XML data, and the operations execute quickly. You can create an XML document from scratch using the tree-based XML parser. For example, here is an XML document that represents catalog information for some songs.

Code Sample 4-18 Build instructions: vbc /r:system.dll /r:system.xml.dll cs4-18.vb

```
<Songs>
   <song format="MP3">
      <title>Eh Cumpari</title>
      <artist>Julius LaRosa</artist>
      <length>149</length>
      <category>Italian-American</category>
   </song>
   <song format="CD">
      <title>Plasticity</title>
      <artist>Front Line Assembly</artist>
      <length>406</length>
      <category>Industrial</category>
   </song>
</Songs>
```

This program creates the aforementioned XML document.

```
Imports System
Imports System.Xml

Module Module1

   Public Function CreateXMLDocument() As XmlDocument
83    Dim objXMLDOM As New XmlDocument()
84    objXMLDOM.AppendChild( _
            objXMLDOM.CreateElement("songs"))
      CreateXMLDocument = objXMLDOM
   End Function

   Public Function AddEntryToDoc(ByVal XMLDoc As XmlDocument, _
                ByVal SongFormat As String, _
                ByVal SongArtist As String, _
                ByVal SongTitle As String, _
                ByVal SongLength As String, _
                ByVal SongCategory As String) As XmlDocument

      Dim objRoot As XmlElement
      Dim objSong As XmlElement
      Dim objSongTitle As XmlElement
      Dim objSongArtist As XmlElement
      Dim objSongLength As XmlElement
```

```
      Dim objSongCategory As XmlElement
      Dim objTmpText As XmlText

85    objRoot = XMLDoc.DocumentElement

86    objSong = XMLDoc.CreateElement("song")
87    objSong.SetAttribute("format", SongFormat)

88    objSongTitle = XMLDoc.CreateElement("title")
89    objTmpText = XMLDoc.CreateTextNode(SongTitle)
90    objSongTitle.AppendChild(objTmpText)
91    objSong.AppendChild(objSongTitle)

      objSongArtist = XMLDoc.CreateElement("artist")
      objTmpText = XMLDoc.CreateTextNode(SongArtist)
      objSongArtist.AppendChild(objTmpText)
      objSong.AppendChild(objSongArtist)

      objSongLength = XMLDoc.CreateElement("length")
      objTmpText = XMLDoc.CreateTextNode(SongLength)
      objSongLength.AppendChild(objTmpText)
      objSong.AppendChild(objSongLength)

      objSongCategory = XMLDoc.CreateElement("category")
      objTmpText = XMLDoc.CreateTextNode(SongCategory)
      objSongCategory.AppendChild(objTmpText)
      objSong.AppendChild(objSongCategory)

92    objRoot.AppendChild(objSong)

      AddEntryToDoc = XMLDoc

   End Function

   Public Sub DisplayXMLDocument(ByVal XMLDoc As XmlDocument)
      Console.WriteLine(XMLDoc.InnerXml)
   End Sub

   Sub Main()
      Dim objSongXMLDoc As XmlDocument

      objSongXMLDoc = CreateXMLDocument()

      objSongXMLDoc = AddEntryToDoc(objSongXMLDoc, _
```

```
                        "MP3", _
                        "Julius LaRosa", _
                        "Eh Cumpari", _
                        "149", _
                        "Italian-American")

        objSongXMLDoc = AddEntryToDoc(objSongXMLDoc, _
                        "CD", _
                        "Front Line Assembly", _
                        "Plasticity", _
                        "406", _
                        "Industrial")

        DisplayXMLDocument(objSongXMLDoc)

    End Sub

End Module
```

Building a new XML document with the DOM begins with the creation of a new `XmlDocument` object, which is the responsibility of the `CreateXMLDocument()` function. This is the root of the document where we perform many different operations, such as creating elements, as shown in line (83). Moving on to line (84), we begin to assemble the top level of the XML document, the `<song>` node where all the song "records" (nodes) will be contained. Then the `XmlDocument` object is returned from the function.

Now the XML document is ready to accept entries. We first need to obtain an `XmlElement` from the root of the XML document using the `DocumentElement` property shown in line (85). We'll need this after we assemble all the elements of the `<song>` node for addition to the XML document.

Next we begin assembling a `<song>` node by creating the needed elements for song format, song title, artist, song length, and musical category. Each of these items is of the `XmlElement` type. To create a new element, we call the `CreateElement()` function of the `XmlDocument` class (specifying a name for the element), which returns an `XmlElement` object. Assembly of the `<song>` node begins in line (86) with the creation of an `XmlElement` with the name `"song"`. Since the `<song>` element has an attribute called `"format"`, we can add that by calling the `SetAttribute()` method of the `XmlElement` class in line (87) and supplying the value for the attribute.

Now that we've established the empty `<song>` node, we can create nested elements for the song's catalog information. Again, we start by creating a new

`XmlElement` object in line ❽❽, this time for the song's title. The song's title will be contained within the `<title></title>` tags. This text is represented in the XML DOM as an `XmlText` object. We create a new instance of this object in line ❽❾ by using the `CreateTextNode()` method of `XmlDocument` and specifying the text as the parameter. Now that we have the `XmlElement` object representing the song title and its associated element text, we need to add it to the document structure. The `AppendChild()` method shown in line ❾⓿ attaches an existing `XmlNode` (`XmlElement` derives from `XmlNode`) to another `XmlElement` or `XmlNode`. The `AppendChild()` method associates the `XmlText` object, which contains the song title text, to the `<title>` `XmlElement`, then the code in line ❾❶ adds the complete `<title>` `XmlElement` to the `<song>` node, represented by `objSong`. This procedure repeats for the artist, song length, and musical category. Once we have all the child elements in place for the `<song>` node, it is added to the root `DocumentElement` `objRoot` in line ❾❷. Then the updated XML document is returned from the function, and the results are displayed to the console using the `InnerXml` property.

The properties and methods of the `XmlDocument`, `XmlElement`, and `XmlText` classes used in this example are outlined in Appendix A.

4.9.2 Loading and Searching Tree-Based XML Documents

The last example showed how to programmatically create an XML document from scratch by starting with a newly initialized `XmlDocument` object. While this is useful for many applications, such as data conversions from flat files to XML (the song information could have originated from a flat-file database), in some situations you'll have to work in the opposite direction: starting with an existing XML document, then reading, searching, and updating its information and saving it back to a file. In this section, we'll explore how to accomplish those tasks by using methods of the `XmlDocument` class.

Reading XML Data without Validation

Reading in XML data is accomplished by using two different methods of the `XmlDocument` object: `Load()` or `LoadXML()`. The `LoadXML()` method loads XML data into an `XmlDocument` object from a string but performs no validation of the data against a Document Type Definition (DTD) or schema. `Load()` reads the XML data from a file. If you wish to validate the data you load against a DTD, you should use the `Load()` method (in conjunction with the `XmlValidatingReader` and `XmlTextReader` classes, which are discussed below in "Reading XML Data with Validation"). The examples in this section use the `Load()` method to process XML data.

Let's look at a quick example of reading an XML file into an XmlDocument object. This example doesn't attempt to validate the data against a DTD; it just takes in a well-formed XML data file. (A *well-formed* XML document is one that adheres to a minimum set of rules so that it can be understood by a parser. This is different than a *valid* XML document, in which the data contained within the XML file is validated against rules outlined in a DTD.)

The sample program uses the Load() method to read in the same XML data file used in Section 4.9.1. (Note that the songs file is a well-formed XML document.) The program then visits each node in the XML document and displays it to the console.

Code Sample 4-19 Build Instructions: vbc /r:system.dll /r:system.xml.dll cs4-19.vb

```
Imports System
Imports System.Xml

Module Module1

   Public Sub DisplayNode(ByVal Nodes As XmlNodeList)

      Dim objNode As XmlNode

      For Each objNode In Nodes
93       If objNode.NodeType = XmlNodeType.Text Then
            Console.WriteLine( _
               objNode.ParentNode.Name & _
               ControlChars.Tab & _
               ControlChars.Tab & _
               objNode.Value)
         End If
94          If objNode.HasChildNodes Then
            DisplayNode(objNode.ChildNodes)
         End If
      Next

   End Sub

   Sub Main()

      Dim objXMLDoc As New XmlDocument()

      Try
```

```
95          objXMLDoc.Load("songs.xml")
96          DisplayNode(objXMLDoc.ChildNodes)
      Catch E As Exception
         Console.WriteLine("ERROR: " & E.Message)
      End Try

   End Sub

End Module
```

Inside the `DisplayNode()` function, we use a `For . . . Each` loop to iterate through each node in the `Nodes` `XmlNodeList` object. For purposes of displaying data, we are interested only in text nodes, which we test for using the `NodeType` property in line 93. If the current node is a text node, we display the name of the node using the `ParentNode` property. The `Value` property returns the text of the node.

An XML document is hierarchical in nature, so it follows that a recursive algorithm should be used to traverse the document. Line 95 uses the `Load()` method to read in the data from the songs file. Then we make the initial call to the `DisplayNode()` function in line 96. This will display the nodes contained in the `ChildNodes` property (an `XmlNodeList`). `ChildNodes`, in this initial call, represents the outermost nodes of the document. If the node contains children (see line 94), we recursively call `DisplayNode()`. This process continues until all nodes in the XML document are visited.

Reading XML Data with Validation

Let's look at a slightly modified example of reading in an XML document, this time validating the XML data against a DTD. The sample below shows the previous XML file of songs with a new DTD section in boldface type that describes the valid data characteristics allowed for the XML file.

```
<?xml version="1.0" encoding="UTF-8"?>
<!DOCTYPE Songs [
   <!ELEMENT Songs (song*)>
   <!ELEMENT artist (#PCDATA)>
   <!ELEMENT category (#PCDATA)>
   <!ELEMENT length (#PCDATA)>
   <!ELEMENT song (title, artist, length, category)>
   <!ATTLIST song
   format (MP3 | LP | CS | CD) #REQUIRED>
   <!ELEMENT title (#PCDATA)>
```

```
]>
<Songs>
   <song format="MP3">
      <title>Eh Cumpari</title>
      <artist>Julius LaRosa</artist>
      <length>149</length>
      <category>Italian-American</category>
   </song>
   <song format="CD">
      <title>Plasticity</title>
      <artist>Front Line Assembly</artist>
      <length>406</length>
      <category>Industrial</category>
   </song>
</Songs>
```

> **TIP:** You don't have to include your DTD and XML in the same file. This example does so for simplicity's sake, but you can specify an external reference to a DTD by substituting this line in place of the inline DTD:
>
> ```
> <!DOCTYPE Songs SYSTEM "your_dtd_file.dtd">
> ```

The DTD allows for any number of song entries and imposes a rule that the format attribute for `<song>` elements must be one of the following: `MP3`, `LP`, `CS`, or `CD`.

The code for reading in an XML document with validation remains much the same as that for no validation, except for how we load the XML file. In the `Main()` subroutine, we change some of the code that loads the XML document, as indicated by the boldface text below.

Code Sample 4-20 Build instructions: vbc /r:system.dll /r:system.xml.dll cs4-20.vb

```
Sub Main()

   Dim objXMLDoc As New XmlDocument()
   Dim objXmlValidatingReader As XmlValidatingReader
   Dim objXmlTextReader As New XmlTextReader("songs2.xml")

   Try
```

```
            objXmlValidatingReader = New _
                XmlValidatingReader(objXmlTextReader)
            objXMLDoc.Load(objXmlValidatingReader)
            DisplayNode(objXMLDoc.ChildNodes)
        Catch E As Exception
            Console.WriteLine("ERROR: " & E.Message)
        End Try

    End Sub
```

Loading validated XML data into an `XmlDocument` object starts with the `XmlTextReader` class. This class is normally used for reading XML data in a stream-based mechanism (see Section 4.9.3), but we are using it to create an `XmlTextReader` object for the constructor of the `XmlValidatingReader` class. Now, instead of passing a file name to the `Load()` method of the `XmlDocument` object, we give `Load()` the `XmlValidatingReader` object that we created. When `Load()` is called, if any errors are found during validation of the XML data, an exception is thrown citing in what line numbers and column numbers the validation errors occurred. In this example, an invalid option was selected for the `format` attribute and the program output this error message (you'll have to modify the XML file and put in an invalid `format` attribute value for an error to be generated):

```
ERROR: The 'format' attribute has an invalid value according to its
  data type.
An error occurred at file:///c:/songs2.xml(13, 8).
```

Searching XML Nodes

How do you locate a particular node in the XML tree? You can use the `SelectNodes()` and `SelectSingleNode()` methods of the `XmlNode` class (which `XmlDocument` inherits) to perform a search and return an `XmlNode` or `XmlNodeList` object that contains the items that matched the query. The query is expressed in a language called XPath, another W3C standard for searching the XML DOM.

> **TECHTALK: XPATH**
> XPath is rather complicated, and discussion of it is really beyond the scope of this book. But you can find all the information you need to know about XPath at *http://www.w3.org/TR/xpath*.

Let's use the previous XML data file of songs and perform a search. The loading code remains the same as the previous example. The new function, `SearchArtist()`, finds all songs matching a specified artist and displays the node contents for each match of the query.

Code Sample 4-21 Build instructions: vbc /r:system.dll /r:system.xml.dll cs4-21.vb

```
Imports System
Imports System.Xml

Module Module1

   Public Sub SearchArtist(ByVal Artist As String, _
                           ByVal XmlDoc As XmlDocument)

      Dim objNodeList As XmlNodeList
      Dim objMatch As XmlNode

      objNodeList = XmlDoc.SelectNodes( _
              "descendant::song[artist='" & Artist & "']")

      For Each objMatch In objNodeList
         Console.WriteLine(objMatch.InnerText)
      Next

   End Sub

   Sub Main()

      Dim objXMLDoc As New XmlDocument()
      Dim objXmlValidatingReader As XmlValidatingReader
      Dim objXmlTextReader As New XmlTextReader("c:\s.xml")

      Try

         objXmlValidatingReader = New _
                 XmlValidatingReader(objXmlTextReader)
         objXMLDoc.Load(objXmlValidatingReader)

         SearchArtist("Front Line Assembly", objXMLDoc)

      Catch E As Exception
         Console.WriteLine("ERROR: " & E.Message)
```

```
      End Try

   End Sub

End Module
```

The boldface code shows the use of the `SelectNodes()` method. The parameter we passed to it is the XPath query string. This query says to return all the nodes that contain an `<artist>` element with the text passed into the function as a parameter. Then we display a string representation of the matching node data using the `InnerText` property of every node in the returned `XmlNodeList`.

`SelectSingleNode()` works the same way, but it's used for returning only one `XmlNode`. Use `SelectSingleNode()` when your query should return only one `XmlNode`.

4.9.3 Reading Stream-Based XML Data

There is an obvious disadvantage to working with XML data using the tree-based DOM method: the entire XML file is read into the DOM memory structure at once. This takes a lot of memory, plus the processing expense of parsing all that data, which also occurs all at once. When dealing with large XML files that contain many records, a more efficient method is required—a stream-based mechanism.

The `XmlTextReader` class is the mechanism used for reading XML data in a stream-based fashion. There are many properties and methods to this class; they are outlined in tables in Appendix A.

The following example demonstrates how to read XML data in a stream-based fashion.

Code Sample 4-22 Build instructions: vbc `/r:system.dll /r:system.xml.dll cs4-22.vb`

```
Imports System
Imports System.Xml

Module Module1

   Sub Main()
      Dim objReader As XmlTextReader = Nothing
```

```
        Try

97          objReader = New XmlTextReader("songs.xml")

98          While objReader.Read()
99              Select Case objReader.NodeType
                    Case XmlNodeType.Element
                        Console.WriteLine("<{0}>", _
                                objReader.Name)
                    Case XmlNodeType.Text
                        Console.WriteLine(objReader.Value)
                    Case XmlNodeType.XmlDeclaration
                        Console.WriteLine( _
                            "<?xml version='1.0'?>")
                    Case XmlNodeType.EndElement
                        Console.WriteLine("</{0}>", _
                                objReader.Name)
                End Select
            End While

        Finally
            If Not (objReader Is Nothing) Then
100                 objReader.Close()
            End If
        End Try

    End Sub

End Module
```

The example begins with creating a new `XmlTextReader` object in line 97. Its constructor is the path to an XML file to load. Data read from an XML file using stream-based methods (like that of the `XmlTextReader` class) read the file node by node. The sample program reads the entire file, so we construct a `While` loop beginning in line 98 to read in each node until the end of the stream is reached.

Many XML files contain different types of nodes. A typical XML file contains nodes such as document declarations (for example, `"<?xml version='1.0'?>"`), text nodes, beginning and ending element nodes, entity references, and so on. Each of these types of nodes can be identified using the `NodeType` property of the `XmlTextReader` class. Using that code in line 99 gives the type of the current node in the stream. The example uses a

`Select . . . Case` block to format the value of the node for display to the console. At the end of the loop, the program checks to see if all nodes have been read from the stream by checking whether the `XmlTextReader` class contains a null reference (`Nothing`). If so, the program closes the stream (see line 100).

4.9.4 Writing Stream-Based XML Data

Just as you can read an XML file using a forward-only, stream-based method, you can also write XML data in a similar manner using the `XmlTextWriter` class. Tables in Appendix A describe the `XmlTextWriter` class properties and methods.

The following code shows a typical use of the `XmlTextWriter` class. Like the earlier example that generates an XML document using the tree-based DOM mechanism, this example writes XML data.

Code Sample 4-23 Build instructions: `vbc /r:system.dll /r:system.xml.dll cs4-23.vb`

```
Sub XmlWriteDemo()
      Dim writer As New _
(101)             XmlTextWriter("sample.xml", Nothing)

(102) writer.Formatting = Formatting.Indented

(103) writer.WriteComment("Stream-XML Write demo")

(104) writer.WriteStartElement("Songs")

(105) writer.WriteStartElement("song")

(106) writer.WriteStartAttribute("", "format", "")
(107) writer.WriteString("MP3")
(108) writer.WriteEndAttribute()

      writer.WriteStartElement("title")
      writer.WriteString("Plasticity")
      writer.WriteEndElement()

      writer.WriteStartElement("artist")
      writer.WriteString("Front Line Assembly")
      writer.WriteEndElement()
```

```
        writer.WriteStartElement("category")
        writer.WriteString("Industrial")
        writer.WriteEndElement()

        writer.WriteStartElement("length")
        writer.WriteString("406")
        writer.WriteEndElement()


        writer.WriteEndElement()

109     writer.WriteEndElement()

        writer.Flush()
        writer.Close()

        Dim doc As New XmlDocument()

        doc.PreserveWhitespace = True
        doc.Load("sample.xml")

        Console.Write(doc.InnerXml)
End Sub
```

The function begins with creating a new `XmlTextWriter` object in line 101, supplying a new file to contain the output. When XML data is routed around networks or contained in persistent storage, it is normally stripped of any insignificant white space. This is, of course, to save storage space, but it has the unfortunate side effect of making the XML text less readable. The default behavior of the `XmlTextWriter` class is to not include any of this white space. This behavior can be changed by setting the `Formatting` property as shown in line 102. This causes XML nodes to be prefixed with indentation to reflect their relative positions in the hierarchy.

We may now begin writing XML nodes to the document. First we write a comment block to the file with the `WriteComment()` method in line 103. Note that the `WriteComment()` method automatically adds the proper formatting (the <!-- --> notation). Moving on, we create the root element for our songs XML file by beginning a node with the `WriteStartElement()` method. It's important to remember that each call to this method must be balanced with a call to the `WriteEndElement()` method. These two calls close off any elements contained within the outermost `WriteStartElement()` and

WriteEndElement() calls. In our example, the <Songs> node is started in line 104 and closed off in line 111.

Each song record in the XML file (we create one song record in this example) begins with a song element, as shown in line 105. The song element has an attribute attached to it, which is the song format. Like the beginning and ending WriteStartElement() and WriteEndElement() methods, we use the WriteStartAttribute() method in line 106 and the WriteEndAttribute() method in line 108 to write an attribute. The text of the attribute is added with a call to the WriteString() method in line 107, which outputs the value of the attribute. Each element for a song (title, artist, and so on) is written using a combination of WriteStartElement(), WriteString(), and WriteEndElement() lines.

This function produces the following output.

```
<!--Stream-XML Write demo-->
<Songs>
   <song format="MP3">
      <title>Plasticity</title>
      <artist>Front Line Assembly</artist>
      <category>Industrial</category>
      <length>406</length>
   </song>
</Songs>
```

4.9.5 Formatting XML Data for Display

XML is great for representing structured data, but by itself it can't be displayed to the user in any meaningful way. XML is human-readable, but typically only by one breed of human—programmers! It would be useful to transform XML data into a more convenient format for display (such as HTML). You can accomplish this by using XSLT (Extensible Stylesheet Transformation) and the XslTransform class.

Here's a small program to demonstrate.

Code Sample 4-24 Build instructions: vbc /r:system.dll /r:system.xml.dll cs4-24.vb

```
Imports System
Imports System.Xml
Imports System.Xml.Xsl

Module Module1
```

```
   Sub Main()
      Dim objXSLT As New XslTransform()

      Try
(110)    objXSLT.Load("songs.xsl")
(111)    objXSLT.Transform("c:\songs.xml", _
                 "songs.htm")
      Catch E As Exception
         Console.WriteLine("ERROR: " & E.Message)
      End Try

   End Sub

End Module
```

In line (110), we load the following XSL file.

```
<?xml version="1.0" encoding="UTF-8"?>
<xsl:stylesheet version="1.0"
xmlns:xsl="http://www.w3.org/1999/XSL/Transform"
xmlns:fo="http://www.w3.org/1999/XSL/Format">
<xsl:template match="/">

<html>
<head>
<title>XslTransform Example</title>
</head>
<body>
<h1>List of Songs</h1>
<table border="1">
<tr>
   <td><b>Title</b></td>
   <td><b>Artist</b></td>
   <td><b>Length</b></td>
   <td><b>Category</b></td>
</tr>

<xsl:for-each select="//Songs/song">
<tr>
   <td><xsl:value-of select="title"/></td>
   <td><xsl:value-of select="artist"/></td>
   <td><xsl:value-of select="length"/></td>
   <td><xsl:value-of select="category"/></td>
```

```
</tr>
</xsl:for-each>
</table>
</body>
</html>
</xsl:template>
</xsl:stylesheet>
```

With one call to the `Transform()` method in line (111), we transform the following XML source file into HTML.

```
<Songs>
   <song format="MP3">
      <title>Eh Cumpari</title>
      <artist>Julius LaRosa</artist>
      <length>149</length>
      <category>Italian-American</category>
   </song>
   <song format="CD">
      <title>Plasticity</title>
      <artist>Front Line Assembly</artist>
      <length>406</length>
      <category>Industrial</category>
   </song>
</Songs>
```

Here's the HTML that results from using the `Transform()` method on the preceding XML file.

```
<html xmlns:fo="http://www.w3.org/1999/XSL/Format">
   <head>
      <META http-equiv="Content-Type"
   content="text/html; charset=utf-8">
      <title>XslTransform Example</title>
   </head>
   <body>
      <h1>List of Songs</h1>
      <table border="1">
         <tr>
            <td>
               <b>Title</b>
            </td>
            <td>
               <b>Artist</b>
```

```
                </td>
                <td>
                    <b>Length</b>
                </td>
                <td>
                    <b>Category</b>
                </td>
            </tr>
            <tr>
                <td>Eh Cumpari</td>
                <td>Julius LaRosa</td>
                <td>149</td>
                <td>Italian-American</td>
            </tr>
            <tr>
                <td>Plasticity</td>
                <td>Front Line Assembly</td>
                <td>406</td>
                <td>Industrial</td>
            </tr>
        </table>
    </body>
</html>
```

Tables in Appendix A give the breakdown of the `XslTransform` class.

4.10 Sending Internet E-mail (System.Web.Mail)

E-mail functionality is easy to include in your .NET Framework applications. The `System.Web.Mail` namespace offers classes that support Internet e-mail messages using the Simple Mail Transfer Protocol (SMTP). You can send e-mail messages in plain text or HTML format and can include file attachments.

The SMTP functionality included in the `System.Web.Mail` namespace requires an available SMTP server. This server must grant appropriate permission to the sender of the e-mail for the message to be properly routed to its destination. The server can include any host on your LAN or on the Internet. You can also use the SMTP server included with IIS 5.0.

The `System.Web.Mail` namespace has three classes that provide all the SMTP functionality you need to send messages: the `SmtpMail`, `MailMessage`, and `MailAttachment` classes. Details about these classes are shown in Tables 4-22 through 4-25. (Note that the `MailMessage` and `MailAttachment` classes have no methods.)

Table 4-22 Property of the `SmtpMail` Class

Property	Description
`SmtpServer`	The hostname of the SMTP server to use. If omitted, the IIS 5.0 SMTP service running on the local machine is used.

Table 4-23 Method of the `SmtpMail` Class

Method	Description	Syntax

`Send`	Sends a mail message using a preassembled `MailMessage` object or a text message with contents specified in the parameters	`Send(ByVal` *`message`* `As MailMessage)`
		
		`Send(ByVal` *`from`* `As String, ByVal` *`to`* `As String, ByVal` *`subject`* `As String, ByVal` *`messageText`* `As String)`

Table 4-24 Properties of the `MailMessage` Class

Property	Description
`Attachments`	A collection (`IList`) of `MailAttachment` objects representing attachments to send with the e-mail message
`Bcc`	A semicolon-delimited list of e-mail addresses that receive a blind carbon copy (BCC) of the e-mail message
`Body`	The body of the e-mail message
`BodyEncoding`	The encoding type of the e-mail body
`BodyFormat`	The content type of the e-mail body: either `MailFormat.Text` or `MailFormat.HTML`
`Cc`	A semicolon-delimited list of e-mail addresses that receive a carbon copy (CC) of the e-mail message
`From`	The e-mail address of the sender

Property	Description
`Headers`	Custom headers to send along with the message
`Priority`	The priority of the e-mail message: `MailPriority.High`, `MailPriority.Low`, or `MailPriority.Normal`
`Subject`	The subject line of the e-mail message
`To`	The e-mail address of the recipient
`UrlContentBase`	The base URL to use for all relative links included in the body of the e-mail message
`UrlContentLocation`	Gets or sets the Content-Location HTTP header for the e-mail message.

Table 4-25 Properties of the `MailAttachment` Class

Property	Description
`Encoding`	The encoding used to encode the e-mail attachment: either `MailEncoding.Base64` or `MailEncoding.UUEncode`
`Filename`	The pathname to the file attachment

Let's move right to a code sample.

Code Sample 4-25 Build instructions: `vbc /r:system.dll /r:system.web.dll cs4-25.vb`

```
Imports System
Imports System.Web.Mail

Module Module1

   Sub Main()

112      Dim objMsg As New MailMessage()
         Dim objAttachment As New _
113                  MailAttachment("c:\samples\mountain.jpg")
```

```
      Try
114          objMsg.To = "someuser@somehost.com"
115          objMsg.From = "vbdotnet@yourorghere.org"
116          objMsg.Priority = MailPriority.High
         objMsg.Subject = _
            ".NET Framework Mail Demonstration"
117          objMsg.BodyFormat = MailFormat.Html
         objMsg.Body = _
            "<h1>.NET Framework Mail Demo</h1>" & _
            "This mail contains an attachment"

118          objMsg.Attachments.Add(objAttachment)

119          SmtpMail.Send(objMsg)

      Catch E As Exception
         Console.WriteLine("ERROR: " & E.Message)
      End Try

   End Sub

End Module
```

This sample assumes that we will use the local SMTP server that IIS 5.0 provides. In line 112 we create a new `MailMessage` object, which will contain addressing information and the message content. Next we create a `MailAttachment` object. In line 113 we specify the path to a file to attach to the message.

> **WARNING:** This code works only on Windows NT, 2000, or XP. Also make sure the file name for the attachment points to an existing file or the message will not be sent.

Now we're ready to set up the message for delivery. Lines 114 and 115 show how to set the e-mail addresses of the recipient and the sender, respectively. Line 116 shows setting the high-priority flag of the message so that compatible e-mail clients can display a special visual indicator to highlight important messages. This particular message will be sent in HTML format, so we specify this in line 117, followed by an HTML string that represents the content of the message. Next we append the `MailAttachment` object to the `Attachments` collection in line 118. The message is sent in line 119 by using the `Send()` method of the static class `SmtpMail` and passing it the `objMsg` object we constructed.

4.11 Summary

We covered a lot of ground in this tour of the .NET Framework Class Library. In spite of all the material presented, we've only scratched the surface of this massive code library. Nonetheless, you learned about several things in this chapter:

- The benefits of using preexisting code
- The different varieties of collections (`System.Collections`); array lists (dynamic arrays), stacks (first-in-first-out lists), queues (first-in-last-out lists), and hashtables (parallel arrays)
- Streams, buffered input/output, and various operations with files and directories
- The `FileSystemWatcher` object, which provides a convenient way to monitor changes to a directory's contents
- The Windows Event Log
- Active Directory Services and LDAP
- Message queues and asynchronous messaging
- Internet-based network communication
- XML and DOM

As a result, after working through this chapter you've learned how to:

- Write applications using a common set of functions
- Handle file I/O using text and binary files
- Perform directory operations
- Write messages to the Windows Event Log for diagnostic purposes
- Work with Active Directory Services by using classes in the `System.DirectoryServices` namespace
- Query information stores on a local computer
- Create and use message queues
- Use sockets as well as high-level HTTP communication

- Create XML documents using DOM as well as stream-based methods
- Locate nodes and transform an XML document to HTML using XSLT
- Send Internet e-mail using the `System.Web.Mail` classes

4.12 What's Ahead

In Chapter 5 we'll start creating components, which are reusable units of code. We'll also talk more about the Common Language Runtime and explain assemblies. In Chapter 6 we'll dive into Web Services, which are considered the most important part of the .NET Framework.

Further Reading

- The .NET Framework SDK documentation (*http://msdn.microsoft.com/library*): This is (at the time of this writing) the best location to turn to for reference material on the entire .NET Framework Class Library.
- *XML—The Microsoft Way* by Peter Aitken: This book is an excellent reference for XML as it relates to the Microsoft platform.

CHAPTER 5

Building .NET Managed Components for COM+

Modern software systems are component-based. Components make large, enterprise-wide software systems easier to manage since system functionality is divided among several components. VB.NET and all other .NET-supported languages have the ability to create these components, which can be used and reused in a variety of projects, including (but not limited to) ASP.NET projects, Windows applications, and unmanaged code (which is code that executes outside the .NET Framework).

This chapter covers the following topics:

- Managed code (the code that runs on the .NET Framework) and runtime environments
- The Common Language Runtime and its role in the .NET Framework
- Just-in-time compilation of managed code
- Code assemblies
- COM+ Component Services and its role in the .NET Framework
- Creation of managed components using VB.NET
- Serviced components, which take advantage of the services provided by COM+ Component Services

5.1 The Concept of Managed Code Execution

Before we get into making .NET components, we need to discuss a .NET concept called *managed code*. Managed code is any source code you compile that targets the .NET Framework. All the code we've examined so far in this book (ASP.NET, console applications, and so on) has been managed code.

The .NET Framework is a runtime environment in which code executes. Internal tasks, such as allocating and freeing memory, and software services (like the kinds discussed in Chapter 4) are handled by the .NET Framework as well. In general terms, a runtime environment enables user programs to take advantage of services provided by the host operating system. A runtime environment also supplies a layer of abstraction between user code and those services, through either an API or some other type of interface. Almost any program you write, regardless of the platform or language, involves interaction with a runtime environment. (An exception to this are programs written in assembly language, in which case the programmer is calling on the services of the microprocessor and memory storage in a direct, low-level fashion.)

Many programs written for the Windows platform use the C++ programming language and its runtime library. Before other languages and development systems became available, this was the only choice for developers making applications for Windows. The C/C++ runtime code shipped as a part of Windows as a series of dynamic link libraries (known as DLLs or `.dll` files). As a result, many Windows applications could be distributed with as little as one file, the `.exe` file that contained the main program code. Since no other files were required, many developers referred to these types of applications as *native code applications* since the preinstalled runtime code was quite small.

As new languages became available for developing Windows applications, new runtime environments needed to be developed. VB developers using version 6.0 or earlier might be aware of special support files that must be installed on the deployment computer in order for VB applications to run. These `.dll` files make up the VB runtime environment. Like the C/C++ runtime code mentioned above, it provides a code wrapper around operating system internals and services.

Some runtime environments provide an additional layer of abstraction over another existing runtime environment. This creates an execution environment that can exist on multiple platforms. Programs targeted to such a runtime don't compile to machine object code. Instead, they compile to another language, referred to as an *intermediate language*. The runtime then executes this intermediate language using an engine built for a particular operating system. The most popular type of intermediate language system is Java. The intermediate language for Java is referred to as *bytecode*. The .NET Framework works in a similar manner. Compiled Microsoft .NET code is referred to as *Microsoft Intermediate Language* (MSIL).

5.2 The Common Language Runtime

The runtime environment for the .NET Framework is called the *Common Language Runtime* (CLR). Managed code execution happens inside the CLR space. The goal of the CLR is to provide an environment that includes language integration, exception handling, security, versioning, deployment, debugging, profiling, and component interaction. Most importantly, all of these features need cross-language support. In other words, all the features mentioned must work in the same manner regardless of the language used.

Metadata makes cross-language integration possible. When you compile .NET managed code, the metadata gets stored along with the object code. Metadata describes to the CLR various types of information (for example, data types, members, and references) used in the code. This data is used by the CLR to "manage" the code execution by providing such services as memory allocation, method invocation, and security enforcement. It also eases deployment since references to other objects are included along with metadata. This ensures that your application contains all up-to-date versions of all dependent components.

5.2.1 The Common Type System

Along with providing information about managed code through metadata, the CLR implements a series of data types that are cross-language compatible. That system of data types is known as the Common Type System (CTS). CTS data types include simple value types, classes, enumerated value types, interfaces, and delegates.

Simple value data types include primitive types as well as user-defined types. Primitive types include integers, Boolean values, and strings. These types are included in the `System` namespace. The data types used thus far in the VB.NET programs in this book are also included in this namespace. When you use these primitive types in your programs, the language you use may already have an equivalent native data type that corresponds to a .NET Framework type. Table 5-1 shows some data types and their VB.NET native language equivalents.

Occasionally you may want to define your own data types. You can do this by using the native features of the language with which you're working. If you're using VB.NET, you can use the `Structure` statement to define a structure. This custom type needs to be type-safe for the CLR, so it's no coincidence that it inherits from the `ValueType` .NET class.

Table 5-1 Primitive Data Types and VB.NET Equivalents

.NET Data Type Class Name (`System` Namespace)	VB.NET Data Type
`Byte`	`Byte`
`SByte`	*Not supported*
`Int16`	`Short`
`Int32`	`Integer`
`Int64`	`Long`
`UInt16`	*Not supported*
`UInt32`	*Not supported*
`UInt64`	*Not supported*
`Single`	`Single`
`Double`	`Double`
`Object`	`Object`
`Char`	`Char`
`String`	`String`
`Decimal`	`Decimal`
`Boolean`	`Boolean`

TECHTALK: STRUCTURES AND CLASSES

Structures and classes are quite similar. They both have members, constructors, events, properties, fields, and constants. They can both implement interfaces as well.

There are some differences. Structures don't allow for inheritance; therefore they are referred to as *sealed*.

> Structures can't have any constructor code, that is, you can't define an overloaded New() subroutine with your own initialization code like you can with a class.
>
> When structures are used in procedure calls, the structure is passed by value (like primitive data types are). Classes, on the other hand, are always passed by reference. Whether to use classes or structures for your user-defined data types depends mostly on the complexity of your data types. Structures are useful for defining relatively simple data types for which the members do not use much memory and no custom initialization code is required. If your design requires more than this, consider defining your custom data type as a class.

Let's quickly look at a VB.NET structure definition. Structure definitions are placed outside of procedure definitions. You can define them at the module level, as shown below.

Code Sample 5-1 Build instructions: vbc /r:system.dll cs5-01.vb

```
Module Module1

❶ Structure Student
    Dim FirstName As String
    Dim LastName As String
    Dim SSN As String
    Dim ClassRank As Integer
  End Structure

  Sub Main()

    Dim udtStudent As New Student()

❷   With udtStudent
      .FirstName = "Matt"
      .LastName = "Crouch"
      .SSN = "888-88-1234"
      .ClassRank = 2
    End With
```

```
    End Sub

End Module
```

The example shows a typical structure definition. The members are enclosed in the `Structure . . . End Structure` block that begins in line ❶. The VB.NET `With . . . End With` statement in line ❷ is used to save some typing. It allows you to refer to the individual members of the structure without fully qualifying the names of the structure members.

Since the VB.NET structures you define automatically inherit from `System.ValueType`, you can treat the value type as a `ValueType` object. As a demonstration, let's create a function that lists all the members of an arbitrary structure at runtime.

Code Sample 5-2 Build instructions: vbc /r:system.dll cs5-02.vb

```
Public Sub ValueTypeDemoFunction(ByVal udt As ValueType)

   Dim mi() As MemberInfo
   Dim srmMemberInfo As MemberInfo

   Dim typTmp As Type
❸  typTmp = udt.GetType(udt.ToString())
❹  mi = typTmp.GetMembers()

   Console.WriteLine("Value Type Information" & _
                     Chr(13) & Chr(10))

   For Each srmMemberInfo In mi
     Console.WriteLine(srmMemberInfo.Name)
   Next

End Sub
```

The function `ValueTypeDemoFunction()` takes a `ValueType` object as its parameter. Thus we can pass a VB.NET structure to this function. The `GetType()` function in line ❸, which is a member of the `System.Object` namespace, returns a `System.Type` object. We use the returned `System.Type` object in line ❹ to get the member names (an array of `System.Reflection.MemberInfo` objects).

If we modify Code Sample 5-1 to add a call to `ValueTypeDemoFunction()` as shown below in boldface text, we'll obtain output similar to Figure 5-1.

```
Sub Main()

   Dim udtStudent As New Student()

   With udtStudent
     .FirstName = "Matt"
     .LastName = "Crouch"
     .SSN = "888-88-1234"
     .ClassRank = 2
   End With

   ValueTypeDemoFunction(udtStudent)

End Sub
```

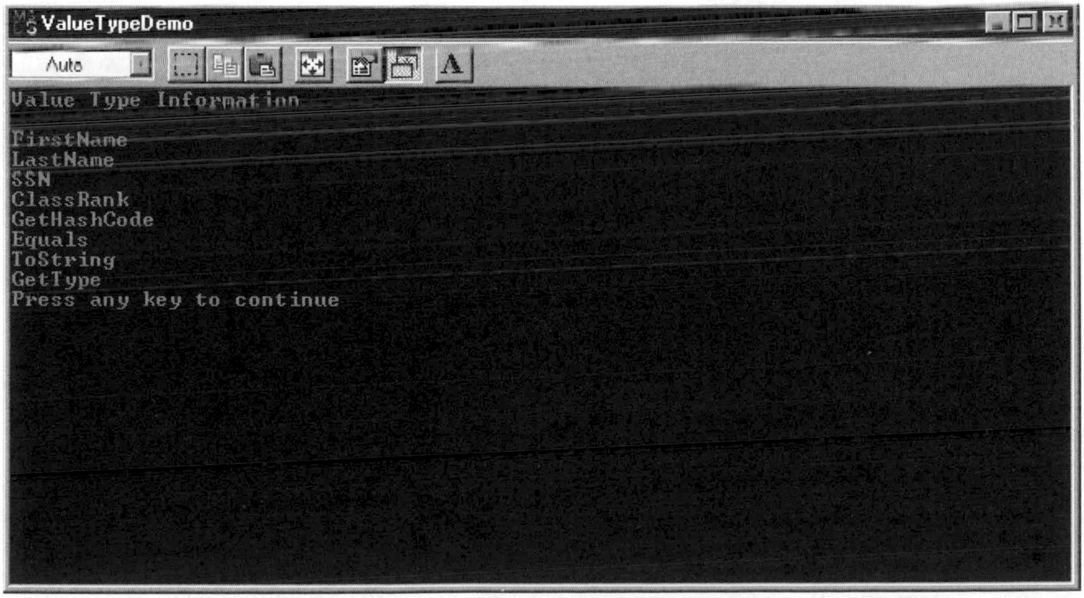

Figure 5-1 Output of the ValueType example

5.2.2 Just-in-Time Code Compilation

Managed code cannot be executed directly by the CPU. It must be converted to native executable code before running. Just-in-time (JIT) compilation compiles MSIL code right at the moment it is needed. Optimizations exist in the JIT compiler to ensure that only code planned for execution gets compiled. The JIT compiler also performs security checks and verifies type-safety.

5.2.3 Code Assemblies

I've mentioned the topic of component-based system architectures before, and now it's time to introduce the .NET Framework concept of this idea. The component (that is, the unit of reuse) in the .NET Framework is the *assembly*. An assembly is a collection of files, typically `.dll` files and any others relating to the assembly, such as resource files. The assembly *manifest* contains metadata relating to version information, security attributes, and external code references. It also contains information on how the pieces in the assembly relate to each other. The assembly manifest, therefore, constructs a logical DLL around the assembly elements.

5.2.4 Application Domains

Modern software systems run applications that are isolated from the internal execution of the operating system and other programs. The reason for this is to protect the operating system from crashing if the application attempts to access memory being used by another application. Another situation that could cause a crash is an internal error in the application that causes the operating system to crash. Fortunately, all versions of Windows offer process protection to prevent this problem. Each application running under Windows has its own memory space, and memory used by other running applications is not visible from any other application.

The .NET Framework extends the capabilities of protected process spaces by building this functionality into the CLR. These protected spaces are known as *application domains*. In addition to the fault tolerance that process isolation provides, application domains can enforce security policies, thereby granting or denying users and groups the right to run the application. Application domains also consume fewer system resources than traditional Windows processes because they can provide fault tolerance by taking advantage of the inherit type-safety of the .NET Framework code.

5.3 COM+ Component Services

The .NET Framework leverages many existing Windows services to make it a more robust application environment. A particular technology that deserves attention is COM+ Component Services. These technologies were the predecessors to the .NET Framework. To see how COM+ Component Services fits into the .NET Framework arena, let's explore a little about these technologies.

5.3.1 Overview of COM

The Component Object Model (COM) was designed to address the shortcomings of conventional object-oriented languages like C++ and traditional binary software distribution of code. COM is about not a particular type of software but rather a philosophy of programming. This philosophy is manifested in the COM specification. The specification explicitly states how a COM object should be constructed and what behaviors it should have.

COM objects are roughly equivalent to normal classes, but COM defines how these objects interact with other programs at the binary level. By *binary*, I mean compiled code, with all the methods and member variables of the class already built into an object. This "binary encapsulation" allows you to treat each COM object as a "black box." You can call the black box and use its functionality without any knowledge of the inner workings of the object's implementation. In the Windows environment, these binary objects (COM objects) are packaged as either DLLs or executable programs. COM is also backed by a series of utility functions that provide routines for instantiating COM objects, process communication, and so on.

COM was the first methodology to address object-oriented software reuse. COM has enjoyed great commercial success; many third-party software vendors provide COM objects to perform a wide range of tasks, from e-mail to image processing. COM is also highly useful for creating components called *business objects*. Business objects are COM objects in the strict sense, but they are used to encapsulate business rules and logic. Typically these business objects are tied to database tables. The objects move around the database according to the business rules implemented in the COM object.

Generally, several smaller business objects work together to accomplish a larger task. To maintain system integrity and to prevent the introduction of erroneous data into the application, transactions are used. A software service called Microsoft Transaction Server (MTS) is used to manage these transactions. We'll cover the function of MTS (and its successor, COM+) in Section 5.3.3.

5.3.2 Overview of Transactions

Simply stated, a transaction is a unit of work. Several smaller steps are involved in a transaction. The success or failure of the transaction depends on whether or not all of the smaller steps are completed successfully. If a failure occurs at any point during a transaction, you don't want any data changes made by previous steps to remain. In effect, you want to initiate an "undo" command, similar to what you would do when using, say, a word processor. A transaction is *committed* when all steps have succeeded. A failed transaction causes a *rollback* to occur (the "undo" operation).

Well-designed transactions conform to *ACID* principles. ACID is an acronym for Atomicity, Consistency, Isolation, and Durability.

- *Atomicity* means that either the operation that the component performs is completely successful or the data that the component operates on does not change at all. This is important because if the transaction has to update multiple data items, you do not want to leave it with erroneous values. If a failure occurs at any step that could compromise the integrity of the system, the changes are undone.
- *Consistency* deals with preserving the system state in the case of a transaction failure.
- *Isolation* means that a transaction acts as though it has complete control of the system. In effect, this means that transactions are executed one at a time. This process keeps the system state consistent; two components executed at the same time that operate on the same data can compromise the integrity of the system.
- *Durability* is the ability of a system to return to any state that was present before the execution of a transaction. For example, if a hard drive crash occurs in the middle of a transaction, you can restore the original state from a transaction log stored on another disk to which the system recorded.

A classic example of a transaction operation is a bank transfer that involves a transfer of funds from one account to another (a credit and a debit). Such a transaction moves through the following steps.

1. Get the amount to be transferred, and check the source account for sufficient funds.
2. Deduct the transfer amount from the source account.
3. Get the balance of the destination account, and add the amount to be transferred to the balance.
4. Update the destination account with the new balance.

Suppose a system failure occurs at step 4. The source account had the transfer amount deducted but the amount was not added to the destination account. Therefore, the money from the source account gets lost. Clearly, this is not good because the integrity of the database has been damaged.

Each of the account transfer's steps can be checked for success or failure. If a failure occurs before all values have been updated, the program needs to undo the deduction made to the source account. That's a rollback. If every step succeeds, the program needs to apply all the changes made to the database. That's when a commit operation is performed.

5.3.3 Automatic Transactions

Transactions have been in widespread use since the early days of enterprise computing. Many database systems include internal support for transactions. Such database systems contain native commands to begin, abort, and commit transactions. This way, several updates to database data can be made as a group, and in the event of a failure, they can be undone. Using a database's internal transaction-processing system is referred to as *manual transaction processing*.

Automatic transactions differ from manual transactions because automatic transactions are controlled by a system external to the database management system (DBMS). Earlier versions of Windows (95/98/NT) provide automatic transaction services using Microsoft Transaction Server (MTS). MTS works by coordinating database updates made by COM components grouped into a logical unit called a *package*. An MTS package defines the boundary of the transaction. Each component in the package participates in the transaction. After a component performs a piece of work (such as updating the database), it informs MTS that it successfully (or unsuccessfully) performed its share of the transaction. MTS then makes a determination to continue based on the success of the last component's signal of success or failure. If the transaction step was unsuccessful, the transaction is aborted immediately, and MTS instructs the DBMS to undo any changes made to data. If the step was successful, the transaction continues with the other steps. If all steps execute successfully, MTS commits the transaction and tells the DBMS to commit changes to the data.

5.3.4 COM+ Applications

With the release of Windows 2000 came the next version of COM, dubbed *COM+*. COM+'s *raison d'être* is the unification of COM and MTS. COM+

also offers performance improvements over MTS by implementing technologies such as *object pooling*, which maintains an active set of COM component instances. Other performance-enhancing features include *load balancing*, which distributes component instances over multiple servers, and *queued components*, which uses Microsoft Message Queue Server to handle requests for COM+ components.

The services that were formerly provided by MTS are known as *COM+ Component Services* in the COM+ model. COM+ Component Services works in a similar manner to MTS. Packages are now referred to as *COM+ applications*. Participating transactional components are grouped into applications in the same way components were grouped into packages under MTS.

Individual COM+ components in an application can be assigned different levels of involvement in an automatic transaction. When setting up COM+ applications, each component can have the levels of automatic transaction support shown in Table 5-2.

Table 5-2 COM+ Automatic Transaction Support Levels

Transaction Support	Description
`Disabled`	No transaction services are ever loaded by COM+ Component Services.
`Not Supported`	This is the default setting for new MTS components. Execution of the component is always outside a transaction regardless of whether or not a transaction has been initiated for the component.
`Supported`	You may run the component inside or outside a transaction without any ill effects.
`Required`	The component must run inside a transaction.
`Required New`	The component needs its own transaction in which to run. If the component is not called from within a transaction, a new transaction is automatically created.

5.3.5 COM+ Security

Security is of paramount importance, especially for applications intended to run on the Internet. In the past, programming security features into an Internet application was largely a manual effort. Often it consisted of custom security schemes that did not necessarily leverage the existing security infrastructure provided by the operating system. Besides being difficult to maintain, such security systems are typically costly to develop.

COM+ Component Services provides a security infrastructure for applications that uses Windows 2000/XP users and groups. COM+ security is declarative, which means you designate which users and groups have permission to access a COM+ application. This is done by defining *roles* for application access.

A role is a defined set of duties performed by particular individuals. For example, a librarian can locate, check out, and shelve books. The person fulfilling the librarian role is permitted to perform such duties under the security policies defined for that role. An administrator is responsible for assigning users and groups to roles. The roles are then assigned to a COM+ application.

This *role-based security* is not only easy to implement (it can be done by the system administrator) but it also typically doesn't require the programmer to work on the components to implement any security code. When a call is made to a component running under COM+ Component Services, COM+ checks the user/group identity of the caller and compares it against the roles assigned to the component. Based on that comparison, the call is allowed or rejected.

You can provide additional security checking by using *procedural security*. This type of security is implemented programmatically using special .NET classes designed for interaction with COM+ Component Services.

5.3.6 .NET Classes and COM+ Component Services

Thus far, our discussions about COM+ Component Services, transactions, and security deal specifically with COM+ components. COM+ predated the .NET Framework and has had much success in enterprise-wide applications developed using Microsoft Visual Studio 6.0. But how does .NET fit into all of this?

COM+ still remains a dominant technology and is a significant part of Windows. The architecture for .NET managed components was designed to take advantage of all the features COM+ Component Services has to offer (object pooling, transaction processing, security, and so on) by providing classes to implement those features. These concepts are very important when developing Web applications, too.

5.4 Using VB.NET to Develop Managed Components

In this section I'll present the concepts you need to understand to build managed components using VB.NET.

5.4.1 Defining Namespaces

Namespaces are a way to hierarchically organize class names. Namespaces become especially useful when the number of classes available to you is quite large. You've been exposed to namespaces quite a bit already in this book. Whenever you write VB.NET code, you use .NET classes in the `System` namespace. For example, when you use the `Console.WriteLine()` command, you are using an assembly called `Console` that exists in the `System` namespace. In the code, `Console` is not fully qualified because it is assumed to be a part of the `System` namespace based on the uniqueness of the name `Console`. You could fully qualify the statement this way:

```
System.Console.WriteLine( . . . )
```

When you create a new .NET assembly (program), a default root namespace is assigned to the assembly. This name is typically the name of your project. However, you are free to assign your own namespace names.

5.4.2 Using the Class Library

Managed components start with a VS.NET project called a *class library*. The class library puts the infrastructure in place for creating an assembly for packing a component. Figure 5-2 shows the selections used to create a new class library project.

You can specify several project properties and options for class library projects. Of particular interest are the root namespace and the assembly name. VB.NET creates default names for both of these options. You can view and modify them by selecting the **Project→Properties** menu. This opens the Property Pages dialog shown in Figure 5-3.

By default, VB.NET assigns the name you specified for the project as the names for the assembly and the root namespace. You can override these default names with better, more descriptive ones. Given these new designations, references to classes inside the assembly would be made in the follow-

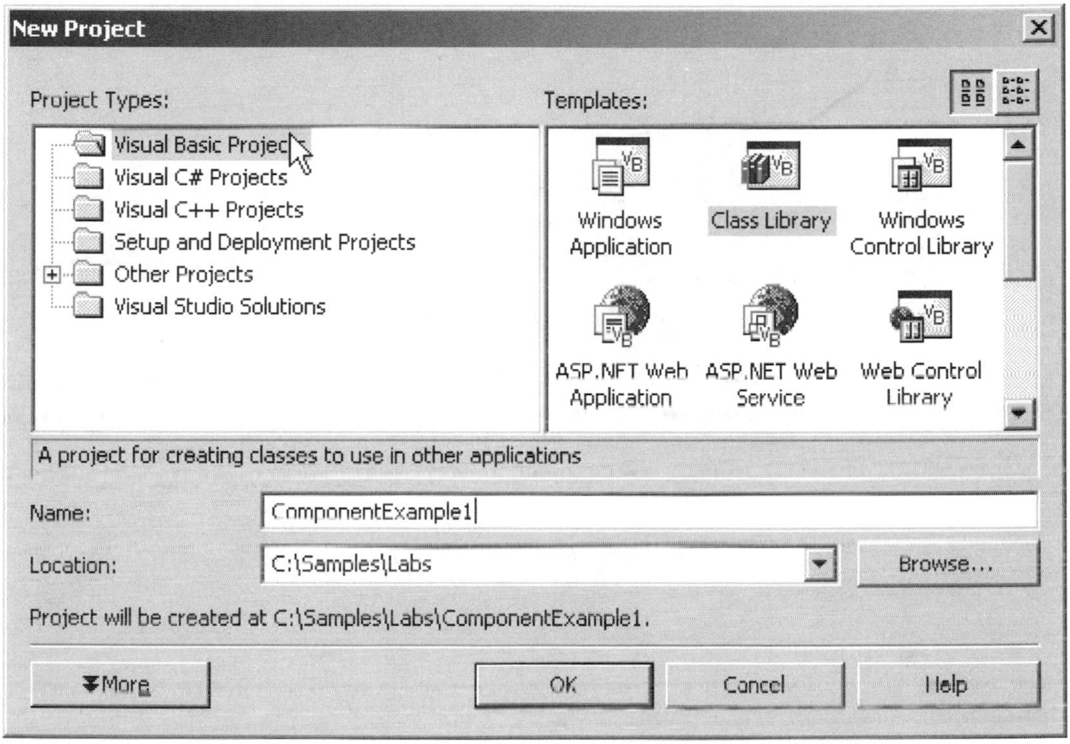

Figure 5-2 Creating a new class library project in VB.NET

ing manner. (This example shows the usage of `Dim` to declare an object for a particular class inside the assembly.)

```
Dim objMyObject As objMyExample.SomeClassInTheAssembly
```

.NET applications that you write need to include a reference to each assembly you wish to use inside the main application. You can add a reference to an assembly by right-clicking on the References folder (see Figure 5-4) and selecting Add Reference . . . . VS.NET displays a dialog with a list of available assemblies (see Figure 5-5). Those assemblies that are a part of the .NET Framework distribution are displayed in the list. To add a reference to another assembly, click the Browse . . . button. Then you'll be able to select the assembly file you need.

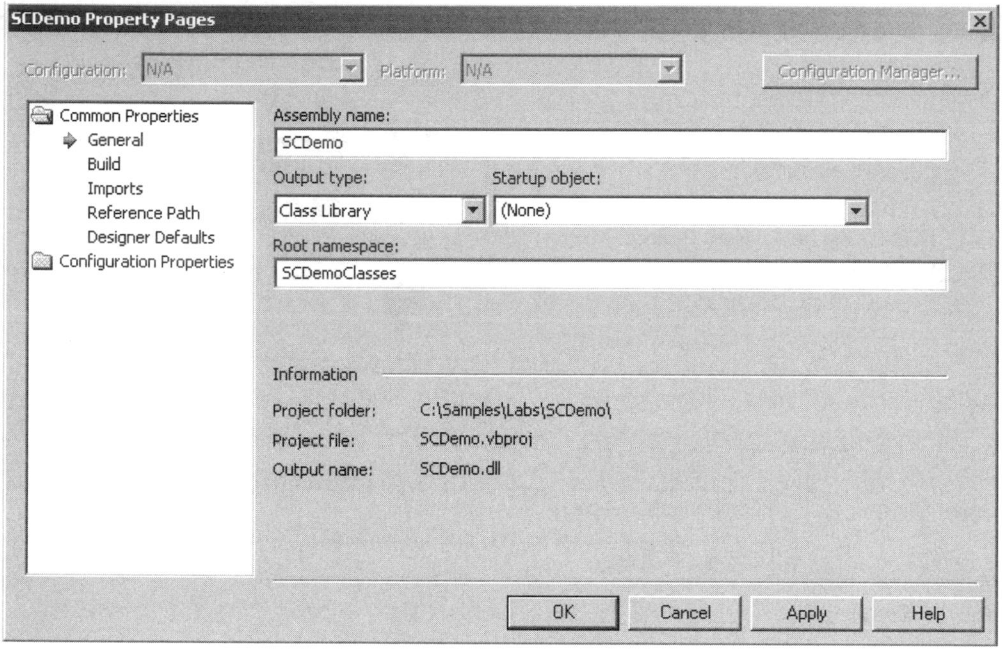

Figure 5-3 The Property Pages dialog

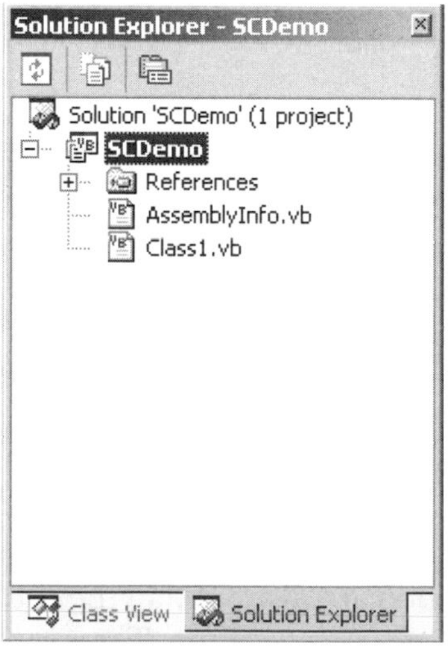

Figure 5-4 The References folder

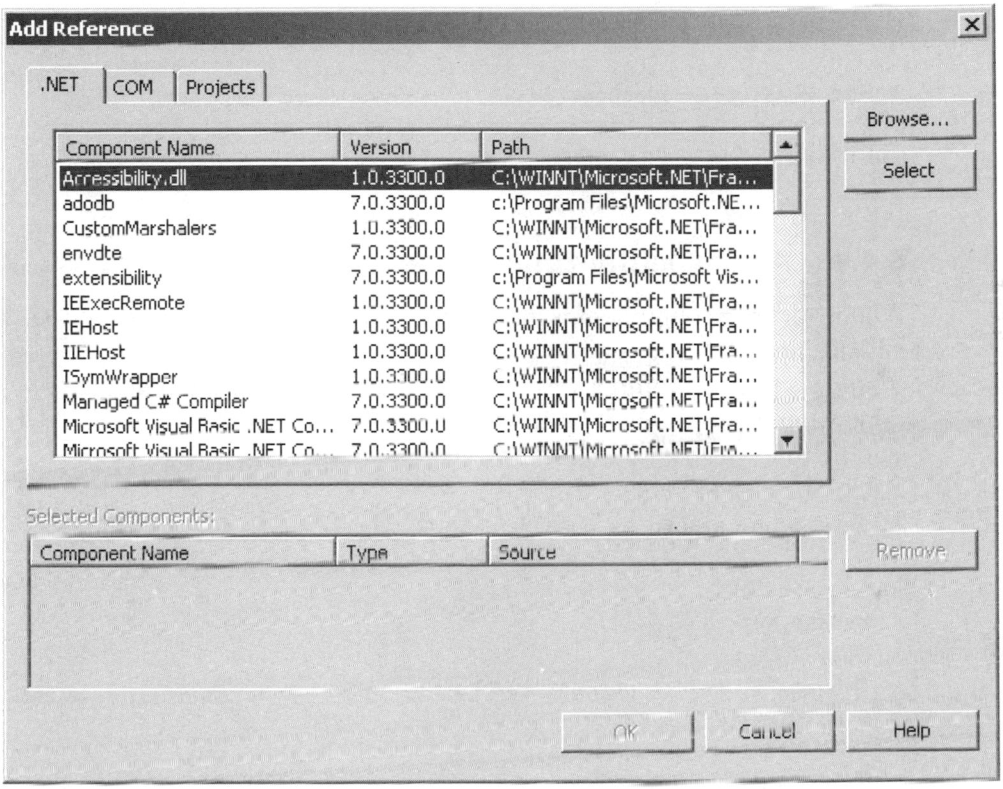

Figure 5-5 The Add Reference dialog

5.4.3 Using Component "Plumbing" Code

When class library projects are started in VB.NET, some stub code is generated for you. A new, "empty" component's "plumbing" code looks something like this:

```
Public Class Class1

End Class
```

The VS.NET IDE adds this code for you for an empty class called `Class1`. A `.vb` file is also generated that contains the class's code (which VS.NET should be displaying in the front-most window). Give the class another name (in the example below, we'll name it `CTaxComponent`) by changing it in the editor and then renaming the class file in the Solution Explorer to `CTaxComponent`. The code should now say:

```
Public Class CTaxComponent

End Class
```

5.4.4 Adding Initialization Code

Whenever your component is instantiated, the `New()` subroutine is called. Any initialization code you require goes here. As an illustration, suppose your class contains a private member variable that you wish to have an initial default value when the component is instantiated. Such initialization code could look like the following.

```
Private m_dblTaxRate As Double

Public Sub New()
   MyBase.New

   ' Specify default percent tax rate
   m_dblTaxRate = 5

End Sub
```

5.4.5 Creating Methods

In Chapter 2 we discussed classes and several class concepts, such as methods. When creating class libraries and components, you'll notice that the same principles apply to components. Methods are simply member functions and subroutines. In order for other .NET applications to access methods you define, you need to expose them by marking them for public access. Here's a public method definition and implementation to illustrate.

```
Public Function CalculatePriceAfterTax( _
   ByVal Amount As Double) As Double

   CalculatePriceAfterTax = Amount * (1 + (m_dblTaxRate / 100))

End Function
```

5.4.6 Creating Properties

Component properties are created in the same way as properties for regular classes. Like methods, they should be marked for public access. The property in the sample code below sets or gets the value of the private class member variable used in the previous example.

```
Public Property TaxRate() As Double
   Get
      TaxRate = m_dblTaxRate
   End Get
   Set(ByVal Value As Double)
      m_dblTaxRate = Value
   End Set
End Property
```

5.4.7 Using the Class Library in an Application

The preceding sections described all the steps required to create a class library that can function as an independent component in another application. Now the class library needs to be tested. You can create another .NET application that references the assembly and write code to call the `CTaxComponent` class. The code below is a simple console application that uses the class library.

```
Imports System
Imports SCDemoClasses
Imports Microsoft.VisualBasic

Module Module1

   Sub Main()
      Dim objTaxComponent As New CTaxComponent()
      Dim dblItemPrice As Double = 9.99
      Dim dblTotalPrice As Double

      With objTaxComponent
         .TaxRate = 7
         dblTotalPrice = _
            .CalculatePriceAfterTax(dblItemPrice)
      End With

      Console.WriteLine("{0} after tax is {1}", _
         FormatCurrency(dblItemPrice), _
```

```
            FormatCurrency(dblTotalPrice))

    End Sub

End Module
```

This code produces the following output (assuming U.S. currency):

```
$9.99 after tax is $10.69
```

> **WARNING:** Before this program can compile and run, a reference to the assembly DLL, `SCDemo` (used in the example), must be added as a reference to the hosting application (the sample console application) using the **Add Reference . . .** command from the menu.

5.5 Serviced Components

Building components and class libraries is a good way to organize your code, but the main advantage of writing class libraries and components for your application is to gain the benefits of COM+ Component Services. With COM+ Component Services, your components can take advantage of automatic transaction processing, object pooling, and role-based security. Components that use COM+ Component Services are called *serviced components*.

Setting up a component to take advantage of these features is not difficult. It requires creating a class library project as shown earlier plus creating several component classes to handle the business logic. Let's discuss an example scenario that uses serviced components.

Suppose that we are writing an ordering and inventory system for a supermarket. The system will track inventory as well as receive orders. Three different types of users will work with this system: Suppliers, Supervisors, and Receiving Clerks. Suppliers enter any orders that we expect to receive into our database. Any products that are ordered must be products that the store normally carries. Supervisors are authorized to add new product types to the database. Receiving Clerks and Supervisors are authorized to receive orders. Line items received from an order will be immediately reflected as available inventory for the supermarket. Figure 5-6 shows the database schema used for

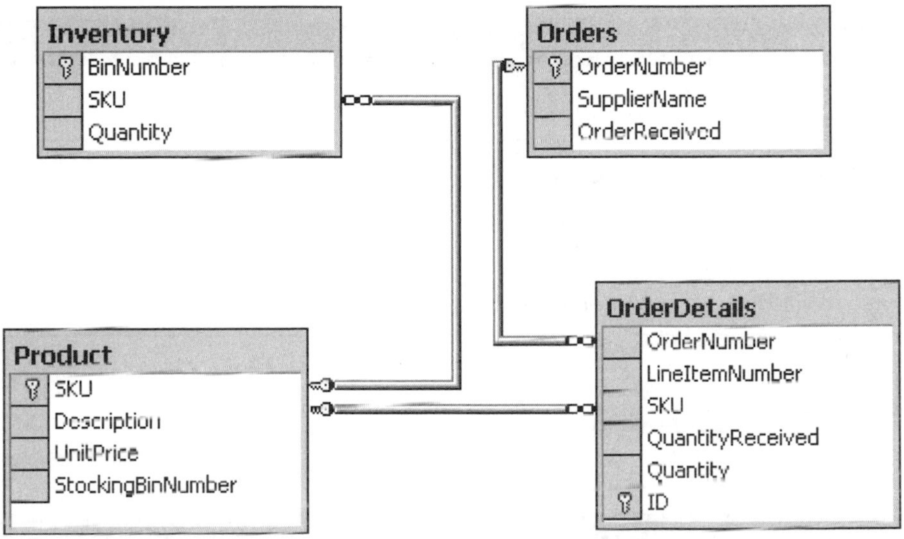

Figure 5-6 Database diagram of a supermarket ordering and inventory system

the ordering and inventory system, showing tables, columns, and foreign key relationships among columns. (Note that this system is simplified for the purposes of the example.) To run the code samples, you will need to create a SQL Server database with these specifications, tables, and relationships. Tables 5-3 through 5-6 list the table column names and data types for the four tables shown in Figure 5-6.

Table 5-3 Column Names and Data Types for the `Inventory` Table

Column Name	Data Type
`BinNumber`	`Varchar(255)`
`SKU`	`Varchar(255)`
`Quantity`	`Int`

Table 5-4 Column Names and Data Types for the `Product` Table

Column Name	Data Type
SKU	Varchar(255)
Description	Varchar(255)
UnitPrice	Decimal
StockingBinNumber	Varchar(255)

Table 5-5 Column Names and Data Types for the `Orders` Table

Column Name	Data Type
OrderNumber	Varchar(255)
SupplierName	Varchar(255)
OrderReceived	Bit

Table 5-6 Column Names and Data Types for the `OrderDetails` Table

Column Name	Data Type
OrderNumber	Varchar(255)
LineItemNumber	Int
SKU	Varchar(255)
QuantityReceived	Int
Quantity	Int
ID	Identity

> **TIP:** Consult your SQL Server documentation about creating a new database and setting up tables if you are not familiar with the process. Recruit the help of a database administrator if you need assistance in obtaining authorization to create a database (if you're in an enterprise/shared database environment). We will discuss database access in detail in Chapter 7.

5.6 Building VB.NET Serviced Components

Now it's time for you to use serviced components to build the supermarket ordering and inventory system outlined in the previous section! You'll work through each step in the process, from designing to coding and then testing the components in an ASP.NET application.

LAB 5-1

AN ORDERING AND INVENTORY SYSTEM MADE WITH SERVICED COMPONENTS

STEP 1. Create a new VB.NET class library project.

a. Open VS.NET and select **File→New→Project.**

b. Highlight Class Library and give the new project the name "SupermarketSystem".

STEP 2. Design the components.

a. Consider the design of your system. First, establish the users of the system and their roles:

- Supervisors (adding new products, receiving orders, updating inventory)
- Receiving Clerks (receiving orders)
- Suppliers (shipping goods to the supermarket and supplying order information)

b. Organize these functions into a series of classes for your class library. Four classes will handle the business logic of the different duties that each user will perform: `Product`, `ReceiveOrder`, `UpdateInventory`, and `CreateOrder`. Lab Figure 5-1 shows the classes and the methods of each class.

Adding a new product to the system, updating inventory, receiving an order, and creating an order all involve operations on the database tier of the application. For some of these operations, database updates can occur in multiple tables. It's important to keep data integrity across these tables. You also want to implement security features so the users perform only the functions that their roles designate. You'll see this functionality develop as you code the components.

STEP 3. Write code for component functionality.

In the process of implementing the components, we'll discuss these topics:

- How to use the `System.EnterpriseServices` namespace and one particular class: the `ServicedComponent` class
- How to use class attributes to specify the type of COM+ support you want your components to have
- How to specify an interface from which to call the components
- How to control the transaction inside the components

a. Create the classes outlined in the specifications in Step 2: `Product`, `ReceiveOrder`, `UpdateInventory`, and `CreateOrder`. For each of these classes, right-click the project in the Solution Explorer and select **Add**

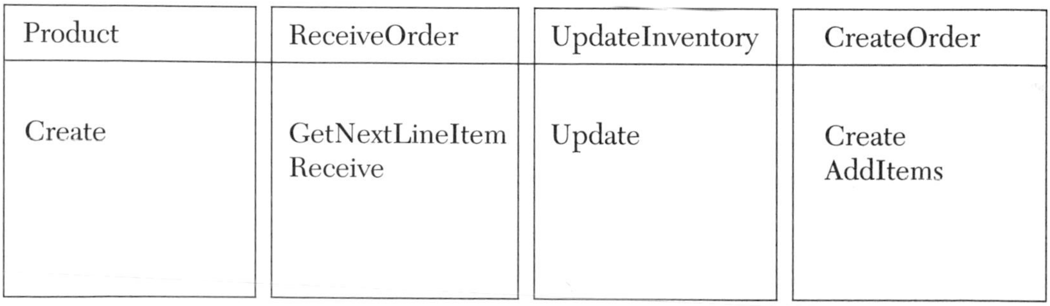

Lab Figure 5-1 The classes and the methods of the Supermarket program

Class . . . from the menu. Name the classes as listed above. VS.NET will "stub out" an empty class definition for each class.

b. Building serviced components requires support from COM+ Component Services. The .NET Framework implements this support through classes in the `System.EnterpriseServices` namespace. VS.NET doesn't include this reference by default, so you'll need to add it yourself. Select **Project→Add Reference** from the menu and select `System.EnterpriseServices` from the list. Click the Select button and then click OK.

c. Now you're ready to add component functionality. Start by adding the following code for the `Product` class (`Product.vb`).

LAB CODE SAMPLE 5-1

```
Imports System
Imports System.Reflection
Imports System.EnterpriseServices
Imports System.Data
Imports System.Data.SqlClient

5 <Assembly: ApplicationName("Supermarket")>
6 <Assembly: ApplicationActivation(ActivationOption.Library)>
7 <Assembly: AssemblyKeyFile("KeyFile.snk")>
8 Namespace Supermarket

9 Public Interface IProduct
  Function Create(ByVal SKU As String, _
               ByVal Description As String, _
               ByVal UnitPrice As Decimal, _
               ByVal StockingBinNumber As String) _
               As Boolean
  End Interface

10 <ConstructionEnabled( _
  [Default]:="Default Construction String"), _
  Transaction(TransactionOption.Required)> _
  Public Class Product
11      Inherits ServicedComponent
12      Implements Supermarket.IProduct

    Public Sub New()

    End Sub
```

```
    Protected Overrides Sub Construct( _
13          ByVal constructString As String)

    End Sub

    Function Create(ByVal SKU As String, _
                ByVal Description As String, _
                ByVal UnitPrice As Decimal, _
                ByVal StockingBinNumber As String) _
                As Boolean _
                Implements Supermarket.IProduct.Create

      Dim objCnn As SqlConnection
      Dim objCmd As SqlCommand
      Dim objParam As SqlParameter
      Dim intRowsReturned As Integer

      Try
        objCnn = New SqlConnection()
        objCnn.ConnectionString = _
"Initial Catalog=Supermarket;Data Source=localhost;uid=sa;pwd="
        objCnn.Open()
        objCmd = objCnn.CreateCommand()
        objCmd.CommandText = _
   "INSERT INTO Product " & _
   "( SKU, Description, UnitPrice, StockingBinNumber ) " & _
   "VALUES ( @sku, @description, @unitprice, @stockingbinnumber )"

        objParam = New SqlParameter()
        With objParam
            .ParameterName = "@sku"
            .SqlDbType = SqlDbType.VarChar
            .Direction = ParameterDirection.Input
            .Value = SKU
        End With
        objCmd.Parameters.Add(objParam)

        objParam = New SqlParameter()
        With objParam
            .ParameterName = "@description"
            .SqlDbType = SqlDbType.VarChar
            .Direction = ParameterDirection.Input
            .Value = Description
        End With
```

```
        objCmd.Parameters.Add(objParam)
        objParam = New SqlParameter()
        With objParam
            .ParameterName = "@unitprice"
            .SqlDbType = SqlDbType.Decimal
            .Direction = ParameterDirection.Input
            .Value = UnitPrice
        End With
        objCmd.Parameters.Add(objParam)

        objParam = New SqlParameter()
        With objParam
            .ParameterName = "@stockingbinnumber"
            .SqlDbType = SqlDbType.VarChar
            .Direction = ParameterDirection.Input
            .Value = StockingBinNumber
        End With
        objCmd.Parameters.Add(objParam)

        intRowsReturned = _
            objCmd.ExecuteNonQuery()
        Create = True
14          ContextUtil.SetComplete()

      Catch E As Exception
        Create = False
15      ContextUtil.SetAbort()
      Finally
        objCnn.Close()
      End Try

    End Function

  End Class

End Namespace
```

This code implements a serviced component. As mentioned before, a serviced component is a .NET class that uses COM+ Component Services. The class becomes a serviced component when it derives from the `System.EnterpriseServices.ServicedComponent` class. Before we talk more about the `ServicedComponent` class, let's first investigate the beginning of the code where some assembly-level attributes are declared.

Making a serviced component requires you to provide information to COM+ Component Services about the component's configuration. First you designate to which package, or COM+ application, the component will belong. That designation is made with the `ApplicationName` assembly-level attribute shown in line ❺. The name for the order and inventory application is "Supermarket". COM+ applications are listed in the Component Services Console.

COM+ Component Services provides a runtime environment for assembly components. You can also control where the components are activated—in the same process as the creator of the object (IIS) or in a separate system process (`dllhost.exe`). You can control application activation by specifying the `ApplicationActivation` assembly attribute shown in line ❻. This code specifies `ActivationOption.Library`, which causes components to be activated in the creator's process. So, if you were running these components inside ASP.NET Web Forms, the creating process would be the Web server, IIS. The `ActivationOption.Server` option provides faster performance; this option, which runs the component in a system process, provides more isolation, so the component's execution won't adversely affect the execution of IIS. One advantage to using `ActivationOption.Library` is to make debugging easier.

The final assembly-level attribute, `AssemblyKeyFile`, specifies a shared name for the assembly (see line ❼). The shared name is sometimes referred to as a *strong name*. A shared name ensures that a name assigned to a component is unique. This is accomplished by using a public/private cryptographic key pair to sign each shared component in the assembly. The public key is then published with the assembly. Besides specifying this attribute in the code, you'll need to actually generate the key file specified for the assembly-level attribute. To do this, use `sn.exe`, the Strong Name Utility. Lab Figure 5-2 shows how this is done.

The usage of `sn.exe`, as shown in Lab Figure 5-2, outputs a `.snk` file. This is the file name that you specify in the `AssemblyKeyFile` attribute in the code (change the path to the location of your generated key file). You must complete this step before you compile your project. These assembly-level attributes appear once in the project's code. The class file in which they appear is irrelevant, but they must be declared once and only once in the assembly code.

> **WARNING:** Never let anybody else have access to your `.snk` file. It contains a private key that is for your use only.

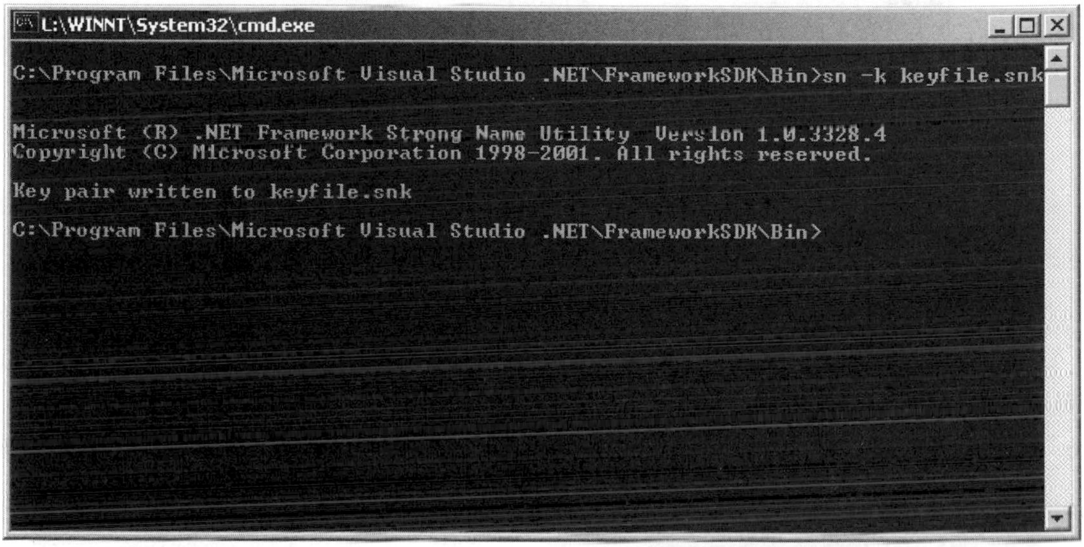

Lab Figure 5-2 Specifying a strong name for the assembly using `sn.exe`

Let's move on to the main part of the component code. Line ❽ defines the `Supermarket` namespace, which will contain all the components for the Supermarket application. Line ❾ declares an interface you'll use in the client application (the ASP.NET Web Form) to call the component. The interface has one function, `Create()`, which you'll use to set up a new product in the `Product` database table.

The component's class definition comes next. The code beginning in line ❿ shows two class-level attributes for the `Product` class. The first one, `ConstructionEnabled`, specifies that the class will be able to use COM+ constructor strings. A constructor string is a string passed into the activation procedure of the component. This string can be specified by a system administrator inside the Component Services Console. A constructor string can contain any information, but typically you'll use it for passing initialization information to the component. If no constructor string is given for the component in the Component Services Console (see Lab Figure 5-3, which shows the Component Services Console dialog box for setting a constructor string), a default constructor string is used by specifying it in the attribute as shown in the continuation of line ❿. The other class-level attribute specifies how the class will participate in transactions. Use the `Transaction` attribute to specify the participation level. In this code, `Transaction` uses

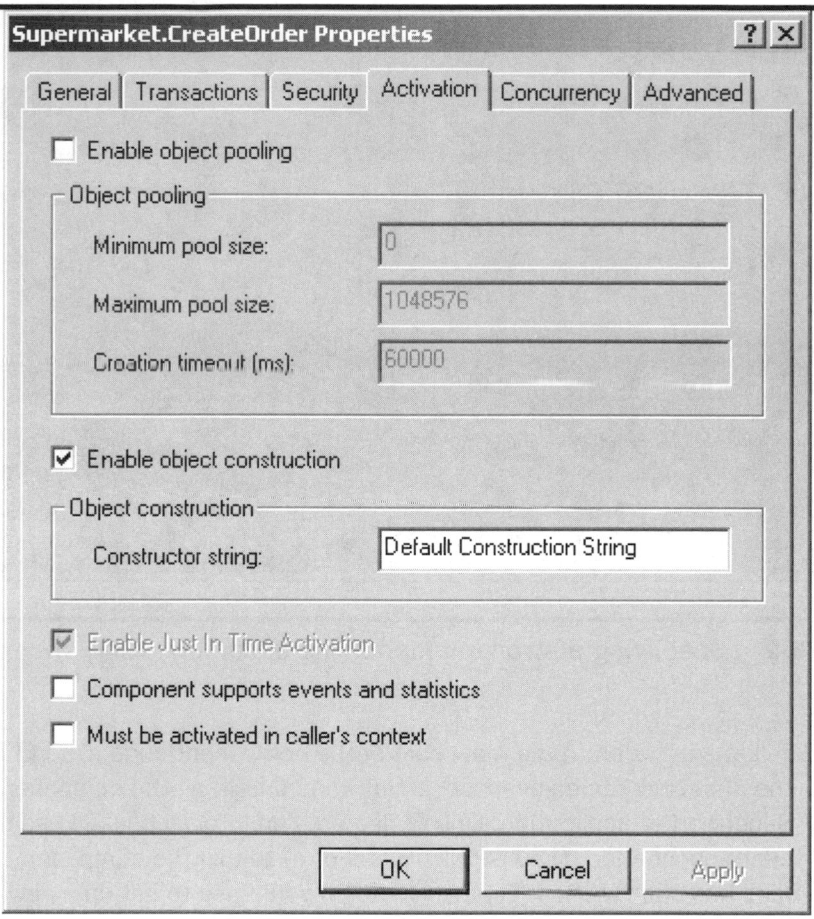

Lab Figure 5-3 Specifying a constructor string in Component Services

`TransactionOption.Required`. This indicates that the `Product` component should participate in an existing transaction if one already exists. If no transaction exists, a new transaction will begin and the `Product` component will execute within the boundaries of that transaction.

The class definition continues with the specification of an inherited class and an `Implements` statement. Since this will be a serviced component, it needs to derive from the `ServicedComponent` class, as shown in line ⓫. In line ⓬ the class implements the `IProduct` interface specified earlier.

Line ⓭ provides implementation support for constructor strings. Since the code specified that the component will have support for constructor strings with the class-level attribute `ConstructionEnabled`, here there is an override method for the `Construct()` sub. This method will be called upon object construction, and the constructor string assigned to the component will be available in the `constructString` variable.

Now follows the implementation of the `Create()` method, which accepts a new product's SKU number, product description, unit price, and stocking bin number. The `Create()` method then executes the appropriate ADO.NET code to insert a new row into the `Product` database table. (ADO.NET code will be discussed in Chapter 7. For now, just be aware that the `Product` component contains this method that will be callable from an ASP.NET Web Form.)

Although the discussion of the ADO.NET code details is deferred, it's important to point out two details in the `Create()` method. These are two methods of the `ContextUtil` object, `SetComplete()` in line ⓮ and `SetAbort()` in line ⓯. These methods cast a vote in the current transaction. Typically, when you have verified that all of the code inside a particular component method has executed successfully, a call to `SetComplete()` is made. This tells COM+ Component Services that a unit of work has succeeded and that database integrity and consistency is assured for updates made by the unit of work. It's a signal that the transaction can continue running. Conversely, if a failure occurs (an exception or other user-defined error or condition), the program needs to cast a "fail" vote for the transaction by calling `SetAbort()`. This will cause COM+ Component Services to stop the transaction and roll back any changes made to the database by previous steps in the transaction.

d. Now that you understand the basic pieces of the `Product` class code, add the code for the remaining classes (`CreateOrder`, `UpdateInventory`, and `ReceiveOrder`). The implementations are all different, of course, but they follow pretty much the same conventions as the `Product` component.

LAB CODE SAMPLE 5-2

```
Imports System
Imports System.Reflection
Imports System.EnterpriseServices
Imports System.Data
Imports System.Data.SqlClient


Namespace Supermarket
```

```
Public Interface ICreateOrder
   Function Create(ByVal OrderNumber As String, _
                   ByVal SupplierName As String) _
                   As Boolean
   Function AddItems(ByVal OrderNumber As String, _
                   ByVal SKU As String, _
                   ByVal Quantity As Integer) _
                   As Boolean
End Interface

<ConstructionEnabled( _
[Default]:="Default Construction String"), _
Transaction(TransactionOption.Required)> _
Public Class CreateOrder
   Inherits ServicedComponent
   Implements ICreateOrder

   Public Sub New()

   End Sub

   Public Function Create(ByVal OrderNumber As String, _
                   ByVal SupplierName As String) _
                   As Boolean _
                   Implements ICreateOrder.Create

      Dim objCnn As SqlConnection
      Dim objCmd As SqlCommand
      Dim objParam As SqlParameter
      Dim intRowsAffected As Integer

      Try
         objCnn = New SqlConnection()
         objCnn.ConnectionString = _
"Initial Catalog=Supermarket;Data Source=localhost;uid=sa;pwd="
         objCnn.Open()
         objCmd = objCnn.CreateCommand()

         objCmd.CommandText = _
 "INSERT INTO Orders " & _
 "( OrderNumber, SupplierName, OrderReceived ) " & _
 "VALUES ( @OrderNumber, @SupplierName, @OrderReceived )"

         objParam = New SqlParameter()
```

```
        With objParam
            .ParameterName = "@OrderNumber"
            .SqlDbType = SqlDbType.VarChar
            .Direction = ParameterDirection.Input
            .Value = OrderNumber
        End With
        objCmd.Parameters.Add(objParam)

        objParam = New SqlParameter()
        With objParam
            .ParameterName = "@SupplierName"
            .SqlDbType = SqlDbType.VarChar
            .Direction = ParameterDirection.Input
            .Value = SupplierName
        End With
        objCmd.Parameters.Add(objParam)

        objParam = New SqlParameter()
        With objParam
            .ParameterName = "@OrderReceived"
            .SqlDbType = SqlDbType.Bit
            .Direction = ParameterDirection.Input
            .Value = False
        End With
        objCmd.Parameters.Add(objParam)

        intRowsAffected = objCmd.ExecuteNonQuery()

        Create = True
        ContextUtil.SetComplete()
    Catch E As Exception
        Create = False
        ContextUtil.SetAbort()
    End Try
End Function

Public Function AddItems(ByVal OrderNumber As String, _
                ByVal SKU As String, _
                ByVal Quantity As Integer) _
                As Boolean _
                Implements ICreateOrder.AddItems

    Dim objCnn As SqlConnection
    Dim objCmd As SqlCommand
```

```
        Dim objParam As SqlParameter
        Dim intMaxLineNumber As Integer
        Dim intRowsAffected As Integer
        Dim objTemp As Object

        Try
           objCnn = New SqlConnection()
           objCnn.ConnectionString = _
"Initial Catalog=Supermarket;Data Source=localhost;uid=sa;pwd="
           objCnn.Open()
           objCmd = objCnn.CreateCommand()

           objCmd.CommandText = _
              "SELECT MAX( LineItemNumber ) " & _
              "FROM OrderDetails " & _
              "WHERE OrderNumber = @OrderNumber"
           objParam = New SqlParameter()
           With objParam
              .ParameterName = "@OrderNumber"
              .SqlDbType = SqlDbType.VarChar
              .Direction = ParameterDirection.Input
              .Value = OrderNumber
           End With
           objCmd.Parameters.Add(objParam)

           objTemp = objCmd.ExecuteScalar()
           If TypeOf objTemp Is DBNull Then
              intMaxLineNumber = 1
           Else
              intMaxLineNumber = CType(objTemp, Integer)
              intMaxLineNumber += 1
           End If

           objCmd = objCnn.CreateCommand()
           objCmd.CommandText = _
              "INSERT INTO OrderDetails " & _
              "( OrderNumber, LineItemNumber, SKU, " & _
              "QuantityReceived, Quantity ) VALUES " & _
              "( @OrderNumber, @LineNumber, @SKU, " & _
              "@QuantityReceived, @Quantity )"
           objParam = New SqlParameter()
           With objParam
              .ParameterName = "@OrderNumber"
              .SqlDbType = SqlDbType.VarChar
```

```
    .Direction = ParameterDirection.Input
    .Value = OrderNumber
End With
objCmd.Parameters.Add(objParam)

objParam = New SqlParameter()
With objParam
    .ParameterName = "@LineNumber"
    .SqlDbType = SqlDbType.Int
    .Direction = ParameterDirection.Input
    .Value = intMaxLineNumber
End With
objCmd.Parameters.Add(objParam)

objParam = New SqlParameter()
With objParam
    .ParameterName = "@SKU"
    .SqlDbType = SqlDbType.VarChar
    .Direction = ParameterDirection.Input
    .Value = SKU
End With
objCmd.Parameters.Add(objParam)

objParam = New SqlParameter()
With objParam
    .ParameterName = "@QuantityReceived"
    .SqlDbType = SqlDbType.Int
    .Direction = ParameterDirection.Input
    .Value = 0
End With
objCmd.Parameters.Add(objParam)

objParam = New SqlParameter()
With objParam
    .ParameterName = "@Quantity"
    .SqlDbType = SqlDbType.Int
    .Direction = ParameterDirection.Input
    .Value = Quantity
End With
objCmd.Parameters.Add(objParam)

intRowsAffected = objCmd.ExecuteNonQuery()

AddItems = True
```

```
            ContextUtil.SetComplete()

         Catch E As Exception
            AddItems = False
            ContextUtil.SetAbort()
         Finally
            objCnn.Close()
         End Try

      End Function

   End Class
End Namespace
```

LAB CODE SAMPLE 5-3

```
Imports System
Imports System.Reflection
Imports System.EnterpriseServices
Imports System.Data
Imports System.Data.SqlClient

Namespace Supermarket

   Public Interface IUpdateInventory
      Function Update(ByVal BinNumber As String, _
                      ByVal SKU As String, _
                      ByVal Quantity As Integer) _
                      As Boolean
      Function GetStockingLocation(ByVal SKU As String) _
                      As String
   End Interface

   <ConstructionEnabled( _
   [Default]:="Default Construction String"), _
   Transaction(TransactionOption.Required)> _
   Public Class UpdateInventory
      Inherits ServicedComponent
      Implements IUpdateInventory

      Public Sub New()

      End Sub
```

```
    Public Function GetStockingLocation( _
            ByVal SKU As String) As String _
            Implements IUpdateInventory.GetStockingLocation

        Dim objCnn As SqlConnection
        Dim objCmd As SqlCommand
        Dim objParam As SqlParameter
        Dim objTemp As Object

        Try
            objCnn = New SqlConnection()
            objCnn.ConnectionString = _
"Initial Catalog=Supermarket;Data Source=localhost;uid=sa;pwd="
            objCnn.Open()
            objCmd = objCnn.CreateCommand()

            objCmd.CommandText = _
                  "SELECT StockingBinNumber " & _
                  "FROM Product WHERE SKU = @SKU"

            objParam = New SqlParameter()
            With objParam
               .ParameterName = "@SKU"
               .SqlDbType = SqlDbType.VarChar
               .Direction = ParameterDirection.Input
               .Value = SKU
            End With
            objCmd.Parameters.Add(objParam)

            objTemp = objCmd.ExecuteScalar()
            If TypeOf objTemp Is DBNull Then
               GetStockingLocation = ""
            Else
               GetStockingLocation = _
                  CType(objCmd.ExecuteScalar(), String)
            End If
            ContextUtil.SetComplete()

        Catch E As Exception
            ContextUtil.SetAbort()
            GetStockingLocation = ""
        Finally
            objCnn.Close()
        End Try
```

```
    End Function

    Private Function InventoryRecExists( _
            ByVal SKU As String, _
            ByVal StockingBinNumber As String) _
            As Boolean

        Dim objCnn As SqlConnection
        Dim objCmd As SqlCommand
        Dim objParam As SqlParameter
        Dim intRowCount As Integer
        Dim objTemp As Object

        Try
            objCnn = New SqlConnection()
            objCnn.ConnectionString = _
"Initial Catalog=Supermarket;Data Source=localhost;uid=sa;pwd="
            objCnn.Open()
            objCmd = objCnn.CreateCommand()

            objCmd.CommandText = _
                    "SELECT COUNT(*) FROM Inventory " & _
                    "WHERE SKU = @SKU AND " & _
                    "BinNumber = @StockingBinNumber"
            objParam = New SqlParameter()
            With objParam
                .ParameterName = "@SKU"
                .SqlDbType = SqlDbType.VarChar
                .Direction = ParameterDirection.Input
                .Value = SKU
            End With
            objCmd.Parameters.Add(objParam)

            objParam = New SqlParameter()
            With objParam
                .ParameterName = "@StockingBinNumber"
                .SqlDbType = SqlDbType.VarChar
                .Direction = ParameterDirection.Input
                .Value = StockingBinNumber
            End With
            objCmd.Parameters.Add(objParam)

            objTemp = objCmd.ExecuteScalar()
            If TypeOf objTemp Is DBNull Then
```

```
                intRowCount = 0
            Else
                intRowCount = CType(objTemp, Integer)
            End If

            If intRowCount > 0 Then
                InventoryRecExists = True
            Else
                InventoryRecExists = False
            End If

            ContextUtil.SetComplete()

        Catch E As Exception
            InventoryRecExists = False
            ContextUtil.SetAbort()
        Finally
            objCnn.Close()
        End Try

    End Function

    Private Sub UpdateInventoryRecord( _
                ByVal BinNumber As String, _
                ByVal SKU As String, _
                ByVal Quantity As Integer)

        Dim objCnn As SqlConnection
        Dim objCmd As SqlCommand
        Dim objParam As SqlParameter
        Dim intRowCount As Integer

        Try
            objCnn = New SqlConnection()
            objCnn.ConnectionString = _
"Initial Catalog=Supermarket;Data Source=localhost;uid=sa;pwd="
            objCnn.Open()
            objCmd = objCnn.CreateCommand()

            objCmd.CommandText = "UPDATE Inventory " & _
                 "SET Quantity = Quantity + @Quantity " & _
                 "WHERE BinNumber = @BinNumber AND SKU = @SKU"

            objParam = New SqlParameter()
```

```
            With objParam
               .ParameterName = "@Quantity"
               .SqlDbType = SqlDbType.Int
               .Direction = ParameterDirection.Input
               .Value = Quantity
            End With
            objCmd.Parameters.Add(objParam)

            objParam = New SqlParameter()
            With objParam
               .ParameterName = "@BinNumber"
               .SqlDbType = SqlDbType.VarChar
               .Direction = ParameterDirection.Input
               .Value = BinNumber
            End With
            objCmd.Parameters.Add(objParam)

            objParam = New SqlParameter()
            With objParam
               .ParameterName = "@SKU"
               .SqlDbType = SqlDbType.VarChar
               .Direction = ParameterDirection.Input
               .Value = SKU
            End With
            objCmd.Parameters.Add(objParam)

            intRowCount = objCmd.ExecuteNonQuery()
            ContextUtil.SetComplete()

         Catch E As Exception
            ContextUtil.SetAbort()
         Finally
            objCnn.Close()
         End Try
      End Sub

      Private Sub InsertInventoryRecord( _
              ByVal BinNumber As String, _
              ByVal SKU As String, _
              ByVal Quantity As Integer)

         Dim objCnn As SqlConnection
         Dim objCmd As SqlCommand
         Dim objParam As SqlParameter
```

```
        Dim intRowCount As Integer

        Try
           objCnn = New SqlConnection()
           objCnn.ConnectionString = _
  "Initial Catalog=Supermarket;Data Source=localhost;uid=sa;pwd="
           objCnn.Open()
           objCmd = objCnn.CreateCommand()

           objCmd.CommandText = _
                "INSERT INTO Inventory " & _
                "( BinNumber, SKU, Quantity ) VALUES " & _
                "( @BinNumber, @SKU,  @Quantity )"

           objParam = New SqlParameter()
           With objParam
              .ParameterName = "@BinNumber"
              .SqlDbType = SqlDbType.VarChar
              .Direction = ParameterDirection.Input
              .Value = BinNumber
           End With
           objCmd.Parameters.Add(objParam)

           objParam = New SqlParameter()
           With objParam
              .ParameterName = "@SKU"
              .SqlDbType = SqlDbType.VarChar
              .Direction = ParameterDirection.Input
              .Value = SKU
           End With
           objCmd.Parameters.Add(objParam)

           objParam = New SqlParameter()
           With objParam
              .ParameterName = "@Quantity"
              .SqlDbType = SqlDbType.Int
              .Direction = ParameterDirection.Input
              .Value = Quantity
           End With
           objCmd.Parameters.Add(objParam)

           intRowCount = objCmd.ExecuteNonQuery()
           ContextUtil.SetComplete()
```

```
        Catch E As Exception
            ContextUtil.SetAbort()
        Finally
            objCnn.Close()
        End Try
    End Sub

    Public Function Update(ByVal BinNumber As String, _
            ByVal SKU As String, _
            ByVal Quantity As Integer) _
            As Boolean _
            Implements IUpdateInventory.Update

        Dim objCnn As SqlConnection
        Dim objCmd As SqlCommand
        Dim objParam As SqlParameter
        Dim strStockingLocation As String
        Dim intRowsAffected As Integer

        Try
            If InventoryRecExists(SKU, BinNumber) Then
                UpdateInventoryRecord( _
                     BinNumber, _
                     SKU, _
                     Quantity)
            Else
                InsertInventoryRecord( _
                     BinNumber, _
                     SKU, _
                     Quantity)
            End If

            Update = True
            ContextUtil.SetComplete()

        Catch E As Exception
            Update = False
            ContextUtil.SetAbort()
        End Try

    End Function
  End Class
End Namespace
```

LAB CODE SAMPLE 5-4

```
Imports System
Imports System.Reflection
Imports System.EnterpriseServices
Imports System.Data
Imports System.Data.SqlClient

Namespace Supermarket

   Public Interface IReceiveOrder
      Function GetNextLineItem(ByVal OrderNumber As String, _
                      ByRef SKU As String) As Integer
      Function Receive(ByVal OrderNumber As String, _
                      ByVal SKU As String, _
                      ByVal LineNumber As Integer, _
                      ByVal QuantityReceived As Integer) _
                      As Boolean
   End Interface

   <ConstructionEnabled( _
   [Default]:="Default Construction String"), _
   Transaction(TransactionOption.Required)> _
   Public Class ReceiveOrder
      Inherits ServicedComponent
      Implements IReceiveOrder

      Public Sub New()

      End Sub

      Private Sub UpdateOrderDeatils( _
                  ByVal OrderNumber As String, _
                  ByVal LineNumber As Integer, _
                  ByVal QuantityReceived As Integer)

         Dim objCnn As SqlConnection
         Dim objCmd As SqlCommand
         Dim objParam As SqlParameter
         Dim objSQLDr As SqlDataReader
         Dim intRowsAffected As Integer

         Try
            objCnn = New SqlConnection()
```

```
            objCnn.ConnectionString = _
"Initial Catalog=Supermarket;Data Source=localhost;uid=sa;pwd="
            objCnn.Open()
            objCmd = objCnn.CreateCommand()

            objCmd.CommandText = _
"UPDATE OrderDetails " & _
"SET QuantityReceived = " & _
"QuantityReceived + @QuantityReceived " & _
"WHERE OrderNumber = " & _
"@OrderNumber AND LineItemNumber = @LineNumber"

            objParam = New SqlParameter()
            With objParam
               .ParameterName = "@QuantityReceived"
               .SqlDbType = SqlDbType.Int
               .Direction = ParameterDirection.Input
               .Value = QuantityReceived
            End With
            objCmd.Parameters.Add(objParam)

            objParam = New SqlParameter()
            With objParam
               .ParameterName = "@OrderNumber"
               .SqlDbType = SqlDbType.VarChar
               .Direction = ParameterDirection.Input
               .Value = OrderNumber
            End With
            objCmd.Parameters.Add(objParam)

            objParam = New SqlParameter()
            With objParam
               .ParameterName = "@LineNumber"
               .SqlDbType = SqlDbType.Int
               .Direction = ParameterDirection.Input
               .Value = LineNumber
            End With
            objCmd.Parameters.Add(objParam)

            intRowsAffected = objCmd.ExecuteNonQuery()

            ContextUtil.SetComplete()

         Catch E As Exception
```

```
            ContextUtil.SetAbort()
        Finally
            objCnn.Close()
        End Try

    End Sub

    Public Function GetNextLineItem( _
            ByVal OrderNumber As String, _
            ByRef SKU As String) _
            As Integer Implements _
            IReceiveOrder.GetNextLineItem

        Dim objCnn As SqlConnection
        Dim objCmd As SqlCommand
        Dim objParam As SqlParameter
        Dim objSQLDr As SqlDataReader

        Try

            objCnn = New SqlConnection()
            objCnn.ConnectionString = _
"Initial Catalog=Supermarket;Data Source=localhost;uid=sa;pwd="
            objCnn.Open()
            objCmd = objCnn.CreateCommand()

            objCmd.CommandText = _
                "SELECT MAX(LineItemNumber), " & _
                "SKU FROM OrderDetails od, Orders o " & _
                "WHERE od.OrderNumber = @OrderNumber AND " & _
                "o.OrderReceived = 0 AND " & _
                "o.OrderNumber = od.OrderNumber GROUP BY SKU"

            objParam = New SqlParameter()
            With objParam
                .ParameterName = "@OrderNumber"
                .SqlDbType = SqlDbType.VarChar
                .Direction = ParameterDirection.Input
                .Value = OrderNumber
            End With
            objCmd.Parameters.Add(objParam)

            objSQLDr = objCmd.ExecuteReader()
            objSQLDr.Read()
```

```
            If Not objSQLDr.IsDBNull(0) Then
               GetNextLineItem = objSQLDr.GetInt32(0)
               SKU = objSQLDr.GetString(1)
            Else
               GetNextLineItem = -1
               SKU = ""
            End If

            ContextUtil.SetComplete()
            objSQLDr.Close()

         Catch E As Exception
            GetNextLineItem = -1
            SKU = ""
            ContextUtil.SetAbort()
         Finally
            objCnn.Close()
         End Try

      End Function

      Public Function Receive(ByVal OrderNumber As String, _
                     ByVal SKU As String, _
                     ByVal LineNumber As Integer, _
                     ByVal QuantityReceived As Integer) _
                     As Boolean _
                     Implements IReceiveOrder.Receive

         Dim objCnn As SqlConnection
         Dim objCmd As SqlCommand
         Dim objParam As SqlParameter
         Dim objInvUpdate As IUpdateInventory
         Dim strBinNumber As String

         Try
            UpdateOrderDeatils(OrderNumber, _
                    LineNumber, _
                    QuantityReceived)

            objInvUpdate = New UpdateInventory()
            strBinNumber = _
               objInvUpdate.GetStockingLocation(SKU)
```

```
            If objInvUpdate.Update(strBinNumber, _
                    SKU, QuantityReceived) Then
               Receive = True
               ContextUtil.SetComplete()
            Else
               Receive = False
               ContextUtil.SetAbort()
            End If

         Catch E As Exception
            Receive = False
            ContextUtil.SetAbort()
         End Try
      End Function

   End Class
End Namespace
```

e. Now that you've entered the main code for the Supermarket COM+ application, it's time to compile it. Choose **Build→Build Solution** from the menu to create the assembly file. In the next step, you'll create a project that references that assembly.

STEP 4. Create the ASP.NET application.

a. Create a new VB ASP.NET project called "SupermarketWeb".

b. Add a reference to `System.EnterpriseServices` to the project by right-clicking the project icon and selecting **Add Reference . . .** from the pop-up menu.

c. Add four new Web Forms (`.aspx` files) and their code-behind files (`.vb` files) to the project, named as follows:

```
Lcs5-5.aspx, Lcs5-5.aspx.vb
Lcs5-6.aspx, Lcs5-6.aspx.vb
Lcs5-7.aspx, Lcs5-7.aspx.vb
Lcs5-8.aspx, Lcs5-8.aspx.vb
```

These Web Forms will test the different components and their functionality.

Product Component Test Web Form

The HTML for the Lcs5-5.aspx file appears below.

LAB CODE SAMPLE 5-5

```
<%@ Page Language="vb"
   AutoEventWireup="false"
   src="Lcs5-05.aspx.vb"
   Inherits="WebForm1"
   Transaction="RequiresNew"%>
<html>
<head>
<title>Create New Product</title>
</head>
<body>

<form id="Form1"
   method="post"
   runat="server">

<p>SKU:
<asp:TextBox
   id=txtSKU
   runat="server">
</asp:TextBox></p>

<p>Description:
<asp:TextBox
   id=txtDescription
   runat="server">
</asp:TextBox></p>

<p>Unit Price:
<asp:TextBox
   id=txtUnitPrice
   runat="server">
</asp:TextBox></p>

<p>Stocking Location:
<asp:TextBox
   id=txtStockLoc
   runat="server">
</asp:TextBox></p>
```

```
<p>
<asp:Button
   id=cmdAddProduct
   runat="server"
   Text-"Add Product">
</asp:Button>

<asp:CompareValidator
   id=CompareValidator1
   runat="server"
   ErrorMessage="You must enter a price (number)"
   Type="Double"
   ControlToValidate="txtUnitPrice"
   Operator="DataTypeCheck">
</asp:CompareValidator></p>

</form>
</body>
</html>
```

ASP.NET Web Forms can run inside the context of a COM+ Component Services transaction. In this ASP.NET Web application, the Web Forms call the serviced components in response to events raised by Web Controls (buttons clicked and so on). Since the ASP.NET Web Form is the initiator of calls made into a COM+ application, the Web Form is considered the root of the transaction. It has the "final vote" as to whether or not the transaction succeeds or fails.

In order to designate that the Web Form will participate in a transaction, you need to set the `Transaction` page attribute (highlighted in bold above). This code specifies the level as `RequiresNew`. This means that the page will always begin a new transaction for any units of work executed during the lifetime of the page.

Here is the code-behind file, `Lcs5-5.aspx.vb`, for the preceding Web Form.

```
Imports SupermarketSystem.Supermarket
Imports System.EnterpriseServices
Imports System.Reflection
Imports System.ComponentModel

Public Class WebForm1
      Inherits System.Web.UI.Page
      Protected WithEvents cmdAddProduct As _
   System.Web.UI.WebControls.Button
      Protected WithEvents txtSKU As _
```

```
System.Web.UI.WebControls.TextBox
   Protected WithEvents txtDescription As _
System.Web.UI.WebControls.TextBox
   Protected WithEvents txtUnitPrice As _
System.Web.UI.WebControls.TextBox
   Protected WithEvents txtStockLoc As _
System.Web.UI.WebControls.TextBox
   Protected WithEvents CompareValidator1 As_
System.Web.UI.WebControls.CompareValidator

   Private Sub Page_Load(ByVal sender As System.Object, _
          ByVal e As System.EventArgs) Handles MyBase.Load

   End Sub

   Private Sub cmdAddProduct_Click( _
      ByVal sender As System.Object, _
      ByVal e As System.EventArgs) _
      Handles cmdAddProduct.Click

      Dim objProduct As IProduct
      Dim bln As Boolean

      objProduct = New Product()
      bln = objProduct.Create(txtSKU.Text, _
               txtDescription.Text, _
               CDec(txtUnitPrice.Text), _
               txtStockLoc.Text)

      If bln Then
            ContextUtil.SetComplete()
      Else
            ContextUtil.SetAbort()
      End If

   End Sub
End Class
```

The `Click` event for the `cmdAddProduct` button calls the `Product` component to add a new product to the database. The code creates a new `Product` object and obtains a reference to the `IProduct` interface. It then calls the `Create()` method. If the call was successful (returned `True`), `SetComplete()` is called to indicate to COM+ that this unit of work in the transaction was successful. If not, `SetAbort()`stops the transaction immediately.

CreateOrder **Component Test Web Form**

The code for the Lcs5-6.aspx file follows below. Note that again the Transaction page attribute is specified and set to RequiresNew.

LAB CODE SAMPLE 5-6

```
<%@ Page Language="vb"
   AutoEventWireup="false"
   src="Lcs5-06.aspx.vb"
   Inherits="SupermarketCreateOrder"
   Transaction="RequiresNew"%>
<html>
<head>
<title>Create New Order</title>
</head>
<body>

<form id="Form1"
   method="post"
   runat="server">

<p>Order number:
<asp:TextBox
   id=txtOrderNumber
   runat="server">
</asp:TextBox></p>

<p>Supplier Name:
<asp:TextBox
   id=txtSupplierName
   runat="server">
</asp:TextBox></p>

<p>
<asp:Button
   id=cmdCreateOrder
   runat="server"
   Text="Add">
</asp:Button></p>

</form>
</body>
</html>
```

The code-behind file, `Lcs5-6.aspx.vb`, contains the following code.

```
Imports System.EnterpriseServices
Imports System.Reflection
Imports SupermarketSystem.Supermarket

Public Class SupermarketCreateOrder
   Inherits System.Web.UI.Page
   Protected WithEvents txtOrderNumber As _
      System.Web.UI.WebControls.TextBox
   Protected WithEvents txtSupplierName As _
      System.Web.UI.WebControls.TextBox
   Protected WithEvents cmdCreateOrder As _
      System.Web.UI.WebControls.Button

   Private Sub Page_Load(ByVal sender As System.Object, _
      ByVal e As System.EventArgs) Handles MyBase.Load

   End Sub

   Private Sub cmdCreateOrder_Click( _
      ByVal sender As System.Object, _
      ByVal e As System.EventArgs) _
      Handles cmdCreateOrder.Click

      Dim objCreateOrder As ICreateOrder
      objCreateOrder = New CreateOrder()

      If objCreateOrder.Create(txtOrderNumber.Text, _
                         txtSupplierName.Text) Then
         ContextUtil.SetComplete()
      Else
         ContextUtil.SetAbort()
      End If
   End Sub
End Class
```

Similar to the test Web Form for the `Product` component, this code creates a `CreateOrder` object using `New`. The program calls the `Create()` method and then calls `SetComplete()` or `SetAbort()` upon success or failure, respectively.

AddToOrder Test Web Form

The HTML code for the AddToOrder Web Form (Lcs5-7.aspx) appears below.

LAB CODE SAMPLE 5-7

```
<%@ Page Language="vb"
   AutoEventWireup="false"
   Codebehind="SupermarketAddToOrder.aspx.vb"
   Inherits="SupermarketWeb.SupermarketAddToOrder"
   Transaction="RequiresNew"%>
<html>
<head>
<title>Add To Order</title>
</head>
<body>

<form id="Form1"
   method="post"
   runat="server">

<p>Order Number:
<asp:TextBox
   id=txtOrderNumber
   runat="server">
</asp:TextBox></p>

<p>SKU:
<asp:TextBox
   id=txtSKU
   runat="server">
</asp:TextBox></p>

<p>Quantity:
<asp:TextBox
   id=txtQuantity
   runat="server">
</asp:TextBox></p>

<p>
<asp:CompareValidator
   id=CompareValidator1
   runat="server"
   ErrorMessage="Quantity must be a whole number!"
```

```
   ControlToValidate="txtQuantity"
   Type="Integer"
   Operator="DataTypeCheck">
</asp:CompareValidator></p>

<p>
<asp:Button
   id=cmdAddToOrder
   runat="server"
   Text="Add To Order">
</asp:Button></p>

</form>
</body>
</html>
```

Here is the associated code-behind file (`Lcs5-7.aspx.vb`). `AddItems()` is a method of the `CreateOrder` component, so the code is very similar to the `CreateOrder` Web Form.

```
Imports System.EnterpriseServices
Imports System.Reflection
Imports SupermarketSystem.Supermarket

Public Class SupermarketAddToOrder
   Inherits System.Web.UI.Page
   Protected WithEvents txtOrderNumber As _
      System.Web.UI.WebControls.TextBox
   Protected WithEvents txtSKU As _
      System.Web.UI.WebControls.TextBox
   Protected WithEvents txtQuantity As _
      System.Web.UI.WebControls.TextBox
   Protected WithEvents CompareValidator1 As _
      System.Web.UI.WebControls.CompareValidator
   Protected WithEvents cmdAddToOrder As _
      System.Web.UI.WebControls.Button

   Private Sub Page_Load(ByVal sender As System.Object, _
        ByVal e As System.EventArgs) Handles MyBase.Load

   End Sub

   Private Sub cmdAddToOrder_Click( _
        ByVal sender As System.Object, _
```

```
        ByVal e As System.EventArgs) _
        Handles cmdAddToOrder.Click

      Dim objCreateOrder As ICreateOrder
      objCreateOrder = New CreateOrder()

      If objCreateOrder.AddItems(txtOrderNumber.Text, _
         txtSKU.Text, CInt(txtQuantity.Text)) Then

         ContextUtil.SetComplete()
      Else
         ContextUtil.SetAbort()
      End If
   End Sub
End Class
```

ReceiveOrder Component Test Web Form

Finally, here is the code (Lcs5-8.aspx) for the Web Form that will receive items for an order.

LAB CODE SAMPLE 5-8

```
<%@ Page Language="vb"
   AutoEventWireup="false"
   src="SupermarketReceiveOrder.aspx.vb"
   Inherits="SupermarketReceiveOrder"
   Transaction="RequiresNew"%>
<html>
<head>
<title>Receive Order</title>
</head>
<body>

<form id="Form1"
   method="post"
   runat="server">

<p>Order Number to Receive:

<asp:TextBox
   id=txtOrderToReceive
   runat="server">
</asp:TextBox>
```

```
<asp:Button
   id=cmdGetOrder
   runat="server"
   Text="Get Order">
</asp:Button></p>

<p>
<asp:Panel
   id=Panel1
   runat="server"
   Width="399px"
   Height="144px"
   Enabled="False">

   <p>
   <asp:Label
   id=lblOrderNumber
   runat="server"
   Width="184px"
   Height="19px">
   </asp:Label></p>

   <p></p><p>
   <asp:Label
   id=lblReceiveSKU
   runat="server"
   Width="183px"
   Height="19px">
   </asp:Label></p>

   <p>
   <asp:Label
   id=lblLineNumberReceive
   runat="server"
   Width="188px"
   Height="19px">
   </asp:Label></p>

   <p>
   <asp:Label
   id=Label1
   runat="server"
   Width="128px"
```

```
    Height="19px">
    Quantity To Receive:
    </asp:Label>

    <asp:TextBox
    id=txtQuantityToReceive
    runat="server">
    </asp:TextBox>

    <asp:Button
    id=cmdReceive
    runat="server"
    Text="Receive">
    </asp:Button>

</asp:Panel></p>

</form>
</body>
</html>
```

This Web Form wraps page elements in a `Panel` Web Control. The panel is initially disabled to avoid displaying or enabling the order information until a valid order number is keyed into the Web Form. Here's the code-behind file (`Lcs5-8.aspx.vb`).

```
Imports System.EnterpriseServices
Imports System.Reflection
Imports SupermarketSystem.Supermarket

Public Class SupermarketReceiveOrder
   Inherits System.Web.UI.Page
   Protected WithEvents cmdGetOrder As _
      System.Web.UI.WebControls.Button
   Protected WithEvents Panel1 As _
      System.Web.UI.WebControls.Panel
   Protected WithEvents lblOrderNumber As _
      System.Web.UI.WebControls.Label
   Protected WithEvents Label1 As _
      System.Web.UI.WebControls.Label
   Protected WithEvents txtOrderToReceive As _
      System.Web.UI.WebControls.TextBox
   Protected WithEvents cmdReceive As _
      System.Web.UI.WebControls.Button
```

```
Protected WithEvents lblReceiveSKU As _
   System.Web.UI.WebControls.Label
Protected WithEvents lblLineNumberReceive As _
   System.Web.UI.WebControls.Label
Protected WithEvents txtQuantityToReceive As _
   System.Web.UI.WebControls.TextBox

Private Sub Page_Load(ByVal sender As System.Object, _
   ByVal e As System.EventArgs) Handles MyBase.Load

End Sub

Private Sub cmdGetOrder_Click( _
   ByVal sender As System.Object, _
   ByVal e As System.EventArgs) _
   Handles cmdGetOrder.Click

   Dim objReceiveOrder As IReceiveOrder
   Dim intLineNumber As Integer
   Dim strSKUToReceive As String

   objReceiveOrder = New ReceiveOrder()

   intLineNumber = _
        objReceiveOrder.GetNextLineItem( _
        txtOrderToReceive.Text, _
        strSKUToReceive)

   If intLineNumber <> -1 Then
      ViewState("OrderToReceive") = txtOrderToReceive.Text
      ViewState("SKUToReceive") = strSKUToReceive
      ViewState("LineNumber") = intLineNumber
      Panel1.Enabled = True
      lblLineNumberReceive.Text = _
           "Line Number: " & intLineNumber
      lblOrderNumber.Text = _
           "Order Number: " & txtOrderToReceive.Text
      lblReceiveSKU.Text = "SKU: " & strSKUToReceive
   Else
      Panel1.Enabled = False
   End If
End Sub

Private Sub cmdReceive_Click( _
```

```
        ByVal sender As System.Object, _
        ByVal e As System.EventArgs) _
        Handles cmdReceive.Click

        Dim objReceiveOrder As IReceiveOrder
        objReceiveOrder = New ReceiveOrder()

        If objReceiveOrder.Receive( _
                ViewState("OrderToReceive"), _
                ViewState("SKUToReceive"), _
                ViewState("LineNumber"), _
                CInt(txtQuantityToReceive.Text)) Then

           ContextUtil.SetComplete()
        Else
           ContextUtil.SetAbort()
        End If
    End Sub
End Class
```

This form uses two `Button` Web Controls, `cmdGetOrder` and `cmdReceive`. This makes a two-step process for receiving items for an order. First, the event handler for `cmdGetOrder` calls `GetNextLineItem()`, taking as input the order number the user entered. If there is a line item to receive for the order, the program displays the line-item information in the `Label` Web Control contained within the `Panel` Web Control. The `Panel` Web Control is then enabled, making the information visible to the user. The line-item information is also copied to the `ViewState StateBag` because the program will need this information on the subsequent post-back that will occur when items are received.

The event handler for `cmdReceive` calls the `Receive()` method. The `Receive()` method updates the `OrderDetails` table as well as the `Inventory` table. Using a transaction in this situation helps point out any discrepancies between quantities in inventory and quantities ordered. The `Receive()` method returns `True` on success and `False` on failure, and the program makes an appropriate call to either `SetComplete()` or `SetAbort()` as a result.

d. Now you need to add a reference to the assembly DLL for the components. Right-click the References folder in the Solution Explorer, select **Add Reference**, browse to the compiled DLL, and select it. Click OK to add the reference to the selected assembly.

STEP 5. Run the application.

a. Now you're ready to build the application. Select **Build→Build Solution** from the menu. Select a start page for the application (like `Lcs5-5.aspx`) by right-clicking on a Web Form in the Solution Explorer and selecting **Set As Start Page** from the menu.

b. Run the application by selecting **Debug→Start Without Debugging.**

c. Test the application by entering some products. Then create a new order, add some items to the order, and run an order-receive process. This should complete a full test.

Something important happened when you first called a component's method inside the assembly. The system performed what is known as a *lazy registration*. A lazy registration automatically places the components in the assembly into a new COM+ application in the COM+ Component Services Console. It does this based on the assembly-level attributes specified in the component assembly code. Lab Figure 5–4 shows the Supermarket COM+ application in the COM+ Component Services Console.

STEP 6. Add role-based security.

a. One of the requirements for the application is that only certain categories of users should be allowed to run certain components. To enable role-based security for the Supermarket COM+ application, right-click on the Supermarket COM+ application icon and select **Properties**. Click the **Security** tab. Check the boxes and radio buttons as shown in Lab Figure 5-5.

b. Now you can set up the user roles (Receiving Clerks, Supervisors, and Suppliers) inside the COM+ Component Services Console. For each role, right-click the Roles folder under the Supermarket application (see Lab Figure 5-6), select **New→Role** from the menu, and assign a name for the role.

c. Assign users to each role by right-clicking the User folder under the role and selecting **New→User** from the menu. Pick a Windows account name(s) or group(s) to assign to the role. Lab Figure 5-7 shows users assigned to the various roles of the Supermarket application.

d. Now you need to assign each role to a component. Right-click a component in the COM+ application and select **Properties** from the menu. Click the **Security** tab. Check **Enforce component level access checks**, and then check the roles you wish to assign to the component, as shown in Lab Figure 5-8.

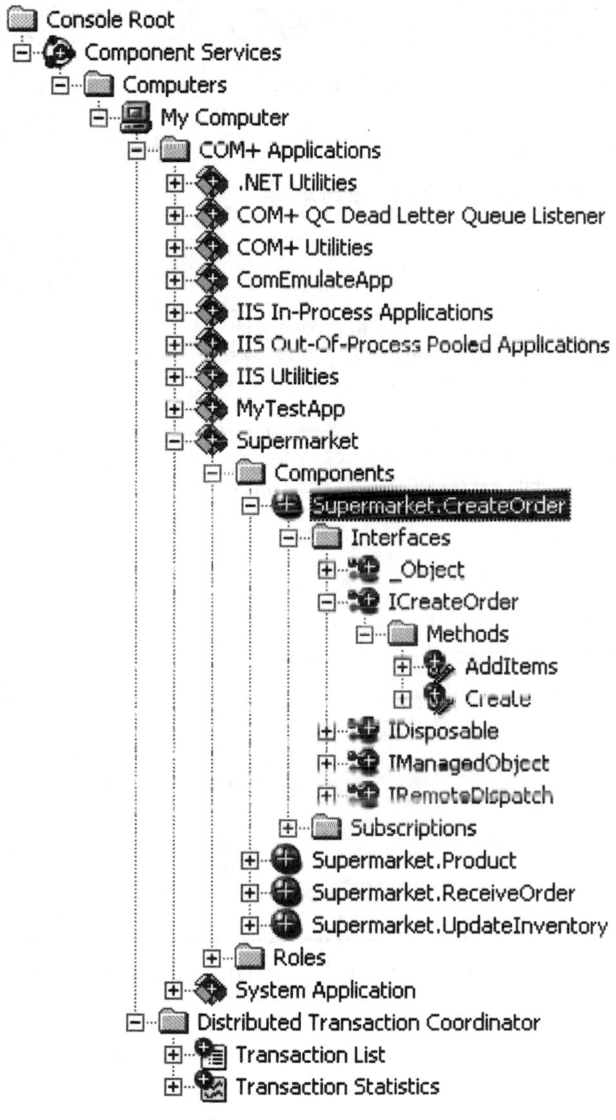

Lab Figure 5-4 The Supermarket application within the COM+ Component Services Console

STEP 7. Test the role-based security.

a. A convenient way to test the role-based security is to call the components from a console application and run the console application in the security

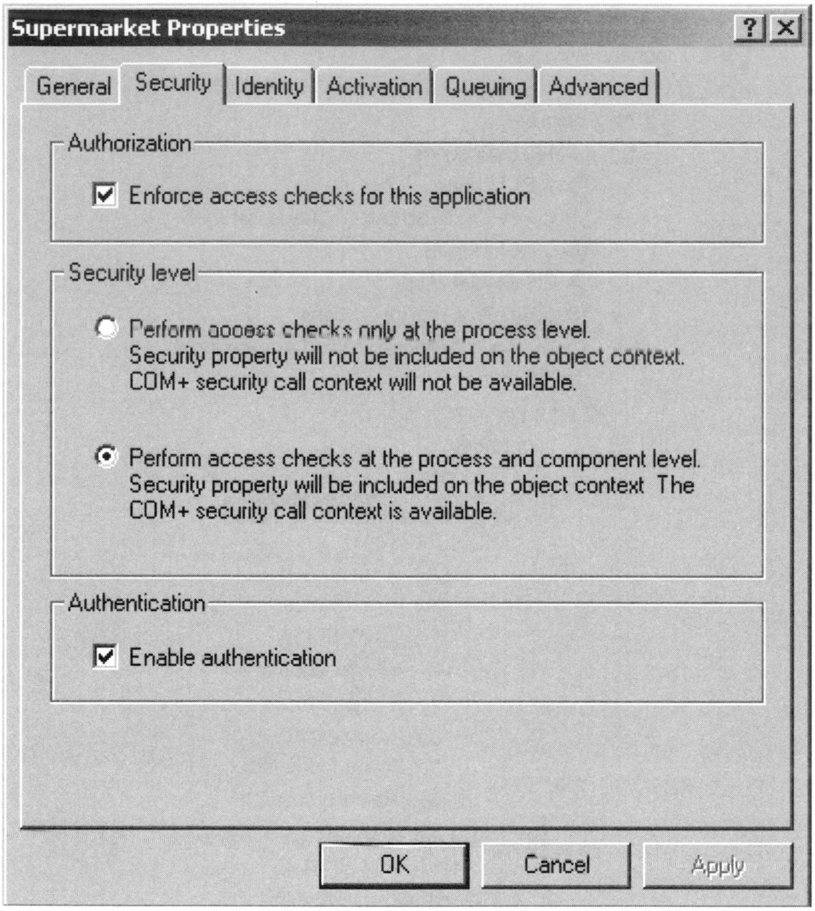

Lab Figure 5-5 Enabling role-based security for the Supermarket application

context of a specific user. Normally, when you run an application from the console, Windows uses the security context of the currently logged-on user. By using the `runas` command, you can run an executable program using any account name (provided, of course, you have the password of that account!). Here's a simple console application you can run to test role-based security.

```
Imports System
Imports SupermarketSystem.Supermarket
Imports System.EnterpriseServices

Module Module1
```

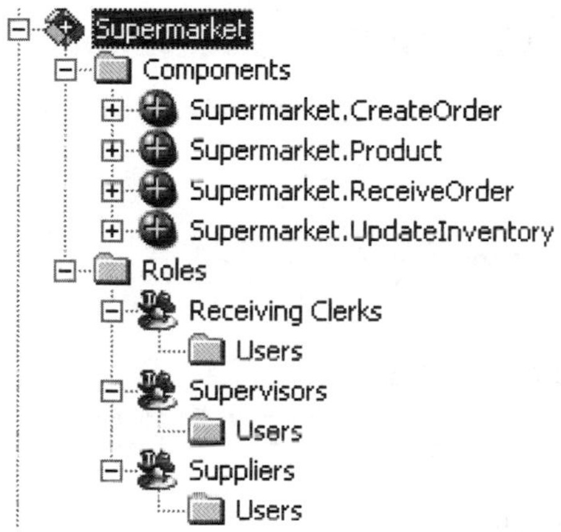

Lab Figure 5-6 Adding roles for the Supermarket application

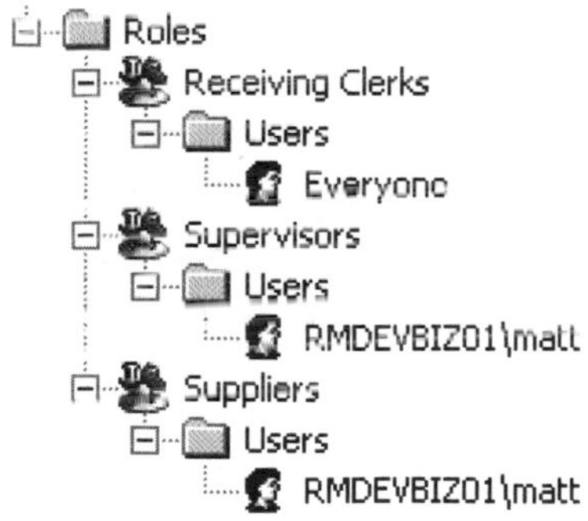

Lab Figure 5-7 Assigning users to roles

```
    Sub Main()
       Dim objCreateOrder As ICreateOrder

       objCreateOrder = New CreateOrder()

       objCreateOrder.Create("834957239-1", "My Supplier")

    End Sub

End Module
```

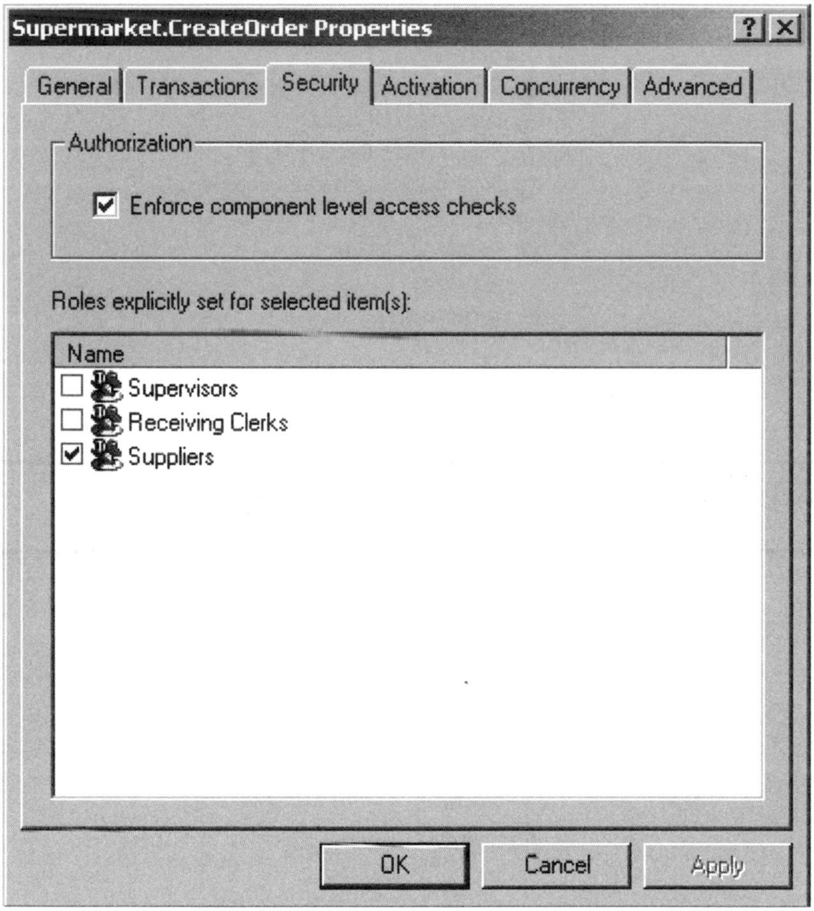

Lab Figure 5-8 Assigning roles to components

Compile this small testing console application and run it using the `runas` command below:

```
runas /user:rmdevbiz01\matt roletester.exe
```

Given the role configuration of the `CreateOrder` component, the username "matt" should be the only user allowed to run the application. Assuming that the user account "matt" has appropriate Windows permissions set to run the program, it should execute without errors.

b. You can also perform a negative test by rerunning the program with an account name not included in the Supplier role.

5.7 Summary

Let's recap what you've learned in this chapter about writing .NET managed components.

- Managed code is application code that executes within the .NET Framework.
- Runtime systems enable application programs you write to access operating system–level services. Several different runtime environments are available for various systems. A runtime environment is usually specific to a programming language.
- Intermediate languages provide an additional layer of abstraction over another existing runtime environment. The goal of intermediate languages is to provide portability of application code across operating systems. The intermediate language for the .NET Framework is called the *Microsoft Intermediate Language* (MSIL).
- The runtime environment for the .NET Framework is called the *Common Language Runtime* (CLR). It supports self-describing code through metadata, a specification for the Common Type System (CTS), just-in-time compilation of code, and the concept of assembly manifests, which describe a packaged set of components, programs, files, and other dependencies an application needs in order to function properly.
- COM is a programming model invented by Microsoft that allows for binary-level software component reuse.
- Transactions provide consistency and data integrity to a software system. By checking the success or failure of smaller atomic tasks that make up the transaction, you can decide whether the transaction should succeed as a whole.
- Windows provides programmers with easy transaction support for their applications through COM+ Component Services. COM+ Component Services provides transaction support, object pooling, and component-level runtime security.
- Components are simply classes at their most basic level. Components have properties and methods, which roughly correspond to member functions and member variables, respectively.
- Serviced components are classes that take advantage of COM+ Component Services. Security is provided by grouping users into roles and assigning those roles to components.

5.8 What's Ahead

In Chapter 6 we'll explore Web Services, the most important part of the .NET Framework. Chapter 7 covers data access with ADO.NET, and we'll wrap up with .NET Web application security topics in Chapter 8.

CHAPTER 6

Building Web Services

Web Services form the most important piece of the .NET Framework. Web Services solve the problems that arise from the design and implementation of distributed software systems. For the first time, software developers can use the Internet as an infrastructure for building applications. Data can flow freely through this infrastructure, unrestrained by incompatibilities of protocols and transport mechanisms. Much as component-based software systems revolutionized the way desktop and server-side applications are developed, so do Web Services make these component-based systems truly distributed. Also, Web Services can be used in any operating system or platform environment, which makes interoperability with other software easy.

This chapter covers the following topics:

- The problems associated with distributed Web application development and how Web Services can solve these problems
- The architecture of Web Services as they relate to ASP.NET
- The Web Service Description Language (WSDL)
- Wire formats (the communication protocols used by Web Services)
- Static and dynamic discovery of Web Services
- Creation of Web Services, including the use of transactions and state management

6.1 The Need for Web Services

Over the course of many years before the days of the Internet, we came to rely on software systems tied to a desktop computer or mainframe. All the functionality of the programs we used was supplied through software installed on the desktop computer's hard drive or, in the case of time-sharing mainframe systems, the software ran on that central computer and displayed information through a terminal console. Each application was usually suited for a particular task, for example, word processing or banking, and had little or no facilities to access external data outside the scope of what the application was designed to handle. And as these applications became more complex and grew in size, so did the effort increase on the part of software developers making these applications.

Another problem associated with these monolithic applications was incompatibilities between network mediums and protocols. Many of these systems, if they were networked at all, used proprietary network mediums and protocols that were generally incompatible with other networks. Hopes of sharing data across these systems were thwarted due to complex interfacing code that would need to be developed in order for communication to take place.

Switching these software systems to component-based architecture solved many of the problems of upgrading, scaling, and interfacing. Many software vendors have been quite successful selling just components to other software developers who make complete applications from them. Components make software development easier because code doesn't need to be written from scratch, it can easily be upgraded, and it provides a logical structure that makes complex, enterprise-wide applications more understandable.

However, component-based software systems are not without their architectural limitations. Many component-based architectures are designed to work within the confines of a single computer, limiting their ability to operate over a network. If distributed capabilities exist, they are typically retrofitted onto the current design, as is the case with COM/DCOM (Distributed COM). Furthermore, the communication protocol used for sending remote procedure calls (RPCs) over the network wire is proprietary and uses network communication channels that are normally not accessible through firewall systems due to security reasons. Web Services aim to solve these problems and make distributed component-based computing practical and usable for all participants.

6.1.1 Standards-Based Functionality (XML and HTTP)

The framework for Web Services is founded in open Internet standards; no part of Web Services uses proprietary technology. HTTP is the substrate for all communications between components and clients of those components. HTTP network traffic flows across firewalls since it uses the same network port as other Web traffic. The payload of these communications is contained inside a special XML data format called the *Simple Object Access Protocol* (SOAP; see Section 6.4.3).

It's important to point out that Web Services are not another component architecture like COM, CORBA, or JavaBeans. Rather, they form a communication method that allows components to communicate with clients and each other. The advantage is that the transport mechanism is decoupled from the component technology. Thus, components using different architectures can talk to each other using the Web Services framework no matter the underlying component architecture. In fact, the client of a Web Service knows nothing about the underlying architecture of the component, nor is the client tightly coupled with the component—and that's a good thing.

6.1.2 Separation of Data from Presentation

Many people already use Web sites to perform specific day-to-day tasks. We use different Web sites to shop for goods and services, manage our finances, arrange for travel, buy and sell stocks, and perform many other tasks. Today these tasks are performed through Web browsers accessing HTML pages. Although it's convenient to have all this information and these services available to use at the click of a mouse, the limitation of these sites becomes apparent: data is tied to an HTML page, which is in turn tied to a computer and a Web browser.

As the Internet grows, users are demanding access to their information while they are away from their desktop computers. Devices such as cell phones, PDAs, sub-notebook computers, and even home refrigerators now have wireless capabilities and can access Internet sites. Since these devices are meant to be portable and/or don't have the computing resources of a full computer (as is the case of the home refrigerator), they have limited screen space. Many devices can display only a few lines of text (typically 15–20 characters each) and cannot display graphics. This makes traditional Web browsing impossible. Thus, the data available on standard Web pages are inaccessible to these wireless devices.

Traditional applications that attempt to use services provided by Web sites also experience limitations. For example, if you want to query the current stock price of a company, you enter the ticker symbol and click the Submit button. The results come in the form of a new HTML page, with graphics, formatting, and other redundant information when all you want is the string containing the stock price. The application would have to perform complex string search operations to parse out the data you need. However, if the Web site exposed that lookup functionality as a Web Service, it would return only the relevant data (the stock price). You could query the service programmatically and use the return value in a manner appropriate for the device you used to access the service.

6.2 Overview of Web Services

Since Web Services are part of ASP.NET and thus the .NET Framework, they share the same architectural benefits as other .NET Framework applications. Web Services are compiled classes (using any .NET-compatible language) just like the classes we have worked with up to this point. These classes are contained within a `.asmx` file. This is how ASP.NET identifies a Web Service.

6.2.1 The .asmx File

The `.asmx` file contains code, such as Visual Basic, that is compiled into a class. This file contains a special page directive that identifies the file to the compiler as a Web Service. Another page directive specifies the name of the Web Service class. To illustrate, here's how an "empty" `.asmx` file looks.

```
<%@ WebService Language="VB" Class="MyWebServiceClass" %>
Imports System.Web.Services
```

The second line denotes that you wish to import the required class libraries that enable Web Services to work. These classes are contained in the `System.Web.Services` namespace.

6.2.2 Web Service Classes and Web Methods

A Web Service begins with a class definition. Web Service classes are just like classes that we've created before but with a couple of distinguishing elements. Let's look at a very simple class definition.

```
Public Class FirstWebService
   Inherits System.Web.Services.WebService

   <WebMethod> Public Function  HelloWorld() As String
```

```
        HelloWorld = "Hello World"
    End Function

End Class
```

The implementation of this method is quite simple and not really important, but the declaration of the member function is key. The class starts by inheriting from `System.Web.Services.WebService`, which is a class that contains support for Web Services. It also exposes ASP.NET intrinsic objects, such as those used for session and state management. The member function `HelloWorld()` contains an attribute class called `<WebMethod>`. This specifics that the member function will be publicly exposed through the Web Service. This attribute class also allows you to define an optional description for the Web method and specify additional parameters that can alter the behavior of the Web method. We'll discuss the specifics shortly

6.3 Web Service Description Language

Building a Web Service is just the first step to distributing component functionality over the Web. You also need a mechanism that allows clients of your Web Service to locate it and learn about its structure. This enables clients to discover what methods are available in the Web Service as well as how to call them.

Web Services have the ability to describe themselves, that is, they can tell clients how to call their methods, what the parameters and types are, and what data types to expect as return values from those methods. This is accomplished by describing the Web Service through an XML data format called *Web Service Description Language* (WSDL).

WSDL describes the methods of a Web Service, the data type definitions, the parameter definitions of each method, the supported wire formats for calling the Web Service, the URL where the Web Service is located, and other supporting information. Below is the WSDL file from the previous example's HelloWorld Web Service.

```
<?xml version="1.0" encoding="utf-8"?>
<definitions xmlns:s=http://www.w3.org/2001/XMLSchema
xmlns:http=http://schemas.xmlsoap.org/wsdl/http/
xmlns:mime=http://schemas.xmlsoap.org/wsdl/mime/
xmlns:tm=http://microsoft.com/wsdl/mime/textMatching/
```

```
xmlns:soap=http://schemas.xmlsoap.org/wsdl/soap/
xmlns:soapenc="http://schemas.xmlsoap.org/soap/encoding/"
xmlns:s0="http://tempuri.org/"
targetNamespace="http://tempuri.org/"
xmlns="http://schemas.xmlsoap.org/wsdl/">
   <types>
      <s:schema attributeFormDefault="qualified"
      elementFormDefault="qualified"
      targetNamespace="http://tempuri.org/">
         <s:element name="HelloWorld">
            <s:complexType />
         </s:element>
         <s:element name="HelloWorldResponse">
            <s:complexType>
               <s:sequence>
                  <s:element minOccurs="1"
                     maxOccurs="1"
                     name="HelloWorldResult"
                     nillable="true"
                     type="s:string" />
               </s:sequence>
            </s:complexType>
         </s:element>
         <s:element name="string"
            nillable="true"
            type="s:string" />
      </s:schema>
   </types>
   <message name="HelloWorldSoapIn">
      <part name="parameters" element="s0:HelloWorld" />
   </message>
   <message name="HelloWorldSoapOut">
      <part name="parameters" element="s0:HelloWorldResponse" />
   </message>
   <message name="HelloWorldHttpGetIn" />
   <message name="HelloWorldHttpGetOut">
      <part name="Body" element="s0:string" />
   </message>
   <message name="HelloWorldHttpPostIn" />
   <message name="HelloWorldHttpPostOut">
      <part name="Body" element="s0:string" />
   </message>
   <portType name="PalindromeTestSoap">
```

```
    <operation name="HelloWorld">
      <input message="s0:HelloWorldSoapIn" />
      <output message="s0:HelloWorldSoapOut" />
    </operation>
  </portType>
  <portType name="PalindromeTestHttpGet">
    <operation name="HelloWorld">
      <input message="s0:HelloWorldHttpGetIn" />
      <output message="s0:HelloWorldHttpGetOut" />
    </operation>
  </portType>
  <portType name="PalindromeTestHttpPost">
    <operation name="HelloWorld">
      <input message="s0:HelloWorldHttpPostIn" />
      <output message="s0:HelloWorldHttpPostOut" />
    </operation>
  </portType>
  <binding name="PalindromeTestSoap"
    type="s0:PalindromeTestSoap">
    <soap:binding
      transport="http://schemas.xmlsoap.org/soap/http"
      style="document" />
    <operation name="HelloWorld">
      <soap:operation
      soapAction="http://tempuri.org/HelloWorld"
      style="document" />
      <input>
        <soap:body use="literal" />
      </input>
      <output>
        <soap:body use="literal" />
      </output>
    </operation>
  </binding>
  <binding name="PalindromeTestHttpGet"
    type="s0:PalindromeTestHttpGet">
    <http:binding verb="GET" />
    <operation name="HelloWorld">
      <http:operation location="/HelloWorld" />
      <input>
        <http:urlEncoded />
      </input>
      <output>
```

```
            <mime:mimeXml part="Body" />
         </output>
      </operation>
   </binding>
   <binding name="PalindromeTestHttpPost"
      type="s0:PalindromeTestHttpPost">
      <http:binding verb="POST" />
      <operation name="HelloWorld">
         <http:operation location="/HelloWorld" />
         <input>
            <mime:content
               type="application/x-www-form-urlencoded" />
         </input>
         <output>
            <mime:mimeXml part="Body" />
         </output>
      </operation>
   </binding>
   <service name="PalindromeTest">
      <port name="PalindromeTestSoap"
         binding="s0:PalindromeTestSoap">
         <soap:address
   location="http://yourserver/Palindrome/PalindromeTest.asmx" />
      </port>
      <port name="PalindromeTestHttpGet"
         binding="s0:PalindromeTestHttpGet">
         <http:address
   location="http://yourserver/Palindrome/PalindromeTest.asmx" />
      </port>
      <port name="PalindromeTestHttpPost"
         binding="s0:PalindromeTestHttpPost">
         <http:address
   location="http://yourserver/Palindrome/PalindromeTest.asmx" />
      </port>
   </service>
</definitions>
```

WSDL is automatically generated by a Web Service when it is invoked by requesting the Web Services URL with this form:

```
http://yourserver/YourWebService.asmx?WSDL
```

> **TECHTALK: THE WSDL WORKING SPECIFICATION**
> Since WSDL is largely hidden from developers of Web Services, you needn't concern yourself with the technical details of WSDL. But if the implementation details are of interest to you, check out the WSDL working specification. WSDL, like SOAP, is currently a W3C "Note," which is a preliminary specification submitted to the W3C organization for purposes of future standardization. WSDL is being developed by Microsoft and IBM. You can find the Note on WSDL at *http://www.w3.org/TR/wsdl.*

6.4 Web Service Wire Formats

Web Services have the flexibility to be invoked in a variety of ways. Since Web Services are URL-addressable resources that exist on Web servers, it follows that any client capable of formulating an HTTP request can be a Web Services client. One of the design goals of the Web Services framework was to make Web Services available to as many different clients (computers, wireless devices, and so on) as possible. Each of these devices has varying capabilities in regards to how it can send requests over HTTP. The aim of Web Services is to accommodate every mechanism available to receive those requests. Let's take a look at the different methods used to call a Web Service, which include HTTP `GET`, HTTP `POST`, and SOAP.

6.4.1 Using HTTP `GET`

An HTTP `GET` is the simplest method for requesting a resource (file, script, or Web Service) from a Web server. `GET` is an HTTP verb that takes a URL as a parameter. To allow for additional data to be sent along with the request (in the form of name–value pairs), `GET` requests are appended to the end of the URL as a CGI-encoded query string, as in this example:

```
http://yourserver/scriptname.aspx?param1=value1&param2=value2
```

Calling a Web Service using this method requires a URL like the following example:

```
http://yourserver/YourWebService.asmx/YourWebMethod?Param1=Value1
```

After the Web Service has finished performing its work, the results are returned to the client using the following format. (This particular Web method returned a Boolean value equal to `True`.)

```
<?xml version="1.0" encoding="utf-8"?>
<boolean xmlns=http://tempuri.org/>True</boolean>
```

The client then parses this XML result and passes it on to whatever program called the Web Service for further processing.

6.4.2 Using HTTP POST

Another method used to request a resource from a Web server is the HTTP `POST` method. Similar in functionality to the `GET` method, HTTP `POST` passes name–value pairs to the server inside the body of the request. To illustrate, here's how an HTTP `POST` request would be formulated (using the previous HTTP `GET` example).

```
POST /yourserver/YourWebService.asmx/YourWebMethod HTTP/1.1
Host: rmdevbiz01
Content-Type: application/x-www-form-urlencoded
Content-Length: length

Param1=value1
```

This is the actual "chunk" of data sent by the client over the network socket. Normally, the HTTP `POST` method is used to send the values a user has entered into an HTML form along with the request. In the case of a Web Service call, the name–value pair mechanism normally used to send input element values is used to send the Web method parameter values.

The response back from the Web Service is in the same format as for the HTTP `GET`.

```
<?xml version="1.0" encoding="utf-8"?>
<boolean xmlns="http://tempuri.org/">True</boolean>
```

6.4.3 Using the Simple Object Access Protocol (SOAP)

Using the HTTP `GET` and `POST` methods provides a simple way to communicate with Web Services, but they have limitations. Both of these methods are restricted by the types of information they can send to Web Services. Since they send only name–value pairs of information, you can't easily extend the types of information you can send with the request. Plus, the name–value pair approach isn't structured, so that makes processing of the request more difficult for the Web Service.

SOAP solves these problems by providing a mechanism for passing Web Service request data in a structured and expandable fashion. You can use a standardized XML schema for passing request data as well as receiving response data.

SOAP is a fairly complex topic, so we'll just touch on the basics of the protocol. Whenever you use VS.NET to build systems that use Web Services, the IDE configures your Web Services and clients to use SOAP for all communications by default. Keeping with the previous examples, here's how a request for a Web method looks when using SOAP.

```
POST /Palindrome/YourWebService.asmx HTTP/1.1
Host: rmdevbiz01
Content-Type: text/xml; charset=utf-8
Content-Length: length
SOAPAction: "http://tempuri.org/IsPalindrome"

<?xml version="1.0" encoding="utf-8"?>
<soap:Envelope
xmlns:xsi=http://www.w3.org/2001/XMLSchema-instance
xmlns:xsd=http://www.w3.org/2001/XMLSchema
xmlns:soap="http://schemas.xmlsoap.org/soap/envelope/">
   <soap:Body>
      <YourWebMethod xmlns="http://tempuri.org/">
         <Param1>Value1</Param1>
      </YourWebMethod>
   </soap:Body>
</soap:Envelope>
```

The XML in boldface shows how the Web method is called. An XML element called `YourWebMethod` contains subelements that specify the parameters and their values. The response received from the Web Service is also encoded using SOAP, as shown below.

```
HTTP/1.1 200 OK
Content-Type: text/xml; charset=utf-8
Content-Length: length

<?xml version="1.0" encoding="utf-8"?>
```

```
<soap:Envelope
xmlns:xsi=http://www.w3.org/2001/XMLSchema-instance
xmlns:xsd=http://www.w3.org/2001/XMLSchema
xmlns:soap="http://schemas.xmlsoap.org/soap/envelope/">
   <soap:Body>
      <YourWebMethodResponse xmlns="http://tempuri.org/">
         <YourWebMethodResult>True</YourWebMethodResult>
      </YourWebMethodResponse>
   </soap:Body>
</soap:Envelope>
```

SOAP returns the value from the Web method as shown in boldface. The XML element `YourWebMethod` shows a return value of `True`.

> **TECHTALK: DETAILS OF SOAP**
> SOAP is a collaborative effort on the part of Microsoft, IBM, Lotus, and UserLand Software, Inc. You can find the W3C "Note" on SOAP at *http://www.w3.org/TR/SOAP.*

6.5 Web Services Discovery

When you create a Web Service, you usually want to tell other users about it. You can accomplish this by using *discovery files*, which provide information about the location of Web Services and their corresponding WSDL. The Web Services framework provides two methods for discovering Web Services: *static discovery* and *dynamic discovery*.

6.5.1 Static Discovery

Static discovery allows you to explicitly define the location of individual Web Services. It also allows you to group together the locations of Web Services into a logical unit. For example, you may have many different Web Services that are related by the type of tasks they perform. Grouping them makes it convenient for users to learn about all of these Web Services at once.

A discovery (`.disco`) file is, not surprisingly, an XML file with a defined schema. Here's how a typical discovery file looks.

```
<?xml version="1.0" ?>
<disco:discovery
```

```
    xmlns:disco="http://schemas.xmlsoap.org/disco"
    xmlns:scl="http://schemas.xmlsoap.org/disco/scl">
    <scl:contractRef
       ref="http://MyWebServer/MyWebService.asmx?WSDL"/>
    <disco:discoveryRef
       ref="SomeFolder/OtherWebService.disco"/>
</disco:discovery>
```

The root element of a discovery file is named `discovery`, which is defined in the `disco` namespace specified by `http://schemas.xmlsoap.org/disco`. There is also a reference to the `scl` (service contract) namespace. Inside the `<discovery>` element appear references to discovery files and the Web Services WSDL files. The boldface text shows a reference to a Web Service called `MyWebService`, with WSDL in the query string. This goes in a `<contractRef>` tag, which belongs to the `scl` namespace. The example also contains a reference to another discovery file, called `OtherWebService.disco`. This goes in a `<discoveryRef>` tag, which belongs to the `disco` namespace.

6.5.2 Dynamic Discovery

Dynamic discovery provides an automatic way to discover multiple Web Services. Unlike static discovery files, dynamic discovery files allow users to discover every available Web Service underneath a given URL. A dynamic discovery file looks like the following code.

```
<?xml version="1.0" encoding="utf-8" ?>
<dynamicDiscovery
xmlns="urn:schemas-dynamicdiscovery:disco.2000-03-17">
<exclude path="_vti_cnf" />
<exclude path="_vti_pvt" />
<exclude path="_vti_log" />
<exclude path="_vti_script" />
<exclude path="_vti_txt" />
<exclude path="Web References" />
</dynamicDiscovery>
```

Dynamic discovery automatically enables the discovery of Web Services in the directory in which the file resides. Notice the `<exclude>` tags in the file. These denote particular directories you do not wish to consider for dynamic discovery. This example excludes from dynamic discovery the directories reserved for use by the FrontPage server extensions.

6.6 Creating a Simple Web Service

You're now ready to develop your first Web Service! In this lab, you'll gain an understanding of Web Service development using VS.NET. Specifically, you'll learn how to:

- Create a new Web Service project in VS.NET
- Create a Web Services class
- Use code-behind techniques to develop Web Services
- Test the Web Service using Internet Explorer and the self-generating test page

LAB 6-1
THE PALINDROME WEB SERVICE

The first Web Service you'll create will check whether a supplied word or phrase is a palindrome (a special word or phrase that, when the letters are reversed, spells the original word, for example, "Anna"). This Web Service will take an input string that contains the word or phrase and return a Boolean `True` value if the string is a palindrome.

STEP 1. Launch VS.NET.

STEP 2. Create a new ASP.NET Web Service project.

a. Select **File→New→Project . . .** from the menu.

b. Highlight the Visual Basic Projects folder under the Project Types list.

c. Select the ASP.NET Web Service icon and assign the name "Palindrome" for the project.

Step 3. Assign names to classes.

a. VS.NET creates some default files for you for the Palindrome Web Service project, which include (among others) a `Global.asax` file, a default `.asmx` file, and a discovery file. Right-click on the `.asmx` file (typically named `Service1.asmx`), select Rename, and rename the file to "`palindrome.asmx`". Once the rename has taken place, notice that the discovery file was also renamed as a result.

b. Since you renamed some files, you need to adjust the default code slightly. The change occurs in the `palindrome.asmx` file. VS.NET defaults the view of this file to the Design View, but you need to modify the file directly in the Source Code Editor. To open the file with the Source Code Editor, right-click the `palindrome.asmx` file and select Open With . . . . The Open With dialog appears with different program selections (see Lab Figure 6-1).

c. Select the Source Code (Text) Editor option from the list and click the Open button. The source file appears and contains the following code (spacing has been added here for readability):

```
<%@ WebService Language="vb"
   Codebehind="Palindrome.asmx.vb"
   Class="Palindrome.Service1" %>
```

This .asmx file is all that's required for your Web Service. VS.NET configures it with the `Codebehind` directive to separate the Web Service code from this file.

d. Because of the file name change, you need to edit the value for the `Class` directive. Change it to read "`Palindrome.Palindrome`".

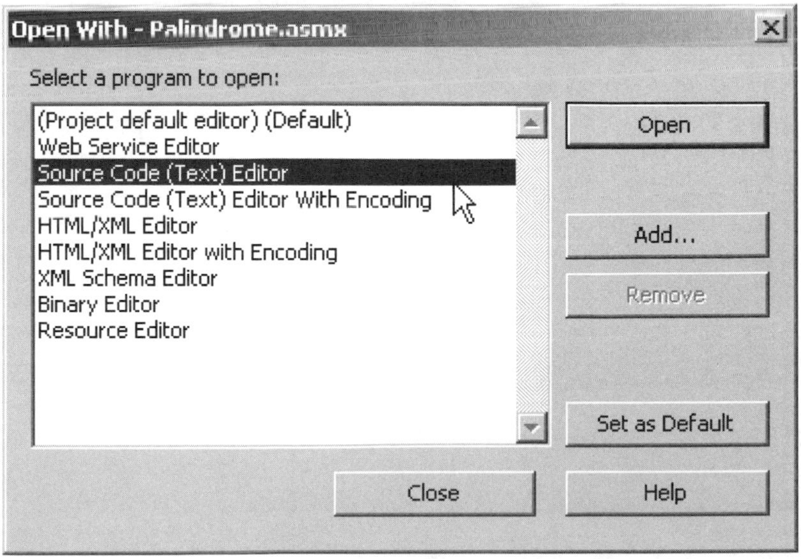

Lab Figure 6-1 The Open With dialog

STEP 4. Enter the Web Service code.

a. Switch to the Design View for the `Palindrome.asmx` file, right-click on it, and select View Code (or double-click in the Design View). This opens the code-behind file, `Palindrome.asmx.vb` (see Lab Figure 6-2).

b. Notice that VS.NET placed some code in the class file that shows how to declare a Web method. It's a very simple one that returns the string "Hello World" to the caller. You won't use this code for your Web Service, so delete that portion.

c. Now you need to edit the name of the class in the remaining code. Change the name from "`Service1`" to "`Palindrome`" to coincide with the changes to file names you made previously.

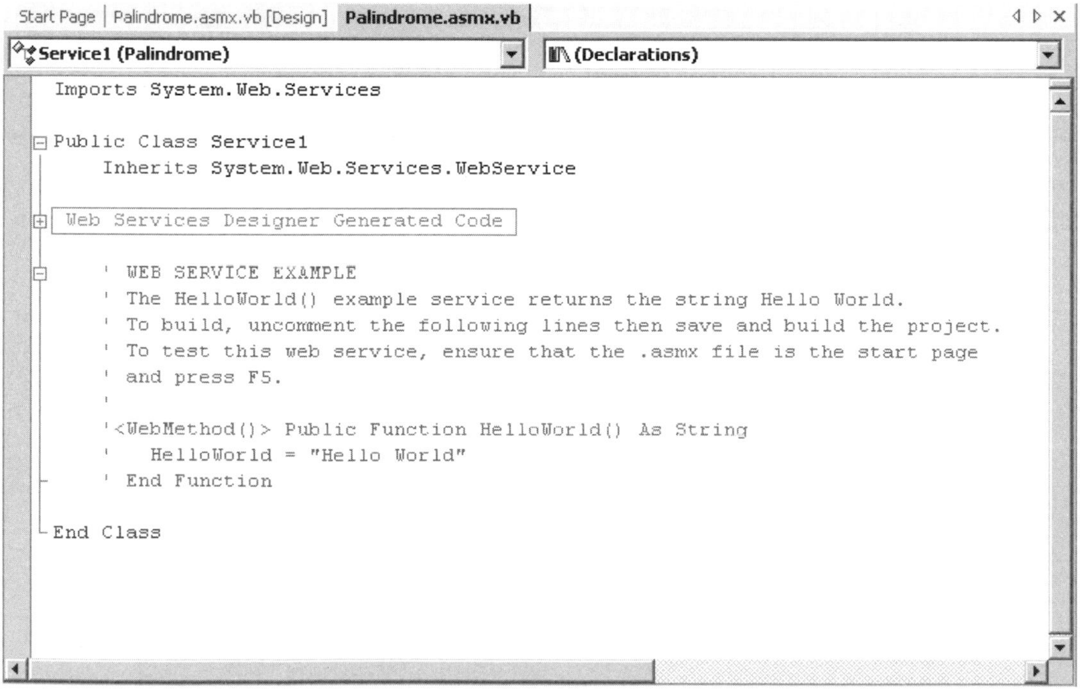

Lab Figure 6-2 Stub code for the Palindrome Web Service

d. It's time to add a Web method of your own. This Web method is called `IsPalindrome()`. Enter the following code.

```
<WebMethod()> Public Function IsPalindrome( _
   ByVal TestString As String) _
   As Boolean

   TestString = Replace(TestString, " ", "")
   TestString = UCase(TestString)
   If StrReverse(TestString) = TestString Then
      IsPalindrome = True
   Else
      IsPalindrome = False
   End If

End Function
```

This code first removes any spaces from the word or phrase and converts the string to all uppercase letters. Removal of spaces is necessary so they won't be considered as part of the palindrome. (A more complete implementation would consider other characters as well, such as punctuation.) Conversion to uppercase letters ensures that case-sensitivity will not be an issue when comparing the reversed string with the original. The VB.NET `StrReverse()` function reverses the candidate string and compares it to the original passed as the parameter to the function. If the values match, the string is a palindrome, and `True` is returned by the Web method.

e. After you've entered all the code, save the project.

STEP 5. Build and test the solution.

a. Select **Build→Build Solution** from the menu bar to build the solution. (If there are errors, recheck the code entry, correct any typos, and build the solution again.)

b. Select **Debug→Start Without Debugging** to run the Web Service. Internet Explorer is launched, and the Web Services test page is displayed (see Lab Figure 6-3). This page tells you, from the automatically generated WSDL, the available Web methods of the Palindrome Web Service. In this case, there's just one: `IsPalindrome()`.

c. Click the `IsPalindrome` hyperlink to open the Palindrome test page (see Lab Figure 6-4).

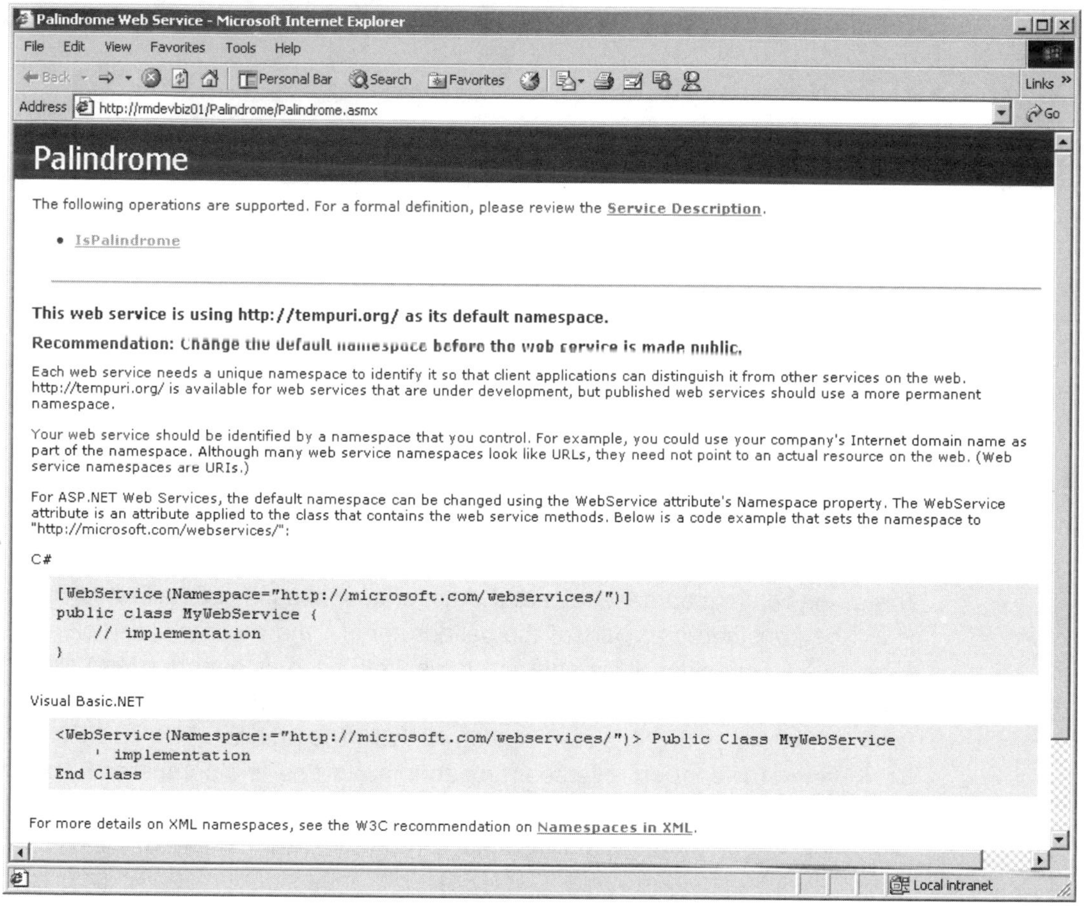

Lab Figure 6-3 The Web Services test page

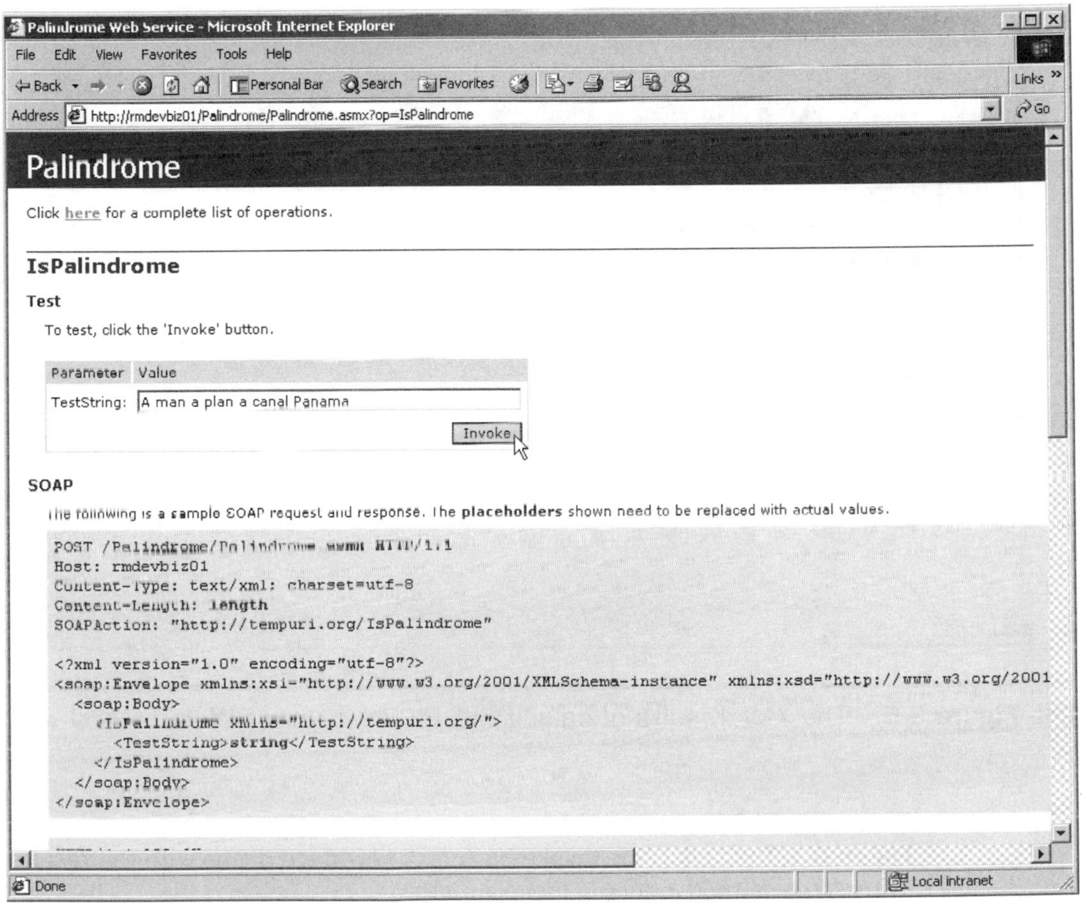

Lab Figure 6-4 Testing the `IsPalindrome()` Web method

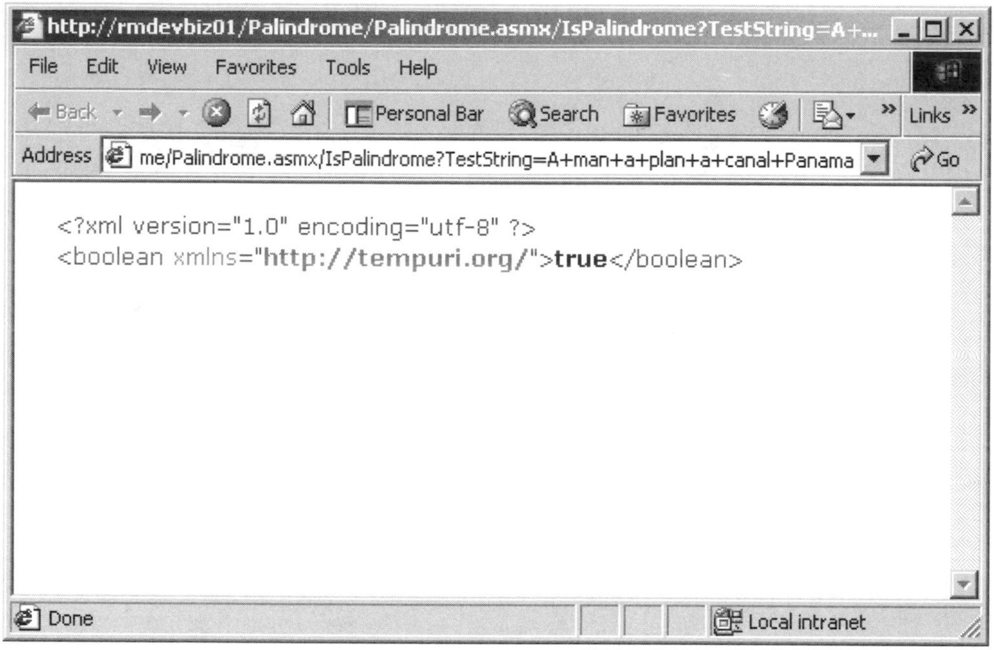

Lab Figure 6-5 The XML results of calling the `IsPalindrome()` Web method

d. To test the `IsPalindrome()` Web method, enter a string as shown in Lab Figure 6-4. Then click the Invoke button. A new page opens with the results of the Web method call (see Lab Figure 6-5).

Congratulations! You've just built a complete, working Web Service. Of course, Web Services for production systems are considerably more complex than this one, but the basic process of construction remains the same.

6.7 Calling Web Services with Proxy Classes

In Lab 6-1 you constructed a Web Service and tested it from the default test pages, but you didn't consume that Web Service from any application you wrote. To efficiently consume a Web Service in another application, you need to use a *proxy class.*

A proxy class is a code class in the usual sense. It acts as a go-between from the Web Service to the client application code. The proxy class is designed in such a way to model the structure of the class that makes up a Web Service. The proxy class itself doesn't perform any type of application logic. Its job is to provide the transport mechanism for moving data between the client application code and the Web Service.

> **TIP:** The source code generated for proxy classes is not necessary to your understanding of Web Services or how to call them. We're covering them here for the sake of completeness.

What does a proxy class look like? To illustrate, let's examine the proxy class for the Palindrome Web Service.

```
Option Explicit On

Imports System
Imports System.Diagnostics
Imports System.Web.Services
Imports System.Web.Services.Protocols
Imports System.Xml.Serialization

Namespace MattsWebServices

<System.Web.Services.WebServiceBindingAttribute( _
Name:="PalindromeSoap", [Namespace]:="http://tempuri.org/")> _

Public Class Palindrome
   Inherits System.Web.Services.Protocols.SoapHttpClientProtocol

   <System.Diagnostics.DebuggerStepThroughAttribute()> _
   Public Sub New()
      MyBase.New()
      Me.Url = "http://localhost/palindrome/Palindrome.asmx"
   End Sub

   <System.Diagnostics.DebuggerStepThroughAttribute(), _
   System.Web.Services.Protocols.SoapDocumentMethodAttribute( _
"http://tempuri.org/IsPalindrome", _
Use:=System.Web.Services.Description.SoapBindingUse.Literal, _
ParameterStyle:= _
```

```
System.Web.Services.Protocols.SoapParameterStyle.Wrapped)>

Public Function IsPalindrome(ByVal TestString As String) _
   As Boolean

   Dim results() As Object = Me.Invoke( _
      "IsPalindrome", New Object() {TestString})
   Return CType(results(0), Boolean)

End Function

<System.Diagnostics.DebuggerStepThroughAttribute()> _
   Public Function BeginIsPalindrome( _
      ByVal TestString As String, _
      ByVal callback As System.AsyncCallback, _
      ByVal asyncState As Object) As _
      System.IasyncResult

            Return Me.BeginInvoke( _
            "IsPalindrome", New Object() {TestString}, _
                 callback, asyncState)

   End Function

<System.Diagnostics.DebuggerStepThroughAttribute()> _
    Public Function EndIsPalindrome( _
         ByVal asyncResult As System.IAsyncResult) As _
         Boolean

       Dim results() As Object = Me.EndInvoke(asyncResult)
       Return CType(results(0), Boolean)
    End Function
  End Class
End Namespace
```

The class starts with a namespace, `MattsWebServices`. The name of this public class is `Palindrome`, which is consistent with the name of the Web Service class. This consistency makes the behavior of the proxy class exactly like that of the Web Service class. The boldface text highlights two important member functions of the proxy class. The first is the constructor, `New()`. This initializes the class and sets the `Url` member variable to the location of the Web Service file. The next member function is the `IsPalindrome()` function itself. The code contained inside this class performs the necessary operation to invoke the `IsPalindrome()` method using SOAP over HTTP.

Although the code for the proxy class looks considerably complex, you don't need to worry about it because VS.NET and the .NET Framework generate this code for you. The .NET Framework contains a utility that parses the WSDL for a Web Service and generates all the proxy class code based on the information contained in the WSDL.

6.8 Creating a Client for a Web Service

To get a feel for using VS.NET to consume Web Services, work through Lab 6-2 to create a new console application that uses the Palindrome Web Service.

LAB 6-2

A CONSOLE APPLICATION FOR THE PALINDROME WEB SERVICE

STEP 1. Create a new VB console application project.

a. See Lab 2-1 if you need a reminder of how to do this. Name the new project "PalindromeTester".

STEP 2. Add a Web reference to the project.

a. After VS.NET creates the new project, switch to the Solution Explorer if it isn't already active.

b. Right-click on the References folder and select **Add Web Reference . . .** from the pop-up menu (see Lab Figure 6-6).

The Add Web Reference dialog appears (see Lab Figure 6-7). Here you can search for Web Services, view the WSDL contracts and documentation for Web Services, and perform elementary testing of those Web Services. You'll be using the Palindrome Web Service, so you need to point to the location of that Web Service. The location of the `.asmx` file depends on where you built the Web Service when you worked through Lab 6-1. For example, if the Web Service were located on the local machine in the `Palindrome` virtual directory, you would enter *http://localhost/Palindrome/palindrome.asmx* as a URL and click the Go button (the curved arrow).

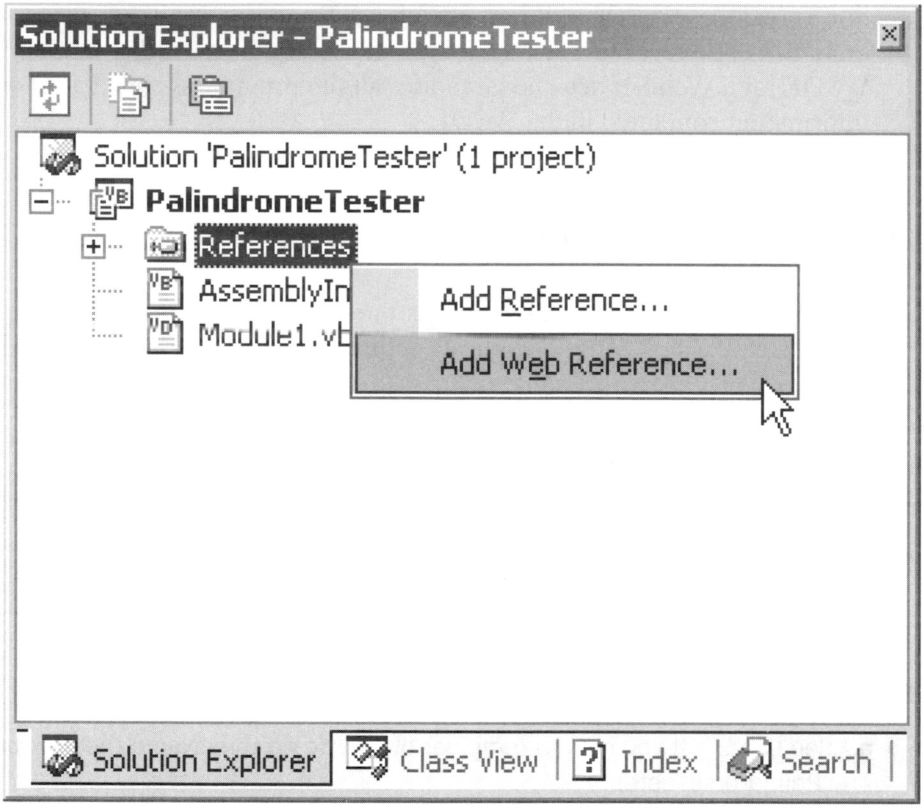

Lab Figure 6-6 Selecting Add Web Reference . . .

c. When you have successfully located the Palindrome Web Service, enter its location as a URL and click the Add Reference button at the bottom of the Add Web Reference window.

STEP 3. Call the Web Service.

a. After you add the Web Service reference to your project, VS.NET automatically generates the proxy class. To see the results, switch to the Class View and expand the hierarchy to see the full view of your project (see Lab Figure 6-8). You can see the generated proxy class code if you double-click on the `Palindrome` class in the Class View.

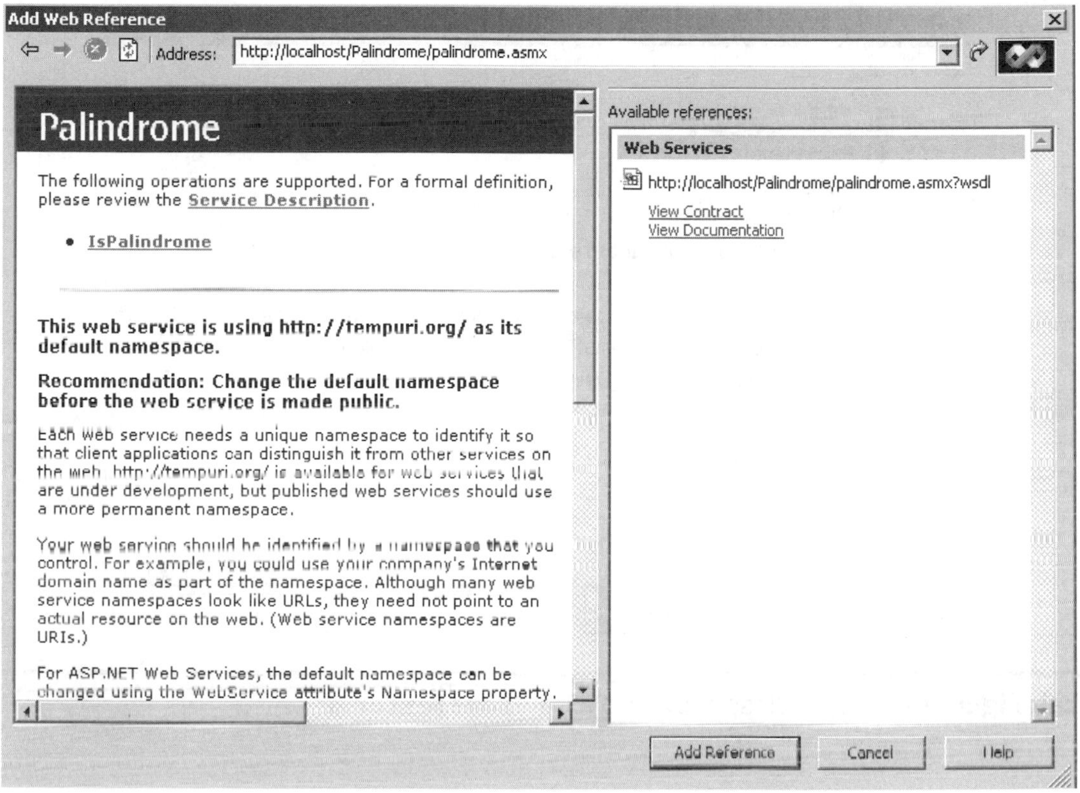

Lab Figure 6-7 The Add Web Reference dialog

b. VS.NET assigns a namespace for the proxy class to reside in by default. In this example, VS.NET chose `localhost` as the namespace, which is the name of the host on which the Web Service exists. You may want to choose another name for this namespace that's meaningful to you. To do this, simply change the `Namespace` statement in the `Palindrome` class file to whatever name you wish. (Be sure to save your changes.)

c. Switch back to the console application's `Main()` subroutine (double-click on `Module1` in the Class View). Inside the `Main()` subroutine, enter the following code.

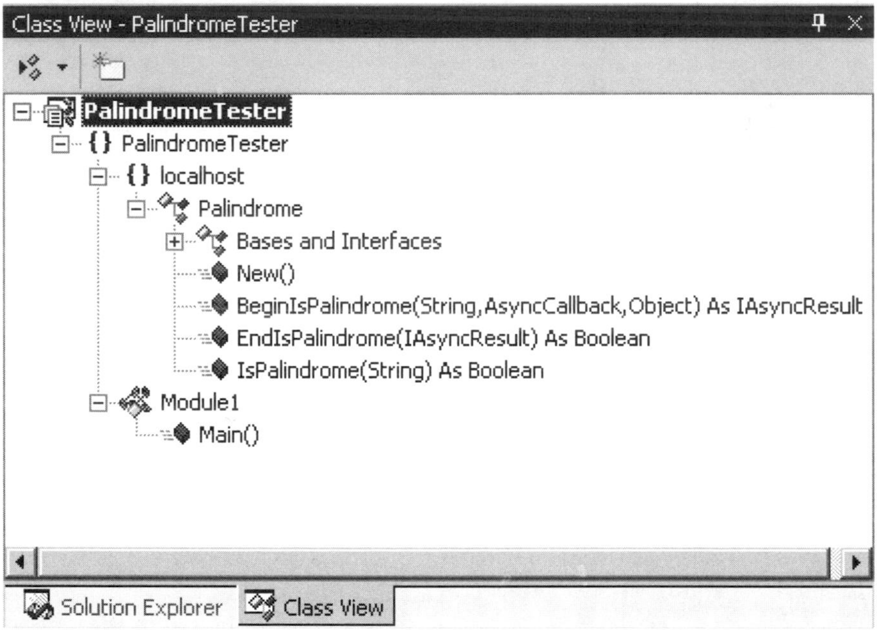

Lab Figure 6-8 The Class View of `PalindromeTester`

```
❶ Dim clsPalindrome As New localhost.Palindrome()
Dim strTestString As String

Console.WriteLine("Palindrome Web Service Client")
Console.Write("Enter a word or phrase: ")
strTestString = Console.ReadLine()

❷ If clsPalindrome.IsPalindrome(strTestString) Then
   Console.WriteLine("{0} is a palindrome!", _
        strTestString)
Else
   Console.WriteLine("{0} is NOT a palindrome!", _
        strTestString)
End If
```

Here's a brief overview of this code. Line ❶ creates a new `Palindrome` class object. Again, this is the proxy class that VS.NET created. The code reads from the console one line that contains the test string. Then in line ❷ the `IsPalindrome()` method is called and the Boolean return value is checked with an `If . . . Then` condition. Then the program outputs an appropriate message according to the results.

d. Run this code in the same fashion as the console applications in Chapter 2 and test it.

6.9 Managing State in Web Services

Earlier in this book we explored options for recording state information in ASP.NET Web Forms. Web Services also provide the same state-management capabilities. The `WebService` class contains many of the same objects that ASP.NET uses, so you are free to exploit those as appropriate.

Let's look at a simple Web Service that saves some state.

Code Sample 6-1

```
<%@ WebService Language="vb"
   Class="StateWebServ" %>

Imports System.Web.Services

Public Class StateWebServ
   Inherits System.Web.Services.WebService

   <WebMethod(True)> Public Function GetSessionCount() _
         As Integer
      If Session("MyCounter") Is Nothing Then
         GetSessionCount = 0
      Else
         GetSessionCount = CInt(Session("MyCounter"))
      End If

   End Function

   <WebMethod(True)> Public Function IncrementSessionCount()
      If Session("MyCounter") Is Nothing Then
         Session("MyCounter") = 1
      Else
         Session("MyCounter") = _
```

```
                CInt(Session("MyCounter")) + 1
        End If
        IncrementSessionCount = CInt(Session("MyCounter"))
    End Function

End Class
```

This code uses the `HttpSessionState` class (`Session`) to maintain a count of how many times the Web Service is used during a session. For every call to `IncrementSessionCount()`, the `MyCounter` variable is incremented and the new value returned. You can read the current session value by calling the `GetSessionCount()` function. Notice that in order to use the `HttpSessionState` class from within your Web Service, you need to specify `True` as the first parameter to the `WebMethod()` attribute.

6.10 Using Transactions in Web Services

Just as ASP.NET can participate in COM+ Component Services transactions, so can Web Services take advantage of the same transactional services. Here's an example of a Web Service that uses transactions.

```
<%@ WebService
    Language="vb"
    Class="SomeWebService" %>

Imports System
Imports System.Web.Services
Imports System.EnterpriseServices

Public Class SomeWebService
    Inherits System.Web.Services.WebService

    <WebMethod(TransactionOption:=TransactionOption.RequiresNew)> _
    Public Sub SomeMethod()

    End Sub

End Class
```

There are two preliminary requirements for using a transaction in a Web Service.

1. You must include the `Imports` statements shown in the `.asmx` file above.
2. The transaction option must be set for Web methods that will execute as part of a transaction. This example uses the `TransactionOption.RequiresNew` option, which will begin a new transaction. In other words, the Web method will act as the root of the transaction. When the code for the Web method finishes executing, it will automatically commit or roll back the transaction based on whether or not an exception inside the Web method was thrown.

6.11 Making an Advanced Web Service

To further explore the use of transactions and sessions inside Web Services, here's another lab exercise. In it you'll return to the Supermarket application you created in Lab 5-1 and enable the `Product` component to use Web Services.

LAB 6-3

AN ENHANCED ORDERING AND INVENTORY SYSTEM

STEP 1. Start VS.NET.

STEP 2. Create a new VB ASP.NET Web Service project.

STEP 3. Create a new Web Service (`.asmx`) file.

a. In the Solution Explorer, right-click on the project and select **Add→Add Web Service** from the menu.

b. Name the file "TransWS.asmx".

STEP 4. Enter the Web Service code.

a. Right-click the Design Area and select **View Code** from the menu.

b. Enter the following code.

```
Imports System
Imports SupermarketSystem.Supermarket
```

```
Imports System.Web.Services
Imports System.EnterpriseServices

Public Class TransWS
   Inherits System.Web.Services.WebService

   <WebMethod(True, TransactionOption.RequiresNew)> _
   Public Sub AddAProduct(ByVal SKU As String, _
                  ByVal Description As String, _
                  ByVal UnitPrice As Decimal, _
                  ByVal StockBinNumber As String)
      Dim objProduct As IProduct
      Dim bln As Boolean

      Try
         objProduct = New Product()
         bln = objProduct.Create(SKU, _
                   Description, _
                   CDec(UnitPrice), _
                   StockBinNumber)
         If bln Then
            If Session("MyCounter") Is Nothing Then
               Session("MyCounter") = 1
            Else
               Session("MyCounter") = _
                    CInt(Session("MyCounter")) + 1
            End If
         End If

      Catch e As Exception
         '* handle error here
      End Try

   End Sub

   <WebMethod(True)> _
   Public Function GetNumProductAdds() As Integer
      If Session("MyCounter") Is Nothing Then
         GetNumProductAdds = 0
      Else
         GetNumProductAdds = CInt(Session("MyCounter"))
      End If
   End Function

End Class
```

This Web Service contains two methods, `AddAProduct()` and `GetNumProductAdds()`. `AddAProduct()`uses the `Product` class to add a new product entry to the `Product` database table. It also increments a session variable by one for every successful operation. `GetNumProductAdds()` returns an integer containing the number of successful products added for the session.

STEP 5. Add a reference to the `SupermarketSystem` assembly.

a. Right-click the References folder and select **Add Web Reference . . .** from the pop-up menu.

b. Browse to the `SupermarketSystem` assembly DLL, select it, and add it to the project.

STEP 6. Build and test the solution.

a. Select **Build→Build Solution** from the menu.

b. Right-click the `TransWS.asmx` file and select **Set As Start Page**.

c. Select **Debug→Start Without Debugging** from the menu. The Web Service test form should appear.

d. Enter in some test values for the `AddAProduct()` method and check for the increment by testing the `GetNumProductAdds()` function.

6.12 Summary

In this chapter, you learned several things about .NET Web Services.

- Web Services are the most important piece in the .NET Framework. They are designed to facilitate the construction of truly distributed and interoperable software systems.
- Web Services use open Internet standards for communication, such as XML and HTTP.
- Web Services allow you to separate content from presentation. In a sense, they allow programmatic access to functionality that would normally be tied to a Web page.
- The Simple Object Access Protocol (SOAP) is the protocol used to communicate with a Web Service. It is a standards-based protocol that uses XML and is transported over HTTP.

- Web Services can use the HTTP `GET` and `POST` communication methods in place of SOAP. However, SOAP is the protocol of choice since it allows the use of complex data types and VS.NET will automatically SOAP-enable any Web Service you create with it.
- A Web Service is a class that derives from `System.Web.Services.WebService`. You expose member functions in the class as callable Web methods by using the `WebMethod()` attribute.
- The Web Service Description Language (WSDL) is an XML schema that a Web Service client uses to determine how to call the Web Service. From the Web Service's WSDL file, you can determine available methods, parameters, and data types.
- Web Service discovery is the process of letting a potential client know what Web Services are available on a particular server. A special XML file called a `.disco` file gives this information.
- Static discovery allows you to explicitly define the location of individual Web Services. It also allows you to group together the locations of Web Services into a logical unit.
- Dynamic discovery allows for an automatic way to discover multiple Web Services. It automatically identifies every Web Service in a particular directory. You also have the option to exclude certain subfolders from the discovery process.
- Web Services can be called inside any .NET managed code. Calls to Web Services can be made through proxy classes. This allows you to treat a Web Service just like a normal class in the program code, making the coding process more intuitive.
- Web Services can use ASP.NET state management using the `Session` and `Application` objects.
- Web Services can participate in a COM+ Component Services transaction by specifying a `TransactionOption` in the `WebMethod()` attribute.

6.13 What's Ahead

The next chapter covers data access with ADO.NET. You'll learn how to use ADO.NET to access SQL Server and add, update, and delete database data. Finally, Chapter 8 discusses various ASP.NET security topics.

CHAPTER 7

Accessing Data with ADO.NET

ActiveX Data Objects.NET (ADO.NET) is Microsoft's latest and most powerful solution for data access. In this chapter, we'll explore how to access data from Microsoft SQL Server 2000 and integrate it with ASP.NET applications. Specifically, we'll cover these topics.

- The history of data access and how it has evolved from flat files to ADO.NET
- The benefits of using ADO.NET
- The important .NET Framework classes of ADO.NET
- Data display using ADO.NET
- The `DataSet` and `DataTable` objects
- The `DataRelation` classes
- Manual database transactions
- Typed `DataSet` objects

7.1 Overview of Data Access on the Web

Unless you are programming a "brochure-ware" Web site, chances are that your site will need to access external data sources. In fact, an interactive Web site without a back-end database is almost unknown. The primary motivation of many Internet and intranet Web sites is to expose corporate data to a wider audience, such as customers or other departments in the organization. Data-access technologies in the Microsoft universe have a long and colorful history, from the earliest file-based data stores to ADO.NET. Let's take a cursory look at this evolutionary path of data access.

7.1.1 Flat Files

Before relational database management systems (DBMSs) were widely adopted, data were stored in flat files. *Flat files* is a catch-all term that refers to any kind of data existing in files that are not part of a DBMS. Most of the time the terms *flat file* and *text file* are used interchangeably to describe data stored in a fixed-length or delimited format. *Fixed-length files* store their data in records separated by a terminating character (typically a carriage return, line feed, or combination of both). Each element of data in the record occupies a fixed number of characters, padded with white-space characters as needed to fill the fixed length. Some flat files delimit each data element with a certain character (commas or horizontal tabs are common), providing the flexibility for the data elements to vary in length.

Flat files are not very flexible as a data-storage solution for several reasons, including the following.

- Flat files limit the kind of data you can store in them since they can contain only textual data.
- Flat files don't work well in multiuser situations (like the Web) because operating systems typically limit the amount of streams that can be opened on a file.
- Problems with data integrity arise out of concurrent updates with flat files.

Thus, using flat files is not a suitable choice for data-enabled Web sites.

7.1.2 Legacy or Mainframe Data

As mentioned previously, the primary motivation for creating data-enabled Web sites is to expose corporate data within the confines of a Web page. More often than not, a corporation already has mission-critical enterprise computer systems installed. These systems are usually old character-based mainframe computers.

Even though the technological capabilities of desktop computers have in many instances exceeded those of mainframe computers, company managers are often reluctant to discontinue the use of mainframe computers. Not only do these systems directly affect the business's bottom line but information technology personnel typically can't justify the cost of converting the legacy data stored in the mainframe to a modern DBMS.

The company managers still want to keep pace with the Web revolution, so they need a way to expose the data to the Web in a way that is minimally intrusive. An arcane process known as *screen scraping* retrieves data from a virtual terminal session with the mainframe. This virtual terminal session is triggered by server-side code invoked from a Web page. The program controlling the terminal session, in turn, passes the "scraped" data back to the browser. It's a slow process, and the ways you can retrieve, update, and assimilate data are limited by the established interface of the mainframe's character-based user programs.

7.1.3 Proprietary Database APIs

In the days of old, database systems shipped with an API that was specific to that particular database system. Attempts at standardization of data access were made, among the most significant being the *Structured Query Language* (SQL). SQL remains the primary language used to describe queries to a database, but the underlying programming models used to access data from application code are fragmented. Some language compilers include support for a technology called Embedded SQL, which allows programmers to place SQL statements inline with the host language (C, Pascal, and so on).

7.1.4 Standard APIs

The possibility of a standard API for data access increased with the introduction of Open Database Connectivity (ODBC). ODBC is a single C-language API used to access relational databases on a wide variety of distributed systems. It freed programmers from having to know the specifics about a particular DBMS in order to interact with the database. For a database to be ODBC-compliant, the database vendor must provide ODBC driver software that translates the ODBC API calls into the native database query language.

ODBC has two main drawbacks.

1. ODBC is designed to be used only with C/C++. The API functions have only a call-level interface compatible with this language. If you program in another language, you probably have to use the native API of the database system.
2. Programming with ODBC is cumbersome at best. ODBC requires many calls to the ODBC API to perform the simplest of operations. Many of the low-level details of database access with ODBC are left to the programmer. Thus, development times for programming with ODBC are considerably longer.

For these reasons, ODBC is rarely used now for programming with databases.

With the introduction of COM and its language-independent architecture, a new version of data-access technology was required to take advantage of COM's architecture. This new technology is known as OLE-DB (OLE stands for Object Linking and Embedding, which is the forerunner technology of COM). OLE-DB communicates with a data provider, which is software that provides access to the physical data. The OLE-DB package that Microsoft distributes comes with a data provider for ODBC drivers. This enables programmers to write OLE-DB code, which communicates with ODBC data sources, using the COM methodology. In addition to providing access to ODBC data sources, OLE-DB providers are available for specific DBMSs. This provides the fastest access to the data. OLE-DB can even talk to data providers for nonrelational database data as well, such as flat files or stores of e-mail messages. Whatever the data source, the programmer's interface remains the same.

7.1.5 ADO

ADO provides an easier programming interface to data sources while still being efficient. The object model of OLE-DB is complicated, so ADO serves as another code "wrapper" around OLE-DB to make programming easier. ADO unifies the functionality of previous data-access methods and reduces the number of objects in the programming interface as well. In the past Microsoft often referred to ADO technology as "Universal Data Access," and this is the company's strategy for the future of access to any kind of data, relational or not.

7.2 ADO.NET: The Next Generation of Data-Access Technology

ADO.NET brings us to the present day. Increasing demands for scalability and performance prompted Microsoft to release the next generation of ADO with ADO.NET. Many benefits come with this upgrade; let's review them.

Flexibility in a Mixed-Platform Environment

The original version of ADO had a disadvantage when it was used among distributed systems. When ADO passed around data between components, it did so using a proprietary network protocol that required COM to function properly. This communication took place over TCP/IP, but over ports that were normally blocked by firewalls. This puts limitations on the ways you can architect Web application systems. It hampered interoperability, which is a key strategy behind the .NET platform.

In ADO.NET, XML and HTTP are used to work around the interoperability problem. Data records are encoded and transported using XML and HTTP. XML is the format of choice for representing structured and hierarchical data, and HTTP can easily be ferried across firewalls along with normal Web traffic. XML is an open standard, so even non-Microsoft platforms can act as receiving points for data that originated from ADO.NET. Likewise, data records can originate from sources other than ADO.NET as long as the XML schema rules are followed.

Intuitive and Innovative Programming Model

Programming in ADO.NET is easy for both new developers and seasoned ones who have previous experience with ADO. Many of the inconsistencies of the ADO programming model have been revised in ADO.NET while keeping much of the same familiar object model. Since ADO.NET is managed code that's part of the .NET Framework Class Library, you can make custom classes for your applications based on (inherited from) those classes of ADO.NET. As you will see in Lab 7-2, you can also create classes that are directly modeled after your data. This makes dealing with data more intuitive since there is no code indirection you need to apply to obtain the data from the data-access API.

High Performance

ADO.NET gets a dramatic performance boost over any previous data-access method. This speed increase is accounted for by the lightweight nature of the XML/HTTP transport and the use of disconnected data. Unlike traditional client/server models of data access that maintain an open data connection for the duration that commands are executed, ADO.NET operates on data retrieved from the server and cached locally on the client computer. After retrieving that initial set of data, any updates made to the data happen locally. After updates are complete, the modified data is marshaled back to the server in one step.

7.3 ADO.NET Programming Objects and Architecture

The architecture of ADO.NET can be divided into two main areas: the `DataSet` class and the .NET Managed Data Provider.

7.3.1 The DataSet Class

Because of ADO.NET's disconnected model, programmers need an architecture that has the capability to represent an in-memory snapshot of a database. This snapshot can have all the functionality of a DBMS including, but not limited to, tables, columns, views, and keys. These capabilities are all included in the `DataSet` class.

Another key concept of the `DataSet` class is its ability to track changes made to itself. Since the `DataSet` object is holding a snapshot of the data in memory and doesn't have an active connection to the database, the change-tracking capability is needed so that you may reconcile any changes made to the data. `DataSet` objects include functionality to check changes made to the `DataSet` object, to check for errors in changed data, and to send modifications to the data back to the database server.

The `DataSet` class makes use of various other objects. The major ones are outlined below.

- **The `DataTable` and `DataTableCollection` objects:** A `DataTable` object is a tabular representation of data. Conceptually, a `DataTable` object is analogous to a table in a database. The table has rows (records) and columns (fields). Just like database tables, a `DataTable` object can have a primary key. You aren't limited to the number of `DataTables` objects that a `DataSet` can hold. All of the `DataTable` objects in a `DataSet` are housed in the `DataTableCollection` object.
- **The `DataRow` and `DataRowCollection` objects:** Each row in a `DataTable` object is represented by a `DataRow` object. The `DataRow` object contains the data that belongs to a particular record. All the `DataRow` objects are kept in the `DataRowCollection` object.
- **The `DataColumn` and `DataColumnCollection` objects:** Just as rows are represented as `DataRow` objects, columns are represented using `DataColumn` objects. `DataColumn` objects can be used to refer to a specific field in a `DataTable` or `DataRow`. When creating new `DataTable` objects, the `DataColumn` object is instrumental in defining the schema of the data to be contained in the `DataTable`. All the `DataColumn` objects reside in the `DataColumnCollection` object.
- **The `DataView` object:** A `DataView` object serves several functions. First, as its name implies, it provides a view of the data in a `DataTable` object. This view can contain a sorted and filtered version of the data. In Chapter 3, `DataView` objects were used for data binding to ASP.NET Web Controls.

- **The `DataRelation` and `DataRelationCollection` objects:** `DataRelation` objects are used to represent foreign key relationships among `DataTable` objects. The `DataRelationCollection` object contains all the `DataRelation` objects in the `DataSet`.

7.3.2 The .NET Managed Data Provider

`DataSet` objects form half of ADO.NET's architecture. They can be used to manipulate data that originated from a variety of formats. But a mechanism to obtain the data from a data source is still needed. That's the job of a .NET Managed Data Provider. It handles connecting to a database, execution of queries, and retrieval of results. These results are used to populate `DataSet` objects.

A .NET Managed Data Provider is made up of four base classes. All .NET Managed Data Providers supplied by Microsoft (and, eventually, third parties) inherit from these classes, listed below.

- **The `Connection` class:** This object is responsible for obtaining a connection to a database and controlling manual transactions.
- **The `Command` class:** This object executes queries and stored procedures.
- **The `DataReader` class:** This object provides fast, forward-only, read-only access to data. This is useful if you need to process a large number of records from a database (for example, a report) but don't need to update the data or have random access to it.
- **The `DataAdapter` class:** This object's job is to populate `DataSet` objects with data retrieved from the database.

As of this writing, the .NET Framework ships with the following Data Providers:

- **The SQL Server .NET Managed Data Provider:** This provider is used for connecting to Microsoft SQL Server 7.0/2000 and Microsoft MSDE (Microsoft Data Engine) database servers.
- **The OLE-DB .NET Managed Data Provider:** This provider is designed to connect to Microsoft SQL Server 6.5 or earlier, Oracle, and Microsoft Access.
- **The ODBC .NET Managed Data Provider:** This driver is used when connecting to database systems that provide only an ODBC driver as an interface.

7.4 Displaying Database Data

In this section we'll look at some code. Let's start with the simplest of ADO.NET code: using the `IDataReader` interface to read data from a single database.

> **TIP:** You need to have SQL Server (7.0 or 2000) installed for this example and the ADO.NET examples following this one. We will be using the example `pubs` database that is present by default on most SQL Server installations. Since some ADO.NET classes are abstract ones (they must be inherited by a .NET Managed Data Provider), we will be mostly focusing on the SQL Server .NET Managed Data Provider and classes in the `System.Data.SqlClient` namespace in our discussions of .NET Managed Data Providers.

7.4.1 The `IDataReader` Interface (`System.Data.IDataReader`)

The `IDataReader` is an interface (an abstract class), so it contains no implementation of its own. Tables 7-1 and 7-2 list the properties and methods, respectively, of the `IDataReader` interface.

The `IDataReader` interface is one of several interfaces that are part of the `System.Data` namespace. Some of the other interfaces included in `System.Data` are `IDataAdapter`, `IDbConnection`, and `IDbCommand`. Why are these interfaces and not classes with implementations? To illustrate the reason, think of what ODBC was trying to accomplish. ODBC was trying to give programmers a common way to write database access code. Regardless of the underlying database used, the code would not change. ADO.NET maintains

Table 7-1 Properties of the `IDataReader` Interface

Property	Description
`Depth`	Sets the depth of nesting for the current row
`IsClosed`	Has a value of `True` if the data reader is closed
`RecordsAffected`	Specifies the number of rows affected by the execution of the SQL statement

Table 7-2 Methods of the `IDataReader` Interface

Method	Description	Syntax
`Close`	Closes the `IDataReader`	–
`GetSchemaTable`	Returns a `DataTable` object with schema data	`GetSchemaTable() As DataTable`
`NextResult`	Gets the next result when reading the results of batch SQL statements	`NextResult() As Boolean`
`Read`	Advances to the next record	`Read() As Boolean`

this same concept by allowing the .NET Managed Data Provider code to implement the various interfaces. This way, when you write ADO.NET application code, you don't refer to specific implemented classes of the .NET Managed Data Provider—you simply call methods and properties of the interface class. For example, the SQL Server .NET Managed Data Provider provides an implementation of the `IDataReader` interface with a class in the `System.Data.SqlClient` namespace called `SqlDataReader`.

To further illustrate and to see your first ADO.NET sample in action, let's look at a piece of code that queries the `authors` table in the `pubs` SQL Server database.

Code Sample 7-1 Build instructions: vbc `/r:system.dll /r:system.data.dll cs7-01.vb`

```
Imports System
Imports System.Data
Imports System.Data.SqlClient
Imports Microsoft.VisualBasic

Module Module1

   Sub Main()

      Try
❶           Dim objCnn As New SqlConnection( _
                  "Initial Catalog=pubs;" & _
                  "Data Source=localhost;uid=sa;pwd=")
```

```
❷          objCnn.Open()

❸          Dim objCmd As IDbCommand = objCnn.CreateCommand()

❹          objCmd.CommandText = _
            "SELECT au_id, au_lname, au_fname FROM Authors"

         Dim objReader As IDataReader = _
❺              objCmd.ExecuteReader()

❻          Do While objReader.Read()
          Console.WriteLine("{0}" & _
          ControlChars.Tab & "{1} {2}", _
❼                objReader.GetString(0),
                objReader.GetString(1), _
                objReader.GetString(2))
         Loop

❽          objCnn.Close()

      Catch e As Exception
         Console.WriteLine("Error: " & e.Message)
      End Try
   End Sub

End Module
```

The code begins with the creation of a new `SqlConnection` object of the `System.Data.SqlClient` namespace in line ❶. The `SqlConnection` class handles connections to an SQL Server. (The class structure is shown in Tables 7-3 and 7-4.) This class implements the `IDbConnection` interface for the SQL Server .NET Managed Data Provider. Its constructor contains a connection string. Connection string syntax is specific to a particular DBMS; SQL Server connection strings typically supply a host name (`Data Source`), a database name (`Initial Catalog`), a user name (`uid`), and a password (`pwd`).

> **WARNING:** To run this sample, you may need to modify the connection string. Typically, the `uid` and `pwd` values need to be changed to a valid user name and password in your SQL Server installation.

Table 7-3 Properties of the `SqlConnection` Class

Property	Description
`ConnectionString`	Specifies the connection string to use when opening an SQL Server database
`ConnectionTimeout`	Sets the maximum time (in seconds) to wait for a successful connection to the database
`Database`	Specifies the name of the database to which to connect
`DataSource`	Specifies the SQL instance to which to connect (configured with the SQL Server Client Network Utility)
`PacketSize`	Sets the size (in bytes) of network packets to use when communicating with SQL Server
`ServerVersion`	Specifies the version of SQL Server
`State`	Gets the current state of the connection: `Broken`, `Closed`, `Connecting`, `Executing`, `Fetching`, or `Open` (`ConnectionState` enumeration)
`WorkstationId`	Specifies the identifier of the database client

Continuing on, we open the connection to the database in line ❷ by using the `Open()` method. After the connection is successfully established, we want to run a query. The first step is to establish a new `SqlCommand` object, a class that implements the `IDbCommand` interface, with the `CreateCommand()` method in line ❸. (The `SqlCommand` object has the properties and methods shown in Tables 7-5 and 7-6.)

The newly created `SqlCommand` object now needs to have a command assigned to it. Setting the `CommandText` property in line ❹, we specify an SQL `SELECT` statement that retrieves the identification number, last name, and first name of each record in the `authors` table. Next, we execute the command by calling the `ExecuteReader()` command in line ❺.

We are now ready to display the data. Beginning in line ❻ we use a `Do While . . . Loop` to read records from the `SqlDataReader` object. The `SqlDataReader` object implements the `IDataReader` interface and adds

Table 7-4 Methods of the `SqlConnection` Class

Method	Description	Syntax

`BeginTransaction`	Starts a database transaction	`BeginTransaction() As SqlTransaction`
		
		`BeginTransaction(ByVal` *`iso`* `As IsolationLevel) As SqlTransaction`
		
		`BeginTransaction(ByVal` *`transactionName`* `As String) As SqlTransaction`
		
		`BeginTransaction(ByVal` *`iso`* `As IsolationLevel, ByVal` *`transactionName`* `As String) As SqlTransaction`

`ChangeDatabase`	Changes the database on an open connection	`ChangeDatabase(ByVal` *`database`* `As String)`
`Close`	Closes the connection to the database	–
`CreateCommand`	Creates a new `SqlCommand` object for the current connection	`CreateCommand() As SqlCommand`
`Open`	Opens a database connection using the `ConnectionString`	–

properties and methods of its own. Documentation for the `SqlDataReader` class is in Appendix B.

The value returned from the `Read()` method of the `SqlDataReader` object will evaluate to `False` when there are no more records to return. So for each record we retrieve, we use the `GetString()` method (see line ❼) to return the value of each field as a string. `GetString()` (and most of the other `Get` methods of the `SqlDataReader` object) takes the ordinal position of the columns

Table 7-5 Properties of the `SqlCommand` Class

Property	Description
`CommandText`	Identifies the SQL/Transact-SQL statement to execute
`CommandTimeout`	Sets the maximum time (in seconds) to wait for the completion of a command
`CommandType`	Determines how to interpret the `CommandText` string: as `StoredProcedure`, `TableDirect`, or `Text` (`CommandText` enumeration)
`Connection`	Specifies the `SqlConnection` to use for execution of this command
`DesignTimeVisible`	Has a value of `True` if the object is visible on a Windows Forms Designer control
`Parameters`	Returns the `SqlParameterCollection`
`Transaction`	Specifies the `SqlTransaction` object to use for the command
`UpdatedRowSource`	Determines how command results are applied to the `DataRow` object when used by the `Update()` method of the `DbDataAdapter`

retrieved in the SQL command (starting with `0`). After all the records are retrieved, we clean up by closing the `SqlDataReader` object with a call to the `Close()` method in line ❽.

7.4.2 Working with Command Parameters

When you construct commands to execute with ADO.NET, you normally supply a value to `CommandText` and execute the command. You can construct the command in two ways. The first method is to supply a formatted string to `CommandText`. You can do this by using a combination of taking values from variables, converting them to strings, and concatenating them to build a Transact-SQL statement. For simple queries, this is a perfectly acceptable way to accomplish this. But as queries become more complex, this method becomes tiresome and prone to errors from a coding standpoint. Plus, strings that are intended to be quoted inside Transact-SQL statements may contain

Table 7-6 Methods of the SqlCommand Class

Method	Description	Syntax
Cancel	Cancels the execution of the current command	–
CreateParameter	Creates a new SqlParameter object	CreateParameter() As SqlParameter
ExecuteNonQuery	Executes the command and returns the number of rows affected by the command's execution	ExecuteNonQuery() As Integer
ExecuteReader	Executes the command and returns an SqlDataReader class so reading of results can begin	ExecuteReader() As SqlDataReader ExecuteReader(ByVal *behavior* As CommandBehavior) As SqlDataReader
ExecuteScalar	Returns the value of the first row and first column after execution of the command; used for stored procedures and aggregate SQL queries that return a single value	ExecuteScalar() As Object
ExecuteXmlReader	Executes the command and returns the results in an XML format in the XmlReader object	ExecuteXmlReader() As XmlReader
Prepare	Creates a prepared version of the command on an instance of SQL Server	–
ResetCommandTimeout	Resets the CommandTimeout property to its default value	–

quotes themselves. This leads to syntax errors in the statement, or worse, erroneous data in your database!

You can avoid these issues by constructing the command the second way: by using `SqlParameter` objects to supply parameters to Transact-SQL statements. Table 7-7 lists the properties of the `SqlParameter` class.

Table 7-7 Properties of the `SqlParameter` Class

Property	Description
`DbType`	Specifies the parameter's `DbType`, which is specific to a particular .NET Managed Data Provider
`Direction`	Determines how the parameter is to be used: as `Input`, `InputOutput`, `Output`, or `ReturnValue` (`ParameterDirection` enumeration)
`IsNullable`	Has a value of `True` if the parameter accepts null values
`Offset`	Sets the offset to the `Value` property for binary and string types
`ParameterName`	Gives the name of the parameter
`Precision`	Sets the maximum number of digits used to represent the `Value` property
`Scale`	Sets the number of decimal places to which the `Value` property is resolved
`Size`	Sets the maximum size (in bytes) of the data within the column
`SourceColumn`	Specifies the name of the source column that is mapped to the `DataSet` object and used for loading or returning the `Value` property
`SourceVersion`	Specifies the `DataRowVersion` to use when loading the `Value` property
`SqlDbType`	Specifies the `SqlDbType` of the parameter (maps to SQL Server data types)
`Value`	Specifies the value of the parameter

To demonstrate how to work with `SqlParameter` objects, let's expand the last example that used the `IDataReader` interface. The modified code looks like this, with the `SqlParameter` code added where shown in boldface type.

Code Sample 7-2 Build instructions: vbc /r:system.dll /r:system.data.dll cs7-02.vb

```
Imports System
Imports System.Data
Imports System.Data.SqlClient
Imports Microsoft.VisualBasic

Module Module1

   Sub Main()

      Try
         Dim objParam As SqlParameter
         Dim objCnn As New SqlConnection( _
     "Initial Catalog=pubs;Data Source=localhost;uid=sa;pwd=")

         objCnn.Open()

         Dim objCmd As IDbCommand = objCnn.CreateCommand()
         objCmd.CommandText = _
         "SELECT au_id, au_lname, au_fname FROM Authors " & _
         "WHERE state = @state AND contract = @contract"

         objParam = New SqlParameter()
         With objParam
            .ParameterName = "@state"
            .DbType = DbType.String
            .Direction = ParameterDirection.Input
            .Value = "CA"
         End With
         objCmd.Parameters.Add(objParam)

         objParam = New SqlParameter()
         With objParam
            .ParameterName = "@contract"
            .DbType = DbType.Boolean
            .Direction = ParameterDirection.Input
            .Value = True
         End With
```

```
            objCmd.Parameters.Add(objParam)

            Dim objReader As IDataReader = _
               objCmd.ExecuteReader()

            Do While objReader.Read()
               Console.WriteLine("{0}" & _
                  ControlChars.Tab & "{1} {2}", _
                  objReader.GetString(0), _
                  objReader.GetString(1), _
                  objReader.GetString(2))
            Loop

            objCnn.Close()

         Catch e As Exception
            Console.WriteLine("Error: " & e.Message)
         End Try
      End Sub

   End Module
```

Whenever you specify a name for the `ParameterName` property of the `SqlParameter` object, it should always be in the following form:

```
@parameter_name
```

Notice the first boldface line, where we set the `CommandText` property. Instead of reading in every record in the `authors` table like we did in the previous example, we use an SQL `WHERE` clause to return records only for those authors who live in California (CA) and have a contract. Names you assign to parameters are arbitrary. The example uses parameter names that are the same as the column names for simplicity.

Now it's time to create the `SqlParameter` objects. After we create an `SqlParameter` object, we proceed to assign values to the class properties. We start with the `ParameterName` property, which is assigned the corresponding parameter name specified in the `CommandText` string. Then the `DbType` needs to be set. Since the `state` column in the `authors` table is a character field, we use the `DbType.String` value to indicate that the parameter's data should be treated as a string. Next we need to specify how the parameter is to be used. In this case, the SQL statement shall treat the value supplied as input, so we specify `ParameterDirection.Input`. Finally, we specify the actual value for the parameter using the `Value` property. The process is repeated for the second parameter, only we assign `DbType.Boolean` for the `DbType` (maps to SQL Server "bit" type) and specify a Boolean `True` for the `Value`.

7.4.3 The `DataGrid` Control Revisited

In Chapter 3, you learned about a Web Control that can display data in various formats: the `DataGrid` Control. You also read a brief mention about the process of data binding, whereby you assign a `DataView` object to Web Controls for purposes of populating them visually. (We'll investigate binding to the `DataGrid` Web Control, but you can bind to several other Web Controls, too.) Now that you've learned some fundamentals about data access with ADO.NET, you can begin to review some examples of binding the `DataGrid` Control to SQL Server database data.

The `DataGrid` Control example in the next section is a simple editable grid. It displays a subset of data from the `authors` table of the `pubs` database, allows users to select a field of data to edit, and updates the database with the new value entered into the field.

7.4.4 Displaying Data in the `DataGrid` Control

The `DataGrid` Control works with template columns, which allow you to specify exactly how data items will appear in the grid. The `TemplateColumn` Control can contain child controls, typically `Label` or `TextBox` Controls. Our first step in the example is to construct a `.aspx` file that contains the HTML for the grid.

Code Sample 7-3

```
<%@ Page Language="vb"
   AutoEventWireup="false"
   Src="WebForm1.aspx.vb"
   Inherits="WebForm1"%>

<html>
<head>
<title>SQL Server Data Binding Example</title>
</head>
<body>
```

```
<form id="Form1"
   method="post"
   runat="server">

❾ <asp:DataGrid
   id=dgMyDataGrid
   DataKeyField="au_id"
   AutoGenerateColumns=false
   runat="server">

<Columns>
❿ <asp:TemplateColumn HeaderText="Author ID">
   <ItemTemplate>
      <asp:Label
         Text='<%# Container.DataItem("au_id") %>'
         id=lblAuthorID
         Runat="server" />
   </ItemTemplate>
</asp:TemplateColumn>

⓫ <asp:TemplateColumn HeaderText="Author Last Name">
   <ItemTemplate>
      <asp:Label
         Text='<%# Container.DataItem("au_lname") %>'
         id=lblAuthorLName
         Runat="server"/>
   </ItemTemplate>

⓬ <EditItemTemplate>
   <asp:TextBox
      Text='<%# Container.DataItem("au_lname") %>'
      ID="txtAuthorLName"
      Runat="server"/>
   </EditItemTemplate>

</asp:TemplateColumn>

⓭ <asp:EditCommandColumn
   EditText="Edit"
   CancelText="Cancel"
   UpdateText="Update"/>

</Columns>
```

```
</asp:DataGrid>


</form>
</body>
</html>
```

The code block beginning in line ❾ shows the definition of the DataGrid Control named dgMyDataGrid. Since we are defining our own template columns, we don't want the DataGrid Control to automatically generate columns from the DataSource, so we set the AutoGenerateColumns property to False. One other property of importance, DataKeyField, states which field to use as a key when updating edited rows (more on this later).

Inside the <Columns> tag, we begin to define the template columns. In the first column, coded in the block that begins in line ❿, we are going to display the contents of the au_id field. So, we use an <ItemTemplate> tag to instruct the DataGrid Control how to display the column data in item (read) mode. A child control, Label, is used to display the data. The data-binding syntax introduced in Chapter 3 is employed again in this example. In this case, the DataItem is the name of the au_id column in the authors table we are going to query.

Moving on to the next column, we display the au_lname field in the code block that starts in line ⓫. The column template for display/item mode is the same as in the previous template column for au_id, except for changes to the ID attribute and the DataItem name.

The au_lname field is one that we wish to edit, so we must provide an <EditItemTemplate> tag in line ⓬ so the DataGrid Control will know how to display data fields in edit mode. Again, it's similar to our previous templates, but we use a TextBox Control instead of a Label Control so the user will be able to type in a new value.

In line ⓭ we specify a special column for the editing controls using the EditCommandColumn Control. This column will display links for invoking editing on a row of data (EditText), canceling an edit (CancelText), and updating the row (UpdateText).

Like most of our ASP.NET pages, we use a code-behind file to perform the database access to SQL Server. In the Page_Load subroutine (see line ⓮ in the code below), we want to retrieve the data from the database. We do this by calling the BindIt() subroutine. This call will occur only when the page does not send a post-back to the server (the first time the page is requested).

The `BindIt()` subroutine that begins in line ⓯ below uses code from the `IDataReader` example. Just to recap the functionality of that code, we establish a connection to SQL Server with the `SqlConnection` object. After establishing a connection, we obtain an `SqlCommand` object. Using `SqlParameter` objects, we build our query to retrieve records for authors who live in California and have active publishing contracts. The `IDataReader` interface we obtain from the `ExecuteReader()` method in line ⓰ can be used to set the `DataSource` property of the `DataGrid` ⓱.

Here's the complete code for the editable `DataGrid` Control.

```
Imports System.Data
Imports System.Data.SqlClient
Imports System.Web
Imports System.Web.UI
Imports System.Web.UI.WebControls

Public Class WebForm1
   Inherits System.Web.UI.Page
   Protected WithEvents dgMyDataGrid As _
      System.Web.UI.WebControls.DataGrid

⓮     Private Sub Page_Load(ByVal sender As System.Object, _
         ByVal e As System.EventArgs) Handles MyBase.Load

      If Not IsPostBack Then
         BindIt()
      End If

   End Sub

⓯     Public Sub BindIt()
      Dim objParam As SqlParameter
      Dim objCnn As New SqlConnection( _
"Initial Catalog=pubs;Data Source=localhost;uid=sa;pwd=")

      objCnn.Open()

      Dim objCmd As IDbCommand = objCnn.CreateCommand()
      objCmd.CommandText = _
         "SELECT au_id, au_lname FROM Authors " & _
         "WHERE state = @state AND contract = @contract"

      objParam = New SqlParameter()
```

```
        With objParam
            .ParameterName = "@state"
            .DbType = DbType.String
            .Direction = ParameterDirection.Input
            .Value = "CA"
        End With
        objCmd.Parameters.Add(objParam)

        objParam = New SqlParameter()
        With objParam
            .ParameterName = "@contract"
            .DbType = DbType.Boolean
            .Direction = ParameterDirection.Input
            .Value = True
        End With
        objCmd.Parameters.Add(objParam)

16      Dim objReader As IDataReader = objCmd.ExecuteReader()

        dgMyDataGrid.DataSource = objReader
17          dgMyDataGrid.DataBind()

    End Sub

18       Private Sub dgMyDataGrid_EditCommand( _
                    ByVal source As Object, _
                    ByVal e As DataGridCommandEventArgs) _
                    Handles dgMyDataGrid.EditCommand

        dgMyDataGrid.EditItemIndex = e.Item.ItemIndex
        BindIt()
    End Sub

19       Private Sub dgMyDataGrid_CancelCommand( _
                    ByVal source As Object, _
                    ByVal e As DataGridCommandEventArgs) _
                    Handles dgMyDataGrid.CancelCommand

        dgMyDataGrid.EditItemIndex = -1
        BindIt()
    End Sub

20       Private Sub dgMyDataGrid_UpdateCommand( _
                    ByVal source As Object, _
```

```
                  ByVal e As DataGridCommandEventArgs) _
                  Handles dgMyDataGrid.UpdateCommand

        Dim lblAuthorID As Label
        Dim txtAuthorLName As TextBox
        Dim objParam As SqlParameter
        Dim objCnn As New SqlConnection( _
    "Initial Catalog=pubs;Data Source=localhost;uid=sa;pwd=")
        Dim intRowsAffected As Integer

21      lblAuthorID = CType(e.Item.FindControl( _
                              "lblAuthorID"), _
                              Label)
22      txtAuthorLName = CType(e.Item.FindControl( _
                              "txtAuthorLName"), _
                              TextBox)

        objCnn.Open()

        Dim objCmd As IDbCommand = objCnn.CreateCommand()
        objCmd.CommandText = _
           "UPDATE Authors SET au_lname = @au_lname " & _
           "WHERE au_id = @au_id"

        objParam = New SqlParameter()
        With objParam
           .ParameterName = "@au_id"
           .DbType = DbType.String
           .Direction = ParameterDirection.Input
23            .Value = lblAuthorID.Text
        End With
        objCmd.Parameters.Add(objParam)

        objParam = New SqlParameter()
        With objParam
           .ParameterName = "@au_lname"
           .DbType = DbType.String
           .Direction = ParameterDirection.Input
24            .Value = txtAuthorLName.Text
        End With
        objCmd.Parameters.Add(objParam)

25      intRowsAffected = objCmd.ExecuteNonQuery()
```

```
        dgMyDataGrid.EditItemIndex = -1
        BindIt()

    End Sub
End Class
```

7.4.5 Editing Data in the DataGrid Control

Now that we have the display of data covered, it's time to add functionality to make the DataGrid Control editable. We need to write event handlers for three events that the DataGrid Control exposes: EditCommand, CancelCommand, and UpdateCommand.

Let's begin with the EditCommand event. First, notice the signature of the event-handler subroutine shown above in line ⓲ and reproduced here.

```
Private Sub dgMyDataGrid_EditCommand( _
            ByVal source As Object, _
            ByVal e As DataGridCommandEventArgs) _
            Handles dgMyDataGrid.EditCommand
```

We use the Handles keyword to designate for which event we are writing an event handler. The event-handling function signature consists of an Object parameter and the DataGridCommandEventArgs parameter. We can determine specifics about the row we are about to edit through the DataGridCommandEventArgs object. Setting the DataGrid Control into edit mode is easy; we simply assign the EditItemIndex property of the DataGrid Control to the index of the row that was selected. The selected row value comes from e.Item.ItemIndex.; Item represents the row object for the event and ItemIndex the ordinal index of that row. With the EditItemIndex property set, we call the BindIt() subroutine again to refresh the display.

We want to give users the opportunity to cancel an edit in progress. They do this by clicking the Cancel button for a row for which the Edit button was previously clicked. When Cancel is clicked, the CancelCommand event is raised, and the event handler is called according to the code block that begins in line ⓳. Canceling the edit is simply a matter of setting EditItemIndex to -1. This returns the DataGrid Control to read mode.

Handling the UpdateCommand event requires two steps, as shown in the code beginning in line ⓴. First we need to find out the values of the edited data items by obtaining references to the edited controls (see lines ㉑ and ㉒ in the code above, reproduced here as well).

```
lblAuthorID = CType(e.Item.FindControl( _
                     "lblAuthorID"), _
                     Label)
txtAuthorLName = CType(e.Item.FindControl( _
                     "txtAuthorLName"), _
                     TextBox)
```

`e.Item` refers to the row in which the event occurred. That row contains child controls that interest us. The `FindControl()` method helps us locate a control based on its identifier. We obtain references to the `Label` Control that holds the `AuthorID` value and the `TextBox` Control that contains the modified value entered for the author's last name. `FindControl()` returns an `Object`, so in order for us to reference that `Object` as the control it's supposed to represent, we use the VB `CType()` function to convert the `Object` to a `Label` Control and a `TextBox` Control.

Now we begin to build an `SqlCommand` to update the database. We use code similar to that in previous examples. In lines ㉓ and ㉔ we see the `String` values of the parameters being set to the value contained in the `Text` property of the `Label` and `TextBox` Controls. Then, after the parameters have been attached to the SQL `UPDATE` command, we use the `ExecuteNonQuery()` method in line ㉕ to execute the update. The final call to the `BindIt()` subroutine refreshes the display.

> **TIP:** Use the `ExecuteNonQuery()` method when you want to execute an `SqlCommand` that does not return row data, such as a utility-like stored procedure, an SQL `INSERT` command, or an SQL `UPDATE` command.

Figure 7-1 shows the editing of a row in the completed data grid.

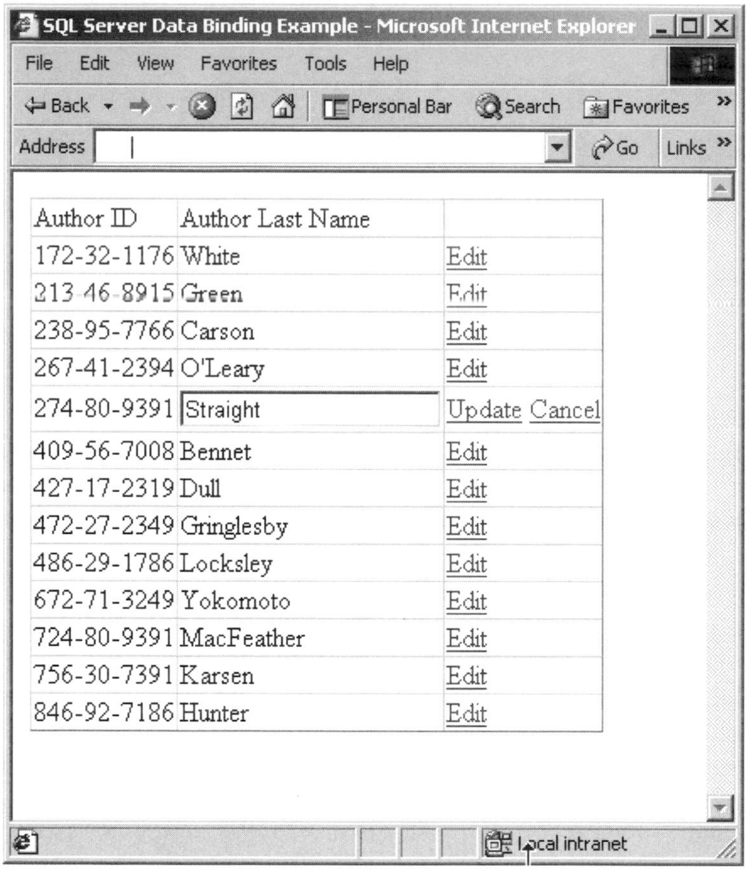

Figure 7-1 Output of the editable data grid example

7.5 Programming with the `DataList` and `DataGrid` Controls

By now you've learned a lot about data-binding techniques using the `DataList` and `DataGrid` Controls. These two Web Controls are useful for a wide variety of Web applications. In this lab, you're going to use the `DataList` and `DataGrid` Controls to implement an online photo gallery! You'll work through constructing the HTML and implementing the code-behind functionality necessary for the upload, browse, and text-annotation features of the photo gallery. The photo gallery created below is simplistic and its feature set is rather rudimentary so you can implement improvements on your own.

LAB 7-1

AN ONLINE PHOTO GALLERY

STEP 1. Create a new VB.NET Web application named "PhotoAlbum".

STEP 2. Create the main Web Form.

a. Make sure the Solution Explorer is active and shown. Right-click on the PhotoAlbum Project icon and select **Add→Add Web Form . . .** from the menu.

b. Name the new Web Form "PhotoMain.aspx". Be sure to set this Web Form as the start page. (Right-click it in the Solution Explorer and select **Set As Start Page**.)

STEP 3. Create a database for the photo gallery.
This project uses an SQL Server database to store photo text annotations. You can set this up in the SQL Server Enterprise Manager Console. You may need to consult the SQL Server documentation to complete these steps.

a. Create a new database called "Photo".

b. Inside the Photo database, create a new table called "PhotoInfo". The PhotoInfo table has three columns with the data types shown below:

- The Filename column: VARCHAR(255) (primary key)
- The PhotoFieldValue column: VARCHAR(255)
- The PhotoFieldName column: VARCHAR(255)

STEP 4. Place and format the Web Controls.
For the visual design of the Web Form, you'll need to create the following:

- A DataGrid Web Control
- A DataList Web Control
- An HTMLInputFile HTML Control
- A Button Web Control
- A Label Web Control
- Other miscellaneous page elements

The DataGrid Control will display text annotations to the photos in a tabular format. This will be an editable data grid so users can change the text annotation entries.

a. Drag a new DataGrid Web Control onto the Web Form and name its ID property "dgPhotoData". This DataGrid Control needs to set the AutoGenerateColumns property to False. The DataGrid code should look something like the following.

```
<asp:datagrid
   id=dgPhotoData
   runat="server"
   Visible="False"
   AutoGenerateColumns=false>
</asp:datagrid>
```

b. Now you need to create template columns for the DataGrid. This DataGrid will ultimately be bound to the PhotoInfo table in the Photo SQL Server database. To create an editable DataGrid you need to add an EditCommandColumn command and some TemplateColumn Controls. Within one of the TemplateColumn Controls, add an ItemTemplate command and an EditItemTemplate command. Here's how the modified DataGrid Control code should look when you're finished making these additions to the previous DataGrid Control code.

```
<asp:datagrid
   id=dgPhotoData
   runat="server"
   Visible="False"
   AutoGenerateColumns=false>

<Columns>
   <asp:TemplateColumn HeaderText="Name">
      <ItemTemplate>
         <%# Container.DataItem("PhotoFieldName")%>
      </ItemTemplate>
   </asp:TemplateColumn>

   <asp:TemplateColumn HeaderText="Value">
      <ItemTemplate>
         <%# Container.DataItem("PhotoFieldValue")%>
      </ItemTemplate>
    <EditItemTemplate>
      <asp:TextBox
         ID="txtEditValue"
         runat="server"
         Text='<%# Container.DataItem("PhotoFieldValue") %>' />
```

```
      </EditItemTemplate>
    </asp:TemplateColumn>

    <asp:EditCommandColumn
       UpdateText="Update"
       CancelText="Cancel"
       EditText="Edit"
       ButtonType=LinkButton/>
</Columns>

</asp:datagrid>
```

Notice that the PhotoFieldValue and PhotoFieldName table columns are bound.

c. Next comes the DataList Control, which will display the photos in a grid format. Drag a new DataList Control onto the Web Form and name it "dlPhotoGrid". Set the properties of the DataList Control to match those shown in the code below.

```
<asp:datalist
   id=dlPhotoGrid
   runat="server"
   HorizontalAlign="Center"
   RepeatColumns="3"
   RepeatDirection="Horizontal"
   BorderColor="Black"
   CellSpacing="1"
   CellPadding="1"
   GridLines="Both"
   BorderWidth="1px">
</asp:datalist>
```

These properties will give the data list gridlines and will display data items in three columns.

d. Now set up the item templates. The code below shows what's required to place an HTML <img> tag in each cell of the DataList Control, plus the styles to use for selected items in the DataList Control. Here's the complete DataList Control implementation.

```
<asp:datalist
   id=dlPhotoGrid
```

```
    runat="server"
    HorizontalAlign="Center"
    RepeatColumns="3"
    RepeatDirection="Horizontal"
    BorderColor="Black"
    CellSpacing="1"
    CellPadding="1"
    GridLines="Both"
    BorderWidth="1px">

<SelectedItemStyle
    BackColor="black"
    ForeColor="white">
</SelectedItemStyle>

<SelectedItemTemplate>
    <img src="<%# Container.DataItem.ToString() %>"><br>
    <asp:Label BackColor="white" ID="lblSelFilename">
    <%# Container.DataItem.ToString() %>
    </asp:Label>
</SelectedItemTemplate>

<ItemTemplate>
    <img src="<%# Container.DataItem.ToString() %>"><br>
    <asp:Button
       CommandName="Select"
       CommandArgument="<%# Container.DataItem.ToString() %>"
       Text="Select"
       Runat="server"/>
    <asp:Label ID=lblFilename>
    <%# Container.DataItem.ToString() %>
    </asp:Label>
</ItemTemplate>
</asp:datalist>
```

To show the cell as "inverted" for items the user selects, the code specifies a `BackColor` of `black` for the `SelectedItemStyle`. Also, the `SelectedItemTemplate` shows that the text should also be displayed as `white` to make it visible against the black background of the cell. The implementation of `ItemTemplate` is similar but includes the specification of `CommandName` and `CommandArgument`, which will be used in the code-behind file that handles events for selection of items.

e. Photos are added to the album via a forms-based file upload (RFC 1867) using the `HtmlInputFile` Control. Place the code below, which contains the required HTML fragment, in the Web Form. This code also includes a `Button` Web Control to accept the file submission. Make sure the controls are named correctly so they match the event handlers in the code-behind file.

```
Select photo to add:
<INPUT id=fAddPhoto
   type=file
   name=fAddPhoto
   runat="server">
<asp:Button
   id=cmdUpload
   runat="server"
   Text="Add Photo">
</asp:Button>
```

f. For the last Web Control, place a `Label` Control in the Web Form, which will be used to display any errors encountered during the use of the photo gallery. Here is the code to enter.

```
<asp:Label
   id=lblErrorMessage
   runat="server"
   Width="461px"
   Height="19px"
   ForeColor="Red"
   Font-Bold="True">
</asp:Label>
```

g. Finally, you need to make one small adjustment to the `<form>` tag: add an attribute, encType, and set it to `multipart/form-data`. This is a requirement for the file upload since IIS needs to know how to decode the form data as well as the Base64-encoded file submission on the server. The code should read as follows.

```
<form id=Form1
   method=post
   encType="multipart/form-data"
   runat="server">
```

STEP 5. Implement the code-behind functionality.

The code-behind file for the Web Form can be roughly divided between these areas of functionality:

- Data-binding code
- Event handlers for the DataList and DataGrid Controls
- Event handler for the Add Photo button
- Miscellaneous support functions

a. Begin with the data-binding code. Your first job is to write a function that will retrieve the images from the directory and bind that data to the DataList Control. Here is that code.

```
Private Sub BindIt()
   Dim strImagePath As String
   Dim aryFileArray As New ArrayList()
   Dim strFilename As String

   strImagePath = Server.MapPath("/images")

   strFilename = Dir(strImagePath & "\*.jpg")
   Do While strFilename <> ""
      aryFileArray.Add("/images/" & strFilename)
      strFilename = Dir()
   Loop

   dlPhotoGrid.DataSource = aryFileArray
   dlPhotoGrid.DataBind()

End Sub
```

The BindIt() subroutine first retrieves the physical path of the /images virtual directory. Then the code uses the VB Dir() function to return .jpg file names in a loop. Each one is added to an array list, which is bound to the DataList Control, dlPhotoGrid.

b. Implement the code shown below to bind the DataGrid Control for the text-annotation data.

```
   Private Sub BindPhotoData(ByVal pKey As String)
      Dim objCnn As New SqlConnection( _
"Initial Catalog=Photo;Data Source=localhost;uid=sa;pwd=")
      Dim objCmd As SqlCommand
      Dim objSqlDR As SqlDataReader

      objCnn.Open()

      objCmd = objCnn.CreateCommand()
```

```
        objCmd.CommandText = _
           "SELECT PhotoFieldName, PhotoFieldValue " & _
           "FROM PhotoInfo WHERE Filename = '" & pKey & _
                "'"
        objSqlDR = objCmd.ExecuteReader()

        dgPhotoData.Visible = True
        dgPhotoData.DataSource = objSqlDR
        dgPhotoData.DataBind()

    End Sub
```

This data-binding code takes a single parameter, pKey, which serves as the value to search for in the PhotoInfo table. That value is the primary key, Filename. The code then builds an SQL statement string for the SqlCommand object and calls ExecuteReader() to obtain a bindable SqlDataReader object.

c. Set up some code for the Page_Load event that binds the DataList Control.

```
    Private Sub Page_Load(ByVal sender As System.Object, _
        ByVal e As System.EventArgs) Handles MyBase.Load

        If Not Page.IsPostBack Then
           BindIt()
        End If
    End Sub
```

d. Next come the various event-handling routines you need to implement. Start with the DataList Control. Implement the event to handle the clicking of the Select button by adding the code below.

```
    Private Sub dlPhotoGrid_ItemCommand( _
            ByVal source As Object, _
            ByVal e As DataListCommandEventArgs) _
            Handles dlPhotoGrid.ItemCommand
        Try

           If e.CommandName = "Select" Then
              dlPhotoGrid.SelectedIndex = e.Item.ItemIndex
              BindIt()
           End If
```

```
            ViewState("filename") = e.CommandArgument

            BindPhotoData(e.CommandArgument)

        Catch Ecpt As Exception
            lblErrorMessage.Text = Ecpt.Message
        End Try
    End Sub
```

This code checks the CommandName (which was specified in the DataGrid Control in the HTML code) and then sets the appropriate SelectedIndex. This was passed to the program from the DataListCommandEventArgs parameter, e. Next, the code needs to save one piece of state information, Filename. This is necessary because a post-back to the server will cause the current file name selection in the DataList Control to become unavailable. The program will need this information when binding the DataGrid Control with BindPhotoData().

e. The next step is the event-handling code for the DataGrid Control. You need to handle events for the Edit, Update, and Cancel links. First, enter this code for the Edit event.

```
    Private Sub dgPhotoData_EditCommand( _
            ByVal source As Object, _
            ByVal e As DataGridCommandEventArgs) _
            Handles dgPhotoData.EditCommand

        dgPhotoData.EditItemIndex = e.Item.ItemIndex
        BindPhotoData(ViewState("filename"))
    End Sub
```

This code causes the DataGrid Control to enter edit mode for the selected row. Data binding needs to happen here, so after setting the EditItemIndex, the code calls BindPhotoData(), using the saved value from the ViewState collection, which was populated when the Select button was clicked for an item in the data list.

f. Implement similar functionality to handle the Cancel selection.

```
    Private Sub dgPhotoData_CancelCommand( _
            ByVal source As Object, _
            ByVal e As DataGridCommandEventArgs) _
            Handles dgPhotoData.CancelCommand
```

```
        Dim strFilename As String
        strFilename = ViewState("filename")
        dgPhotoData.EditItemIndex = -1
        BindPhotoData(strFilename)
    End Sub
```

This time, simply set the EditItemIndex to −1 to return the DataGrid Control to the read mode.

g. Now add the code for the Update event.

```
    Private Sub dgPhotoData_UpdateCommand( _
            ByVal source As Object, _
            ByVal e As DataGridCommandEventArgs) _
            Handles dgPhotoData.UpdateCommand

        Dim txtEditedValue As TextBox
        Dim strFilename As String

        Try
            Dim objCnn As New SqlConnection( _
    "Initial Catalog=Photo;Data Source=localhost;uid=sa;pwd=")
            Dim objSqlCmd As SqlCommand
            Dim intRows As Integer
            Dim objParam As SqlParameter

            txtEditedValue = CType( _
                    e.Item.FindControl("txtEditValue"), _
                    TextBox)

            strFilename = ViewState("filename")

            objCnn.Open()

            Dim objCmd As IDbCommand = objCnn.CreateCommand()
            objCmd.CommandText = _
        "UPDATE PhotoInfo SET PhotoFieldValue = @newValue " & _
        "WHERE Filename = @filename"

            objParam = New SqlParameter()
            With objParam
                .ParameterName = "@newValue"
                .DbType = DbType.String
                .Direction = ParameterDirection.Input
                .Value = txtEditedValue.Text
```

```
            End With
            objCmd.Parameters.Add(objParam)

            objParam = New SqlParameter()
            With objParam
                .ParameterName = "@filename"
                .DbType = DbType.String
                .Direction = ParameterDirection.Input
                .Value = strFilename
            End With
            objCmd.Parameters.Add(objParam)

            intRows = objCmd.ExecuteNonQuery()

            dgPhotoData.EditItemIndex = -1
            BindPhotoData(strFilename)

        Catch Ecpt As Exception
            lblErrorMessage.Text = Ecpt.Message
        End Try

    End Sub
```

This code is considerably more complex, but the concepts should be familiar since we have covered all of them in previous examples. To get the value that the user typed into the editable field in the data grid, the code obtains a reference to the `TextBox` Control defined in the `EditItemTemplate`. The `Text` property of this `TextBox` Control contains the value that the user entered. Next the database connection opens and the code begins building the command for the `SqlCommand` object. `SqlParameter` objects set values for the `PhotoFieldValue` and `Filename` columns in the SQL statement. The `SqlParameter` objects are added to the command, the command is executed, and then the `EditItemIndex` is reset to –1, placing the DataGrid Control back into read mode.

h. Add the event handler for the Add Photo button, which copies the uploaded photo to the server's `/images` directory. It also initializes (adds) a new row to the `PhotoInfo` table. Here is the code.

```
    Private Sub cmdUpload_Click( _
        ByVal sender As System.Object, _
        ByVal args As System.EventArgs) _
        Handles cmdUpload.Click
```

```
    Dim strFilePath As String
    Dim objCnn As New SqlConnection( _
"Initial Catalog=Photo;Data Source=localhost;uid=sa;pwd=")
    Dim objSqlCmd As SqlCommand

    Try
       objCnn.Open()
       objSqlCmd = objCnn.CreateCommand()
       objSqlCmd.CommandText = _
    "INSERT INTO PhotoInfo " & _
    "(PhotoFieldName, PhotoFieldValue, Filename) " & _
    "VALUES ('Caption', '', '" & "/images/" & _
    GetFilenameFromPath(fAddPhoto.PostedFile.FileName) & _
    "')"

       strFilePath = Server.MapPath("/images")

       If Not IsNothing(fAddPhoto.PostedFile) Then

          If Right(fAddPhoto.PostedFile.FileName, 4) <> _
                ".jpg" Then
             Throw New BadImageFormatException( _
                "Not a JPEG file")
          End If

          fAddPhoto.PostedFile.SaveAs(strFilePath & _
                "\" & _
                GetFilenameFromPath( _
                fAddPhoto.PostedFile.FileName))

          objSqlCmd.ExecuteNonQuery()
          lblErrorMessage.Text = ""
       End If

       BindIt()

    Catch E As Exception
       lblErrorMessage.Text = E.Message
    End Try

 End Sub
```

The code first sets up the database connection and creates an SQL INSERT statement for the PhotoInfo table. Next the program checks to see if there is a valid file to upload by inspecting the `PostedFile` property of the `fAddPhoto` object (an `HtmlInputFile` class). If so, the program checks the file extension to see if a `.jpg` file is being submitted. An exception defined in the code, `BadImageFormatException`, is thrown upon receiving a non-`.jpg` file (or no file). When an acceptable file is submitted, it is saved to the `/images` virtual directory with the `SaveAs()` method. The SQL `INSERT` statement is executed, and the function terminates.

i. Finally, implement the `BadImageFormatException` class and also a support function, `GetFilenameFromPath()`, that returns just the file name of a fully qualified system path. The code appears below.

```
Public Class BadImageFileException
   Inherits Exception

   Sub New()
      MyBase.New()
   End Sub

   Sub New(ByVal message As String)
      MyBase.New(message)
   End Sub

   Sub New(ByVal message As String, _
           ByVal inner As Exception)
      MyBase.New(message, inner)
   End Sub

End Class

   Private Function GetFilenameFromPath( _
                    ByVal pFilename As String)
      GetFilenameFromPath = Mid(pFilename, _
              InStrRev(pFilename, "\") + 1)
   End Function
```

The complete code for the code-behind file is listed below.

```
Imports System
Imports System.Data
Imports System.Data.SqlClient

Public Class NotImageFileException
```

```
    Inherits Exception

    Sub New()
       MyBase.New()
    End Sub

    Sub New(ByVal message As String)
       MyBase.New(message)
    End Sub

    Sub New(ByVal message As String, _
            ByVal inner As Exception)
       MyBase.New(message, inner)
    End Sub

End Class


Public Class PhotoMain
    Inherits System.Web.UI.Page
    Protected WithEvents Panel1 As _
       System.Web.UI.WebControls.Panel
    Protected WithEvents cmdUpload As _
       System.Web.UI.WebControls.Button
    Protected WithEvents dlPhotoGrid As _
       System.Web.UI.WebControls.DataList
    Protected WithEvents dgPhotoData As _
       System.Web.UI.WebControls.DataGrid
    Protected WithEvents lblErrorMessage As _
       System.Web.UI.WebControls.Label
    Protected WithEvents fAddPhoto As _
       System.Web.UI.HtmlControls.HtmlInputFile

    Private Sub Page_Load( _
                ByVal sender As _
                System.Object, _
                ByVal e As System.EventArgs) _
                Handles MyBase.Load

       If Not Page.IsPostBack Then
          BindIt()
       End If
    End Sub
```

```
Private Function GetFilenameFromPath( _
          ByVal pFilename As String)
   GetFilenameFromPath = Mid(pFilename, _
          InStrRev(pFilename, "\") + 1)
End Function

Private Sub BindPhotoData(ByVal pKey As String)
   Dim objCnn As New SqlConnection( _
"Initial Catalog=Photo;Data Source=localhost;uid=sa;pwd=")
   Dim objCmd As SqlCommand
   Dim objSqlDR As SqlDataReader

   objCnn.Open()

   objCmd = objCnn.CreateCommand()
   objCmd.CommandText = _
          "SELECT PhotoFieldName, PhotoFieldValue " & _
          "FROM PhotoInfo WHERE Filename = '" & pKey & _
          "'"
   objSqlDR = objCmd.ExecuteReader()

   dgPhotoData.Visible = True
   dgPhotoData.DataSource = objSqlDR
   dgPhotoData.DataBind()

End Sub

Private Sub BindIt()
   Dim strImagePath As String
   Dim aryFileArray As New ArrayList()
   Dim strFilename As String

   strImagePath = Server.MapPath("/images")

   strFilename = Dir(strImagePath & "\*.jpg")
   Do While strFilename <> ""
      aryFileArray.Add("/images/" & strFilename)
      strFilename = Dir()
   Loop

   dlPhotoGrid.DataSource = aryFileArray
   dlPhotoGrid.DataBind()

End Sub
```

```
 Private Sub cmdUpload_Click( _
    ByVal sender As System.Object, _
    ByVal args As System.EventArgs) _
    Handles cmdUpload.Click

    Dim strFilePath As String
    Dim objCnn As New SqlConnection( _
"Initial Catalog=Photo;Data Source=localhost;uid=sa;pwd=")
    Dim objSqlCmd As SqlCommand

    Try
       objCnn.Open()
       objSqlCmd = objCnn.CreateCommand()
       objSqlCmd.CommandText = _
       "INSERT INTO PhotoInfo " & _
       "(PhotoFieldName, PhotoFieldValue, Filename) " & _
       "VALUES ('Caption', '', '" & "/images/" & _
       GetFilenameFromPath(fAddPhoto.PostedFile.FileName) & _
       "')"

       strFilePath = Server.MapPath("/images")

       If Not IsNothing(fAddPhoto.PostedFile) Then

          If Right(fAddPhoto.PostedFile.FileName, 4) <> _
                  ".jpg" Then
             Throw New BadImageFormatException( _
                 "Not a JPEG file")
          End If

          fAddPhoto.PostedFile.SaveAs(strFilePath & _
                  "\" & _
                  GetFilenameFromPath( _
                  fAddPhoto.PostedFile.FileName))

          objSqlCmd.ExecuteNonQuery()
          lblErrorMessage.Text = ""
       End If

       BindIt()

    Catch E As Exception
       lblErrorMessage.Text = E.Message
    End Try
```

```
End Sub

Private Sub dgPhotoData_EditCommand( _
        ByVal source As Object, _
        ByVal e As DataGridCommandEventArgs) _
        Handles dgPhotoData.EditCommand

   Dim strFil As String
   dgPhotoData.EditItemIndex = e.Item.ItemIndex
   strFil = ViewState("filename")
   BindPhotoData(ViewState("filename"))
End Sub

Private Sub dgPhotoData_CancelCommand( _
        ByVal source As Object, _
        ByVal e As DataGridCommandEventArgs) _
        Handles dgPhotoData.CancelCommand

   Dim strFilename As String
   strFilename = ViewState("filename")
   dgPhotoData.EditItemIndex = -1
   BindPhotoData(strFilename)
End Sub

Private Sub dgPhotoData_UpdateCommand( _
        ByVal source As Object, _
        ByVal e As DataGridCommandEventArgs) _
        Handles dgPhotoData.UpdateCommand

   Dim txtEditedValue As TextBox
   Dim strFilename As String

   Try
      Dim objCnn As New SqlConnection( _
"Initial Catalog=Photo;Data Source=localhost;uid=sa;pwd=")
      Dim objSqlCmd As SqlCommand
      Dim intRows As Integer
      Dim objParam As SqlParameter

      txtEditedValue = CType( _
              e.Item.FindControl("txtEditValue"), _
              TextBox)

      strFilename = ViewState("filename")
```

```
            objCnn.Open()

            Dim objCmd As IDbCommand = objCnn.CreateCommand()
            objCmd.CommandText = _
         "UPDATE PhotoInfo SET PhotoFieldValue = @newValue " & _
         "WHERE Filename = @filename"

            objParam = New SqlParameter()
            With objParam
                .ParameterName = "@newValue"
                .DbType = DbType.String
                .Direction = ParameterDirection.Input
                .Value = txtEditedValue.Text
            End With
            objCmd.Parameters.Add(objParam)

            objParam = New SqlParameter()
            With objParam
                .ParameterName = "@filename"
                .DbType = DbType.String
                .Direction = ParameterDirection.Input
                .Value = strFilename
            End With
            objCmd.Parameters.Add(objParam)

            intRows = objCmd.ExecuteNonQuery()

            dgPhotoData.EditItemIndex = -1
            BindPhotoData(strFilename)

         Catch Ecpt As Exception
            lblErrorMessage.Text = Ecpt.Message
         End Try

      End Sub

      Private Sub dlPhotoGrid_ItemCommand( _
               ByVal source As Object, _
               ByVal e As DataListCommandEventArgs) _
               Handles dlPhotoGrid.ItemCommand
         Try

            If e.CommandName = "Select" Then
               dlPhotoGrid.SelectedIndex = e.Item.ItemIndex
```

```
                BindIt()
            End If

            ViewState("filename") = e.CommandArgument

            BindPhotoData(e.CommandArgument)

        Catch Ecpt As Exception
            lblErrorMessage.Text = Ecpt.Message
        End Try
    End Sub

End Class
```

STEP 6. Run the program.

a. Operation of the photo gallery should be straightforward. When the application launches, the photos in the designated directory are displayed in the data list. Click the Select button to bind the text-annotation data.

b. Change the data by clicking on the Edit link and typing a new value into the field. Cancel the edit by clicking Cancel.

c. To add a photo, click Browse . . . and select a `.jpg` file, then click Add Photo to add the chosen photo to the gallery.

STEP 7. Improve the photo gallery (optional).

This application is very simplistic. Here are some suggestions of useful features you can add on your own for more practice.

- Give the photo gallery a more aesthetically pleasing look. By adjusting the styles of the `DataGrid` and `DataList` Controls, you can change the colors, fonts, and other visual elements to your liking.
- Add support for more types of text annotation. Currently, the Caption is the only supported annotation. By changing the code that saves the image file, add functionality by creating rows in the `PhotoInfo` table for various items like dates and additional notes.
- Add a way for users to delete photos from the photo gallery.
- Modify the photo gallery so the images all display in a fixed thumbnail size. Add code so that when the thumbnail is clicked, the full-size image is displayed in a separate window.

These are a few suggestions. With your knowledge of Web Controls, you should be able to think up many more. Get creative!

7.6 Working with the DataSet and DataTable Objects

Data access is an expensive operation. Substantial computational power is consumed when connecting, retrieving, and updating databases. Also, as applications demand more and more scalability, greater pressure is placed on the common bottleneck in the enterprise—data access. Couple these facts with the number of users accessing the data simultaneously, and you can quickly ascertain that data access needs to be streamlined.

ADO.NET introduces new concepts in enterprise data access. ADO.NET alleviates the problems mentioned above by implementing a disconnected model for data access. This involves taking a "snapshot" of database data, transferring it to the client, and then immediately disconnecting. The client then proceeds to query and update this "downloaded" data. When changes have been completed (if any), the client then "uploads" the changed data to the server. The server then reconciles any changes to the database automatically. This procedure greatly decreases the use of system resources for data access.

Since ADO.NET has the ability to take a "snapshot" of the database data, it can also retrieve information about the schema of the data. ADO.NET can represent tables, columns, keys, and relations in memory, as well as data. Many times, programmers think of ADO.NET as a way to build an in-memory database. That's an accurate description of the `DataSet` and `DataTable` objects, which are the topics of this section.

7.6.1 The DataSet Class Summary

Tables 7-8 and 7-9 present the properties and methods of the `DataSet` class.

Table 7-8 Properties of the `DataSet` Class

Property	Description
`CaseSensitive`	Has a value of `True` if string comparisons within the `DataSet` object are case-sensitive
`DataSetName`	Specifies the name of the `DataSet` object
`DefaultViewManager`	Returns a `DataViewManager` object used for filtering, searching, and navigating records
`EnforceConstraints`	Has a value of `True` if constraint rules are to be considered when attempting any update operation

(continued)

Table 7-8 Properties of the DataSet Class *(continued)*

Property	Description
ExtendedProperties	Returns a collection of custom information supplied by the user
HasErrors	Has a value of True if there are errors in any of the rows of the DataSet object
Locale	Specifies the geographic region and rules to govern DataSet operations (a CultureInfo object)
Namespace	Specifies the namespace of the DataSet object
Prefix	Specifies the XML prefix that aliases the namespace of the DataSet object
Relations	Specifies the collection of DataRelation objects used in the DataSet object
Site	Sets the System.ComponentModel.ISite for the DataSet object
Tables	Specifies a collection of DataTable objects contained in the DataSet object

Table 7-9 Methods of the DataSet Class

Method	Description	Syntax
AcceptChanges	Commits all changes (updates the data source)	–
BeginInit	Begins the initialization of a DataSet object	–
Clear	Removes all data from the DataSet object	–
Clone	Creates a copy of the DataSet object along with all the underlying objects	Clone() As DataSet

Method	Description	Syntax
Copy	Creates a copy of the data and structure of the DataSet object	Copy() As DataSet
EndInit	Ends the initialization of a DataSet object	–
GetChanges	Returns a DataSet object containing all changes made to it since it was last loaded or since AcceptChanges was called	GetChanges() As DataSet GetChanges(ByVal *rowStates* As DataRowState) As DataSet
GetXml	Returns the XML string of the data stored in the DataSet object	GetXml() As String
GetXmlSchema	Returns the XSD schema for the XML representation of the data stored in the DataSet object	GetXmlSchema() As String
HasChanges	Has a value of True if the DataSet object has changes to any of its rows	HasChanges() As Boolean HasChanges(ByVal *rowStates* As DataRowState) As Boolean
InferXmlSchema	Infers the XML schema from the specified source into the DataSet object	InferXmlSchema(ByVal *stream* As Stream, ByVal *nsArray()* As String) InferXmlSchema(ByVal *fileName* As String, ByVal *nsArray()* As String) InferXmlSchema(ByVal *reader* As TextReader, ByVal *nsArray()* As String) InferXmlSchema(ByVal *reader* As XmlReader, ByVal *nsArray()* As String)

(continued)

Table 7-9 Methods of the `DataSet` Class *(continued)*

Method	Description	Syntax

`Merge`	Merges this `DataSet` object with another `DataSet` object	`Merge(ByVal` *`rows()`* `As DataRow)`
		
		`Merge(ByVal` *`dataSet`* `As DataSet)`
		
		`Merge(ByVal` *`table`* `As DataTable)`
		
		`Merge(ByVal` *`dataSet`* `As DataSet, ByVal` *`preserveChanges`* `As Boolean)`
		
		`Merge(ByVal` *`rows()`* `As DataRow, ByVal` *`preserveChanges`* `As Boolean, ByVal` *`missingSchemaAction`* `As MissingSchemaAction)`
		
		`Merge(ByVal` *`dataSet`* `As DataSet, ByVal` *`preserveChanges`* `As Boolean, ByVal` *`missingSchemaAction`* `As MissingSchemaAction)`
		
		`Merge(ByVal` *`table`* `As DataTable, ByVal` *`preserveChanges`* `As Boolean, ByVal` *`missingSchemaAction`* `As MissingSchemaAction)`

`ReadXml`	Reads XML schema and data into the `DataSet` object	`ReadXml(ByVal` *`stream`* `As Stream) As XmlReadMode`
		
		`ReadXml(ByVal` *`fileName`* `As String) As XmlReadMode`

Method	Description	Syntax
		ReadXml(ByVal *reader* As TextReader) As XmlReadMode ReadXml(ByVal *reader* As XmlReader) As XmlReadMode ReadXml(ByVal *stream* As Stream, ByVal *mode* As XmlReadMode) As XmlReadMode ReadXml(ByVal *fileName* As String, ByVal *mode* As XmlReadMode) As XmlReadMode ReadXml(ByVal *reader* As TextReader, ByVal *mode* As XmlReadMode) As XmlReadMode ReadXml(ByVal *reader* As XmlReader, ByVal *mode* As XmlReadMode) As XmlReadMode
ReadXmlSchema	Reads an XML schema into the DataSet object	ReadXmlSchema(ByVal *stream* As Stream) ReadXmlSchema(ByVal *fileName* As String) ReadXmlSchema(ByVal *reader* As TextReader) ReadXmlSchema(ByVal *reader* As XmlReader)
RejectChanges	Undoes all changes made to the DataSet object since the last call to AcceptChanges	–

(continued)

Table 7-9 Methods of the `DataSet` Class *(continued)*

Method	Description	Syntax
`Reset`	Rolls back the `DataSet` object to its original state	–
`WriteXml`	Writes XML schema and data from the `DataSet` object	`WriteXml(ByVal stream As Stream)WriteXml(ByVal fileName As String)` `WriteXml(ByVal reader As TextReader)WriteXml(ByVal reader As XmlReader)` `WriteXml(ByVal stream As Stream, ByVal mode As XmlWriteMode)WriteXml (ByVal fileName As String, ByVal mode As XmlWriteMode)WriteXml (ByVal reader As TextReader, ByVal mode As XmlWriteMode)WriteXml (ByVal reader As XmlReader, ByVal mode As XmlWriteMode)`

`WriteXmlSchema`	Writes the `DataSet` object structure as an XML schema	`WriteXmlSchema(ByVal stream As Stream)`
		
		`WriteXmlSchema(ByVal fileName As String)`
		
		`WriteXmlSchema(ByVal reader As TextReader)`
		
		`WriteXmlSchema(ByVal reader As XmlReader)`

7.6.2 The `DataTable` Class Summary

One of the objects in the `DataSet` is the `DataTable`, which represents a store of data in tabular form. A `DataTable` object corresponds to a table in a database and in many respects has the same behaviors and characteristics. The properties and methods of the DataTable class are shown in Tables 7-10 and 7-11, respectively.

Table 7-10 Properties of the DataTable Class

Property	Description
CaseSensitive	Has a value of True if case-sensitive comparisons are enabled for strings in the DataTable object
ChildRelations	Specifies a collection of child relations for the DataTable object
Columns	Specifies a collection of columns for the data table
Constraints	Identifies the constraints assigned to the DataTable object
DataSet	Returns the DataSet object that contains the DataTable object
DefaultView	Returns the default view of the DataTable object; used for some data-binding situations
DisplayExpression	Gets or sets the expression that will return a value used to represent this table in the user interface
ExtendedProperties	Specifies a collection of customized user properties
HasErrors	Has a value of True if any rows in the data table contain errors
Locale	Specifies the geographic region and rules to govern DataTable operations (a CultureInfo object)
MinimumCapacity	Sets the minimum number of rows (starting size) for the data table
Namespace	Specifies the namespace for the XML representation of the data stored in the DataTable object
ParentRelations	Specifies a collection of parent relations for the DataTable object
Prefix	Specifies the XML prefix that aliases the namespace of the DataTable object

(continued)

Table 7-10 Properties of the `DataTable` Class *(continued)*

Property	Description
`PrimaryKey`	Specifies the array of columns that make up the primary key for the data table
`Rows`	Specifies a collection of rows of the data table
`Site`	Specifies the `System.ComponentModel.ISite` for the `DataTable` object
`TableName`	Sets the name of the `DataTable` object

Table 7-11 Methods of the `DataTable` Class

Method	Description	Syntax
`AcceptChanges`	Commits all the changes made to this table since the last time `AcceptChanges` was called.	–
`BeginInit`	Begins the initialization of a `DataTable` object that is used on a form or used by another component. The initialization occurs at runtime.	–
`BeginLoadData`	Turns off notifications, index maintenance, and constraints while loading data.	–
`Clear`	Clears the `DataTable` object of all data.	–
`Clone`	Clones the structure of the `DataTable` object, including all `DataTable` schemas and constraints.	–

Method	Description	Syntax
Compute	Computes the given expression on the current rows that pass the filter criteria.	Compute(ByVal *expression* As String, ByVal *filter* As String) As Object
Copy	Copies both the structure and data for this DataTable object.	–
EndInit	Ends the initialization of a DataTable object that is used on a form or used by another component. The initialization occurs at runtime.	–
EndLoadData	Turns on notifications, index maintenance, and constraints after loading data.	–
GetChanges	Gets a copy of the DataTable object containing all changes made to it since it was last loaded or since AcceptChanges was called.	GetChanges() GetChanges(ByVal *rowStates* As DataRowState) As DataTable
GetErrors	Gets an array of DataRow objects that contain errors.	GetErrors() As DataRow()
ImportRow	Copies a DataRow object into a DataTable object, preserving any property settings as well as original and current values.	ImportRow(ByVal *row* As DataRow)
LoadDataRow	Finds and updates a specific row. If no matching row is found, a new row is created using the given values.	LoadDataRow(ByVal *values()* As Object, ByVal *fAcceptChanges* As Boolean) As DataRow
NewRow	Creates a new DataRow object with the same schema as the table.	NewRow() As DataRow

(continued)

Table 7-11 Methods of the `DataTable` Class *(continued)*

Method	Description	Syntax
`RejectChanges`	Rolls back all changes made to the table since it was loaded or since the last time `AcceptChanges` was called.	–
`Reset`	Resets the `DataTable` object to its original state.	–

`Select`	Gets an array of `DataRow` objects.	`Select()`
		
		`Select(ByVal` *`filterExpression`* `As String) As DataRow()`
		
		`Select(ByVal` *`filterExpression`* `As String, ByVal sort As String) As DataRow()`
		
		`Select(ByVal` *`filterExpression`* `As String, ByVal` *`sort`* `As String, ByVal  As` *`recordStates`* `DataViewRowState) As DataRow()`

7.6.3 Creating `DataSet` and `DataTable` Objects

Let's look at a code sample that creates a `DataSet` object and two `DataTable` objects.

Code Sample 7-4 Build instructions: vbc /r:system.dll /r:system.xml.dll /r:system.data.dll cs7-04.vb

```
Imports System
Imports System.Xml
Imports System.Data
```

```
Imports Microsoft.VisualBasic

Module Module1

    Sub Main()

        Dim objDS As DataSet
        Dim objDT As DataTable
        Dim objDC As DataColumn
        Dim aDC(1) As DataColumn

(26)    objDS = New DataSet("Supermarket")

(27)    objDT = New DataTable("Product")
(28)    With objDT.Columns
            .Add("ProductSKU", _
                  Type.GetType("System.String"))
            .Add("ProductDescription", _
                  Type.GetType("System.String"))
        End With
(29)    objDS.Tables.Add(objDT)

(30)    aDC(0) = objDT.Columns("ProductSKU")
(31)    objDT.PrimaryKey = aDC

        objDT = New DataTable("Inventory")
        With objDT.Columns
            .Add("InventoryRecordNum", _
                  Type.GetType("System.Int32"))
            .Add("InventorySKU", _
                  Type.GetType("System.String"))
            .Add("InventoryQuantity", _
                  Type.GetType("System.Int32"))
            .Add("InventoryBinNumber", _
                  Type.GetType("System.String"))
            .Add("InventoryExpirationDate", _
                  Type.GetType("System.DateTime"))
        End With
        objDS.Tables.Add(objDT)

        aDC(0) = objDT.Columns("InventoryRecordNum")
        objDT.PrimaryKey = aDC

        With objDT.Columns("InventoryRecordNum")
```

```
(32)            .AutoIncrement = True
(33)            .AutoIncrementSeed = 1
(34)            .AutoIncrementStep = 1
         End With

         Console.WriteLine("DataSet contains these tables:")
(35)        For Each objDT In objDS.Tables
            Console.WriteLine("-" & objDT.TableName & "-")
            For Each objDC In objDT.Columns
               Console.WriteLine(objDC.ColumnName & _
                                ControlChars.Tab & _
                                objDC.DataType.ToString())
            Next
            Console.WriteLine()
         Next
      End Sub

End Module
```

We begin the code with the creation of a new `DataSet` object in line (26) called `Supermarket`. The `DataSet` object will contain two tables. The first one is created in line (27). The new `DataTable` object, `objDT`, does not contain any fields (columns), so we must specify some. All of the columns for the `DataTable` object are kept in the collection referenced by the `Columns` property.

Working with Columns

Columns in a table are represented by the `DataColumn` class. The `DataColumn` class contains the properties shown in Table 7-12.

As mentioned earlier, the `Product` object created in line (27) needs some columns. We can do that by referencing the `Columns` property of the `DataTable` object. This property is a `DataColumnCollection`, so we can simply use the `Add()` method in the code block that begins at line (28) to create two new `DataColumn` objects. We supply two parameters to the `Add()` method: the name of the column and a `System.Type` that represents the data type the column will hold. Both of the columns in the `Product` table will hold strings, so we use the `System.String` type for both columns. Once all the columns are created for the table, we add the table to the `DataSet` object by adding the `DataTable` object to the `Tables` collection (`DataTableCollection`) in line (29).

Table 7-12 Properties of the DataColumn Class

Property	Description
AllowDBNull	Has a value of True if database NULL values are allowed for this column
AutoIncrement	Has a value of True if a new unique number is generated for this column when a new row is added
AutoIncrementSeed	Sets the value to use as a start value for AutoIncrement columns
AutoIncrementStep	Sets the value to use as an increment for AutoIncrement columns
Caption	Specifies the column's caption text
ColumnMapping	Determines how column data will be represented in XML (the MappingType of the column): Attribute, Element, Hidden, or SimpleContent
ColumnName	Specifies the name of the column
DataType	Sets the data type of the column
DefaultValue	Sets the default value for the column
Expression	Specifies the expression used to filter rows, calculate the values in a column, or create an aggregate column
ExtendedProperties	Specifies a collection of custom user information
MaxLength	Sets the maximum length of a text column in characters
Namespace	Specifies the namespace of the column
Ordinal	Sets the ordinal position of the column in the collection of columns (DataColumnCollection)
Prefix	Specifies the XML prefix that aliases the namespace of the DataColumn object

(continued)

Table 7-12 Properties of the `DataColumn` Class *(continued)*

Property	Description
`ReadOnly`	Has a value of `True` if the column's data can't be changed once a row has been created
`Table`	Returns the `DataTable` object to which the column belongs
`Unique`	Has a value of `True` if the values in each row of the column must be unique

Setting the Primary Key

Primary keys are a way to uniquely identify rows in a table. The `DataTable` class can define one or more columns to serve as the primary key for the table data. The first step in setting the primary key for the table is to make an array of `DataColumn` objects. At the beginning of the code sample, notice that we declare an array of `DataColumn` objects (an array of size 1). This array will hold the `DataColumn` objects that will comprise the primary key. In line ㉚, we set the single element of that array (index `0`) to the `ProductSKU` column. This column becomes the primary key. Then in line ㉛ we set the `PrimaryKey` property to the column array we constructed.

Next in the code we repeat the process of creating a new table, adding columns, and setting a primary key for the `Inventory` table.

One characteristic that the `Inventory` table has that the `Product` table does not is an auto-incrementing column. In the example the auto-incrementing column will populate a sequential, unique number for each row added to the table. We set up an auto-incrementing column by first setting the `AutoIncrement` property of the `DataColumn` object to `True` in line ㉜. Then we specify the increment seed, which is an arbitrary number to begin the sequence, in line ㉝. We also set an increment step value, `AutoIncrementStep`, which is the value that gets added to the previous increment value (see line ㉞).

Displaying `DataSet` Information

Now that we've created the beginnings of a `DataSet`, we can display the information about the `DataTable` objects we've added. The code block beginning in line 35 shows the use of a nested loop that retrieves information for each `DataTable` object in the `DataSet` (using the `DataTableCollection`) and each `DataColumn` object in those `DataTable` objects (using the `DataColumnCollection`). Code within these loops outputs each `DataTable` object's name as well as column name and type information.

7.6.4 Adding Data to a DataTable Object

No data have been inserted yet into the `DataTable` objects. Actions on the data inside a `DataTable` object happen within the `DataRow` object. (See Appendix B for information on the properties and methods of the `DataRow` class.)

Adding data to a `DataTable` object is fairly easy. The code below shows how to add a record (a `DataRow` object) to the `Product` table we constructed in the previous example.

```
Public Sub AddNewProduct( _
        ByVal pProductTable As DataTable, _
        ByVal pProductSKU As String, _
        ByVal pProductDescription As String)

    Try
        Dim dr As DataRow

36      dr = pProductTable.NewRow()
37      dr.Item("ProductSKU") = pProductSKU
38      dr.Item("ProductDescription") = pProductDescription
39      pProductTable.Rows.Add(dr)

    Catch E As Exception
        Console.WriteLine("ERROR: " & E.Message)
    End Try

End Sub
```

The `AddNewProduct()` subroutine takes a `DataTable` object and two `String` values as parameters. The code begins at line 36 with the creation of a new `DataRow` object. We cannot use the `New()` method to create a new `DataRow()` object, so we use the `NewRow()` method of the `DataTable` class. This creates a `DataRow` object that has the same column structure as the `DataTable` object.

Once we've created the `DataRow` object, we can assign values to its columns. In lines 37 and 38 we assign to the `DataRow` object the two `String` parameters defined earlier. We reference the columns in the data row using the `Item` property. The `Item` property can take an ordinal index or a column name (specified as a `String`). The new data that we supply to the `DataRow` object does not get appended to the table until the `DataRow` object is added to the `Rows` collection in line 39.

7.6.5 Displaying Data in a `DataTable` Object

Displaying data in a `DataTable` object is also easy. It involves nested loops that iterate through each row and each column of every row. Here is some sample code to illustrate.

```
Public Sub ListTableContents(ByVal pTable As DataTable)

   Try
      Dim dc As DataColumn
      Dim dr As DataRow
      Dim obj As Object

40    For Each dc In pTable.Columns
         Console.Write(dc.ColumnName & _
                          ControlChars.Tab)
      Next
      Console.WriteLine()

41    For Each dr In pTable.Rows
42       For Each obj In dr.ItemArray
            Console.Write(obj.ToString() & _
                    ControlChars.Tab)
         Next
         Console.WriteLine()
      Next

   Catch E As Exception
      Console.WriteLine("ERROR: " & E.Message)
   End Try

End Sub
```

For clarity of the output, in the code block beginning in line ⓸⓪ we include code to display all the column names in the DataSet object before displaying any row data. In line ⓸⓵ we start the outer loop that iterates through all the DataRow objects in the DataSet object. The DataRow class contains the ItemArray property (see line ⓸⓶), which is an array of System.Object and holds the values contained in the DataRow object. The inner loop converts each of those object values to a System.String for display in the console.

7.6.6 Loading and Updating DataSet Objects with the IDataAdapter Interface

Loading a DataSet object from a database is a common operation with ADO.NET, which allows you to update the DataSet object and then send back the changed data to the database. The IDataAdapter interface (see Tables 7-13 and 7-14), in combination with other ADO.NET classes such as the DataTable and DataRow objects, makes this relatively easy. It also offers a lot of editing flexibility, as illustrated in the example below.

Table 7-13 Properties of the IDataAdapter Interface

Property	Description
MissingMappingAction	Indicates or specifies whether unmapped source tables or columns are passed with their source names in order to be filtered or to raise an error. Can be Error, Ignore, or Passthrough (MissingMappingAction enumeration).
MissingSchemaAction	Indicates or specifies whether missing source tables, columns, and their relationships are added to the DataSet schema, are ignored, or cause an error to be raised. Can be Add, AddWithKey, Error, or Ignore (MissingSchemaAction enumeration).
TableMappings	Indicates how a source table is mapped to a DataSet table.

Table 7-14 Methods of the `IDataAdapter` Interface

Method	Description	Syntax
`Fill`	Adds or refreshes rows in the `DataSet` object to match those in the data source using the `DataSet` name and creates a `DataTable` object named `Table`	`Fill(ByVal` *`dataSet`* `As DataSet) As Integer`
`FillSchema`	Adds a `DataTable` object named `Table` to the specified `DataSet` object and configures the schema to match that in the data source based on the specified `SchemaType`	`FillSchema(ByVal` *`dataSet`* `As DataSet, ByVal` *`schemaType`* `As SchemaType) As DataTable()`
`GetFillParameters`	Gets the parameters set by the user when executing an SQL SELECT statement	`GetFillParameters() As IDataParameter()`
`Update`	Calls the respective `INSERT`, `UPDATE`, or `DELETE` statements for each inserted, updated, or deleted row in the specified `DataSet` object from a `DataTable` object named `Table`	`Update(ByVal` *`dataSet`* `As DataSet) As Integer`

Code Sample 7-5 Build instructions: vbc /r:system.dll /r:system.data.dll /r:system.xml.dll cs7-05.vb

```
Imports System
Imports System.Data
Imports System.Data.SqlClient
Imports System.Xml

Module Module1

    Sub Main()

        Dim objCnn As SqlConnection
```

```
        Dim ds As DataSet
        Dim da As SqlDataAdapter
        Dim cb As SqlCommandBuilder
        Dim dt As DataTable

        ds = New DataSet("TestDataSet")

        objCnn = New SqlConnection( _
    "Initial Catalog=pubs;Data Source=localhost;uid=sa;pwd=")

43      da = New SqlDataAdapter("SELECT * from authors", _
             objCnn)
44      cb = New SqlCommandBuilder(da)
45      da.UpdateCommand = cb.GetUpdateCommand()

46      da.Fill(ds, "authors")

        Dim dr As DataRow
        dt = ds.Tables("authors")

47      AddHandler da.RowUpdated, AddressOf OnRowUpdated

48      For Each dr In dt.Rows
           dr.BeginEdit()
           If dr.Item("contract") = True Then
              dr.Item("contract") = False
           Else
              dr.Item("contract") = True
           End If
           dr.EndEdit()
        Next

        '* Uncomment this line
        '* to "undo" changes
49          'dt.RejectChanges()

50          da.Update(ds, "authors")


    End Sub

51      Public Sub OnRowUpdated(ByVal Source As Object, _
                 ByVal E As SqlRowUpdatedEventArgs)
        Console.WriteLine("row updated: " & _
```

```
                    E.Row.Item("au_id"))
    End Sub

End Module
```

This example shows how we can use the `SqlDataAdapter` to populate a `DataSet` object. After establishing a new connection to the SQL Server database with the `SqlConnection` object, we create a new `SqlDataAdapter` object in line ㊸. Any `SqlDataAdapter` object must supply a `SelectCommand` so that the `SqlDataAdapter` object may populate the `DataSet` object. The constructor in line ㊸ shows the first parameter as the SQL `SELECT` statement used to populate the `DataSet` object (with one `DataTable` object). The second parameter shows the use of the `SqlConnection` object we've created.

Whenever we make changes to a `DataSet` object, we typically want those changes reflected in the associated database on the server. We need to tell the `DataAdapter` interface how to update the data, via an SQL statement. We could supply an SQL `UPDATE` statement and set the `UpdateCommand` property, but ADO.NET provides us with an automatic way to generate an otherwise complex SQL statement. We build these commands using the `SqlCommandBuilder` class (see Tables 7-15 and 7-16).

Table 7-15 Properties of the `SqlCommandBuilder` Class

Property	Description
`DeleteCommand`	SQL statement used to delete records
`InsertCommand`	SQL statement used to insert records
`SelectCommand`	SQL statement used to select records
`UpdateCommand`	SQL statement used to update records

Table 7-16 Method of the `SqlCommandBuilder` Class

Method	Description	Syntax
`Dispose`	Frees the resources used by the `SqlDataAdapter` object	`Dispose(ByVal` *`disposing`* `As Boolean)`

Line ❹❹ shows the use of SqlCommandBuilder. We supply the SqlDataAdapter in the constructor. Since the program will be updating rows in the authors table, we generate an UpdateCommand and assign it to the SqlDataAdapter in line ❹❺.

To fill a DataSet object with values, we call the Fill() method of the SqlDataAdapter in line ❹❻. The DataSet object we are filling is supplied as the first parameter. When a fill operation occurs using this call, a new DataTable object is added to the Tables collection of the DataSet object. The name of that DataTable object is specified as the second parameter (named "authors" in the example for consistency).

The SqlDataAdapter class can raise the events shown in Table 7-17 when certain changes occur to the data. We can show that rows have been updated by adding an event handler for the RowUpdated event. We do this in line ❹❼ by using the AddHandler statement. We supply the address of the event-handling function OnRowUpdated(). This way, the event will be raised every time a row in the DataSet object is modified.

This example program will iterate through each row in the authors table of the sample pubs database. To demonstrate updating rows, the For . . . Each loop that begins in line ❹❽ will retrieve the value of the contract field in the authors table. The editing process uses the BeginEdit() and EndEdit() functions of the DataRow object. This enables us to make changes to the data in a row and then either commit or roll back those changes. To begin the editing process, we call BeginEdit(). Next, the Item collection is used to get the Boolean value of the contract column. The editing process reverses any True value to False and vice versa. At this point (and any other point during the alteration of DataRow values), we may opt to call CancelEdit()(not shown in this code). This would undo any changes made to the column values of the DataRow object. When changes are finalized, EndEdit() is called to indicate that changes made to the DataRow object are complete and should be committed to the database once at the appropriate time, for example, when AcceptChanges() is called. Even though we don't explicitly call

Table 7-17 Events of the SqlDataAdapter Class

Event	Description
OnRowUpdated	Raises the RowUpdated event
OnRowUpdating	Raises the RowUpdating event

AcceptChanges(), changes are committed in the code when the Update() method is called.

Now that changes have been made to the rows, a decision needs to be made whether or not to accept the changes made to the DataSet object. At line 49 we can call RejectChanges(), which will undo all changes made to the DataSet object and leave the database data untouched. The code calls the Update() method of the SqlDataAdapter in line 50. Update() makes an implicit call to AcceptChanges() and it also raises the RowUpdated event, which we trap with our OnRowUpdated() subroutine in line 51. OnRowUpdated() simply displays a line in the console for every row updated, showing the value of the au_id field. Information about the updated row is contained in the SqlRowUpdatedEventArgs class

7.6.7 Filtering and Sorting Data with the DataView Class

The DataView class aids in formatting data that exists in a DataTable object. You can use DataView objects for sorting, filtering, and searching data. The properties and methods of the DataView class appear in Tables 7-18 and 7-19, respectively.

Table 7-18 Properties of the DataView Class

Property	Description
AllowDelete	Has a value of True if deletes from the DataView object are allowed
AllowEdit	Has a value of True if edits of the DataView object are allowed
AllowNew	Has a value of True if new rows are allowed to be added to the DataView object
ApplyDefaultSort	Has a value of True if the default sorting method is to be used
Count	Returns the number of records in the DataView object
DataViewManager	Gets the DataView object associated with this view
Item	Returns a row of data from a specified table

Property	Description
RowFilter	Specifies the filtering expression
RowStateFilter	Specifies the row state filter with these values: Added, CurrentRows, Deleted, ModifiedCurrent, ModifiedOriginal, None, OriginalRows, and Unchanged (DataViewRowState enumeration)
Sort	Specifies the sort expression
Table	Specifies the DataTable object to use for the view

Table 7-19 Methods of the DataView Class

Method	Description	Syntax
AddNew	Adds a new row.	AddNew() As DataRowView
BeginInit	Begins the initialization of a DataView object that is used on a form or used by another component. The initialization occurs at runtime.	–
Delete	Deletes a row with the specified index.	Delete(ByVal *index* As Integer)
Dispose	Frees resources used by the DataView object.	–
EndInit	Ends the initialization of a DataView object that is used on a form or used by another component. The initialization occurs at runtime.	–

(continued)

Table 7-19 Methods of the `DataView` Class *(continued)*

Method	Description	Syntax

`Find`	Finds a row or array of rows in the `DataView` object by the specified primary key.	`Find(ByVal` *`key`* `As Object) As Integer`
		
		`Find(ByVal` *`key()`* `As Object) As Integer`

`GetEnumerator`	Returns an enumerator for this `DataView` object.	`GetEnumerator() As IEnumerator`

A `DataView` object represents a "copy" of sorts of the data in a `DataTable` object. The following example demonstrates techniques for sorting, filtering, and searching data in the `authors` table.

Code Sample 7-6 Build instructions: vbc /r:system.dll /r:system.data.dll /r:system.xml.dll cs7-06.vb

```
Imports System
Imports System.Data
Imports System.Data.SqlClient
Imports System.Xml
Imports Microsoft.VisualBasic

Module Module1

   Sub Main()

      Dim objCnn As SqlConnection
      Dim ds As DataSet
      Dim da As SqlDataAdapter

      Try
         ds = New DataSet("TestDataSet")

         objCnn = New SqlConnection( _
  "Initial Catalog=pubs;Data Source=localhost;uid=sa;pwd=")

         da = New SqlDataAdapter("SELECT * from authors", _
            objCnn)
```

```
      da.Fill(ds, "authors")

      ListTableContents(ds.Tables("authors"))

   Catch E As Exception
     Console.WriteLine("ERROR: " & E.Message)
   End Try
End Sub

Public Sub ListTableContents(ByVal pTable As DataTable)

   Try
      Dim dc As DataColumn
      Dim dr As DataRow
      Dim obj As Object
      Dim dv As DataView
      Dim intRowIndex As Integer
      Dim intFoundIndex As Integer
      Dim aSearchValues(2) As String


      For Each dc In pTable.Columns
         Console.Write(dc.ColumnName & _
                       ControlChars.Tab)
      Next
      Console.WriteLine()

52    dv = New DataView(pTable)
      With dv
53       .Sort = "au_fname, au_lname"
54       .RowFilter = "Contract = 0"
55       .RowStateFilter = _
         DataViewRowState.OriginalRows
      End With

56    For intRowIndex = 0 To dv.Count - 1
57          dr = dv.Item(intRowIndex).Row
         For Each obj In dr.ItemArray
            Console.Write(obj.ToString() & _
                            ControlChars.Tab)
         Next
      Next

      Console.WriteLine(ControlChars.NewLine)
```

```
58             aSearchValues(0) = "Michel"
            aSearchValues(1) = "DeFrance"
            intFoundIndex = dv.Find(aSearchValues)

            dr = dv.Item(intFoundIndex).Row
            For Each obj In dr.ItemArray
               Console.Write(obj.ToString() & _
                     ControlChars.Tab)
            Next

         Catch E As Exception
            Console.WriteLine("ERROR: " & E.Message)
         End Try

      End Sub

   End Module
```

This example, in regards to the `Main()` function, is similar to the other ADO.NET examples. It establishes a connection to the database using the `SqlConnection` object and populates a `DataSet` object with data from the `authors` table of the `pubs` database. Then, `ListTableContents()` is called, which contains the `DataView` sample code.

`ListTableContents()`creates a `DataView` object from the data contained in the `DataTable` object. In line 52 the constructor for the `DataView` class is a `DataTable` object. This automatically generates a `DataView` object that contains all the columns and data from the `DataTable` object.

Sorting the data involves assigning an expression to the `Sort` property of the `DataView` class in line 53. The expression syntax used for the `Sort` property matches that of an SQL `ORDER BY` clause. For the example, we specify the `au_fname` and `au_lname` fields as the sort fields. If desired, we could use `ASC` or `DESC` keywords to specify an ascending or a descending sort order, respectively.

The `DataView` class can also filter rows. To do this, we set the `RowFilter` property in line 54. The `RowFilter` property is a string expression that corresponds to an SQL `WHERE` clause. In the example, we choose to include only rows in the `DataView` object that have the `contract` field set to `False` (`0`).

Another way we can filter rows in a `DataView` object is by the row state. The `RowStateFilter` property shown in line 55 allows us to include only original rows, deleted rows, modified rows, and so on. The example sets up a filter that will include only original, unmodified rows in the `DataView` object using the `OriginalRows` value from the `DataViewRowState` enumeration.

Next comes displaying the rows in the `DataView` object. We use a `For . . .` loop beginning in line ❺❻ and an ordinal index to reference each row. A reference to an individual `DataRow` object is made by using the index from the `For . . .` loop, `intRowIndex`, and using it to reference a `DataRowView` object. `DataRowView` contains a property called `Row` that returns the `DataRow` object that corresponds to that index (see line ❺❼). We display the data for the row using the techniques from the previous examples.

Now we'll examine the code for locating particular items in the `DataView` object with the `Find()` method. Some preliminary setup is required to use the `Find()` method, and that setup involves how we specify the values for which to search. First, in order for a search to return valid results, the `DataView` object must be previously sorted (using the `Sort` property). In effect, this establishes the sort keys. The `Find()` method can then accept a string array of search values. The ordering of the strings in the array beginning in line ❺❽ is parallel to the columns specified in the `Sort` property in line ❺❸. This form of the `Find()` method, which locates a single row, returns the index of the row in the `DataView` object. Once the index is returned from the `Find()` method, we can use that index in the same manner we did before to obtain a reference to the `DataRow` objects for display purposes.

7.7 Maintaining Data Integrity with the `DataRelation` Class

`DataSet` objects have rich functionality, and they are not limited to just `DataTable` objects and `DataView` objects. As mentioned before, the `DataSet` object can be used to implement an in-memory database. This is meant in the strict sense of the word since databases normally contain tables that are linked to one another and have certain restrictions on the type of data that the tables can accept. These are called *foreign keys* and *constraints*, respectively. In ADO.NET, we refer to these concepts in a generic sense with their functionality provided by the `DataRelation` class (see Tables 7-20 and 7-21) and the `Constraint` class (which we won't discuss further).

Maintaining data integrity is an important function of any database system. Data in the database are expected to be valid for the type of objects modeled. For example, consider the `DataSet` example with the `DataTable` class in Section 7.6.3. Two tables were created, one called `Product` and one called `Inventory`. The `Product` table is used to describe different items that the supermarket stocks. The `Inventory` table is used to represent what quantities of certain products the supermarket currently has in stock. The `Product` table is meant to store information (SKU, product description, price) about a particular product offering. Since this table is to be used as a master list of the types

Table 7-20 Properties of the `DataRelation` Class

Property	Description
`ChildColumns`	Returns the `DataColumn` objects of this relation
`ChildKeyConstraint`	Gets the `ForeignKeyConstraint` for the relation
`ChildTable`	Returns the child table of this relation
`DataSet`	Returns the `DataSet` object to which the `DataRelation` object belongs
`ExtendedProperties`	Returns the customized property collection
`Nested`	Has a value of `True` if `DataRelation` objects are nested
`ParentColumns`	Returns an array of `DataColumn` objects that are the parent columns of this `DataRelation` object
`ParentKeyConstraint`	Returns the `UniqueConstraint` of the parent column
`ParentTable`	Returns the parent `DataTable` object of this `DataRelation` object
`RelationName`	Specifies the name of the `DataRelation` object

Table 7-21 Method of the `DataRelation` Class

Method	Description	Syntax
`CheckStateForProperty`	Checks for a valid `DataRelation` object	—

of products, it follows that these products are the only ones that can exist in the `Inventory` table. We can enforce this rule using the `DataRelation` class, as shown in the code below.

Code Sample 7-7 Build instructions: vbc /r:system.dll /r:system.data.dll /r:system.xml.dll cs7-07.vb

```
Imports System
Imports System.Xml
Imports System.Data
Imports Microsoft.VisualBasic

Module Module1

   Sub Main()

      Dim objDS As DataSet
      Dim objDT As DataTable
      Dim objIT As DataTable
      Dim objDC As DataColumn
      Dim aDC(1) As DataColumn
      Dim objProduct_SKU As DataColumn
      Dim objInventory_SKU As DataColumn

      objDS = New DataSet("Supermarket")

      objDT = New DataTable("Product")
      With objDT.Columns
         .Add("ProductSKU", _
                  Type.GetType("System.String"))
         .Add("ProductDescription", _
                  Type.GetType("System.String"))
      End With
      objDS.Tables.Add(objDT)

      aDC(0) = objDT.Columns("ProductSKU")
      objDT.PrimaryKey = aDC

      objDT = New DataTable("Inventory")
      With objDT.Columns
         .Add("InventoryRecordNum", _
                  Type.GetType("System.Int32"))
         .Add("InventorySKU", _
                  Type.GetType("System.String"))
         .Add("InventoryQuantity", _
                  Type.GetType("System.Int32"))
         .Add("InventoryBinNumber", _
                  Type.GetType("System.String"))
```

```
   .Add("InventoryExpirationDate", _
            Type.GetType("System.DateTime"))
End With
objDS.Tables.Add(objDT)

aDC(0) = objDT.Columns("InventoryRecordNum")
objDT.PrimaryKey = aDC

With objDT.Columns("InventoryRecordNum")
   .AutoIncrement = True
   .AutoIncrementSeed = 1
   .AutoIncrementStep = 1
End With
```

59

```
objProduct_SKU = _
objDS.Tables("Product").Columns("ProductSKU")
objInventory_SKU = _
objDS.Tables("Inventory").Columns("InventorySKU")
objDS.Relations.Add(New DataRelation( _
                    "fk_ProductSKU", _
                    objProduct_SKU, _
                    objInventory_SKU))

Console.WriteLine("DataSet contains these tables:")
For Each objDT In objDS.Tables
   Console.WriteLine("-" & objDT.TableName & "-")
   For Each objDC In objDT.Columns
      Console.WriteLine(objDC.ColumnName & _
                     ControlChars.Tab & _
                     objDC.DataType.ToString())
   Next
   Console.WriteLine()
Next

objDT = objDS.Tables("Product")
objIT = objDS.Tables("Inventory")
```

60

```
objDS.EnforceConstraints = True
AddNewProduct(objDT, "82312A", "BATTERY-4PKG AA")
AddNewProduct(objDT, "4088", "TOMATOES-ROMA")
AddNewInventory(objIT, _
                "4088", _
                100, _
                "123-45", _
```

```
                    DateAdd(DateInterval.Day, 10, Now()))

    ListTableContents(objDT)
    ListTableContents(objIT)

End Sub

Public Sub AddNewInventory( _
        ByVal pInventoryTable As DataTable, _
        ByVal pProductSKU As String, _
        ByVal pQuantity As Integer, _
        ByVal pBinNumber As String, _
        ByVal pExpire As Date)

    Try
        Dim dr As DataRow

        dr = pInventoryTable.NewRow()
        dr.Item("InventorySKU") = pProductSKU
        dr.Item("InventoryQuantity") = pQuantity
        dr.Item("InventoryBinNumber") = pBinNumber
        dr.Item("InventoryExpirationDate") = pExpire
        pInventoryTable.Rows.Add(dr)

    Catch E As Exception
        Console.WriteLine("ERROR: " & E.Message)
    End Try

End Sub

Public Sub AddNewProduct( _
        ByVal pProductTable As DataTable, _
        ByVal pProductSKU As String, _
        ByVal pProductDescription As String)

    Try
        Dim dr As DataRow

        dr = pProductTable.NewRow()
        dr.Item("ProductSKU") = pProductSKU
        dr.Item("ProductDescription") = pProductDescription
        pProductTable.Rows.Add(dr)

    Catch E As Exception
```

```
            Console.WriteLine("ERROR: " & E.Message)
        End Try

    End Sub

    Public Sub ListTableContents(ByVal pTable As DataTable)

        Try
            Dim dc As DataColumn
            Dim dr As DataRow
            Dim obj As Object

            For Each dc In pTable.Columns
                Console.Write(dc.ColumnName & _
                        ControlChars.Tab)
            Next
            Console.WriteLine()

            For Each dr In pTable.Rows
                For Each obj In dr.ItemArray
                    Console.Write(obj.ToString() & _
                            ControlChars.Tab)
                Next
                Console.WriteLine()
            Next

        Catch E As Exception
            Console.WriteLine("ERROR: " & E.Message)
        End Try

    End Sub

End Module
```

With this code we've modified the previous `DataSet` example somewhat. The boldface text shows the additions to the code. The code block that begins in line ❺❾ shows the process of adding a new `DataRelation` object to the `DataSet` object. Creating a new `DataRelation` object involves linking two table columns together. The first step is obtaining two `DataColumn` objects to the `ProductSKU` and `InventorySKU` columns. Then, using the `Relations` collection of the `DataSet` object, we use the `Add()` method to add a new `DataRelation` object to the collection. The `DataRelation` constructor accepts three parameters: an arbitrary name to assign to the `DataRelation` object, a parent DataColumn object, and a child DataColumn object. The parent DataColumn object in this example is the ProductSKU column. This is the parent because it contains the reference data that all other tables will use. The InventorySKU column is the child column.

The modified DataSet example contains a new subroutine in the code block beginning in line 60, AddNewInventory(), which adds a DataRow object to the Inventory table and is much like the AddNewProduct() subroutine. But unlike the AddNewProduct() subroutine, AddNewInventory() allows insertion of a new DataRow object into the Inventory table only on the condition that the InventorySKU column already exists in the Product table. If not, an exception is thrown by ADO.NET. This block of code also shows the addition of data to the two DataTable objects. Notice the EnforceConstraints property of the DataSet object. This property should be set to True to ensure that the DataRelation applied to the DataSet object will be considered when adding rows to the DataSet object. The code proceeds to add two new products and then an inventory record. We are using a SKU that should exist in the Product table ("4088"), so the AddNewInventory() call should succeed.

7.8 Using Manual Database Transactions

We've discussed transactions before—how important they are for maintaining database integrity and how support for automatic transactions is provided in COM+ Component Services. In addition to this transaction support, ADO.NET provides its own support in the form of manual transactions, that is, transactions that you control programmatically using the SqlTransaction class and the SqlConnection class. Tables 7-22 and 7-23 outline the property and methods of the SqlTransaction class. (Such details for the SqlConnection class were presented earlier in Tables 7-3 and 7-4.)

Table 7-22 Property of the SqlTransaction Class

Property	Description
IsolationLevel	Specifies the IsolationLevel for this transaction: Chaos, ReadCommitted, ReadUncommitted, RepeatableRead, Serializable, or Unspecified (IsolationLevel enumeration)

Table 7-23 Methods of the `SqlTransaction` Class

Method	Description	Syntax
`Commit`	Commits the database transaction	–
`Rollback`	Rolls back the current transaction	`Rollback()` `Rollback(ByVal` *`transactionName`* `As String)`
`Save`	Creates a save point in the transaction to which a rollback can return	`Save(ByVal` *`savePointName`* `As String)`

Let's examine a demonstration of manual database transactions. Again, we are using the SQL Server `pubs` database to show how we would enter information for a book. Since the `pubs` database enforces various foreign key constraints on its tables, we need to make sure that valid publisher data exists for the book title we are entering. Since a foreign key constraint exists between the `pub_id` field in the `titles` table and the `pub_id` field in the `publishers` table, performing an SQL `INSERT` into the `titles` table with a nonexistent `pub_id` will cause an error to be raised. An incident such as this should prompt a rollback procedure to return the database to a valid state. Miscellaneous system failures, such as a lost database connection, should also cause a rollback to occur. It's the responsibility of the code to execute a commit or rollback at the appropriate time when using manual transactions.

Let's look at the code.

Code Sample 7-8 Build instructions: `vbc /r:system.dll /r:system.data.dll cs7-08.vb`

```
Imports System
Imports System.Data
Imports System.Data.SqlClient

Module Module1

    Sub Main()
```

```
      Dim objCnn As SqlConnection
      Dim objCmd As SqlCommand
      Dim objTrans As SqlTransaction

      Try
         objCnn = New SqlConnection( _
  "Initial Catalog=pubs;Data Source=localhost;uid=sa;pwd=")
         objCnn.Open()

61       objTrans = objCnn.BeginTransaction()

         objCmd = New SqlCommand()
         objCmd.Connection = objCnn
62          objCmd.Transaction = objTrans

         objCmd.CommandText = "INSERT INTO publishers " & _
      "(pub_id, pub_name, city, state, country) VALUES " & _
      "('9909', 'Addison-Wesley Professional', " & _
      "'Boston', 'MA', 'USA')"
      objCmd.ExecuteNonQuery()

         objCmd.CommandText = "INSERT INTO authors " & _
      "(au_id, au_lname, au_fname, phone, contract) VALUES " & _
      "('888-88-1234', 'Crouch', 'Matt', '317-555-1212', 1)"
         objCmd.ExecuteNonQuery()

         objCmd.CommandText = "INSERT INTO titles " & _
           "(title_id, title, type, pub_id) VALUES " & _
           "('PC7777', 'Web Programming with ASP and COM', " & _
           "'popular_comp', '9909')"

         objCmd.ExecuteNonQuery()

63       objTrans.Commit()

              Console.WriteLine("Book information added.")

      Catch e As Exception
64       objTrans.Rollback()
         Console.WriteLine("ERROR: " & e.Message)
         Console.WriteLine("All records rolled back.")

      Finally
         objCnn.Close()
```

```
        End Try

    End Sub

End Module
```

In this example, we are connecting to an SQL Server database and executing several SQL `INSERT` statements using an `SqlCommand` object. Each of these steps is a potential failure point—a failure that could cause database integrity to be compromised. So, we use a `Try . . . Catch . . . Finally` structure to group all the database operations. This gives us a centralized location (in the `Catch` block) to trap errors and execute the `Rollback()` method as part of the cleanup procedure.

Beginning with the database connection, we initiate a new transaction with the `BeginTransaction()` method of the `SqlConnection` object in line ❻❶. This returns an `SqlTransaction` object, which we'll use to control the transaction. The next step is to create a new `SqlCommand` object for the SQL `INSERT` statements. Once the `SqlCommand` object is created, we need to tell the object that executed commands should be under the control of a transaction. We do this in line ❻❷ by assigning the `Transaction` property to the `SqlTransaction` object created by `BeginTransaction()`. We then proceed with three different SQL `INSERT` statements: one record each for publishers, authors, and titles. Assuming that no errors occur in any of these statements, we commit the transaction by calling the `Commit()` method of the `SqlTransaction` object in line ❻❸. This makes our modifications to the database. If an exception occurs (ADO.NET will raise exceptions whenever database or other errors occur), we call the `Rollback()` method in line ❻❹ to undo any modifications that would have been made to the database by successful `SqlCommand` operations.

7.9 Working with Typed `DataSet` Objects

So far, our discussions about `DataSet` objects have focused on using the `DataRowCollection` and `DataColumnCollection` classes of the `DataTable` class to reference the record data. For example, the `DataRow` object contains a `Columns` property, which is a collection of `DataColumn` objects. You can use ordinal indexes and string identifiers to obtain individual column data from the collection. While this is a perfectly acceptable approach to accessing data, ADO.NET provides a much more intuitive method for accomplishing the same goal through the use of typed `DataSet` objects.

One of the most powerful features of the .NET Framework lies in the extensibility of the class libraries. Many of the classes in the .NET Framework can be extended through inheritance. The `DataSet` is one such class. By creating new application-specific classes that inherit from the `DataSet` class, you can access table, column, and row information in a strongly typed fashion, that is, you can reference objects by name rather than using a collection-based index. Another benefit gained from using typed `DataSet` objects is the productivity enhancement received when using the VS.NET IDE. The editor offers help via IntelliSense with method and property names for the typed `DataSet` object.

VS.NET provides powerful graphical tools to aid in the construction of typed `DataSet` objects. In Lab 7-2 you'll learn how to use VS.NET to create typed `DataSet` classes. The lab uses the SQL Server `pubs` database. You'll examine the process of generating the code for the new classes and write a small program to demonstrate the use of the new typed `DataSet` class.

LAB 7-2
VS.NET AND TYPED DataSet OBJECTS

STEP 1. Launch VS.NET.

STEP 2. Create a new VB console application project.

- **a.** Enter a name for the project in the `Name` text box.
- **b.** Click on the OK button to create the new project.

STEP 3. Connect to a database.

- **a.** Select **Tools→Connect To Database . . .** from the menu. The Data Link Properties appears as shown in Lab Figure 7-1.
- **b.** Select an appropriate server in the server name drop-down list.
- **c.** Specify logon information (Windows or SQL Server account) and a user name and password if appropriate.
- **d.** Select the `pubs` database from the database selection drop-down list.
- **e.** Click the Test Connection button to verify the connection to the database, then click OK to finish the database setup.

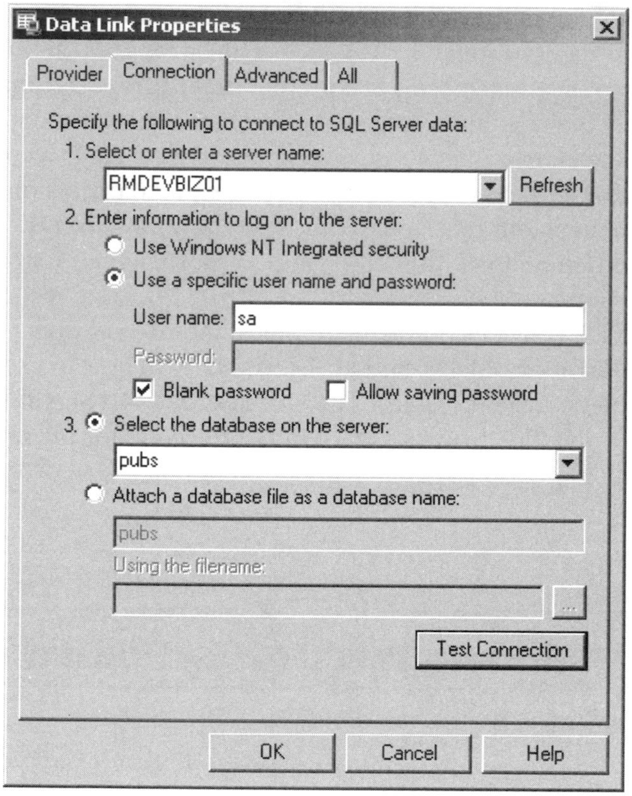

Lab Figure 7-1 The Data Link Properties dialog

This process establishes a data environment for your project. In the Server Explorer, you'll see a reference to the SQL Server to which you connected. Lab Figure 7-2 shows the `Tables` node expanded, revealing the familiar tables of the `pubs` database.

STEP 4. Add the XSD file and generate the `DataSet` object.

a. Select **File→Add New Item . . .** from the menu. Select the DataSet icon and enter a name for the XSD file (`PubsDS.xsd` is used in Lab Figure 7-3). Click the Open button to create the XSD file.

The XSD file is an XML schema used to describe a `DataSet` object. VS.NET uses this XML schema to generate the typed `DataSet` classes. Initially, this file is "blank" (contains no table definition data). To add a

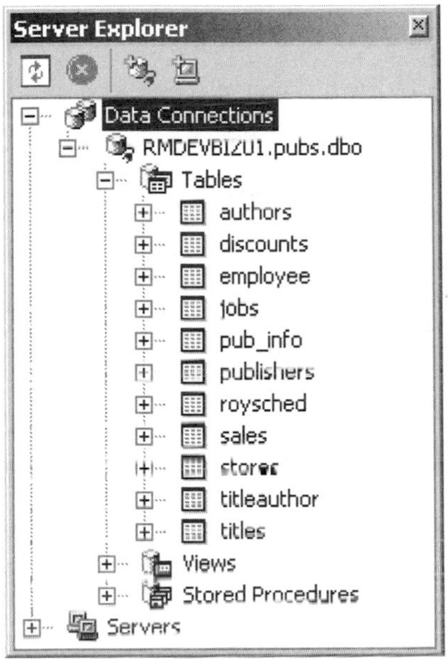

Lab Figure 7-2 The Server Explorer dialog showing the tables of the pubs database

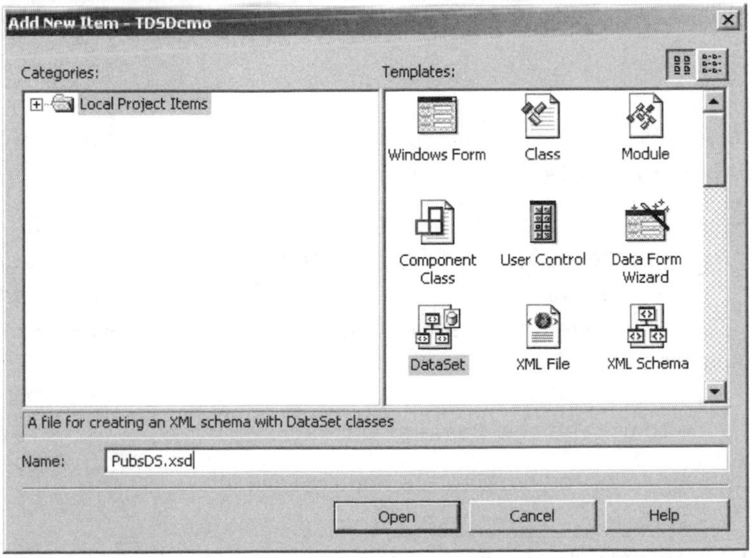

Lab Figure 7-3 The Add New Item dialog

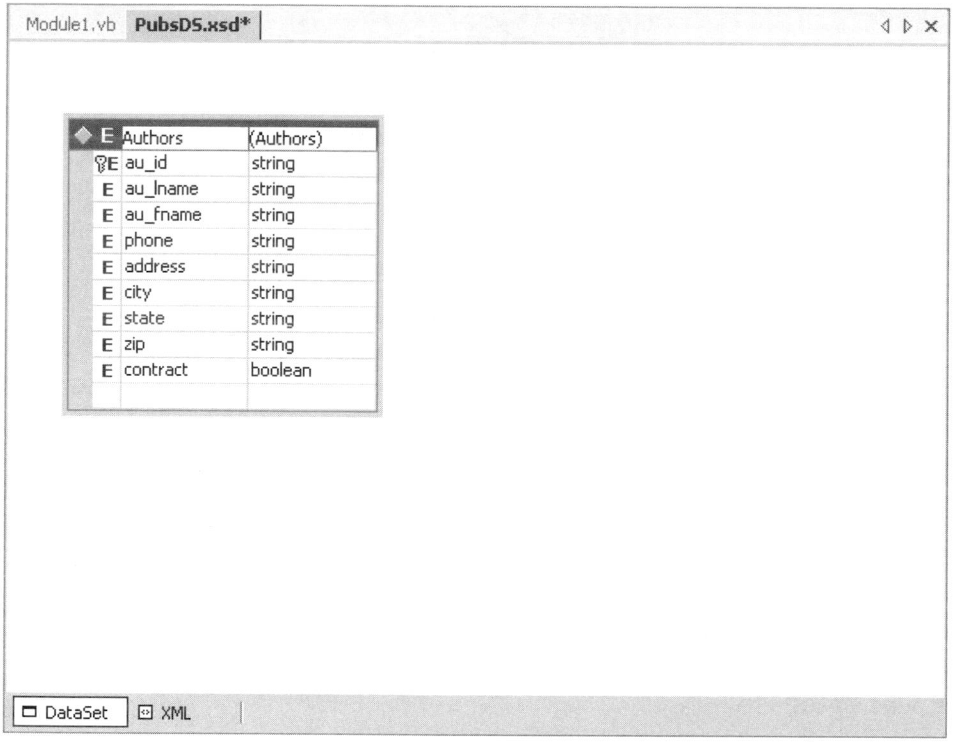

Lab Figure 7-4 The `authors` `DataSet` object in the XSD Design View

table definition to the file, you need to select a table from the Server Explorer and drag it to the Design View of the XSD file.

b. Select the `authors` table from the Server Explorer and drag it to the designer surface of the XSD file. The table appears as shown in Lab Figure 7-4.

A new class is generated as a result of adding the `authors` table to the XSD file. Lab Figure 7-5 shows the Class View of the `PubsDS` class that was created.

STEP 5. Add code to use the new `DataSet` object.

a. Add the following code to the `Module1.vb` file.

```
Imports System
Imports System.Data
Imports System.Data.SqlClient
```

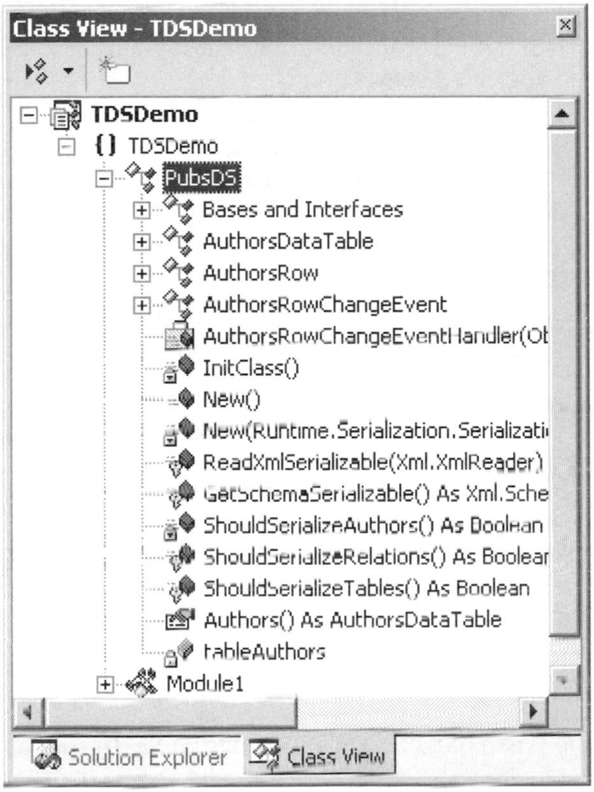

Lab Figure 7-5 Class view showing the PubsDS class

```
Imports Microsoft.VisualBasic

Module Module1

   Sub Main()
      Dim objDA As SqlDataAdapter
      Dim objPubsDS As PubsDS
      Dim objAuthor As PubsDS.AuthorsRow

      Try
         objDA = New SqlDataAdapter( _
             "SELECT * FROM authors", _
  "Initial Catalog=pubs;Data Source=localhost;uid=sa;pwd=")

         objPubsDS = New PubsDS()
```

```
            objDA.Fill(objPubsDS, "Authors")

            For Each objAuthor In objPubsDS.Authors.Rows
               Console.WriteLine( _
                   objAuthor.au_id & _
                   ControlChars.Tab & _
                   objAuthor.au_lname)
            Next

         Catch e As Exception
            Console.WriteLine("ERROR: " & e.Message)
         End Try

      End Sub

   End Module
```

The code follows these main steps for the typed `DataSet` object.

1. Create a new `SqlDataAdapter` object.
2. Declare a new instance of the typed `DataSet` object (using the `New` statement).
3. Fill the typed `DataSet` object using the `SqlDataAdapter` object.
4. Access the typed `DataSet` row data.

The code declares an object called `objAuthor`, which represents a single row in the `authors` table of the typed `DataSet` object. The `For . . . Each` loop uses the `objAuthor` object as an iterator. Notice that when code is entered in the VS.NET IDE, IntelliSense shows the columns of the `authors` table as class member variables (see Lab Figure 7-6). VS.NET automatically built this class and added the appropriate stub code to handle the application logic behind the properties.

STEP 6. Run the application.

a. Select **Debug→Start Without Debugging** (or hit Ctrl-F5) to run the application. The output should look something like that shown in Lab Figure 7-7.

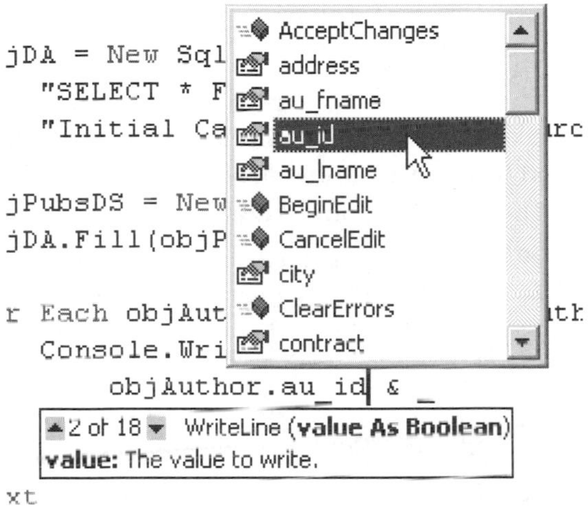

Lab Figure 7-6 IntelliSense showing columns of the authors table as class member variables

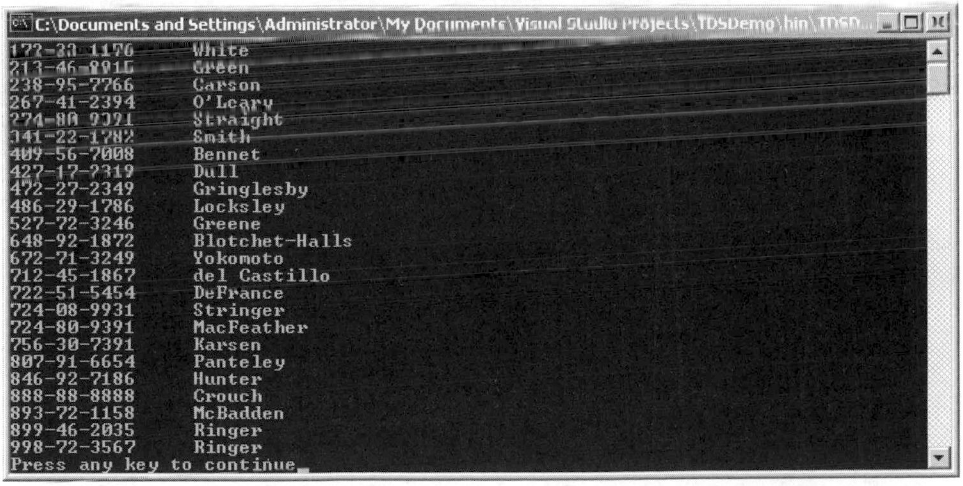

C:\Documents and Settings\Administrator\My Documents\Visual Studio Projects\TDSDemo\bin\TDSD...
White
Green
238-95-7766 Carson
267-41-2394 O'Leary
Straight
Smith
409-56-7008 Bennet
427-17-2319 Dull
472-27-2349 Gringlesby
486-29-1786 Locksley
527-72-3246 Greene
648-92-1872 Blotchet-Halls
672-71-3249 Yokomoto
712-45-1867 del Castillo
722-51-5454 DeFrance
724-08-9931 Stringer
724-80-9391 MacFeather
756-30-7391 Karsen
807-91-6654 Panteley
846-92-7186 Hunter
888-88-8888 Crouch
893-72-1158 McBadden
899-46-2035 Ringer
998-72-3567 Ringer
Press any key to continue

Lab Figure 7-7 Output of the typed DataSet application

7.10 Summary

Here are some critical points to remember about accessing data with ADO.NET.

- Data-access technologies from Microsoft have followed an evolutionary path that includes technologies such as Embedded SQL, ODBC, OLE-DB, ADO, and now ADO.NET.
- ADO.NET brings many performance and architectural enhancements, including XML-based data marshalling, an intuitive programming model, and high scalability due to the disconnected fashion in which data is handled.
- The architecture of ADO.NET includes the `DataSet` class and the .NET Managed Data Provider. The `DataSet` class and its related classes, the `DataTable`, `DataRow`, and `DataColumn` classes, create an in-memory representation of database data. The .NET Managed Data Provider is the piece that talks to the database and supplies the `DataSet` object with data.
- The `IDataReader` interface and the SQL Server implementation of that interface, `SqlDataReader`, provides quick and efficient read-only access to data. It's typically used for applications that need forward-only access to record data in `DataTable` objects. The `SqlConnection` object is used to establish a physical connection to an SQL Server.
- ASP.NET Web Controls, like the `DataGrid` Control, can be bound with data using the `SqlDataReader` object. The `DataGrid` Control can also allow for editing of the data, using a combination of intrinsic functionality and the `SqlCommand` class for handling the updates.
- The `DataSet` object is made up of a collection of `DataTable` objects. `DataTable` objects in turn are comprised of `DataRow` and `DataColumn` objects. The `DataView` class is used for filtering, searching, and sorting data contained in `DataTable` objects.
- The `DataRelation` class is used to set up relationships between `DataColumn` objects in different `DataTable` objects. The `DataRelation` class is used to model the functionality of foreign keys in databases.
- Manual transactions are those types of transactions that have direct support in ADO.NET. In SQL Server, you explicitly control the transaction by using the methods of the `SqlTransaction` class rather than using a declarative method such as COM+ Component Services provides.

- The typed `DataSet` object is a user-defined class that inherits from the `DataSet` class. The typed `DataSet` object allows you to refer to row data in a `DataTable` object as class member variables rather than using a collection-based index.

7.11 What's Ahead

The final chapter of this book deals with cryptography and security, two very important topics in Web application programming. ASP.NET provides many different security features, several of which can be implemented without application code. Chapter 8 also briefly covers cryptography concepts and demonstrates how to use the .NET Framework's cryptographic class libraries to encrypt and decrypt data.

CHAPTER 8

Securing .NET Applications

Keeping unwanted visitors out of your site is essential, and there are a number of ways to ensure that intruders stay clear. If your site is used for a commercial purpose and if financial transactions are taking place, security is paramount. Protecting the privacy of users and preventing access to sensitive system resources are equally important.

Protecting the site comes down to two tasks you need to accomplish as the site administrator.

1. Provide a way to restrict site access so that only authenticated users can visit the site.
2. Make sure that the data transmitted between the Web user and the Web server cannot be intercepted by a third party.

Robust security is achieved by taking appropriate measures at many different levels. A secure system involves implementing the following processes.

- **Authentication** is the process by which the system determines a user's identity. The user has to prove his or her identity to the system. The most common type of authentication in use is the combination of a user name and password. The system accepts the identity of the user based on the assumption that only the user knows his or her password. Other means of authentication include biometric devices (fingerprints, retinal scans, voice prints, and so on). Authentication is the first step of any diligent security process.
- **Authorization** is the process of determining which resources an authenticated user can access and how those resources can be used. Users of a multiuser system have varying levels of privileged use

assigned to them. The most common type of authorization deals with how files can be accessed. For example, some users may be able to read a particular file but not write to it. This must be configurable by the system administrator or another trusted person.

- **Impersonation** is the process of taking a user's identity and having it assume the identity of another user or entity. From a practical administration standpoint, this simplifies the work required in authentication on public servers. It removes the need to assign user accounts to anonymous users since you can have a shared account for public-access use.

Windows, IIS, and ASP.NET work in concert to implement secure Web applications and services. Authentication and authorization work at both the Windows and IIS layers of the Web application model. Using various combinations of security controls placed in multiple layers enables you to create very secure applications.

8.1 Windows Security

The Windows operating system is designed in such a way that any action you perform on the computer involves a security check. It follows that whenever you are working inside the Windows environment you (the user) should have an identity. This is your user account (or user name). These user names are stored in a user accounts database.

The user accounts database can exist in two different areas. The first is on the server itself. When a user attempts to gain access to this server, the security check is performed against the database residing on the server. The accounts in this database are referred to as *local user accounts*. The other area in which the user accounts database may live is on a machine called the primary domain controller (PDC). The job of the PDC is to authenticate users on a local area network. This local area network may contain several servers. Collectively, these servers are logically grouped into a domain. The job of the PDC is to provide a centralized area for authentication to occur for machines in the domain. If a user wishes to gain access to a particular server's resources within the domain, the user need only log into the PDC. Windows determines what type of authentication to perform (local or on a domain) by determining whether or not the user elected to log into a domain.

8.1.1 File/Object System Security

Windows can secure many different types of resources. These include but are not limited to files, directories, services, and registry keys. Any object on the Windows system contains privileges associated with it in an access control list (ACL). The ACL contains a list of security identifiers (SIDs) that correspond to a user account. When a request for a resource is made, the currently logged-in user is matched against the user SIDs in the ACL for the resource. The system then decides whether or not to grant access.

Most of our discussion about securing ASP.NET applications and services is based on protecting files and directories. Introduced in Windows NT (and used in Windows) is the NT File System (NTFS). NTFS is a proprietary storage mechanism for storing files on disk volumes. Prior to the first version of Windows NT, files were stored using the File Allocation Table (FAT) method. This technology has been used since the early days of DOS, a single-user operating system. Since Windows NT was introduced as a multiuser operating system, a new file system was necessary to implement the required security protections of a multiuser system. NTFS allows you to assign many different security attributes to files, including which users are allowed to access which files and in what ways (for example, read, write, execute).

8.1.2 User Rights, Groups, and Policies

Windows identifies users by account names and groups. A user is identified by a unique user name. Users can be clustered into groups. Users in a group share common characteristics and access capabilities. Groups enable system administrators to assign security rights on a group level instead of assigning security rights to each individual user.

A user right is a permission granted by the security system to perform a specific task. There are several different types of security rights. (You can see all the types from the Windows User Management Console.) For instance, you can assign the user right "Log on locally" to a user or group. The "Log on locally" user right grants a user or group the ability to access the server from another computer on the network.

User rights are associated with a particular resource on a particular Windows system. For example, a file in the NTFS file system contains information regarding access permissions for every group and user on the server or domain. This system allows you to just associate the user credentials with a user account. The resource permissions and privileges associated with Windows resources can then be traced back to a user account.

8.2 IIS Authentication and Authorization Security

IIS implements its own authentication mechanisms and controls how to authenticate users. Listed below are the various ways you can implement authentication in IIS.

8.2.1 Anonymous Access

IIS provides the ability for an anonymous user to access files on the Web server without having to supply his or her credentials (like a user name and a password). By default, IIS enables this type of access. Were it not enabled, the user's Web browser would pop up a dialog box asking for a user name and password. With anonymous access enabled, IIS performs retrieval of files by using a special Windows user account (sometimes referred to as the *Web guest account*) that is set up to have guest privileges to the Web files. This account is created upon installation of IIS. It is named `IUSR_`*`MachineName`*, where `MachineName` is the name of the Windows server. The password is also configured automatically, making the entire authentication process transparent to the user.

Anonymous access to system resources on your server may give you a bit of pause. With so much media focus on "crackers" obtaining access to sensitive corporate information, it is no surprise that securing anonymous access is at the top of the Web master's list of priorities. Theoretically, the very fact that a Windows account is used to gain access to any file on the Windows system could be a problem. Could that same account used for anonymous access be used to gain control of other files or services critical to the server? It is possible, but the answer is generally no. The list below explains why.

- The `IUSR_`*`MachineName`* account is assigned Guests permissions only. This means that the anonymous access account is a member of the default Windows group called Guests. The Guests account has very limited permissions. In a typical installation, users in the Guests group just have read-only permission (or execute permission, if the account needs to run `.aspx` files) to files that are visible in the Web server filespace (that is, files in virtual directories or the Web root directory).
- IIS allows Web users to view files in the virtual directory spaces only. A Web user cannot specify a URL that points to a directory outside of this virtual directory space to gain access to a file.
- If for some reason, through covert cracking techniques or otherwise, the unauthorized user does know the path of a protected file, the per-

missions set on the file will not include accounts in the Guests group. Thus, the system will deny access.

8.2.2 BASIC Authentication

The most common type of authentication for Web servers to perform is BASIC Authentication. This is the security implemented in the HTTP protocol. BASIC Authentication uses the HTTP response headers to signal that a user name and password are required to access the Web page. To see how this works, let's investigate the HTTP exchange that transpires during BASIC Authentication.

First, a request is made for a document, so an HTTP `GET` command is issued by the browser that looks something like this (simplified for clarity):

```
GET /passwd.aspx HTTP/1.0
```

IIS sees that the file, `passwd.aspx`, is protected from Guest access, so it returns a 401 status code in the HTTP response. The 401 status code indicates that password authorization is required to access the file.

```
HTTP/1.1 401 Authorization Required
Server: Microsoft IIS/5.0
Date: Sun, 08 Apr 2001 03:46:51 GMT
Content-Type: text/html
Cache-control: private
```

The 401 HTTP status code triggers a password dialog box to appear in the user's browser. Now the user needs to send the user name and password information. When this information is entered, the user name and password are concatenated into a single string separated by a colon (`:`). This string is then encoded using the Base64 encoding algorithm. The encoded string is placed inside the HTTP header with the following request:

```
GET /passwd.asp HTTP/1.0
Authorization: BASIC Base64encodedstring
```

The header shows what is appended to the HTTP request. `Base64encodedstring` contains the Base64-encoded version of the user name and password string. If the user is granted access, which means that the user name and password supplied match a user with credentials to access the file, a normal 200 status code is returned along with the contents of the request.

```
HTTP/1.1 200 OK
Server: Microsoft IIS/4.0
```

```
Date: Sun, 08 Apr 2001 03:46:51 GMT
Content-Type: text/html
Cache-control: private

[Contents of request go here]
```

It is important to understand that using BASIC Authentication transmits the user name and password data over the network, which makes it vulnerable to interception. Crackers have several network-monitoring tools that can "sniff" network packets as they are transmitted. These packets can contain the password information. Even though the password is encoded using Base64, this format can easily be decoded programmatically by using a cracking tool. You can change the type of authentication used by the Web server by using the IIS configuration tools.

8.2.3 Integrated Windows Authentication

Integrated Windows Authentication provides strong security. The name of this type of security stems from how authentication is performed. In a nutshell, the user is "challenged" for permission to access a protected resource when a previous attempt to access the protected file failed due to the user's current credentials not being adequate to access the resource. The user sends back a response to the server with credentials that are expected to allow access to the resource. Using this method, passwords are not transmitted over the network in any form. Thus, the user's Web browser does not prompt for a user name and password. Instead, the Web browser uses the user name and password that the user logged in with to the local workstation. If an account with the same user name exists on the Web server and this account has permission to access the file requested, the file is delivered. This security authorization happens using a network connection separate from the HTTP network stream.

Using Integrated Windows Authentication is not the best choice in all situations for two reasons.

1. Internet Explorer is the only browser that supports Integrated Windows Authentication. If your target audience may be using different types of Web browsers, you should not use Integrated Windows Authentication.
2. Many Internet users have Internet access only through a proxy/firewall. This may create a problem with the network connection used for the authentication.

In light of these two facts, Integrated Windows Authentication is useful only in an intranet setting where persistent connections are more reliable.

8.2.4 Digest Authentication

Digest Authentication involves authenticating users using hashes. A *hash* is a fixed-length value (the length depends on what level of security is specified) that is derived from a chunk of data using a secret data string. The security of a hash relies on the fact that it is extremely unlikely that two chunks of data would ever hash to the same value using the same secret data string. Digest Authentication works by having the user recreate a hash with the same value as a hash created on the server.

Hashes will be covered in greater detail in the coming sections on cryptography.

8.2.5 Authentication by IP Address and Domain

IIS also has the ability to restrict access to resources based on a user's IP address or Windows domain name. Access by this method is exclusive. By default, all IP addresses and domain names are allowed to access resources on the IIS server. You may specify a list of IP addresses (single addresses or subnets) and domain names that are not allowed to access content on the Web server. This can be assigned on a per-file or per-directory basis.

8.3 A Crash Course in Cryptography

Secure communications work on the principle of cryptography, which is the process of applying a mathematical formula to a message in order to scramble it. This makes it unreadable to anyone who does not have the decryption key. A *key* is a piece of data that the mathematical encryption formula uses to encrypt the data. Keys vary in length. The longer the length of the key, the more secure the message is. Commercial-grade encryption uses a key that is 128 bits in length.

Until recently, software that used cryptography bound for sale in international markets (outside the United States and Canada) could use up to 40-bit encryption only. The 40-bit standard of encryption has been in use for a number of years. But with the advent of new computer technologies and faster processors, cracking a message by "brute force" (that is, by trying every possible key) has become frighteningly simple. Even garden-variety computers equipped with fast Pentium processors can break a 40-bit key in a matter of hours. The U.S. government's concern with national security has now resulted in the switch to 128-bit encryption. Even the most powerful computers on the planet cannot crack this key within any reasonable time. Having more powerful encryption is important domestically as well. Currently, this is the only method that can be used to ensure that credit card and bank account information is kept private.

8.3.1 Symmetric Cryptography

In general, there are two methods for encrypting a message. The first method, symmetric cryptography, involves using a single key to encrypt and decrypt a message. The sender and receiver of the message both have the encryption/decryption key. The method for information exchange is straightforward.

1. The sender composes a message and encrypts the data using the key.
2. The message is sent to the receiver, who uses the same key to decrypt the message.

However, this simple method of exchanging messages has a major flaw in terms of the logistics used in distributing the key. Since the key itself cannot be encrypted, it is vulnerable to interception—at which point, the system breaks down.

8.3.2 Public Key Cryptography

The second method of encrypting a message solves the problem raised with single-key cryptography by using two keys. One key is used for encrypting the message, and the other is used for decrypting the message. The keys are referred to as the *public key* and the *private key*, respectively. Here's how the system works.

1. The public and private keys are generated using an algorithm that relates the two with a factoring formula. Using this formula, it is possible (however, very, very unlikely) to determine the private key from the public key. As the length of the key increases from, say, 40 bits to 128 bits, the likelihood of discovering the private key diminishes to impossibility.
2. The public key is distributed to anyone who wants it. The recipients of the public key are now ready to send messages to the holder of the private key.

3. The sender encrypts a message using the public key and sends it to the holder of the private key. Using the decryption algorithm, the receiver uses the private key to decrypt the message.

The level of security that an encryption scheme offers relies on two factors: (1) the continued secrecy of the private key and (2) the length of the keys. Some weaker encryption schemes rely on a secret algorithm. These are never good encryption schemes because the program used to implement the secret algorithm is subject to reverse engineering. This would expose the process used for encryption and decryption. The most popular public/private key encryption scheme used is the RSA (from RSA Data Security, Inc., named after its creators, Ron Rivest, Adi Shamir, and Len Adelman). The RSA algorithm is common knowledge in the information technology world, but its strength comes from the use of large keys that are impossible to crack using current hardware in a reasonable amount of time. Incidentally, the RSA encryption algorithm is used to uniquely identify the publisher of a strong named assembly.

8.3.3 Hashes and Digital Signatures

Digital signatures are the electronic counterpart to handwritten signatures. They work by reversing the normal roles of the public and private keys. To "sign" a message, the sender takes the private key and the message and generates a digest of the message. This message digest is created using what is known as a *one-way hash algorithm*. The one-way hash ensures that the complete message cannot be derived from the message digest alone. The message digest is then appended to the original message, just as you would add a "wet-ink" signature to a paper document.

The recipient uses the sender's public key to verify the signature. If this is successful, the recipient knows that the message actually came from the expected sender. Digital signatures also provide a method to see whether the message has been tampered with. Since the message digest was created from a message that the sender originally composed, an altered message would produce a digital signature different from the original message. The recipient's encryption software can verify that the message received is the original one by using the sender's public key.

8.3.4 Digital Certificates

Certificates, an application of digital signatures, can act as containers for public/private key pairs. The first step in configuring IIS to use Secure Sockets Layer (SSL) connections is to obtain a certificate from a certificate authority. One of the jobs of a certificate authority is to verify the legitimacy of the company or person applying for a certificate. The third party is necessary because without one, anyone could create a forged certificate that falsifies the identity of the person creating the certificate.

Receiving certificates from a third party may seem like a good solution that shows impartiality, but how can you trust the third party? You can trust it because the certificate authority attaches a digital signature to the certificate. When you receive your certificate from the certificate authority, you also need to retrieve the certificate authority's public key. In this way, you can verify that the certificate is valid. This concept is known as the *chain of trust*, since any certificate issued by a certificate authority can be verified as legitimate by tracing the lineage of intermediate certificate authorities back to the root certificate authority. Internet Explorer can store these digital certificates in the "Internet Options" area.

8.4 Implementing Data Encryption (`System.Security.Cryptography`)

The .NET Framework SDK includes classes for performing data encryption. These classes are part of the `System.Security.Cryptography` namespace. Shipping with these classes are several implementations of industry-standard cryptographic algorithms.

As an example, let's implement a small program that will

1. Encrypt a file with a randomly generated encryption key
2. Save the key to a key file
3. Read the key back from the key file
4. Decrypt the encrypted file to a new file

This program uses the RC2 encryption algorithm (invented by Ron Rivest for RSA Data Security, Inc.). RC2 is a symmetric encryption algorithm. Recall that symmetric encryption algorithms use the same key for encryption and decryption. Here's the code for our program.

Code Sample 8-1 Build instructions: `vbc /r:system.dll /r:system.security.dll cs8-01.vb`

```
Imports System
Imports System.IO
Imports System.Security
```

```
Imports System.Security.Cryptography
Imports System.Text

Module Module1

    Private m_bytKey as Byte()
    Private m_bytIV as Byte()

    Sub Main()

        EncryptFile("test.txt", "Encrypted.txt")
        DecryptFile("Encrypted.txt", "Decrypted.txt")

    End Sub

    Private Sub ReadKeyFile()

        Dim fsInput As New FileStream("keyfile.key", _
            FileMode.Open, FileAccess.Read)
        Dim bytearrayinput(fsInput.Length - 1) As Byte
            fsInput.Read(bytearrayinput, 0, bytearrayinput.Length)

        m_bytKey = bytearrayinput

    End Sub

    Private Sub ReadIVFile()

        Dim fsInput As New FileStream("ivfile.iv", _
            FileMode.Open, FileAccess.Read)
        Dim bytearrayinput(fsInput.Length - 1) As Byte
        fsInput.Read(bytearrayinput, 0, bytearrayinput.Length)

        m_bytIV = bytearrayinput

    End Sub

    Private Sub SaveKeyFile()

        Dim fsKeyFile As New FileStream("keyfile.key", _
                FileMode.Create, FileAccess.Write)
        fsKeyFile.Write(m_bytKey, 0, m_bytKey.Length)
        fsKeyFile.Flush()
        fsKeyFile.Close()
```

```
End Sub

Private Sub SaveIVFile()

   Dim fsKeyFile As New FileStream("ivfile.iv", _
        FileMode.Create, FileAccess.Write)
   fsKeyFile.Write(m_bytIV, 0, m_bytIV.Length)
   fsKeyFile.Flush()
   fsKeyFile.Close()

End Sub

Public Sub EncryptFile(ByVal pstrInFile As String, _
        ByVal pstrOutFile As String)

   Dim fsInput As New FileStream(pstrInFile, _
        FileMode.Open, FileAccess.Read)
   Dim fsEncrypted As New FileStream(pstrOutFile, _
        FileMode.Create, FileAccess.Write)

   Try

❶     Dim RC2Prov As New RC2CryptoServiceProvider()
      RC2Prov.EffectiveKeySize = 128
      RC2Prov.GenerateKey()
      RC2Prov.GenerateIV()

      Dim RC2Encrypt As ICryptoTransform = _
❷           RC2Prov.CreateEncryptor()

❸     Dim cryptostream As New CryptoStream(fsEncrypted, _
         RC2Encrypt, CryptoStreamMode.Write)

      Dim bytearrayinput(fsInput.Length - 1) As Byte
      fsInput.Read(bytearrayinput, 0, bytearrayinput.Length)

❹     cryptostream.Write(bytearrayinput, 0, _
         bytearrayinput.Length)
         cryptostream.Close()

❺     m_bytKey = RC2Prov.Key
      m_bytIV = RC2Prov.IV
      SaveKeyFile()
      SaveIVFile()
```

```
      Catch E as CryptographicException
         Console.WriteLine(E.Message)
      End Try

   End Sub

   Public Sub DecryptFile(ByVal pstrInFile As String, _
         ByVal pstrOutFile As String)

      Dim RC2Prov As New RC2CryptoServiceProvider()

❻     ReadKeyFile()
      ReadIVFile()
      RC2Prov.EffectiveKeySize = 128
      RC2Prov.Key() = m_bytKey
      RC2Prov.IV = m_bytIV

❼     Dim fsread As New FileStream(pstrInFile, _
         FileMode.Open, _
         FileAccess.Read)

❽     Dim RC2Decrypt As ICryptoTransform = _
         RC2Prov.CreateDecryptor()

❾     Dim cryptostreamDecr As New CryptoStream(fsread, _
         RC2Decrypt, CryptoStreamMode.Read)

❿     Dim fsDecrypted As New StreamWriter(pstrOutFile)
      fsDecrypted.Write( _
         New StreamReader(cryptostreamDecr).ReadToEnd)
      fsDecrypted.Flush()
      fsDecrypted.Close()

   End Sub

End Module
```

Our first point of interest in this program is the `EncryptFile()` function in line ❶, where we see the creation of an `RC2CryptoServiceProvider` object. This class provides a wrapper for the Windows cryptographic server provider for the RC2 algorithm. Tables 8-1 and 8-2 show the properties and methods, respectively, of the `RC2CryptoServiceProvider` class.

Table 8-1 Properties of the `RC2CryptoServiceProvider` Class

Property	Description
`BlockSize`*	Gets or sets the block size (in bits) of the cryptographic operation
`EffectiveKeySize`	Gets or sets the effective size (in bits) of the secret key used by the RC2 algorithm
`FeedbackSize` *	Gets or sets the feedback size (in bits) of the cryptographic operation
`IV` *	Gets or sets the initialization vector for the symmetric algorithm
`Key` *	Gets or sets the secret key for the symmetric algorithm
`KeySize` **	Gets or sets the size (in bits) of the secret key used by the RC2 algorithm
`LegalBlockSizes` *	Gets the block sizes that are supported by the symmetric algorithm
`LegalKeySizes` *	Gets the key sizes that are supported by the symmetric algorithm
`Mode` *	Gets or sets the mode for operation of the symmetric algorithm
`Padding` *	Gets or sets the padding mode used in the symmetric algorithm

* Inherited from `SymmetricAlgorithm`.
** Inherited from `RC2`.

The `System.Security.Cryptography` classes are high-level classes that inherit base functionality from other classes. For example, the `RC2CryptoServiceProvider` class inherits much of its functionality from the base class `RC2`, which in turn inherits from the `SymmetricAlgorithm` class. These base classes are provided to organize cryptographic functionality and also to allow programmers to implement their own functionality by deriving from base classes. For example, programmers could devise their own symmetric cryptographic algorithm by inheriting from `SymmetricAlgorithm` and providing an implementation based on that class.

Table 8-2 Methods of the `RC2CryptoServiceProvider` Class

Method	Description	Syntax
`CreateDecryptor`	Creates a symmetric RC2 decryptor object	`CreateDecryptor(ByVal` *`rgbKey()`* `As Byte, ByVal` *`rgbIV()`* `As Byte) As ICryptoTransform`
`CreateEncryptor`	Creates a symmetric RC2 encryptor object	`CreateEncryptor(ByVal` *`rgbKey()`* `As Byte, ByVal` *`rgbIV()`* `As Byte) As ICryptoTransform`
`GenerateIV`	Generates a random initialization vector to be used for the algorithm	–
`GenerateKey`	Generates a random key to be used for the algorithm	–
`ValidKeySize` °	Determines whether the specified key size is valid for the current algorithm	–

° Inherited from `SymmetricAlgorithm`.

Let's return to the code. After the `RC2CryptoServiceProvider` object is created, we initialize the object with a new symmetric key and a special value called an *initialization vector*. We use the `GenerateKey()` and `GenerateIV()` methods to do this. Both of these generated values are random—this provides better security over password-derived keys, which can be guessed. We also use the `EffectiveKeySize` property to set the size of the key to 128 bits. This is the largest allowed key size for the RC2 algorithm. In line ❷, we use the `CreateEncryptor()` method of the `RC2CryptoServiceProvider` class to obtain an `ICryptoTransform` interface. This interface defines the basic operations of cryptographic transformations. The members of this interface are used to perform the actual encryption and decryption of blocks of data. For the example, we pass the `ICryptoTransform` interface as one of the parameters to the constructor of the `CryptoStream` object in line ❸. The encrypting and decrypting of data is accomplished through the use of this class. (See Tables 8-3 and 8-4 for details on the `CryptoStream` class.) The `CryptoStream` object inherits from the familiar `Stream` class, so writing data to the stream to

Table 8-3 Properties of the `CryptoStream` Class

Property	Description
`CanRead`	Gets a value indicating whether the current `CryptoStream` object is readable
`CanSeek`	Gets a value indicating whether the current `CryptoStream` object is seekable
`CanWrite`	Gets a value indicating whether the current `CryptoStream` object is writable
`Length`	Gets the length in bytes of the stream
`Position`	Gets or sets the position within the current stream

encrypt it should be easily understood. Along with the `ICryptoTransform` interface that we passed to the constructor, we provide a previously created, writable `FileStream` object, which corresponds to the output file (the file to which the encrypted contents will be written).

The encryption process begins reading in the contents of the input file (cleartext) into a `Byte` array. The actual encryption happens in line ❹, when the `Write()` method of the `CryptoStream` object is used to dump the contents of the input `Byte` array to the output (encrypted) file.

As a final step, we want to persist (save) the key and the initialization vector to files for later use. The code block beginning in line ❺ shows how to access the values of the `Key` and `IV` properties of the

Table 8-4 Methods of the `CryptoStream` Class

Method	Description	Syntax
`FlushFinalBlock`	Updates the underlying data source or repository with the current state of the buffer, then clears the buffer	–
`Seek`	Sets the position within the current stream	–
`SetLength`	Sets the length of the current stream	–

`RC2CryptoServiceProvider` class (inherited from `SymmetricAlgorithm`) for use by the `SaveKeyFile()` and `SaveIVFile()` methods. These methods use the `FileStream` object to write the key and the initialization vector, respectively, to disk.

Decryption of the data follows a similar process. It begins in the code block that starts in line ❻ with retrieving the key and the initialization vector from the files, setting the key size, and setting the `Key` and `IV` properties for the `RC2CryptoServiceProvider` object ❻. Line ❼ opens a `FileStream` object to the encrypted data. Line ❽ obtains the `ICryptoTransform` interface for use by the `CryptoStream` object. In line ❾, the program reads in (decrypts) the data from the opened stream. The code beginning in line ❿ takes the resulting stream and uses a `StreamReader` object to read the contents of the stream and immediately dump it to another file using the `StreamWriter()` method.

> **WARNING:** This sample does not provide any security for the saved symmetric key or the initialization vector. If these files are compromised, the encrypted data can be read by an unauthorized party. These files can be protected by encrypting their contents (by possibly using a public-key/asymmetric system) or by forbidding their access by other means (for example, Windows file security).

8.5 ASP.NET Authentication Security

As stated before, authentication is the process of allowing certain users access to privileged resources. ASP.NET accomplishes this through authentication providers. At this writing, there are three different authentication providers: Forms-Based, Windows, and Passport.

8.5.1 The Forms-Based Authentication Provider

The Forms-Based Authentication Provider uses developer-made HTML forms to collect user identification information (for example, a user name and password). Whenever a user requests a privileged resource for which the current user credentials do not suffice, a client-side redirection to an HTML form can be made. At this time, user credentials are collected for the resource at the login page. If the login passes, the user is allowed access to the resource.

The Forms-Based Authentication Provider works by using browser cookies. For each request to a protected Web site, ASP.NET checks to see if there is an authentication ticket attached to the request. This authentication ticket is in the form of a browser cookie. Upon a successful login, a cookie is generated with the user's identity. You can set an expiration time on the authentication ticket, which is useful if a user logs in and then leaves his or her desk. The time-out period will expire and the user will need to repeat the login process. The data contained in the authentication ticket is also usually encrypted, which prevents another indomitable user from accessing the contents.

You can build a Forms-Based Authentication system quite easily; most of the steps require the configuration of a special file called the `web.config` file. The `web.config` file resides in the root of the ASP.NET application. There is only one `web.config` file per application, and its use is optional. Here is how a sample `web.config` file looks.

```
<?xml version="1.0" encoding="utf-8" ?>
<configuration>

   <system.web>

      <compilation defaultLanguage="vb" debug="true" />
      <customErrors mode="RemoteOnly" />

      <authentication mode="Forms" />
      <authorization>
         <allow users="*" />
      </authorization>

      <trace enabled="false"
       requestLimit="10"
       pageOutput="false"
       traceMode="SortByTime"
       localOnly="true" />

      <sessionState
       mode="InProc"
       stateConnectionString="tcpip=127.0.0.1:42424"
       sqlConnectionString=
"data source=127.0.0.1;user id=sa;password="
       cookieless="false"
       timeout="20"
      />
```

```
        <globalization
         requestEncoding="utf-8"
         responseEncoding="utf-8" />

    </system.web>

</configuration>
```

As you can see, this is an XML file. The `web.config` file is used to store security settings for an ASP.NET application. There are two particularly interesting sections in the file (set in boldface type) that relate to using the Forms-Based Authentication Provider: the `<authentication>` and `<authorization>` tags. Here you can list specific users who will be allowed to access the site. But first, let's make the changes needed to configure the Forms-Based Authentication Provider. Here are some modifications that set up the initial configuration.

```
<authentication mode="Forms">
   <forms name="Ch8-Auth"
    path="/"
    loginUrl="cs8-03.aspx"
    protection="All"
    timeout="20">
   </forms>
</authentication>
```

The `mode` attribute designates which authentication provider to use. In this case, it's the Forms-Based Authentication Provider called `Forms`. Below the `authentication` node is the `forms` node. The value of the `name` attribute is the name that will be assigned to the authentication ticket.

The `path` attribute specifies the virtual path for which the authentication ticket is valid. You may specify a particular directory within the site, or if the entire site is for members only, you can specify `"/"` as shown. This protects the entire site.

The `loginUrl` attribute specifies where the login page is located. This is the Web Form used to collect the user's identity information. The minimum requirements for such a form are two text fields (one for the user name, one for the password) and a submit button. We'll implement this page shortly.

The `protection` attribute specifies how much security you want applied to the authentication ticket. In the sample, we use the value `"All"` to indicate that the authentication ticket should be encrypted and that data validation should be performed on the ticket based on specific optional settings. Data validation of the ticket is useful for Web farm situations, where you want all machines that are replicating content for the site to be able to validate and decrypt tickets using common keys.

The `timeout` attribute specifies how long the authentication ticket is valid. The time is expressed in minutes.

Now that we've configured Forms-Based Authentication, we need to specify some users to allow into the site. Let's modify the `web.config` file again to include user account information.

```
<authentication mode="Forms">
   <forms name="Ch8-Auth"
     path="/"
     loginUrl="cs8-03.aspx"
     protection="All"
     timeout="20">
    <credentials passwordFormat="Clear">
       <user name="mcrouch" password="secret"/>
       <user name="jsmith" password="secret"/>
    </credentials>
   </forms>
</authentication>
```

The `<credentials>` node set in boldface type contains the user accounts information, which are pairs of user names and passwords. Notice the attribute called `passwordFormat`. The value for this is `Clear`, which signifies that the passwords assigned to each user in the `<credentials>` section are stored in cleartext format. You can specify two other options: `SHA` or `MD5`. These correspond respectively to the SHA and MD5 hash algorithms used to encrypt passwords. For simplicity in this example, we store our passwords in cleartext.

> **WARNING:** Storing user account passwords using the `Clear` method is not recommended. Although specific browser requests for the `web.config` file are always explicitly denied by IIS, it does not stop a user who has legitimate access to the Web server files from reading the `web.config` file and retrieving passwords. For this reason, you should always store passwords in the hashed format.

Let's say we want to access the following page. The HTML code is shown first, followed by the code-behind file.

Code Sample 8-2

```
<%@ Page Language="vb"
   AutoEventWireup="false"
   Src="cs8-02.aspx.vb"
   Inherits="secret"%>
<html>
<body>

<form id="Form1"
   method="post"
   runat="server">

<h1>Welcome
<asp:Label id=lblUser
   runat="server">
</asp:Label>
!</h1>

<p>You have successfully logged into our site!
</p>

<p>
<asp:Button id=btnLogOut
   runat="server"
   Text="Log Out">
</asp:Button>
</p>

</form>
</body>
</html>
```

```
Imports System.Web
Imports System.Web.Security

Public Class secret
   Inherits System.Web.UI.Page
   Protected WithEvents lblUser As _
      System.Web.UI.WebControls.Label
```

```
   Protected WithEvents btnLogOut As _
      System.Web.UI.WebControls.Button

   Private Sub Page_Load(ByVal sender As System.Object, _
      ByVal e As System.EventArgs) _
      Handles MyBase.Load

      lblUser.Text = HttpContext.Current.User.Identity.Name

   End Sub

   Private Sub btnLogOut_Click(ByVal sender As System.Object, _
      ByVal e As System.EventArgs) _
      Handles btnLogOut.Click

      FormsAuthentication.SignOut()
      Response.Redirect("cs8-03.aspx")

   End Sub
End Class
```

Now we need to construct a login Web Form. Here's a simple login form with an accompanying code-behind file.

Code Sample 8-3

```
<%@ Page Language="vb"
   AutoEventWireup="false"
   Src="cs8-03.aspx.vb"
   Inherits="login"%>
<html>
<body>

<form id="Form1"
   method="post"
   runat="server">
<h1>Authorization Required</h1>

<p>You need to supply a user name and
password to access this site.</p>

<p>User name:
<asp:TextBox id=txtUsername
   runat="server">
```

```
</asp:TextBox>
</p>

<p>Password:
<asp:TextBox
   id=txtPassword
   runat="server"
   TextMode="Password">
</asp:TextBox>
</p>

<p>
<asp:Button id=btnLogin
   runat="server"
   Text="Login">
</asp:Button>

<asp:Label id=lblInvalidLogin
   runat="server"
   ForeColor="Red">
</asp:Label>
</p>

</form>
</body>
</html>
```

The login form is pretty straightforward. It contains two text fields (one for the user name and one for the password), a submit button, and a `Label` Control to display an invalid login message. In the code-behind file, authentication is performed when the user clicks the submit button.

```
Imports System.Web
Imports System.Web.Security

Public Class login
   Inherits System.Web.UI.Page
   Protected WithEvents txtUsername As _
      System.Web.UI.WebControls.TextBox
   Protected WithEvents txtPassword As _
      System.Web.UI.WebControls.TextBox
   Protected WithEvents lblInvalidLogin As _
      System.Web.UI.WebControls.Label
```

```
    Protected WithEvents btnLogin As _
        System.Web.UI.WebControls.Button


    Private Sub btnLogin_Click(ByVal sender As Object, _
        ByVal e As System.EventArgs) _
        Handles btnLogin.Click

        If FormsAuthentication.Authenticate(txtUsername.Text, _
                txtPassword.Text) Then
            FormsAuthentication.RedirectFromLoginPage( _
                txtUsername.Text, False)
        Else
            lblInvalidLogin.Text = "Invalid Login.  Try again!"
        End If
    End Sub
End Class
```

Part of the authentication process uses the `FormsAuthentication` class. The `FormsAuthentication` class is outlined in Tables 8-5 and 8-6.

The login screen appears when the user tries to make a request for a resource (for example, `cs8-02.aspx`) and doesn't have an authentication ticket. The user is then redirected to `cs8-03.aspx`, which is our login page. The authentication happens inside the `btnLogin_Click` subroutine. We first call the `Authenticate()` method, supplying the user name and password entered into the `TextBox` Controls. `Authenticate()` returns `True` and generates the authentication ticket if the user enters the correct password for the given user name. Also, `RedirectFromLoginPage()` is called to redirect the user back to the original page he or she requested (`cs8-02.aspx`).

Table 8-5 Properties of the `FormsAuthentication` Class

Property	Description
`FormsCookieName`	Returns the configured cookie name used for the current application
`FormsCookiePath`	Returns the configured cookie path used for the current application

Table 8-6 Methods of the `FormsAuthentication` Class

Method	Description	Syntax
`Authenticate`	Attempts to validate the credentials against those contained in the configured credential store, given the supplied credentials	`Authenticate(ByVal` *`name`* `As String, ByVal` *`Password`* `As String) As Boolean`
`Decrypt`	Returns an instance of a `FormsAuthenticationTicket` class, given an encrypted authentication ticket obtained from an HTTP cookie	`Decrypt(ByVal` *`encryptedTicket`* `As String) As String`
`Encrypt`	Produces a string containing an encrypted authentication ticket suitable for use in an HTTP cookie, given a `FormsAuthenticationTicket`. object	`Encrypt(ByVal` *`ticket`* `As FormsAuthenticationTicket) As String`

`GetAuthCookie`	Creates an authentication cookie for a given user name	`GetAuthCookie(ByVal` *`username`* `As String, ByVal` *`createPersistentCookie`* `As Boolean) As HttpCookie`
		
		`GetAuthCookie(ByVal` *`username`* `As String, ByVal` *`createPersistentCookie`* `As Boolean, ByVal` *`strCookiePath`*`) As HttpCookie`

`GetRedirectUrl`	Returns the redirect URL for the original request that caused the redirect to the logon page	`GetRedirectUrl(ByVal` *`username`* `As String, ByVal` *`createPersistentCookie`* `As Boolean) As String`

(continued)

Table 8-6 Methods of the `FormsAuthentication` Class *(continued)*

Method	Description	Syntax
`HashPasswordForStoringInConfigFile`	Produces a hash password suitable for storing in a configuration file, given a password and a string identifying the hash type	`HashPasswordForStoringInConfigFile(ByVal` *`password`* `As String, ByVal` *`passwordFormat`* `As String) As String`
`Initialize`	Initializes `FormsAuthentication` by reading the configuration and getting the cookie values and encryption keys for the given application	

`RedirectFromLoginPage`	Redirects an authenticated user back to the originally requested URL	`RedirectFromLoginPage(ByVal` *`username`* `As String, ByVal` *`createPersistentCookie`* `As Boolean)`
		
		`RedirectFromLoginPage(ByVal` *`username`* `As String, ByVal` *`createPersistentCookie`* `As Boolean, ByVal` *`strCookiePath`* `As String)`

`RenewTicketIfOld`	Conditionally updates the sliding expiration on a `FormsAuthenticationTicket` object	`RenewTicketIfOld(ByVal` *`tOld`* `As FormsAuthenticationTicket) As FormsAuthenticationTicket`
`SetAuthCookie`	Creates an authentication ticket and attaches it to the cookie's collection of the outgoing response but does not perform a redirect	`SetAuthCookie(ByVal` *`username`* `As String, ByVal` *`createPersistentCookie`* `As Boolean)`

Method	Description	Syntax
		`SetAuthCookie(ByVal` *`username`* `As String, ByVal` *`createPersistentCookie`* `As Boolean, ByVal` *`strCookiePath`* `As String)`
`SignOut`	Removes the authentication ticket	–

The `cs8-02.aspx` Web Form also contains a logout button. Inside the event handler for the logout button we find this code.

```
Private Sub btnLogOut_Click(ByVal sender As System.Object, _
   ByVal e As System.EventArgs) _
   Handles btnLogOut.Click

   FormsAuthentication.SignOut()
   Response.Redirect("cs8-03.aspx")

End Sub
```

When the user clicks the button, the code calls the `SignOut()` method, which expires the authentication ticket immediately. Then we use the `HttpResponse` class `Redirect()` method to perform a client-side redirect to the login page.

8.5.2 The Windows Authentication Provider

The Windows Authentication Provider allows the use of Windows users accounts and groups to authenticate visitors to a Web site. Generally, no code is required on your part to use this authentication.

As before, the `web.config` file configures this security. Here is a sample `web.config` file set up for the Windows Authentication Provider.

```
<?xml version="1.0" encoding="utf-8" ?>
<configuration>
```

```
   <system.web>
      <authentication mode="Windows" />
      <identity impersonate="true" />
      <authorization>

         <allow users="RMDEVBIZ01\Joe,RMDEVBIZ01\matt"
            roles="RMDEVBIZ01\SpecialGroup" />
         <deny users="*" />

      </authorization>

   </system.web>

</configuration>
```

This particular `web.config` file uses Windows security to allow only certain users into the site. After setting the authentication mode to `"Windows"`, we designate users and groups (roles) that are allowed into the site. The `<allow>` node is for designating who is allowed to access the site. The `users` attribute contains a comma-separated list of user account names that are permitted to access the site. The `roles` attribute contains a comma-separated list of Windows group names. Users within those groups are allowed access to the site. The `<deny>` node lists users who should not have access to the site. The wildcard character (*) indicates that all users should be denied access (except for the users and roles explicitly allowed in the `<allow>` node).

8.5.3 The Microsoft Passport Authentication Provider

No doubt you've heard of services such as MSN Hotmail, the free e-mail service from Microsoft. Hotmail, along with its associated services (MSN Messenger and so on), use a service called Microsoft Passport. Passport is a centralized authentication service that allows users to visit multiple Web sites and be authenticated on each of them by logging in only once.

Discussion of implementing Passport is beyond the scope of this text. Using the Passport service requires additional software downloads and there are fees involved. However, you can find all sorts of information about implementing Passport on your site by visiting *http://www.passport.com/business*.

8.6 Summary

Here's a summary of the important points covered in this chapter.

- Windows, IIS, and ASP.NET work in concert to implement secure Web applications and services. Authentication and authorization work at both the Windows and IIS layers of the Web application model.
- Windows can secure many different types of resources. These include but are not limited to files, directories, and services.
- Any object on the Windows system, be it a file, service, or registry key, contains privileges associated with it in access control lists (ACLs).
- IIS provides authentication and authorization services using a variety of schemes, including anonymous access, BASIC Authentication, Integrated Windows Authentication, Digest Authentication, and authentication by IP address and/or domain.
- Cryptography is the process of applying a mathematical formula to a message in order to scramble it. The strength of a particular encryption algorithm lies in the size of the keys used to encrypt the data. Encryption is the process of taking unencoded data (cleartext) and converting it to scrambled data (ciphertext).
- Symmetric cryptography involves the use of a single key for both encryption and decryption of the data. Symmetric encryption algorithms are a good choice for bulk data encryption since they tend to be fast.
- Asymmetric cryptography uses two keys; one for encrypting the data and one for decrypting the data. The two keys are mathematically related. Asymmetric cryptography is sometimes referred to as public-key cryptography since the encryption key portion of the key pair, called the public key, can be used by anyone to encrypt data intended for the recipient. The recipient is the only keeper of the decryption key, called the private key.
- One-way hashes are used to generate a fixed-length digest of a variable-length message. Hash algorithms are designed to produce unique hash values for any given input. Generating hash values involves reversing the roles of the public and private keys. The private key is used to generate the message digest. An outside party can use the originator's public key to verify the authenticity of the hash. Hashes used in this way are referred to as digital signatures.

- The `System.Security.Cryptography` namespace contains classes to perform cryptographic operations. One such class is the `RC2CryptoServiceProvider` class, which implements the industry-standard RC2 encryption algorithm.
- The `web.config` file, located at the root of the ASP.NET application, configures application authentication using a variety of techniques, including the use of Windows, Forms-Based, and Passport Authentication Providers.

I would like to thank you for reading this far. You must enjoy ASP.NET and VB.NET programming as much as I do. Good luck with all your programming endeavors, and thanks for your support!

APPENDIX A

.NET Framework Class Library Reference Tables

This appendix contains the following tables, which provide information on the methods and properties of classes in the .NET Framework Class Library. The tables are listed below in alphabetical order by class name to assist you in finding the information you want.

Table A-1 Properties of the ArrayList Class

Property	Description
Capacity	Gets or sets the number of elements that the array list can contain
Count	Gets the number of elements actually contained in the array list
IsFixedSize	Gets a value indicating whether the array list has a fixed size
IsReadOnly	Gets a value indicating whether the array list is read-only
IsSynchronized	Gets a value indicating whether access to the array list is synchronized (thread-safe)
Item	Gets or sets the element at the specified index
SyncRoot	Gets an object that can be used to synchronize access to the array list

Table A-2 Methods of the `ArrayList` Class

Method	Description	Syntax
`Add`	Adds an object to the array list.	`Add(ByVal` *`value`* `As Object) As Integer`
`AddRange`	Adds multiple elements to an array list that come from a collection (a list class that implements `ICollection`). Items are placed at the end of the list.	`AddRange(ByVal` *`c`* `As ICollection`

`BinarySearch`	Uses a binary search algorithm to locate a specific element in the sorted array list or a portion of it.	`BinarySearch(ByVal` *`value`* `As Object) As Integer`
		
		`BinarySearch(ByVal` *`value`* `As Object, ByVal` *`comparer`* `As IComparer) As Integer`
		
		`BinarySearch(ByVal` *`index`* `As Integer, ByVal` *`count`* `As Integer, ByVal` *`value`* `As Object, ByVal` *`comparer`* `As IComparer) As Integer`

`Clear`	Removes all elements from the array list.	–
`Clone`	Creates a shallow copy of the array list.	`Clone() As Object`
`Contains`	Determines whether an element is in the array list.	`Contains(ByVal` *`item`* `As Object) As Boolean`

`CopyTo`	Copies the array list or a portion of it to a one-dimensional array	`CopyTo(ByVal` *`array`* `As Array)`
		
		`CopyTo(ByVal` *`array`* `As Array, ByVal` *`arrayIndex`* `As Integer)`

Method	Description	Syntax
		`CopyTo(ByVal index As Integer, ByVal array As Array, ByVal arrayIndex As Integer, ByVal count As Integer)`

`GetEnumerator`	Returns an enumerator that can iterate through the array list.	`GetEnumerator() As IEnumerator`
		
		`GetEnumerator(ByVal index As Integer, ByVal count As Integer) As IEnumerator`

`GetRange`	Returns an array list that represents a subset of the elements in the source array list.	`GetRange(ByVal index As Integer, ByVal count As Integer) As ArrayList`
`IndexOf`	Searches the array list (linear) for the first occurrence of the object. Form 2 searches the array list starting from the specified element. Form 3 returns the first occurrence of the object from the specified index that occurs the specified number of times in the array list.	Form 1: `IndexOf(ByVal value As Object) As Integer` Form 2: `IndexOf(ByVal value As Object, ByVal startIndex As Integer) As Integer` Form 3: `IndexOf(ByVal value As Object, ByVal startIndex As Integer, ByVal count As Integer) As Integer`
`Insert`	Inserts an element into the array list at the specified index.	`Insert(ByVal index As Integer, ByVal value As Object)`
`InsertRange`	Inserts the elements of a collection into the array list at the specified index.	`InsertRange(ByVal index As Integer, ByVal c As ICollection)`

(continued)

Table A-2 Methods of the `ArrayList` Class *(continued)*

Method	Description	Syntax
`LastIndexOf`	Form 1 returns the zero-based index of the last occurrence of a value in the array list. Form 2 returns the last occurrence of the specified object starting from the specified starting index. Form 3 searches the array list for the last *count* number of occurrences starting from the specified starting index.	Form 1: `LastIndexOf(ByVal` *`value`* `As Object) As Integer` Form 2: `LastIndexOf(ByVal` *`value`* `As Object, ByVal` *`startIndex`* `As Integer) As Integer` Form 3: `LastIndexOf(ByVal` *`value`* `As Object, ByVal` *`startIndex`* `As Integer, ByVal` *`count`* `As Integer) As Integer`
`Remove`	Removes the first occurrence of a specific object from the array list.	`Remove(ByVal` *`obj`* `As Object)`
`RemoveAt`	Removes the element at the specified index.	`RemoveAt(ByVal` *`index`* `As Integer)`
`RemoveRange`	Removes a range of elements from the array list.	`RemoveRange(ByVal` *`index`* `As Integer, ByVal` *`count`* `As Integer)`

`Reverse`	Reverses the order of the elements in the array list or a portion of it.	`Reverse()`
		
		`Reverse(ByVal` *`index`* `As Integer, ByVal` *`count`* `As Integer)`

`SetRange`	Copies the elements of a collection over a range of elements in the array list.	`SetRange(ByVal` *`index`* `As Integer, ByVal` *`c`* `As ICollection)`

`Sort`	Sorts the elements in the array list or a portion of it. All elements must be the same type.	`Sort()`
		
		`Sort(ByVal` *`comparer`* `As IComparer)`

Method	Description	Syntax
		Sort(ByVal *index* As Integer, ByVal *count* As Integer, ByVal *comparer* As IComparer)
ToArray	Copies the elements of the array list to a new array.	ToArray() As Object() ToArray(ByVal *type* As Type) As Array
TrimToSize	Sets the capacity to the actual number of elements in the array list.	–

Table A-3 Properties of the Stack Class

Property	Description
Count	Returns the number of stack elements
IsReadOnly	Checks whether the stack is read only
IsSynchronized	Gets a value indicating whether access to the stack is synchronized (thread-safe)
SyncRoot	Gets an object that can be used to synchronize access to the stack

Table A-4 Methods of the Stack Class

Method	Description	Syntax
Clear	Clears all items from the stack	–
Clone	Returns a shallow copy of the stack object	Clone() As Object
Contains	Returns True if the stack contains the object element	Contains(ByVal *obj* As Object) As Boolean

(continued)

Table A-4 Methods of the `Stack` Class *(continued)*

Method	Description	Syntax
`CopyTo`	Copies the elements in the stack to an existing array	`CopyTo(ByVal` *`array`* `As Array, ByVal` *`index`* `As Integer)`
`GetEnumerator`	Returns an `IEnumerator` for the stack	`GetEnumerator() As IEnumerator`
`Peek`	Returns the top stack element without removing it	`Peek() As Object`
`Pop`	Removes the top element of the stack	`Pop() As Object`
`Push`	Puts an object onto the top of the stack	`Push(ByVal` *`obj`* `As Object)`
`ToArray`	Copies the stack to a new array	`ToArray() As Object()`

Table A-5 Properties of the `Queue` Class

Property	Description
`Count`	Gets the number of elements contained in the queue
`IsReadOnly`	Gets a value indicating whether the queue is read-only
`IsSynchronized`	Gets a value indicating whether access to the queue is synchronized (thread-safe)
`SyncRoot`	Gets an object that can be used to synchronize access to the queue

Table A-6 Methods of the `Queue` Class

Method	Description	Syntax
`Clear`	Removes all objects from the queue	–
`Clone`	Creates a shallow copy of the queue	`Clone() As Object`
`Contains`	Determines whether an element is in the queue	`Contains(ByVal` *obj* `As Object)`
`CopyTo`	Copies the queue elements to an existing one-dimensional array, starting at the specified array index	`CopyTo(ByVal` *array* `As Array, ByVal` *index* `As Integer)`
`Dequeue`	Removes and returns the object at the beginning of the queue	`Dequeue() As Object`
`Enqueue`	Adds an object to the end of the queue	`Enqueue(ByVal` *obj* `As Object)`
`GetEnumerator`	Returns an enumerator that can iterate through the queue	`GetEnumerator() As IEnumerator`
`Peek`	Returns the object at the beginning of the queue without removing it	`Peek() As Object`
`ToArray`	Copies the queue elements to a new array	`ToArray() As Object()`

Table A-7 Properties of the `Hashtable` Class

Property	Description
`Count`	Gets the number of `Hashtable` items
`IsFixedSize`	Returns `True` if the hashtable has a fixed size
`IsReadOnly`	Returns `True` if the hashtable is read-only
`IsSynchronized`	Gets a value indicating whether access to the hashtable is synchronized (thread-safe)

(continued)

Table A-7 Properties of the `Hashtable` Class *(continued)*

Property	Description
`Item`	Gets or sets the value associated with the specified key
`Keys`	Gets an `ICollection` containing the keys in the hashtable
`SyncRoot`	Gets an object that can be used to synchronize access to the hashtable
`Values`	Gets an `ICollection` containing the values in the hashtable

Table A-8 Methods of the `Hashtable` Class

Method	Description	Syntax
`Add`	Adds an entry to the hashtable	`Add(ByVal` *`key`* `As Object, ByVal` *`value`* `As Object)`
`Clear`	Delete all entries in the hashtable	–
`Clone`	Creates a shallow copy of the hashtable	`Clone() As Object`
`Contains`	Tests to see if a key exists in the hashtable	`Contains(ByVal` *`key`* `As Object) As Boolean`
`ContainsKey`	Determines whether the hashtable contains a specific key	`ContainsKey(ByVal` *`key`* `As Object) As Boolean`
`ContainsValue`	Tests to see if a specific value exists in the hashtable (warning: slow for large sets of data)	`ContainsValue(ByVal` *`value`* `As Object) As Boolean`
`CopyTo`	Copies the hashtable entries to a one-dimensional array starting at the specified index	`CopyTo(ByVal` *`array`* `As Array, ByVal` *`arrayIndex`* `As Integer)`

Method	Description	Syntax
`GetEnumerator`	Returns an enumerator that can iterate through the hashtable	`GetEnumerator() As IDictionaryEnumerator`
`GetObjectData`	Implements the `ISerializable` interface and returns the data needed to serialize the hashtable	`GetObjectData(ByVal` *`info`* `As SerializationInfo, ByVal` *`context`* `As StreamingContext)`
`OnDeserialization`	Implements the `ISerializable` interface and raises the deserialization event when the deserialization is complete	`OnDeserialization (ByVal` *`sender`* `As Object)`
`Remove`	Removes the item with the specified key from the hashtable	`Remove(ByVal` *`key`* `As Object)`

Table A-9 Properties of the `StreamReader` Class

Property	Description
`BaseStream`	Returns the stream object
`CurrentEncoding`	Gets the character encoding

Table A-10 Methods of the `StreamReader` Class

Method	Description	Syntax
`Close`	Closes the file associated with the stream	–
`DiscardBufferedData`	Throws away the current data in the `StreamReader` class	–
`Peek`	Returns the next character from the stream but does not advance the file pointer	`Peek() As Integer`
`Read`	Reads the next character from the stream; returns "–1" at the end of the stream	`Read() As Integer`
`ReadLine`	Reads one line of characters from the stream	`ReadLine() As String`
`ReadToEnd`	Reads the entire contents of the stream	`ReadToEnd() As String`

Table A-11 Properties of the `StreamWriter` Class

Property	Description
`AutoFlush`	Causes all output bound for the stream to be written immediately when the value is `True`
`BaseStream`	Returns the underlying stream object
`Encoding`	Gets the encoding in which the output is written
`FormatProvider` (inherited from `TextWriter`)	Gets an object that controls formatting
`NewLine` (inherited from `TextWriter`)	Gets or sets the line terminator string used by the current `TextWriter` class

Table A-12 Methods of the `StreamWriter` Class

Method	Description	Syntax
`Close`	Closes the open stream.	–
`Flush`	Forces all buffered output to be written to the stream.	–
`Write`	Writes data to the stream. Form 1 writes a single `Char` to the stream. Form 2 writes a `Char` array to the stream. Form 3 writes a string object to the stream. Form 4 writes a portion of a character array to the stream, starting at the specified index and continuing for the specified count.	Form 1: `Write(ByVal` *`value`* `As Char)` Form 2: `Write(ByVal` *`buffer()`* `As Char)` Form 3: `Write(ByVal` *`value`* `As String)` Form 4: `Write(ByVal` *`buffer()`* `As Char, ByVal` *`index`* `As Integer, ByVal` *`count`* `As Integer)`

`WriteLine` (inherited from `TextWriter`)	Writes data to the stream with an ending new line character. The various syntaxes show the use of different data types.	`WriteLine()`
		
		`WriteLine(Boolean)`
		
		`WriteLine(Char)`
		
		`WriteLine(Char())`
		
		`WriteLine(Decimal)`
		
		`WriteLine(Double)`
		
		`WriteLine(Int32)`
		
		`WriteLine(Int64)`
		
		`WriteLine(Object)`
		
		`WriteLine(Single)`
		
		`WriteLine(String)`

Table A-12 Methods of the `StreamWriter` Class *(continued)*

Method	Description	Syntax
		`WriteLine(UInt32)`
		`WriteLine(UInt64)`
		`WriteLine(String, Object)`
		`WriteLine(String,Object())`
		`WriteLine(Char(), Int32, Int32)`

Table A-13 Properties of the `FileStream` Class

Property	Description
`CanRead`	Returns a value of `True` if the stream supports read operations
`CanSeek`	Returns a value of `True` if the stream supports random access seeking
`CanWrite`	Returns a value of `True` if the stream supports write operations
`Handle`	Gets the operating system file handle for the file that the current `FileStream` object encapsulates; used with COM interoperability with unmanaged code
`IsAsync`	Returns a value of `True` if the file supports asynchronous read/write operations
`Length`	Sets the length of the stream in bytes
`Name`	Specifies the name supplied to the `FileStream` constructor
`Position`	Designates the current position of the stream

Table A-14 Methods of the `FileStream` Class

Method	Description	Syntax
`BeginRead`	Begins an asynchronous read	`BeginRead(ByVal` *`array()`* `As Byte, ByVal` *`offset`* `As Integer, ByVal` *`numBytes`* `As Integer, ByVal` *`userCallback`* `As AsyncCallback, ByVal` *`stateObject`* `As Object) As IAsyncResult`
`BeginWrite`	Begins an asynchronous write	`BeginWrite(ByVal` *`array()`* `As Byte, ByVal` *`offset`* `As Integer, ByVal` *`numBytes`* `As Integer, ByVal` *`userCallback`* `As AsyncCallback, ByVal` *`stateObject`* `As Object) As IAsyncResult`
`Close`	Closes the file and releases any resources associated with the current file stream	–
`EndRead`	Waits for the pending asynchronous read to complete	`EndRead(ByVal` *`asyncResult`* `As IAsyncResult) As Integer`
`EndWrite`	Ends an asynchronous write, blocking until the I/O operation has completed	`EndWrite(ByVal` *`asyncResult`* `As IAsyncResult)`
`Flush`	Clears all buffers for this stream and causes any buffered data to be written to the underlying device	–
`Lock`	Prevents access by other processes to all or part of a file	`Lock(ByVal` *`position`* `As Long, ByVal` *`length`* `As Long)`

(continued)

Table A-14 Methods of the `FileStream` Class *(continued)*

Method	Description	Syntax
`Read`	Reads a block of bytes from the stream and writes the data in a given buffer	`Read(ByVal` *`array()`* `As Byte, ByVal` *`offset`* `As Integer, ByVal` *`count`* `As Integer) As Integer`
`ReadByte`	Reads a byte from the file and advances the read position one byte	`ReadByte() As Integer`
`Seek`	Sets the current position of this stream to the given value	`Seek(ByVal` *`offset`* `As Long, ByVal` *`origin`* `As SeekOrigin) As Long`
`SetLength`	Sets the length of this stream to the given value	`SetLength(ByVal` *`value`* `As Long)`
`Unlock`	Allows access by other processes to all or part of a file that was previously locked	`Unlock(ByVal` *`position`* `As Long, ByVal` *`length`* `As Long)`
`Write`	Writes a block of bytes to this stream using data from a buffer	`Write(ByVal` *`array()`* `As Byte, ByVal` *`offset`* `As Integer, ByVal` *`count`* `As Integer)`
`WriteByte`	Writes a byte to the current position in the file stream	`WriteByte(ByVal` *`value`* `As Byte)`

Table A-15 Methods of the `File` Class

Method	Description	Syntax
`AppendText`	Opens up a `StreamWriter` class that allows for appending of text to an existing file or a new file with the specified path.	`AppendText(ByVal` *`path`* `As String) As StreamWriter`
`Copy`	Copies an existing file to a new file. Form 2 offers a Boolean overwrite flag. If `True`, any existing destination file is overwritten.	Form 1: `Copy(ByVal` *`sourceFileName`* `As String, ByVal` *`destFileName`* `As String)` Form 2: `Copy(ByVal` *`sourceFileName`* `As String, ByVal` *`destFileName`* `As String, ByVal` *`overwrite`* `As Boolean)`
`Create`	Creates the specified file and returns a `FileStream` class for the file. Form 2 specifies a maximum buffer size for the returned `FileStream` class.	Form 1: `Create(ByVal` *`path`* `As String) As FileStream` Form 2: `Create(ByVal` *`path`* `As String, ByVal` *`bufferSize`* `As Integer) As FileStream`
`CreateText`	Creates a new text file and returns a `StreamWriter` class for the new file.	`CreateText(ByVal` *`path`* `As String) As StreamWriter`
`Delete`	Deletes the specified file.	`Delete(ByVal` *`path`* `As String)`
`Exists`	Returns `True` if the specified file exists.	`Exists(ByVal` *`path`* `As String) As Boolean`

(continued)

Table A-15 Methods of the `File` Class *(continued)*

Method	Description	Syntax
`GetAttributes`	Gets the `FileAttributes` of the file on the fully qualified path. `FileAttributes` is an enumeration with these members: `Archive`, `Compressed`, `Device`, `Directory`, `Encrypted`, `Hidden`, `Normal`, `NotContentIndexed`, `Offline`, `ReadOnly`, `ReparsePoint`, `SparseFile`, `System`, `Temporary`	`GetAttributes(ByVal` *`path`* `As String) As FileAttributes`
`GetCreationTime`	Gets the date and time the specified file was created.	`GetCreationTime(ByVal` *`path`* `As String) As DateTime`
`GetLastAccessTime`	Gets the date and time that the specified file was last accessed.	`GetLastAccessTime(ByVal` *`path`* `As String) As DateTime`
`GetLastWriteTime`	Gets the date and time that the specified file was last written to.	`GetLastWriteTime(ByVal` *`path`* `As String) As DateTime`
`Move`	Moves the source file to the destination file, which can have a different name.	`Move(ByVal` *`sourceFileName`* `As String, ByVal` *`destFileName`* `As String)`

`Open`	Opens a `FileStream` class for the specified path.	`Open(ByVal` *`path`* `As String, ByVal` *`mode`* `As FileMode) As FileStream`
		
		`Open(ByVal` *`path`* `As String, ByVal` *`mode`* `As FileMode, ByVal` *`access`* `As FileAccess) As FileStream`

Method	Description	Syntax
		`Open(ByVal` *path* `As String, ByVal` *mode* `As FileMode, ByVal` *access* `As FileAccess, ByVal` *share* `As FileShare) As FileStream`
`OpenRead`	Creates a new file that is read-only.	`OpenRead(ByVal` *path* `As String) As FileStream`
`OpenText`	Opens an existing text file and returns a `StreamReader` class for the file.	`OpenText(ByVal` *path* `As String) As StreamReader`
`OpenWrite`	Opens a file for writing, returning a `FileStream` path.	`OpenWrite(ByVal` *path* `As String) As FileStream`
`SetAttributes`	Sets the specified `FileAttributes` for the specified file.	`SetAttributes(ByVal` *path* `As String, ByVal` *fileAttributes* `As FileAttributes)`
`SetCreationTime`	Sets the date and time the file was created.	`SetCreationTime(ByVal` *path* `As String, ByVal` *creationTime* `As DateTime)`
`SetLastAccessTime`	Sets the date and time the specified file was last accessed.	`SetLastAccessTime(ByVal` *path* `As String, ByVal` *lastAccessTime* `As DateTime)`
`SetLastWriteTime`	Sets the date and time that the specified file was last written to.	`SetLastWriteTime(ByVal` *path* `As String, ByVal` *lastAccessTime* `As DateTime)`

Table A-16 Properties of the `FileInfo` Class

Property	Description
`Attributes`	Gets or sets file attributes (inherited from `FileSystemInfo`)
`CreationTime`	Gets the date and time the specified file was created (inherited from `FileSystemInfo`)
`Directory`	Gets the instance of the parent directory
`DirectoryName`	Gets the file's full path
`Exists`	Returns `True` if the specified file exists
`Extension`	Specifies the file name extension (inherited from `FileSystemInfo`)
`FullName`	Gets the full file/directory path (inherited from `FileSystemInfo`)
`LastAccessTime`	Gets the date and time that the specified file was last accessed (inherited from `FileSystemInfo`)
`LastWriteTime`	Gets the date and time that the specified file was last written to (inherited from `FileSystemInfo`)
`Length`	Gets the size of the current file or directory
`Name`	Gets the name of the file

Table A-17 Methods of the `FileInfo` Class

Method	Description	Syntax
`AppendText`	Opens up a `StreamWriter` class that allows for appending of text to an existing file or a new file with the specified path.	`AppendText() As StreamWriter`
`CopyTo`	Copies an existing file to a new file. Form 2 offers a Boolean overwrite flag. If `True`, any existing destination file is overwritten.	Form 1: `CopyTo(ByVal` *`destFileName`* `As String) As FileInfo`

Method	Description	Syntax
		Form 2: `CopyTo(ByVal` *`destFileName`* `As String, ByVal` *`overwrite`* `As Boolean) As FileInfo`
`Create`	Creates the specified file and returns a `FileStream` class for the file.	`Create() As FileStream`
`CreateText`	Creates a new text file and returns a `StreamWriter` class for the new file.	`CreateText() As StreamWriter`
`Delete`	Deletes the specified file	–
`MoveTo`	Moves the source file to the destination file, which can have a different name.	`MoveTo(ByVal` *`destFileName`* `As String)`

`Open`	Opens a `FileStream` class for the specified path.	`Open(ByVal` *`mode`* `As FileMode) As FileStream`
		
		`Open(ByVal` *`mode`* `As FileMode, ByVal` *`access`* `As FileAccess) As FileStream`
		
		`Open(ByVal` *`mode`* `As FileMode, ByVal` *`access`* `As FileAccess, ByVal` *`share`* `As FileShare) As FileStream`

`OpenRead`	Creates a new file that is read-only.	`OpenRead() As FileStream`
`OpenText`	Opens an existing text file and returns a `StreamReader` class for the file.	`OpenText() As StreamReader`

(continued)

Table A-17 Methods of the `FileInfo` Class *(continued)*

Method	Description	Syntax
`OpenWrite`	Opens a file for writing, returning a `FileStream` path.	`OpenWrite() As FileStream`
`Refresh` (inherited from `FileSystemInfo`)	Refreshes the state of the object.	–

Table A-18 Properties of the `FileSystemWatcher` Class

Property	Description
`EnableRaisingEvents`	Turns on (`True`) and turns off (`False`) file change notification.
`Filter`	Gets or sets the filter used to determine what subset of files to monitor for changes.
`IncludeSubdirectories`	Specifies whether subdirectories are to be included (`True`) when monitoring for changes.
`InternalBufferSize`	Sets the size (in bytes) of the buffer to use to store change data. Should be a minimum of 4096 bytes (4K) and a multiple of that value for best performance.
`NotifyFilter`	Gets or sets the type of changes to monitor. Can be any of the following: `Attributes`, `CreationTime`, `DirectoryName`, `FileName`, `LastAccess`, `LastWrite`, `Security`, and `Size`.
`Path`	Specifies the directory path to watch.
`SynchronizingObject`	Specifies the object used to marshal the event-handler calls issued as a result of a directory change.

Table A-19 Methods of the `FileSystemWatcher` Class

Method	Description	Syntax
`BeginInit`	Starts the file watching for the component used on a Windows Form or by another component	–
`EndInit`	Stops the file watching for the component used on a Windows Form or by another component	–
`OnChanged`	Called when a file change occurs	`OnChanged(ByVal` *`e`* `As FileSystemEventArgs)`
`OnCreated`	Called when a file is created	`OnCreated(ByVal` *`e`* `As FileSystemEventArgs)`
`OnDeleted`	Called when a file is deleted	`OnDeleted(ByVal` *`e`* `As FileSystemEventArgs)`
`OnError`	Called when `InternalBufferSize` is exceeded	`OnError(ByVal` *`e`* `As ErrorEventArgs)`
`OnRenamed`	Called when a file is renamed	`OnRenamed(ByVal` *`e`* `As RenamedEventArgs)`
`WaitForChanged`	Synchronously watches for file system changes	`WaitForChanged(ByVal` *`changeType`* `As WatcherChangeTypes) As WaitForChangedResult` `WaitForChanged(ByVal` *`changeType`* `As WatcherChangeTypes, ByVal` *`timeout`* `As Integer) As WaitForChangedResult`

Table A-20 Methods of the `Directory` Class

Method	Description	Syntax
`CreateDirectory`	Creates the specified directory. Any subdirectories that don't already exist as part of the path are created.	`CreateDirectory(ByVal` *`path`* `As String) As DirectoryInfo`

`Delete`	Deletes a directory and all of its contents.	`Delete(ByVal` *`path`* `As String)`
		
		`Delete(ByVal` *`path`* `As String, ByVal` *`recursive`* `As Boolean)`

`Exists`	Returns `True` if the specified directory exists.	`Exists(ByVal` *`path`* `As String) As Boolean`
`GetCreationTime`	Gets the creation date and time of a directory.	`GetCreationTime(ByVal` *`path`* `As String) As DateTime`
`GetCurrentDirectory`	Gets the current directory.	`GetCurrentDirectory() As String`

`GetDirectories`	Returns an array of the subdirectories in the current directory.	`GetDirectories(ByVal` *`path`* `As String) As String()`
		
		`GetDirectories(ByVal` *`path`* `As String, ByVal` *`searchPattern`* `As String) As String()`

`GetDirectoryRoot`	Returns the root of the specified path.	`GetDirectoryRoot(ByVal` *`path`* `As String) As String`
`GetFiles`	Returns the files in the specified directory.	`GetFiles(ByVal` *`path`* `As String) As String()`

Method	Description	Syntax
		GetFiles(ByVal *path* As String, ByVal *searchPattern* As String) As String()
GetFileSystemEntries	Returns an array of file system entries in the specified path.	GetFileSystemEntries (ByVal *path* As String) As String() GetFileSystemEntries (ByVal Path As String, ByVal *searchPattern* As String) As String()
GetLastAccessTime	Gets the last accessed date and time of the specified directory.	GetLastAccessTime(ByVal *path* As String) As DateTime
GetLastWriteTime	Gets the last date and time the directory was written to	GetLastWriteTime(ByVal *path* As String) As DateTime
GetLogicalDrives	Retrieves the names of all the logical drives (disks and network drives).	GetLogicalDrives() As String()
GetParent	Retrieves the parent directory of the specified path.	GetParent(ByVal *path* As String) As DirectoryInfo
Move	Moves the specified directory and all of its contents to a new location.	Move(ByVal *sourceDirName* As String, ByVal *destDirName* As String)
SetCreationTime	Sets the creation time of the specified directory.	SetCreationTime(ByVal *path* As String, ByVal *creationTime* As DateTime)
SetCurrentDirectory	Sets the current directory.	SetCurrentDirectory(ByVal *path* As String)

(continued)

Table A-20 Methods of the `Directory` Class *(continued)*

Method	Description	Syntax
`SetLastAccessTime`	"Touches" the specified directory by changing the date and time it was last accessed.	`SetLastAccessTime(ByVal` *`path`* `As String, ByVal` *`lastAccessTime`* `As DateTime)`
`SetLastWriteTime`	Sets the date and time a directory was last written to.	`SetLastWriteTime(ByVal` *`path`* `As String, ByVal` *`lastWriteTime`* `As DateTime)`

Table A-21 Properties of the `DirectoryInfo` Class

Property	Description
`Attributes`	Gets or sets file attributes (inherited from `FileSystemInfo`)
`Exists`	Returns `True` if the directory exists
`Extension`	Specifies the file name extension (inherited from `FileSystemInfo`)
`FullName`	Gets the full path of the directory (inherited from `FileSystemInfo`)
`LastAccessTime`	Gets or sets the last accessed time (inherited from `FileSystemInfo`)
`LastWriteTime`	Gets or sets the time when the current file or directory was last written to (inherited from `FileSystemInfo`)
`Name`	Gets the name of the class instance
`Parent`	Gets the parent directory of a specified subdirectory
`Root`	Gets the root portion of a path

Table A-22 Methods of the `DirectoryInfo` Class

Method	Description	Syntax
`Create`	Creates a directory.	—
`CreateSubdirectory`	Creates the specified subdirectory. Any subdirectories that don't already exist as part of the path are created.	`CreateSubdirectory(ByVal` *`path`* `As String) As DirectoryInfo`

`Delete`	Deletes a directory and all its contents.	`Delete()`
		
		`Delete(ByVal` *`recursive`* `As Boolean)`

`GetDirectories`	Returns an array of the subdirectories in the current directory.	`GetDirectories() As DirectoryInfo()`
		
		`GetDirectories(ByVal` *`searchPattern`* `As String) As DirectoryInfo()`

`GetFiles`	Returns the files in the specified directory.	`GetFiles() As FileInfo()`
		
		`GetFiles(ByVal` *`searchPattern`* `As String) As FileInfo()`

`GetFileSystemInfos`	Retrieves an array of strongly typed `FileSystemInfo` objects.	`GetFileSystemInfos() As FileSystemInfo()`
		
		`GetFileSystemInfos(ByVal` *`searchPattern`* `As String) As FileSystemInfo()`

`MoveTo`	Moves a `DirectoryInfo` object and its contents to a new path.	`MoveTo(ByVal` *`destDirName`* `As String)`

Table A-23 Properties of the EventLog Class

Property	Description
EnableRaisingEvents	Returns True if the EventLog object can receive notifications (EntryWritten events)
Entries	Specifies the contents of the Event Log
Log	Sets the name of the log to read or write to
LogDisplayName	Returns the friendly name of the log
MachineName	Sets the name of the computer to read and write events to
Source	Specifies the source name to register with the Event Log
SynchronizingObject	Gets or sets the object used to marshal the event handler calls issued as a result of an EventLog entry written event

Table A-24 Methods of the EventLog Class

Method	Description	Syntax
CreateEventSource	Registers an application name with the Event Log.	CreateEventSource(ByVal *source* As String, ByVal *logName* As String) CreateEventSource(ByVal *source* As String, ByVal *logName* As String, ByVal *machineName* As String)
Delete	Removes a registered Event Log.	Delete(ByVal *logName* As String) Delete(ByVal *logName* As String, ByVal *machineName* As String)
DeleteEventSource	Removes a registered event source from the Event Log.	DeleteEventSource(ByVal *source* As String)

Method	Description	Syntax
		`DeleteEventSource(ByVal` *`source`* `As String, ByVal` *`machineName`* `As String)`

`Exists`	Returns `True` if the specified Event Log exists.	`Exists(ByVal` *`logName`* `As String) As Boolean`
		
		`Exists(ByVal` *`logName`* `As String, ByVal` *`machineName`* `As String) As Boolean`

`GetEventLogs`	Creates an array of the Event Logs.	`GetEventLogs() As EventLog()`
		
		`GetEventLogs(ByVal` *`machineName`* `As String) As EventLog()`

`LogNameFromSourceName`	Gets the name of the log to which the specified source is registered.	`LogNameFromSourceName (ByVal` *`source`* `As String, ByVal` *`machineName`* `As String) As String`

`SourceExists`	Checks to see if the specified event source is already registered.	`SourceExists(ByVal` *`source`* `As String) As Boolean`
		
		`SourceExists(ByVal` *`source`* `As String, ByVal` *`machineName`* `As String) As Boolean`

`WriteEntry`	Writes an entry in the Event Log. Various forms of this function are shown.	`WriteEntry(ByVal` *`message`* `As String)`
		
		`WriteEntry(ByVal` *`message`* `As String, ByVal` *`type`* `As EventLogEntryType)`
		
		`WriteEntry(ByVal` *`source`* `As String, ByVal message As String)`

(continued)

Table A-24 Methods of the `EventLog` Class *(continued)*

Method	Description	Syntax
		WriteEntry(ByVal *message* As String, ByVal *type* As EventLogEntryType, ByVal *eventID* As Integer) WriteEntry(ByVal *source* As String, ByVal *message* As String, ByVal *type* As EventLogEntryType) WriteEntry(ByVal *message* As String, ByVal *type* As EventLogEntryType, ByVal *eventID* As Integer, ByVal *category* As Short) WriteEntry(ByVal *source* As String, ByVal *message* As String, ByVal *type* As EventLogEntryType, ByVal *eventID* As Integer) WriteEntry(ByVal *message* As String, ByVal *type* As EventLogEntryType, ByVal *eventID* As Integer, ByVal *category* As Short, ByVal *rawData()* As Byte) WriteEntry(ByVal *source* As String, ByVal *message* As String, ByVal *type* As EventLogEntryType, ByVal *eventID* As Integer, ByVal *category* As Short) WriteEntry(ByVal *source* As String, ByVal *message* As String, ByVal *type* As EventLogEntryType, ByVal *eventID* As Integer, ByVal *category* As Short, ByVal *rawData()* As Byte)

Table A-25 Properties of the `DirectoryEntry` Class

Property	Description
`AuthenticationType`	Specifies the authentication to use when connecting to Active Directory Services.
`Children`	Gets a `DirectoryEntries` object that represents the child nodes of the current node in the directory.
`Guid`	Obtains the globally unique identifier (GUID) of the `DirectoryEntry` object.
`Name`	Gets the name of the object as used by Active Directory Services.
`NativeGuid`	Gets the GUID of the `DirectoryEntry` object from the provider.
`NativeObject`	Gets the native Active Directory Services Interface (ADSI) object.
`Parent`	Gets the parent object of the current directory node.
`Password`	Specifies the password to use when accessing password-protected directory resources.
`Path`	Specifies the path to the directory entry.
`Properties`	Gets a `PropertyCollection` object that contains properties for the current directory entry.
`SchemaClassName`	Gets the name of the schema used for this directory entry.
`SchemaEntry`	Gets the `DirectoryEntry` object that holds schema information for this entry. An entry's `SchemaClassName` determines what properties are valid for it.
`UsePropertyCache`	Gets or sets a value indicating whether the cache should be committed after each operation.
`Username`	Gets or sets the user name to use when authenticating the client.

Table A-26 Methods of the `DirectoryEntry` Class

Method	Description	Syntax
`Close`	Closes the `DirectoryEntry` object and releases system resources	–
`CommitChanges`	Saves changes made to Active Directory Services	–

`CopyTo`	Creates a copy of this entry as a child of the specified parent	`CopyTo(ByVal` *`newParent`* `As DirectoryEntry) As DirectoryEntry`
		
		`CopyTo(ByVal` *`newParent`* `As DirectoryEntry, ByVal` *`newName`* `As String) As DirectoryEntry`

`DeleteTree`	Deletes the current entry and its entire subtree from the Active Directory Services hierarchy	–
`Invoke`	Calls a method on the native Active Directory Services	`Invoke(ByVal` *`methodName`* `As String, ByVal` *`ParamArray args()`* `As Object) As Object`

`MoveTo`	Moves this entry to the specified parent	`MoveTo(ByVal` *`newParent`* `As DirectoryEntry)`
		
		`MoveTo(ByVal` *`newParent`* `As DirectoryEntry, ByVal` *`newName`* `As String)`

`RefreshCache`	Loads the property values for this directory entry into the property cache	`RefreshCache()`
		
		`RefreshCache(ByVal` *`propertyNames()`* `As String)`

`Rename`	Changes the name of this directory entry	`Rename(ByVal` *`newName`* `As String)`

Table A-27 Properties of the `DirectorySearcher` Class

Property	Description
`CacheResults`	Returns `True` if the results are cached on the client machine
`ClientTimeout`	Sets the maximum amount of time (in seconds) for the client to wait for results
`Filter`	Specifies the Lightweight Directory Access Protocol (LDAP) filter string to use for searching
`PageSize`	Sets the search page size
`PropertiesToLoad`	Gets the set of properties retrieved during the search (defaults to the `Path` and `Name` properties)
`PropertyNamesOnly`	Returns `True` if search results are to contain only values that are assigned
`ReferralChasing`	Gets or sets how referrals are chased
`SearchRoot`	Designates the starting point for searches in Active Directory Services
`SearchScope`	Specifies the scope of the search observed by the server
`ServerPageTimeLimit`	Sets the time limit the server observes to search an individual page of results
`ServerTimeLimit`	Specifies the maximum amount of time (in seconds) that the server is allowed to search
`SizeLimit`	Sets the number of results to which to limit a search
`Sort`	Gets the property on which the results are sorted

Table A-28 Methods of the `DirectorySearcher` Class

Method	Description	Syntax
`FindAll`	Returns a collection of search results	`FindAll() As SearchResultCollection`
`FindOne`	Returns only the first resulting match	`FindOne() As SearchResult`

Table A-29 Properties of the `SearchResult` Class

Property	Description
`Path`	Gets the path for this `SearchResult` object
`Properties`	Gets a `ResultPropertyCollection` of properties set on this object

Table A-30 Method of the `SearchResult` Class

Method	Description
`GetDirectoryEntry`	Gets the `DirectoryEntry` object that matches with the `SearchResult` object

Table A-31 Properties of the `SearchResultsCollection` Class

Property	Description
`Count`	Counts the number of `SearchResult` objects in the collection
`Handle`	Gets the handle returned by `IDirectorySearch::ExecuteSearch` (called by `DirectorySearcher`)
`Item`	Gets the `SearchResult` object in the collection at the specified index
`PropertiesLoaded`	Gets the `DirectorySearcher` properties that were specified before the search was executed

Table A-32 Methods of the `SearchResultsCollection` Class

Method	Description	Syntax
`Contains`	Indicates whether the specified `SearchResult` object is in the collection	`Contains(ByVal` *`result`* `As SearchResult) As Boolean`
`CopyTo`	Copies `SearchResult` objects in the collection to an array beginning with the specified index	`CopyTo(ByVal` *`results()`* `As SearchResult, ByVal` *`index`* `As Integer)`
`IndexOf`	Retrieves the index of a specified `SearchResult` object in this collection	`IndexOf(ByVal` *`result`* `As SearchResult) As Integer`

Table A-33 Property of the Static `MessageQueue` Class

Property	Description
`EnableConnectionCache`	Returns `True` if connections to the message queue are to be cached

Table A-34 Methods of the Static `MessageQueue` Class

Method	Description	Syntax
`ClearConnectionCache`	Clears the connection cache	–

`Create`	Creates a new queue (transactional or not) at the specified path on a Microsoft Message Queues server	`Create(ByVal` *`path`* `As String) As MessageQueue`
		
		`Create(ByVal` *`path`* `As String, ByVal` *`transactional`* `As Boolean) As MessageQueue`

(continued)

Table A-34 Methods of the Static `MessageQueue` Class (continued)

Method	Description	Syntax
`Delete`	Deletes a queue	`Delete(ByVal` *`path`* `As String)`
`Exists`	Returns `True` if the supplied path points to a valid queue	`Exists(ByVal` *`path`* `As String) As Boolean`
`GetMachineId`	Get the GUID of the Microsoft Message Queue computer	`GetMachineId(ByVal` *`machineName`* `As String) As Guid`
`GetMessageQueue Enumerator`	Creates a `MessageEnumerator` object for a dynamic listing of the public queues on the network	`GetMessageQueue Enumerator() As MessageEnumerator`
`GetPrivateQueuesBy Machine`	Gets all the private queues on the specified computer	`GetPrivateQueuesBy Machine(ByVal` *`machineName`* `As String) As MessageQueue()`

`GetPublicQueues`	Retrieves all the public queues on the network according to the criteria specified in the `MessageQueueCriteria` object	`GetPublicQueues() As MessageQueue()`
		
		`GetPublicQueues (ByVal` *`criteria`* `As MessageQueue Criteria) As MessageQueue()`

`GetPublicQueuesBy Category`	Retrieves all the public queues on the network that belong to the specified category	`GetPublicQueuesBy Category(ByVal` *`category`* `As Guid) As MessageQueue()`
`GetPublicQueuesBy Label`	Retrieves all the public queues on the network that carry the specified label	`GetPublicQueuesBy Label(ByVal` *`label`* `As String) As MessageQueue()`

Method	Description	Syntax
GetPublicQueuesByMachine	Retrieves all the public queues that reside on the specified computer	GetPublicQueuesByMachine(ByVal *machineName* As String) As MessageQueue()

Table A-35 Properties of the Instance MessageQueue Class

Property	Description
Authenticate	Returns True if the queue accepts only authenticated messages.
BasePriority	Sets the base priority for the queue that is used to route messages.
CanRead	Returns True if messages can be read from the queue.
CanWrite	Returns True if messages can be written to the queue.
Category	Specifies the queue category.
CreateTime	Gets the creation date/time for the queue.
DefaultPropertiesToSend	Specifies the message property values to be used by default when the application sends messages to the queue.
DenySharedReceive	Returns True if the MessageQueue instance has exclusive access to receive messages from the queue.
EncryptionRequired	Returns True if the queue will accept only encrypted messages.
FormatName	Gets the unique queue name generated at the time of the queue's creation.
Formatter	Gets or sets the formatter used to serialize an object into or deserialize an object from the body of a message read from or written to the queue.

(continued)

Table A-35 Properties of the Instance `MessageQueue` Class *(continued)*

Property	Description
`Id`	Gets the unique ID for the queue.
`Label`	Gives the queue description.
`LastModifyTime`	Gives the date and time the queue's properties were last modified.
`MachineName`	Specifies the machine name at which the queue is located.
`MaximumJournalSize`	Sets the maximum size of the journal queue.
`MaximumQueueSize`	Sets the maximum size of the queue.
`MessageReadPropertyFilter`	Gets or sets the property filter for receiving or peeking messages.
`Path`	Specifies the path of the current queue. Pointing to a different queue requires changing this property to a new path.
`QueueName`	Sets the friendly name that identifies the queue.
`ReadHandle`	Sets the native handle used to read messages from the queue.
`SynchronizingObject`	Gets or sets the object that marshals the event-handler call resulting from a `ReceiveCompleted` or `PeekCompleted` event.
`Transactional`	Gets a value indicating whether the queue accepts only transactions.
`UseJournalQueue`	Returns `True` if received messages are copied to the journal queue.
`WriteHandle`	Gets the native handle used to send messages to the message queue.

Table A-36 Methods of the Instance `MessageQueue` Class

Method	Description	Syntax

`BeginPeek`	Starts an asynchronous peek operation. Completion of the operation is signaled through events.	`BeginPeek() As IAsyncResult`
		
		`BeginPeek(ByVal` *`timeout`* `As TimeSpan) As IAsyncResult`
		
		`BeginPeek(ByVal` *`timeout`* `As TimeSpan, ByVal` *`stateObject`* `As Object) As IAsyncResult`
		
		`BeginPeek(ByVal` *`timeout`* `As TimeSpan, ByVal` *`stateObject`* `As Object, ByVal` *`callback`* `As AsyncCallback) As IAsyncResult`

`BeginReceive`	Starts an asynchronous receive operation. Completion of the operation is signaled through events.	`BeginReceive() As IAsyncResult`
		
		`BeginReceive(ByVal` *`timeout`* `As TimeSpan) As IAsyncResult`
		
		`BeginReceive(ByVal` *`timeout`* `As TimeSpan, ByVal` *`stateObject`* `As Object) As IAsyncResult`
		
		`BeginReceive(ByVal` *`timeout`* `As TimeSpan, ByVal` *`stateObject`* `As Object, ByVal` *`callback`* `As AsyncCallback) As IAsyncResult`

(continued)

Table A-36 Methods of the Instance `MessageQueue` Class *(continued)*

Method	Description	Syntax
`Close`	Closes the message queue.	–
`EndPeek`	Stops the asynchronous peek operation.	`EndPeek(ByVal` *`asyncResult`* `As IAsyncResult) As Message`
`EndReceive`	Stops the asynchronous receive operation.	`EndReceive(ByVal` *`asyncResult`* `As IAsyncResult) As Message`
`GetAllMessages`	Returns all the messages in the queue.	`GetAllMessages() As Message()`
`GetEnumerator`	Returns the enumerator for the objects in the queue.	`GetEnumerator() As IEnumerator`
`GetMessage Enumerator`	Creates an enumerator for queue messages.	`GetMachineId(ByVal` *`machineName`* `As String) As Guid`

`Peek`	Returns a copy of the next message in the queue without removing (receiving) it.	`Peek() As Message`
		
		`Peek(ByVal` *`timeout`* `As TimeSpan) As Message`

`PeekBy CorrelationId`	Peeks a message that matches a given correlation identifier.	`PeekByCorrelationId (ByVal` *`correlationId`* `As String) As Message`
		
		`PeekByCorrelationId (ByVal` *`correlationId`* `As String, ByVal` *`timeout`* `As TimeSpan) As Message`

`PeekById`	Peeks at a message matching the identifier.	`PeekById(ByVal` *`id`* `As String) As Message`

Method	Description	Syntax
		PeekById(ByVal *id* As String, ByVal *timeout* As TimeSpan) As Message
Purge	Deletes all messages from the queue.	–
Receive	Overloaded. Receives the first message in the queue, removing it from the queue.	Receive() As Message Receive(ByVal *transaction* As MessageQueueTransaction) As Message Receive(ByVal *timeout* As TimeSpan) As Message Receive(ByVal *timeout* As TimeSpan, ByVal *transaction* As MessageQueueTransaction) As Message
ReceiveBy CorrelationId	Receives a message matching the correlation identifier.	ReceiveByCorrelationId (ByVal *correlationId* As String) As Message ReceiveByCorrelationId (ByVal *correlationId* As String, ByVal *transaction* As MessageQueueTransaction) As Message ReceiveByCorrelationId (ByVal *correlationId* As String, ByVal *timeout* As TimeSpan) As Message

(continued)

Table A-36 Methods of the Instance `MessageQueue` Class *(continued)*

Method	Description	Syntax
		`ReceiveByCorrelationId (ByVal` *`correlationId`* `As String, ByVal` *`timeout`* `As TimeSpan, ByVal` *`transaction`* `As MessageQueueTransaction) As Message`

`ReceiveById`	Receives a message matching the identifier.	`ReceiveById(ByVal` *`id`* `As String) As Message`
		
		`ReceiveById(ByVal` *`id`* `As String, ByVal` *`transaction`* `As MessageQueueTransaction) As Message`
		
		`ReceiveById(ByVal` *`id`* `As String, ByVal` *`timeout`* `As TimeSpan) As Message`
		
		`ReceiveById(ByVal` *`id`* `As String, ByVal` *`timeout`* `As TimeSpan, ByVal` *`transaction`* `As MessageQueueTransaction) As Message`

`Refresh`	Refreshes all queue properties.	–
`ResetPermissions`	Resets queue permissions to default OS values.	–

`Send`	Sends an object to the queue.	`Send(ByVal` *`obj`* `As Object)`
		
		`Send(ByVal` *`obj`* `As Object, ByVal` *`transaction`* `As MessageQueueTransaction)`

Method	Description	Syntax
		Send(ByVal *obj* As Object, ByVal *label* As String) Send(ByVal *obj* As Object, ByVal *label* As String, ByVal *transaction* As MessageQueueTransaction)
SetPermissions	Adds permissions to the current set. This controls who has access rights to queue properties and messages in the queue.	SetPermissions(ByVal *dacl* As AccessControlList) SetPermissions(ByVal *ace* As MessageQueue AccessControlEntry) SetPermissions(ByVal *user* As String, ByVal *rights* As MessageQueueAccess Rights) SetPermissions(ByVal *user* As String, ByVal *rights* As MessageQueue AccessRights, ByVal *entryType* As Access ControlEntryType)

Table A-37 Properties of the `TCPClient` Class

Property	Description
`Active`	Indicates whether the TCP connection is still active (true/false value)
`Client`	Retrieves the underlying `Socket` object
`LingerState`	Sets the connection linger option
`NoDelay`	Causes a delay to be invoked when send and receive buffers are full if the value is set to `True`
`ReceiveBufferSize`	Sets the size of the receive buffer
`ReceiveTimeout`	Sets the time-out value (in milliseconds) of the connection
`SendBufferSize`	Specifies the size of the send buffer
`SendTimeout`	Sets the send time-out value (in milliseconds) of the connection

Table A-38 Methods of the `TCPClient` Class

Method	Description	Syntax
`Close`	Closes the TCP connection	–
`Connect`	Opens a connection to a TCP server	`Connect(ByVal` *`remoteEP`* `As IPEndPoint)`
		`Connect(ByVal` *`address`* `As IPAddress, ByVal` *`port`* `As Integer)`
		`Connect(ByVal` *`hostname`* `As String, ByVal` *`port`* `As Integer)`
`GetStream`	Gets the stream used to read and write data to the server	`GetStream() As NetworkStream`

Table A-39 Properties of the `TcpListener` Class

Property	Description
`Active`	Gets or sets a value that indicates whether the listener's socket has been bound to a port and started listening
`LocalEndpoint`	Gets the active end point for the local listener socket
`Server`	Gets or sets the underlying network socket

Table A-40 Methods of the `TcpListener` Class

Method	Description	Syntax
`AcceptSocket`	Accepts an incoming socket connection request	`AcceptSocket() As Socket`
`AcceptTcpClient`	Accepts an incoming connection request	`AcceptTcpClient() As TcpClient`
`Pending`	Determines whether there are pending connection requests	`Pending() As Boolean`
`Start`	Starts listening to network requests	–
`Stop`	Closes the network connection	–

Table A-41 Properties of the `WebRequest` Class

Property	Description
`ConnectionGroupName`	Specifies the connection group for the class
`ContentLength`	Sets the content length (in bytes) of the request data
`ContentType`	Specifies the MIME type of the request being sent
`Credentials`	Specifies the network credentials needed when requesting files that require authentication
`Headers`	Specifies a collection of HTTP headers
`Method`	Determines the HTTP protocol method used for the request (for example, `GET`, `POST`, `HEAD`)
`PreAuthenticate`	Indicates whether to preauthenticate the request
`Proxy`	Sets the network proxy to use for the request
`RequestUri`	Gets the URI of the Internet resource associated with the request when overridden in a descendant class
`Timeout`	Sets the time-out value for the request

Table A-42 Methods of the `WebRequest` Class

Method	Description	Syntax
`Abort`	Cancels a request in progress	–

`BeginGetRequestStream`	Provides an asynchronous version of the `GetRequestStream` method	`BeginGetRequestStream(`
		
		`ByVal` *`callback`* `As AsyncCallback, ByVal` *`state`* `As Object) As IAsyncResult`

Method	Description	Syntax
`BeginGetResponse`	Begins an asynchronous request for an Internet resource	`BeginGetResponse(ByVal` *`callback`* `As AsyncCallback, ByVal` *`state`* `As Object) As IAsyncResult`

`Create`	Initializes a new `WebRequest` object instance with the given URI scheme	`Create(ByVal` *`requestUriString`* `As String) As WebRequest`
		
		`Create(ByVal` *`requestUri`* `As Uri) As WebRequest`

`CreateDefault`	Initializes a new `WebRequest` object instance with the given URI scheme	`CreateDefault(ByVal` *`requestUri`* `As Uri) As WebRequest`
`EndGetRequestStream`	Returns a `Stream` object for writing data to the Internet connection	`EndGetRequestStream (ByVal` *`asyncResult`* `As IAsyncResult) As Stream`
`EndGetResponse`	Returns a `WebResponse` object	`EndGetResponse(ByVal` *`asyncResult`* `As IAsyncResult) As WebResponse`
`GetRequestStream`	Returns a `Stream` object for writing data to the Internet resource	`GetRequestStream() As Stream`
`GetResponse`	Returns a response to an Internet request	`GetResponse() As WebResponse`
`RegisterPrefix`	Registers a `WebRequest` descendant for the specified URI	`RegisterPrefix(ByVal` *`prefix`* `As String, ByVal` *`creator`* `As IWebRequestCreate) As Boolean`

Table A-43 Properties of the `WebResponse` Class

Property	Description
`ContentLength`	The content length of the received data (in bytes)
`ContentType`	The MIME type of the data being received
`Headers`	The collection of HTTP header name–value pairs from the response
`ResponseUri`	The URI of the Internet resource that responded to the request

Table A-44 Methods of the `WebResponse` Class

Method	Description	Syntax
`Close`	Closes the response stream	–
`GetResponseStream`	Returns the data stream (`System.IO.Stream` object) from the Internet resource	`GetResponseStream() As Stream`

Table A-45 Properties of the `XmlDocument` Class

Properties	Description
`Attributes`*	Returns an `XmlAttributeCollection` containing the attributes of the node
`BaseURI`	Gets the base URI of the current node
`ChildNodes`*	Returns the children of the node
`DocumentElement`	Return the root `XmlElement` for the document
`DocumentType`	Gets the node containing the DOCTYPE declaration
`FirstChild`*	Returns the first child of the node
`HasChildNodes`*	Gets a value indicating whether this node has any child nodes

Properties	Description
Implementation	Returns the XmlImplementation object for the current document
InnerText*	Gives the XML text representing the node and all its children
InnerXml	Gives the XML text representing the children of the current node
IsReadOnly	Returns True if the current node is read-only
Item*	Returns the specified child element
LastChild*	Returns the last child of the node
LocalName	Gets the local name of the node
Name	Returns the qualified name of the node
NamespaceURI*	Returns the namespace URI of this node
NameTable	Gets the XmlNameTable associated with this implementation
NextSibling*	Returns the next node
NodeType	Returns the type of the current node
OuterXml*	Returns the XML text representing the node and all its children
OwnerDocument	Gets the XmlDocument to which the current node belongs
ParentNode*	Returns the parent of this node
Prefix*	Specifies the namespace prefix of this node
PreserveWhitespace	Indicates to preserve white space if set to True
PreviousSibling*	Returns the previous node
Value*	Specifies the value of the node
XmlResolver	Sets the XmlResolver to use for resolving external resources

* Inherited from XmlNode.

Table A-46 Methods of the `XmlDocument` Class

Method	Description	Syntax
`AppendChild`	Adds the specified node to the end of the list of children of this node.	`AppendChild(ByVal` *`newChild`* `As XmlNode) As XmlNode`
`CloneNode`	Creates a duplicate of the node.	`CloneNode(ByVal` *`deep`* `As Boolean) As XmlNode`

`CreateAttribute`	Creates an `XmlAttribute` with the specified name.	`CreateAttribute(ByVal` *`name`* `As String) As XmlAttribute`
		
		`CreateAttribute(ByVal` *`qualifiedName`* `As String, ByVal` *`namespaceURI`* `As String) As XmlAttribute`
		
		`CreateAttribute(ByVal` *`prefix`* `As String, ByVal` *`localName`* `As String, ByVal` *`namespaceURI`* `As String) As XmlAttribute`

`CreateCDataSection`	Creates an `XmlCDataSection` containing the specified data.	`CreateCDataSection(ByVal` *`data`* `As String) As XmlCDataSection`
`CreateComment`	Creates an `XmlComment` containing the specified data.	`CreateComment(ByVal` *`data`* `As String) As XmlComment`
`CreateDocumentFragment`	Creates an `XmlDocumentFragment`.	`CreateDocumentFragment() As XmlDocumentFragment`
`CreateDocumentType`	Returns a new `XmlDocumentType` object.	`CreateDocumentType (ByVal` *`name`* `As String, ByVal` *`publicId`* `As String, ByVal` *`systemId`* `As String, ByVal` *`internalSubset`* `As String) As XmlDocumentType`

Method	Description	Syntax
CreateElement	Creates an XmlElement object.	CreateElement(ByVal *name* As String) As XmlElement CreateElement(ByVal *qualifiedName* As String, ByVal *namespaceURI* As String) As XmlElement CreateElement(ByVal *prefix* As String, ByVal *localName* As String, ByVal *namespaceURI* As String) As XmlElement
CreateEntity Reference	Creates an XmlEntityReference with the specified name.	CreateEntityReference (ByVal *name* As String) As XmlEntityReference
CreateNode	Creates an XmlNode.	CreateNode(ByVal *nodeTypeString* As String, ByVal *name* As String, ByVal *namespaceURI* As String) As XmlNode CreateNode(ByVal *type* As XmlNodeType, ByVal *name* As String, ByVal *namespaceURI* As String) As XmlNode CreateNode(ByVal *type* As XmlNodeType, ByVal *prefix* As String, ByVal *name* As String, ByVal *namespaceURI* As String) As XmlNode

(continued)

Table A-46 Methods of the `XmlDocument` Class *(continued)*

Method	Description	Syntax
`CreateProcessingInstruction`	Creates an `XmlProcessingInstruction` with the specified name and data.	`CreateProcessingInstruction(ByVal` *`target`* `As String, ByVal` *`data`* `As String) As XmlProcessingInstruction`
`CreateSignificantWhitespace`	Creates an `XmlSignificantWhitespace` node.	`CreateSignificantWhitespace(ByVal` *`text`* `As String) As XmlSignificantWhitespace`
`CreateTextNode`	Creates an `XmlText` node with the specified text.	`CreateTextNode(ByVal` *`text`* `As String) As XmlText`
`CreateWhitespace`	Creates an `XmlWhitespace` node.	`CreateWhitespace(ByVal` *`text`* `As String) As XmlWhitespace`
`CreateXmlDeclaration`	Creates an `XmlDeclaration` node with the specified values.	`CreateXmlDeclaration(ByVal` *`version`* `As String, ByVal` *`encoding`* `As String, ByVal` *`standalone`* `As String) As XmlDeclaration`
`GetElementById`	Gets the `XmlElement` with the specified identifier.	`GetElementById(ByVal` *`elementId`* `As String) As XmlElement`

`GetElementsByTagName`	Returns an `XmlNodeList` containing a list of all descendant elements that match the specified name.	`GetElementsByTagName(ByVal` *`name`* `As String) As XmlNodeList`
		
		`GetElementsByTagName(ByVal` *`localName`* `As String, ByVal` *`namespaceURI`* `As String) As XmlNodeList`

Method	Description	Syntax
ImportNode	Imports a node from another document to the current document.	ImportNode(ByVal *node* As XmlNode, ByVal *deep* As Boolean) As XmlNode
InsertAfter	Inserts the specified node immediately after the specified reference node.	InsertAfter(ByVal *newChild* As XmlNode, ByVal *refChild* As XmlNode) As XmlNode
InsertBefore	Inserts the specified node immediately before the specified reference node.	InsertBefore(ByVal *newChild* As XmlNode, ByVal *refChild* As XmlNode) As XmlNode
Load	Loads the specified XML data (from a Stream, a String, a TextReader, or an XmlReader)	Load(ByVal *inStream* As Stream) Load(ByVal *filename* As String) Load(ByVal *txtReader* As TextReader) Load(ByVal *reader* As XmlReader)
LoadXml	Loads the XML document from the specified string.	LoadXml(ByVal *xml* As String)
Normalize	Puts all XmlText nodes in the full depth of the subtree underneath this XmlNode into a "normal" form where only markup (for example, tags, comments, processing instructions, CDATA sections, and entity references) separates XmlText nodes—there are no adjacent XmlText nodes.	–
PrependChild	Adds the specified node to the beginning of the list of children of this node.	PrependChild(ByVal *newChild* As XmlNode) As XmlNode

(continued)

Table A-46 Methods of the `XmlDocument` Class *(continued)*

Method	Description	Syntax
`ReadNode`	Creates an `XmlNode` object based on the information in the `XmlReader`. The reader must be positioned on a node or attribute.	`ReadNode(ByVal` *`reader`* `As XmlReader) As XmlNode`
`RemoveAll`	Removes all the children and/or attributes of the current node.	–
`RemoveChild`	Removes the specified child node.	`RemoveChild(ByVal` *`oldChild`* `As XmlNode) As XmlNode`
`ReplaceChild`	Replaces the `oldChild` child node with `newChild` node.	`ReplaceChild(ByVal` *`newChild`* `As XmlNode, ByVal` *`oldChild`* `As XmlNode) As XmlNode`

`Save`	Saves the XML document to the specified location or stream.	`Save(ByVal` *`outStream`* `As Stream)`
		
		`Save(ByVal` *`filename`* `As String)`
		
		`Save(ByVal` *`writer`* `As TextWriter)`
		
		`Save(ByVal` *`writer`* `As XmlWriter)`

`SelectNodes`	Selects a list of nodes matching the XPath expression.	`SelectNodes(ByVal` *`xpath`* `As String) As XmlNodeList`
`SelectSingleNode`	Overloaded. Selects the first `XmlNode` that matches the XPath expression.	`SelectSingleNode(ByVal` *`xpath`* `As String) As XmlNode`

Method	Description	Syntax
`Supports`	Tests whether the DOM implementation implements a specific feature.	`Supports(ByVal` *`feature`* `As String, ByVal` *`version`* `As String) As Boolean`
`WriteContentTo`	Saves all the children of the `XmlDocument` node to the specified `XmlWriter`.	`WriteContentTo(ByVal` *`w`* `As XmlWriter)`
`WriteTo`	Saves the `XmlDocument` node to the specified `XmlWriter`.	`WriteTo(ByVal` *`w`* `As XmlWriter)`

Table A-47 Properties of the `XmlElement` Class

Property	Description
`Attributes`	Gets an `XmlAttributeCollection` containing the list of attributes for this node
`HasAttributes`	Returns `True` if the current node has any attributes
`InnerText`	Specifies the concatenated values of the node and all its children
`InnerXml`	Specifies the XML text representing the children of this node
`LastChild`	Returns the last child of the node
`LocalName`	Returns the local name of the current node
`Name`	Returns the qualified name of the node
`NamespaceURI`	Returns the namespace URI of this node
`NextSibling`	Gets the `XmlNode` immediately following this element
`NodeType`	Returns the type of the current node
`OwnerDocument`	Returns the `XmlDocument` to which this node belongs
`Prefix`	Specifies the namespace prefix of this node

Table A-48 Methods of the `XmlElement` Class (Inherits `XmlNode`)

Method	Description	Syntax
`CloneNode`	Make a copy of the node	`CloneNode(ByVal` *deep* `As Boolean) As XmlNode`

`GetAttribute`	Returns the attribute value for the specified attribute name	`GetAttribute(ByVal` *name* `As String) As String`
		
		`GetAttribute(ByVal` *localName* `As String, ByVal` *namespaceURI* `As String) As String`

`GetAttributeNode`	Returns the specified attribute as an `XmlAttribute`	`GetAttributeNode (ByVal` *name* `As String) As XmlAttribute`
		
		`GetAttributeNode (ByVal` *localName* `As String, ByVal` *namespaceURI* `As String) As XmlAttribute`

`GetElementsByTagName`	Returns an `XmlNodeList` containing a list of all descendant elements that match the specified name	`GetElementsByTagName (ByVal` *name* `As String) As XmlNodeList`
		
		`GetElementsByTagName (ByVal` *localName* `As String, ByVal` *namespaceURI* `As String) As XmlNodeList`

`HasAttribute`	Checks the element/node for the specified attribute	`HasAttribute(ByVal` *name* `As String) As Boolean`

Method	Description	Syntax
		HasAttribute(ByVal *localName* As String, ByVal *namespaceURI* As String) As Boolean
RemoveAll	Removes all the attributes and children of the current node	–
RemoveAllAttributes	Clears all attributes from the current element/node	–
RemoveAttribute	Removes the specified attribute	RemoveAttribute(ByVal *name* As String) RemoveAttribute(ByVal *localName* As String, ByVal *namespaceURI* As String)
RemoveAttributeAt	Removes the attribute node with the specified index from the element	RemoveAttributeAt (ByVal *i* As Integer) As XmlNode
RemoveAttributeNode	Removes an XmlAttribute	RemoveAttributeNode (ByVal *oldAttr* As XmlAttribute) As XmlAttribute RemoveAttributeNode (ByVal *localName* As String, ByVal *namespaceURI* As String) As XmlAttribute
SetAttribute	Sets the value of the specified attribute	SetAttribute(ByVal *name* As String, ByVal *value* As String)

(continued)

Table A-48 Methods of the XmlElement Class (Inherits XmlNode) *(continued)*

Method	Description	Syntax
		SetAttribute(ByVal *localName* As String, ByVal *namespaceURI* As String, ByVal *value* As String) As String
SetAttributeNode	Adds a new XmlAttribute	SetAttributeNode (ByVal *newAttr* As XmlAttribute) As XmlAttribute SetAttributeNode (ByVal *localName* As String, ByVal *namespaceURI* As String) As XmlAttribute
WriteContentTo	Writes the data contained in the current node and all its children to the XmlWriter	WriteContentTo(ByVal *w* As XmlWriter)
WriteTo	Saves the current node to the specified XmlWriter	WriteTo(ByVal *w* As XmlWriter)

Table A-49 Properties of the XmlText Class

Property	Description
LocalName	Gets the name of the current node without the namespace prefix
Name	Gets the name of the node
NodeType	Gets the type of the current node
Value	Gets or sets the value of the node

Table A-50 Methods of the `XmlText` Class

Method	Description	Syntax
`CloneNode`	Creates a copy of the `XmlText` object as an `XmlNode`.	`CloneNode(ByVal deep As Boolean) As XmlNode`
`SplitText`	Splits the text of the node into two nodes at the specified offset. Both split parts remain as siblings of the current node.	`SplitText(ByVal offset As Integer) As XmlText`
`WriteContentTo`	Saves all the children of the node to the specified `XmlWriter`.	`WriteContentTo(ByVal w As XmlWriter)`
`WriteTo`	Saves the node to the specified `XmlWriter`.	`WriteTo(ByVal w As XmlWriter)`

Table A-51 Properties of the `XmlTextReader` Class

Property	Description
`AttributeCount`	Returns the number of attributes on the current node
`BaseURI`	Gets the base URI of the current node
`CanResolveEntity`	Returns `True` if the reader can parse and resolve entities
`Depth`	Returns the depth of the current node in the XML document
`Encoding`	Returns the encoding attribute for the document
`EOF`	Returns `True` if the `XmlReader` is positioned at the end of the stream
`HasAttributes`	Returns `True` if the current node has any attributes
`HasValue`	Returns `True` if the node can have the `Value` property set
`IsDefault`	Returns `True` if the current node is an attribute and the value of the attribute was generated from the default value defined in the DTD or schema

(continued)

Table A-51 Properties of the XmlTextReader Class *(continued)*

Property	Description
IsEmptyElement	Returns True if the node is an empty element
Item	Returns the value of the attribute
LineNumber	Gets the current line number in the stream
LinePosition	Gets the current line (column) position
LocalName	Returns the name of the node minus the namespace prefix
Name	Gets the qualified name (with namespace) of the current node
Namespaces	Returns True if namespace support is to be used
NamespaceURI	Gets the namespace URI (as defined in the W3C Namespace Specification) of the node on which the reader is positioned
NameTable	Returns the XmlNameTable associated with this implementation
NodeType	Gets the type of the current node
Normalization	Returns True if white space normalization is to be performed
Prefix	Returns the namespace prefix associated with the current node
QuoteChar	Returns the quotation mark character used to enclose the value of an attribute node
ReadState	Returns the state of the reader
Value	Returns the text value of the current node
WhitespaceHandling	Specifies how white space is handled
XmlLang	Returns the current xml:lang scope
XmlResolver	Sets the XmlResolver used for resolving DTD references
XmlSpace	Returns the current xml:space scope

Table A-52 Methods of the `XmlTextReader` Class

Method	Description	Syntax
`Close`	Changes the `ReadState` to `Closed` and closes the stream	–

`GetAttribute`	Returns the value of an attribute	`GetAttribute(ByVal` *`i`* `As Integer) As String`
		
		`GetAttribute(ByVal` *`name`* `As String) As String`
		
		`GetAttribute(ByVal` *`localName`* `As String, ByVal` *`namespaceURI`* `As String) As String`

`GetRemainder`	Gets the remainder of the buffered XML	`GetRemainder() As TextReader`
`IsStartElement`	Tests whether the current content node is a start tag	`IsStartElement() As Boolean`
`LookupNamespace`	Resolves a namespace prefix in the current element's scope	`LookupNamespace (ByVal` *`prefix`* `As String) As String`

`MoveToAttribute`	Moves to the specified attribute	`MoveToAttribute (ByVal` *`i`* `As Integer)`
		
		`MoveToAttribute (ByVal` *`name`* `As String) As Boolean`
		
		`MoveToAttribute (ByVal` *`localName`* `As String, ByVal` *`namespaceURI`* `As String) As Boolean`

(continued)

Table A-52 Methods of the `XmlTextReader` Class *(continued)*

Method	Description	Syntax
`MoveToContent`	Checks whether the current node is a content node and moves to a node that has content if the current node doesn't	`MoveToContent() As XmlNodeType`
`MoveToElement`	Moves to the element that contains the current attribute node	`MoveToElement() As Boolean`
`MoveToFirst Attribute`	Moves to the first attribute	`MoveToFirst Attribute() As Boolean`
`MoveToNext Attribute`	Moves to the next attribute	`MoveToNext Attribute() As Boolean`
`Read`	Reads the next node from the stream	`Read() As Boolean`
`ReadAttribute Value`	Parses the attribute value into one or more `Text` and/or `EntityReference` node types	`ReadAttributeValue() As Boolean`
`ReadBase64`	Decodes Base64 and returns the decoded binary bytes	`ReadBase64(ByVal` *`array()`* `As Byte, ByVal` *`offset`* `As Integer, ByVal` *`len`* `As Integer) As Integer`
`ReadBinHex`	Decodes BinHex and returns the decoded binary bytes	`ReadBinHex(ByVal` *`array()`* `As Byte, ByVal` *`offset`* `As Integer, ByVal` *`len`* `As Integer) As Integer`

Method	Description	Syntax
`ReadChars`	Reads the text contents of an element into a character buffer	`ReadChars(ByVal` *`buffer()`* `As Char, ByVal` *`index`* `As Integer, ByVal` *`count`* `As Integer) As Integer`
`ReadElementString`	Reads simple, text-only elements	`ReadElementString() As String`
`ReadEndElement`	Checks that the current content node is an end tag and advances the reader to the next node	–
`ReadInnerXml`	Reads all the XML content as a string	`ReadInnerXml() As String`
`ReadOuterXml`	Reads all the XML that includes the current node and all its children	`ReadOuterXml() As String`
`ReadStartElement`	Checks that the current node is an element and advances the reader to the next node	–
`ReadString`	Reads the contents of an element or a text node as a string	`ReadString() As String`
`ResolveEntity`	Resolves the entity reference for `EntityReference` nodes	–
`Skip`	Skips the current element	–

Table A-53 Properties of the `XmlTextWriter` Class

Property	Description
`Formatting`	Indicates how the output is formatted: `Formatting.Indented` or `Formatting.None`
`Indentation`	Specifies how many `IndentChars` to write for each level in the hierarchy when `Formatting` is set to `Formatting.Indented`

Table A-53 Properties of the `XmlTextWriter` Class *(continued)*

Property	Description
`IndentChar`	Specifies the character (for example, `ControlChars.Tab`) to use for indenting when `Formatting` is set to `Formatting.Indented`
`Namespaces`	Returns `True` if namespace support is to be used
`QuoteChar`	Specifies the character to use to quote attribute values
`WriteState`	Gets the state of the writer
`XmlLang`	Gets the current `xml:lang` scope
`XmlSpace`	Gets an `XmlSpace` representing the current `xml:space` scope

Table A-54 Methods of the `XmlTextWriter` Class

Method	Description	Syntax
`Close`	Closes the stream	–
`Flush`	Flushes buffered output to the stream	–
`LookupPrefix`	Returns the closest prefix defined in the current namespace scope for the namespace URI	`LookupPrefix(ByVal` *`ns`* `As String) As String`
`WriteAttributes`	Writes out all the attributes found at the current position in the `XmlReader`	`WriteAttributes (ByVal` *`reader`* `As XmlReader, ByVal` *`defattr`* `As Boolean)`
`WriteAttributeString`	Writes an attribute with the specified value	`WriteAttribute String(ByVal` *`localName`* `As String, ByVal` *`value`* `As String)`

Method	Description	Syntax
`WriteBase64`	Encodes the specified binary bytes as Base64 and writes out the resulting text	`WriteBase64(ByVal` *`buffer()`* `As Byte, ByVal` *`index`* `As Integer, ByVal` *`count`* `As Integer)`
`WriteBinHex`	Encodes the specified binary bytes as BinHex and writes out the resulting text	`WriteBinHex(ByVal` *`buffer()`* `As Byte, ByVal` *`index`* `As Integer, ByVal` *`count`* `As Integer)`
`WriteCData`	Writes out an XML `<![CDATA[...]]>` block containing the specified text	`WriteCData(ByVal` *`text`* `As String)`
`WriteCharEntity`	Forces the generation of a character entity for the specified Unicode character value	`WriteCharEntity (ByVal` *`ch`* `As Char)`
`WriteChars`	Writes text in the specified buffer	`WriteChars(ByVal` *`buffer()`* `As Char, ByVal` *`index`* `As Integer, ByVal` *`count`* `As Integer)`
`WriteComment`	Writes out an XML comment containing the specified text	`WriteComment(ByVal` *`text`* `As String)`
`WriteDocType`	Writes the `DOCTYPE` declaration with the specified name and attributes	`WriteDocType(ByVal` *`name`* `As String, ByVal` *`pubid`* `As String, ByVal` *`sysid`* `As String, ByVal` *`subset`* `As String)`
`WriteElementString`	Writes an element containing a string value	`WriteElement String(ByVal` *`localName`* `As String, ByVal` *`value`* `As String)`

(continued)

Table A-54 Methods of the `XmlTextWriter` Class *(continued)*

Method	Description	Syntax
`WriteEndAttribute`	Closes the previous `WriteStartAttribute` call	–
`WriteEndDocument`	Closes any open elements or attributes and puts the writer back in the `Start` state	–
`WriteEndElement`	Closes one element and pops the corresponding namespace scope	–
`WriteEntityRef`	Writes out an entity reference	`WriteEntityRef (ByVal` *`name`* `As String)`
`WriteFullEndElement`	Closes one element and pops the corresponding namespace scope	–
`WriteName`	Writes out the specified name, ensuring it is a valid `Name` according to the XML specification	`WriteName(ByVal` *`name`* `As String)`
`WriteNmToken`	Writes out the specified name, ensuring it is a valid `NmToken` according to the XML specification	`WriteNmToken(ByVal` *`name`* `As String)`
`WriteNode`	Copies everything from the reader to the writer and moves the reader to the start of the next sibling	`WriteNode(ByVal` *`reader`* `As XmlReader, ByVal` *`defattr`* `As Boolean)`
`WriteProcessing Instruction`	Writes out a processing instruction with a space between the name and text	`WriteProcessing Instruction(ByVal` *`name`* `As String, ByVal` *`text`* `As String)`

Method	Description	Syntax
`WriteQualifiedName`	Writes out the namespace-qualified name	`WriteQualifiedName(ByVal` *`localName`* `As String, ByVal` *`ns`* `As String)`

`WriteRaw`	Writes raw XML markup	`WriteRaw(ByVal` *`data`* `As String)`
		
		`WriteRaw(ByVal` *`buffer()`* `As Char, ByVal` *`index`* `As Integer, ByVal` *`count`* `As Integer)`

`WriteStartAttribute`	Writes the start of an attribute	`WriteStartAttribute(ByVal` *`prefix`* `As String, ByVal` *`localName`* `As String, ByVal` *`ns`* `As String)`

`WriteStartDocument`	Writes the XML declaration	`WriteStartDocument()`
		
		`WriteStartDocument(ByVal` *`standalone`* `As Boolean)`

`WriteStartElement`	Writes the specified start tag	`WriteStartElement(ByVal` *`prefix`* `As String, ByVal` *`localName`* `As String, ByVal` *`ns`* `As String)`
`WriteString`	Writes the given text content	`WriteString(ByVal` *`text`* `As String)`

(continued)

Table A-54 Methods of the `XmlTextWriter` Class *(continued)*

Method	Description	Syntax
`WriteSurrogateCharEntity`	Generates and writes the surrogate character entity for the surrogate character pair	`WriteSurrogateCharEntity(ByVal lowChar As Char, ByVal highChar As Char)`
`WriteWhitespace`	Writes out the specified white space	`WriteWhitespace(ByVal ws As String)`

Table A-55 Property of the `XslTransform` Class

Property	Description
`XmlResolver`	Used to resolve DTD and schema location references

Table A-56 Methods of the `XslTransform` Class

Method	Description	Syntax

`Load`	Loads the XSLT stylesheet to use for the transformation of XML	`Load(ByVal stylesheet As IXPathNavigable)`
		`Load(ByVal url As String)`
		`Load(ByVal stylesheet As XmlReader)`
		`Load(ByVal stylesheet As XPathNavigator)`
		`Load(ByVal stylesheet As IXPathNavigable, ByVal resolver As XmlResolver)`

Method	Description	Syntax
		`Load(ByVal url As String, ByVal resolver As XmlResolver)`
		`Load(ByVal stylesheet As XmlReader, ByVal resolver As XmlResolver)`
		`Load(ByVal stylesheet As XPathNavigator, ByVal resolver As XmlResolver)`

`Transform`	Transforms the specified XML data using the loaded XSLT stylesheet and outputs the results	`Transform(ByVal input As IXPathNavigable, ByVal args As XsltArgumentList) As XmlReader`
		`Transform(ByVal inputfile As String, ByVal outputfile As String)`
		`Transform(ByVal input As XPathNavigator, ByVal args As XsltArgumentList) As XmlReader`
		`Transform(ByVal input As IXPathNavigable, ByVal args As XsltArgumentList, ByVal output As Stream)`

(continued)

Table A-56 Methods of the `XslTransform` Class *(continued)*

Method	Description	Syntax

		`Transform(ByVal` *`input`* `As XPathNavigator, ByVal` *`args`* `As XsltArgumentList, ByVal` *`output`* `As TextWriter)`
		
		`Transform(ByVal` *`input`* `As XPathNavigator, ByVal` *`args`* `As XsltArgumentList, ByVal` *`output`* `As XmlWriter)`

Table A-57 Property of the `SmtpMail` Class

Property	Description
`SmtpServer`	The hostname of the SMTP server to use. If omitted, the IIS 5.0 SMTP service running on the local machine is used.

Table A-58 Method of the `SmtpMail` Class

Method	Description	Syntax

`Send`	Sends a mail message using a preassembled `MailMessage` object or a text message with contents specified in the parameters	`Send(ByVal` *`message`* `As MailMessage)`
		
		`Send(ByVal` *`from`* `As String, ByVal` *`to`* `As String, ByVal` *`subject`* `As String, ByVal` *`messageText`* `As String)`

Table A-59 Properties of the `MailMessage` Class

Property	Description
`Attachments`	A collection (`IList`) of `MailAttachment` objects representing attachments to send with the e-mail message
`Bcc`	A semicolon-delimited list of e-mail addresses that receive a blind carbon copy (BCC) of the e-mail message
`Body`	The body of the e-mail message
`BodyEncoding`	The encoding type of the e-mail body
`BodyFormat`	The content type of the e-mail body; either `MailFormat.Text` or `MailFormat.HTML`
`Cc`	A semicolon-delimited list of e-mail addresses that receive a carbon copy (CC) of the e-mail message
`From`	The e-mail address of the sender
`Headers`	Custom headers to send along with the message
`Priority`	The priority of the e-mail message: `MailPriority.High`, `MailPriority.Low`, or `MailPriority.Normal`
`Subject`	The subject line of the e-mail message
`To`	The e-mail address of the recipient
`UrlContentBase`	The base URL to use for all relative links included in the body of the e-mail message
`UrlContentLocation`	Gets or sets the Content-Location HTTP header for the e-mail message.

Table A-60 Properties of the `MailAttachment` Class

Property	Description
`Encoding`	The encoding used to encode the e-mail attachment: either `MailEncoding.Base64` or `MailEncoding.UUEncode`
`Filename`	The pathname to the file attachment

APPENDIX B

ADO.NET Class Library Reference Tables

This appendix contains the following tables, which provide information on the methods and properties of classes in ADO.NET. The tables are listed below in alphabetical order by class name to assist you in finding the information you want.

Table B-1 Properties of the `IDataReader` Interface

Property	Description
`Depth`	Sets the depth of nesting for the current row
`IsClosed`	Has a value of `True` if the data reader is closed
`RecordsAffected`	Specifies the number of rows affected by the execution of the SQL statement

Table B-2 Methods of the `IDataReader` Interface

Method	Description	Syntax
`Close`	Closes the `IDataReader`	–
`GetSchemaTable`	Returns a `DataTable` object with schema data	`GetSchemaTable() As DataTable`
`NextResult`	Gets the next result when reading the results of batch SQL statements	`NextResult() As Boolean`
`Read`	Advances to the next record	`Read() As Boolean`

Table B-3 Properties of the `SqlConnection` Class

Property	Description
`ConnectionString`	Specifies the connection string to use when opening an SQL Server database
`ConnectionTimeout`	Sets the maximum time (in seconds) to wait for a successful connection to the database
`Database`	Specifies the name of the database to which to connect
`DataSource`	Specifies the SQL instance to which to connect (configured with the SQL Server Client Network Utility)
`PacketSize`	Sets the size (in bytes) of network packets to use when communicating with SQL Server
`ServerVersion`	Specifies the version of SQL Server
`State`	Gets the current state of the connection: `Broken`, `Closed`, `Connecting`, `Executing`, `Fetching`, or `Open` (`ConnectionState` enumeration)
`WorkstationId`	Specifies the identifier of the database client

Table B-4 Methods of the `SqlConnection` Class

Method	Description	Syntax

`BeginTransaction`	Starts a database transaction	`BeginTransaction() As SqlTransaction`
		
		`BeginTransaction(ByVal` *`iso`* `As IsolationLevel) As SqlTransaction`
		
		`BeginTransaction(ByVal` *`transactionName`* `As String) As SqlTransaction`

(continued)

Table B-4 Methods of the `SqlConnection` Class *(continued)*

Method	Description	Syntax
		`BeginTransaction(ByVal` *`iso`* `As IsolationLevel, ByVal` *`transactionName`* `As String) As SqlTransaction`
`ChangeDatabase`	Changes the database on an open connection	`ChangeDatabase(ByVal` *`database`* `As String)`
`Close`	Closes the connection to the database	–
`CreateCommand`	Creates a new `SqlCommand` object for the current connection	`CreateCommand() As SqlCommand`
`Open`	Opens a database connection using the `ConnectionString`	–

Table B-5 Properties of the `SqlCommand` Class

Property	Description
`CommandText`	Identifies the SQL/Transact-SQL statement to execute
`CommandTimeout`	Sets the maximum time (in seconds) to wait for the completion of a command
`CommandType`	Determines how to interpret the `CommandText` string: as `StoredProcedure`, `TableDirect`, or `Text` (`CommandText` enumeration)
`Connection`	Specifies the `SqlConnection` to use for execution of this command
`DesignTimeVisible`	Has a value of `True` if the object is visible on a Windows Forms Designer control

Property	Description
Parameters	Returns the SqlParameterCollection
Transaction	Specifies the SqlTransaction object to use for the command
UpdatedRowSource	Determines how command results are applied to the DataRow object when used by the Update() method of the DbDataAdapter

Table B-6 Methods of the SqlCommand Class

Method	Description	Syntax
Cancel	Cancels the execution of the current command	–
CreateParameter	Creates a new SqlParameter object	CreateParameter() As SqlParameter
ExecuteNonQuery	Executes the command and returns the number of rows affected by the command's execution	ExecuteNonQuery() As Integer
ExecuteReader	Executes the command and returns an SqlDataReader class so reading of results can begin	ExecuteReader() As SqlDataReader ExecuteReader(ByVal *behavior* As CommandBehavior) As SqlDataReader
ExecuteScalar	Returns the value of the first row and first column after execution of the command; used for stored procedures and aggregate SQL queries that return a single value	ExecuteScalar() As Object

(continued)

Table B-6 Methods of the `SqlCommand` Class *(continued)*

Method	Description	Syntax
`ExecuteXmlReader`	Executes the command and returns the results in an XML format in the `XmlReader` object	`ExecuteXmlReader() As XmlReader`
`Prepare`	Creates a prepared version of the command on an instance of SQL Server	–
`ResetCommandTimeout`	Resets the `CommandTimeout` property to its default value	–

Table B-7 Property of the `SqlDataReader` Class

Property	Description
`FieldCount`	Specifies the number of columns in the current row

Table B-8 Methods of the `SqlDataReader` Class

Method	Description	Syntax
`GetBoolean`	Gets the value of the specified column as a `Boolean`	`GetBoolean(ByVal` *`i`* `As Integer) As Boolean`
`GetByte`	Gets the value of the specified column as a `Byte`	`GetByte(ByVal` *`i`* `As Integer) As Byte`

Method	Description	Syntax
`GetBytes`	Reads a stream of bytes from the specified column offset into the buffer as an array starting at the given buffer offset	`GetBytes(ByVal` *`i`* `As Integer, ByVal` *`dataIndex`* `As Long, ByVal` *`buffer()`* `As Byte, ByVal` *`bufferIndex`* `As Integer, ByVal` *`length`* `As Integer) As Long`
`GetChar`	Gets the value of the specified column as a single character	`GetChar(ByVal` *`i`* `As Integer) As Char`
`GetChars`	Reads a stream of characters from the specified column offset into the buffer as an array starting at the given buffer offset	`GetChars(ByVal` *`i`* `As Integer, ByVal` *`dataIndex`* `As Long, ByVal` *`buffer()`* `As Char, ByVal` *`bufferIndex`* `As Integer, ByVal` *`length`* `As Integer) As Long`
`GetDataTypeName`	Gets the name of the source data type	`GetDataTypeName(ByVal` *`i`* `As Integer) As String`
`GetDateTime`	Gets the value of the specified column as a `DateTime` object	`GetDateTime(ByVal` *`i`* `As Integer) As DateTime`
`GetDecimal`	Gets the value of the specified column as a `Decimal` object	`GetDecimal(ByVal` *`i`* `As Integer) As Decimal`
`GetDouble`	Gets the value of the specified column as a double-precision floating point number	`GetDouble(ByVal` *`i`* `As Integer) As Double`
`GetFieldType`	Gets the data type of the object	`GetFieldType(ByVal` *`i`* `As Integer) As Type`
`GetFloat`	Gets the value of the specified column as a single-precision floating point number	`GetFloat(ByVal` *`i`* `As Integer) As Single`
`GetGuid`	Gets the value of the specified column as a globally unique identifier (GUID)	`GetGuid(ByVal` *`i`* `As Integer) As GUID`

(continued)

Table B-8 Methods of the `SqlDataReader` Class *(continued)*

Method	Description	Syntax
`GetInt16`	Gets the value of the specified column as a 16-bit signed integer	`GetInt16(ByVal` *`i`* `As Integer) As Short`
`GetInt32`	Gets the value of the specified column as a 32-bit signed integer	`GetInt32(ByVal` *`i`* `As Integer) As Integer`
`GetInt64`	Gets the value of the specified column as a 64-bit signed integer	`GetInt64(ByVal` *`i`* `As Integer) As Long`
`GetName`	Gets the name of the specified column	`GetName(ByVal` *`i`* `As Integer) As String`
`GetOrdinal`	Gets the column ordinal, given the name of the column	`GetOrdinal(ByVal` *`name`* `As String) As Integer`
`GetSqlBinary`	Gets the value of the specified column as an `SqlBinary`	`GetSqlBinary(ByVal` *`i`* `As Integer) As SqlBinary`
`GetSqlBoolean`	Gets the value of the specified column as an `SqlBoolean`	`GetSqlBoolean(ByVal` *`i`* `As Integer) As SqlBoolean`
`GetSqlByte`	Gets the value of the specified column as an `SqlByte`	`GetSqlByte(ByVal` *`i`* `As Integer) As SqlByte`
`GetSqlDateTime`	Gets the value of the specified column as an `SqlDateTime`	`GetSqlDateTime(ByVal` *`i`* `As Integer) As SqlDateTime`
`GetSqlDecimal`	Gets the value of the specified column as an `SqlDecimal`	`GetSqlDecimal(ByVal` *`i`* `As Integer) As SqlDecimal`
`GetSqlDouble`	Gets the value of the specified column as an `SqlDouble`	`GetSqlDouble(ByVal` *`i`* `As Integer) As SqlDouble`
`GetSqlGuid`	Gets the value of the specified column as an `SqlGuid`	`GetSqlGuid(ByVal` *`i`* `As Integer) As SqlGuid`

Method	Description	Syntax
`GetSqlInt16`	Gets the value of the specified column as an `SqlInt16`	`GetSqlInt16(ByVal i As Integer) As SqlInt16`
`GetSqlInt32`	Gets the value of the specified column as an `SqlInt32`	`GetSqlInt32(ByVal i As Integer) As SqlInt32`
`GetSqlInt64`	Gets the value of the specified column as an `SqlInt64`	`GetSqlInt64(ByVal i As Integer) As SqlInt64`
`GetSqlMoney`	Gets the value of the specified column as an `SqlMoney`	`GetSqlMoney(ByVal i As Integer) As SqlMoney`
`GetSqlSingle`	Gets the value of the specified column as an `SqlSingle`	`GetSqlSingle(ByVal i As Integer) As SqlSingle`
`GetSqlString`	Gets the value of the specified column as an `SqlString`	`GetSqlString(ByVal i As Integer) As SqlString`
`GetSqlValue`	Gets an object that is a representation of the underlying `SqlDbType Variant`	`GetSqlValue(ByVal i As Integer) As Object`
`GetSqlValues`	Gets all the attribute columns in the current row	`GetSqlValues(ByVal values() As Object) As Integer`
`GetString`	Gets the value of the specified column as a `String`	`GetString(ByVal i As Integer) As String`
`GetValue`	Gets the value of the specified column in its native format	`GetValue(ByVal i As Integer) As Object`
`GetValues`	Gets all attribute columns in the collection for the current row	`GetValues(ByVal values() As Object) As Integer`
`IsDBNull`	Gets a value indicating whether the column contains nonexistent or missing values	`IsDBNull(ByVal i As Integer) As Boolean`

Table B-9 Properties of the SqlParameter Class

Property	Description
DbType	Specifies the parameter's DbType, which is specific to a particular .NET Managed Data Provider
Direction	Determines how the parameter is to be used: as Input, InputOutput, Output, or ReturnValue (ParameterDirection enumeration)
IsNullable	Has a value of True if the parameter accepts null values
Offset	Sets the offset to the Value property for binary and string types
ParameterName	Gives the name of the parameter
Precision	Sets the maximum number of digits used to represent the Value property
Scale	Sets the number of decimal places to which the Value property is resolved
Size	Sets the maximum size (in bytes) of the data within the column
SourceColumn	Specifies the name of the source column that is mapped to the DataSet object and used for loading or returning the Value property
SourceVersion	Specifies the DataRowVersion to use when loading the Value property
SqlDbType	Specifies the SqlDbType of the parameter (maps to SQL Server data types)
Value	Specifies the value of the parameter

Table B-10 Properties of the DataSet Class

Property	Description
CaseSensitive	Has a value of True if string comparisons within the DataSet object are case-sensitive
DataSetName	Specifies the name of the DataSet object
DefaultViewManager	Returns a DataViewManager object used for filtering, searching, and navigating records
EnforceConstraints	Has a value of True if constraint rules are to be considered when attempting any update operation
ExtendedProperties	Returns a collection of custom information supplied by the user
HasErrors	Has a value of True if there are errors in any of the rows of the DataSet object
Locale	Specifies the geographic region and rules to govern DataSet operations (a CultureInfo object)
Namespace	Specifies the namespace of the DataSet object
Prefix	Specifies the XML prefix that aliases the namespace of the DataSet object
Relations	Specifies the collection of DataRelation objects used in the DataSet object
Site	Sets the System.ComponentModel.ISite for the DataSet object
Tables	Specifies a collection of DataTable objects contained in the DataSet object

Table B-11 Methods of the DataSet Class

Method	Description	Syntax
AcceptChanges	Commits all changes (updates the data source)	–
BeginInit	Begins the initialization of a DataSet object	–
Clear	Removes all data from the DataSet object	–
Clone	Creates a copy of the DataSet object along with all the underlying objects	Clone() As DataSet
Copy	Creates a copy of the data and structure of the DataSet object	Copy() As DataSet
EndInit	Ends the initialization of a DataSet object	–
GetChanges	Returns a DataSet object containing all changes made to it since it was last loaded or since AcceptChanges was called	GetChanges() As DataSet GetChanges(ByVal *rowStates* As DataRowState) As DataSet
GetXml	Returns the XML string of the data stored in the DataSet object	GetXml() As String
GetXmlSchema	Returns the XSD schema for the XML representation of the data stored in the DataSet object	GetXmlSchema() As String
HasChanges	Has a value of True if the DataSet object has changes to any of its rows	HasChanges() As Boolean HasChanges(ByVal *rowStates* As DataRowState) As Boolean

Method	Description	Syntax

`InferXmlSchema`	Infers the XML schema from the specified source into the `DataSet` object	`InferXmlSchema(ByVal` *`stream`* `As Stream, ByVal` *`nsArray()`* `As String)`
		
		`InferXmlSchema(ByVal` *`fileName`* `As String, ByVal` *`nsArray()`* `As String)`
		
		`InferXmlSchema(ByVal` *`reader`* `As TextReader, ByVal` *`nsArray()`* `As String)`
		
		`InferXmlSchema(ByVal` *`reader`* `As XmlReader, ByVal` *`nsArray()`* `As String)`

`Merge`	Merges this `DataSet` object with another `DataSet` object	`Merge(ByVal` *`rows()`* `As DataRow)`
		
		`Merge(ByVal` *`dataSet`* `As DataSet)`
		
		`Merge(ByVal` *`table`* `As DataTable)`
		
		`Merge(ByVal` *`dataSet`* `As DataSet, ByVal` *`preserveChanges`* `As Boolean)`
		
		`Merge(ByVal` *`rows()`* `As DataRow, ByVal` *`preserveChanges`* `As Boolean, ByVal` *`missingSchemaAction`* `As MissingSchemaAction)`

(continued)

Table B-11 Methods of the `DataSet` Class *(continued)*

Method	Description	Syntax

		`Merge(ByVal` *dataSet* `As DataSet, ByVal` *preserveChanges* `As Boolean, ByVal` *missingSchemaAction* `As MissingSchemaAction)`
		
		`Merge(ByVal` *table* `As DataTable, ByVal` *preserveChanges* `As Boolean, ByVal` *missingSchemaAction* `As MissingSchemaAction)`

`ReadXml`	Reads XML schema and data into the `DataSet` object	`ReadXml(ByVal` *stream* `As Stream) As XmlReadMode`
		
		`ReadXml(ByVal` *fileName* `As String) As XmlReadMode`
		
		`ReadXml(ByVal` *reader* `As TextReader) As XmlReadMode`
		
		`ReadXml(ByVal` *reader* `As XmlReader) As XmlReadMode`
		
		`ReadXml(ByVal` *stream* `As Stream, ByVal` *mode* `As XmlReadMode) As XmlReadMode`
		
		`ReadXml(ByVal` *fileName* `As String, ByVal` *mode* `As XmlReadMode) As XmlReadMode`

Method	Description	Syntax

		`ReadXml(ByVal reader As TextReader, ByVal mode As XmlReadMode) As XmlReadMode`
		
		`ReadXml(ByVal reader As XmlReader, ByVal mode As XmlReadMode) As XmlReadMode`

`ReadXmlSchema`	Reads an XML schema into the `DataSet` object	`ReadXmlSchema(ByVal stream As Stream)`
		
		`ReadXmlSchema(ByVal fileName As String)`
		
		`ReadXmlSchema(ByVal reader As TextReader)`
		
		`ReadXmlSchema(ByVal reader As XmlReader)`

`RejectChanges`	Undoes all changes made to the `DataSet` object since the last call to `AcceptChanges`	–
`Reset`	Rolls back the `DataSet` object to its original state	–
`WriteXml`	Writes XML schema and data from the `DataSet` object	`WriteXml(ByVal stream As Stream)WriteXml(ByVal fileName As String) WriteXml(ByVal reader As TextReader)WriteXml(ByVal reader As XmlReader) WriteXml(ByVal stream As Stream, ByVal mode As XmlWriteMode)WriteXml (ByVal fileName As String, ByVal mode As XmlWriteMode)WriteXml`

(continued)

Table B-11 Methods of the `DataSet` Class *(continued)*

Method	Description	Syntax
		(ByVal *reader* As TextReader, ByVal *mode* As XmlWriteMode)WriteXml (ByVal *reader* As XmlReader, ByVal *mode* As XmlWriteMode)
`WriteXmlSchema`	Writes the `DataSet` object structure as an XML schema	WriteXmlSchema(ByVal *stream* As Stream) WriteXmlSchema(ByVal *fileName* As String) WriteXmlSchema(ByVal *reader* As TextReader) WriteXmlSchema(ByVal *reader* As XmlReader)

Table B-12 Properties of the `DataTable` Class

Property	Description
`CaseSensitive`	Has a value of `True` if case-sensitive comparisons are enabled for strings in the `DataTable` object
`ChildRelations`	Specifies a collection of child relations for the `DataTable` object
`Columns`	Specifies a collection of columns for the data table
`Constraints`	Identifies the constraints assigned to the `DataTable` object
`DataSet`	Returns the `DataSet` object that contains the `DataTable` object
`DefaultView`	Returns the default view of the `DataTable` object; used for some data-binding situations

Property	Description
DisplayExpression	Gets or sets the expression that will return a value used to represent this table in the user interface
ExtendedProperties	Specifies a collection of customized user properties
HasErrors	Has a value of True if any rows in the data table contain errors
Locale	Specifies the geographic region and rules to govern DataTable operations (a CultureInfo object)
MinimumCapacity	Sets the minimum number of rows (starting size) for the data table
Namespace	Specifies the namespace for the XML representation of the data stored in the DataTable object
ParentRelations	Specifies a collection of parent relations for the DataTable object
Prefix	Specifies the XML prefix that aliases the namespace of the DataTable object
PrimaryKey	Specifies the array of columns that make up the primary key for the data table
Rows	Specifies a collection of rows of the data table
Site	Specifies the System.ComponentModel.ISite for the DataTable object
TableName	Sets the name of the DataTable object

Table B-13 Methods of the `DataTable` Class

Method	Description	Syntax
`AcceptChanges`	Commits all the changes made to this table since the last time `AcceptChanges` was called.	–
`BeginInit`	Begins the initialization of a `DataTable` object that is used on a form or used by another component. The initialization occurs at runtime.	–
`BeginLoadData`	Turns off notifications, index maintenance, and constraints while loading data.	–
`Clear`	Clears the `DataTable` object of all data.	–
`Clone`	Clones the structure of the `DataTable` object, including all `DataTable` schemas and constraints.	–
`Compute`	Computes the given expression on the current rows that pass the filter criteria.	`Compute(ByVal` *`expression`* `As String, ByVal` *`filter`* `As String) As Object`
`Copy`	Copies both the structure and data for this `DataTable` object.	–
`EndInit`	Ends the initialization of a `DataTable` object that is used on a form or used by another component. The initialization occurs at runtime.	–
`EndLoadData`	Turns on notifications, index maintenance, and constraints after loading data.	–

Method	Description	Syntax

`GetChanges`	Gets a copy of the `DataTable` object containing all changes made to it since it was last loaded or since `AcceptChanges` was called.	`GetChanges()`
		
		`GetChanges(ByVal` *`rowStates`* `As DataRowState) As DataTable`

`GetErrors`	Gets an array of `DataRow` objects that contain errors.	`GetErrors() As DataRow()`
`ImportRow`	Copies a `DataRow` object into a `DataTable` object, preserving any property settings as well as original and current values.	`ImportRow(ByVal` *`row`* `As DataRow)`
`LoadDataRow`	Finds and updates a specific row. If no matching row is found, a new row is created using the given values.	`LoadDataRow(ByVal` *`values()`* `As Object, ByVal` *`fAcceptChanges`* `As Boolean) As DataRow`
`NewRow`	Creates a new `DataRow` object with the same schema as the table.	`NewRow() As DataRow`
`RejectChanges`	Rolls back all changes made to the table since it was loaded or since the last time `AcceptChanges` was called.	–
`Reset`	Resets the `DataTable` object to its original state.	–

`Select`	Gets an array of `DataRow` objects.	`Select()`
		
		`Select(ByVal` *`filterExpression`* `As String) As DataRow()`

(continued)

Table B-13 Methods of the `DataTable` Class *(continued)*

Method	Description	Syntax

		`Select(ByVal` *`filterExpression`* `As String, ByVal sort As String) As DataRow()`
		
		`Select(ByVal` *`filterExpression`* `As String, ByVal` *`sort`* `As String, ByVal  As` *`recordStates`* `DataViewRowState) As DataRow()`

Table B-14 Properties of the `DataColumn` Class

Property	Description
`AllowDBNull`	Has a value of `True` if database NULL values are allowed for this column
`AutoIncrement`	Has a value of `True` if a new unique number is generated for this column when a new row is added
`AutoIncrementSeed`	Sets the value to use as a start value for `AutoIncrement` columns
`AutoIncrementStep`	Sets the value to use as an increment for `AutoIncrement` columns
`Caption`	Specifies the column's caption text
`ColumnMapping`	Determines how column data will be represented in XML (the `MappingType` of the column): `Attribute`, `Element`, `Hidden`, or `SimpleContent`
`ColumnName`	Specifies the name of the column
`DataType`	Sets the data type of the column

Property	Description
`DefaultValue`	Sets the default value for the column
`Expression`	Specifies the expression used to filter rows, calculate the values in a column, or create an aggregate column
`ExtendedProperties`	Specifies a collection of custom user information
`MaxLength`	Sets the maximum length of a text column in characters
`Namespace`	Specifies the namespace of the column
`Ordinal`	Sets the ordinal position of the column in the collection of columns (`DataColumnCollection`)
`Prefix`	Specifies the XML prefix that aliases the namespace of the `DataColumn` object
`ReadOnly`	Has a value of `True` if the column's data can't be changed once a row has been created
`Table`	Returns the `DataTable` object to which the column belongs
`Unique`	Has a value of `True` if the values in each row of the column must be unique

Table B-15 Properties of the `DataRow` Class

Property	Description
`HasErrors`	Has a value of `True` if there are errors in a columns collection
`Item`	Gives the data stored in a specified column in the row
`ItemArray`	Specifies an array of all the values for this row
`RowError`	Specifies the custom error description for a row
`RowState`	Gets the current state of the row: `Added`, `Deleted`, `Detached`, `Modified`, or `Unchanged` (`DataRowState` enumeration)
`Table`	Specifies the `DataTable` object to which the row belongs

Table B-16 Methods of the `DataRow` Class

Method	Description	Syntax
`AcceptChanges`	Commits all the changes made to this row	–
`BeginEdit`	Begins an edit operation	–
`CancelEdit`	Cancels any changes made to the row data	–
`ClearErrors`	Clears the errors for the row	–
`Delete`	Deletes the row	–
`EndEdit`	Ends the edit occurring on the row	–

`GetChildRows`	Gets the child rows of the `DataRow` object	`GetChildRows(ByVal` *`relation`* `As DataRelation) As DataRow()`
		
		`GetChildRows(ByVal` *`relationName`* `As String) As DataRow()`
		
		`GetChildRows(ByVal` *`relation`* `As DataRelation, ByVal` *`version`* `As DataRowVersion) As DataRow()`
		
		`GetChildRows(ByVal` *`relationName`* `As String, ByVal` *`version`* `As DataRowVersion) As DataRow()`

`GetColumnError`	Gets the error description for a column	`GetColumnError(ByVal` *`column`* `As DataColumn) As String`

Method	Description	Syntax

		`GetColumnError(ByVal` *`columnIndex`* `As Integer) As String`
		
		`GetColumnError(ByVal` *`columnName`* `As String) As String`

`GetColumnsInError`	Returns an array of `DataColumn` objects that have errors	`GetColumnsInError() As DataColumn()`

`GetParentRow`	Gets the parent row of the `DataRow` object	`GetParentRow(ByVal` *`relation`* `As DataRelation) As DataRow`
		
		`GetParentRow(ByVal` *`relationName`* `As String) As DataRow`
		
		`GetParentRow(ByVal` *`relation`* `As DataRelation, ByVal` *`version`* `As DataRowVersion) As DataRow`
		
		`GetParentRow(ByVal` *`relationName`* `As String, ByVal` *`version`* `As DataRowVersion) As DataRow`

`GetParentRows`	Gets all parent rows of a `DataRow` object	`GetParentRows(ByVal` *`relation`* `As DataRelation) As DataRow()`
		
		`GetParentRows(ByVal` *`relationName`* `As String) As DataRow()`

(continued)

Table B-16 Methods of the `DataRow` Class *(continued)*

Method	Description	Syntax

		`GetParentRows(ByVal` *`relation`* `As DataRelation, ByVal` *`version`* `As DataRowVersion) As DataRow()`
		
		`GetParentRows(ByVal` *`relationName`* `As String, ByVal` *`version`* `As DataRowVersion) As DataRow()`

`HasVersion`	Has a value of `True` if a specified version exists for the `DataRow` object	`HasVersion(ByVal` *`version`* `As DataRowVersion) As Boolean`

`IsNull`	Has a value of `True` if the specified column contains a null value	`IsNull(ByVal` *`column`* `As DataColumn) As Boolean`
		
		`IsNull(ByVal` *`columnIndex`* `As Integer) As Boolean`
		
		`IsNull(ByVal` *`columnName`* `As String) As Boolean`
		
		`IsNull(ByVal` *`column`* `As DataColumn, ByVal` *`version`* `As DataRowVersion) As Boolean`

`RejectChanges`	Rejects all changes made to the row since `AcceptChanges` was called	–

Method	Description	Syntax
SetColumnError	Sets the error description for a column	SetColumnError(ByVal *column* As DataColumn, ByVal *error* As String) SetColumnError(ByVal *columnIndex* As Integer, ByVal *error* As String) SetColumnError(ByVal *columnName* As String, ByVal *error* As String)
SetParentRow	Sets the parent row of the DataRow object	SetParentRow(ByVal *parentRow* As DataRow) SetParentRow(ByVal *parentRow* As DataRow, ByVal *relation* As DataRelation)
SetUnspecified	Sets the value of a DataColumn object with the specified name to unspecified	SetUnspecified(ByVal *column* As DataColumn)

Table B-17 Properties of the `IDataAdapter` Interface

Property	Description
`MissingMappingAction`	Indicates or specifies whether unmapped source tables or columns are passed with their source names in order to be filtered or to raise an error. Can be `Error`, `Ignore`, or `Passthrough` (`MissingMappingAction` enumeration).
`MissingSchemaAction`	Indicates or specifies whether missing source tables, columns, and their relationships are added to the `DataSet` schema, are ignored, or cause an error to be raised. Can be `Add`, `AddWithKey`, `Error`, or `Ignore` (`MissingSchemaAction` enumeration).
`TableMappings`	Indicates how a source table is mapped to a `DataSet` table.

Table B-18 Methods of the `IDataAdapter` Interface

Method	Description	Syntax
`Fill`	Adds or refreshes rows in the `DataSet` object to match those in the data source using the `DataSet` name and creates a `DataTable` object named `Table`	`Fill(ByVal` *`dataSet`* `As DataSet) As Integer`
`FillSchema`	Adds a `DataTable` object named `Table` to the specified `DataSet` object and configures the schema to match that in the data source based on the specified `SchemaType`	`FillSchema(ByVal` *`dataSet`* `As DataSet, ByVal` *`schemaType`* `As SchemaType) As DataTable()`
`GetFillParameters`	Gets the parameters set by the user when executing an SQL SELECT statement	`GetFillParameters() As IDataParameter()`

Method	Description	Syntax
`Update`	Calls the respective `INSERT`, `UPDATE`, or `DELETE` statements for each inserted, updated, or deleted row in the specified `DataSet` object from a `DataTable` object named `Table`	`Update(ByVal` *`dataSet`* `As DataSet) As Integer`

Table B-19 Properties of the `SqlCommandBuilder` Class

Property	Description
`DeleteCommand`	SQL statement used to delete records
`InsertCommand`	SQL statement used to insert records
`SelectCommand`	SQL statement used to select records
`UpdateCommand`	SQL statement used to update records

Table B-20 Method of the `SqlCommandBuilder` Class

Method	Description	Syntax
`Dispose`	Frees the resources used by the `SqlDataAdapter` object	`Dispose(ByVal` *`disposing`* `As Boolean)`

Table B-21 Events of the `SqlDataAdapter` Class

Event	Description
`OnRowUpdated`	Raises the `RowUpdated` event
`OnRowUpdating`	Raises the `RowUpdating` event

Table B-22 Properties of the `DataView` Class

Property	Description
`AllowDelete`	Has a value of `True` if deletes from the `DataView` object are allowed
`AllowEdit`	Has a value of `True` if edits of the `DataView` object are allowed
`AllowNew`	Has a value of `True` if new rows are allowed to be added to the `DataView` object
`ApplyDefaultSort`	Has a value of `True` if the default sorting method is to be used
`Count`	Returns the number of records in the `DataView` object
`DataViewManager`	Gets the `DataView` object associated with this view
`Item`	Returns a row of data from a specified table
`RowFilter`	Specifies the filtering expression
`RowStateFilter`	Specifies the row state filter with these values: `Added`, `CurrentRows`, `Deleted`, `ModifiedCurrent`, `ModifiedOriginal`, `None`, `OriginalRows`, and `Unchanged` (`DataViewRowState` enumeration)
`Sort`	Specifies the sort expression
`Table`	Specifies the `DataTable` object to use for the view

Table B-23 Methods of the `DataView` Class

Method	Description	Syntax
`AddNew`	Adds a new row.	`AddNew() As DataRowView`
`BeginInit`	Begins the initialization of a `DataView` object that is used on a form or used by another component. The initialization occurs at runtime.	–
`Delete`	Deletes a row with the specified index.	`Delete(ByVal` *`index`* `As Integer)`
`Dispose`	Frees resources used by the `DataView` object.	–
`EndInit`	Ends the initialization of a `DataView` object that is used on a form or used by another component. The initialization occurs at runtime.	–

`Find`	Finds a row or array of rows in the `DataView` object by the specified primary key.	`Find(ByVal` *`key`* `As Object) As Integer`
		
		`Find(ByVal` *`key()`* `As Object) As Integer`

`GetEnumerator`	Returns an enumerator for this `DataView` object.	`GetEnumerator() As IEnumerator`

Table B-24 Properties of the `DataRelation` Class

Property	Description
`ChildColumns`	Returns the `DataColumn` objects of this relation
`ChildKeyConstraint`	Gets the `ForeignKeyConstraint` for the relation
`ChildTable`	Returns the child table of this relation
`DataSet`	Returns the `DataSet` object to which the `DataRelation` object belongs
`ExtendedProperties`	Returns the customized property collection
`Nested`	Has a value of `True` if `DataRelation` objects are nested
`ParentColumns`	Returns an array of `DataColumn` objects that are the parent columns of this `DataRelation` object
`ParentKeyConstraint`	Returns the `UniqueConstraint` of the parent column
`ParentTable`	Returns the parent `DataTable` object of this `DataRelation` object
`RelationName`	Specifies the name of the `DataRelation` object

Table B-25 Method of the `DataRelation` Class

Method	Description	Syntax
`CheckStateForProperty`	Checks for a valid `DataRelation` object	–

Table B-26 Property of the `SqlTransaction` Class

Property	Description
`IsolationLevel`	Specifies the `IsolationLevel` for this transaction: `Chaos`, `ReadCommitted`, `ReadUncommitted`, `RepeatableRead`, `Serializable`, or `Unspecified` (`IsolationLevel` enumeration)

Table B-27 Methods of the `SqlTransaction` Class

Method	Description	Syntax
`Commit`	Commits the database transaction	–
`Rollback`	Rolls back the current transaction	`Rollback()` `Rollback(ByVal` *`transactionName`* `As String)`
`Save`	Creates a save point in the transaction to which a rollback can return	`Save(ByVal` *`savePointName`* `As String)`

Bibliography

Printed Resources

Aitken, Peter G. 2002. *XML—The Microsoft Way*. Boston, MA: Addison-Wesley.

Anderson, Richard, et al. 2001. *Professional ASP.NET*. Birmingham, U.K.: Wrox Press.

Crouch, Matt J. 2000. *Web Programming with ASP and COM*. Boston, MA: Addison-Wesley.

Thai, Thuan L., and Hoang Q. Lam. 2001. *.NET Framework Essentials*. Sebastopol, CA: O'Reilly & Associates.

Tittel, Ed. 2000. *XML for Dummies*. Foster City, CA: IDG Books Worldwide.

Online Resources

Microsoft COM+ Web site, *http://www.microsoft.com/complus*.

Microsoft GotDotNet Web site, *http://www.gotdotnet.com/*.

Microsoft Internet Information Server Web site, *http://www.microsoft.com/windows2000/technologies/web/default.asp*.

Microsoft MSDN Library Web site, *http://msdn.microsoft.com/library/default.asp* (includes the *Visual Basic Language Reference* and *Design Guidelines for Class Library Developers* as part of the .NET Framework SDK documentation).

Microsoft .NET Web site, *http://www.microsoft.com/net*.

University of Illinois Common Gateway Interface Web site, *http://hoohoo.ncsa.uiuc.edu/cgi*.

Index

Note: Italicized page locators indicate tables/figures.

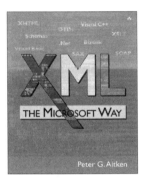

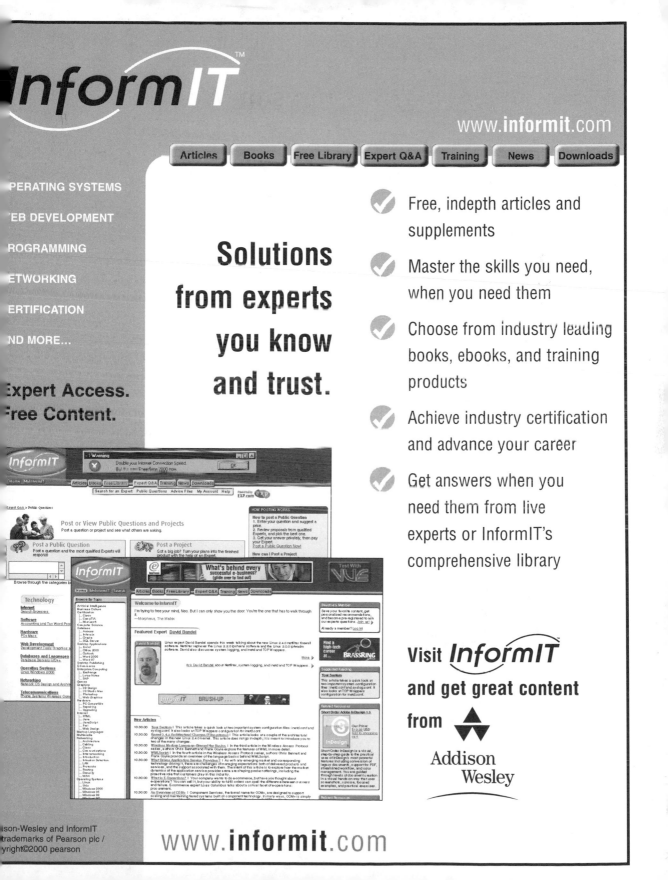